Corrections

IN

America

Corrections
IN
America

ROBERT M. CARTER
University of Southern California

RICHARD A. McGEE
American Justice Institute

E. KIM NELSON
University of Southern California

J. B. LIPPINCOTT COMPANY
Philadelphia   New York   Toronto

ISBN 0-397-47317-6
Library of Congress Catalog Card Number 74-34158

Printed in the United States of America

1 3 5 7 9 8 6 4 2

Library of Congress Cataloging in Publication Data

Carter, Robert Melvin
   Corrections in America.

   Includes bibliographical references and index.
   1. Corrections — United States. I. McGee,
Richard A., joint author. II. Nelson, Elmer K., joint
author. III. Title.
HV9304.C37   364.6'0973   74-34158
ISBN 0-397-47317-6

Contents

Foreword

Corrections in America is designed for those who desire to find within the covers of a single volume an overview of the origins, processes, organization and contemporary trends of corrections in America. Thus, this text deals with the total spectrum of management, control and treatment of juvenile and adult offenders both in institutions and in community programs. It is not intended to be a critique of correctional programs nor a theoretical treatise on correctional philosophy and practice.

Corrections is part of the system of criminal justice administration in the United States and its political subdivisions. The correctional establishment is fragmented by political jurisdictions on the federal, state and local levels. In practice, it is further subdivided on a basis of ascending degrees of criminal responsibility, from child to juvenile to adult. Other fractionalizations along philosophical and functional lines are apparent in such areas as pretrial detention, probation, parole, correctional schools, reformatories, camps, farms and security prisons.

The complexity of programs, practices, institutions and philosophies in corrections places the casual observer in a position analogous to the fable of the blind man and the elephant. Most of us in criminal justice — academician, administrator, practitioner and researcher alike — touch but one part of the correctional apparatus and therefore may have a distorted notion of the whole.

FOREWORD

Whether the user of this text is a graduate or undergraduate student or in the criminal justice system at any point from law enforcement through corrections, we trust this volume will provide him a useful perspective of corrections in America.

Robert M. Carter
Richard A. McGee
E. Kim Nelson

Los Angeles
Sacramento
January, 1975

Preface

The problems of crime bring us together. Even as we join in common action, we know there can be no instant victory. Ancient evils do not yield to easy conquest. We cannot limit our efforts to enemies we can see. We must, with equal resolve, seek out new knowledge, new techniques and new understanding.

Thus spoke President Lyndon Johnson in a message to the Congress of the United States on March 9, 1966, in which he announced the formation of a President's Commission on Law Enforcement and Administration of Justice in America.

The authors of *Corrections in America* modestly claim to do little more than describe the origins, organization and trends of corrections in America. In reality, this text represents a fixing, not an exhorting; a positioning, not a proselytizing; indeed, the "bringing together" mentioned above. In this regard, authors Carter, McGee and Nelson have made a considerable contribution to our knowledge and awareness of corrections by developing a careful and coordinated statement of the correctional process in America today.

And they have made yet another, more subtle and significant achievement. From an awareness of where we are, we can develop an appreciation of where we should be going; and this, in President Johnson's words, enables us to seek out "new knowledge, new techniques and new understanding."

This is probably the greatest achievement of the text. While we have slipped the grip of gravity and reached the moon, while we have found solutions to many persistent ills, we have not, in the field of corrections or in the total criminal justice system, progressed much beyond the claims and hopes of our pioneering predecessors. The Statement of Principles of the American Correctional Association, made at its founding meeting in Cincinnati, in 1870, still represents a challenge to modern practitioners.

The reasons for this are, perhaps, related to the lack of concentrated, continuous concern and the cost of improving programs. Until such time as all of us become aware of and accept the fact that the purpose of corrections is the protection of society, including the offender himself, and until we value that purpose sufficiently — only then will we move drastically and dramatically beyond what is being done today and what has been done in the not-too-distant past.

Perhaps the time has come when we who are or are about to become practitioners can no longer wait to be sedately and serenely pushed in the direction of public opinion. We must now take specific strides in the direction we discern as having the most hope of progress. Most correctional administrators and practitioners are public servants, but perhaps there is a need for the servant to assume greater responsibility in leadership.

It is my submission that *Corrections in America* offers not so much a blueprint for progress as a launching platform for such efforts. It is essential that our thoughts be brought beyond a description of the here-and-now, for we bear, as citizens, a heavy responsibility for the total criminal justice system. As a renowned British statesman once said:

> The harm done by wrongdoing is the responsibility of a relatively few members of society. But the harm done by improper methods of treatment of the offender when better methods are known or achievable — that is the responsibility borne by all members of society.*

This challenge is inherent and implicit within the words of this text.

That such a clear, concise statement depicting corrections in America today and suggesting where corrections should be tomorrow should come from these authors is not unexpected. Each has been, at various times in his career, equally at home teaching in the classroom or working in the corrections system.

Dr. E. Kim Nelson, Dean of the Center for Public Affairs and the School of Public Administration, University of Southern California, and Chairman of the Research Council of the National Council on Crime and Delinquency,

---

*Sir Herbert Morrison, Home Secretary, Great Britain, 1940.

has experience as a teacher, a line practitioner and a correctional administrator. Dean Nelson was Associate Director of the President's Commission on Law Enforcement and Administration of Justice in 1966–1967, and he headed the Commission's Task Force on Corrections. He was elected to the prestigious National Academy of Public Administration in 1971. I have been privileged to know him in my successive roles as student, subordinate and successor in a new correctional institution he brought into operation in my native land. He, like his colleagues, has an international reputation that is richly deserved.

Richard A. McGee, President of the American Justice Institute, has, throughout my life and the lives of many practitioners throughout the world, been a guiding light in the field of corrections. He has served as Director of Education in the Federal Bureau of Prisons; as the first Warden of New York City Penitentiary, Rikers Island; as Deputy Commissioner of Corrections for New York City; and, subsequently, Director of Public Institutions in the state of Washington. In 1944, he became the Director of the California Department of Corrections and was the administrator who brought California to acknowledged leadership status in the total field. He, too, enjoys well-deserved international renown. Of considerable significance to readers of this text is the fact that Richard McGee was the Editor-in-Chief of the *Manual of Correctional Standards* and Chairman of the Committee on Standards for the American Correctional Association when that *Manual* underwent its far-reaching revision of 1959.

Robert M. Carter, Director of the Center for the Administration of Justice and Professor of Public Administration, University of Southern California, is one of the most prolific writers on corrections in America today. But he is more than an academician and philosopher. He has worked as a line correctional officer at San Quentin and as a United States Probation and Parole Officer. He was the first Director of the San Francisco Crime Commission. His research experience is probably best known for his work in the now-famed San Francisco project, the Study of the Federal Probation and Parole System in 1968. Subsequent to that, he served as Research Administrator in the Washington State Department of Institutions.

That these men have come together to develop a text on American corrections is not so much remarkable as it is rewarding and not so much a surprise as it is a significant contribution to our understanding and to our subsequent efforts as students and practitioners.

The author of *Folsom Prison Blues* wrote, "If they freed me from that prison, if that railroad train was mine, I'd like to move it on a little further down the line." This is the challenge of our correctional process. As supporters or

PREFACE

participants of a total criminal justice system, we have our dreams, ideals, achievements and aspirations. At the same time, we have our failings, our sins and our confessions. This text represents, in part, a confession as to where we are and what we have achieved and an indication of to what we might aspire. To that extent and for all of us, we have a clearer picture of how far we have moved the correctional train down the line, the direction in which it should go and how much further our journey will take us.

John Braithwaite
Deputy Commissioner (Programs),
Canadian Penitentiary Service
President, American Correctional Association

1 Foundations of Corrections in America

The term "corrections" has a special meaning in the American system of criminal justice. It is used to designate the programs and the agencies which have legal authority for the custody or supervision of persons who have been convicted of a criminal act by the courts. Thus, corrections includes the jails and work camps operated by county governments for the confinement of misdeameanants. It includes prisons, large and small, which are administered through the state governments, as well as the network of institutions for youth and adults which make up the Federal Bureau of Prisons. Also included are detention homes and reformatories for juvenile offenders, and probation and parole programs through which offenders of various ages and both sexes are supervised while living in the community.

On any given day in the United States about a million and a half convicted offenders are under the control of this extensive network of agencies. Approximately three million offenders pass through the corrections system of the United States in a year. The total yearly operating budget of the agencies involved, almost all of them within federal, state or county governments, is about one and a half billion dollars. The enormous diversity and the fragmentation of the services included in American corrections is revealed in the following quotation from the report of the 1966 President's Commission on Law Enforcement and Administration of Justice:

> "Corrections," America's prisons, jails, juvenile training schools, and probation and parole machinery, is the part of the criminal justice system that the public sees least of and knows least about. It seldom gets into the news unless there is a jail break, a prison riot, or a sensational scandal involving corruption or brutality in an institution or by an official. The institutions in which about a third of the corrections population lives are situated for the most part in remote rural areas, or in the basements of police stations or courthouses. The other two-thirds of the corrections population are on pro-

bation and parole, and so are widely, and on the whole invisibly, dispersed in the community. Corrections is not only hard to see; traditionally, society has been reluctant to look at it. Many of the people, juvenile and adult, with whom corrections deals are the most troublesome and troubling members of society. The misfits and the failures, the unrespectable and the irresponsible. Society has been well content to keep them out of sight.

Its invisibility belies the system's size, complexity, and crucial importance to the control of crime. Corrections consists of scores of different kinds of institutions and programs of the utmost diversity in approach, facilities, and quality.[1]

American corrections represents one of the most controversial and volatile areas to be found in the national public policy arena. It often is asserted that corrections really does not correct most of the offenders committed to it, indeed that it further criminalizes many of them. Penal programs frequently are criticized for being brutal and dehumanizing for the inmates subjected to them. Probation and parole programs frequently are charged with leniency in their supervision of offenders, and with a failure to protect the public through rigorous controls. State legislatures often find themselves in heated debate concerning the length and severity of prison sentences, the conditions of confinement for inmates, the use of corporal punishment, the laws which govern parole and the authority of the parole board, and numerous other prickly issues which appear to be chronic dilemmas since they continually reappear in spite of persistent efforts to resolve them.

No doubt the most emotionally inflammatory issue of all is that of capital punishment in which efforts to abolish and efforts to reinstate the death penalty see-saw back and forth within many states, and most recently, in the U. S. Congress. Few would regard capital punishment as "correctional" in character, but nevertheless its administration is the responsibility of correctional officials and, like it or not, they must contend with it as a part of the environment in which they carry out their duties.

The primary purpose of this book is to describe the operations and the administration of American corrections; to illuminate its problems, needs, and dilemmas; to indicate the developmental trends and reforms which seem to point the way to an improved system in the future. Before turning to these matters, however, it may be useful to examine briefly the historical roots of the contemporary system and to identify the major philosophical movements which have influenced the development of our prisons, reformatories, probation and parole programs. Our focus will be upon American corrections, but some attention will be given to the ways in which the United States' correctional practices have been derived from other countries.

We shall be brief and selective, discussing only the historical events and philosophical positions which seem most pertinent to the situation in which American corrections finds itself today.

Historical Perspective

Primitive men, of course, did not think of crime and punishment in the legalistic and bureaucratic ways familiar to us. There were no statutory crimes, no police, no courts, no prisons, although anthropologists have discovered fascinating equivalents of these institutionalized products of modern society. Prehistoric man thought of good and evil in supernatural terms. Those who acted in a manner destructive to others tended to be viewed as possessed by evil spirits, which were "exorcised," typically by the death or mutilation of the offender.

The earliest responses to acts which we would now define as criminal took the form of efforts to exact revenge by the victim, or members of his family or his friends. As tribal societies matured, became more cohesive and developed collective norms and sanctions, there came to be more and more social controls over the revenge process. Taboos developed against permitting individuals to exact private retribution. Tribunals comprised of leaders and elders appeared to determine questions of guilt and innocence. There was concern for the formal settlement of injuries and grievances in order to break the chain of retaliatory acts, the "blood feuds" which perpetuated crimes of vengeance through generations of warring families.

The primary method through which primitive peoples responded to acts regarded as criminal was to severely punish the offender for the injuries he had inflicted upon others. The extremes of brutality, and the great ingenuity with which pain and fear were institutionalized in various forms of torture and capital punishment, make this long period of prehistory a ghastly commentary on the human propensity for cruelty, for responding to criminal deviance and terror with social controls of even greater ferocity.

Mutilation, burning, crucifixion, dismemberment, and boiling in oil are examples of a veritable encyclopedia of punishments which were administered in different periods of history and in widely disparate cultures. The unhappy victims of these retaliatory cruelties ranged from hardened recidivists to first offenders, from perpetrators of heinous to petty crimes, and included the young and the old of both sexes. For those who have an appetite for documentation of man's inhumanity to man, *The History of Capital Punishment* by John Laurence Pritchard offers informative reading.[2]

Some themes and evolutionary trends run through this period of fearsome punishment. The motivation for punishment in primitive groups often was to placate powerful spirits, to maintain the protection of capricious and potentially vengeful gods. It is a great irony that harsh punishment was so often justified by religious doctrine and, even under Christianity (as in the case of the Inquisition), administered by clerical officers.[3]

Early Reformist Approaches

Gradually the process of punishing offenders became less oriented to supernatural forces and increasingly was justified by rational argument and philosophical postulates. During the latter part of the eighteenth century a hedonistic interpretation of crime and punishment developed in England and Europe. Later designated as the "Classical School of Criminology," this highly rational point of view argued strongly against the arbitrary and unequal infliction of punishment.

Cesare Beccaria presented this position in its clearest form, maintaining that all persons who violated a particular law should receive an identical punishment. Those who belonged to the classical school believed that the pain associated with punishment should exceed the pleasure obtained from violating the law. The concept of letting the punishment fit the crime became a major basis for the legal and penological systems of the western world. It was also the major rationale for the use of imprisonment as punishment. It seemed logical that the period of incarceration could be varied to match the seriousness of the offense. To these early reformers, the prison appeared to be an humanitarian innovation of the greatest importance.

Neo-classicists made various exceptions to the basic concept, such as asserting that children and lunatics should not be punished for their crimes in the same manner as normal adults, but the classical point of view suited the needs of an increasingly rational society very well, and became the dominant frame of reference for the application of criminal punishments in the nineteenth and twentieth centuries. It also served to some extent to mitigate the excesses of brutality which characterized the earlier period. And, as we have noted, it provided ideological underpinnings for the use of incarceration in the nineteenth and twentieth centuries.

During the nineteenth century, the classical position came to be challenged by a variety of philosophical movements which shared the common feature of asserting the criminal was not wholly responsible for his acts. Although enormously varied in its explanations of criminal behavior, this so-called "Positive School of Criminology" was built upon the premises of determinism in place of the concepts of free will which supported the classical movement. Those committed to deterministic theories believed that criminal acts were determined, at least in part, by forces beyond the control of the individual who committed them. Advocates of the free-will philosophy believed that individuals have control over their own conduct and therefore are accountable for the choices they make, including decisions to commit criminal acts. Classicists and positivists often qualify their arguments in such a fashion as to reduce differences, but the underlying polarities suggested above nevertheless have tended to oppose each other in the evolution of public policy regarding the problem of crime.

Variations on the Theme

During the past two centuries the positive school of criminology has subdivided into several subordinate schools of thought which have generated as much discussion and controversy as the more fundamental argument between the concepts of free will and determinism. Cesare Lombroso and fellow Italians, Garfolo and Ferri, advanced highly specific theories which stated that there are innate differences between criminals and law-abiding persons, and that the former may be distinguished by the presence of moral and physical anomalies or "stigmata." Lombroso, for example, set forth an elaborate typology of criminals, including those who are morally insane, those who are criminals through passion and a variety of other subtypes. The great contribution of the Italian criminologists was to focus attention on the *criminal* instead of the *crime*, which had been the preoccupation of the classicists.

In the succeeding years there were many other morphological explanations of criminality, but gradually these ideas fell into disrepute and were replaced by somewhat more sophisticated and empirically based theories asserting that mental deficiency or emotional aberration constituted the predilections of criminal behavior. The literature of criminology is filled with quite elaborate propositions (and a considerable volume of research data of varying quality) to support the notion that some kind of psychic or cognitive deficiency or aberration accounts for the presence of crime in society.

Some of these theories were highly specific with regard to the relationship between a particular kind of individual defect and a particular kind of criminal behavior. Individuals who received rejection and hostility from parents and other "authority figures" were said to become pathologically angry and

5

predatory in their dealings with society. Rapists were said to reflect impotence and insecurity with females by committing their criminal acts. Alcoholic offenders were said to be immature personalities who reacted to the frustrations of life in self-destructive ways.

Other theories were gross and over-arching in nature, e.g., the argument of H. H. Goddard shortly after the turn of the last century that "feeble-mindness" as an inherited characteristic is the basic cause of criminality because of the inability of the persons so afflicted to understand the requirements of laws and to monitor their own behavior accordingly. As with so many theories of criminality, this belief that all criminals are feeble-minded and all feeble-minded persons are potentially criminal gradually gave way to contradictory evidence, here the mental testing movement which provided a factual rebuttal to Goddard's position.[4]

The positivistic school which has been most indigenous to the United States, and which exerts the greatest influence on correctional policies today, is mainly a sociological contribution to criminology. While much too large and diverse to summarize here, sociologists and social-psychologists have gathered extensive information about the incidence and characteristics of criminal behavior and have advanced a variety of theoretical explanations for crime, some of which have had clear implications for the design and management of correctional programs.

Societal Explanations

Like the earlier psychiatric and psychometric explanations of crime, sociological theories have been deterministic in the sense that they find the origin of criminal acts largely outside of the willful impulses of the individual offender. Sociologists have tended to downgrade the importance of individual pathology, aberration, or defect, and to discover the bases of crime in the cultural and social processes which influence all of us from birth. It is argued that individuals learn to become criminals just as they learn to participate in the legitimate activities of their particular social group.

Sociological perspectives on the origin of crime suggest strategies for the prevention and rehabilitation of criminal behavior which are vastly different from the theories which attribute such behavior to some form of individual defect. Sociologists, for example, have argued that the concentration of offenders within a prison creates a culture favorable to learning criminal modes of behavior, thus subverting the objectives of the correctional system. In later chapters when we describe the content of particular correctional methods and programs, it may be useful for the reader to consider the implications of these approaches for theories of crime causation. Although the connection between theories of causation and theories of intervention is seldom made explicit, almost all of those who work within the correctional field tend to operate consciously or otherwise, from some preconceptions about the cause of the criminal behavior which they are attempting to modify.

The Continued Search for Alternatives to Brutality — The Rise of Incarceration

Civilized man has had little success in his attempts to develop methods for handling criminals outside of the use of corporal and capital punishment. One approach which needs no lengthy discussion here is the banishment or transportation of offenders from their homeland to a distant penal colony. Many European countries experimented with this method in the seventeenth and eighteenth centuries. The obvious motive of "out of sight out of mind" doubtlessly inspired such experiments. Almost without exception, they were carried out under the conditions of extreme cruelty. Detailed accounts of these events reveal another wretched chapter in human misery and failure to solve the problem of criminality.

England experimented extensively with transportation of offenders, and, indeed, British use of this method reached its height during the colonization of North America. Many of our American ancestors came to this continent as convicted felons, perhaps as many as a hundred thousand. The use of "the new world" as a receptacle for rejects from British society did not end until the American Revolution in 1776. Australia served a similar purpose for the mother country.

The major alternative to corporal and capital punishment, however, has been the use of varying lengths of confinement as a punishment for criminal behavior.

American Applications

Although most of us tend to think of the prison and the reformatory as the normal and appropriate institutions for dealing with offenders, the use of this technique for sentenced offenders is relatively recent. Prior to the second half of the nineteenth century, penal institutions were used primarily to confine those awaiting trial or the imposition of corporal or capital punishment.

As we have seen, the use of incarceration as punishment had its beginnings in humanitarian efforts to avoid the extremes of brutality which had characterized earlier penalties. The Quakers must be credited with leading this movement in America (following the example of British penal reformers, notably John Howard) by making the first "penitentiary" in the new world. The Walnut Street Jail became an institution for the confinement of convicted felons within the Commonwealth of Pennsylvania in 1790. The task, which faced these early advocates of penal reform is dramatically revealed in the following description of the Walnut Street Jail a few years prior to its designation as a prison:

> It is represented as a scene of promiscuous and unrestricted intercourse, and universal riot and debauchery. There was no labor, no separation of those accused, but yet untried, nor even of those confined for debt only, from convicts sentenced for the foulest crimes; no separation of color, age or sex, by day or by night; the prisoners lying promiscuously on the floor, most of them without anything like bed or bedding. As soon as the sexes were placed in different wings, which was the first reform made in the prison, of thirty or forty women then confined there, all but four or five immediately left it; it having been a common practice, it is said, for women to cause themselves to be arrested for fictitious debts, that they might share in the orgies of the place. Intoxicating liquors abounded, and indeed were freely sold at a bar kept by one of the officers of the prison. Intercourse between the convicts and persons without was hardly restricted. Prisoners tried and acquitted were still detained till they should pay jail fees to the keeper; and the custom of garnish was established and unquestioned; that is, the custom of stripping every newcomer of his outer clothing, to be sold for liquor, unless redeemed by the payment of a sum of money to be applied to the same object. It need hardly be added, that there was no attempt to give any kind of instruction, and no religious service whatsoever.[5]

For the first time, imprisonment at hard labor became an actual alternative to harsh physical punishment, and Pennsylvania became a place for experimentation with the use of incarceration. The humanitarian spirit of the Quakers generated the belief that imprisonment in and of itself was sufficient punishment. Thus, we see again the hedonistic (pleasure-pain) philosophy, now expressed through the imposition of periods of incarceration deemed to be sufficiently painful to overcome the presumed pleasures associated with the commitment of the offense for which confinement was ordered.

The early "Pennsylvania System" of penology placed a heavy emphasis upon solitary confinement and the belief that long reflection upon past misdeeds (the "penitence" which gave rise to the term "penitentiary"), would lead to reformation and the ability to refrain from crime at the end of the period of confinement.

Although some work was required of the inmates incarcerated under this system, and certain carefully selected contacts were permitted with persons outside of the prison, the emphasis was upon the solitary confinement of each inmate within the small world of his prison cell. Obviously this early approach to the correction of offenders did not rest upon any very sophisticated ideas concerning the cause of crime, stressing instead the concept that criminal acts stem from moral and spiritual breakdown. The appropriate way to deal with such conduct was to remove the culprit from society, and place him in an austere and disciplined environment within which to meditate his way to an upright life.

This philosophy was adopted by other Pennsylvania institutions, notably the Eastern Penitentiary in Philadelphia, known locally as Cherry Hill. Here the "silent system" reached its most refined form, and a major question of public policy had to do with whether prisoners should be allowed to work within their cells or, alternatively, should be forced to spend all their time reflecting upon past misdeeds. The crusading zeal with which Pennsylvania penal leaders approached their work is well indicated in the following quotation from the *Journal of Prison Discipline and Philanthropy* published in that time:

> The thorough separation . . . must not be misunderstood . . . to mean, as has been charged, "perpetual solitude," or "total isolation from the world." It is not society in itself, or intercourse with his fellow-men that is denounced by the system, but is association and companionship with criminals, — with the depraved and wicked, — which it is believed . . . should be utterly prohibited. The social intercourse under this system, is, in point of fact, abundantly sufficient for the health, both of body and mind . . . We give them that of the virtuous, the intelligent and the good (visitors), who not only make it their business to see that they have the bodily comforts to which they are entitled; but who are desirous of promoting their reformation with a view to their own real good through the remaining term of their lives, and to securing society against renewed depredations from them after their discharge; and above all, that they may be instrumental, under the divine blessing, in bringing these poor wanderers and outcasts, into a true sense of their past sinfulness, that they may in condescending mercy, be yet brought, by repentance and amendment of life, to work out their soul's salvation.[6]

9

In the early 1800s a second major school of thought concerning the use of incarceration began to develop in American penal circles. This movement, which came to be known as the Auburn System of penology, began as an effort to follow the lead of the Pennyslvania Quakers in using confinement as an alternative to capital and corporal punishment.

Because of continuing doubts about the Pennsylvania system of solitary confinement (which was carried out in very small and dark cells) New York penologists began to experiment with congregate work programs for inmates during the day, followed by solitary confinement at night. Soon a lively argument developed between advocates of the Pennsylvania and the New York systems, with the Boston Society for the Improvement of Prison Discipline supporting the Auburn approach and opposing the Philadelphia Society's advocacy of solitary penitence.

As time went by, the Auburn system began to dominate the American scene, perhaps because of the much higher cost of building institutions which followed the Pennsylvania emphasis on individual confinement, as well as the economic advantages of a congregate inmate work program. On the other hand, European visitors who came from many countries to observe the two American experiments generally favored the Pennsylvania system and tended to incorporate it into the institutional programs of their countries. Perhaps their reactions resulted from a belief that the Pennsylvania penologists were more faithful to their "old world" mentors than were the New York innovators.

The Reformatory Movement

Following several decades of debate concerning the relative advantages and disadvantages of the two first American modes of incarceration, other ideas found their way into practice in this country, notably the so-called "Irish System" through which inmates confined on an indeterminate sentence could earn their way to release by hard work and conformity with institutional discipline.

This last philosophy formed the basis for programs of institutions established specifically for juvenile offenders and usually called "reformatories." These institutions were euphemistically referred to as schools rather than prisons, but the regime of the typical reformatory was as harsh as that of most adult prisons, and, indeed, some of the most cruel and repressive practices in the chronicles of American penology are to be found in descriptions of the handling of youthful offenders.

Thus, incarceration came to be the dominant "correctional" method in America. While originating in humanitarian revulsion concerning the brutality of earlier approaches, the prisons and reformatories built in each of the American states soon developed their own ways of punishing and humiliating those committed to them. When applied in real life, the belief that incarceration alone was sufficient failed to realize its supporters' claims. The strong custodial requirements of both the Pennsylvania and the Auburn systems tended to deprive inmates of their individuality as human beings. The efforts of guards, who were responsible for maintaining control over the offenders committed to them, usually led to harsh disciplinary codes which in turn often brought a return to rigorous physical punishment.

The Continued Search for Alternatives to Brutality—The Rise of Probation and Parole

Perhaps the most encouraging aspect in the evolution of correctional programs is the search for alternatives, not only to corporal and capital punishment, but also to the use of incarceration. Although the public tends to be preoccupied with the institutional aspect of American corrections, about two-thirds of the offenders now under correctional supervision are living in the community and are on either probation or parole.

Probation is the suspension of a criminal's sentence, conditional upon the offender observing the law and whatever specific conditions are imposed upon him by the court. It is, therefore, a genuine alternative to institutional confinement. Parole, on the other hand, is the suspension of a portion of an institutional sentence in order that the offender may be returned to his community to determine if he is able to avoid criminal activity, and as in the case of probation, observe whatever specific conditions are stipulated by the paroling authority.

Paroling has its roots in the practice of early Anglo-Saxon courts of suspending the imposition of sentences upon the assurance of the criminal that he would "keep the peace." This practice is interwoven with the historic procedure of release on recognizance and on bail. John Augustus, a Boston shoemaker, is usually credited with developing the role of the probation officer in America. In 1841, Augustus undertook to act as surety for the release of a drunkard into his care. In the following years, he performed this service for many hundreds of offenders.

The use of probation for both adult and juvenile offenders had spread to all of the states by the early 1900s, and it was made available to the federal

11

courts in 1925. Probation officers and administrators during the years between then and now have struggled with the extraordinarily difficult task of attempting to provide protection for the community through their supervision of probationers, while at the same time attempting to help and rehabilitate those same individuals.

As probation found its origin in the concept of the suspended sentence, parole grew out of the idea of the indeterminate or indefinite sentence which was inaugurated in Europe in the early 1800s and brought to America as a part of the "ticket of leave" or conditional-pardon movement around 1870. This Irish System of penology was adopted by the Elmira Reformatory in New York and subsequently was incorporated into the correctional systems of all of the states and the federal government.

Parole boards perform a quasi-judicial function in the granting and revocation of parole, and have often found themselves subject to public outrage when charged with leniency, typically when an offender released on parole commits a new crime. Since there never have been enough institutional beds to care for more than a fraction of the offenders committed to prison during the total length of their sentences, parole has long been an essential though controversial part of the correctional system of this country.

The improvement of the ability of parole boards to make wise predictions about the future behavior of offenders released on parole, and the development of more effective techniques for supervising such persons once they are released to the community, represent major challenges for the correctional system of the future.

The Philosophical Mix of Contemporary Corrections

In this first chapter, we have attempted to note some of the historical developments, the ideological and theoretical perspectives, and the individual contributions which have created the programs, techniques, and organizations which today comprise the American system of corrections. Professor Daniel Glaser has offered a classification of the major philosophical positions which may help us to obtain an overall perspective.

Glaser suggests that the ultimate purpose of all correctional activity centers around three basic ideas which have developed throughout its long history. He expresses these ideas in three words: revenge, restraint, and reform.

Revenge, as we have seen, describes the long panorama of events from prehistory to about the middle of the eighteenth century, in which retribution or retaliation was the major motivation for actions taken against those perceived as criminals. These penalities also had the subordinate purpose of deterring others from crime.

The second "R" of Restraint was the product of the classical school of criminology and was the philosophical basis for the use of incarceration to contain offenders, with the goal of helping them to adopt law-abiding attitudes and behaviors. The philosophy of Restraint also undergirded the development of probation and parole in the sense that both of these techniques seek to place some controls and establish some limits around the activities of offenders subjected to them.

The third "R" of Reform evolved out of the Positive School of Criminology and led to a great variety of efforts to rehabilitate individual offenders, whether through education, psychotherapy, vocational training, or some other method designed to remedy a defect presumed to have caused the criminal conduct. The treatment programs which developed in American prisons and reformatories in the late 1800s and early 1900s reflect this goal of seeking to reform the criminal rather than to exact revenge or restrain him from further misconduct. Probation and parole programs also are fashioned around a rationale of reform through their efforts to meet the needs and problems of individual offenders in counseling, education, job-finding, and other forms of community-based treatment.

Thus, it may be said that both institutional and community correctional programs currently represent a mosaic in which all of the three philosophical modalities mentioned above appear in varying degrees and combinations. Given these quite different and frequently contradictory goals, it is small wonder that those who administer correctional programs have been called "managers of dilemma."

Succeeding chapters of this book will reflect the authors' belief that corrections is now entering a new period, a fourth "R", which might be described as the goal or philosophy of Reintegration of offenders into the community. One feature shared by the philosophical positions described earlier is that they focus entirely upon the individual transgressor. Whether revenge, restraint, or reform was the object of public policy, there is no doubt that its target was the criminal.

The concept of Reintegration or resocialization of offenders starts from the premise that change must occur not only within the individual offender but within the social context in which he lives and seeks to adjust to the forces around him. Advocates of Reintegration assert that the power of correctional programs to produce significant change in the behavior of offenders can be vastly increased if that change is sanctioned and reinforced by other significant persons and institutions in their lives. Just as prisons have often been highly efficient in training and socializing inmates into criminal behavior, so communities (and hopefully some penal institutions, too) can be seen as networks of influence for legitimate and noncriminal patterns of behavior. In this model, then, correctional personnel must be skillful in bringing about change, not only in the offender but within his family structure, among those who relate to him as peers, and in the institutions within which he must develop successful modes of participation, i.e., the world of education, work, recreation, and neighborhood life.

Overview of the Book

This chapter has provided a broad, historical perspective on the ideas, events, and persons which have contributed to the American system of corrections. The chapters which follow focus upon particular areas of the correctional field, and particular issues which are important to corrections in its present phase of development.

Attention is given to the relationship of corrections to the other major parts of the criminal justice system, the courts, and the police. Recent efforts to divert some offenders away from the justice system and toward other types of service are discussed and appraised.

Chapters are devoted to each major segment of corrections: probation, parole, juvenile institutions, adult prisons, and the ubiquitous, still barbarous jails.

Chapters 10 and 11 treat, respectively, the organization of American corrections, and the leadership and management processes extant within the network of public organizations which makes up our correctional system.

Chapter 12 discusses the increasingly important, and controversial, subject of the legal rights of offenders who are under the control of correctional agencies.

Chapter 13 examines the political context within which corrections carries on its work, giving attention to the increasingly complex field of forces with which correctional officials must contend.

Finally, Chapter 14 looks ahead to the future of corrections in this country, attempting to extrapolate from current trends a portrait of the system as it will exist at the beginning of the twenty-first century, or thereabouts.

NOTES

[1]*The Challenge of Crime in a Free Society,* The President's Commission on Law Enforcement and Administration of Justice, Washington. D.C.: U. S. Government Printing Office, 1967, p. 159.

[2]John Laurence Pritchard, *The History of Capital Punishment,* Port Washington, New York: Kennikat Press.

[3]Harry Elmer Barnes and Negley T. Teeters, *New Horizons in Criminology,* 2nd edition, New York: Prentice Hall, 1951.

[4]Edwin H. Sutherland and Donald R. Cressey, *Criminology,* 9th edition, Philadelphia: J. B. Lippincott Company, 1970, p. 54.

[5]F. C. Gray, *Prison Discipline in America,* London: J. Murray, 1847, pp. 15–16.

[6]*Journal of Prison Discipline and Philanthropy,* 1862, p. 26.

2 Corrections as a Component of the Criminal Justice System

Corrections is one part of a set of institutional arrangements, activities, and processes which collectively are referred to as the criminal justice system. Corrections is a subsystem of the criminal justice system. Two other subsystems, law enforcement and the judicial process, operationally may be distinguished from corrections, but all three are interrelated. Although this text is concerned with corrections in the United States and therefore focuses upon probation, correctional institutions, and parole, it is important to recognize system relationships. The failure to do so in the past has been dysfunctional and has generated many of the difficulties now confronting American justice.

How are the three major subsystems of criminal justice related? Perhaps an analogy relating to America's exploration of the moon will be useful. Although it is clear that activities *on* the lunar surface — the landing, exploration of mountains and craters, setting up experiments, and lifting off for return to Earth — were the most newsworthy, dramatic, and seemingly challenging to man, these activities were but part of incredibly complicated and detailed processes which comprised the "moon exploration system." The activities on the moon may be seen as a subsystem, but there were two other significant, less attention-receiving sets of events or subsystems. These were the blast-off from Cape Kennedy and the flight *to* the moon and the return flight *from* the moon which culminated in a splash-down in the Pacific Ocean. Just as blast-off, activities on the moon, and splash-down are related, so too are the events in the criminal justice system and its subsystems. To think of law-enforcement, judicial, or correctional activities occurring in a vacuum, independent and apart from one another, is no more rational than thinking of man's exploration of space *solely* in terms of a safe return to this planet.

It is true that the justice system in America is not as orderly as the space exploration system which has taken us from this planet, but that does not make it any less of a system if by system we mean "a set or arrangement of things so related or connected as to form a unity or organic whole." It has become increasingly popular to speak and write about the "nonsystem" of criminal justice, but the "non" aspect must be related to such notions as efficiency, effectiveness, coordination, agreement as to goals and objectives, and the like; the "system" does exist, even if all of its activities are not systematic, orderly, and smooth-flowing.

It is equally true that there is not a single system of criminal justice in the United States. Each level of government, indeed each jurisdiction, has its own unique way of doing things. These many systems/subsystems, all established to enforce the standards of conduct believed necessary for the protection of individuals and the preservation of the community, are a collectivity of thousands of law-enforcement agencies and a multiplicity of courts, prosecution and defense agencies, probation and parole departments, correctional institutions, and related community-based organizations. It is clear that the American system(s) of criminal and juvenile justice sacrifices much in the way of efficiency and effectiveness in order to protect the individual and to preserve local autonomy.

The many systems of justice in existence in the United States in the 1970s are not the same as those which emerged following the American Revolution. Although American legal arrangements have traditionally tried to insure justice for all citizens, the systems have not developed or evolved uniformly or consistently or, for that matter, always in the same direction. Parts of our system, such as trial by jury and the principle of bail, are relatively old and date back to our European heritage in general and the English common law in particular, while probation and parole began in the nineteenth century, and the juvenile court is a twentieth century innovation. Some of the innovations and changes in our systems have been generated by judicial decisions and legislative enactments; others have evolved more by chance than by design.

Coupled with the numerous criminal and juvenile justice systems in the United States and their uneven development is the separation of functions within the systems. There are similar components in all systems ranging from police at input, through prosecution and courts, to correction at outgo. Although these major components and subcomponents are interwoven and interdependent one with the other, they typically function independently and autonomously. This separateness of functions, which on one hand prevents the possibility of a "police state," on the other leads to some extraordinarily complex problems. Not the least of these is that the systems of justice are not really integrated, coordinated, and effective entities, but rather are fragmented collections of agencies tied together by the processing of an increasing number of adult and juvenile offenders. They are marked by an unequal quality of justice, inadequate funding, manpower, and training resources, shortages in equipment and facilities, lack of relevant research and evaluation to provide some measure of effectiveness and, until recently, a general indifference and apathy on the part of the public which the systems were designed to serve.

These many problems notwithstanding, the criminal justice system has as its basic goals the prevention and reduction of crime. The system, fragmented though it may be and with its many imperfections, works to prevent and reduce crime in three basic ways:

deterrence: posing a threat of apprehension and consequent penalties

incapacitation: removing individuals from places where they might commit further crimes or subjecting them to supervision which makes it difficult for them to do so

rehabilitation: treatment by correctional agencies[1]

Different agencies in the justice system focus upon one or more of these techniques. The police, for example, are generally concerned with deterrence and incapacitation; corrections is concerned with rehabilitation and reintegration. Reintegration into the community on one hand and incapacitation by removal from the community on the other represent different perspectives of appropriate responses to crime and generate considerable philosophical debate and operational conflict between law-enforcement and correctional agencies as to how best to accomplish the basic goals of the justice system. Similarly, conflict may exist between courts and corrections. The courts increasingly are reviewing the internal operations and decisions of correctional institutions and paroling authorities because of concern over the rights of prisoners. Correctional and parole administrators find that they are no longer the final authority for correctional operations; their decisions and actions are subject to judicial review. These kinds of conflicts not only produce ambivalence among the citizenry but also within those legislative bodies which must make policy decisions and allocations of limited fiscal resources. Given also the lack of adequate data on the effectiveness of one approach to crime in contrast to some other, decision making about the justice system is frequently responsive to specific newsworthy incidents such as violence in an institution or the killing of a police officer—rather than to carefully calculated strategies and plans.

Aside from these conflicts over the identification of and techniques for achieving basic goals, it is possible to construct models of the criminal justice system. These models enable the viewer to examine the complicated and diverse set of activities and processes which collectively represent our efforts to address the challenge of crime. Perhaps the best-known criminal justice system model is that developed for the President's Commission on Law Enforcement and Administration of Justice (see Fig. 2-1). This model generally portrays the movement of cases through the justice system, indicates the relative volume of cases disposed of at various points in the system, and distinguishes between felonies, petty offenses, and juvenile offenses.[2]

The Commission model and other justice system flow charts are useful for they provide an overview of the justice system, but they may be misleading in that there is at least an implication that offenders move in an orderly, horizontal fashion from left to right and that the system operates both efficiently and effectively. As relates to the horizontal flow, it is clear that some offenders leave the system for reasons such as insanity or certification as to addict status, that some change the tracking patterns midway through the system, such as the juvenile offender who is certified to adult court, while others, after a successful appeal, may backtrack in the system to a new trial or resentencing. Then too, some offenders are in several "places" in the system at the same time, such as the offender who is on parole from a state institution and is concurrently confined in a local jail for a misdemeanor offense committed after release from prison.

System charts also suffer a shortcoming in that they generally do not portray the many decision makers located within the justice system and the alternatives available to these decision makers. Alternatives are everywhere: obviously, police may choose to arrest or not arrest, the district attorney may choose to prosecute or not, the jury may choose to convict or acquit, the judge to order probation, jail, or imprisonment for the convicted offender. There are many other decision makers, not as visible perhaps, who are of considerable importance in the administration of justice. Nationwide, it is certain that the identity of all the decision makers is generally not known and that the criteria for selection of alternatives throughout the system are ill-defined and often inconsistent.

Further, system charts, despite their orderliness, cannot reflect the real and potential conflicts which exist in the justice system because of the various levels of government involved in processing the criminal offender. The police are at the local, city level; the police administrator is normally appointed by city officials. The sheriff operates at the county level and is elected to office. The prosecuting attorney, public defender, and the judge may be elected or appointed and are normally county or state employees. And in corrections, the patterns of organization and the levels of government operat-

FIGURE 2–1

A General View of the Criminal Justice System

Police   Prosecution   Courts

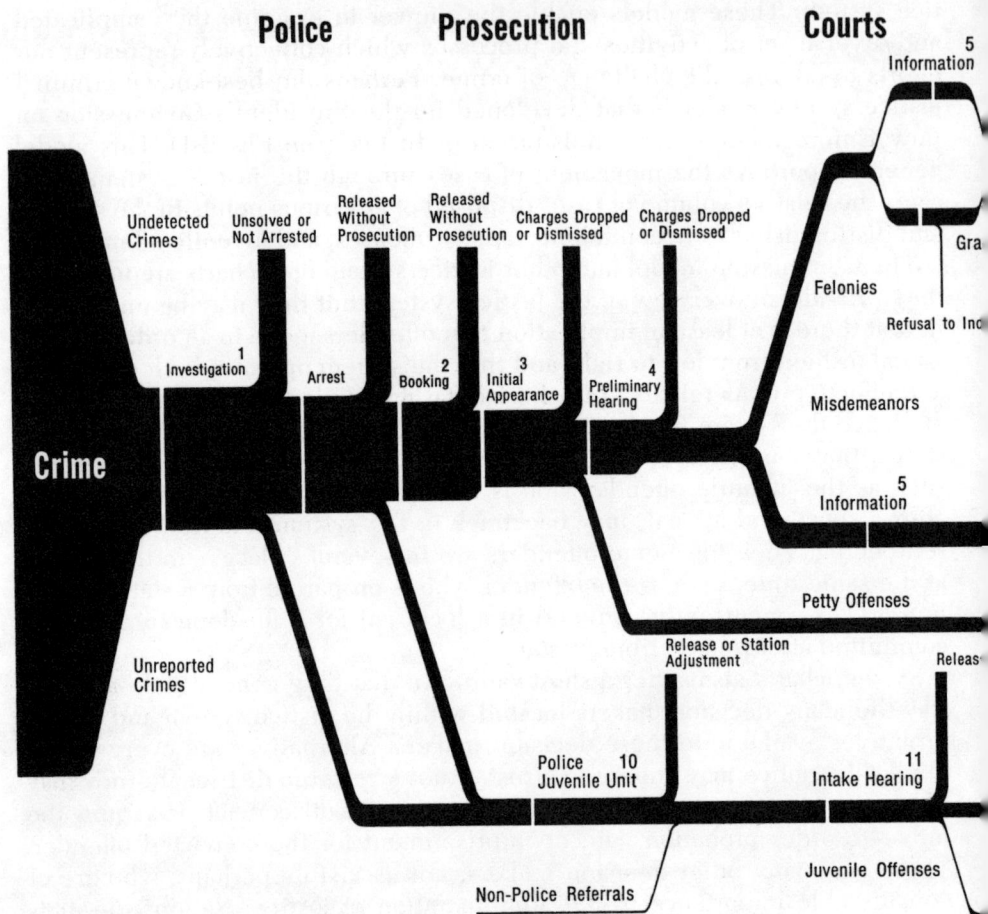

5
Information

Undetected Crimes   Unsolved or Not Arrested   Released Without Prosecution   Released Without Prosecution   Charges Dropped or Dismissed   Charges Dropped or Dismissed

Gra

Felonies

Refusal to Ind

1 Investigation   Arrest   2 Booking   3 Initial Appearance   4 Preliminary Hearing

Misdemeanors

Crime

5
Information

Petty Offenses

Release or Station Adjustment   Releas

Unreported Crimes

Police   10
Juvenile Unit

11
Intake Hearing

Juvenile Offenses

Non-Police Referrals

This chart seeks to present a simple yet comprehensive view of the movement of cases through the criminal justice system. Procedures in individual jurisdictions may vary from the pattern shown here. The differing weights of line indicate the relative volumes of cases disposed of at various points in the system, but this is only suggestive since no nationwide data of this sort exists.

Source: President's Commission on Law Enforcement and Administration of Justice, *The Challenge of Crime in a Free Society*. Washington, D.C.: U.S. Government Printing Office, 1967.

1 May continue until trial.

2 Administrative record of arrest. First st which temporary release on bail may be available.

3 Before magistrate, commissioner, or ju peace. Formal notice of charge, advice rights. Bail set. Summary trials for pe offenses usually conducted here withou further processing.

4 Preliminary testing of evidence against defendant. Charge may be reduced. No separate preliminary hearing for misder in some systems.

5 Charge filed by prosecutor on basis of information submitted by police or cit Alternative to grand jury indictment; o used in felonies, almost always in misdemeanors.

6 Reviews whether Government evidence sufficient to justify trial. Some States grand jury system; others seldom use

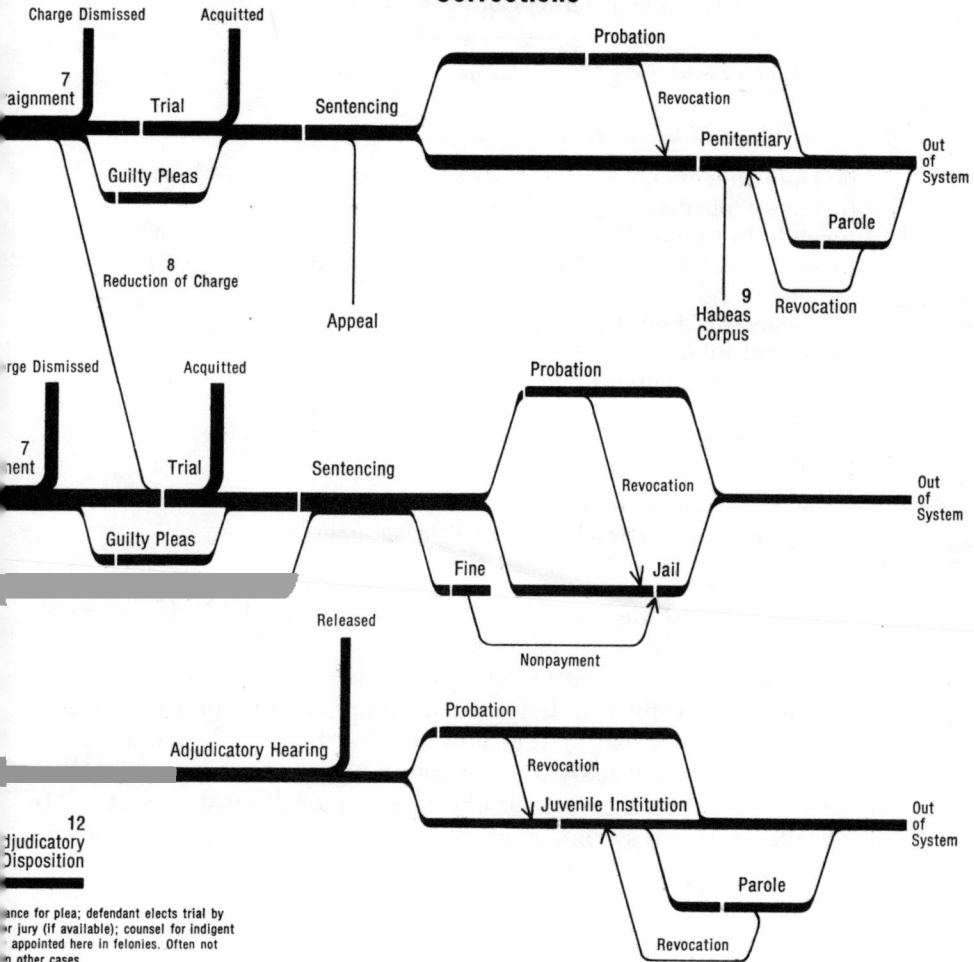

Corrections

Charge Dismissed   Acquitted

Probation

7

aignment   Trial   Sentencing

Revocation

Penitentiary   Out of System

Guilty Pleas

Parole

8
Reduction of Charge

Appeal

9
Habeas   Revocation
Corpus

rge Dismissed   Acquitted

Probability — Probation

7

nent   Trial   Sentencing

Revocation   Out of System

Guilty Pleas

Fine   Jail

Released

Nonpayment

Probation

Adjudicatory Hearing

Revocation

Juvenile Institution   Out of System

12
djudicatory
Disposition

Parole

ance for plea; defendant elects trial by
ir jury (if available); counsel for indigent
  appointed here in felonies. Often not
n other cases.

Revocation

may be reduced at any time prior to
  return for plea of guilty or for other

ge on constitutional grounds to legality
ntion. May be sought at any point in

ften hold informal hearings, dismiss or
many cases without further processing.

on officer decides desirability of further
ction.

agency, social services, counselling,
 care, etc., for cases where
atory handling not needed.

21

Level of Government Responsible
for Administering Correctional Services*

Type of Service	Local	State-Local Combination	State
Juvenile Detention	40	2	8
Juvenile Probation	24	20	6
Juvenile Institutions	0	0	50
Juvenile Aftercare (Parole)	2	5	43
Misdemeanant Probation	13	11	16
Adult Probation	11	13	26
Local Adult Institutions and Jails	43	1	6
Adult Institutions	0	0	50
Parole	0	0	50

*See Appendix III for detailed state-by-state organization.

ing correctional services are extremely diverse. The above table, for example, provides data on the level of government responsible for administering specific correctional services in the 50 states.[3]

Cooperation and coordination between agencies at different levels of government are difficult at best; system flow charts cannot reflect the dimensions of these problems. Finally, these various system diagrams cannot provide significant data on efficiency or effectiveness of the justice system. In short, the reader will find system charts to be useful in obtaining a broad picture of the justice system, but there must be unequivocal recognition that a systematic diagram does not automatically translate into an orderly, efficient, effective, or even just processing of offenders through the justice system.

Examples of System Relationships

There has been an earlier description of the justice system as a set of institutional arrangements, activities, and processes. Implicit in this perspective is the basic point that a significant change in one part of the system will produce changes in other parts. This is true, regardless of whether the change is motivated by activities within agencies of the system or external to it, such as legislative enactments. If the police, for example, increase the number of arrests, more cases may be processed by prosecuting and defense attorneys, and there may be increases in cases handled judicially and by correctional authorities. Similarly, if the courts change their sentencing patterns and thereby alter the ratio of convicted offenders ordered to community supervision or institutionalization, that change will obviously have impact on the correctional system. The changes may not occur immediately and they may impact parts of the system not directly connected to one another on a system chart. Thus, a significant increase in arrests by major law-enforcement agencies may impact upon the size and nature of the prison population in a state a year or so after the increase in police activity. Conversely, the introduction of relevant community crime-prevention programs may reduce the number of cases entering the justice system and months or years later alter the size and nature of the prison and parole populations.

From a systemwide perspective, it is clear that corrections is a recipient of offenders; it does not select them. As the National Advisory Commission on Criminal Justice Standards and Goals noted:

> Corrections inherits any inefficiency, inequity and improper discrimination that may have occurred in any earlier step of the criminal justice process. Its clients come to it from other subsystems; it is the constant heir to their defects.[4]

This phenomenon presents unique problems for corrections; if indeed the criminal justice system is the last resort for coping with social problems, it follows that corrections is the last resort for the justice system.

The relationship between corrections and the criminal justice system may also be illustrated by examining a concept called diversion. Given major impetus by the 1967 President's Commission on Law Enforcement and Administration of Justice[5] and reinforced and emphasized by the 1973 National Advisory Commission on Criminal Justice Standards and Goals,[6] diversion generally is described in one of two ways: a process which *minimizes penetration of the offender into the criminal justice system* or *as an alternative to entry into the criminal justice system*. Diversion, however defined, has long been part of the American criminal justice process. For example, if one accepts the "alternative to entry" definition, there is a long precedent of police officer discretion as relates to decisions to arrest or not arrest. Indeed, nationwide, approximately one-half of all juveniles arrested are "counseled and released" or are "handled within the department." These juveniles are clearly diverted *from* entry into the juvenile justice system, even if a majority of them are not diverted *to* some other system as an alternative.

If, on the other hand, the "minimize penetration" perspective is utilized and we view the criminal justice system as one in which offenders are sequentially arrested, charged, prosecuted, convicted, and sentenced to prison, any behavior on the part of criminal justice system personnel, be it in the law-enforcement, judicial, or correctional components, which terminates the sequence short of completion of the prison sentence could be classified as diversion. And, in fact, police frequently release offenders without arrest, prosecutors for a variety of reasons do not always prosecute, judges use probation far more often than imprisonment, and paroling authorities release prison inmates before completion of the sentences. Thus, even under the "minimize penetration" concept, diversion has long been part of our justice system heritage.

Regardless of which definition is utilized, the increased use of diversion by the agencies comprising the criminal justice system will have significant impact upon corrections. If substantial numbers of offenders are diverted by local law-enforcement to community-based agencies, there will be reduced inputs to prosecution, adjudication, and correctional agencies. Lessened inputs will alleviate some of the backlog in the judicial system and reduce caseload pressures in probation and parole and the size of institutional populations. While these occurrences are desirable, increased diversion may also leave the justice system and ultimately corrections with a unique clientele of hardened, recalcitrant, difficult offenders under supervision and in custody. These offenders may have complex problems requiring long-range treatment; they may represent a major threat to their communities; and in addition to creating major management problems, these offenders may require new and different programs, facilities, and staff for treatment. In short, extensive utilization of diversion may significantly change the justice system population and alter the system itself.

Further, diversion from the justice system implies the use of community resources—non-justice-system agencies and personnel. As programs and offenders are moved to these non-justice organizations, new organizational models and roles will be required for both justice and non-justice-system personnel. Law enforcement agencies increasingly may follow the recommendations of both the President's Commission on Law Enforcement and Administration of Justice and the National Advisory Commission on Criminal Justice Standards and Goals and create Youth Service Bureaus.[7] Traditional roles too may change. The probation and parole officer traditionally has provided individual counseling and guidance to his caseload. But as the use of diversion to community agencies increases, the probation or parole officer may be required to become a catalyst and seek to activate a community and its caretakers to absorb the offender as a member of that community. This would require a complete knowledge of community resources as well as a diagnosis of clientele needs. There would be an emphasis on reducing the alienation of the offender from his community by impairing the continued maintenance of a criminal identity and encouraging a community identity. The officer would no longer find employment for the offender, but instead would direct him into the normal channels of job seeking in the community. Residential, marital, medical, financial, or other problems would be addressed by assisting the offender to engage those community resources which deal with these problem areas. This new role, then, might be one of insuring a process of community, not correctional absorption.

Concurrent with the new role for probation and parole officers might be the increased use of volunteers, paraprofessionals, lay probation and parole advisors, new locations for and different types of correctional facilities. All of this may require, for corrections as well as other justice agencies, an additional allocation and/or reallocation of resources. And resources are all-inclusive—personnel, management and logistic support, time and money, research, administrative commitment to innovation and creativity, and a tolerance for the errors which may occur.

In summary, the student of corrections must bear in mind that probation, correctional institutions, and parole do not operate in a vacuum devoid of influences of law-enforcement and judicial agencies. And, just as corrections is influenced by actions in other parts of the justice system, so too are those other parts impacted upon by corrections. There are conflicts among these many agencies—some of them philosophical and relating to basic goals of the justice system, others quite specific and perhaps concerning individual offenses and offenders—but, and it cannot be overemphasized, the system must be seen as a totality of interdependent agencies, personnel, and programmatic activities impacting upon one another and seeking to insure justice for all.

The National Advisory Commission on Criminal Justice Standards and Goals devoted the first chapter of its report on Corrections to "Corrections and the Criminal Justice System."[8] Because of the importance of recognizing and understanding the relationship of corrections to the total justice system, that chapter is reproduced in its entirety as Appendix I.

NOTES

[1]*Task Force Report: Science and Technology*, The President's Commission on Law Enforcement and Administration of Justice, Washington, D.C.: U.S. Government Printing Office, 1967, p. 55.

[2]Reprinted from *The Challenge of Crime in a Free Society,* The President's Commission on Law Enforcement and Administration of Justice, Washington, D.C.: U.S. Government Printing Office, 1967, pp. 8–9.

[3]*Corrections,* National Advisory Commission on Criminal Justice Standards and Goals, Washington, D.C.: U.S. Government Printing Office, 1973, pp. 610–14.

[4]*Ibid.,* p. 5.

[5]See, for example, *The Challenge of Crime in a Free Society,* pp. 78–89 and *Task Force Report: Juvenile Delinquency and Youth Crime,* The President's Commission on Law Enforcement and Administration of Justice, Washington, D.C.: U.S. Government Printing Office, 1967, pp. 396–99.

[6]*Corrections,* pp. 73–97 and *Courts,* National Advisory Commission on Criminal Justice Standards and Goals, Washington, D.C.: U.S. Government Printing Office, 1973, pp. 27–41.

[7]*The Challenge of Crime in a Free Society,* pp. 78–89 and *Community Crime Prevention,* National Advisory Commission on Criminal Justice Standards and Goals, Washington, D.C.: U.S. Government Printing Office, 1973, pp. 51–83.

[8]*Corrections,* pp. 1–14.

3 Correctional Institutions for Delinquent Youth: An Overview

This chapter is devoted primarily to a general discussion of *public* institutions serving delinquent children and younger adolescents. These facilities are of two major classifications depending upon their principal purposes. There are those for the temporary confinement of juveniles while awaiting further dispositions. The second general classification of juvenile institutions are those to which boys and girls are committed by order of a juvenile court. The latter have been called reform schools, correctional schools, or by other less descriptive designations.

Since corrections as a part of the criminal justice system is the focus of this text, no effort will be made to cover numerous kinds of public residential schools, such as those for the mentally retarded, the deaf, and the blind. Neither will we discuss the related and sometimes overlapping subject of residential institutions and schools for the homeless, neglected, or otherwise socially, educationally, or psychologically maladjusted juveniles who by legal definitions are not delinquent.

The term "juvenile delinquency" has such widespread use in contemporary writings that it has taken on many meanings. In the context of corrections, these two words require more precise definition. A juvenile is a young person who has not yet reached his or her majority. In most states of the United States this will mean persons who have not yet reached their eighteenth birthday. In terms of the law governing responsibility for one's unlawful behavior the division point between those whom the law treats as juveniles and those treated as responsible adults varies from state to state.[1] In some states, it is the sixteenth, in others the seventeenth, and in still others, the eighteenth birthday. Expressed in more specific terms, if a young person commits a delinquent act which would be defined as a crime if the person were an adult, he will be treated as an adult if he has passed his six-

27

teenth birthday in New York State, his eighteenth in California, and seventeenth if he is in Texas or Illinois.

The term "delinquent act" in this context is a legal expression. It means an illegal act which, if committed by a person older than the age at which adult responsibility is established by law, would be a crime. It is often a matter of chance, however, whether an individual juvenile presented to the juvenile court is actually labeled a delinquent or a dependent or a neglected child. As a consequence, many of the boys and girls found in correctional institutions are not delinquents by the above legalistic definition.

The legal philosophy of the juvenile court is expressed by the Latin phrase *parens patriae.* In effect, this means that the court may substitute itself in a sense for a responsible parent or guardian and may choose to make any child who is dependent or neglected a ward of the court in order to provide supervision and protection for the child. This being the case, it has not been uncommon in many jurisdictions for juveniles who have been charged with delinquent acts to be mixed somewhat indiscriminately with nondelinquents in the populations of public correctional institutions.

Neglected and dependent children are normally made the responsibility of welfare agencies. Delinquent juveniles normally become the responsibility of correctional agencies which may include juvenile probation departments, local juvenile detention homes, and special institutions for delinquents, whether they be operated by cities, counties, or states. Despite these general statements, there is great variability in actual practice from one political subdivision of government to another as to where responsibility for the care and treatment of the juvenile is placed. Generally speaking, the leadership in the juvenile justice field opposes the formal commitment of any juvenile to a correctional institution, unless that juvenile had been made a ward of the juvenile court because of a delinquent act. A document entitled *Institutions Serving Delinquent Children—Guides and Goals,* has this to say on the subject:

> Only children who have been officially adjudicated "delinquent" should be committed to training schools for delinquents.
> Although certain things are true of all delinquent children, it cannot be said too often that there is no uniform personality type to which all or most so-called "delinquent" children belong.[2]

Recent trends in most jurisdictions in the United States are strongly away from committing juvenile delinquents to institutions unless there appears to be no workable alternative or unless there is a clear need to take this course in the interest of public protection as well as for the protection of the child. This trend is especially evident for the younger delinquents.

Historical Development

In our early history when the populations of the colonial settlements were small, the placement of neglected and delinquent children in foster homes or in houses run by private agencies, usually with a religious orientation, was the prevalent practice. "Binding out" or indenturing of neglected children to persons, families, or private societies was a common practice inherited from England. As the size of the settlements increased and cities developed, "houses of correction" and "work houses" were established. In the earlier years, however, there was little effort made to separate children from adults, the mad from the sane, the convicted from the unconvicted, or even the men from the women.

Since children naturally elicit more public sympathy than adults these were the first to be separated from the unclassified rabble of the socially neglected or unwanted. The first institutions for juvenile delinquents were generally referred to as "reform schools." The word "reform" obviously has a religious connotation, but it is equally obvious that from the outset these institutions, while falling far short of what we would consider decent standards today, had as their objective the reform, rehabilitation, and social reintegration of their wards.

In the beginning, there was no clear differentiation between the delinquent and the neglected and dependent child. The forerunners of nineteenth and twentieth century American juvenile reformatories had their inception mainly in philanthropic enterprises. It was not until after the first quarter of the nineteenth century that governments began to take over the responsibility by erecting and operating public institutions which we have more recently begun to refer to as correctional training schools for juveniles. The first such institution, known as the "House of Refuge for Delinquents" was opened in New York City in 1825, under the management of a private society. This facility went through numerous stages of development and was not finally abandoned until 1935. Following the lead of New York, other states followed in rapid succession. By 1866 twelve states had erected juvenile reformatories and nine others had institutions referred to as "houses of refuge."

By 1972 each of the fifty states, the federal government, the District of Columbia, the Commonwealth of Puerto Rico, and the Virgin Islands all had some kind of an institution or institutions for the care and training of juvenile delinquents. They are listed in the *National Directory of Public Training Schools Serving Delinquent Children* issued by the U.S. Department of Health, Education, and Welfare, under numerous names, such as Training School for Boys, Residential Group Center, State Industrial School, Forestry Camp, or by less descriptive names, such as Children's Village, School for Boys, Jubilee Lodge, and Pines Ranch.

Incidence of Juvenile Delinquency — Perspectives and Indicators

The literature of juvenile delinquency is replete with estimates and speculation concerning the amount of delinquent behavior by the 10- to 17-year age group in the population. Besides the recorded arrests, petitions filed, and court commitments, there are literally millions of delinquent acts committed each year which either are not recorded or which never come to the attention of the authorities at all and, therefore, do not appear in any public records. In order to discuss the American correctional training school in perspective, it is necessary to know something about the total juvenile population and to understand the route by which a limited number of that population finds its way into such facilities.

Since most of the clientele for these institutions will come principally from the 14- to 17-year age group, it is interesting to note that this component of the population of the United States has been growing steadily in recent years. In 1960 it was 11,411,000; in 1965, 14,164,000; and in 1970, 15,900,000. The National Center for Educational Statistics forecasts that this population will increase by 1975 to 16,918,000, and that it will reach a peak of 16,922,000 in 1977, and will then begin a gradual decline, falling to 15,791,000 in 1980. We may conclude, then, that the eligible age population which feeds the juvenile justice system will not begin to decrease significantly in the 1970–1980 decade.

It is not the intent of this discussion to attempt to engage in a sophisticated exercise in forecasting the incidence of juvenile delinquency, but for those who would like to delude themselves that the problem will go away in the near future, it is important to understand how improbable such an event is. There are some indicators, as a matter of fact, which might cause one to expect an increase in the phenomenon of juvenile delinquency for reasons other than the numbers in the young age group in the population. For example, the widespread use of narcotic and psychedelic drugs and of alcohol by the young is having and will continue to have the effect of increasing the incidence of delinquency. The failure of our society to deal promptly and constructively with the minority group ghettos of the inner cities is another negative indicator. The increased participation of women and girls in the economic life and their increasing freedom of movement and behavior is already causing an increase in the participation of the female sex in criminal and delinquent behavior. This can probably be expected to grow rather than decrease for some time to come.

The most extensive and thorough study made so far on the extent of juvenile delinquency is reported in the book entitled *Delinquency in a Birth Cohort* by Wolfgang, Figlio, and Sellin.[3] This cohort is made up of all of the boys born in 1945, who lived in Philadelphia from their tenth to eighteenth birthdays. The boys were traced through school records of the nearly ten thousand making up the cohort. In their juvenile careers 35 percent of them incurred one or more police contacts. This delinquent group was further subdivided into single offenders, multiple offenders, and chronic offenders. About 50 percent of the juveniles who committed a single offense, according to the records, later committed a second one. It was found that 18.7 percent of the total cohort had committed two or more delinquent acts. On the other hand, most of them did not continue with delinquent behavior, but 6.3 percent were identified as chronic, repetitive offenders. Extrapolating from this finding, one could postulate that every sixteenth boy born in each year will become a chronic juvenile delinquent.

Assuming a peak of slightly less than 17 million teenage children in the 14- to 17-year group in 1976, of which approximately one-half (8½ million) will be boys, and accepting the Philadelphia study findings as representative of the nation, it can be estimated that we will have in the population of the country nearly three million adolescent boys, each of whom will commit one or more delinquent acts, known to the police before they are 18 years old. Perhaps even more important than this is the fact that 6.3 percent of these boys, or 189,000, will be chronic habitual offenders. It is principally from this group that the juvenile justice system will select the temporary residents of the country's correctional institutions. The importance of these facts is further emphasized when one realizes that it is from this same group that most of the adult criminal population is recruited.

No birth cohort study of delinquency among girls has ever been made. Delinquency among adolescent girls appears to be on the increase in recent years, but there are some significant differences between the delinquency of boys and girls. Girls commit fewer offenses than boys. Their delinquent behavior tends to be less violent and a great many of their acts resulting in arrests are committed either in concert with male associates or are drug or sex involved. Girl delinquents are more often than not runaways whose behavior involves irregular sexual conduct. They differ from the male delinquents in another significant way—very few of them become adult criminals.

Arrests and Dispositions

Arrest records of juveniles can be very misleading, because many police contacts are not recorded as arrests. Petitions filed in the juvenile courts are likewise misleading because most of the decisions with respect to the disposition of minor cases are made without the case ever reaching that point.

The Bureau of Criminal Statistics in California reports that in 1972 there were 353,232 arrests of juveniles. Of these, 155,249 were released by the police, and slightly less than 200,000 were referred to the probation departments for further processing. Out of this number, only 47,754 petitions were filed in the juvenile court. Of these 14,000 were dismissed by the juvenile court, and about 500 were remanded to adult courts to be tried as adults. About 29,000 were declared wards of the court, and only 1,460 of them were committed to the California Youth Authority to be placed in state correctional institutions.

The 1972 Uniform Crime Reports issued by the FBI for 2,430 police agencies in the United States report the following:

Total arrests of boys under 18 years of age   786,418
Total arrests of girls under 18 years of age   224,669

Hence, expressed in rounded numbers, for each girl arrested, three boys were taken into police custody. In 1972, 27 percent of all arrests were of persons under 18 years of age.[4] It also appears that youth crime has been increasing faster than total crime.[5] One should be cautioned again that crime statistics are hard to interpret, and those concerning juveniles are especially subject to misinterpretation. Recording varies as do police practices from one jurisdiction to another. Furthermore, it is generally known that such statistics as are available tend to be racially and economically skewed, because middle and upper class delinquency tends to be handled on an informal basis and not recorded in any official records.

In 1971, 1,125,000 juvenile delinquency cases, excluding traffic offenses, were handled by 2,900 juvenile courts.[6] About 58 percent of these were disposed of without filing formal petitions.[7] Since the famous *Gault* decision, 387 U.S. 1, in 1967, there has been more formality introduced into juvenile court proceedings with a related increase in the number of actual petitions filed.

These figures indicate quite clearly that the system from arrest to disposition cycles out most of the cases before they get to the point of commitment to a correctional institution. To recapitulate, there are in the United States over 1,000,000 persons under 18 years of age arrested by the police each year, as indicated by the published statistics for the first part of the 1970–1980 decade. In 1971 the total admissions to training schools, ranches and camps, halfway houses, and group homes were about 85,000.[8] Recognizing the probable inaccuracies of both the arrest and commitment figures, it is nevertheless safe to say that only about 8 percent of the juveniles arrested are committed to residential institutions. The California figures indicated that about 4 percent of juvenile arrests are so committed in that state.

At this writing in 1974, some states[9] are making positive efforts to eliminate entirely the large centralized state operated correctional institutions and to substitute for them greater use of probation, local camps and schools, halfway houses, and group homes. There is no reason to suppose, however, that some institutional care for adjudicated delinquents will disappear from the American scene in the foreseeable future.

Temporary Detention Facilities[10]

Institutions for the temporary detention of juveniles pending disposition are not so much correctional institutions as they are shelters for juveniles who have been apprehended by the police for any reason, ranging on the one hand from running away from home, abandonment by parents and uncontrolled incorrigiblity to the commission of serious offenses, like burglary, arson, assault, and homicide on the other. The former are often referred to as PINS or MINS meaning "persons (or minors) in need of supervision." Many of the PINS group are disposed of informally by the police, probation officers, or welfare agencies without being referred to the juvenile court. In those cases in which no suitable placement can be found immediately the boy or girl may be referred to the court with the possibility of making the case a ward of the court and arranging placement with some public agency or a private charity.

Juveniles arrested and charged with delinquent acts which would have been crimes had the offenders been adults present a somewhat different problem as far as temporary detention is concerned. Some are released to the custody of parents or guardians after police booking, but there are always a few whose behavior and personal circumstances are such that confinement pending disposition seems imperative as a measure of public protection or to prevent the offender from absconding before the probation staff and the court can review the case. In well-organized jursidictions the decision to detain more than a few hours pending a court hearing will be made by an intake officer who is usually a member of the probation staff and the residential facility will usually, but not always, be under the administrative jurisdiction of the probation department. These juvenile detention facilities are somewhat analogous to the local jails in the adult system. Unlike the jails, however, they usually are not managed by a police agency such as the county sheriff.

Unfortunately, there are many hundreds of counties in America that are too small to maintain separate facilities for juvenile detention. As a consequence, the available alternative too often is the county jail. Most states have laws prohibiting the comingling of persons under 18 years of age with adults in such jails, but when there are often only from none to half a dozen persons of both sexes confined at a time, it is easy to understand the temptation to jail managers to ignore the law.

Of the 722 juvenile facilities in the United States on June 30, 1971, 303 were detention centers, 18 were small temporary shelters, and 17 were reception or diagnostic centers.[11] With 3,020 counties in the United States and only 338 facilities for the temporary detention of juveniles it is apparent that probably less than 10 percent of the counties in the country have access to suitable facilities for the temporary detention of that small proportion of juveniles requiring this kind of service. Fortunately, the average length of stay in temporary care facilities for juveniles is short. The 1971 census[12] reported the average to be 14 days.[13]

According to the *National Jail Census* there were 7800 juveniles confined in American jails in March, 1970. This practice is widely condemned but continues to persist.

Contemporary Correctional Facilities for Adjudicated Delinquents

In 1972 there were 384 public training schools for delinquent boys and girls in the United States. As of June 30, 1971, there were 42,642 children in residence in these schools, of which 8,430 were girls.[14] Many of these schools are coeducational, especially for the ages under fifteen. Somewhat less than half are operated under the auspices of some agency of state government, a few under public school systems, and another substantial number under the jurisdiction of country and city governments. For example, the Los Angeles County Probation Department, besides operating a number of juvenile detention homes, also maintains 10 camps and schools operating with capacities just under 100 residents each.

Nationally, the state schools have varying capacities ranging from as few as 18 or 20 to as high as 500 or 600. Juvenile correctional schools for wards under 18 years of age are generally considered much too large if they exceed 400, and the present preference seems to be for total institutional capacities of 100 to 300 with recommended individual living units of not more than 20. In 1971 a national survey[15] indicated that 60 percent of the 192 training schools had designed capacities of 150 or more. In contrast, however, fully one-third of all public juvenile institutions has authorized space for fewer than 25 persons.

The current trend, as we noted earlier, is against any more institutionalization of committed juvenile delinquents than is absolutely necessary. The thrust of change is toward small institutional units with less than 100 capacity located in metropolitan areas as near as possible to the neighborhoods in which the families of the wards reside.

Length of Institutional Stay in Institutions for Committed Delinquents

The law usually permits the confinement of adjudicated juvenile delinquents in correctional institutions until they reach the age of majority and sometimes even longer. The national survey previously quoted reports that the average length of stay in training schools in the fiscal year 1971 was 8.7 months, 7.2 months in halfway houses and group homes, and 6.6 months in ranches and camps. There is great variability around these norms. Some cases may spend only a few weeks in custody pending a more appropriate placement, while others may be retained for many months or even several years. The practice in this regard varies considerably from one jurisdiction to another also.

The authority to release wards from the institutions is provided by law in many different ways in the various jurisdictions. Sometimes the power to authorize a discharge or parole is vested in the committing court; sometimes the superintendents of institutions have such power; sometimes there is a commission or authority similar to an adult parole board; sometimes the power is vested in the commissioner or director of the public agency of which the institution is a part.

Most jurisdictions provide for some degree of supervision of cases after release and for the power to recommit releasees if public protection or the needs of the individual warrant it. The 1971 national survey reports that of the 67,558 total admissions to training schools, 12,556 were returnees from aftercare/parole.

The discretionary power of the releasing authority over the lives of delinquent inmates and parolees is very great indeed. There is a growing concern over the possibilities for abuse of power or of unreasonable disparities in these decisions from time to time and place to place. The need for criteria to guide these decision makers is recognized by most students of the problem. Such factors as behavior and attitude within the institution, the estimated probability of the ward committing another serious offense, the availability of an appropriate home for the ward upon release, of a program of education or work, and other factors having to do with the ward's personality, and the environment in which he must live when released are matters to be considered.

Unfortunately, because most correctional training institutions, especially for older boys, have been grossly overcrowded, it should come as no surprise that institution adminstrators are often torn between the conflicting issues of readiness for release on the part of the wards and availability of space for incoming wards. Hence, it sometimes happens that many cases are pushed out by population pressure rather than released on the basis of good professional judgment. Conversely, when a institution is substantially below its optimum operational quota there is sometimes a tendency to keep cases a few months longer than they would ordinarily be kept, either for disciplinary reasons or because professional staff people would like to see the ward complete some program on which he has embarked.

Since no one has established with any degree of scientific certainty what the optimum length of institutional stay of a given classification of wards is, it is understandable that the subjective conclusions of administrators and parole boards may be as much influenced by practicalities of administration as by professional judgment.

There also has crept into the administration of public training schools for delinquents more than a little of the philosophy and practice of adult prison systems where punishment is measured in terms of length of institutional incarceration. As a consequence, a 15-year-old juvenile who has been involved with adults in an armed robbery, but who has no previous delinquency record, may well be kept a much longer time than another boy of the same age who has a long record of petty theft, shoplifting, and car stealing, but whose instant offense is a minor burglary.

In any event, aside from the manner in which the decisions to release are made, when that decision is arrived at in a given case it is the responsibility of the management of the central system and of the institution to help the ward and his parents or guardians to make a plan for release which should involve at the very least a place of residence, a means of support, and a program of education or work.

After release, a good system will provide for supervision by a case worker whose responsibility should be to see that the release plan is carried out or modified in a rational fashion, and also to make sure that the released ward conforms to the conditions laid down for his release. Generally speaking, these conditions of release include, above all else, that the ward refrain from criminal and delinquent behavior, that he make himself available to his after-care supervisor, that he not abscond from the jurisdiction, and that he make a serious effort to carry put the program which he agreed upon when he was released.

Age and Sex of Residents of Training Institutions for Juveniles

The 1971 census[16] of juvenile facilities revealed an amazingly wide range of ages among their residents. One should not be surprised to find that 25 percent of the temporary care centers had boys and girls under 8 years of age, but to some it may seem incredible that 8 percent of 141 training institutions for boys had some residents under 8, and 31 percent had cases under 11. Conversely, 7 percent of these same schools had male residents 21 and older, and 46 percent had some between 18 and 20 years of age.

The national census did not provide an actual age distribution of the resident populations of the institutions surveyed. Neither did it address the question of the ages of the boys and girls at the time of admission. In order to give the reader a better idea of the age distribution at first admissions to a single system the following table is reproduced from the 1973 annual report of the California Youth Authority.

It is worthy of special note that of 1296 boys received from the juvenile courts, only 22 were under 14 years of age, and of the 158 girls received there were no 12-year-olds and only six 13 year-olds. The mean age of the boys was 16.2 years, and of the girls 16.6.

In California, a very severe screening process occurs from the time of apprehension by the police to an eventual commitment to a state correctional school. In 1972 out of each 1,000 juvenile felony level arrests, only 11 were committed to a correctional school under the jursidiction of the California

Age at Admission of First Commitments Placed Under Youth Authority Custody by the Juvenile Court
1973

Age at Admission	Total		Males		Females°	
	Number	Percent	Number	Percent	Number	Percent
12 years	2	0.1	2	0.2	---	---
13 years	26	1.8	20	1.5	6	3.7
14 years	97	6.6	76	5.9	21	9.4
15 years	261	17.8	223	17.2	38	17.0
16 years	452	30.8	398	30.6	54	24.2
17 years	527	36.0	488	37.7	45	20.2
18 years	96	6.6	86	6.6	23	10.3
19 years	3	0.3	3	0.3	20	9.0
20 years	---	----	---	---	10	4.5
21 years or over	---	----	---	---	6	2.7
Totals	1,454	100.0	1,296	100.0	158	100.0

°Juvenile and Criminal Courts

Youth Authority. Three others, all over 17 years of age, had committed such serious offenses that the juvenile court signed a waiver of jurisdiction and turned them over to a criminal court to be tried as adults.

Correctional institutions for juvenile delinquents are often criticized because substantial numbers of their graduates later become adult criminals and are committed to prison. This is not so surprising when one realizes what a small proportion of delinquent juveniles are actually committed to state correctional institutions.

Systems of Correctional Schools for Juveniles

State Government Patterns

Every state in the United States has within the framework of state government at least one correctional training school for juvenile delinquents. If there are only two such schools, usually one will be for boys and the other for girls. There is a growing tendency to operate some schools on a coeducational basis. Some of the more populous states like California, Florida, New York, and Texas have a diversity of separate institutions operated by the state governments. The state authority responsible for the general management of these facilities often has been a board of trustees appointed for terms by the governor. This governing body will usually be authorized by law to appoint the director of the system, and generally to act somewhat like a board of directors of a corporation. This organizational pattern is being discontinued rapidly. The current trend is toward a single statewide administrator, usually appointed by the governor of the state.

This administrator, who may be known by the title of director, commissioner, or some other appropriate designation, sometimes heads a separate agency of state government or more often this youth agency is a division of a larger one. In Minnesota, the Division of Youth Conservation is a part of the State Department of Corrections, which has overall responsibility for adult prisons, reformatories, and parole services, as well as those for youthful offenders. In Wisconsin, the Division of Corrections is a part of an overall Department of Health and Social Services, and Youth Services is a subdivision of the Division of Corrections. In California, the Department of the Youth Authority has the status of a separate department but is part of a cabinet level agency known as the Health and Welfare Agency. In New York, the Division for Youth is a relatively independent agency, and is a division of the executive department which at least nominally is headed by the governor. In Texas, the State Youth Services is under the jurisdiction of a board (Texas Youth Council) which is appointed by the governor, and which in turn appoints the director. In Florida, the Division of Youth Services is a part of an overall agency known as the Department of Health and Rehabilitative Services, and the director is appointed by the governor.

In the changes taking place in many of the states, it appears that the trend is in the direction of consolidating state youth services as a division of a department of correctional services. In addition to this trend, there is another one which involves the establishment, especially in the larger jurisdictions, of "umbrella" agencies which incorporate a number of departments having like or related services and responsibilities. For example, all the state "people serving" departments are placed in an agency at the cabinet level under some such title as "health and welfare agency." This agency would tend to include, in addition to youth and adult corrections, such departments as public health, health care services, mental hygiene, public welfare, and vocational rehabilitation. Parallel with this kind of consolidation there will usually be several other clusters of departments. Under this plan each umbrella agency made up of a cluster of departments will be headed by a cabinet level administrator.

Local Government Patterns

Because of the historical evolution of our increasingly urbanized and industrialized society, many of the correctional services for juveniles tended in the past to develop first at the local rather than the state levels of government. As a consequence, many cities and counties encompassing large metropolitan populations developed institutions of their own before the state governments recognized the need or were willing to provide the necessary financial support. For example, while the Missouri Department of Corrections maintains five correctional training schools and camps for juvenile delinquents, Kansas City maintains three facilities and several group homes under the general jurisdiction of the Juvenile Division of the 16th Judicial Circuit Court. The city of St. Louis maintains a training school for boys and one for girls under the jurisdiction of the Department of Children's Services. The state of California, on the other hand, operates some 16 separate institutions, reception centers, and camps, but the probation departments in California's 58 counties operate more than 50 separate facilities for delinquent boys and girls.

There is still another pattern found in some states, like Pennsylvania, where the State Department of Public Welfare maintains nine juvenile training schools under various names, but, in addition, there are three other schools under private management which are subsidized either by state or county government.

The Central Administration of a Juvenile Correctional System

In spite of the great diversity of organizational patterns for the administration of juvenile correctional training facilities, there appears to be an emerging consensus among progressive leaders in the field that responsibility for the administration of these facilities and programs should be vested in a single, competent, professional administrator appointed and holding office without regard to partisan political affiliation. Placing the management function of these highly sensitive and complex facilities and programs under a part-time lay board of trustees is contrary to contemporary administrative theory. The lay board appointed by the governor or other elected executive has little or no validity except as a somewhat ineffective device for protecting the appointed administrator from direct political interference. On the other hand, it is as likely to have the effect of keeping in office a person who ought to be removed as of preventing an able and competent adminstrator from being replaced because of political patronage. In addition to this, one should always be mindful that the governor and the legislature hold the trump cards in any event, because of their control of the budget.

In spite of the objections to an administrative board with power to make policy and to hire and fire personnel, there is much to be said for advisory committees of citizens serving on a nonpaid basis who are in a position to render both advice and support to the single administrator whose power and authority derives from the law and the appointing power which he serves.

The administrator in charge of the central administrative functions of a system containing training schools for juveniles will normally have certain powers and responsibilities vested in him by the statutes as follows:

1. He will be the appointing power of all personnel, including the superintendents of institutions in the system, and will be free to delegate some of these responsibilities to subordinate officers if he chooses to do so.

2. Court commitments of wards will be made to the care and custody of the director of the central agency and not to specific institutions.

3. He will have the authority and the responsibility for classifying wards and assigning them to such institutions and programs as are indicated on a basis of the needs of individual wards and the resources available in the department.

4. He will have the authority and responsibility to establish basic policies within the framework of the law for the management of the institutions under his jurisdiction.

5. He will be expected to formulate and publish guidelines and rules and regulations concerning all important functions coming under his general purview.

6. He will be empowered to employ specialized, functional staff to assist him in carrying out his duties.

7. He will be responsible for developing the annual (or biennial) budget for the entire operation and for justifying its provisions to the fiscal authorities of his administration and to the legislative body.

8. He is in effect responsible for carrying out all laws relating to his responsibilities, keeping appropriate records, and for being the person ultimately responsible for the guidance of personnel under his jurisdiction and for the care and welfare of wards committed to his custody.

This kind of clear-cut administrative arrangement is still not widely prevalent, except in the very large and populous states. For an analysis of state laws on this subject, see *Juvenile Delinquency: A Comparative Analysis of Legal Codes in the United States*, by Rosemary Sarri and Mark M. Levin.

Diversification of Institutions

In a small jurisdiction having only one correctional training school for juveniles, all functions of reception, classification, care and treatment and other appropriate program elements are of necessity carried out on the premises of one facility. Many jurisdictions, on the other hand, as has been previously indicated, have a variety of institutional facilities. In those jurisdictions where this is the case the general practice is to provide different kinds of programs in different institutions for different classifications of wards. The first most common subdivision is on a basis of sex, providing one institution for the boys and one for the girls, or sometimes two for boys and one for girls. For the younger wards, especially those under 15 years of age, it is becoming increasingly common to operate coeducational training schools with boys and girls participating in the same general programs and separated only in the actual living quarters.

Beyond these rather rudimentary bases for diversifying facilities within the system, the next most common breakdown is by age. In boys' institutions in particular, where some juvenile court wards are sometimes kept in custody until age 21, there are very valid reasons for separating the more mature boys over 17 years of age from those younger. The older ones are actually young men rather than children. In addition to this, the older ones are often those who have been returned one or more times as parole violators and may have become by all practical standards sophisticated young criminals or are grossly maladjusted personalities. To mix these youths with immature boys between 13 and 16 years of age may be damaging to the younger ones, not only because of the undesirable influence of the older boys, but also the older ones are stronger and often exploit the younger ones in many undesirable ways.

In addition to diversification by age, it is important to point out that in every delinquent population as highly selected as this institutional population is, there tends to be a disproportionate number of personality deviates who ought to be under the management, care, and treatment of highly specialized personnel. Some of these deviates may already be well-developed sex perverts, individuals who have occasional psychotic episodes, or others who are so alienated to normal human associations that they cannot live successfully in a group without engaging in violent behavior. In addition to these, there will be a few individuals who defy classification. They are neither sane nor insane. They may be normal in most aspects but abnormal in some specific kind of behavior. As a consequence, in a large system there is a need for a small specialized institution for these kinds of deviated personalities, or they might be transferred to a special division of the mental hospital system. Another alternative is to provide in one of the regular training schools in the system a specialized branch especially designed and staffed for the care, treatment, and management of this very difficult group of wards. A great many of the scandals growing out of the mistreatment or alleged mistreatment of wards arises from the fact that the system has not provided in a professional and intelligent manner for dealing with this extraordinarily difficult group of young people.

A few jurisdictions have followed at least to some extent a very different pattern of diversification from that indicated in the paragraphs above. Instead of diversified institutions on the basis of age, sex, and personality classification, institutions have been established in various parts of the state or of a large county to serve different geographical areas. There are some arguments in favor of the latter approach; the principal one being that of keeping children near their families and communities rather than shipping them off, sometimes hundreds of miles away from home. This argument has validity, however, only for that part of the institutional population which is made up of reasonably normal children. In a very large state system some combination of the two approaches is desirable.

There should always be provision in the statutes for removing from the populations of the training schools individuals who obviously should have been subjected to some alternative disposition. For example, from time to time, a boy or a girl who has been made the ward of the juvenile court for some delinquent act and has not been adequately diagnosed at the intake level turns out to be so mentally retarded that a more appropriate disposition would have been commitment to an institution for the mentally retarded. Occasionally, one of these young people may be found to be psychotic and should have been placed in a mental hospital. There even have been rare cases of children who for all functional purposes are blind and whose behavior is more related to their bad eyesight than their delinquency. It is obviously not possible for a system of institutions designed to deal with ordinary delinquent behavior to establish specialized facilities or programs for all of these unusual cases that have been misdiagnosed and misunderstood. The law usually provides either for the return of such wards to the committing court for an alternative disposition or the administrator of the system may be empowered to effect a transfer on his own authority.

A few jurisdictions maintain one or more diagnostic centers, where each case is received and after a brief period of observation is assigned to one of the regular institutions. This plan *inter alia* insures a more prompt identification of persons who do not belong in the system.

Characteristics of Residents of Correctional Institutions for Youth

Earlier in this chapter, the age and sex of training school resident populations in the nation have been discussed briefly. There are no recent national reports on other characteristics, such as ethnic origin, intelligence, emotional stability, education, economic status, offenses committed, previous delinquency records, and similar kinds of information. Such data on a nationwide basis might not be too significant anyway, because of the regional differences in laws, practices, and characteristics of the general population. Some information on these matters from the 1973 report[17] of the California Youth Authority is interesting but cannot be considered to be entirely representative of the training institution populations of the nation. There were a total of 1,464 juvenile court wards committed to California State training institutions during the 1973 calendar year. These represented a commitment rate of 65.1 boys and girls per each 100,000 of the youth population in the ages of 10 to 17 years. This rate had dropped from a high of 190.7 in 1961. Only 170 of the 1,464 commitments were girls. Since there are so few girls in the sample, the data below are for the male admissions only.

Age

These data are shown in the table on page 38. About two-thirds of the cases are concentrated in the 15, 16, and 17-year age groups. In some states, the mean age will be one and a half to two years younger, but one should remember that in California the upper age of the juvenile courts' jurisdiction is up to the eighteenth birthday, and not the sixteenth, or seventeenth, as in some other states.

Ethnic Origins

Of the 1973 admissions, 43 percent were white (Caucasian), 20 percent Mexican-American, 34 percent black, and 3 percent other. As is common throughout the country, the minority ethnic groups are overrepresented in proportion to their numbers in the general population. Over the previous decade there have been no significant changes in these proportions.

An interesting trend reported is that 15 percent of the admissions in 1965 were for crimes of violence, but that in 1973 this had increased to 34 percent.

Only about 5 percent of the boys received had no known previous record, 43.6 percent had known records but had no institutional commitments, 30.6 percent had one prior commitment, and 21 percent had two or more priors.

**Offense or Reason for Commitment of First Commitments
Placed Under Youth Authority Custody
1973**

Offense or Reason for Commitment	Males Juvenile Court	
	Number	Percent
Homicide	67	5.2
Robbery	239	18.4
Assault and Battery	168	13.0
Burglary	196	15.1
Theft (except Auto)	76	5.9
Auto Theft	111	8.6
Forgery and Checks	3	0.2
Sex Offenses	73	5.6
Narcotics and Drugs	64	4.9
Road and Driving Laws	10	0.8
Escape from County Facilities	108	8.3
County Camp Failure	23	1.8
Incorrigible and Runaway	31	2.4
Foster Home Failure	53	4.1
Other	74	5.7
Total	1,296	100.0

The training schools operated by the California Youth Authority are obviously used principally as the last resort alternative for repetitive juvenile offenders.

Educational Achievement

About 2,500 cases admitted to California Youth Authority institutions were given a series of educational tests in 1973 with the following results:

In reading comprehension, 6.5 percent were below the third grade, 26 percent were rated between grades three and five, 26.4 percent between grades six and eight, 28 percent grades nine to eleven, and 13.1 percent grade twelve and above. The mean grade level was 8.0. Expressed another way, about half of the cases admitted to the California Youth Authority in 1973 were under the eighth grade level in reading comprehension. Only

45

about 2 percent of this group are under age fourteen, so normally, almost all of them should have been near the eighth grade level or above. In basic arithmetic skills, the group tested even lower with a mean grade level of 5.9.

Program Characteristics — National Scene

In view of the fact that most residents are of school age, the programs in juvenile training schools place special emphasis on education and training. It is wrong to assume, however, that one can successfully transplant a conventional junior and senior high school curriculum into these specialized schools.

Some of the special difficulties in designing educational programs for them include the fact that most of the residents are school dropouts, and besides being educationally retarded, they tend to have a psychological distaste for formal classroom learning. With few exceptions they have the basic intellectual capacity to learn, but environmental factors in their homes, communities, and the public schools have fostered negative attitudes. Most of them have never developed normal reading habits and skills. A large proportion of the wards newly admitted are found by standardized tests to be several years retarded in reading skills and a significant number are functionally illiterate. It is believed by many correctional educators that this deficiency in reading is the principal single challenge to the school program.

The school programs are faced with unique problems, however, which are unrelated to the educational deficiencies of the student body. As has been mentioned previously, the average length of stay is short, and since the reception process may consume several weeks, most of the boys and girls probably will not spend more than six months in school, and for many, it will be much less. Unlike a regular public school, the students are constantly entering and leaving the institution so that instruction cannot be organized efficiently on a term basis. In order to make maximum use of the time classes must be very small and the instruction highly individualized. This kind of situation calls for a very high teacher-student ratio and the use of expensive teaching equipment. It is evident that the unit cost of such an educational program is substantially greater than that of a regular public school.

Vocational training is generally regarded as an essential part of correctional training programs. The short average length of stay and the high cost of shop equipment, instructors, and buildings tend to nullify any really effective vocational training in training schools for juveniles. Accordingly, these programs are more akin to industrial arts courses in junior and senior public high schools. Their principal values in this context are exploratory in help-ing students discover their specialized abilities and interests. They can also serve as incentives to master reading comprehension and simple math-ematics.

Most juvenile training schools in the country fall far short of providing any really viable educational programs for their wards. The 1971 survey, *Chil-dren in Custody*[18] reports some skeletal but revealing facts. In the 384 train-ing schools, 6 had no education programs, 76 had academic classes only, 3 had vocational only, and 299 reported having both academic and vocational training. Of those having academic programs, 56 of them provided such schooling as was available "only in the community," which presumably means that some of the residents were permitted to go out of the institution to attend the public schools.

Of the 302 schools reporting some vocational training, 86 of them had no facilities for the purpose except in the community.

The most frequent size of training schools in the country is between 70 and 100 capacity, and the halfway houses and group homes are all small. It is, therefore, understandable that educational programs within these facili-ties must be very limited.

Counseling and Social Case Work

Almost by definition, juveniles passing through correctional training schools are socially maladjusted. The educational deficiencies of these chil-dren previously mentioned are more often than not merely symptoms of un-stable homes, poverty, disease, and neglect. Besides, they are adolescents going through the maturing process which is painful and difficult enough under reasonably normal conditions. The personnel of the whole institution from the superintendent to night supervisor in the living units are in the position of acting as best they can as surrogate parents. In this respect they all have a role as counselors, but because of the severe personal problems presented by most of the wards, and the fact that they must be prepared and helped to make the adjustments to a new life when released, the need for professional social case workers should be obvious.

The 1971 census (*Children in Custody*) reports that of 44,626 full-time and part-time staff positions in 722 public detention and correctional facilities for delinquent juveniles, there were only 1,471 social worker positions. Con-sidering the fact that on June 30, 1971, there were in all these facilities a to-tal of 57,239 residents, and that turnover of cases especially in the temporary detention facilities is extraordinarily high, it appears that the availability of professional social worker services is meager indeed. More than half a million boys and girls pass through these facilities each year. Even the 85,000 adjudicated cases who annually pass through the residential correctional schools would be load enough for all the less than 1,500 social workers in the total system.

Medical, Psychiatric, and Psychological Services

It appears from the national records *(Children in Custody)* that on June 30, 1971 there were only 29 full-time psychiatrists and 268 psychologists in the entire national establishment of facilities for juvenile delinquents. This means, of course, that most of the 722 facilities reported had no full-time psychiatric service and only about three out of eight facilities had a full-time psychologist. Speaking generally, it is clear that with few exceptions medical services are provided by part-time or contract personnel. Except in the few institutions which have full-time psychiatrists, the part-time service will be used more for diagnosis than in treatment. Even where a full-time psychiatrist is employed, the workload is likely to be so heavy that even he will be involved more in diagnosis, prescribing medication, and counseling staff than he will in treating patients in conventional ways.

General Services

There are many other necessary functions to be carried on in any residential correctional institution which need only be mentioned in the context of this chapter. They include recreation, feeding, housing, clothing, visiting, religious programs, maintenance of buildings and grounds, record keeping, general administration, and so on and on.

Personnel

In 1971 there were 39,521 full-time positions in all the detention and correctional training facilities in the United States. Of these, 4,441 were administrative, 28,165 were treatment and educational, and 6,915 were operational and maintenance personnel. For those interested in the opportunities for employment in educational and treatment positions, these were divided as follows: 16,583 were cottage staff, 3,475 were academic teachers, 984 were vocational teachers, 1,471 were social workers, 544 were recreation personnel, 268 were psychologists, and 29 were psychiatrists. When these statistics are examined state-by-state, one finds wide disparity from one state to another.[19]

Costs

As has been estimated earlier, these small facilities with relatively rich staff-resident ratios are expensive from the budget standpoint. The unit costs have increased dramatically in the past 25 or 30 years for reasons unrelated to economic inflation. At one time a man and wife were employed to operate a "cottage" with 15 to 25 or more residents. They were paid as little as $100 a month each, plus their food and living quarters. They got relatively little time off except an occasional weekend and a two-week annual leave. With the advent of civil service, 40-hour weeks, and fringe benefit packages up to 25 or 30 percent of wages, the cost of operating a small living unit was increased by three- to five-fold without taking into account any increase in dollar wages. During the same period, the unit dollar costs of buildings and equipment increased about ten-fold.

The total cost including operational and capital expenditures in fiscal year 1971 was $456,000,000. Operating expenditures alone were $409,000,000. The average annual per capita cost was about $7,000. This varied from about $17,500 in Alaska and $15,500 in Connecticut to $3,250 in Mississippi and $3,260 in Arkansas. It is probable that by 1976 all of these costs will have increased by at least 20 percent.

It is important to note here that annual per capita cost can be misleading because of the wide variation of average length of stay of the residents in different kinds of facilities and in different regions of the country. For example, if the average length of stay in a correctional training school is four months, obviously the annual per capita cost will be shared by three residents, and if it is 6 months, the cost per case will be only one-half of the per capita annual cost. In temporary detention facilities where the average length of stay is only 14 days for the country as a whole and varies from state to state from 4 days in Hawaii and Oklahoma to 37 days in the District of Columbia, and 27 days in Michigan, it would seem to be far more meaningful to compute basic unit costs on a daily basis and to convert these into costs per case processed.

Finally, in this context it is worthy of note that part of the general movement in this country toward reducing length of stay in institutions and toward substituting "community-based" correctional programs for incarceration is motivated as much by the great cost of institutionalization as by humanitarian and professional considerations.

NOTES

[1]William H. Sheldon, Ph.D., M.D., *Varieties of Delinquent Youth*, New York: Harper & Brothers, 1949, p. 899.

[2]*Institutions Serving Delinquent Children—Guides and Goals*, Washington, D.C.: U.S. Department of Health, Education, and Welfare, Children's Bureau, in cooperation with National Association of Training Schools and Juvenile Agencies. Children's Bureau Publication No. 360–1957.

[3]Marvin E. Wolfgang, Robert M. Figlio, and Thorsten Sellin, *Delinquency in a Birth Cohort*, Chicago and London: The University of Chicago Press, 1972, p. 327.

[4]*Uniform Crime Reports* (1972). Federal Bureau of Investigation, U.S. Department of Justice, Washington, D.C.

[5]National Advisory Commission on Criminal Justice Standards and Goals. *Corrections*. Chapter 8, pages 247–263.

[6]U.S. Department of Health, Education, and Welfare, *Juvenile Court Statistics 1971* (1972), p. 2.6.

[7]*Ibid.*

[8]*Children in Custody*, Washington, D.C.: U.S. Department of Justice, Law Enforcement Assistance Administration, National Criminal Justice Information and Statistics Service, page 10, Table 7A.

[9]Andre Rutherford, *The Dissolution of the Training Schools in Massachusetts*, Columbus, Ohio: The Academy for Contemporary Problems, March 1974. See also Lloyd E. Ohlin, Robert B. Coates, and Alden D. Miller, *Radical Correctional Reform: A Case Study of the Massachusetts Youth Correctional System*, Harvard University Educational Review, February, 1974.

[10]For a more exhaustive discussion of juvenile detention see Rosemary Sarri and Mark M. Levin, *Juvenile Delinquency: A Comparative Analysis of Legal Codes in the United States*, published by National Institute of Law Enforcement and Criminal Justice, Ann Arbor, Mich.: University of Michigan.

[11]*Children in Custody.*

[12]*Children in Custody.*

[13]*Children in Custody.*

[14]*Children in Custody.*

[15]*Children in Custody.*

[16]*Children in Custody*, Tables 9 and 10.

[17]California Youth Authority, Health & Welfare Agency, *Annual Report—Program Description and Statistical Summary*, 1973.

[18]*Children in Custody*, Table B-17.

[19]*Children in Custody*, Table B-19.

4 Correctional Institutions for Delinquent Youth: Organization and Programs

Administrative Organization

An institutional facility for delinquents, like a mental hospital or a prison, is sometimes referred to as a "total institution." This means an establishment in which substantially all of the needs of the residents are provided for within the institution. A regular community secondary school is maintained to provide only for the educational and to some extent cultural and social needs of its students, but their other requirements are met by the home and the community. The correctional training school is, in and of itself, a community.

The administrative organization and the program of the school must be designed and maintained with this concept in mind. These institutional communities have permanence and continuity even though the residents are temporary. Cultural patterns of behavior are passed on from one generation of wards to the next and are reinforced by the management and the staff of the institution whose incumbency is many times that of the average ward's time in residence.

Each institution is normally headed by an appointive officer who in the United States usually bears the title of superintendent. He is, of course, responsible to the parent organization of which he is a part and is also sworn to uphold the laws and the Constitution of the United States and of the state in which he is employed.

Superintendents of correctional training schools throughout the United States tend to come from a wide variety of backgrounds. Many of them have little direct preparation for their jobs; have often had virtually no relevant administrative experience; tend to be less than skillful in dealing with the general public and with the political forces affecting the governmental structure of which they are a part.[1] Consequently, the quality of their performance is often inadequate, except in the few jurisdictions with a strong parent organization and an established tradition of professional career service in this field. Their professional background is more often than not from that of public education, social work, probation services, law enforcement, and here and there one sees former athletic coaches, retired army officers, psychiatric nurses, and occasionally persons with no apparent professional qualifications occupying these extremely demanding and sensitive positions.

There is at present no well-organized training ground for administrators of training schools for juvenile delinquents. There are many reasons why this particular type of public institution is under general attack because of its alleged ineffectiveness, but it may very well be that a substantial share of the responsibility for the alleged failure of some of these institutions rests with the quality of their leadership.

The U.S. Department of Health, Education, and Welfare and the National Association of Training Schools and Juvenile Agencies in the publication *Institutions Serving Delinquent Children* have this to say about the qualifications of a superintendent of such an institution:

> The superintendent should have the training and experience that will command the respect of the entire staff, particularly the various professional persons who make up the core of the institutional treatment program. He should have demonstrated in his experience his ability as an administrator, his understanding of the treatment function and his capacity to make effective use of all professional personnel. He should be selected from leaders in social work, clinical or social psychology, psychiatry, education, related fields in child development, and should have a record of understanding and successful work with children. The superintendency requires administrative skills of the highest order, particularly those which will effectively coordinate the specialized efforts and talents of the professional people heading up the various departments in the institution.
>
> Graduation from college and the completion of graduate training in one of the fields indicated above are educational requirements. In addition to a thorough knowledge of the principles and practices of institutional management, he should have five or more years of successful supervisory or administrative experience, at least two of which should have been in institutions or agencies dealing primarily with youths on a 24-hour basis.[2]

The Assistant Superintendent

Even in very small training schools there is usually a second in command who acts as the assistant and alter ego to the superintendent. Ideally, he should be a younger man, with qualifications similar to those of the superintendent, who might be expected to aspire to the rank of superintendent, either in the same school or in another one in the system.

He should be prepared to act for the superintendent in his absence, and also to carry out other administrative duties on a day to day basis. Usually his duties will involve overseeing the smooth functioning of the daily program. While he may have primary responsibility for some specialized functions like personnel management, inmate discipline, or institutional security, he is a generalist; under the guidance of the superintendent he is a coordinator and a facilitator rather than a functional specialist.

The Housekeeping Functions

Since the training school is a 24-hour, seven-days-a-week operation, it is obvious that there is a group of management functions that are basic and only indirectly related to the training and correctional missions of the institution. Shelter, food, clothing, and orderly social living must be provided and maintained, not only for humanitarian reasons but also because other programs of education, training, and treatment cannot function without them.

In large institutions direction of these housekeeping functions is often placed under a person with a title such as chief of management services. He would be responsible to the superintendent for fiscal accounting, acquisition, storage and issuing of supplies, food service, physical plant maintenance, the wards' personal money and property, and any other related matters not specifically assigned to other department or division managers. His subordinates will be such occupational specialists as bookkeepers, cooks, storekeepers, and tradesmen.

The Chief Group Supervisor

This person may be the assistant superintendent, or in larger operations he may report to the assistant superintendent. He will usually be responsible for the coverage of all posts according to the daily and weekly plan. The largest group of employees under his supervision will be the group supervisors assigned to living quarters and other activities not covered by professional specialists such as teachers or nurses.

If he is also the chief disciplinary officer, he will be responsible for the investigation and review of all cases in which any other employee of the institution makes a formal charge against a ward for a violation of institutional rules. Since this is a most sensitive area of institutional administration, he will usually not be given responsibility or authority to order any kind of pun-

53

ishment without the written approval of the superintendent or assistant superintendent.

The Supervisor of Education

Since most of the wards in a training school are of school age and the younger ones are subject to compulsory school attendance laws, it is essential that each institution maintain a certified elementary and secondary school curriculum and that the supervisor be a qualified school principal. Such regular and specialized teachers as are needed should get their professional direction and supervision from him.

The principal will usually report directly to the superintendent, but in a very large institution he may report to an assistant superintendent who is responsible for all educational, vocational training and related treatment and ward activity programs.

The Chief of Medical and Health Services

Institutions with over 400 wards should have a full-time medical doctor in charge of these services. He will normally report directly to the superintendent. In small institutions where the workload cannot justify a full-time physician, it is common to employ a part-time doctor who will be on call for emergencies and who will spend an hour or so a day at the facility as required.

Because there must be an infirmary for those not sick enough to warrant transfer to a hospital outside the facility, and further, because medical equipment, supplies, and records must be kept under professional oversight, at least one resident nurse or medical technician should be on duty at all times.

Dental equipment should also be available to institutions with a resident population of 100 or more, and either a full-time or part-time dentist provided, depending on the workload. In very small institutions, an outside dentist may be employed to visit the premises about once a week to conduct examinations. Those needing dental care may be transferred, if necessary, to his private office for treatment.

Other Professional Services

It is customary to provide religious guidance and opportunities for worship by arranging for the part-time services of chaplains from the major religious groups in the outside community.

The services of social caseworkers, psychologists, psychiatrists, and other professional specialists are often brought in from outside the regular institutional staff, unless specialized programs requiring their services on a full-time basis are incorporated into the ongoing program.

Part-time employees and unpaid volunteers are necessary to round out the personnel services of these relatively small institutions. It is very important, however, that these persons who are not regular members of the personnel team be supervised by some professionally responsible official or employee who is familiar with the routine program of the institution, and who also personally knows the wards being treated, trained, or otherwise serviced.

The Institutional Program

In this context program simply means all of the activities of the institution which are intended to provide for the health and welfare of the wards, and to educate, train, counsel, treat, or otherwise influence them toward that degree of social adjustment which will help them to return to normal community living without resorting to further delinquent behavior.

Because of the community nature of such residential schools, no part of the total program can be completely separated or insulated from the others. It is the responsibility of the schools' management to plan, schedule, and facilitate the total program so that each subordinate part—dining, sleeping, schooling, working, playing, and the like—can be carried on to the optimum advantage without one function interfering with another.

For purposes of clarity in discussing the totality of the institutions' activities the usual program elements are listed and briefly described in the following sections.

Reception and Classification

Most training schools for delinquent wards will have nearly 200 percent turnover per year. This is assuming an average length of residential stay of about six months. Accordingly, an institution with an average daily population of 300 wards can expect to receive about 600 cases per year. These wards will usually have spent from a few hours to several weeks in a detention home awaiting disposition by the court if they are new cases. Others may be former wards being returned for parole violation or they may have been on probation and are being remanded to the institution for some violation.

In some of the larger state systems, such as California, the ward will have been received initially at a "reception clinic" at a central point in the state, where he will have been studied, tested, and programmed by a staff of spe-

55

cialists for a period of from one to three weeks before being transferred to the institution where he usually will be confined until released. In the latter case the reception process at the training school is greatly simplified because most of the professional elements of the process will have been completed.

In this context, reception is a series of routine processes involved in the physical transference of the custody of the ward from the transportation officer to the receiving officer at the institution: checking the validity of the commitment papers, escorting the ward to a place in the institution where he will await further processing, and so on. The ward at this point becomes the responsibility of the receiving institution. He will be entered in the records of the institution. His property and clothing will be checked. Some of his possessions he may retain, some will be placed in safekeeping, and some sent to his home. He will be given a preliminary medical examination, bathed, and outfitted in appropriate clothing. In some facilities there is a reception cottage where he will be kept for a few days until all other arrangements for living and programming have been determined. In other settings he may be assigned directly to one of the living units of the institution where he will remain pending further developments in his institutional progress.

The word classification as used in corrections has a specialized meaning. It does not necessarily mean deciding what class or group in which the ward is to be placed. While there are many similarities among the wards entering these institutions, it is important for the management to know as much as possible about the individual characteristics of each ward received in order to provide an intelligent program for him. There will usually be records accompanying a new arrival in the form of probation officer reports. These are sometimes extensive and informative, but often they may be extremely meager with respect to information about family, health, school, and items of that kind. Consequently, it is important during the first week or ten days after a ward is received to develop a case file in which all of the pertinent information about him is obtained and filed in a systematic manner. The process involves correspondence with family, school, and sometimes with former employers, intensive interviewing of the ward, psychological tests to measure school achievement, general intelligence, and specialized abilities, an analysis of previous delinquent behavior, and, finally, a preliminary appraisal of the ward's attitude toward the world around him.

On the basis of this kind of thoroughgoing case information, the institution personnel will decide on the various elements of the new arrival's program. These elements include housing, school, medical treatment, special counseling, recreational activities, and qualifications for entry into any and all programs within the resources of the institution. Initial classification is very important, but it is the beginning of a continuing process which goes on until the ward is finally discharged.

Clothing and Personal Property

Some training schools remove all personal items of clothing and property from the possession of the new ward and provide instead a prescribed uniform and such personal items as toilet articles and the like. In other institutions wards may be permitted to keep their own clothing, including shoes if they are suitable. Since most of the youngsters will come from poor families, their clothing and other personal articles are more often than not barely worth preserving. Conversely, administrative problems are often generated by the presence in the institution of a few inmates with valuable and unusual items of clothing, for example, leather jackets, expensive boots, and so on. Jealousies and fights often develop over possession of such articles. For purposes of this brief discussion it is only important to point out that the management of the institution must promulgate and enforce some reasonable rules with respect to personally owned clothing.

Cash in the hands of institutional wards can also create special problems. Accordingly, the most common practice is to prohibit the possession of currency by correctional institution wards and to maintain an individual trust account for each resident. From this he can authorize expenditures and deposits much like a bank account.

Valuables such as expensive rings, watches, and other jewelry are usually retained for safekeeping by the property officer if their estimated value exceeds some established amount, like $20.

Generally speaking, the policy in training schools is to make life for the wards as normal as is possible in an institutional setting. Accordingly, personal possessions which can be very important, especially to young people, should be permitted to the extent that they do not interfere with the good order and security of the institution.

Living Quarters

The question of whether wards should be housed in individual rooms or in open dormitories is a continuing source of debate among institutional managers. Because dormitories are less expensive to construct initially, there are probably far more wards in institutions for boys housed in open dormitories than in single rooms. (The opposite is the case for living quarters for girls.) There are some boys who because of their personal habits and individual idiosyncrasies cannot be successfully maintained in open dormitories. It is considered preferable, cost aside, for each ward to have an individual room. On the other hand, where a dormitory system exists there usually will be some individual rooms for special kinds of cases. As far as possible, individual rooms for training school wards normally avoid the conventional cell-like characteristics common in jails and prisons for adults. They are most likely to be in one or two-story buildings.

The living units, whether dormitories, individual rooms, or combinations of both, are often too large for effective control. Recent studies recommend living units providing for not more than 20 residents. In connection with each living unit there must, of course, be adequate facilities for toilets, bathing, and individual locker space for clothing and personal possessions. There will normally be a common room, sometimes referred to as a dayroom, for such activities as television viewing and table games. Reading and studying will usually be carried on in the individual rooms, if they are available. In the case of dormitory housing there will generally be a space separate from both the dayroom and the sleeping quarters where reading and studying can be carried on without interference or disturbance.

One cannot overemphasize the importance of the living quarters units, because at least half or more of a resident's time during each week will be spent there.

Food and Dining

Long ago, Napoleon is reputed to have said that "an army marches on its stomach!" In a residential institution and especially one for young, growing adolescents, food assumes a level of importance in the minds of the wards surpassing almost everything else. Most well-administered systems will have a well-planned food control system which will insure an adequate, nutritious, attractively served diet.

The most common contemporary practice for serving food in these institutions is to provide cafeteria-style service in central dining rooms. Because of the necessity for controlling the items in the ration, this operation must be carefully supervised. Tables, chairs, table settings, and the like should be as normal and noninstitutional in character as possible.

On the other hand, in larger institutions, especially those for the 14- to 17-year-old age groups, it is sometimes difficult to maintain order. As a result, a considerable amount of regimentation is often imposed. It is also considered wise by most administrators of training schools to design the feeding facilities so as to avoid congregating too large a number of wards in the same dining room at the same time. More than 50 or 60 is usually thought to be too many.

Recreation

Leisure time activities become unusually important in institutions for adolescent wards. In institutions with 50 or more residents there will usually be a large recreation room, sometimes fully-equipped as a gymnasium, providing opportunities for organized sports and also seating space for spectators. Such a room or gymnasium is particularly important in cold climates where opportunities for outdoor activities are sharply limited by the weather. There will usually be either a full-time or part-time personnel member assigned to supervise and organize the activities in this space.

Recreation in youth institutions is regarded not only as normal, healthy use of otherwise idle time, but as an educational and character-building activity as well. It is therefore an important part of the training school program.

Education and Training

The correctional training school is a residential school, not a penal institution. Hence, vocational and academic educational programs constitute the core around which the entire program is built. A large proportion of training school wards are educationally handicapped or retarded. They usually have been behavior problems in the public schools and have tended to be school failures for a variety of reasons. Some have had home conditions which discouraged school achievement or at best have done nothing to reinforce it. Others have been habitual truants or have attended schools in which the quality of instruction was grossly inferior.

Whatever the reasons, the average 14- to 16-year-old delinquent arriving at a correctional training school already has become hostile to school and schoolteachers. He resents discipline and authority figures and arrives in the classroom prepared to resist rather than to cooperate. He is already about four years behind the normal grade level of his own age group in public schools. This is especially true in reading skills.

The need for highly specialized teachers and unique programs of motivational instruction is all too obvious. Unfortunately, few public correctional training schools are equipped to provide this quality of teaching and educational guidance. Aside from the qualifications of teachers, the teacher-student ratio is often too great for even the most able and inspired teacher to be minimally effective. Small classes of less than 15 and much individualized tutoring and counseling are indicated for these kinds of students.

Makers of budgets very often argue that standards in the public schools their own children attend are not only good enough, but perhaps too good for delinquents who are public charges. This is obviously a shortsighted and self-defeating attitude, but it is one which the training school administrator must meet and counteract if he can.

It should be borne in mind also that students in these schools rarely remain there longer than one full school year. The most intensive effort possible to counteract, at least in part, the educational failures of the past ought to be the major thrust of the educational effort.

To avoid leaving an overly pessimistic impression in the reader's mind, mention should be made of the fact that an occasional boy or girl in these schools displays unexpected ability and energy. There are always some each year who finish high school, and a rare one now and then who goes on to finish college or a vocational course leading to a better social and economic life.

Vocational and trade training always have been emphasized in correctional training schools from their very beginning. This has been the case partly because of the general history of failure of the wards in elementary and secondary schools, and partly from a somewhat naive belief that "shopwork" doesn't require much, if any, ability to read, write, and figure. This is true only to the extent that shopwork calls for such simple mechanical and repetitive tasks as are common in assembly line manufacturing. This training in semiskilled tasks is best given on the job at the time of employment rather than in a school setting.

Trade training leading to journeyman standing in the skilled crafts cannot be carried out successfully in correctional schools, partly because of the short periods of institutional stay, and partly because small residential schools cannot possibly provide the diversity of mechanical equipment, the specialized instructors, and the normal conditions of production which exist in free society.

The recent trend is to emphasize skills in reading and understanding written directions and in computation and measurement skills common to most trades. The actual shop experiences made available in the institutions are therefore to be regarded as exploratory more than as skill developing. These courses or work assignments can be of very short duration so that the student can test his specialized mechanical capacities and his natural interests.

To be most effective these production experiences are accompanied by related counseling that will motivate the ward to pursue after release an occupation best suited to his capacities and interests.

Work Assignments

Most newly admitted wards have never had a regular job with prescribed hours and duties. Many have never even had regular home chores which they had been required to perform. If they are to survive and live normal lives they must be prepared for the time when they will have to enter the world of economic employment. In short, they must learn to work.

Accordingly, it is normal practice to require each boy or girl to perform some regular daily tasks. No matter how meager the educational facilities of the institution may be, there are many kinds of tasks which must be carried out just to maintain the institution and service its programs. For example, merely preparing, serving, and handling the food seven days a week generates a great variety of jobs, ranging from mopping floors and washing dishes to assisting the cooks and the meat cutter. Other similar and obvious kinds of jobs are involved in maintenance of the grounds and gardens, repairs to buildings and equipment, interior painting, clerical work, and serving as helpers in the school, library, recreation field, and so on.

Agricultural programs have been common in connection with these institutions in the past, but farming and animal husbandry enterprises have been discontinued in most institutions for juveniles and even in many for adults. This is partly because they are no longer an economic asset and also because most wards and inmates of these facilities are city-born and bred and normally return to city life after release. If suitable land is available, small vegetable garden plots are sometimes maintained, but are justified for general educational purposes rather than as a significant source of food supply.

Clinical and Counseling Services

It is normal practice in training schools which are large enough to warrant it to have a special department of clinical services usually headed by a clinical psychologist, or a graduate social worker. If the department is headed by a psychiatrist, medical services are sometimes included, but otherwise medical services are usually coordinated by the superintendent or his assistant.

The functions of the nonmedical clinical services include:

1. Planning the institutional program of each ward.

2. Recommending to the superintendent or assistant superintendent each child's assignment to living quarters, school, recreation, and work. In short, prescribing the so-called treatment program for each individual ward.

3. Reviewing periodically the progress and development for each child.

4. Serving on a review board to determine the disposition of the more serious disciplinary charges which may be brought against any ward.

5. Recommending the time and conditions under which wards may be released for placement outside the institution.

Upon admission, and continuing during each ward's institutional stay, he is normally assigned to a single caseworker or advisor whose duty it is to act as an advisor and to serve as a link between the ward and the management and other members of the staff, as well as with his family and outside associations.

If a psychiatrist is available, he will provide diagnostic and treatment services for a limited number of special cases. Beyond that his role may be more useful and effective as an advisor and teacher of regular staff personnel who are in constant contact with the institution's population.

Medical Services

Schools with an average daily population of 400 or more can justify a full-time resident physician and such supporting nurses and technicians as may be necessary. Smaller schools must usually be content with part-time services. Besides ministering to the sick, medical personnel should be responsible for all routine medical examinations, overseeing the general health and sanitation of the institution, providing for corrective surgery, and contracting for outside specialists like optometrists and dentists. They will also make whatever arrangements are needed with outside hospitals and specialized clinics. Instead of the hospital section found in large institutions, an appropriately equipped doctor's treatment room and a few hospital beds for infirmary use are usually adequate.

Religion

In institutions with resident populations of 400 or more, at least one full-time chaplain is usually provided. The particular religious group with which he is affiliated will depend on the predominant faith represented in the institution population. His role as a chaplain is not the normal pastor-congregation relationship, but rather that of coordinating the religious needs of all the residents and making available to each of them volunteer religious counselors of their faith of choice. A place or places for religious services usually are provided for groups that are numerous enough to warrant them.

Chaplains and visiting clergymen are often very helpful also as counselors and as liaison persons with the families of wards.

Visiting and Correspondence

Visits to wards, especially by parents and other relatives, are very important to the morale of the youngsters and also tend to sustain and reinforce family ties. Appropriate space is usually provided in each institution for these visits to take place in as informal an atmosphere as possible without jeopardizing the safety of the institution or the welfare of the wards. Except in a few special cases where the family relationship is a detrimental one, visiting is actively encouraged and not regarded as a special privilege.

The writing of letters to family and friends is also encouraged in most cases. Some controls are usually imposed to prevent abuses, such as the writing of nuisance letters, or conversely, the receipt of letters which contain contraband drugs or other illegal and grossly objectionable material. Except for security reasons, the practice of reading and censoring mail is being discontinued in most correctional institutions.

Even communication by telephone is now being permitted in many correctional institutions for both juveniles and adults.

Furloughs and Home Visiting

It is not uncommon practice to permit residents of training schools to make visits to their homes, if home conditions and the adjustment of the ward involved appear to justify it. Such visits may involve only a Sunday ride with the family or a home visit of a few days. There is always apprehension that the ward will either get into further trouble or that he may not return voluntarily. However, where good judgment has been used in granting and arranging such visits, unfavorable outcomes are rare.

Special logistical problems present more difficulties than delinquent behavior in most instances. The training school is often many miles from a ward's home, the family does not have a car or money for travel, or there is no suitable place for the ward to sleep at home. To be sure of the family situation, an employee of the institution or of the parent system should visit the home. This may be either too expensive or even wholly impractical for other reasons. As a result, furloughs and home visits, even when clearly desirable, are not permitted as frequently as might be hoped or expected.

63

Discipline

The word discipline in the context of correctional institution management means conformance to rules and acceptable standards of behavior. Violation of these rules and standards is a breach of discipline and cannot be ignored if the responsible leadership in the institution is to maintain control. Loss of control by constituted authority, especially in a community of behavioral deviates, can only result in a state of anarchy and chaos.

Ideally, the interpersonal relationships among wards and staff and the general cultural mores of the community would be ordered in such a manner that infractions would be relatively rare and minor in severity. This ideal situation will be sought by the institutional administration in differing ways depending on the skill, philosophy, and style of the management.

Some old style administrators used very repressive methods and depended almost exclusively upon fear of punishment as a means of maintaining order and discipline. Many rigid and petty rules were made and enforced. Corporal punishment, lockups, and deprivation of normal food allowances were in common use in some juvenile institutions until very recently.

Corporal punishment is prohibited by law in most states today, and other brutal and unnecessary disregard of contemporary standards of basic human rights are rejected as unnecessary, self-defeating, and inhumane. This does not mean that deliberate misbehavior by residents of correctional training schools can or should be tolerated or ignored.

Rules and guidelines for behavior should be simply stated and of such a character as to "make sense," not only to the staff, but to the average ward as well. There will usually be no rigid penalty applied to each offense, except that any charge for an overt infraction of the code of conduct will be made in writing and the offender will be given a hearing by the superintendent or his assistant in minor matters, and in more serious cases the hearing will be held before a disciplinary committee of at least three persons appointed by the superintendent. This method protects against personal and whimsical decisions being made by a single individual and satisfies at least in essence the basic democratic principle that an accused person is entitled to "due process of law."

Dispositions may range from a finding of not guilty or a dismissal of the charge with a warning, to the withholding of some prized privilege for a short period, transfer to a more secure housing unit, or the withholding of release dependent upon a prescribed period of acceptable behavior.

Serious crimes committed by wards while in residence are ordinarily referred to the prosecuting attorney in the jurisdiction where the institution is located. Such offenses are rare, but they do occur. They include possession of an illegal weapon, e.g., a firearm, assault with a weapon upon a staff person or another ward, forcible rape, and homicide.

Modern psychology holds that rewards for good behavior are more effective in the maintenance of discipline than punishment for misconduct. There are solid research findings in support of this theory.[3] This clearly implies not that punishments should be abandoned, but that the whole institutional program should be designed to provide a system for giving rewards rather than merely for threatening punishment for nonconformance.

Runaways

Training schools for nondangerous juvenile offenders are usually "open institutions." In the correctional context this means a residential facility which is not surrounded by a wall or security fence manned with armed guards as is common practice in prisons for adult felons. Furthermore, since juvenile court commitments are, under the law, civil cases, the use of lethal force in preventing an escape would also be illegal.

As a result of these facts and the further tendency of young adolescents to behave impulsively, runaways from training schools are very common. The school's management is faced, therefore, with finding some middle ground between undesirable and excessive regimentation and long hours of locked confinement on the one hand, and a degree of openness and freedom of movement which makes the temptation to run away all too easy on the other.

Good morale on the part of both employees and residents, active and interesting programs, and a well-trained staff of sufficient size on all shifts are the best preventive methods. Wards also need to be impressed with the consequences of unauthorized absences. They should know that there is less than one chance in a hundred of not being caught, that new offenses, such as burglaries and car theft, which are common accompanying offenses during a runaway episode, are new crimes which will bring them further unfortunate results. But in spite of all the negative aspects of escape, even when well understood by the offender, some surely will go anyway.

Since runaways are to everybody's disadvantage, it is a recognized responsibility of management to try to prevent them without turning the training school into a high security prison. In some jurisdictions running away from a correctional training school is in and of itself a delinquent act and is so defined in the law. In that case the offender can be returned to juvenile court for further disposition, or if he is beyond the age jurisdiction of the juvenile court he might be charged with escape and tried as an adult. This is unlikely, however, unless the offender has committed some other crime in connection with the escape.

The more common disposition of escapes or attempted escapes from juvenile facilities is return to the institution or transfer to another more secure one in the system. The episode will be regarded as an act revealing instability which calls for appropriate changes in program and quite possibly a delay in his release date.

The Physical Plant

The most visible and permanent feature of any residential institution is its buildings, its site, and its physical equipment. Consequently, discussions of training schools for delinquents usually begin at this point. Even worse, planners faced with the need for a new institution too often begin by commissioning an architect to plan the buildings before the site is selected or the elements of the program are determined and designed.

The *program* determines the *design* — not the other way around. The basic requirements of the design, such as number and kinds of residents, location, cost limitations, and architectural style are important, but experience has demonstrated that if costly errors and omissions are to be avoided, a design document sometimes several hundred pages in length must be prepared in advance describing each element of the program and the space and equipment needs of each. These elements extend from such mundane matters as sewage disposal and power supply to strictly programmatic items, such as classrooms, visiting rooms, chapel, and vocational shops.

Space limitations prevent further discussion of details of institutional design. Mention of a few general concepts is necessary, however.

Location

Many existing training schools are severely handicapped because of their locations in remote rural settings. To the political visitor from a crowded metropolis, like New York, Chicago, or Los Angeles, a boys' institution 200 miles away in a beautiful and benign countryside may seem like an idyllic *retreat*. Unfortunately, a training school for juvenile delinquents is *not a retreat*. It is a place where the residents are sent against their will. With few exceptions they are city boys; they are lonely and frightened. Their families are poor and too far away to visit.

From the standpoint of the management, these small institutions are dependent upon outside resources. Part-time doctors, dentists, and clergymen are often not easily available. Many full-time staff do not want to live in an isolated community because of lack of educational opportunities for their children and entertainment and cultural advantages for themselves. Even deliveries of consumable supplies present annoying logistical problems. Without further elaboration it should be clear that remote rural settings for correctional institutions of all kinds in this day of population concentration in urban areas present disadvantages far outweighing any real or imagined advantages.

The actual site of an institution should be as near public transportation lines providing access to the communities from which its residents originate as practicable. It does not follow that it should sacrifice all other program needs by placing the facility in a skyscraper in the center of a slum. An atmosphere of openness should be fostered by keeping the buildings well-spaced and preferably no higher than two stories. There should always be enough open land around the buildings so that neighbors, undesirable or otherwise, can be kept far enough away so that neither the neighbors nor the institution will encroach on each other. How far will depend on the specifics of the situation, but 200 feet is probably a reasonable distance to deviate from in either direction, depending on special site conditions.

Size

Speaking in general terms, these institutions operate best if they are small enough to enable the superintendent and his assistant to personally recognize and know something about each ward. Since the turnover is so rapid, this becomes virtually impossible if the daily population exceeds 100 to 150. Also the larger an institution becomes, the more regimentation will inevitably occur.

Early concepts of children's institutions were built around the idea of trying to simulate family life. This was the "cottage" plan with each cottage managed by a husband and wife team who were called "cottage parents." The size of each cottage varied from a capacity of eight or ten to as many as 25. This plan never worked well, and for practical reasons has long since been abandoned, except for the vestigial use of the word cottage as a name for individual housing units.

The 40-hour work week for employees sounded the death knell of the cottage system. Since there are 1095 eight-hour shifts in a year and with various holidays, vacations, and sick leave, an employee works only about 230 eight-hour shifts per year. Hence, it takes almost five full-time employees to provide continuous coverage of one post assignment. Obviously, the simulated child-parent relationship between wards and living quarters supervisors could not survive under these circumstances.

The response to these changed conditions of personnel assignment in these institutions has taken several forms; first, small living units of twenty or less, second, assignment of counselors to individual wards, and third, keeping each institution small enough so that it can be run as a totality rather than as an aggregation of bureaucratic departments.

A further factor arguing for small institutions is the current conviction that these facilities should be as close as possible to the home communities of the wards. Only small institutions can be distributed throughout a metropolitan area in a way that will meet this criterion.

Financing

Small institutions adequately programmed and fully staffed become very costly to operate. This argues for limiting the use of institutional care to an absolute minimum consistent with public safety and humanitarian needs. This objective can be approached in two ways: first, by sending no juvenile to an institution unless there is no acceptable alternative, and second, by limiting the length of stay of each ward to as short a time as possible.

The emerging practice is to use the residential settings as diagnostic and backup resources to community treatment. It is probable then that whatever agency operates the probation and parole supervision services in a community should also operate the residential facilities so that they become resources for the community-based programs and not separate administrative entities.

Another unfortunate aspect of the financing problem arises because in a given state there may be many and diverse funding sources. For example, in California, the state government operates and finances the state schools and 58 separate county governments operate and finance the probation departments and the local detention homes and training schools. There are many variations of this pattern in the other states, but everywhere there is a continuing controversy over the question of which unit of government should pay for what correctional services.

Simple logic points toward state governments taking over the total responsibility for both management and financing. On the other hand, it is clear that insofar as practicable all correctional programs and especially those for youth should be carried out at the community level. State and federal participation could, of course, be limited to standard setting and subsidy financing, but this has serious limitations, partly because of the uneven distribution of population with the result that there are numerous counties which are both poor and sparsely populated. At this writing there has been no statewide resolution of this problem anywhere in the country.

General Trends

Specific trends have been mentioned in the preceding sections of this chapter, but speaking generally, it seems clear at this juncture in history that the following futurist statements can be ventured:

1. The incidence of serious juvenile delinquency will not decline much before 1980 and may increase some, especially among girls.

2. Confinement of juvenile delinquents who have not reached their seventeenth birthday in large central training schools is a practice rapidly disappearing from the American correctional scene.

3. Alternatives to long periods of institutional treatment of juvenile delinquents are developing but have not yet fully matured. It appears that these will take form in many varieties of community-based programs designed to intervene in disordered lives in such ways as to deflect them from adult criminality and provide for a better level of public protection without resorting to self-defeating penal measures.

4. Such residential facilities as will persist will be for backup resources to community programs and for the treatment of severely maladjusted and hazardous cases.

5. There will probably be an increasing use of volunteer workers in the field during the next decade.

6. There will be many continuing efforts to reorganize the juvenile justice system in all of its aspects throughout the country in the immediate years ahead.

7. The problem of financing juvenile correctional services will be studied and tampered with but will probably not be resolved in any really rational way for many years. Unit costs will not decrease.

8. State governments will assume increasing responsibility for both operation and financing of programs for juvenile delinquents, but the actual operation of these efforts will be based more and more in the populous communities of the states.

NOTES

[1]E. K. Nelson and Catherine H. Lovell, *Developing Correctional Administrators*, Washington, D.C.: Joint Commission on Correctional Manpower and Training, 1969.

[2]*Institutions Serving Delinquent Children*, Washington, D.C.: U.S. Department of Health, Education and Welfare and the National Association of Training Schools and Juvenile Agencies.

[3]Carl Jesness, Comparative Effectiveness of Two Institutional Programs for Delinquents, *Child Care Quarterly*, 1 (1971), published by Behavioral Publications, New York City.

5 Jails

Of all the criminal justice agencies falling under the broadly defined rubric of corrections, jails are the oldest, most numerous, most criticized, and most stubbornly resistant to reform. They process more cases per day and touch more human lives than any other, but despite their obvious importance as a part of the total system, they owe their continued state of retarded development principally to archaic state and local laws, uneven and wide geographical distribution, petty political vested interests, and public apathy.

Historically, these local places of confinement were used almost exclusively for the detention of accused persons who could not make bail during the interval between arrest and judicial disposition. This remains their primary function. On any given day slightly over one-half of the population of the 4,037 local jails in the United States is being held pending further disposition. Others are serving sentences usually ranging from a few days to one year for committing relatively minor offenses. In a few states jails are still used for long-term offenders serving sentences up to 99 years.

According to the only nationwide jail census[1] ever made in the United States, there were on March 15, 1970, 160,863 persons confined in local jails. Of these, 153,063 were adults and 7,800 were juveniles. Fifty and nine-tenths percent of the adults and 66.1 percent of the juveniles were classified as "not convicted." This category includes persons under appeal or awaiting sentencing, pretrial detainees, and others who are either not yet arraigned, or who are being held for other authorities, such as parole boards, or other jurisdictions. A few persons in the "not convicted" group obviously are both convicted and sentenced, but are temporarily confined in a local jail awaiting further judicial processing or transfer to state or federal prisons. Some others may be awaiting removal to a civil institution, such as a mental hospital.

There are also various types of sentenced prisoners in local jails. Many states have laws prohibiting sentences to county jails in excess of one year.

The one-year penalty is usually considered the maximum term for a misdemeanor. This is the reason for the "year-and-a-day" sentence commonly used in the federal system and in some states. It is the minimum term for a felony to be served in a federal penitentiary. In some states, however, felons may be sentenced to county jails for relatively long terms ranging up to 99 years.

The national jail census referred to above reports that on March 15, 1970, there were 58,600 persons serving sentences of less than one year, and 10,496 with sentences in excess of one year in the nation's local jails. In some cases the latter arise from the sum of two or more sentences for separate offenses which have been ordered to be served consecutively. Some states, such as California, follow a practice of sentencing some convicted felons to a period of years under probation supervision, and, in addition, require that part of the term before release to community supervision be served in the county jail.

States in which more than 10 percent of the sentenced county jail population on March 15, 1970 was serving sentences in excess of one year include Alabama, Georgia, Louisiana, Massachusetts, Nebraska, New York, Ohio, Pennsylvania, South Carolina, Tennessee, Texas, and Wisconsin. In Pennsylvania, there were 2,400 persons serving sentences in county institutions, 1,514 of whom had sentences of more than one year. In the nation as a whole, 15 percent of all sentenced jail inmates were serving terms longer than one year.

Considering the deplorable physical conditions and program deficiencies in most county jails, it is at least a questionable practice to sentence any human being to such facilities for more than a few months. In fact, some authorities advocate that local jails be used for preadjudication detention only and that *all* sentenced defendants be transferred to state or regional facilities owned and operated by the state governments.

In Alaska, Connecticut, Delaware, and Rhode Island there are no county jails. The state governments operate the jails for both the convicted and the not convicted. In Vermont, three months is the maximum legal county jail sentence.

Despite the fact that there are many persons serving jail sentences of a year or more, it is important to observe that most sentences are very short. There are no national statistics on this subject which reveal accurately the amount of time served by the total cohort of persons released from local jails during a year. Such fragmentary information as is available in census data relates to the resident jail population on a given day which provides no clue to the numbers of prisoners who are admitted and released over a period of time.

An unpublished report (1974) from the Sheriff of Los Angeles County indicates that over a two-year period 52 percent of those released from County Jail served two days or less and 80 percent ten days or less.[2] The two-day sentences, no doubt, are accounted for, in the main, by street drunks who are arrested and "released when sober." Eliminating the "disorderly person" categories, the remainder of sentenced misdemeanants who have committed such offenses as burglary, assault, petty theft, fraud, weapons offenses, and drug possession, also serve relatively short terms, probably averaging 90 days or less. It should be noted, however, that one prisoner serving 180 days occupies the same space and requires about the same maintenance costs as 18 persons serving ten days each.

In an article entitled "Our Sick Jails" appearing in *Federal Probation*, March 1971, Richard A. McGee states: "As a practical matter, however, we find the local jail being occupied principally by drunks, addicts, and petty thieves. And as for the women, if the prostitutes were eliminated from the jail populations, most of the women's quarters would be virtually empty most of the time."[3]

Based on a very rough estimate, about 7 percent of the 3 million persons, more or less, who pass through these jails each year are charged with or convicted of felonies, and 93 percent are misdemeanants. It can be seen readily enough that the problem of jail administration, aside from holding a few felons awaiting disposition by the courts, is that of managing a miscellaneous array of persons charged with or convicted of offenses of a relatively minor nature. Only a very few of these are incarcerated for periods of six months to one year. A 1966 study of two large counties in California revealed that about one-third of the sentenced prisoners on a given day were serving terms of 30 days or less, one-third one month to three months, and one-third over 90 days up to and including one year.[4]

> One month in jail may not seem long either to the judge or the sheriff, but to the prisoner it may be the longest 720 hours in his life, and just one of those hours could include the most damaging experience in his lifetime. Contrariwise, short stays in jail are a way of life for thousands of deteriorated middle-aged alcoholics and petty offenders. A 1963 study of some 7,000 inmates in five New York county penitentiaries showed that over 20 percent were serving a term which was their tenth or more.[5]

The Not Convicted

As noted earlier, slightly more than one-half of the resident jail population on a given day is made up of persons not convicted. This can be misleading in terms of the numbers of persons passing through these institutions over one year's time because literally hundreds of thousands of persons arrested and booked into jail may stay any length of time from a few hours to one year or more before the judicial process disposes of each case by dismissal, transfer, or sentence. Hence, despite the fact that the national jail population of unadjudicated cases on a specified day is less than 80,000 adults and 5,000 juveniles, it is estimated that as many as 3,000,000 or more accused persons may be admitted to them in a single year.

There are no general terms by which this mass of humanity can be described except that each individual has been arrested for some allegedly illegal act and booked into jail pending further processing. The range is from the alcoholic tramp to the freshly arrested robber, and from the professional racketeer to the otherwise respectable citizen taken into custody for drunk driving. The most frequent arrests are for public drunkenness, drug law violations, and of disorderly adolescent youths. About one in twenty will be female and approximately one-third of the males will be persons under 18 years of age.

Laws in many states either prohibit confining juveniles in jails for adults or require that they be housed separately from adults. But most jails are small, old, poorly designed, and inadequately staffed, and it is not uncommon for juveniles to be mixed with adults or housed in quarters which are even more deplorable than those used for adults. Of the 4,037 jails surveyed in 1970, 70 percent received juveniles. There were 765 institutions which had the authority to retain juveniles serving sentences of one year or less, and 67 jails were reported as holding juveniles serving sentences in excess of one year.

Women inmates are usually quartered separately from men, but in small jails of less than 75 capacity, they are so few in number that they too are often kept under the most miserable conditions. In a few of the large populous jurisdictions, separate jails are maintained for women prisoners. There are, however, only about a dozen of these in the entire country.

The Organization of Jails — Who Runs Them?

As noted previously, the local jails are run by state governments in Alaska, Connecticut, Rhode Island, and Delaware, but there is an extraordinary variety of management structures throughout the country. The most common arrangement is for the sheriff of each county to maintain one or more jails for detention cases and short-term sentenced prisoners.

It has also been common practice for many city governments to maintain jails under the jurisdiction of the municipal police. These city-run police jails have been used chiefly for initial booking of most arrests before arraignment and for the service of very short sentences for violations of city ordinances. Their principal clients have tended to be drunks and street prostitutes. Sentences to these police jails rarely exceed six months; over 90 percent are less than 30 days, and three-fourths less than 15 days.

Except for temporary lockups for holding arrested persons less than 48 hours, jails operated by the municipal police are going out of use in most parts of the country. For example, there were 3,767 persons serving sentences in city jails in California on September 29, 1960, but on September 26, 1968, there were only 530 such persons.[6] Even where there is no logical geographic basis, some cities persist in keeping the city jail. The City and County of San Francisco present the most blatant example, in which the sheriff's detention jail and the police jail are on adjoining floors of the Hall of Justice.

Another variation of administrative arrangement is found in some counties where the county sheriff operates the jail for the "not convicted," and the facilities for sentenced county prisoners are placed under the county probation department or an independent manager appointed by the county's governing board. In the latter case, these facilities are often given some different name, such as "County Industrial Farm" "Rehabilitation Center," or "County Farm."

In a few states sheriffs operate the detention jails, and the state government runs one or more camps or farms for misdemeanants. The Indiana State Farm at Greencastle is an example.

Another system exists in New York City where all accused persons after arraignment are turned over by the police to a City Department of Correction which runs not only the city prisons (detention jails), but also the facilities on Rikers Island for sentenced misdemeanants. New York City under its "home rule" charter does not have the conventional form of county government, and the elective office of sheriff has been abolished.

Whether the adminstration of jails should remain in the hands of any police agency, including elected county sheriffs, is a question that is being asked more and more frequently. The President's Commission on Law Enforcement and Administration of Justice comments on the subject:

> Most jails continue to be operated by law-enforcement officials. The basic police mission of apprehending offenders usually leaves little time, commitment, or expertise for the development of rehabilitative programs, although

notable exceptions demonstrate that jails can indeed be settings for correctional treatment. Many law-enforcement officials, particularly those administering large and professionalized forces, have advocated transfer of jails to correctional control.

The most compelling reason for making this change is the opportunity it offers to integrate the jails with the total corrections network, to upgrade them, and to use them in close coordination with both institution and community-based correctional services. As long as jails are operated by law-enforcement officials, no matter how enlightened, it will be more difficult to transform them into correctional centers. As a major step toward reform, jails should be placed under the control of correctional authorities who are able to develop the needed program services. The trend should be away from the isolated jail and toward an integrated but diversified system of correctional facilities.[7]

In its exhaustive report of a survey of the county jails of Illinois, The Center for Studies in Criminal Justice at the Law School of the University of Chicago observes: "The law enforcement psychology of a policeman is to put offenders into *jail;* the rehabilitative psychology of a correctional worker should be to prepare an inmate to get *out* of jail as a law-abiding citizen. This psychological contradiction is worth pondering."

The National Advisory Commission on Criminal Justice Standards and Goals in its 1973 report recommends the following: "All local detention and correctional functions, both pre- and postconviction, should be incorporated within the appropriate State system by 1982."

Jail Standards

Since most jails are still operated by counties and cities which are political subdivisions of state governments, it is logical to assume that the states would have both the right and an inherent responsibility to exercise some supervisory power over them. In practice, only 21 states in 1973 had laws directing an appropriate state agency, such as the department of corrections, to set detailed standards for jail operation. In many states where such laws still exist, however, the state has no effective way of forcing local jurisdictions to comply with such set standards. In only 13 of the states does the government have authority to enforce compliance. In 23 states there is no statutory provision for state inspection, establishment of standards, enforcement of standards, or authority to enforce standards.[8]

In New York State the State Commission of Corrections is provided for in the constitution. It has the power to establish standards, to inspect all local places used for the detention of offenders, and to order any such facility closed if after reasonable notice it fails to comply. In practice, this enforcement power has rarely been invoked. In any event these standards are usually minimal and tend to be limited largely to basic legal rights of prisoners, health, sanitation, food, disciplinary actions, and so on.

It is the opinion of most observers and students of this problem that the basic issue militating against raising standards is that of cost. The remedy would seem to lie either in total state support and management or in state subsidies to be paid contingent upon state standards being met.

One chapter in a text such as this cannot discuss in detail all of the matters which quite properly might be the subject of standard setting for jail management. But some indication of the complexity of the problem can be revealed by simply enumerating the major items to be covered. The following list is neither exhaustive nor complete, but may give the reader a closer view of the problems of jail management:

1. Legal bases for jail management and organization.
2. Legal rights of persons confined in jail.
3. Receiving procedures.
4. Release procedures.
5. Transportation of prisoners between jails and to and from court.
6. Rules and regulations for inmate conduct.
7. Disciplinary procedures.
8. Segregation: legal requirements, of females, of juveniles, of sentenced and unsentenced persons, of witnesses, of disciplinary cases, of sex offenders, of work releasees.
9. Records system.
10. Personnel standards and employee training.
11. Rules and regulations for jail personnel.
12. Emergency procedures for: fire, escapes, riots, crimes by inmates, epidemics, and other unusual events.
13. Security; segregation and special custodial provisions for high-risk cases, custodial supervision, prisoner movements, key control, firearms and tear gas, tool control, contraband control, use of physical force, lighting.
14. Health and medical services.
15. Sanitation.
16. Heating and ventilation.
17. Limitations on overcrowding.

18. Inmate privileges: mail, visits, telephone, canteen, personal property and clothing, radios, television, moving pictures.

19. Social and educational services: classification, counseling, school, library, religion, recreation, hobbies.

20. Work programs: maintenance work, industries, agriculture, work furlough.

Such a list might serve as an outline of chapter titles for a textbook on jail administration or of a manual of jail standards.[9] Until very recently little has been written in this field, and we still find most small jails and even some of the larger ones operating principally by a system of unwritten customs passed on from one generation of prisoners and jail personnel to the next.

Special Problems and Issues

It should be clear to the reader at this point that the often discussed "jail problem" is, in fact, a complex multiplicity of problems and issues which are easy to address rhetorically.But if this approach were either useful or effective, most of the difficulties would have been overcome a half century ago by the eloquence of such writers as Charles Dickens,[10] John Howard,[11] Thomas Mott Osborne,[12] Joseph F. Fishman,[13] and many others. Furthermore, such an approach is beyond the scope of this textbook. Instead it will be the purpose of this section to identify the problems and to discuss possible responses to them.

Uneven Geographical Distribution of the Population and Archaic Local Jurisdictional Boundaries

The Problem

In the early years of our country's development, states were divided into counties, and county governments established county seats mainly for the convenience of farmers. The basic concept was that in most instances, a citizen farmer should be able to travel to and from the county seat by horse and buggy between daylight and darkness, or if not, that he should not be so far away that he would be required to spend more than one night away from home. In some of the states which were admitted to the Union after the development of railroads and improved highways, many of the counties were much larger, particularly those which contained much agriculturally unproductive desert or mountain land.

Once county lines were established and local governments became politically entrenched, changing those lines was for all practical purposes virtually impossible. Consequently, in the light of the extraordinary industrial expansion and urbanization of our population in the last 100 years, there is little rationality to the way in which county boundaries are drawn. For example, in California, Los Angeles County covers 4,069 square miles with a population of over 7 million, while Alpine County located in the northern and mountainous region of the state covers 727 square miles and has a population of around 485. Illinois, with a total area of 55,748 square miles, is divided into 102 counties. The total population of the state is 11,113,976, while Cook County, which contains the city of Chicago, is 954 square miles in area and has a population of 5,493,529.

It is not the purpose of this discussion to deal with the multiplicity of governmental, political, and social problems growing out of this archaic organizational structure of local government. But since we are dealing with jails, which in most states are institutions of local government, this factor must be mentioned because it presents one of the difficulties that lies at the root of our failure to address the jail problem in a sensible way.

Not only are some county jails in great metropolitan cities becoming too large, overcrowded, and virtually unmanageable, but conversely, hundreds of local jails are so small that acceptable management and program services are impossible or at least impracticable to achieve.

In the national jail census of March 15, 1970, 4,037 jails contained 160,863 inmates which is an average population of slightly less than 40 persons per jail. Thirty-five hundred twenty-two of the jails were designed to hold fewer than 100 inmates. Three hundred seventy-four had capacities of 100 to 299, and 131 were designed for 300 or more inmates.

Of 160 jails surveyed in Illinois in 1967–68, 45 city jails and eight county jails were completely vacant 25 percent of the time; 24 city and four county jails were empty more than 50 percent of the time, while at the same time, the large metropolitan jails were overcrowded from 50 to 80 percent most of the time.

Possible Solutions

Short of a complete reorganization of local government in most of the 50 states, it would appear that there are two possible approaches to this problem:

1. *Regionalization.* Without changing county lines, it is possible for state legislatures to establish jail regions encompassing as large an area and a population as might be practicable in terms of distances and organizational size. Such districts might be operated as special districts with their own governing boards, like large school districts.

Some states have provided for contractual relationships between counties and between counties and municipalities. The contractual relationship between a county and a city within its boundaries is often easily worked out. Conversely, contractual relationships between counties for the operation of jails is rarely practicable. The obstacles lie chiefly with local politics, on the one hand, and the question of capital outlay moneys on the other.

In the event of any regional arrangement, it would be necessary for practical reasons to maintain temporary lockups near county courthouses for persons awaiting judicial disposition. Central regional jails would be used primarily for persons serving sentences, and to a lesser extent for longer-term confinement of a small number of persons awaiting disposition. Such an arrangement would necessitate an extensive network of transportation.

2. *Regionalization Under State Government Administration.* This may well be the most logical and expeditious way of dealing with the problem, because the state administrative agency would then be free to adjust jurisdictional lines among regions as conditions might dictate. The principal stumbling block to this approach is usually thought to be the political jealousies of local governments and the resistance to turning over what has traditionally been a local function to state government. This is undeniably a real and significant factor. But, should the state assume management of these institutions, it would probably be called upon to assume full responsibility for financial support as well. State governments are hesitant to increase their budgets in this way, but if they were willing to assume this responsibility, it would be a strong incentive to local governments and local taxpayers to relinquish this function which has little appeal to local pride anyway.

Under any regional scheme of administration and financial support, it would always be necessary to provide temporary lockups for police convenience when persons are arrested and booked during the night, on weekends and holidays, when courts are not available, and when arrangements for transportation to a central facility might be both difficult and inadvisable. Even in New York City the police maintain detention pens in the police precincts, but they are prohibited by law from keeping a person in this kind of confinement for more than 48 hours or until the next "court day." Such substations and temporary lockups are even more necessary in extremely large and populous areas. These facilities should, of course, meet minimum standards of health and safety, but their basic function is one of custodial security and managerial convenience.

There is another side to the regional concept. Too often administrative and custodial convenience has led local governments in large metropolitan areas to permit their local jails to become excessively large. This is especially bad, because such jails process so many people in short periods of time that the inmate population becomes almost anonymous as far as the staff and management are concerned. There have been instances in which men have become virtually lost in these facilities, especially if they are uneducated and have neither family nor lawyer. Large jurisdictions, like Cook County, Illinois, and Los Angeles County, California, would be better advised to maintain completely separate jails for people serving sentences longer than ten days and to decentralize the detention jails throughout the metropolitan areas in keeping with a related plan of decentralization of the trial courts.

Jail Size

Approximately one-half of all the local jails in the United States have a designed capacity of less than 25 inmates, and many of these are unoccupied part of the time. The impracticality of maintaining even the most rudimentary standards of security, health, classification, and professional management in these kinds of facilities will be apparent even to the most inexperienced observer. Except for temporary safekeeping for a few hours or at most for three days, these small jails might well be eliminated altogether.

Another 25 percent of the nation's local jails have an average daily occupancy of more than 24 but less than 50 inmates. Since most of these facilities must also accept women and juveniles, the convicted and the not convicted, the untried felon and the sentenced misdemeanant, it is clear that no matter how well-intentioned the management might be, such jails are usually unable to maintain acceptable standards of segregation, security, and health, to say nothing of programs for the orderly reintegration of their charges into normal community life. It is the opinion of most experienced students of jail administration that wherever regionalization is practicable, general purpose jails with a normal capacity of less than 50 should be abolished, consolidated, or converted to other use. This means that approximately 75 percent of all local city and county jails in the country should be eliminated, primarily because they are too small to successfully carry out their functions and meet even rock bottom minimum standards.

Related to the question of designed capacity is the factor of jail population fluctuations. Many more misdemeanants are arrested on weekends and holidays than on other days. Hence, it is not uncommon in some communities to find nearly twice as many inmates in a small jail on Monday morning than will be there on the following Thursday or Friday. There are also seasonal fluctuations. The presence of large numbers of seasonal farm workers or of nonresident construction laborers in a community will have the effect of swelling the jail population. A large jail system can accommodate itself to these population peaks and valleys much more readily than the small jail in a rural county seat.

Small jails with designed capacities of less than 50 inmates present their own peculiar problems. Conversely, large jails in metropolitan urban areas are beset with problems relating to overcrowding, mass handling of human beings, lack of financial support, and concentrations of too many offenders in one facility. The result, more often than not, is regimentation together with callous and cavalier attitudes toward the basic legal and human rights of both the accused and the convicted.

Only 131 of the more than 4,000 local jails in the country have designed capacities of 300 or more inmates. However, a few of these are very much larger than this. For example, in Illinois, the Cook County Jail is designed for 1,300 and usually has an average daily population of over 2,000. Cook County House of Correction for sentenced persons is planned for 1,800. The Dallas, Texas County Jail has an average daily population of about 1,500. Fulton County (Atlanta) Georgia has four local jails with average populations of 300 to 650. Dade County, Florida (Miami) Jail has a population of between 900 and 1,000. Los Angeles County, California has 24 separate city and county jails with estimated average daily populations ranging from four in the Beverly Hills police jail to 3,267 in the central County Jail, and 2,781 in the Hall of Justice detention jail. Los Angeles County also maintains a separate women's jail for between 800 and 900 inmates.

In New York State there are 76 local jails with a total daily population of about 17,000, but nearly 12,000 of these are in nine institutions operated by the New York City Department of Corrections. The Manhattan House of Detention for Men (The "Tombs") was at the time of the 1970 census 100 percent overcrowded.

Overcrowding

It is interesting to note that while overcrowding is common in all local jails, it is the large metropolitan jails that suffer most in this respect. Of the 131 jails of 300 or more capacity listed in the 1970 census, 38, or 29 percent, had average daily populations in excess of their designed capacities. Since the bulk of the jail population of the country is confined in these big city/county complexes, it is fair to say that most defendants committed to local jails will find themselves occupying less space per person than generally accepted standards would require. A further sad commentary on this matter is that the jails for the "not convicted" are more likely to suffer from overcrowding than are those for sentenced prisoners.

The legal thesis that a defendant is to be regarded "as innocent until proven guilty" appears in a most incongruous light in this situation. Conditions of treatment for prisoners are strangely reversed in our system of jails and prisons. The best conditions are likely to exist in state and federal prisons for long-term convicted and sentenced felons. They become progressively worse in jails for sentenced misdemeanants, and finally, tend to be worst of all in facilities for persons accused but not yet found guilty.

Overcrowding is most noticeable in the actual living quarters of jails where management is often forced to put two or even three men in a small cell designed for one, and in open barracks-type quarters beds are pushed closer together. The final resort of the desperate jailer is to install double and sometimes triple deck bunks. This may reduce the living space per man to as little as 20 square feet or even less. Seventy-two square feet per occupant in dormitories and one person per single cell of about the same area is usually regarded as acceptable.

The evils of overcrowding are too numerous to discuss in detail, but suffice it to say that there is probably no environment in which too many people living in too little space is more damaging. It creates psychological tensions leading to disciplinary problems; it makes staff supervision more difficult; it encourages abnormal sex behavior; it makes sanitary standards difficult to maintain; it prevents adherence to good practice in the separation of individuals and groups who should not be associated; and under some circumstances, it might even be held to be unconstitutional on the grounds of "cruel and unusual punishment."

As stated previously, one usually thinks of overcrowding in relation to living quarters, but it is important to remember that excessive numbers of prisoners place other kinds of strains on the total operation. For example, the workload of personnel is increased; feeding facilities will be inadequate; space and time for exercise will be cut down; and visiting facilities will become overtaxed, as will medical services and other programs of education, counseling, and so on.

The roots of most riots and mutinies in jails are to be found in conditions stemming from overcrowding.

Lack of Professional Management

Since most of the county and city jails are operated by county sheriffs or municipal police departments, it is inevitable that they will be managed and staffed chiefly by deputy sheriffs and policemen who are rarely trained to carry out correctional functions. In addition, sheriffs are usually elected because they present themselves to the electorate as good policemen, not as good correctional managers. Similarly, municipal police are appointed and trained in the functions and philosophy of police agencies. As a result, persons placed in direct charge of jails usually are not only untrained for the function, but are very often uninterested and unsympathetic to the needs of the assignment. It should be emphasized that this is not necessarily true in all instances. Some jails operated within the framework of sheriffs' departments do have reasonably adequate management. Unfortunately this is the exception rather than the rule.

An even worse condition exists in some states, such as Illinois, where sheriffs are not permitted to succeed themselves. Consequently, what skills and attitudes might have been learned by experience are lost because of artificial turnover in leadership.

The National Sheriffs' Association has recognized the need for training in jail management, and, in 1970 published a 220-page document entitled *Manual on Jail Administration*. Generally speaking, this is a good manual. That its provisions have not been implemented in any significant degree is the real problem.

The U.S. Bureau of Prisons has developed a jailer's correspondence course.[14]

Personnel Problems

As inferred above, professional policemen ordinarily do not prefer to be assigned to jail duty. This being the case, it is a common practice for the sheriff or police administrator responsible for the jail in his jurisdiction to assign personnel to jail duty who, for one reason or another, have been inadequate in their assignments as patrolmen. Another unfortunate practice observed in some jurisdictions is that of assigning new recruit policemen and deputies to jail duty precisely because it is unpopular duty for the more mature and experienced officers.

The pay level of employees assigned to jail duty also creates a serious problem in the recruitment of competent and trainable persons. These levels are substantially better in the large cities and populous counties than in the small jurisdictions. The 1970 national jail census states that: "The average

84

monthly earnings of full-time employees is almost 50% higher in cities over 25,000 population . . . ." The variability in salary levels in various parts of the country is also of interest in this respect. The 1970 national jail census reports as follows: "The highest average salaries are paid in the District of Columbia ($849), California ($760), New York ($745) and Wisconsin ($705). The lowest are found in Arkansas ($338), South Dakota ($350), West Virginia ($369), Idaho and South Carolina ($380), North Dakota ($392), and Mississippi ($397).

"Over 30% of the full-time equivalent work force is located in only two states—New York and California with 4,477 and 4,474 employees, respectively."

In addition to low pay, a further problem arises because most jails are undermanned as measured by the relationship between the number of inmates and the number of employees. The ratio of inmates to full-time equivalent employees averages 5.6 for the United States. It is also of special interest that some of the states with the lowest salaries also had the poorest ratio between employees and inmates. For example, in Mississippi, there were 11.44 inmates per employee, 10.63 in Idaho, and 10.22 in Texas. On the other end of the continuum, Hawaii had one full-time employee to 1.31 inmates, and the ratio was 2.7 in Massachusetts, 3.27 in Maine, 3.40 in the District of Columbia, and 3.43 in New Hampshire.

It should be reemphasized that in jurisdictions maintaining a 40-hour week with normal holidays, vacation, and sick leave, it takes almost five full-time employees to cover one post around the clock and throughout the year. Consequently, in a jurisdiction that has a ratio of ten inmates per employee and in a jail with an average daily population of 100, there would be an average of only two employees on duty at a time. Since there would probably be more employees on duty during the day than at night, it would be inevitable that on some shifts in such a jail there would be only one employee on duty. Under these circumstances, it is inevitable that most of the jail functions, other than keeping the front door locked, would be carried out by prisoners and not by employees.

Since there are so many very small jails in the country, it is also very probable that jails with fewer than 15 or 20 inmates are left entirely uncovered during some hours of the day. This kind of reckless disregard for public safety and for the health and safety of inmates is intolerable to say the least.

A few large jurisdictions, such as New York City, have a separate civil service class of correctional officers. They are recruited for this profession, are given training in the knowledge and skills they will be required to perform, and work out their career development within the correctional system rather than in the police system. In some other large jurisdictions in which jails are operated within the framework of a sheriff's department, a separate civil service classification for jail officers has also been adopted. Unfortunately, in most cases, this movement has been motivated not by the professional needs of corrections, but by the unfortunate fact that the average pay of correctional officers has tended to be lower than that of police officers, and by fiscal and personnel analysts who are seeking another way to save on the counties' payroll costs.

Correctional officers, municipal police, and municipal firemen tend to be recruited from the same pool of available manpower. Accordingly, unless the entry levels of pay of all three classifications in a given city or county are essentially equivalent, that classification which receives the lowest pay will almost certainly, on the average, get poorer quality personnel. Certainly the duties and working conditions of firemen, jailers, and policemen are different and may attract the interests of different kinds of prospective employees. Nevertheless, sound public policy should dictate that these pay levels be kept approximately equal.

No matter what the size or nature of a jail operation may be, it is essential that there be an orientation period for new recruits and incentives offered by management to encourage continuous upgrading by education and training throughout the careers of these public servants.

Archaic and Unsuitable Buildings

Buildings which are required to be both secure and fireproof are expensive to construct. Public funds for capital construction are difficult to obtain in most jurisdictions, and where it has been necessary to float bond issues by popular election, the voters are much more likely to want to go in debt for public buildings, for schools, hospitals, offices, and courthouses than they are for the replacement, or even the modernization, of old jails. The national jail census of 1970 reports that in the 3,319 county and urban institutions in jurisdictions with 25,000 population or more there are approximately 100,000 cells, and that one of every four of these has been in use for longer than fifty years, including more than 5,000 cells that are over 100 years old.

The census also reports that 86 percent of these institutions provide no facilities for exercise or other recreation for their inmates. Nearly 90 percent have no educational facilities, only one-half provide medical facilities, one in four has no visiting facility, and 47 are without an operating flush toilet (see table on p. 90). Many small jails are located in the basements of courthouses or other county buildings which would almost surely be declared unfit for human habitation if that same space were proposed for occupancy by other classes of citizens.

There are, of course, some jails which are modern, fireproof, secure, well-equipped, uncrowded, and adequately staffed, but these are so few that they can be counted on one's fingers, probably with some digits to spare.

Overuse of Jail Detention

As noted previously, over one-half of the adults and two-thirds of the juveniles held in jails on a given day are classified as "not convicted." A small percentage of these have been arrested and booked so recently (usually less than 48 hours) that they have not yet been arraigned before a magistrate. A still smaller number, such as murder cases, may have been denied bail. The overwhelming majority, however, are being held because of their inability to pay the premium on a "bail bond" or to put up a cash bond.

The Eighth Amendment of the U.S. Constitution says in part "Excessive bail shall not be required . . . ." Since the purpose of the bail bond is to ensure the appearance of the defendant in court when required, the amount of the cash bail prescribed in a specific case tends to be related to the severity of the offense rather than to the financial resources of the defendant. As a result, bail set as low as $25 is out of reach of a person who is penniless, jobless, and friendless. One-half to two-thirds of the persons held in most jails for more than 72 hours pending disposition probably fall into these categories.

Experiments in many jurisdictions in recent years have shown conclusively that jail populations can be drastically reduced without unusual risk to the public safety by instituting a few relatively simple procedures.

1. Use of Citations

Many persons arrested for misdemeanors can be issued a citation ordering the appearance of an individual before a magistrate at a given time. We are all familiar with this practice in connection with ordinary traffic violations. It can also be applied to a host of other minor offenses, such as disorderly conduct, simple assault and battery, petty theft, trespassing, and so on. An extension of the ordinary issuance of a citation by an arresting officer is what is often referred to as a "stationhouse" citation. In this case the arrested person is brought to the police station where a superior officer interviews the individual, checks on his residence, employment, and identity, and on a selective basis issues a citation at that point rather than confining the individual in jail.

2. Release on Own Recognizance

In this situation the accused may have been confined in jail, but when he is produced before a magistrate for arraignment and the setting of bail, the judge may, if the individual is unable to post cash bail, release him on his own recognizance, that is, on his personal promise to appear in court when ordered to do so. Obviously, this calls for some screening process, and unless a system is set up for establishing criteria for release on OR and assigning appropriate personnel to interview the defendant before his appearance in court and to check on his reliability, the judge will not have any basis for making a judgment, other than the unverified statement of the defendant. The small amount of personnel time needed to carry out this relatively straightforward task represents a financial outlay which is infinitesimal in comparison with the cost of confining the individual involved in jail for a period of days or weeks. Experiments with this practice indicate that the percentage of those released on OR who fail to appear is actually less than that of those who have posted a cash bail and forfeited the amount by nonappearance.

Even in felony cases, more than 8 percent of persons charged with a felony and referred to the criminal trial court are dismissed before trial, presumably on the grounds that the prosecuting attorney has concluded that he would be unable to get a conviction if the case went to trial. In addition, another 6 percent are acquitted by the court. This has led to the conclusion that a substantial number of persons charged with felony at the point of arrest might have been dropped earlier in the process had the case been examined at intake to the jail by a deputy district attorney. An experiment with precisely this approach is being initiated in Santa Clara County, California at the time of this writing.

Another problem of which most jailers complain is that judges and prosecutors are not on duty on weekends, holidays, or during the evening hours of working days. As a result, many people are held in jail awaiting the convenience of the courts and the prosecutors.

3. Giving Priority on Trial Court Calendars to Cases Confined in Jail as Opposed to Those Who Are Out on Bail

Admittedly, this presents some problem in the scheduling of court cases and requires a very close relationship and coordination between the jail administrator and the court adminstrator. Where practiced, however, this procedure can have a significant effect upon the length of time that persons stay in jail awaiting court disposition.

4. Alternative Programs for Special Categories of Offenders Who Are Now Processed Through the Jails in Large Numbers

This whole subject will be discussed in Chapter 6. The most numerous and obvious offenders occupying jail space are the chronic alcoholics. The establishment of detoxification and rehabilitation programs outside the jail system for these cases could have a dramatic effect in reducing jail populations. This is not necessarily a solution to the chronic street "drunk," but it can have the effect of transferring the problem to health authorities where it more properly belongs.

Unfortunately, the local jail in the American system tends to be a kind of human wastebasket for our attempts to deal with the total spectrum, not only of crime and criminals, but of a vast horde of humanity composed of social nuisances and economic misfits for which society has not yet devised more appropriate programs.

Lack of Minimal Programs for the Preservation of Physical and Mental Health

Admittedly, the basic purpose of the local jail is the secure custodial confinement of persons accused of all kinds of serious crimes and minor misdemeanors, and others who have been convicted and given short sentences. On the other hand, under the American system of jurisprudence, persons accused of crime are to be treated as innocent until proven guilty. Consequently, the majority of inmates confined in local jails must be regarded under the law as innocent even though accused, and they retain all of the rights of a free citizen except those which are necessarily abridged by confinement in jail while awaiting disposition by the judicial processes. Beginning with this premise, the accused person confined in jail has a basic right to the protection of his life and of his mental and physical health. This implies nutritious food, sanitary surroundings, and available medical service as an irreducible minimum. In addition, he is entitled to legal representation and to reasonable access to family and legitimate friends through correspondence and visits. Physical exercise and materials for reading and writing are absolute musts, even though the accused is to be confined only a few days.

The facts as revealed by the 1970 national jail census present a depressing picture even in the face of these rudimentary basic standards of care. In the 3,319 jails in counties with populations of over 25,000 people, the following facts are of interest:

Total Institutions	Recreational Facilities		Educational Facilities		Medical Facilities		Visiting Facilities		Toilets	
	Without	With	Without	With	Without	With	Without	With	Without	With
3319	2869	450	2961	358	1627	1692	684	2455	47	3272
100%	86.4	13.6	89.2	10.8	49.	51.	26.	74.	1.4	98.6

Perhaps the most incredible figures revealed in this table are that almost one-half of these jails have no medical facilities whatever, and that there are still 47 jails in the United States without flush toilets.

The number of diabetic and heart disease cases who die in jails each year because of inadequate or nonexistent medical services is unknown, but even a reading of the public newspapers makes it abundantly clear that such incidents occur with dismal regularity. These are the dramatic occurrences that only serve to punctuate other health deficiencies, such as the spread of infectious diseases, the neglect of untreated venereal disease, or even the failure to kill the vermin which infest the bodies and clothing of substantial numbers of deteriorated inmates.

Prisoners who must spend more than a few days in jail, whether awaiting judicial disposition or serving sentences, should be entitled to certain minimum services beyond the bare necessities of life. This is not because of the unrealistic expectation that each person released will have been remade or rehabilitated. Rather it is because when a society, for reasons believed necessary for the maintenance of law and order, takes away the liberty of an accused or convicted person for a limited period of time, that society has an obligation to the affected person, as well as to its own larger self-interest, to take the necessary steps to preserve, if not to enhance, that person's capacity to function as a free member of society after release. A healthy democratic society cannot afford to maintain institutions and programs which damage rather than sustain its own members.

Hence, reasonable opportunities for self-improvement for jail inmates should be maintained by giving them access to reading material, exercise and recreation, productive occupation, counseling, religious worship, and protection against destructive associations while confined. In general, it is in these kinds of program resources that local jails are most glaringly deficient.

Part-Time Sentences

In an effort to prevent jail sentences of a few months from causing loss of employment, a practice has gradually evolved in many parts of the country which permits selected inmates to serve their sentences on a part-time basis. Another motivation for this kind of sentencing arose during World War II when there was a serious labor shortage.

The practice has taken different forms:

1. *Weekend Sentences.* This kind of sentence usually prescribes that a convicted defendant serve a number of Saturdays and Sundays in jail, thus permitting him to continue his regular employment during the week. While this type of penalty may be assessed for almost any kind of offense, it is most frequently applied in cases of persons convicted and sentenced for driving while intoxicated. Weekend sentences have a strong appeal to some judges and also to welfare administrators who realize that the loss of employment and income to a breadwinner may very well result in the family being placed on relief. The practice is not popular with jail administrators because of problems arising from checking defendants in and out of a security area. This is seen as an administrative nuisance, and also increases the risk that such movements may provide opportunities for smuggling contraband. Such sentences might be more widely employed if jails had specially designed and separate quarters for this limited number of special cases.

2. *Work and Educational Furloughs.* This kind of sentence permits the prisoner to leave the jail during working hours and to spend the remainder of his time on weekends, holidays, and nights in the jail. Informal and very limited use of such furloughs extends back to the nineteenth century, but the first legislative act authorizing them was passed by the Wisconsin Legislature in 1913. This law is widely known as the "Huber Law." During World War II, the practice was extended to many other states and was justified under the "duration of the war" emergency acts of the federal and state governments.

In 1957 the California Legislature enacted its first work furlough statute, despite the fact that the practice had been employed on rather flimsy grounds in many of the agricultural counties for a number of years, dating back to World War II. It was widely publicized throughout the country in the mid-1950s, and by July 1, 1972, there was only a handful of states which had not enacted a statute authorizing work release for prisoners sentenced both to state and local institutions.

Even the U.S. Congress enacted a law in 1965 authorizing work release for prisoners in federal penitentiaries. There is wide variability in the detailed provisions of these statutes and equally wide disparity in the manner and extent to which the laws are implemented.

As of April 1, 1972, a nationwide survey of work release conducted by the American Justice Institute under a grant from the Law Enforcement Assistance Administration[15] revealed that there were then 522 counties in the United States making use of work release, that about 22,000 persons had been granted such release during the previous twelve months, and that 4,600 persons in the whole country were on work release status on a given day. Five states—California, Florida, Massachusetts, North Carolina, and Wisconsin—accounted for over one-half of the misdemeanant work releases in the country.

These facts indicate that while there has been great expansion in this practice by local jails in recent years, it obviously has not been fully implemented.

Work release is usually justified primarily as a vehicle for offender rehabilitation. But in fact, it is often justified by local jail administrators chiefly because it is a program which costs very little—a few jurisdictions have even been able to turn a profit from it by charging the prisoners for their keep while confined in jail, thus relieving the county of the expense.

One of the principal administrative problems with work release is the lack of special quarters for persons serving such sentences. The second problem relates to the necessity for having some specialized personnel to administer the program. Budget restrictions tempt jail administrators to try to run work release programs without the addition of specialized personnel. The problems of maintaining relationships with employers and families, arranging transportation, handling the moneys involved make it almost essential that a viable work furlough program be administered by a specially qualified person who has these duties as his major responsibility. In a few jurisdictions the work release program is administered by the probation department rather than by the sheriff.

While these programs are usually referred to as work release, they are often appropriately used for releasing persons to continue their education. For example, to interrupt a college or vocational education course by a 60-day jail sentence might very well delay a person's education a whole year or perhaps discourage him from continuing at all.

There are other variations of part-time sentences which are not widely practiced. They include such things as requiring the prisoner to do certain work for the victim of his crime as a measure of restitution. Occasionally a judge has given a sentence requiring that an offender engage in some public service for a specified number of hours where such service is related to the nature of his offense. For example, an offender convicted of vandalism for breaking windows and desecrating walls in a school building might be required to correct his damages in that school district or to do other work in compensation for his acts.

Of all the part-time sentences in use in the country at this time, the work and educational release programs are by far the most commonly practiced.

Financial Problems

Local jails, embedded as they are in the governmental structure of counties and cities, suffer in a unique way from the financial problems common to all local governments in the United States. The taxing power of government in this country, especially during the last half century, has been shifting upward in the governmental hierarchies. Early in our national history most of the taxes collected were levied by local governments. In this decade the principal tax burden on the citizenry originates with the federal government, followed by state governments, and, finally, by counties and cities. This is not the appropriate place to discuss the economic and political reasons for this shift. But the simple fact is that local governments, limited as they are chiefly to property taxes and in a lesser degree to sales taxes, are all having difficulty in supporting local government services from these sources. Consequently, some of the money collected by the federal government and by state governments filters down to local governments in the form of various kinds of subsidies and subventions. The local service which is most popular and most uniquely demanded is public education. Schools receive support from all three levels of government. This is also true of public welfare, hospitals, public health, and similar services which are more universally supported by voters.

Until very recently, no subsidies or subventions for criminal justice agencies have been provided by the federal government or state governments. Within the broad structure of criminal justice agencies, including courts, police, and corrections, the local jail is at the bottom of that neglected group of public services. Except in Alaska, Connecticut, Rhode Island, Delaware, and Vermont where, as has been noted previously, the state governments have taken over the management as well as the support of local jails, very little financial assistance comes from the higher levels of government.

Perhaps one of the reasons for this unhappy situation is that jails have no constituency, and the idea of spending money to improve services for law violators appears to the average citizen and his political representatives as an extraordinarily low priority item.

State governments have gradually taken over prison and parole services for adult felons, as well as state institutions for delinquents committed by the juvenile courts. In many jurisdictions this very fact has encouraged some of the local jurisdictions to commit convicted defendants to state institutions for no better reason than that they did not wish to assume the financial burden of taking care of the cases at the local level. It was this phenomenon which was referred to by the State Director of Corrections as "shipping the bodies to the money" which served as the principal motivation for the enactment of the Probation Subsidy Act of 1963 in California.

It is becoming more and more apparent that the problem of enforcing minimum standards and providing adequate financial support for local jails will not be solved or even substantially improved unless state governments either provide a substantial proportion of the financial support accompanied by enforceable standards or that the state governments assume the management and support of these functions in their entirety.

The National Advisory Commission on Criminal Justice Standards and Goals which issued its massive document on "Corrections" on January 23, 1973, has this to say on the subject: "All local detention and correctional functions, both pre- and postconviction, should be incorporated within the appropriate State system by 1982."[16]

NOTES

[1]U. S. Law Enforcement Assistance Administration and U. S. Bureau of the Census, *Local Jails*, Washington, D. C.: U. S. Government Printing Office, 1973.

[2]Unpublished report of Los Angeles, California Sheriff's Department, 1974.

[3]Richard A. McGee, "Our Sick Jails," *Federal Probation* 35 (March 1971): 3–8.

[4]The President's Commission on Law Enforcement and Administration of Justice, *Task Force Report: Corrections*, Washington, D. C.: U. S. Government Printing Office, 1967, Chapter 7.

[5]*Ibid.*

[6]Unpublished data, Bureau of Criminal Statistics, Sacramento, California: California Department of Justice.

[7]The President's Commission on Law Enforcement and Administration of Justice, *Task Force Report: Corrections*, p. 79.

[8]American Bar Association Commission on Correctional Facilities and Services, Statewide Jail Standards and Inspection Systems Project, *Survey of State Standards and Inspection Legislation for Jails and Juvenile Detention Facilities: Preliminary Report*, Washington, D. C.: American Bar Association, August 1972.

[9]See Illinois Department of Corrections, Bureau of Detention Facilities and Jail Standards, *Illinois County Jail Standards*, Springfield, Ill.: July 1971. See also National Sheriffs' Association, *Manual on Jail Administration: A Handbook Designed to Ease the Difficult Task of the Jail Administrator*, Washington, D. C., 1970, and Califor-

nia Board of Corrections, *A Study of California County Jails*, Sacramento, Calif., April 1970.

[10]Charles Dickens, *American Notes*, 1842.

[11]John Howard, *The State of the Prisons in England and Wales, with Preliminary Observations and an Account of Some Foreign Prisons and Hospitals*, London, 1777.

[12]Thomas Mott Osborne, *Society and Prisons*, New Haven, 1916.

[13]Joseph F. Fishman, *Crucibles of Crime*, New York, 1923.

[14]U. S. Bureau of Prisons, *The Jail: Its Operation and Management*, Nick Pappas, ed., Washington, D. C.: U. S. Department of Justice, 1970.

[15]*Ordering Time to Serve Prisoners: A Manual for the Planning and Administering of Work Release*, Washington, D. C.: U. S. Department of Justice Law Enforcement Assistance Administration, Technical Assistance Division, 1973.

[16]National Advisory Commission on Criminal Justice Standards and Goals, *Corrections*, Washington, D. C.: U. S. Department of Justice, 1973, Standard 9.2, p. 292.

6 Correctional Institutions for Adult Offenders: An Overview

As was pointed out in an earlier chapter, the definition of adult as viewed by criminal law varies from state to state. In this context an adult is a person who in the eyes of the law is held responsible as an individual for his behavior, and if charged with a criminal offense, his case is disposed of as if he were a responsible adult and not an immature adolescent or a child.[1] In some states the dividing line is the sixteenth birthday, in others the seventeenth, and in some the eighteenth. In a few states a court of initial jurisdiction, whether it be the juvenile court or the adult criminal court, may waive jurisdiction so that an adult under twenty-one years of age can be treated as a juvenile, or conversely, a person under the juvenile court age may be treated as an adult.

Accordingly, this chapter will deal with prisons, penitentiaries, reformatories, and other correctional institutions for convicted defendants whom the law and the court have dealt with as adults. With few exceptions, these institutions are operated either by state governments or the federal government. Local jails, while used primarily for the confinement of adult persons as noted in Chapter 5, will not be discussed here.

This chapter being an overview of correctional institutions for adults, the organization, management, and programs in such institutions today will not be considered here but will be developed in greater detail in Chapter 7.

State prisons in some jursidictions may be used for the confinement of persons convicted of serious misdemeanors, but generally speaking, state and federal prisons and correctional institutions are used for the confinement of persons convicted of offenses which have been defined by the law and by the court as felonies.

In California, the statutory definition of a felony is: "A crime which is punishable with death or by imprisonment in the State prison."[2]

96

Brief History of American Prisons

The history of the measures which various societies have used as punishments for violating criminal laws is fascinating, if one is addicted to horror stories. Death by every conceivable means from burning at the stake to the electric chair; brutal beatings and whippings, physical mutilations, such as branding and blinding, and amputation of extremities; drawing and quartering; hangings in the public square; deportation to faraway colonies; public degradation by whipping through the streets and by locking in the stocks in a public place. All of these are well-known to even the most casual reader of history.

In England, from which America has inherited most of its legal doctrine, the death penalty was still retained as punishment for 160 different offenses as late as the close of the eighteenth century.

The revulsion against physical brutality which accompanied the rise of democratic thinking and the revolutionary movements of the eighteenth century dictated the necessity for finding some means of punishing most convicted criminals other than by execution or physical brutality. Our forefathers appear to have built prisons and penitentiaries because they could think of no better substitute.[3] Jails and prisons were, of course, not unknown. In fact, tourists of today may visit the tomb in Rome where the Apostle Paul was confined awaiting disposition of his case. The point is that these jails, prisons, and places of involuntary incarceration were not used as a means of punishment, but primarily as places of temporary detention, just as the county jails of today serve that function. The old prison at Ghent, Belgium, erected in 1772, is probably the oldest institution in Europe built for the confinement of convicted criminals.

Thus it is fair to say that the development of penal institutions for the punishment of offenders began to develop about the time of the American Revolution. History records that in March, 1787, two years before the final ratification of the Constitution, a small group of Philadelphia citizens met at the home of Benjamin Franklin to discuss the problem of public punishment in Pennsylvania. Dr. Benjamin Rush, one of the signers of the Declaration of Independence, presented a paper setting forth the unfortunate state of affairs and proposing a new program for the treatment of criminals. It is interesting to note how many of the ideas presented in that paper persist to the present day.

He proposed the establishment of a prison which would include in its program: a) classification of prisoners for housing, b) a rational system of prison labor to make the prison self-supporting, including gardens to provide

97

food and outdoor exercise for the prisoners, c) individualized treatment for convicts according to whether the crimes arose from passion, habit, or temptation, and d) indeterminate periods of punishment. In the same year, as an outgrowth of this meeting, the Philadelphia Society for Alleviating the Miseries of Public Prisons was organized and, as a result of its efforts, on April 5, 1790, the Pennsylvania Legislature passed an act which is regarded as the beginning of the modern system of prison administration in America. During this period Pennsylvania abolished the brutal code of corporal punishment, mutilation, and degradation which had been in vogue, not only in that state, but throughout the American colonies under English rule, and by 1800 the death penalty was applicable in only two crimes, murder and treason. Fines or imprisonment had been substituted for mutilation and degradation in all other crimes. Here we see the inauguration of a new method of dealing with convicted criminals, not only for Pennsylvania, but ultimately for the whole nation.

It would be a mistake to assume that these reforms came into being suddenly. There had been previous experiments in Europe, and even in America. William Penn had established a penal system in Pennsylvania based on these principles 100 years previously. However, this code lasted for only 36 years, 1682 to 1718, when with the death of William Penn the Colony reverted to the harsher English code.

For the purpose of this brief discussion, the nearly 200 years of penological history in America can be divided into six parts, each identified by certain dominant characteristics. It should be pointed out, however, that each of these periods passed on to its successors some of its special flavor, so that the American prison in the last quarter of the twentieth century retains some of the features of all of the preceding periods. The six periods may be identified as follows:

1. 1790 to 1830, the Early American Prison
2. 1830 to 1870, the Pennsylvania and Auburn Systems
3. 1870 to 1900, the Reformatory System
4. 1900 to 1945, the Industrial System
5. 1945 to 1965, Post-World War II Reconstruction
6. 1965 to the present, a period of rigorous reappraisal and groping for alternatives

The first period, 1790 to 1830, was one of pioneer makeshift methods. The simple housing classification into "night rooms" and a few handicraft industries quickly lost credence and any effectiveness they might have had, owing to overcrowding, idleness, incompetent personnel, and lack of administrative leadership. It is interesting to note that many of the county jails and so-called industrial farms for misdemeanants at the present time are not unlike these early American prisons and suffer from some of the same maladies.

The second period, 1830 to 1870, witnessed the development and the decline of two competing systems of prison discipline. These are usually identified as the Pennsylvania System and the Auburn System (New York State). The Pennsylvania System was built around the idea of separate confinement in individual cells at all times with the prisoner occupied with handicraft labor. This was to be supplemented by moral and religious instruction, and "prison visiting" by responsible volunteers from the honest citizenry. Prisoners were not only prohibited from speaking to each other, but every possible method was used to keep them from looking upon each other's face. The latter was accomplished by placing a hood of black gauzelike cloth over each man's head whenever he was taken from his cell to the infirmary or to church. On the other hand, the Auburn System advocated separate confinement at night only, and permitted labor in congregate workshops during the day under enforced silence. Noncommunication with rigid discipline and punishment to enforce it, and religious instruction as the rehabilitative agent were the theoretical bases of both systems. Actually, hard work was probably the most effective ingredient of both.

Remnants of both the Pennsylvania and Auburn Systems prevail to this day in concepts of segregation of different types of prisoners from each other and confinement in individual cells; even the silence rule has been enforced in some institutions, especially in large congregate dining rooms, until very recently.

The third period, 1870 to 1900, was characterized by the rise of the reformatory system with its program of education, trade training, the earning of credits and marks, and the indeterminate sentence and parole. The reformatory movement was a triumph of the idea that treatment of prisoners should be reformative and educational, as well as punitive. It called for reformative measures through education and vocational training, as well as through religion. This approach was described by one prison writer as "pedagogical penology."[4]

The first reformatory in the United States was opened at Elmira, New York in 1876. It is interesting to note, however, that this institution with its classical reformatory program was reserved for young men from 16 to 30 years of age who were serving their first prison term. It also provided one of the early examples of the indeterminate sentence. A reformatory sentence had a maximum but no minimum, and prisoners could be released on parole before the maximum if their behavior warranted it. Reformatories were established in rapid succession in twelve other states within the next 25 years. By 1913, when Connecticut established its reformatory at Cheshire, the movement had lost its impetus. In fact, the whole program failed to outlive many of its own founders.

On the other hand, many of the ideas which were essential ingredients of the reformatory movement were extended to the management of all state prisons for youths and adults. For example, the indeterminate sentence for all persons committed to state prisons in California was enacted in 1917, but no state reformatories have ever been built in that state. Remnants of the grading system were still to be found in San Quentin Prison as late as 1945. The word "rehabilitation" replaced the word "reform" and took on broader connotations.

The chief contribution of the reformatory period to modern correctional practice was the introduction of indeterminacy in sentencing, of parole laws, and of "good time" credits for good behavior. By 1900 every state in the Union had at least one prison for adults. There was some effort to provide incentives for good behavior through "good time" credits and parole. Some lip service was given to rudimentary education programs, but generally, the only regular personnel, other than guards and work supervisors, who concerned themselves to any great degree with the concepts of rehabilitation and the preparation of the prisoner for reintegration into normal society were the chaplains, and they were often part-time and unpaid.

As new prisons were provided in the newly admitted states of the Union and in the South after the Civil War, both the work programs and discipline and the architectural features of the buildings more nearly represented the Auburn rather than the Pennsylvania system. The latter was more widely imitated in Europe than in the United States.

During the period 1900 to 1945, the industrial prison was characterized by emphasis upon "hard labor" and industrial and agricultural production aimed at reducing the rising costs of these institutions. This rising cost was brought about not only by the increasing unit cost per prisoner, but by the burgeoning of the whole prison population. For example, in 1850 there were only 6,737 persons in American prisons. By 1890 this had increased to 45,233, and by 1935 there were about 137,000 men and women in state prisons, reformatories, and other kinds of facilities for convicted felons.

The period between 1935 and 1945 was unstable and abnormal for prisons because the Great Depression of the 1930s resulted in a great increase in prison population and World War II began having its effect as early as 1939. By 1945 the prison population of the country had dropped temporarily by about one-third in many jurisdictions, only to rise again at an even more rapid rate in the following three decades.

This great increase in prison population not only stretched the buildings and physical plants to the bursting point, but also shocked state legislatures with increasing costs. It was perhaps a very normal reaction for political and lay leaders to demand that ways be found to make it possible for this small army of ablebodied men and women to contribute to their own support. Work was the order of the day, and the value of prison production which had been declining between 1885 and 1895 increased to 34 million dollars in 1905, and to 71 million dollars in 1932.

Undoubtedly some trade training was accomplished in the course of employment in prison industries, but the managers of these industries did not regard training as their primary objective. For them industries were established and operated chiefly to make money for the state and to maintain prison discipline. When challenged by labor leaders, industrialists, and reformers, the euphemistic excuse for the industries was that they not only made money, but they taught the prisoners "habits of industry." On the other hand, if the alternative is complete idleness and physical and mental deterioration, any excuse is probably good enough.

A large number of the problems surrounding prison industries have stemmed from the claim that prison labor competes unfairly with private labor and that it depresses the market in any product in which prison production is significantly large. The extensive history of this subject reveals many practices which did exploit the prisoner and also corrupted the system. Most of these questionable practices had been eliminated by 1935 by restrictive state and federal legislation. These matters will be discussed in greater detail later in Chapter 7.

The death knell of prison industries as the core of an institutional program was really sounded by the passage of a number of federal laws. The Hawes-Cooper Act passed in 1929 divested prison production of its interstate character by making the products subject to state laws upon arrival at destination. Many of the populous industrialized states had laws prohibiting the sale of prison-made products on the open market. Consequently, if a state which had no such laws shipped its products like sisal rope and cotton cloth to another state, they could not be sold there because it would violate that state's laws. The Ashurst-Sumners Act passed in 1935 prohibited transportation companies from accepting prison products for transportation to any other state in violation of the laws of that state and provided for the labeling of all prison products in interstate commerce. The effect of these statutes was greatly accentuated by the deep economic depression of 1929 to 1933. It made state legislatures more responsive than usual to the protests of organized labor and related organized businesses. As a result, in rapid succession 29 states passed laws restricting the sale of prison products to government use only. Some exceptions were made for farm products, but in 1935, 33 states had virtually prohibited the sale of prison products on the open market, and by 1940 every state had passed some type of restrictive law limiting the free sale of prison-made products on the open market. On October 14, 1940, the President signed an act further restricting the movement of prison-made products in interstate commerce.

Prison industries had a brief revival between 1941 and 1945 with the establishment of special "war industries" in most prisons across the country. These industries were involved in producing goods or services in support of the war effort. An opinion of the U.S. Attorney General set aside for the duration of the national emergency the provisions of a presidential executive order signed by Theodore Roosevelt in 1905 which prohibited using the labor of state prisoners to produce goods or services for the federal government. Once the war was over, these industries had no market and were quickly forced out of business. Prison industries did not die in the following period, but it has been an uphill fight for survival, and industrial production programs in most state prisons employ but a small fraction of the population and contribute relatively little to their financial support. The war industries program prolonged the life of the industrial prison by at least a decade.

The post-World War II period from 1945 to 1965 was an agonizing time of readjustment characterized by unprecedented increases in prison populations and destructive idleness and overcrowding, accompanied by frequent riots and disturbances. Twenty years may seem like an inordinately long time to be characterized as a "postwar" period, but it should be pointed out that the Korean conflict, the war in Southeast Asia, and the "Cold War" in Europe have had a continuing effect on the social climate, economy, and political institutions of this country, even until today.

The year 1965 is chosen as the beginning of the contemporary period, not because of some historical event, but rather because it became clear about that time that the growing disenchantment with prison terms as the disposition of choice for most criminal cases was being translated into action throughout the land. For example, in 1960 in California, 28.3 percent of all felons sentenced in the Superior Courts were committed to prison. This percentage had been fairly constant for many years. By 1965 this percentage had dropped to 23.3 percent, and by 1972 it had declined to 9.8 percent.

In the years immediately following 1945, prison populations, which had dropped dramatically during the war years, began to increase at an accelerated rate. Except for the expansion of the U.S. Bureau of Prisons, there had been little prison construction during the depression years of the 1930s, and almost none during the war. Normally, from the time a new prison is authorized, it takes from three to seven years to go through the process of fund appropriation, equipping, and activation. Consequently, states whose prisons were already filled to capacity in 1930 found themselves 15 to 20 years behind in construction needs in the period between 1945 and 1955.

The problem was compounded by the fact that notoriously underpaid prison employees had deserted their work for higher wages in war industries, and many of those of military age had gone into the services. New postwar recruits were inexperienced and untrained. The workweek for prison custodial officers in some jurisdictions was still as high as 48 hours – in some places before the war it had been as high as 72 hours. The general adoption of the 40-hour week in both private and public employment put an unprecedented strain on prison budgets. Changing from a 48-hour week to a 40-hour week called for a 20 percent increase in staff in order to maintain the same level of service. Food and other commodity prices had also increased. This sudden escalation of costs together with increased prison populations was more than most state legislatures were willing to provide for. From the standpoint of prison administrators, the postwar "catch up" period was more than a process of reconstruction – it was a struggle for survival by crisis management in many jurisdictions.

The decade following World War II presented prison administrators with numerous handicaps, none of which was unfamiliar, but which when combined provided the formula for inevitable disaster. In summary, the typical situation was this:

Substandard budgets;
Untrained personnel;
Not enough custodial staff;
Gross overcrowding, sometimes to the extent of 100 to 150 percent in excess of capacity;
Institutions which had grown too large for safe and efficient management;
Gross idleness, owing partly to the collapse of the war industries and partly to overcrowding and shortage of personnel;
Deteriorated physical plants which were not only old, but which had not been maintained properly during the Depression or during the War because of material shortages;
Conflicts in philosophy between old-line prison managers and newly recruited executives and professional personnel;

Parole boards who were often insensitive to the effects of their decisions on prison morale;

Lack of educational and rehabilitative programs to occupy the prisoners' time and to provide a sense of hope. Despair is the father of anger and frustration. Angry mobs of idle young men are the stuff from which mutiny and riot are made.

The dam burst in the old state prison at Trenton, New Jersey at 11:30 P.M. on March 29, 1952. The men in the segregation wing mutinied, smashed their toilets and almost everything else breakable. Their excuse was that one of their number had not been given needed medical treatment. They took no hostages, however, and they were quickly brought under control. Two weeks later, April 15, a real riot started when the men in one of the shops seized four employees as hostages, barricaded themselves in the print shop, and demanded that an outside agency investigate the prison and the parole system. Shortly after, the Rahway Prison Farm a few miles away also erupted, and by Thursday noon the inmates had seized nine hostages, wrecked the dormitory of which they had taken control, and begun negotiations based on a list of demands. They held out for five days before surrendering.

While this was going on, the huge state prison at Jackson, Michigan exploded into the most disastrous riot in American prison history up to that time.[5]

As noted previously, the weaknesses and chronic problems of the system were nationwide. Riots, like many other highly publicized events, are also contagious. The fire had actually started a year earlier in other smaller, less publicized prisons, but the real blaze was sparked by the Trenton and Jackson blowups. Then, in rapid succession, one prison after another fell prey to riots, mutinies, disturbances, fires, and strikes. During the remainder of 1952 through 1955, one disturbance after another occurred in Louisiana, Montreal, Canada, North Carolina, Idaho, Georgia, Kentucky, California, Massachusetts, Chillicothe, Ohio (federal reformatory), Menard, Illinois, Utah, Ohio, New Mexico, Pennsylvania, Arizona, Washington, Minnesota, and Alcatraz (federal). Almost everyone experienced at least some form of prisoner rebellion.

The American Prison Association created a special committee on riots in 1953. Its chairman was Richard A. McGee, Director of Corrections of California, and its members included such well-known officials as James V. Bennett, Director of the Federal Bureau of Prisons; Sanford Bates of New Jersey; Austin MacCormick, former Commissioner of Corrections of New York City; Joseph Ragen, Warden of Stateville, Illinois; Will C. Turnbladh, Executive Director of the National Council on Crime and Delinquency. The committee stated in its report that riots "should be looked upon as costly and dramatic symptoms of faulty prison administration."

The committee listed as the bases of this maladministration the following factors:

A. Inadequate financial support, and official and public indifference.
B. Substandard personnel.
C. Enforced idleness.
D. Lack of professional leadership and professional programs.
E. Excessive size and overcrowding of institutions.
F. Political domination and motivation of management.
G. Unwise sentencing and parole practices.

It is noteworthy that this committee, made up of key national leaders in prison administration of that time, offered no fundamental changes in the system—only that it be better supported and made safer and more efficient. Questioning of the system itself was to come later, as we shall see. It is doubtful that prisoner leaders of prison rebellions actually expect anything but public attention and a few brief hours of sweet revenge against the agents of constituted authority, to be followed inevitably by retaliation and punishment, sometimes including violent death for some of the guilty and a few of the innocent.

No one wishes to accept the idea that violent insurrections among the most irresponsible of our convicted criminals can result in needed reforms. But the historical fact has been that after the harsh clamping down of disciplinary control in prisons where such control has been temporarily lost, responsible political leaders do move in with money and resources to correct obvious deficiencies. That we must have violence, bloodshed, and millions of dollars worth of property damage before most state governments are moved to bring about reforms is a sad commentary on the erratic course of prison administration in this country.

The decade following the riots and related chaotic conditions in American prisons generally saw renewed efforts to repair the aftermath of the disturbances and to reorganize state systems of prison management. Increases in prison populations resulted in substantial efforts to expand physical plants and to improve the overall administrative direction of the correctional systems. Frequent turnover in top management with changes in state governors continued to be a problem, but civil service and training programs for personnel were greatly expanded.

Except for the federal system and in a very few states, overcrowding and excessive inmate idleness were continuing problems which actually got worse instead of better in some institutions. There were attempts to find alternatives to incarceration in oversized central state prisons. For example, California expanded its forestry camp program to the extent that for a time about 3,000 men were assigned to forty 80-man camps which in turn were supported by three medium-sized institutions known as Conservation Centers. Specialized institutions, or segments of general prisons, were established for the confinement of mentally ill and mentally abnormal prisoners. Some beginning efforts were made to extend "work furlough" programs to state and federal prisons. Unfortunately, because most prisons are located far from employment opportunities, this movement gained much more impetus in county jails than it did in prisons.

Developments in California during the postwar period deserve special attention, because it was there that the most massive effort was made to compensate for past neglect, and to meet the needs of a general population growth unequaled in the history of the nation. The population of the state in 1900 was 1,485,053 and by 1940 had increased to 6,907,387. The estimated number of people in the state in 1945 was 8,500,000, and the decennial census of 1950 reported 10,586,223 residents. By 1960 the figure was 15,717,204, and in 1970 it was 19,953,134.

The first prison was established in a group of tar paper shacks on San Quentin Point in San Francisco Bay in 1850, and had grown by accretion rather than plan until, in the depths of the Depression in 1934, it held some 6,000 prisoners in a physical plant with a normal capacity of 2,700.

In 1880 a second prison had been started near Folsom on the edge of a granite quarry on the American River, 22 miles from Sacramento. Until 1940 San Quentin and Folsom were the only prisons for adult males in the state, except for a few small road camps. A third open-style institution at Chino, California had been authorized and some construction begun, but it was not activated until a year later and then only for a few hundred men. In 1940 these two high-security prisons held a combined population of 8,900. About 150 women prisoners were confined in the California Institution for Women at a remote location in the Tehachapi Mountains. This was the prison system of what was soon to become the most populous of the states.

When Earl Warren became Governor in 1943, he was keenly aware of the inadequacy of the system and resolved to move as quickly and aggressively as possible. Fortunately for all concerned, the war had caused the prison population to decline from a high of 9,300 in 1939, to a low of 5,400 by the end of 1944. In a limited degree this allowed some time for planning, law changes, and reorganization.

Since 1879 the prisons had been under the administrative direction of a part-time lay board of five members, each serving a ten-year term.

It is beyond the scope of this chapter to recount all the events of this period in California's prison history. Suffice it to say that the legislature created a new department of state government to administer the system, and brought in an experienced prison administrator from outside the state to head the new Department of Corrections.[6] The resident population of the correctional institutions for adults grew from the low of 5,400 in December, 1944 to 25,500 on June 30, 1964.

A diversified system of 12 major institutions and 42 camps was created. Personnel were blanketed into civil service, and training programs were inaugurated. A full spectrum of programs for inmates was developed and put into effect, ranging from improved medical services and professional food management through vocational and academic education, revitalized industries, recreation, and case counseling. Each newly admitted case was studied and classified in regional reception centers.

Despite massive efforts to implement the kinds and quality of prison programs which professional leaders had been advocating since the famous Declaration of Principles of 1870, the sheer pressure of numbers prevented many programs from serving more than a fraction of the prisoners. The overcrowding problem was not solved until after 1965, when the population began to decline as a result of the increased use of probation. This had the related effect of reducing the proportion of prisoners who could be trusted in open institutions and camps.

In addition to the increased spending of public funds, legislators and fiscal staff analysts began insisting on facts to show that these new and expanded programs were producing results in terms of reduced criminal behavior by released prisoners.

The Director had been advocating research for these purposes for years, but it was not until 1957 that the legislature finally authorized the formal establishment of a Division of Research in the central office of the Department. This was the first unit of its kind in the country which devoted itself to actual research studies rather than the mere keeping of administrative statistics. Thus scientific evaluation of correctional programs by qualified research personnel gained its first solid foothold in an operational department. The rigorous and objective appraisal of performance is a concept which is receiving growing acceptance in contemporary corrections.

The Contemporary Period beginning about 1965 has been marked by several significant developments. The President's Commission on Law Enforcement and Administration of Justice, which published its landmark reports in 1966, focused national attention upon the whole crime problem and the public agencies charged with its control. For the first time the "systems" approach to these agencies enabled everyone to view the prison in perspective, in relationship to courts, prosecutors, police, jails, probation, parole, and juvenile agencies and facilities. Planners and analysts began trying to define the roles of all these diverse functions and institutions and to see at last the real meaning of their interrelationships.

During this same period, nearly half of the states and the federal government continued to revise their criminal laws. Most states tended to follow the general plan of the *Model Penal Code* developed by the American Law Institute. A substantial number of states have enacted new codes. In others, Criminal Law Revision Commissions are still at work. These codes are significant in relation to prisons because of their effects on sentencing and parole, and also on the organizational structures of state government which administer prisons and correctional programs.

Another characteristic of this period has been the explosion of "case law" brought about by numerous court decisions affecting the constitutional rights of prisoners and parolees (see Chapter 12).

In addition, there has been intense interest in prisons by the so-called New Left groups which appear to be anarchistic and revolutionary in character. Since many of the leaders of these movements have been in prison, their interest and hostility is understandable. Furthermore, the apparent strategy of these groups is always to attack institutions in which disruption of constituted authority seems to be easiest. First, it was universities, then military induction centers and politcal conventions, and later prisons. The massive rebellion and riot at New York's Attica Prison[7] in September, 1971 had many of the same characteristics as the riots of the early 1950s, but its distinctive feature was the demands of its leaders for the presence of leaders and lawyers identified with militant revolutionary groups. It is believed by some of those close to the scene that some of the riot leaders actually had the visionary belief that the rebellion in Attica might spark a nationwide revolution among the minorities, and the disillusioned youth of the country.

What was accomplished was the deaths of 43 persons and irreparable damage to other people and property. Reforms were admittedly needed in the New York system and were, in fact, already underway; but revolutionaries do not want reforms. They seek destruction of a system with the fanatical belief that a better system can be built on the ashes of the old.

Another development has taken place quietly, but has had a far more dramatic effect on prisons than anything which had happened to them before in this century. Because of the use of alternatives to prison sentences for convicted felons, the proportion of eligibles actually sent to prison has been dropping steadily in most jurisdictions since about 1960. This has been most dramatic in California where a state probation subsidy went into effect in 1965. There the proportion of felons sentenced to prison has dropped from 28.3 percent in 1960, to 9.8 percent in 1972. Comparative statistics are difficult to obtain and even more difficult to interpret, but, generally speaking, it is fair to say that throughout the country, courts are moving toward a policy of not sentencing men and women to prison except as a last resort for most property and drug abuse offenses. Consequently, prison populations more and more tend to be composed of individuals convicted of crimes of personal violence, or of other kinds of offenders whose patterns of crime are such that no other disposition seems tenable.

Following the 1966 reports of the President's Commission on Law Enforcement and Administration of Justice, Congress enacted the so-called Safe Streets Act of 1968, which created in the U.S. Department of Justice the Law Enforcement Assistance Administration (LEAA) and provided for substantial monetary grants-in-aid to the states for the improvement of police, courts, and corrections. Each state was required by the Act to create a state criminal justice planning agency to administer the distribution and monitoring of these federal funds.

A special division within the LEAA was also created with some grant funds to encourage and support experimentation and research in the whole spectrum of criminal justice administration.

During its first five years, LEAA was plagued by frequent turnover among top level administrators which resulted in lack of consistent policy direction. By 1974, the agency had distributed over 3 billion dollars. What the longer-term effect of this federal intervention will be on the efficiency and quality of the total system, and more especially on correctional programs, will probably not be clear for years to come.

One of the recent productions of this federal effort is of special interest to corrections in general and to prisons in particular. In October, 1971 the Attorney General appointed a National Commission on Criminal Justice Standards and Goals. Four massive documents containing recommendations and commentary were issued in 1973.[8] The volume on corrections contains 129 specific "standards and goals."

Of these, the following are of special significance in their possible effects on conventional prisons and prison systems:

Rights of Offenders

Special emphasis is given to the rights of prisoners, such as access to courts, protection against personal abuse, medical care, nondiscrimination, rehabilitation, grievance procedures, exercise of religious beliefs and practices.

Diversion from the Criminal Justice Process

The concept here is that from the time an offender commits an illegal act until final disposition of the case, there should be an organized procedure to explore alternative courses to formal processing through the conventional criminal justice steps of arrest, conviction, and sentence, to final discharge. Admittedly, many cases present no acceptable alternatives, but considering the many thousands of offenses involving alcoholism, drug abuse, prostitution, minor thefts, simple assaults, and so on, it is argued that remedies other than criminal prosecution often serve society better and relieve the criminal justice system of a load it is usually ill-equipped to deal with.

Institution Programs

Other sections of the report which are relevant to correctional institutions for adults include such subjects as classification of offenders, planning new institutions, inmate rehabilitation programs, and prison industries.

The emphasis of this part of the report is on smaller prisons which are located closer to population centers and which have full programs of work and education.

Related Standards and Goals

Other sections emphasize the need for improved personnel programs, including training; professional management at all levels of administration; research, statistics, and information systems; and improved statutory frameworks for corrections as a whole.

It is apparent that the need and desirability of large central "fortress type prisons" are being questioned. What the outcome may be in the remainder of this century is far from clear. The movement toward alternatives to prison, such as probation, and the strengthening of those alternatives will be slow, partly because the required capital outlay will be difficult to obtain, and partly because of political resistance to the adoption of correctional programs which appear to be both lenient and ineffective in controlling crime. The public continues to demand its measure of punishment, if not its "pound of flesh."

The term "fortress prison" has become a cliché in recent years and calls for definition. Conventional state and federal prisons built during the past 100 years have tended to be located in relatively remote rural areas and constructed of stone, steel, and concrete, surrounded by walls, security fences, and armed guard towers. They have grown to unmanageable size with capacities ranging from 1,000 to 5,000 inmates. It is these massive piles of badly planned, badly located, and oversized prisons which are now under criticism in this country. Smaller prisons with capacities of 100 to 400 inmates, located near or in metropolitan areas, and planned as a part of rational correctional programs are being promoted for the containment and management of that portion of the correctional clientele which cannot be prudently placed in open institutions or under community supervision. It is nonetheless inevitable that some of these newer facilities must be as custodially secure as is necessary to restrain their occupants.

Nevertheless, we embark on the fourth quarter of this century knowing that the "fortress prison" as a correctional institution has probably run its course. It will, no doubt, survive for a long time, but its uses will diminish, and its residents will be selected from the eligible output of the criminal courts on a basis of the perceived severity of their offenses or on the repetitiveness of less serious crimes.

American Prison Systems

Military Prisons

Each of the three armed services maintains facilities for the confinement of its own personnel who are charged with or convicted of violations of the "Uniform Code of Military Justice." This Code covers all kinds of offenses, from absence without leave to murder. If a service person violates the criminal law in a civil jurisdiction in the continental United States, normally he will be turned over to the civil authorities for disposition. If convicted of a serious crime, he will often be given a dishonorable discharge and left to the civil authorities.

On the other hand, his offense may be in a foreign country or on a military reservation where the military will assume full jurisdiction. Or the offense, wherever committed, may be one which is a violation of military law but not of civil law, in which case the military judicial system must deal with the matter. By far the most common offenses in this category are unauthorized absence and desertion.

As a result of the need to have a system of sanctions to support military discipline, each major military post maintains the equivalent of the county jail in the civil system. In the Army and Air Force they are called "stockades," and the Navy calls them "brigs." In addition, the Army maintains a disciplinary barracks at Fort Leavenworth for the more serious offenders convicted by military courts. Most of them will be given dishonorable discharges from the service, although the possibility is held open for some of them to be restored to active duty. The Air Force maintains no such institution and, as needed, uses the Army facility.

The Army, the Air Force, and the Navy each maintains a facility for personnel convicted by their military courts but who are given an opportunity during a short retraining period to be restored to active duty.

The Navy has a disciplinary barracks at Portsmouth, New Hampshire, and also a counterpart to the Army's retraining facility. The Marine Corps, being a part of the Department of the Navy, uses the same facilities, and Marine Corps guards are commonly used to man the Navy's brigs and disciplinary barracks.

Some military cases with long sentences for serious crimes are transferred to the prisons of the U.S. Bureau of Prisons of the U.S. Department of Justice to serve out their time before release to civilian life. These cases will have exhausted all normal opportunities for sentence reduction or of restoration to honorable service.

The U.S. Bureau of Prisons, U.S. Department of Justice

The Criminal Code of the United States includes prohibitions against almost every offense defined as a crime in state codes, and a few which are exclusively federal crimes, such as counterfeiting U.S. currency, smuggling, treason, and crimes on the high seas. Until about 1900 persons convicted of federal civil crimes served their sentences in state or county institutions under contractual arrangements with the federal government.

The proliferation of federal criminal laws resulting in more and more federal prisoners grew steadily with the increase in interstate commerce, but it was the Eighteenth Amendment and the Volstead Act designed to enforce the prohibition against illegal liquor traffic that swelled the federal prison population to such proportions that the government found it necessary to develop and expand its own prison system.

The three original federal prisons at Leavenworth, Atlanta, and McNeil Island reported administratively to a deputy attorney general whose controls were essentially fiscal and legal. In 1930, Congress authorized by statute the creation of the U.S. Bureau of Prisons in the U.S. Department of Justice. Sanford Bates of Massachusetts was appointed the first Director by President Herbert Hoover. During the ensuing years the system has been expanded to its present size with 43 institutions and some 23,000 prisoners. Because of the great federal market for the products of prison industries, these institutions have less idleness than most state prisons. The physical plants of the federal prisons are relatively new, well-maintained and well-staffed.

The system is what its name implies, a prison bureau, not a unified correctional system. The Federal Parole Board is an agency completely independent of the Bureau, and the parolees are supervised by probation officers attached to 93 U.S. District Courts. The federal system, like many of the states, suffers because many of its institutions are isolated from major population centers and from the homes of the inmates.

State Prisons

Nationwide statistics on state prison populations are not readily available, and even those published from time to time by the U.S. Census Bureau and the U.S. Department of Justice are incomplete and difficult to interpret. This is partly because of different laws and varying practices in the 50 states, the District of Columbia, and the Commonwealth of Puerto Rico. For example, as mentioned previously, the dividing line between adult and juvenile is not uniform. In Florida and New York[9] there will be a significant number of inmates between the ages of 16 and 18 in the adult system of correctional institutions. In California, there will be virtually none in this age bracket, and a considerable number of inmates between 18 and 22 years of age will be in the institutions of the Department of the Youth Authority rather than those of the Department of Corrections. Furthermore, some states commit a few misdemeanants to state prisons, and as seen in Chapter 5, some state laws permit the sentencing of felons to county jails.

According to the best information available for the year 1973, there were about 190,000 adults serving sentences in state prison systems, the District of Columbia, and Puerto Rico. Of these, about 6,500 were women.

While the ratio of women to men in prison varies somewhat from state to state, women in state prisons in the country as a whole have accounted for 3 to 4 percent of the total for many years, despite the fact that in recent years there appears to have been an increase in crimes by women.

The resident population of state prisons per 100,000 of general population varies amazingly from state to state. For example, in 1974, the number of inmates per 100,000 population in Washington was 80.8, in Georgia 214.2, in California 100.0, in Illinois 54.0, Pennsylvania 63.9, Wisconsin 61.7, and Florida 137.3.

The Prison Clientele

We have observed the gross facts of how many persons there are in American prisons, reformatories, and other correctional institutions for adults, but this information is of limited value to those who attempt to understand these institutions as living establishments which, in one way or another, serve a complex array of humanity. They cannot be described in any general terms, except that the residents have all been convicted of serious crimes and have been sentenced to serve some amount of time in involuntary incarceration.

The following descriptive facts about these people are generally correct, but will vary in emphasis and degree from one state or one geographical region to another.

Age of Adult Prisoners

The median age of the adult resident population in American prisons is about 30 years for both men and women. Since they all grow older by six months to 40 years after admission, the median age of those admitted in any given year is about 27 to 27.5 years. Twenty-two to 25 percent of the resident population will be under 25 years of age. Only about one out of five of them will be over 45 years old. In short, men and women in these institutions are predominantly young adults of which about 96 percent are males.

There are also some variations in age in relationship to the crime for which they are sentenced. For example, those committed for sex offenses against children are the oldest group, with a median age as much as five years above the average, while car thieves, with a median age of about 20 years, are a good ten years younger than the average prisoner. Another interesting fact is that offenders under 25 years of age who have been convicted of some kind of theft, including robbery and burglary, are poorer risks on parole than others nearly ten years older whose crimes have been sex offenses, homicide, and manslaughter. One outstanding exception to this pattern is the fraudulent check passer whose median age is likely to be about 28 years and who competes with the car thief for first place among those least likely to succeed on parole.[10]

From the standpoint of the institution administrator and his staff, it is also significant to note that the age group most prone to take part in riots, criminal assaults, and irresponsible and reckless behavior in prison is most likely to include those under age 25 who have long sentences and well-established delinquent and criminal histories.

Crimes for Which Sentenced

Most state criminal codes define scores of acts made crimes by law. The most common felonies for which defendants may be sentenced to prison, however, are relatively few, and their most common element, plainly speaking, is simply *stealing,* or in more professional language, "crimes vs. property." Crimes against the person, such as homicide, assault, rape, kidnapping, and armed robbery are most feared by the citizenry, and carry more severe penalties, and a person convicted of any crime of personal violence is more likely to go to prison than to suffer a lesser penalty.

For example, in one state in 1972, one-third of all those convicted of robbery in any degree got prison sentences, and while there were three times as many burglaries as robberies, only one out of twelve of the burglars went to state prison. Only one out of twenty drug violators got prison sentences.

As a result of this selective sentencing, a state prison system in this decade will have in its daily resident population a preponderance of persons whose crimes have been threats against the personal safety of their victims, and whose sentences as individuals may not be longer or shorter than they would have been a generation ago. But the average time to be served by the prison population as a whole will be substantially longer.

Of the 5,664 prisoners received in the California Department of Corrections in 1972, 43 percent had committed robberies or crimes of personal violence, and the remaining 57 percent had been convicted of crimes against property. Because of the accumulation of longer-term prisoners, however, 56 percent of the resident population on June 30, 1973 was composed of persons sentenced for such crimes as robbery, kidnapping, homicide, rape, assault, and sex perversion. More than one-half of these were convicted of robberies. Of the total resident population of 20,793, 1,256 men were serving life sentences.

Socioeconomic and Ethnic Background

With rare exceptions, men and women found in prison come from poor and socially disadvantaged families. This does not mean that poverty and deprivation are causes of crime, but is merely to state the statistical fact that the economically deprived and the ethnic minorities contribute disproportionately to those sentenced to prison terms. In California, the male prison population on June 30, 1973, was 49 percent white American, 32 percent black, and 17 percent American of Mexican descent. The remaining 2 percent were mostly Orientals and American Indians.

In this classification there was an interesting difference between women and men prisoners. Only 11 percent of the women were of Mexican descent, 30 percent were black, 56 percent white, and less than 3 percent other.

The ethnic distribution of prisoners in custody in the institutions of the New York State Department of Correctional Services[11] reveals the following: of a total of 12,998 inmates, 51.5 percent were black, 35.4 percent were white, 12.8 percent were of Puerto Rican origin, and 0.3 percent other.

Of the 7,848 inmates of the above total who had been committed from New York City, slightly over 60 percent were black and the remaining 40 percent were about equally divided between Anglos and Puerto Ricans. Of the remainder from "upstate" New York, 61 percent were white, 36 percent black, and only 3 percent other, including Puerto Rican.

The pattern of overrepresentation of minorities, and especially of blacks, in prison populations is common throughout the United States, especially in the South and the industrial-commercial urban centers of the North. The factor of ethnicity tends to be overemphasized because of its surface visibility. When this matter is examined in other countries in which the nation's population is essentially homogeneous, it becomes apparent that social and economic deprivation is the essential ingredient — not ethnic origin.

Educational Levels of Prisoners

As one might expect, adult prisoners, coming as they do principally from the lower economic classes, are also below average in educational achievement. The actual school grade placement in a state like California which has compulsory school attendance and well-supported public schools will be higher than that of another state with poorly supported schools and limited economic resources. Reliable information on this subject is not available on a nationwide basis, but the following facts from the California system are indicative. These facts are based on actual test scores — not on inmates' statements of school attendance.

Among the more than 16,000 inmates tested, the median grade placement was 7.8 which means that less than one-half of this group had the equivalent of a common school education. Nearly 4 percent, or 600, were illiterate. Thirty-one percent tested sixth grade or less. At the upper end of the distribution only 6.4 percent tested at the twelfth grade or above. The popular notion that prisons are filled with highly intelligent, clever criminals is obviously a myth manufactured by fiction writers.

Occupational Skills of Prisoners

As they arrive at the intake gate, prisoners are not only poor and undereducated, but they are even more inadequate in the vocational skills and abilities needed to make an honest living. As we will see in the next section, many of them have spent much of their time getting in and out of juvenile institutions, jails, and prisons, when they might have been learning a productive occupation. Many have never held a regular job for as long as six months. They often lack job skills, and do not know how to either get a job or to keep one. In addition, one-third of them are further handicapped by habits of drug and alcohol abuse.

Criminal Histories of Prisoners

Here again, the 1973 prisoner population of the California Department of Corrections is used as an example, but it is important to make two precautionary points. First, resident prison population on a given day is what the warden has to deal with, but because of the accumulation of long-term repeaters in the system, these figures should not be confused with recidivism rates of a longitudinal cohort of prisoners released during a specified period of time, like one quarter or one year. Second, and more obviously, there will be variations in the proportions of these groups from state to state and region to region.

Perhaps the most startling fact to be observed here is that only one in eight of the total male resident population has had no previous commitment to any juvenile correctional institution, local jail, or prison. These are the true "first offenders" as measured by the criteria of no sentences of any kind involving institutional incarceration as a juvenile or an adult.

It is interesting to note that nearly one-third of the women fall in the "no prior commitment" category, and only 19 percent of them have been in prison before.

Returning to the male residents, we find that nearly one-half of them have previously been sentenced to jail or to juvenile institutions. Nearly 40 percent have been in prison before. More than one in five have served one prior prison sentence, about one-tenth of them have had two priors, 4.5 percent three priors, and 3.5 percent four or more.

This seems to be the place to correct an often repeated bit of misinformation. The unsupported statement that 80 percent of the prisoners in American prisons are recidivists has appeared in print frequently in recent years. This leads the unwary reader to assume either that 80 percent of men released from prison come back to prison, or that 80 percent of those in prison have been in prison before. *Neither statement is even close to the truth.* The generally accepted definition of a *prison* is a penal institution for the confinement of convicted felons. Using the California figures, 39.1 percent of the men in the state prisons on June 30, 1973 had served a previous prison term, either in California or elsewhere. On the second question, "What proportion of all the men released in a given year return to prison?" one must add the further query "in what period of time?" Several studies indicate that about one-third return to prison either as parole violators or on new offenses, or both, within three years after release. Others will commit minor crimes and be given jail sentences. From available evidence, mostly from California research, it can be concluded that out of a random cohort of 1,000 men released from prison in a given year, about 500 of them will return to prison or be sentenced to a jail term of three months or more within the following five years.

Some interpret this evidence as a failure of the prison as a reformative agent. But when one looks at the unpromising characteristics of the client group, the 50 percent who stay out of serious crime may represent remarkable success rather than the opposite. Whether or not prison rather than other influences can be given credit for this modest "success" is, of course, another question.

Sentences and Time Served

No subject in correctional administration is more misunderstood by the general public than that of the actual length of time to be served in confinement after a prison sentence has been imposed by a criminal court. This confusion has stemmed from the philosophy of the late nineteenth-century Reformatory movement which held that the primary purpose of a reformatory sentence was reformation of the offender which could not be predicted at the time of sentence. Hence, the sentence had to be indeterminate to permit discretion on the part of the correctional managers so that release could be authorized at a future time when they were convinced the inmate had been "reformed or rehabilitated." This concept of indeterminacy in sentencing has been widely adopted in one form or another in every state.

The law of the state or the federal government defines the limits of the discretion given to the sentencing judge or delegated to the correctional administrator or to a separate parole board. In its simplest form, the judge is permitted to fix an exact term of imprisonment of not less than a stated minimum nor more than a maximum, and the prison authorities are permitted to grant not more than some limited amount of time off for good behavior. For example, a judge might impose a sentence of two years on a convicted burglar. If the "good time" statute permitted five days a month off for good behavior, and assuming no "good time" was forfeited, the man would be discharged in 24 months less 120 days, or in approximately 20 months.

A common variation of this method involves a statutory authorization for a parole board to fix a parole date at something less than the court's sentence but at a point higher than a statutory minimum. For example, if the state law fixed a six-month minimum term for burglary in the above case, the parole board might fix the man's prison term at 18 months instead of 24 months, so he would be eligible for release in 18 months minus 90 days. But during the period between release at the expiration of 15 months and 24 months, he would be under parole supervision and subject to revocation and return to prison if he violated the conditions of his parole.

In a true indeterminate sentence, there would be neither a minimum nor a maximum, and the actual fixing of the term of confinement and the period of postinstitutional parole supervision would be delegated to a parole board. Most lawmakers have been unwilling to go the whole distance, and in states having indeterminate sentences, the law affecting each offense will usually set a minimum, supposedly to protect the public, and a maximum to protect the prisoner from excessively harsh punishment.

There are many other variations of the indeterminate concept, such as permitting the sentencing judge to fix a maximum less than the one provided by the statute, or permitting him to fix both a minimum and a maximum, leaving as little or as much latitude as he chooses to the parole board. A further plan allows the judge to fix a sentence which is within legal limits and then to divide the sentence into thirds. The first third less "good time" must be served in confinement; during the second third, the parole board has discretion to release on parole. The last third is a kind of automatic parole which the man serves in the free community, but his freedom can be rescinded if he violates the prescribed parole conditions.

It is fair to say at this writing that prison sentencing as seen nationally is in a state of confusion and that there are strong voices speaking for reform. Such reform is impeded, not because any thoughtful student of the subject believes that indeterminate sentences are either just or effective. The real stumbling block lies in finding an alternative which can address successfully the problem of disparities in the sentencing practices of a multiplicity of trial court judges.

Definite sentences, even with some limited latitude for good behavior credits and parole, have been thoroughly discredited in the past because the lenient judge may impose a sentence of a few months, while a punitively minded one in another court in the same system might give a term of ten years for the same crime under similar circumstances.[12]

The answer probably will be found by setting up a special appellate court in each state with power to monitor all sentencing practices and to alter those which deviate irrationally from acceptable norms.

From the standpoint of the manager of a prison or a prison system, there are two major factors affecting both his budget and the development of reasonable and effective programs. One is the number and kinds of cases he receives each year, and the other is the length of time they stay before parole or discharge. For example, if the median length of stay in an institution is 24 months and if for any reason, or wholly without reason, the decision makers should increase this to 30 months, it takes no higher mathematics to see that the prison administration will need to provide 25 percent more space and eventually a 25 percent increase in budget.

There is substantial variability in length of stay of those sentenced to prison from state to state, even with similar laws and systems. The most unfortunate aspect of all this is that there is no convincing evidence that increasing or decreasing the average time served has any effect on the recidivism rate.

The Study of Time Served and Parole Outcome[14] previously alluded to has this to say on pages 6 and 7:

> Some isolated studies are available on the relation between time served and recidivism. The State of Washington made a policy decision in 1958 to reduce the overall median time served in prison. A ten-month reduction over a three-year period produced no appreciable change in recidivism rates. In California, two matched groups on parole were selected for having committed misdemeanors while under supervision, and one group was jailed locally and then continued while the other was revoked and returned to prison. There was no difference in the recidivism rates of the two groups after a follow-up, despite the fact that the jail group served 7 months and the prison group served 20 months on the average.
>
> In sum, it must be noted that our store of knowledge on the effects of time served in prison on recidivism is indeed small. In general, the studies which have been conducted have not tended to show that increase in the duration of imprisonment brings a corresponding increase in special deterrence of those so punished; neither do they demonstrate a "worsening" effect. If, however, any significant relation does exist between the amount of time served and recidivism it is more likely to be that an increase in time served will be associated with a decrease in success rates on parole. The studies conducted are spotty and in almost all cases lack sufficient control for other factors which might bear upon the result.

The nationwide information on time served of over 100,000 cases taken from the same study is reproduced here:

Median Months Served by Offense Categories, Mean, Standard Deviation, and Time Served by Mid-Sixty Percent for Each Category

Offense	Median Time Served	Range in Months of Mid-60 percent of Cases	Standard Deviation	Mean
Homicide	58.6	23–121	72.3	79.3
Forcible Rape	49.5	20–106	63.9	68.7
Armed Robbery	33.1	17–62	40.2	44.4
Other Sex Offenses	25.4	12–47	32.6	34.4
Unarmed Robbery	24.8	13–43	29.3	32.1
Statutory Rape	22.6	11–51	36.0	34.9
Manslaughter	20.8	11–42	27.2	29.3
Narcotics Offenses	19.9	10–40	23.3	27.3
Burglary	16.2	9–29	23.0	22.3
Aggravated Assault	15.4	7–30	24.4	22.7
Check Fraud	14.7	9–24	15.4	18.9
Vehicle Theft	13.8	8–23	16.2	18.0
Other Theft, Larceny	12.8	8–22	16.9	17.3
Other Fraud	12.2	8–21	13.6	16.0

The above table includes cases from all of the 50 states and the District of Columbia between the years 1965 and 1970. What the data do not reveal is the variability in length of sentences for similar offenses from one state to another. Failure to publish this information is explained on the grounds that great differences in laws, in judicial practice, in parole board policy, and in sectional variables would make the findings subject to misinterpretation. This is no doubt true, but a careful examination of the differences which have no explanation, except those in the biases of decision makers, is usually not welcomed by the officials responsible.

There can be no question at this point in our history that many convicted criminals must be sent to prison, but since only 3 or 4 percent of them are justifiably kept in for life, it must be frankly admitted at this stage of our development that there is no firm, widely accepted consensus about how long most prisoners should be confined, given a set of relevant facts about each case.

Without question there is consensus that violent crimes against the person should be treated more severely than crimes against property. The table on page 121 makes it quite clear that of the 14 crime classifications, homicide and forcible rape are regarded as much more serious than the third ranking offense of armed robbery, and that nonthreatening crimes like car theft, larceny, and fraud are very clearly at the bottom of the list. However, an examination of the range of time served reveals a further significant fact: there is substantial overlapping throughout the 14 classifications. For example, note that the twentieth percentile of those sentenced for homicide is 23 months, and the eightieth percentile of vehicle theft cases is also 23 months. In other words, one-fifth of the homicide cases served less time than the upper 20 percent of those sentenced for car theft.

Diversified Correctional Institutions for Adults

Because of the heterogeneous nature of the prison population of every state, the practice has developed over the years of establishing specialized institutions for different classes of inmates who ought to be kept separate from each other, either for practical management reasons, because they require differential programs, or because one group is thought to have a contaminating effect on the members of another group.

In a small state like Arizona, for example, there is only one state prison for adults located near the town of Florence. But even here young, relatively unsophisticated male inmates are kept in a separate compound, and the women are housed in a separate structure across the road from the main prison. Psychotic prisoners of whatever age or sex are transferred to the state mental hospital.

In more populous states with standing prison populations of several thousand, and running up to as many as 25,000, the opportunity has been presented for much further diversification. In such states one usually will find a pattern such as the following:

One institution for adult women;
One or two for young adults above the juvenile court age with most of its residents being under age 25. Heavy emphasis in such a facility will usually be on education and vocational training. It is the modern descendant of the reformatory of the late nineteenth century.
One high security prison for long-term, high-risk cases, most of whom will be men with extensive criminal histories;

One or more open type institutions for men who represent little risk of escape or of future crimes of violence;

One or more medium-security institutions for average types of men whose risk of escape or rebellion, while real, does not present any unusual threat to public safety. The great bulk of a state's prison population is likely to fall in this category. Hence, this kind of prison can be replicated in several convenient locations in the state.

One or two specialized mental hospital type security prisons for the mentally ill prisoner and for a miscellaneous classification of inmates who are not psychotic by medical definition nor insane according to legal standards, but who nevertheless behave in irrational, unpredictable, and often dangerous ways. These men need psychiatric treatment, diagnosis, and management. The Medical Facility at Vacaville, California, the Medical Center for Federal Prisoners at Springfield, Missouri, and the New York Facility at Mattewan are examples of this type of specialized institution.

Reception Centers

In a few large systems, one or more reception centers for processing and initial classification are in use. Usually, these may be separate sections of other conveniently located institutions.

Farms and Camps

In many American prisons, farmland attached to the main institution is worked by men residing in the main buildings or in special barracks located some distance from the central complex. In other cases small separate buildings are located on a farm which has no physical connection to the grounds of a central institution. This latter practice is still common in the South and the Midwest, but farm production is gradually being reduced in Northern and Eastern industrialized states.

Forestry camps located in publicly owned forests or in wild park lands are common in such states as California, Washington, and Pennsylvania. These are essentially work camps, with men housed in barracks of either permanent or portable construction. They will usually operate at a strength of 60 to 100 workers, but some, such as those operated by the U.S. Bureau of Prisons in connection with military bases, may contain as many as 250 to 400 men at a time.

Road camps in which prisoners were used either for road construction or maintenance were common in some states until about 1930, and a very few persist to this day. They came into general public disrepute because of the "chain gangs" of the Southeast, but even when operated under humanitarian management, they were forced out of business, partly by the opposition of organized labor and road contractors, and perhaps more importantly by the invention and widespread use of labor-saving road-building machinery.

Prisons for adult felons have been undergoing constant change and reexamination ever since (except for the death penalty) they became accepted as the ultimate criminal sanction. The philosophical and political ferment surrounding the subject has been more active in recent years than at any time in this century. Without doubt prisons are here to stay, but their characteristics and their uses are changing and will continue to do so in response to social, political, and economic developments in our society.

NOTES

[1]Noah Weinstein, *Legal Rights of Children,* Reno, Nevada: National College of Juvenile Court Judges, 1974.

[2]California Penal Code, Section 17.

[3]David Rothman, *Discovery of the Asylum,* Boston, Mass: Little, Brown, 1971.

[4]Blake McKelvey, Ph.D., *American Prisons,* Chicago: University of Chicago Press, 1936.

[5]John Bartlow Martin, *Break Down the Walls,* New York: Ballantine Books, 1954.

[6]Richard A. McGee, one of the authors of this text, was selected on a competitive basis to head the new department. He remained head of the state's correctional system until June 1967.

[7]See Russell G. Oswald, *Attica—My Story,* Garden City, N. Y.: Doubleday, 1972, p. 418. See also the Official Report of the New York State Special Commission on Attica, *Attica,* New York: Bantam Books, Inc., 1972, p. 533.

[8]National Advisory Commission on Criminal Justice Standards and Goals, *Police; Courts; Corrections: Community Crime Prevention,* Washington, D. C.: U. S. Department of Justice, 1973.

[9]The New York State Department of Correctional Services reported as of December 31, 1969, that about one-sixth of its resident population was composed of inmates between 16 and 17 years old, and 28 percent of the total were under 21 years of age.

[10]Don M. Gottfredson, M. D. Neithercutt, Joan Nuffield, and Vincent O'Leary, *Four Thousand Lifetimes: A Study of Time Served and Parole Outcomes,* Davis, Calif.: Research Center, National Council on Crime and Delinquency.

[11]Unpublished Report of the New York State Department of Correctional Services, December 31, 1969. Report dated September 1, 1971.

[12]See Marvin E. Frankel, *Criminal Sentences—Law Without Order,* New York: Hill and Wang, 1973, p 124. See also Walter S. Carr and Vincent J. Connelly, *Sentencing Patterns and Problems,* an annotated bibliography, American Judicature Society, 1973.
[13]*Ibid.*

Foot NotE's

(1 page 122) Corz In Am, RoB Cantrz

7 Institutions for Adult Offenders: Organization, Management, and Program

Since separate prisons, like those at Auburn and Philadelphia, were established as reasonably self-contained units, much of the organizational structure, terminology, and tradition of these institutions has persisted down to the present time. Each prison will invariably have a chief executive in charge, but the precise manner in which the system is organized above him has undergone many changes over the years. Whether this head man reports to a board or to a single executive in the governor's cabinet, or whether he is a patronage politician or a career civil servant are all important issues, but for purposes of this section we will assume that he is in command and subject to law and higher policy, much like a ship captain manages his crew and cargo in and out of port.

The most common title of the prison chief in the United States is "warden," although many are now using the title of superintendent. Outside of the United States, the title is usually some variation of the word director or governor.

Since the early prisons were principally custodial, there was some resemblance between the civil prison and a military fort. In any event, prisons for adults have a long-established tradition of using military rank titles for custodial personnel or guards. They have even copied to some extent the military-police type of uniform dress. With the introduction of many more noncustodial personnel into prison programs, there is now agitation to abolish both military titles and military style uniforms.

Depending on the size of the prison and the diversity of the institution's programs, the warden will invariably have one associate executive and usually two to four. Figure 7–1 divides the principal functions of the institution into four groupings under four associate wardens or superintendents. Above this structure the warden will usually have an administrative assistant to help him with miscellaneous routine tasks associated with his office.

126

The personnel training officer is a special case. Some institutions may not employ such a staff specialist, but, as in all well-managed organizations, personnel training is an essential management function in prison administration. The training officer does not fit well under any of the associates for two reasons. First, he is concerned about training and employee development in all departments of the institution, and, second, he serves as an excellent channel of unofficial communication from the rank and file personnel to the top man. To function on as high a professional level as possible, he should be included as a member of the warden's staff conferences.

Now, let us look briefly at the other numerous functions involved in prison management. One must bear in mind here that a prison is a community in which several hundred or even two or three thousand human beings live 24 hours a day without the relief of holidays, vacations, or weekends in the country. It is a closed community for its inmates, and unlike a hospital, the "shut-ins" are not sick; they are young with all of the appetites and energy of youth, they are of one sex, and they are there against their will.

In addition to inmates, there are workers. For every two to six inmates there will be one such employee. There are also vendors and suppliers and visitors who come and go. Just keeping such an establishment operating smoothly from day to day and month to month is undoubtedly one of the most challenging managerial tasks in modern society. No discussion of the subject in such a context as this can hope to do more than give the reader some appreciation of the complexity of the problem.

Management Services

Budgets and Accounts

Since a prison is a public institution, its operating funds must come from appropriations provided by the legislative body. In some states the legislatures meet for only a few months every other year, in others they meet annually for a part of each year, and in some of the very large states they will be in session longer and more often. Whatever the local practice may be, each institution must prepare a biennial or an annual budget. This of necessity must be done months in advance of the legislative session which will review it in great detail and approve, disapprove, or modify it before the beginning of the next fiscal year.

It is through the instrumentality of the budget process that most of the future planning is done, and any warden who leaves this function entirely to

FIGURE 7–1

Organization and Functional Chart of a Typical Institution for Adult Prisoners

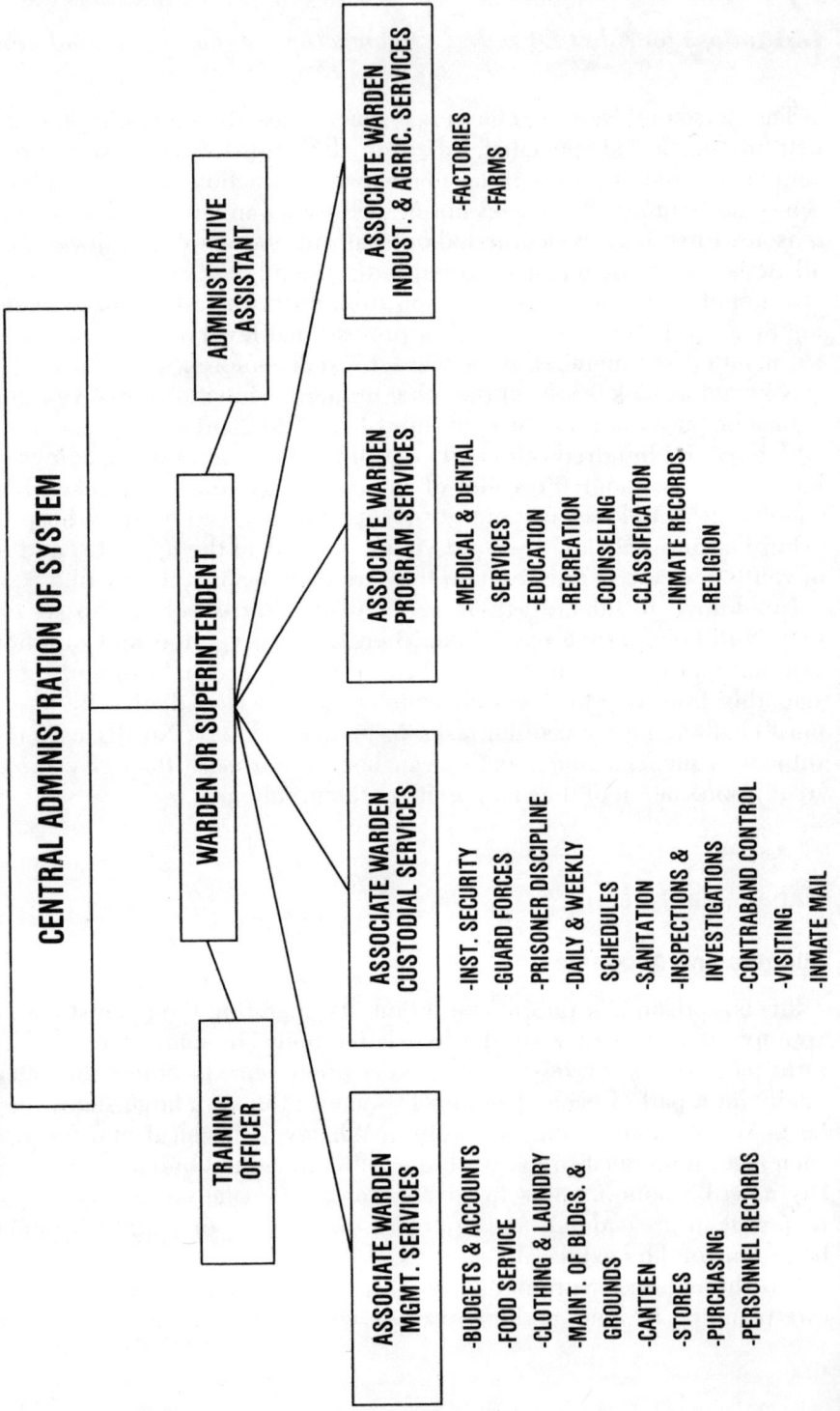

CENTRAL ADMINISTRATION OF SYSTEM

ADMINISTRATIVE ASSISTANT

WARDEN OR SUPERINTENDENT

TRAINING OFFICER

ASSOCIATE WARDEN INDUST. & AGRIC. SERVICES
-FACTORIES
-FARMS

ASSOCIATE WARDEN PROGRAM SERVICES
-MEDICAL & DENTAL SERVICES
-EDUCATION
-RECREATION
-COUNSELING
-CLASSIFICATION
-INMATE RECORDS
-RELIGION

ASSOCIATE WARDEN CUSTODIAL SERVICES
-INST. SECURITY
-GUARD FORCES
-PRISONER DISCIPLINE
-DAILY & WEEKLY SCHEDULES
-SANITATION
-INSPECTIONS & INVESTIGATIONS
-CONTRABAND CONTROL
-VISITING
-INMATE MAIL

ASSOCIATE WARDEN MGMT. SERVICES
-BUDGETS & ACCOUNTS
-FOOD SERVICE
-CLOTHING & LAUNDRY
-MAINT. OF BLDGS. & GROUNDS
-CANTEEN
-STORES
-PURCHASING
-PERSONNEL RECORDS

his bookkeeping staff does so at his own and his institution's peril. There will usually be departmental and budget control officers between the warden and the governor and the legislature, but the grass roots job of planning the future needs of the prison and writing convincing justifications for these requirements must be well done at the operating level or administrative miscarriages and even disaster may result.

A correctional institution will have one of the most complex budgets in state government. It will contain not only salaries and wages of personnel, office supplies and items of that sort, which are common in all public budgets, but will have to include all the items required to feed, clothe, and shelter hundreds of human beings, plus all their other needs for medical care, education, recreation, and scores of incidentals.

Once a budget is approved by the legislature and signed by the governor, the prison manager and his subordinates then become accountable for spending the funds according to need and the limitations set by the legislature and the central government. Mismanagement of public funds, even when unintentioned, is likely to be looked upon as a worse dereliction of duty than almost anything else except gross neglect of duty or downright criminality.

The casual observer may think that managing 1,000 prisoners is the warden's number one task, which, in fact, it is, but mismanaging a five-to-ten-million-dollar-a-year budget is a sure route to administrative oblivion.

Besides the appropriated public funds, there are other moneys for which the prison managers are responsible. Prisoners have small sums of money which must be kept in a trust fund. This is almost like running hundreds of small checking accounts in a bank. It is not uncommon for several million dollars a year to pass through such a trust account. Prisoners are not permitted to have cash in their possession.

If an institution has manufacturing industries which sell their products to other state agencies, here is yet another group of fiscal accounts not unlike those maintained by a private business.

Most institutions operate a canteen where inmates may buy small items like tobacco, candy, stationery, and hobby materials. This becomes another management function where money is handled and accounts must be kept.

Purchasing Supplies and Stores

The prison must acquire a staggering variety of commodities which range from drugs for the hospital to carloads of flour for the bakery, and from typewriters for the offices to coal for the power house. While some of the major purchasing is usually done by a state central bureau of purchasing, no matter how it is done the institution must arrange for deliveries to the site and for the accounting and secure warehousing of the merchandise. Just the raw food alone is a major problem. Assuming that the daily cost of unprepared food per inmate per day is $1.00 and there is a daily resident population of 1,200 inmates, $8,400 worth of food products alone must be delivered and handled each week.

Food Service

Next to maintaining order and security within the prison, the management of food preparation and service is probably the principal and most sensitive function of the institution. This is not the place to go into a detailed or technical discussion of the subject. But if Napoleon's army "marched on its belly," it can be said just as truly that much of the morale of a prison rests on the same part of the anatomy. Since the prisoners have no opportunity to get relief from the monotony of the daily fare, they are seldom completely satisfied with the food, even though it is often of better quality and nutritional value than they are accustomed to in the free community. For this reason, it is of great importance that menus be planned, not only for balance and variety, but the food must be well-prepared and served in as attractive a manner as circumstances permit.

The assumption that a low-paid cook with such prisoner help as may be available will do this job adequately is all too common and always disastrous in the long run. A well-run prison system, even if it has only two or three institutions, will employ a well-trained "food manager" to oversee the whole program of planning, regulating, supervising, purchasing, and final delivery to the prisoner's plate. Experience has demonstrated that this kind of approach to feeding prisoners pays off not only in morale but often in actual dollar costs.

Personnel Management

Since the employee payroll is clearly a fiscal management function, it is normal to place the personnel records and related details such as appointment documents, scheduling, disciplinary records, and the like among the other general management functions. This does not mean that the warden, each of his associates, and unit chiefs do not have personnel management responsibilities. The warden himself is basically a manager of people. The prisoners are people, the employees are people, his submanagers are people, his superiors, the public, the inmate families—all are people. This may be stating the obvious, but it is worth emphasizing because the warden and the system of which he is a part can do their basic job of controlling and directing the prisoners only by managing the other people who influence the behavior of the prisoners.

Maintenance of Buildings, Equipment, and Grounds

The total cost of a new prison of medium size at contemporary prices will run about $25,000 per inmate. Hence, an institution with a capacity of 1,000 is worth about $25,000,000. Such a physical plant must be serviced with electricity, heat, water, sewage, and expendable supplies such as bedding, tools, and paint, and on through hundreds of practical and necessary items. A competent building maintenance engineer, a corps of tradesmen and scores of inmate helpers are needed to operate this complex set of interrelated functions.

All of this might be taken for granted but plant maintenance takes on special importance in prison management, when one asks himself what the consequences might be if the electrical supply should fail at a crucial moment? Suppose the power house breaks down some night when the temperature is subfreezing? Or the sewage line from a cell building gets clogged up at 5:00 A.M., and a hundred toilets begin overflowing? There are obviously hundreds of possibilities for plant and equipment failure in a prison, just as in any other modern plant, but they take on added significance in prison because of the nature of the situation and the residents. Coupled with this, there is also the ever present chance that some prisoner or group of them may sabotage some service as a cover up for escape or as a diversion in a plan for mass rebellion.

Inmate Property

The management of money, jewelry, watches, tools, clothing, books, and a whole host of such items which are the personal possessions of prisoners may seem to the uninitiated to be a rather minor consideration in the administration of a prison. The prison administrator or prison employee who behaves as if these matters were of little or no importance will suffer the consequences in the form of bad inmate morale, frequent complaints from prisoners and their families, the development of petty rackets and trafficking among prisoners, as well as incidents of personal violence because of thefts or failures to pay debts owed by one prisoner to another.

We have already mentioned the question of money, which the prisoner either has on his person at the time of his admission, or is sent to him from persons outside the institution afterwards, or is earned by him while in prison. In this country it is generally the accepted practice to prohibit the personal possession of cash by any inmate of a prison. Instead his money is placed in a trust account to which is added any new receipts and from which is subtracted any sums which he sends home or spends for merchandise or for other purposes while confined. It is also common to discourage individual inmates from having excessively large balances in their trust accounts. This presents no great problem ordinarily because it is rare indeed that a prisoner will have more than a two or three hundred dollar balance at a time, and more often than not his balance may be in sums of less than $10.00. Sometimes prisoners inherit money or receive large payments for one reason or another. When this occurs the prisoner is normally encouraged either to send the money home or to open an interest-bearing savings account in a bank of his choice.

Expensive rings, watches, and other nonmonetary valuables are ordinarily taken from the incoming prisoner and are either kept in a vault pending the prisoner's release or are transferred to some member of his family or to a friend designated by the inmate. The personal possession of any item having a dollar value of more than $50.00 by a prison inmate is likely to make him the target for theft or for gambling or other illicit trading.

On the question of clothing, most adult prisons for men do not permit prisoners to wear their civilian clothes. The practice of requiring prisoners to wear uniforms which are degrading has largely disappeared in this country. Here we refer to the old-fashioned practice of providing outer garments made of grey and white horizontal-striped denim and unattractive caps made from salvaged material in the prison tailor shops. Finally, the practice of printing the prisoner's commitment number in large letters on the back of his shirt and jacket has also been largely discontinued. Some institutions wherein custodial control is of less concern than it is in maximum security facilities permit prisoners to keep their own shoes after they are thoroughly searched for contraband, and a few are beginning to permit them to have civilian slacks and sport shirts to wear during nonworking hours. Here there is the continual pull between management's desires to maintain as tight a control as possible on the behavior of the inmate population and at the same time permit them to maintain a degree of personal choice and individuality. Whether clothing is personally owned by each prisoner or whether it is issued by the institution, the problem of controlling the clothing, preventing its theft, and illicit trading in these articles is an ever present one, both to the management and the prisoners.

Another item of special concern is the possession of goods and instruments for making hobby items. This kind of merchandise, if not carefully regulated, can result in frequent morale and disciplinary problems.

Educational supplies and equipment constitute another classification of inmate property which create no serious problem, unless some of the items are relatively expensive. A portable typewriter, for example, is admittedly an educational piece of equipment, but it is also subject to being put to misuse and may be irreparably damaged by a disgruntled prisoner who becomes angered at its owner if he refuses to make it available for some illicit use.

Another class of inmate property is made up of that miscellaneous group of items of merchandise which are offered for sale in most prison canteens. Ordinarily the prison management will limit the amount of money that any one prisoner can spend per month to some sum like $15.00 or $20.00. On the other hand, if only 10 percent of the prison population can spend as much as $15.00 or $20.00 in the canteen for toilet articles, candy, specialty food and the like, there will probably be another 25 percent or 30 percent of the population who have no money whatsoever. Stealing canteen items from each other and even gang hijacking of canteen items are not uncommon among prisoners. Generally, prison managers consider the availability of canteen merchandise an important factor in maintaining morale, but conversely, the very presence of this merchandise, especially in any large quantities, can and does often result in a variety of disciplinary problems.

It is not the intention of this section to describe in monotonous detail precisely how the problems surrounding inmate property should be addressed. It is important, however, for one who would understand something about the economic and social life of the prisoners that the control and protection of the property of individual inmates has many ramifications of concern to everyone in the prison from the warden to the most economically destitute resident of the facility.

Custodial Services

Since the security prison is populated by people who are there against their will, and these same people have demonstrated by their previous behavior in free society that at least in some areas of behavior they are prone to rebel against conforming to the norms, the first order of business in a prison is to maintain order and peace. This function is usually described as custody, but it is far more complex than merely preventing riots and escapes. In the traditional prison of the recent past the custodial and security functions have been headed by an experienced and mature officer known in some systems as the "deputy warden" or even "principal keeper." In the old-fashioned prison with little or no program except work, this deputy was the autocrat of practically everything that went on inside the prison. The warden was often a political appointee who sometimes had a background in prison management but more often than not this was not the case. He was more likely to be an ex-policeman, a retired military man, a businessman, a former member of the legislature, or a defeated candidate who had political influence with the governor.

In these circumstances the man who really "ran" the inside operations almost of necessity had to be a strong, shrewd man who had a practical knowledge of how to survive in what was both a dangerous and unstable environment. These old-time deputy wardens have their counterparts in the despotic ship captains of fictional fame, like Hornblower, Queeg, and Captain Bligh. Happily that day is almost past, but vestiges of the old practices still persist in a very few locations.

One of these old-time deputies who had survived for more than twenty years under a succession of seven or eight politically appointed wardens once explained to this writer how he had "managed" his bosses over the years. It went something like this:

> When a warden would get fired or quit, I was usually acting warden for a few days or even months before the new appointee arrived. I never went after the appointment myself, because I figured I was better off in the second spot. I also made sure that none of my subordinates, like the Captain (head guard) had any chance for it either. When the new warden arrived I would tell him "You know I've been here a long time. I know the cons, I know the employees, and I know the people in this town. I'll be glad to stay on if you want me to and to carry out any policies or orders you want!" He would always thank me and say, "Well, I wish you would stay for awhile at least. Of course, I'll be making some changes which we'll talk about in a few days." Like all of them he would have some screwy ideas he'd picked up from reading the newspapers or from his political friends. Sometimes, too, he would have what he thought was inside information coming from former employees or ex-cons. Pretty soon, he'd start telling me to change certain things. I would never argue with him about it but just say, "Yes, sir! When do you want me to start?" Usually I knew something bad would happen from it, and when it did, it usually scared the old man. Then, I'd have another talk with him and suggest that he just let me run things on the inside, while he took care of matters down at the capitol, the newspapers and the budget and stuff like that. Sometimes I'd have to give a little on certain appointments, firings and promotions and things like that, but he knew and I

knew that the place would blow up and he'd get the sack unless he gave me a free hand.

Then giving his ego a little stroke, he concluded by saying:

You know the state really owes me a lot for keeping the lid on this joint all these years.

In passing, it may be said that the old system did "keep the lid on" most of the time, but at what expense in terms of human values no one can ever really know. One would have to write a novel to tell how it worked, but in short, it was accomplished by letting the toughest and strongest among the prisoners actually run things by brutal treatment of the dissidents and by allowing a whole system of special privileges for the controlling cliques. What privileges? Special food, visits, housing, clothing, sex, and in a few cases on record of clandestine absences during the night. In such a prison the outward image was that of a "tough" prison where escapes and disturbances were few and the costs low. On the inside official discipline was lax, but the corrupt convict society was kept under control by the worst elements of its membership.

Happily, with the advent of civil service for personnel and the establishment of central state departments of corrections under professional leadership, the old system of internal controls of adult prisons has almost passed from the scene. It still remains in a few places and in at least one state (Louisiana) even to the extent of supplying convict guards with firearms.

In the modern prison the associate warden in charge of custodial services is still the most powerful single officer next to the warden, but now many of the functions and related personnel, as shown by Figure 7–1, are under the control of other associates who are on an equal level with the associate warden. Many decisions concerning his functions, such as the daily schedule, sanitation, visiting, etc., must of necessity be shared with others, and the warden is clearly the single officer in command, and even he does not have a completely free hand if there is a strong head of the state's whole correctional system.

Now, let us look briefly at the principal functions classified as "custodial."

The Guard Force

More than half of the employees of a prison for adults usually will belong to this miscellaneous classification. They are not only the perimeter guards and the police force of the institution, but they have many operational functions. For this reason they are usually referred to in most systems now as "correctional officers" rather than guards. The old stereotype of the prison guard sitting in a wall tower with a rifle on his lap is no more true today than is that of Captain Hornblower on the bridge of a sailing vessel true to modern seafaring. Correctional officers are in closer direct contact with the inmates than anyone else in the institution. They count them in the housing buildings, get them up in the morning, move them to their meals, supervise their conduct and maintain order in dining halls, recreation yards, visiting rooms. Most general working parties are supervised by them. The journeyman correctional officer under the direction of his own hierarchical supervision is the only real correctional generalist in the institution. Other personnel tend to be specialists of many varieties. The correctional officer may be assigned very often to duties which also require some technical skills, such as substituting for the bakery foreman when he is on leave, or acting as foreman in a section of an industrial factory, or directing the work of a farm crew.

The task of assigning, directing, and scheduling this force is usually the duty of the associate warden — custody's principal assistant who may have a variety of titles. Where military titles are used he often is called the captain. There will usually be intermediate titles for those superior officers in charge of night shifts or special sections of the institution.

Prisoner Discipline

This function is listed as one of the principal duties of the associate warden of custody but it should be clear that every employee of the institution from the warden down has a degree of responsibility here. Since discipline must be defined as "conformance to standards of conduct," each prisoner may be said to share in this matter too, at least to the extent of controlling himself and influencing by acceptable means the behavior of his fellows. The term "punishment" is often coupled with and even confused with the word "discipline." This is faulty and careless thinking because punishment is only the last resort in enforcing or achieving discipline.

Most conformance in prison as elsewhere is achieved either by internal personal controls or by the discomfort resulting from disapproval by superiors and peers. In order for a prisoner or his supervisors to have some formal guide to acceptable conduct, there must be a set of rules and regulations which are usually promulgated by the headquarters office and particularized as necessary for each institution. It is obvious, then, that both employee and inmate must be made aware of these rules.

When there is a flagrant violation of a rule calling for a more formal action than an on-the-spot reprimand, there must be a procedure in the prison for bringing the matter to the attention of higher authority. This is like a police officer's arrest report. In an earlier day the deputy warden or some assigned disciplinary officer received the report, listened to the prisoner's defense if any, and meted out some penalty usually in the form of deprivation of some privilege or a period of confinement in a punishment cell.

Because of the arbitrary nature of this process, the courts have begun in recent years to lay down some rules designed to protect the inmate's constitutional right to a reasonable degree of "due process." As a consequence, most well-run prisons today maintain a disciplinary committee before whom an accused prisoner has a right to appear, to hear the charges, to be faced by his accuser, and in some circumstances to be represented by counsel.

More often than not this committee is chaired by the prison's chief custodian. The committee will ordinarily have at least three members and seldom more than five. The other members may include one of the prison doctors, the chief of classification, or any other superior officer the warden may assign. Since this is obviously a rather cumbersome and time-consuming process, only the most serious offenses are likely to be referred. They would normally be offenses which might result in the loss of good behavior credits or disciplinary lockup.

The most common offenses usually fall under the head of stealing, assault, refusal to obey orders, sex perversion, possession of contraband, or attempted escape. If an offense is a serious felony under the civil law the case will usually be referred to the local district attorney for investigation. The offender is usually placed in temporary lockup, pending prosecution. The prison staff will, of course, assist in such investigations.

Investigations

Violations of rules or statutes frequently occur without the management knowing who may be responsible. Evidence may be uncovered revealing that drugs, weapons, or other contraband have been smuggled into the institution. More often than not, the violator is a dishonest employee. All such incidents must be thoroughly investigated to ensure the safety and security of the prison. The associate warden of custody will normally be responsible for directing such inquiries.

Besides the occasional dishonest employee, other likely channels for smuggling contraband may be visitors, delivery men, vendors, contractors' employees, and the mail. The chief custodian must be continuously alert to prevent this kind of activity.

Prisoners' Mail and Visiting

Modern prison administrators encourage the maintenance of constructive relationships between prisoners and families and legitimate friends. Because of the risks to institutional security, both visits and mail in the past were restricted to a point where security, necessary though it is, interfered with the important objective of returning prisoners to free society with as many legitimate ties and supports as possible. Some institutions in the past allowed only one letter per week per inmate and that only one page in length, and all incoming and outgoing mail was recorded, read, and censored. This took a great deal of staff time and accomplished relatively little in the protection of institutional security.

The practice in more liberal institutions today is to pay the postage on a limited number of letters per week, usually three to five, and then permit the inmate to write as many letters as he wishes to at his own expense. Letters are usually recorded and sent to the mailroom without being sealed to avoid the possibility of contraband materials being enclosed, but the letters are not read unless there is some special reason to suspect improper communications or the inclusion of materials in violation of laws governing the United States mails. Incoming mail, of necessity, must be opened in order to prevent the smuggling of contraband, particularly dangerous drugs. Money must be removed and credited to the inmate's trust account.

Certain communications between prisoners and correspondents is considered to be confidential. Therefore, outgoing mail may be sealed and incoming mail unopened for certain specific kinds of correspondence, such as from the prisoner's lawyer, the courts, the governor of the state, and the head of the department of corrections.

Visiting represents a somewhat more difficult problem, because of the danger of visitors bringing in not only drugs but weapons. As a consequence, the visiting room is usually in a neutral area not inside of the security interior of the prison and not outside of the guarded perimeter of the institution. It is difficult to provide for the body-searching of visitors, especially of women. As a consequence, in high-security institutions prisoners are usually given a very thorough search when returning from the visiting room to the security area.

Visitors must of necessity be restricted to certain hours of the day and sometimes to days of the week, but generally speaking, most institutions now permit much more frequent and longer visits, especially with members of their families.

Some prisons now permit incoming telephone calls to prisoners from members of the family or attorneys. These of necessity have to be made by appointment. Outgoing collect telephone calls are also permitted in some institutions.

In open minimum-security institutions both visiting and other kinds of communication are usually permitted on a much more liberal basis than in high-security institutions.

Conjugal visiting is common in most Latin American and many European countries. Only a few states in this country permit such visits, and then only on a very limited scale.

Program Services

Classification

The term "classification" in correctional institutions has a special connotation. It does not mean dividing the prisoners into classes. The term was borrowed originally from the mental hospital field, and what the term has come to mean in corrections is that a case study of each individual is made, which is participated in by all of the professional personnel that the institution provides. Based on this study, individual recommendations are developed with respect to the manner in which the case should be managed in the system. For example, the prisoner's criminal record will be examined in detail, his educational background and achievements will be studied, and his social history will be reviewed. The results of a battery of educational, psychiatric, and psychological tests will be evaluated. Then, based on all of the information which will be recorded in an "admissions summary" the decision makers and clinicians of the institution or correctional system will make a judgment as to what to do with the individual in relationship to the resources available in the system. As indicated earlier, in a system large enough to have a diversified system of institutions the first judgment to be made after admission will be the choice of the institution in which he will serve his sentence. At this particular institution further judgments will be made as to the degree of custodial security required in his case, his assignment to living quarters, to work, to educational or vocational programs, to medical or psychiatric treatment, or to any other services or program which seem best suited to his individual case.

In most well-run modern institutions the initial judgments for programming each newly admitted individual are made by a classification committee. This committee may be headed by the warden or superintendent himself or by the associate warden for program services. Other members of the committee might include such staff members as the associate warden of custody, the chief of the classification and counseling services, the psychiatrist, the supervisor of education, and sometimes the chaplains.

As time goes on, inmates may be brought back to the classification committee for reclassification. This is especially true if transfer to another institution is suggested or if the degree of custody is to be reduced.

The concept of individual study and treatment of prison inmates is a most rational one. The failure to implement the idea tends to lie in the inability of the correctional system to provide all of the specialized resources that might be necessary to carry out the recommendations growing out of the classification process. For example, it is a futile exercise to recommend that a prisoner receive psychiatric treatment if there is no psychiatrist, or that he learn the plumber's trade if there is room for only 15 trainees in this course with a waiting list of 45.

Medical and Health Services

In our organizational chart (Figure 7–1), medical and dental services have been included under the functions which are under the general supervision of the associate warden in charge of program services. In some institutions the chief medical officer reports directly to the warden or superintendent.[1] The only rationale for this administrative arrangement is that the chief medical officer of the institution very often receives a higher salary than the associate warden.

Any correctional institution with a daily population of 500 or more inmates will normally have a hospital and all the necessary diagnostic equipment, as well as an operating room and appropriate wards and hospital rooms. If the institution has included in its population all levels of custodial risks the hospital will normally be placed in the maximum security area for the obvious reason that even the most dangerous prisoner is as likely to need hospital services as anyone else.

Sometimes if an institution is located within a short motor vehicle drive from a fully equipped public hospital, some of the more expensive and unusual medical services may be supplied there. This will only be possible, however, if the general public hospital has a security ward. Otherwise it becomes necessary to post a guard on some of the prisoner patients around the clock. This is not altogether safe and it can be very expensive. As a consequence, most prison administrators much prefer to have all of the hospital and medical services provided for within the confines of the prison.

Since a hospital must be covered continuously, it is normally necessary to have both custodial and nursing personnel on duty all the time. This can also be very expensive, especially if the number of patients in the hospital at any given time is very small.

In an institution for prisoners serving relatively long terms, some prisoners can be trained and used as technicians and nurses. On the other hand, in order to make sure of maintaining an acceptable level of professional services, it is important that there be some qualified nurses employed. Most prisons nowadays find it both safe and desirable to employ some women nurses, partly because male nurses are extremely rare in the profession. Where male nurses are necessary, some prison systems find it satisfactory to employ men who have been trained as medical technicians in the military services.

In every institution with a large population that has a well-equipped hospital it is necessary and common practice to hold a daily "sick line." This enables any prisoner having symptoms to report them at a scheduled time for whatever outpatient treatment the doctor may prescribe. This daily sick line, while an absolute necessity, presents certain custodial and administrative problems, because every prison has its hypochondriacs and malingerers. However, the safe policy for a well-run medical service is to suffer the annoyance of the malingerer rather than to run the risk of denying medical treatment to inmates who are really sick.

Since no institution is likely to be large enough to afford a full spectrum of medical specialists, it is desirable and, in fact, almost necessary to have contractual arrangements with private physicians and nearby general hospitals for part-time and occasional services. This is especially true of ophthalmologists, neuro-surgeons, and other highly specialized medical practitioners. This need for specialized services is one of the most valid arguments for locating prisons near metropolitan areas.

Dental Services

A large proportion of the men and women received in prisons have neglected their teeth. As a consequence, every prison must have a dental service where the very least that should be done is to prevent the prisoners'

141

teeth from degenerating even further during the time they are incarcerated. In some locations it has proven very worthwhile to establish dental laboratories for the production of dental prostheses. This also provides an opportunity for vocational training for a limited number of prisoners who are interested and capable.

Psychiatric Services

Much emphasis was placed for many years on the desirability of providing psychiatric diagnostic and treatment services for prisoners on the assumption that criminality had its primary roots in mental illness. This idea has been largely exploded in recent years but, nevertheless, there is a small percentage of the prisoners who enter the gates of adult correctional institutions who are actually psychotic, or whose behavior is so atypical that psychiatric diagnosis and interpretation are almost essential. As far as treatment is concerned, the one-to-one doctor-patient relationship in psychiatric treatment is virtually impossible except for a bare handful of prisoners. The psychiatrist's role then becomes, first, one of diagnosis, second, of treating a very limited number of cases, third, of developing group therapy for other appropriate classifications and, finally, training and advising other personnel of the institution.

In most systems grossly mentally ill prisoners may be transferred to public mental hospitals. This is not an altogether satisfactory arrangement, because mental hospitals frequently do not have adequate security for some of these prisoners, but perhaps the more important factor is that an unselected general prison population will have amongst its members a mere handful of such psychiatric inmates, while the real problem is a much larger group of prisoners whom one commentator has called the "neither sane nor insane." These are individuals who may be described by a variety of psychiatric labels but whose behavior whether in prison or out is so bizarre, unusual, and unacceptable that psychiatric intervention seems obvious. Even if modern psychiatry may not offer much in the way of a cure of these cases, it is important that other personnel of the institution who must manage these individuals and make decisions concerning them have the advantage of the psychiatrist's specialized knowledge.

Academic Education and Vocational Training

As has been pointed out earlier, a large percentage approaching half of the population of a prison system lacks a full common school education. In a society which depends so much on written materials and instructions, and in

142

which labor-saving machinery has crowded the "hewers of wood and the drawers of water" out of the labor market, it follows that, if the prison program is to contribute to the reintegration of releasees into free society, every effort should be made to bring them up as close to a common school education level as possible. A further factor of great importance, especially in some areas of the country, is the fact that substantial proportions of the prison population are essentially illiterate in the English language, and a few of them neither speak it nor understand it. The importance of overcoming this handicap cannot be overestimated.

Another factor associated with the residents of correctional institutions both for juveniles and adults is that a substantial proportion of them, even though native-born Americans, are nonreaders. As a consequence, it would be justifiable to require all prisoners of normal intelligence to attend school virtually on a full-time basis until they have attained at least a seventh-grade level in common school subjects.

We have previously observed also that most young men on first entering prison have a deplorable work record. The need, therefore, of establishing within each institution opportunities for vocational training and the development of job skills is obvious. One of the great weaknesses of vocational training in most institutions has been that they fail to keep abreast of the fast-moving technologies of the workaday world. One method employed by some institutions is to maintain an active vocational trade advisory committee, whose members will make frequent inspections of such training programs as are available and insure that they are up-to-date in both methods and equipment.

One should not expect miracles from vocational training in the institutions for several reasons. First, many of the students are not highly motivated; second, most of them will not be in prison long enough to become full-fledged journeymen; third, any vocational training effort carried on in a school situation without actual job experience is to that extent artificial and incomplete; fourth, when a prisoner is released he must of necessity find gainful employment if he is not to return to crime, and too often placement in the occupation in which he has learned some skills may not be available. In spite of these obvious difficulties, however, vocational training is one of the more essential segments of a prison program. This is especially true when one considers that too often the alternative is complete idleness or playing dominoes in the recreation area. In any event, most prisoners suffer from lack of self-esteem. The acquisition of any skill, no matter of what value in the marketplace, helps to fill a human need.

Library Services

As has been said previously, a large proportion of the young men entering prison are retarded in reading and have not developed the reading habit. Each institution should maintain a library of up-to-date books, magazines, and newspapers. Such a library in order to serve its purpose ought to have a balanced collection made up partly of fiction books which will be read basically as a pastime, and a nonfiction collection for those who want to pursue and enlarge upon their technical knowledge. Most institutions do maintain some kind of a collection of books which they call a library. Very often, the books are castoffs that have been donated to the institution, and the library more often than not is managed by prisoners with very little direction from anyone else. This cannot properly be called a functioning library. A library should be managed by a trained, professional librarian, and there must be budgetary funds provided for renewing and keeping the collection up-to-date. Since prisoners have little else to do during their leisure hours, reading is far easier to encourage in this setting than in almost any other segment of society.

Recreation

The thoughtless or reactionary citizen is likely to react negatively to the idea of recreation for prisoners by such comments as "Criminals aren't sent to prison to be entertained." Perhaps so, but neither are they sent there to be destroyed. Only two or three percent of those who enter American prisons die there. More than half of them return to the streets in less than two years. As has been pointed out elsewhere, very little of their time is occupied by work. If men, and especially young men, are not to atrophy and deteriorate in both mind and body, they must have activity.

In the days of the industrial prison when there was relatively little idleness, the need for physical exercise was not so important, but even then the need for avocational and recreational pursuits to renew the human spirit and maintain an acceptable level of mental health was always recognized by prison administrators as an essential part of a prison program.

Athletic games have been common in prisons for many years, but they have severe limitations because only a few prisoners can be active participants in baseball, football, basketball, volleyball, boxing, and wrestling. Furthermore, they all require space and equipment. Swimming is refreshing and good exercise but the prisons in the United States which have swimming pools either indoor or outdoor can probably be numbered on the fingers of one hand. Many prisoners are not attracted by any kind of games and seem to prefer noncompetitive exercise which partly accounts for the popularity of weightlifting.

Climate also restricts outdoor activities in cold seasons. Accordingly, a large building of fieldhouse proportions is needed but seldom provided, especially in institutions for young men under 25 years of age.

Other kinds of nonphysical recreation may take the form of hobby crafts, chess, dominoes, and checkers. Playing cards are prohibited in some places because of their frequent use in gambling, which often results in fights and other disciplinary problems. Inmates can gamble anyway with other games, so playing cards are sometimes allowed if the games are closely supervised.

Radios are now permitted in most places but are best controlled if a central receiving set is installed and several channels piped to each cell or bed and received through earphones. This cuts down on annoying noise and eliminates the problem of thefts and trading in individually owned portable transistor sets. Television is popular but appropriate places for group viewing are sometimes not available. Weekly or semiweekly movies are also common, but their showing in darkened auditoriums or dining rooms presents disciplinary problems in some institutions.

For those inmates who enjoy reading, the availability of books and periodicals is one of the more acceptable and inexpensive recreational resources.

Finally, constructive use of the excess of leisure time in prisons is or should be a prime concern of administrators of contemporary prisons.

Counseling and Case Management

The term "counseling" is frequently misunderstood in this connection, because it is likened to the counseling of an attorney, the advice of one's chaplain, or the teaching at mother's knee. A legislator once expressed his abysmal ignorance of this subject by commenting to this writer that he felt that a "counselor" had to be an inspired man, and he doubted if we could employ an inspired man in the state civil service. Actually, in the prison setting each prisoner needs someone to guide him in carrying out the program which the institution has set for him. He may get some miscellaneous advice from his work supervisor or from the chaplain or from the disciplinary officer, but the counselor should be regarded as a case manager who will be assigned 50 or 60 cases, each of whom he will see occasionally to see that the man is on course. He will also make himself available for solicited advice from the inmate and will act as an official representative of the inmate in his relationships with other services in the institution. In a small institution with two or three hundred inmates the warden or superintendent and his immediate staff may well meet this need, but in large institutions, unless a counseling service is provided, the ordinary prisoner who incurs no disciplinary reports and is generally a tractable member of the population may go along for months or years doing nothing but eating three meals a day and getting older.

Religion

The earliest efforts made to treat prisoners with Christian humanity and to provide opportunities for reform and rehabilitation were made by members of the clergy. We have only to call to mind that it was the Quakers who initiated the Pennsylvania System, and in the 200 years intervening, volunteer clergymen and organized groups such as the Salvation Army and Volunteers of America have patiently persisted in their efforts to give service to the poor and economically disadvantaged, including the inmates of jails and prisons. Most of the early efforts of the clergy, aside from the conduct of religious worship, have gradually been taken over by lay professional workers, but religion continues to have an important role in prison programs. Normally, in the United States, each major institution will have at least two chaplains. One will usually be a member of the Roman Catholic Church and the other, one of the major Protestant groups. In some sections of the country there are enough Jewish inmates to warrant a Jewish chaplain, and other chaplains are ordinarily permitted to visit on a confidential basis prisoner members of their congregation. During the last 25 years or thereabouts most well-organized prison systems provide for salaried chaplains, special places of worship in the form of chapels and altars, and an advisory committee of religious leaders who oversee the whole program.

Besides being the minister of his faith, the chaplain serves another function which cannot be administered nearly so well by any other personnel. The prisoner who is a member of a religious faith will usually feel that he can speak confidentially to the chaplain about almost any subject, whereas he might be hesitant to discuss the same matter with a prison official or a counselor. The chaplains also serve as a very useful channel of communication between the prisoners' families and the prisoners, and can usually be especially useful in the case of deaths in the families, divorces, and other disruptions of personal relationships.

A few large prison systems maintain advisory committees on institutional religion, usually composed of prominent church leaders of the principal sectarian groups in the state. Its chief function is to assist the administration to establish and maintain standards for religious observances in the institutions.

Inmate Housing

Historically in American prisons the rooms where the prisoners slept, kept their personal effects, and spent much of their leisure time constituted the very heart of the institution. In the Pennsylvania System the prisoner also ate, worked, and exercised in the same space. In the original prison at Cherry Hill in Philadelphia each room or cell also had an outdoor walled space about 8 feet wide and 16 feet long where the prisoner was allowed to sit or pace up and down a few hours a day if the weather permitted. The cells themselves were 8 feet by 12 feet with 10-foot ceilings—substantially larger than the typical one-man cell of recent construction which will usually be about 6 or 7 feet wide and 8 feet deep with ceilings usually lower than 8 feet.

The cells in the Auburn-type cell buildings were smaller and built in double tiers back-to-back with corridors between the fronts of the cells and the outside walls. This type of cell construction is generally considered more secure than "outside" cells because the cell occupants do not have access to outside walls or windows.[2,3]

In the early prisons there would usually be from 20 to 50 cells in a "cell house" on a single floor. As time went on, growing populations forced wardens to begin putting two or more prisoners in each cell, and as new prisons were built the cell buildings were designed for more and more cells. This latter development was encouraged chiefly on a cost basis—cheaper to build and cheaper to supervise. Perhaps one of the most notorious examples is the south cell block of San Quentin which as originally built contained 1,000 cells 4½ feet by 10 feet and stacked 5 tiers high. To make the situation even worse, 2,000 men were often crowded into this space during the period of maximum overcrowding which occurred in the 1930s.

The State Prison at Jackson, Michigan, built in 1926, contained 4,764 cells. The disastrous riots mentioned earlier had their genesis in many evils, not the least of which was overcrowded and too large prisons.

Leaders in the correctional administration have finally begun to make their voices heard so that once again standards are being promoted calling for housing units designed for 25 to 50 inmates and institutions of 400 to 600 maximum capacity.

The use of congregate dormitories designed like army barracks were in common use from the beginning in boys' correctional schools, and because the cost of construction per inmate occupant is substantially less than for cell construction, many prisons for adult men built since about 1930 have been designed partially for dormitory housing. Such housing has proven fairly satisfactory for farm workers, forestry camps and other minimum security facilities for inmates who require relatively little supervision. With these exceptions dormitory housing is no longer recommended. Speaking generally, the recommended housing for adult prisons for both men and women now is individual cells or rooms arranged in such a way that the enclosed common space—dayrooms and the like—does not serve more than 25 to 50 inmates, with a strong preference for the smaller number.[4]

The only possible argument for larger units is that they are somewhat less costly to build, and more importantly, from the standpoint of unit cost, the custodial supervision of very small units is several times greater. For example, let us compare in a somewhat oversimplified way one cell building of 200 capacity with 8 units of 25 prisoners each. If one correctional officer were assigned to each 25-man unit constantly for 24 hours a day every day in the year it would require 40 positions, while by assigning two men continuously to the 200-man building the budget requirement would be 10 positions. If each position with salaries and fringe benefits costs $10,000 per year, it can be seen that housing supervision for 200 men in one case would cost $100,000 per year and in the other $400,000.

Aside from the safety and cost factors, numerous small housing units are most important because they provide the means for classification and segregation of the usual miscellaneous assortment of inmates. Much of the damage which the prison experience may cause to the individual prisoner arises because of indiscriminate associations with his fellows. These contaminating influences are most likely to take place in the housing units rather than in shops, working parties and classrooms where there is constant supervision and purposeful activity. In addition, employees assigned to small units can develop a personal knowledge of each inmate in his unit and under proper professional guidance can become in fact a "correctional" officer and not merely a custodian.

Work Programs—Institutional Maintenance

Industries, Agriculture, and Maintenance

In the organizational chart (Figure 7–1), it is suggested that an associate warden or someone of that rank be in charge of industrial and agricultural services which maintain activities wherein the inmates produce products for sale either to other agencies or to the institution itself. Closely related to this, however, are all of the maintenance functions which have been mentioned in passing, principally in connection with the functions of the division of management services. No matter how the various inmate work assignments of the institution may be organized for purposes of functional management, we have chosen here to discuss maintenance work separate from industries because of the historical background and controversial nature of the latter. This will become apparent in the text beginning on page 152.

Food Service

Food service normally in an institution with a medium-sized population will require about 10 percent of the inmates to do the work necessary to handle, process, prepare, and serve three meals a day. This is the most active and persistent work function in every institution. Some of the workers and their supervisors will report for work as early as four o'clock in the morning, and others may be engaged in clean-up work and preparation for the next morning as late as seven or seven-thirty in the evening. This assumes that all of the work involved in baking the bread, cutting the meat, preparing the vegetables, cooking the food, washing the dishes, and mopping the floors is done within the confines of the institution. In some small institutions this workload is reduced by buying bread and pastries from commercial bakeries, buying ready-cut meat from butchers, etc. As a matter of fact, there is one small institution in Sweden where the meals are prepared by a commercial vendor and brought to the institution for service. This makes some sense in that institution because of a very active production industry (parts for portable homes), and it is therefore considered more rational to employ the prisoners in that kind of work rather than in food service in which very few of them are likely to be employed after release. The opposite situation exists in most American prisons where every opportunity to give each inmate a day's work needs to be exploited in order to prevent and avoid the decaying influences of the alternative which is almost total idleness.

Clothing and Laundry

It is obvious that prisoners' clothing must be supplied, stored, repaired, and laundered. In addition to this, it is necessary to launder bedding, towels, and other similar items. Most institutions accordingly maintain a laundry adequately equipped with modern machinery. A few institutional systems maintain an industrial laundry not only to do their own work, but also that of other institutions, such as hospitals, school cafeterias, and even other correctional institutions in the same system. This latter is not a common practice, chiefly because of the difficulties of transportation, losses, and pilferage.

Maintenance of Buildings and Grounds

This function has been mentioned earlier because of its special importance in prison administration, but in another context it is very important as a means of employing the time of a considerable number of prisoners and to a limited extent providing opportunities for actual job training for some of them. The work involves all of the building crafts from masonry to electricity, the operation of a power plant, the repair of machinery. Aside from the skilled crafts, there is a multiplicity of unskilled and semiskilled jobs, such as landscape gardening, mowing the grass, disposing of the garbage, and washing the windows.

Clerical Functions

Every office in the institution from that of the chaplain to the bookkeeper to the warden has routine clerical tasks which can well be done by some of the better-educated prisoners. These assignments are usually regarded as prize jobs from the prisoner's standpoint, as they are clean, indoors, and their bosses are civilians who have access to the official power structure of the institution. These kinds of assignments are appropriate for a limited number of prisoners, but care needs to be exercised by a wise superintendent to prevent the occupants of these jobs from becoming the recipients of a variety of special privileges. Another important precaution is that they should not be assigned to work where they have control over fiscal records or of confidential records of personnel or other inmates.

There is one case on record where a prisoner serving some 30 years in aggregated sentences was assigned to the inmate record office. He managed to remove enough information from his own record to reduce his sentence by some 20 years, and then maneuvered to get himself transferred to another institution. It appeared from his record that he was almost ready to be discharged, and he was, in fact, released immediately. This is an unusual and flagrant case but it cannot be emphasized too strongly that there are many records in institutions which should be kept out of the hands of prisoners because of the danger of manipulation and petty blackmail.

Unfortunately, in most adult prisons of today if there is no other work for prisoners except general maintenance assignments, at least half of the population will be idle. It is probable that all of the work done by the 50 percent that are assigned to maintenance could easily be done by 30 percent of the population if they were required to work eight hours a day.

Since the work day of the employees is eight hours from the time they report in the morning until they go home in the afternoon, the prisoners work day must be fitted inside the employees' work day which means that part of the eight hours is consumed going to the place of work, taking an hour out for lunch, going back again to work, and returning to the housing buildings a half hour before quitting time for the afternoon count, so the prisoner who puts in more than six hours a day is the exception and not the rule. In addition to this, when institutions have much idleness the work assignments are overassigned, which means that if it takes a crew of 10 to do a certain task there may well be 15 to 20 persons assigned to the job.

This kind of a situation instead of teaching habits of industry gives lessons in how to look busy while not doing anything.

Agricultural Assignments

As we have seen from the previous review of the history of American prisons, the idea of gardens, animal husbandry, and general farm production as a means of occupation, outdoor exercise, and prison support has been attractive in our society from the very beginning. A generation ago it was sort of a rule of thumb that a small or medium-sized prison should have at least one acre of productive farm land per inmate. In some of the Southern states, like Louisiana, this formula has been exceeded by many fold. Conversely, in California, Folsom Prison had virtually no farm land because it was built next to a granite quarry with the idea in 1880 that it was an appropriate occupation for prisoners to prepare granite rock for the construction of state buildings. The California Institution for Men at Chino, on the other hand, originally had 2,600 acres of farm land and leased another 5,000 acres of grazing land when it was first established. It has been common practice in most institutions located in rural areas to maintain a dairy herd, even though it was often necessary to purchase the feed rather than to produce it on the land. The raising of hogs with the idea that they would consume the edible garbage from the prison dining room was common.

As time goes on, most agricultural enterprises in connection with prisons, especially in the industrial states, have proven to be a losing proposition. Agriculture more and more has become highly specialized, and the products are produced at the lowest possible production cost, using every known labor-saving device and planting only the products that grow best on the available land. It turns out that in most areas almost any product that can be produced on available state-owned land with prison labor can be purchased on the open market for less than it can be produced at the prison. Many prison administrators delude themselves on this subject, because they fail to compute all of the costs. For example, the production of a poultry flock capable of producing the egg supply of a single institution of about 2,000 population will barely support the salary of a civil service employee to supervise the inmates. This takes no account of the food, the interest on the capital invested, nor the taxes which would have to be paid if the land and the operations were owned privately. Another argument against most agricultural enterprises is that most prisoners now come from metropolitan areas and very few of them are going to be employed in agriculture after release. As a consequence, there is very little in agricultural enterprises which can be demonstrated to have both training and economic value.

Industries

As was pointed out earlier, manufacturing industries in American state prisons had been dealt a severe blow by restrictive federal legislation. Had it not been for the Second World War, the production of these industries would have been reduced to a mere trickle by 1940.

Because of the controversy which has raged on the subject of the competition of prison labor with private enterprise, it will be useful to review here very briefly some of the systems for making use of productive prison labor in the past.

Contract System

Under this arrangement, the labor of the prisoners was contracted to a private manufacturer who provided the buildings, the equipment and the supplies, and actually operated the factory. The only responsibility of the prison management under this system was to supply a guaranteed number of days and hours of prison labor for which the contractor paid the administration an agreed upon amount. This system was subject to many abuses and temptations to corruption. By the turn of the century most states had outlawed the contract system of prison labor. The State of California included in its Constitution of 1879 a section prohibiting the State from contracting the labor of prisoners to a private person or corporation.

Piece-Price System

Under this arrangement the factories and shops were operated by the prison management and the private contractor supplied the materials and equipment and paid the institution at some agreed upon rate per piece. This system was not unlike the home labor piecework systems which have generally been referred to in the literature as sweat shops. This system has also been outlawed in most jurisdictions. It may still be found operating in some European countries.

The Lease System

Here the workers were removed from the prison and their labor leased on an hourly or daily rate basis to contractors engaged in kinds of enterprises where the labor was hard and unpopular. Some of the types of enterprises included salvaging of pitch from stumps in jungle swamps for the recovery of turpentine. Prisoners were also used on sugar cane plantations and later, by road contractors. The lease system had been abolished by statute in every state of the Union by 1936.

Generally speaking, the men employed in the contract, piece-price, and lease systems received no pay or at best a pittance, and the conditions of labor were brutal and oppressive.

Public or State Account System

Under this plan no private entrepreneurs were involved. The state operated the factories, provided the personnel, the funds, and the supplies, but sold the products on the open market. In most of the states where this system was in vogue preference was usually given to products used by farmers. For example, in Minnesota and Wisconsin, rope, binder twine, and farm machinery were heavily emphasized. In California, the production of burlap bags which under the statute could be sold only directly to farmers was a major industry at San Quentin. Other products which were widely manufactured under the state account system were workingmen's clothing, brushes and brooms, and similar articles which used a limited amount of machinery and in which the standards of workmanship are relatively low.

This system is still legal in many states, but because of the prohibition against shipping prison-made goods across state lines, the market has been severely curtailed. In addition to this, the introduction of labor-saving machinery and automated processes in private enterprise has also made it difficult, if not impossible, for the prison factories to compete with private manufacturers.

The State Use System

This plan is similar to the state account system, except that the products may not be sold to anyone other than the state itself or its political subdivisions. The state is prohibited from selling any of these products to any private person.

Such prison industries as do exist today almost invariably operate under the state use plan. There are a few minor exceptions, notably in the disposition of surplus and waste products from the industries and agriculture.

Because of the limited market for any specialized products, it has become virtually impossible for state use industries to operate manufacturing enterprises that are sufficiently specialized to compete successfully on a price basis with private enterprise. One type of industry which persists is the manufacture of furniture. This is partly because state governments have a constant need for office furniture especially, and partly because in spite of much improved machinery furniture manufacture still requires a substantial component of hand labor. Another industry that persists is the manufacture of automobile license plates for the state departments of motor vehicles. The states' advantage here is that this is in effect a state monopoly. Other kinds of products manufactured under the state use system include soaps, clothing and bedding, mattresses, institution beds, and canned goods for state institutions.

Public Works and Ways System

This plan involved prison labor to build and maintain roads, carry on reforestation and fire prevention work and to construct buildings within existing prisons. In the highly unionized industrial states the use of prison labor in building construction is practically a thing of the past. It is still done to some extent in the states that are basically rural. The most active use of this plan in the states where there are opportunities for it, such as California and Pennsylvania, involves men working in forestry camps.

Generally speaking, about the only viable system of any consequence left is the state use system.

Hobbies, Arts and Crafts

Hobby shops are not regarded as industries and are usually authorized by special statute and exempted from the restrictions on prison labor. Under this arrangement individual prisoners are permitted to purchase certain materials for purposes of producing various arts and crafts products. These products are usually sold at the store near the visiting section within each prison. The products include leather craft, drawings and paintings, handweaving, inexpensive jewelry, etc. These products make no money for the state. The inmates do the work principally during their idle time, and these arts and crafts programs are justified basically for their recreational values.

Prison industries as they exist today and as we have known them in the past are, unfortunately, no longer a major or a vital part of prison programs. Certainly some small state use industries will persist, as well as some of the public works programs. Until a whole new program is designed and hundreds of restrictive statutes are repealed, manufacturing enterprises in prisons cannot be expected to thrive. Substitutes must be found for occupying the prisoner's time and using his mental and physical energies. It is probable that the most likely alternatives will be found in the developing of training programs of all kinds. Unfortunately, such programs not only will contribute nothing to reducing the per capita cost of running the prison, but because of the necessity of employing skilled teachers besides using much valuable space and equipment, such activities will add substantially to per capita cost. Whether or not such programs will reduce recidivism and hence reduce costs in the long run has yet to be demonstrated.

Prison Architecture

The design plans for prisons for adults are as variable as those for hospitals, hotels, or military forts. For those who would pursue the matter further there is an extensive literature both historical and contemporary on the subject.[5,6,7,8]

For our purpose in this text it will suffice to identify and comment briefly on the more typical plans. Generally, one can say there are two major design schemes – open plans and closed or security plans.

Open or Campus Plans

The open plan is characterized by the absence of physical structures designed to prevent escape, such as walls, elevated guard towers, security windows, and heavy prison locks. This kind of plan for inmates requiring a minimum of custodial restraint is most often seen as an adjunct or annex to a security prison; for example, as a farm workers' dormitory, a forestry camp, or a prerelease center for those soon to be discharged or paroled. Some independent institutions are either truly open or are of modified open design. Most women's prisons, and a few men's prisons in large systems are also of this general class.

The buildings comprising the open institution tend to be arranged on the site somewhat like those on a college campus. Housing buildings, dining rooms, workshops, administration building, schoolrooms, hospital, and so on will for the most part be independent, freestanding structures, and traffic from one to the other will usually be outdoors rather than through corridors, tunnels, and enclosed yards, as is often the case in coventional security prisons.

The California Institution for Men at Chino; the Correctional Center at Fox Lake, Wisconsin; the Robert F. Kennedy Youth Center (federal) at Morgantown, West Virginia; and the State Penitentiary at Vienna, Illinois are examples of campus plans of institutions for adult male felons. Some of them have been built very recently. It should be noted, however, that they are all in systems which have other conventional institutions of higher security. The absence of oppressive architecture in these facilities is always impressive to the humanitarian visitor, but one should not be led to the conclusion that anything more than a fourth to a half of a state's convicted adult male felons can safely be managed in prisons of open design. Another caution on open institutions is also in order. In spite of the elimination of armed perimeter walls or fences, the per capita cost of operating an open facility usually will not be found to be less than for conventional prisons. In fact, the exact opposite is often the case, but the difference is unlikely to be substantial.

The Wheel Plan

It is probably fair to state that Eastern Penitentiary built in Philadelphia in 1821 was the first major prison in America which was designed as a total facility and planned to facilitate a reformative theory of penal treatment. John Haviland, a young English architect, prepared the plans under the direction of the Pennsylvania Quakers.

The overall plan resembles a wagon wheel in which the hub is a large circular rotunda containing most of the administrative space; and the cell buildings, of which there are seven, emanate from the hub like thick spokes. The whole was surrounded by a rectangular masonry wall with an elevated guard tower at each corner. This plan or modifications of it can be seen at Trenton, New Jersey; Leavenworth, Kansas (federal); and in several other countries, including England, Germany, and Japan.

The wheel plan was ideally suited to the solitary program of the initial institution from the standpoint of management and had in addition the virtue of being compact and relatively easy to supervise. With the introduction of congregate dining, industrial factories, classrooms, and outdoor recreation, the plan was less adaptable, although some prisons of rather recent origin retained the scheme for the cell buildings and the dining room but added other separate buildings in an enlarged walled or fenced area.

The Telephone Pole Plan

This plan is so named because the skeletal scheme resembles a telephone pole with a number of crossarms. The pole is a long central corridor like a main street with most of the buildings attached to it. The first major prison built by the Federal Bureau of Prisons in 1932 was designed by Architect Alfred Hopkins and constructed on a site near Lewisburg, Pennsylvania. It was first of a series of similar "telephone pole" type institutions built in the following 25 years, principally by the Federal Bureau and the State of California.

The plan is especially functional from the engineering standpoint because of the economy of the distribution of the facilities for sewage, water, heat, ventilation, and electricity by means of a utility tunnel under the main corridor. From the standpoint of security and inmate traffic it is also efficient, because most of the institution's daily activities can be carried on without the inmates going outside the security enclosures of the buildings themselves. Its disadvantages relate, first, to the rather confining atmosphere of the whole establishment, and second, to the problem of the segregation of different classifications of inmates in a plant which is essentially a single unified facility made up of numerous related parts.

The Self-Enclosing Plan

The essential characteristic of the self-enclosing plan is that of a hollow square or rectangle. Buildings are connected and arranged so as to enclose a central courtyard. Medieval monasteries were often designed in this fashion. The Federal Bureau of Prisons built a series of federal correctional institutions on this plan in the period between 1935 and 1940. By American standards of that time these were regarded as small facilities with capacities of about 500 men. The plan even for as few as 400 or 500 inmates presents problems for the convenient movement of people and materials from one part of the institution to another, because most of the internal traffic must take place around or across the large open courtyard in all kinds of weather. The courtyard also becomes the recreation field and the access to the windows and doors of the enclosing buildings creates many problems. In short, the plan in its simplest form works well for very small institutions of less than 300 capacity if two secondary enclosures are provided—one a fenced area for a recreation field and another for shops, warehouse, heating plant and similar utilitarian appurtenances. For larger populations the self-enclosing plan is only workable if the total institution is divided into two or more quadrangles, which produces another kind of a scheme.

The Quad Plan

This multiple quadrangle plan is in effect a compromise between the management and program advantages of a small institution of 400 or 500 and the construction and operational economies of large institutions with capacities running up to 2,000. The State Prison at San Luis Obispo, California, opened in 1961, is the most noteworthy example of this concept. The plan there is contained in a very large square with the cell buildings forming the outer enclosure but other buildings containing office space, classrooms, kitchen and dining room, maintenance shops, industrial factories, laundry and hospital, all included in a cross which divides the whole facility into four quadrangles. Thus, an overly large institution can be operated as far as its inmates are concerned as if it were four relatively small facilities with differing programs in each.

The Vertical Plan

The high rise or vertical plan has not been widely used except for jails in urban settings. It is like the telephone pole plan, except that the corridor is replaced by a bank of elevators and stairs, and the buildings are stacked on top of one another as floors instead of wings.

The most notable recent example of this plan is to be found in the Federal Correctional Center at Morgantown, West Virginia, opened in 1972. It is some 15 stories high, and except for emergency stairs all traffic of inmates, staff, and material is by elevator. The rationale for such a prison located in a rural area is hard to understand. Such construction is not inexpensive and elevators in prison or jail buildings are notoriously unreliable and expensive to man and operate.

The Panopticon

The concept of the panopticon prison was first advanced by the English philosopher and law reformer Jeremy Bentham in the late eighteenth and early nineteenth centuries. The cell buildings were to be circular in plan with the cells arranged in tiers around the outside wall. The cell fronts were to be glass or open grills, so that each prisoner would be under constant observation by a guard stationed in a guard post in the center of the circular floor. Besides the supposed custodial control provided, Bentham's theory was that if men developed the habit of decorous and conforming behavior over a long period of close supervision these habits would carry over to later life. That such a theory was without either practical or scientific validity hardly requires further discussion now two centuries later.

The panopticon prison was never built in England, but several such institutions were built in Holland and Spain and adaptations of the plan were constructed elsewhere in Europe. The plan would hardly be worthy of mention in relationship to American prison architecture had the State of Illinois not built such a prison at Statesville near Joliet, Illinois, in the period between 1916 and 1924. It is composed of four circular cell buildings each four tiers high. These housing structures are connected by enclosed passageways to another one-story circular building which contains the mess halls, kitchen, and related service space. In the intervening years the plan has been modified by the addition of other conventional buildings, including shops, factories, hospital, administration, and various other structures. The whole complex is surrounded by a concrete wall mounted by some 14 guard towers.

There is one other notable example of this circular plan in the Western Hemisphere at Pine Island, Cuba. It is doubtful that this plan will ever be employed again in America.

Of the many basic schemes for prison plans the three which are currently most favored are a) the campus plan, especially for open, minimum-security purposes; b) the telephone pole plan for medium and high security; and c) the courtyard plan for relatively small minimum- and medium-security type inmates.

It is unlikely that the radial or wheel plan will be much used in the future, and the high-rise facility will probably be restricted principally to urban settings where land is scarce and expensive.

Prison Perimeters

The enclosures around the buildings and grounds of prisons traditionally have been of masonry. The term "prison walls" has become a symbol of prison in our language. "Stone walls do not a prison make . . ." and so on. During the past three or four decades, however, most prison enclosures in the United States have not been of stone or concrete. Partly because of our high labor costs "chain link" fencing now seems to be much preferred. For high-security institutions with armed guard posts, double fences spaced about 10 feet apart are common. Fences also have the virtue of being relatively easy to move if future need should arise.

As a final comment, it is important to emphasize environmental influences on human behavior and attitudes. Prison designers are finally becoming aware of the fact that prisons are not only places to hold convicted offenders in custody for limited periods but are also places where human beings live.

The Prison Community

Prisons, like jails, prisoner of war camps, military barracks, mental hospitals, monasteries, and similar self-contained, 24-hours-a-day, 7-days-a-week facilities have been referred to as "total institutions."[9] In such institutions the residents are usually there more or less against their will. They are segregated in varying degrees from the free society; they are under the close supervision and control of employees of the governing authority; and are deprived of many but not all prerequisites of a normal life. The emphasis on control and segregation from free society will vary, depending on the purpose of the institution. Of all "total institutions" none is so nearly absolute in its separateness from the larger society as the prison.

Each prison is, therefore, a community which develops its own culture and mores made up of formal and informal controls to which the prisoner must learn to make an accommodation if he is to survive the period of his membership. Volumes have been written on this subject, and it would be presumptuous to attempt in the few paragraphs which can be allotted to the subject here to do more than make the reader conscious of some of the conditions and forces at work in the prison culture.[10]

It is important to emphasize first of all that the prison community is not made up entirely of the 24-hour-a-day residents. For each member of the resident population there will be a corps of employees who come and go on their 40-hour-a-week schedule. Depending on the size of the institution and the nature of its programs, the ratio of employees on the payroll to inmates will vary from one-to-one to one-to-six. The members of this employee group play a variety of roles, some formal and some informal.

The custodial security staff are from the resident's standpoint the most significant, because they are the most numerous and the most ever present. Doctors, dentists, teachers, counselors, maintenance personnel, and industrial foremen are often spoken of as civilian personnel as opposed to the uniformed custodial officers. These specialized and professional employees are a part of the fabric of social control but are not regarded by the resident population in the same way that they look upon the correctional officers or guards. Each of these employees, no matter what his occupation or his role in the prison community may be, is another human being involved in the complexities of human relationships in the institutional community. They are all in a sense authority figures, but the warden or superintendent, his subcommanders and department heads, are seen as the possessors of a superior power often magnified in the prisoner's mind. Except for the few very intelligent and experienced members of the resident population, there is often little realization that the prison is very much a subordinate part of a larger society in a superior government structure.

There are other part-time members of the prison community often overlooked in discussion of this subject. For example, there are the prisoner's visitors. These will usually be close friends, members of his immediate family, or his defense attorney. They represent, in a sense, a bridge between the closed society of the prison and the parent society. There are also those who engage in regular correspondence with the prisoners. There is still an additional group which presumably has no direct relationship with the prisoners but they, nevertheless, come and go and are often the targets of manipulation. These are the delivery men, vendors, specialized repairmen, and others who have reason to enter the confines of the prison but who are not regular employees.

Another characteristic of prison communities with the exception of an almost negligible number of experimental institutions is that the resident population is of a single sex. Even if it should become acceptable practice to keep both men and women in the same institutions, they would still be essentially one-sex communities, because as has been pointed out previously, only about 4 percent of the inmates of prisons are women. This single-sex characteristic gets a great deal of attention from outside observers, partly because of the opportunities and motivations for homosexuality, and partly because of the continuing debate all over the world about the question of permitting conjugal visiting in men's institutions. When one looks at the question more carefully there are other effects arising from the single-sex prison community other than the deprivation of sexual gratification. The emphasis among the residents on physical strength, personal courage, and masculinity is apparent among prisoners just as it is in military establishments and boys' schools. There are other concomitants of the problem, however. Some of these can be seen in the crudeness of manners, excessive obscenity and profanity in speech, carelessness about personal appearance and cleanliness, and covert contempt for authority.

Another persistent characteristic of American prisons is the overrepresentation of racial and ethnic minorities. Even as long ago as 1940, as revealed by the census data of that time, nearly 30 percent of the total populations of American prisons was made up of nonwhites, as compared with less than 10 percent of the nation's total population. In some states, as pointed out earlier in this chapter, the Negro prisoner population actually exceeds that of the whites of European stock, and in a few states, the inmates of Latin American origins comprise 15 percent to 20 percent of the prison population.

Because of the cultural heritages of these ethnic groups, the prison culture is necessarily influenced by their presence. There is a strong tendency of these groups to segregate themselves if the prison management permits it, and in any event they will congregate in informal situations in exercise yards and recreation areas.

There has been a further tendency in recent years for them to create informal organizations to advance some pseudoreligious or militant political cause. White inmates sometimes join these groups or form counter groups of their own. Their leaders are likely to be of the antisocial type described later in this chapter.

Until the last 10 years or so, these groups were usually content to cause disruptions in the prison routine and to fight among themselves, but the latest phenomenon is for them to style themselves "political prisoners" and with encouragement from free members of the "New Left" to assault and even assassinate members of the prison staff. In maximum-security prisons where these "outlaws" tend to be concentrated, their presence and their subversive behavior has had a profound effect upon the social mores of these institutions.

The question is often asked, "What is it like to be a prisoner?" No good answer can be given to that question, because what the experience will be like will depend to a large extent on what kind of a person the prisoner is. Many novelists and exprisoners have attempted in their writings to picture the life of the prisoner in terms of his relationships with his fellows and his keepers. Perhaps no one from Fëdor Dostoevski[11] to the present day has been able to interpret prison life in all of its complexities or in ways that would be true statements of the emotional experience of the millions of other individuals who have survived similar experiences. Stated in its starkest language, prison life is sterile. It is lonely; it is monotonous. In spite of all this, each prisoner must survive physically, emotionally, and mentally his 24 hours of each day like every other human being. How he does this will depend as much upon himself as upon the abnormal culture of which he is temporarily a member.

As we have said, each prisoner is an individual and "must do his time" in his own way. Whether he does it by escaping into fantasy, by occupying himself with distracting activities, by becoming a member of a gang of associates who fight authority and prey upon other prisoners, or conversely, by joining the authority group in the hope of rewards in the form of special privileges or personal protection, or by any other means that may be available, he must find some way to survive as best he can in a culture in which he is essentially an unwilling member.

Some efforts have been made to shed some light on this mixture of humanity by classifying prisoners into types, based upon the way in which each general type plays the role of prisoner in making his accommodation to the social situation. Perhaps the most practical effort to do this has been by Clarence Schrag.[12] He originally used such prisoner argot labels as "Square John," "Right Guy," "Con Politician," and "Outlaw." He later used more sociological terms to describe these types of prisoners.

The following summary of this classification may be interesting and hopefully revealing:

> *Prosocial offenders* are most frequently convicted of violent crimes or naive property offenses—homicide, assault, forgery, and the like. Few have a previous record of criminality. Their criminal careers are initiated relatively late in life. Many of their offenses seem to be associated with real or imagined misbehavior on the part of a spouse or of close friends.
> In prison these offenders maintain close ties with family and civilian associates. They are sympathetic and cooperative in their contacts with the authorities. They are supportive of prison regulations, believe in the efficacy of punishment, show guilt feelings regarding their offenses, and expect to pay for their crimes in order to renew civilian life with a clean slate. They are generally naive about criminal techniques and have little knowledge of, or contact with, organized crime and underworld activities. Once released from prison, their prospects for success are good. However, early release seems to be more advantageous than prolonged treatment in prison.
> *Antisocial offenders*, those strongly committed to the inmate code, present a diametrically opposed picture on most issues. They are highly recidivistic. Their delinquent careers are usually initiated at an early age. In most cases their careers progress through several stages—truancy, school dropout, petty theft in gangs, and instrumental theft entailing contacts with "fences" and other organized criminals—culminating in patterns of aggressive criminality, including armed robbery, other assaults, and burglary. Crime is for many of these offenders a mode of life. However, they rarely achieve positions of prominence in organized crime. Their abilities are ordinarily better adapted to the field of direct action than to the affairs of management.
> While in prison the antisocial offenders continue their close association with

criminalistic elements and their conflict with the agents of authority. They are generally regarded as "hardened criminals" and "real cons." Their philosophy of life tends to alleviate any feelings of guilt and to solidify the opposition of inmates against the officials. Because of their demeanor, they are likely to get long sentences and assignments to menial chores in the institution. Although their prospects for success after release are never very great, they do seem to profit from vocational training, group discussions, counseling, and other treatment programs.

Pseudosocial offenders, by contrast, are involved primarily in subtle, sophisticated, profit-motivated crimes, such as fraud, embezzlement, confidence games, professional forgery, and so on. Onset of criminality is relatively late, and it may occur after a position of social respectability has already been attained. Not many cases have a record of juvenile delinquency. Educational and occupational histories are far superior to those of antisocial offenders. Family and community backgrounds are often middle class, though there are frequent signs of inconsistent parental discipline and family discord. It seems that their facility in role playing is acquired at an early age, and these offenders are commonly described as being congenial individuals who have extraordinary skills in interpersonal relations.

These offenders continue in prison to display their chameleonic skills in shifting their allegiance from inmates to staff members and vice versa. They have a vast repertoire of social roles and are highly pragmatic in fitting the role to the occasion. This enables them to exploit the conflicts and contradictions that are inherent in the prison community. Their strategic position between staff members and many of the inmates enables them to play the role of moderator in numerous disputes, resulting in important rewards, including short sentences, reduced custody, and favored prison assignments. Participation in treatment programs is likewise common. After release, however, the recidivism rate is quite high, depending upon the degree of supervision and the pattern of offenses in which the pseudosocial criminal was previously involved.

The fourth type of response pattern is that of *the asocial offender*. Offenders of this type are often involved in crimes characterized by the use of bizarre methods without clear motive or reason. Severe behavioral disturbances are frequently shown at an early age, although the first arrest may be considerably delayed. Social skills and ability to use symbols are generally retarded. Direct and immediate aggression is a favorite means of solving problems. The careers of these offenders are marked by their egocentric and extrapunitive behavior, their apparent inability to profit from mistakes made or to plan for the future, and their distrust of personal ties of any kind. Perhaps the most striking findings in the social backgrounds of asocial individuals, however, is the evidence of early parental rejection and the frequency with which these persons are reared in institutions or shifted from one foster home to another.

Asocial offenders are the prison's main troublemakers. Their conduct records are distinguished by a large number of involvements in riots, escape plots, and assaults upon both inmates and officers. Their style of life inclines them towards violence and rebellion. Yet their undisciplined aggressions and their lack of capacity for cooperative enterprise means that most of their attempts to subvert the official system are destined to fail. These offenders resist any kind of intervention, and their voluntary participation in treatment programs is uncommon. Nor is there evidence that prison treatment is beneficial. Recidivism rates are extraordinarily high.

The above descriptions of typical orientations towards staff and inmate norms indicate a lack of consensus or complementarity. Asocial inmates reject both codes and adopt a nihilistic mode of response. Meanwhile pseudo-social prisoners play it cool. They exploit normative conflicts and ambiguities to their own advantage. They utilize their role playing skills in a relentless game of pragmatism. Antisocial criminals, by contrast, are reared in an environment consistently at odds with the legal order. They accordingly attach themselves to inmate norms that are largely a counteraction against prevailing middle class standards. Prosocial offenders, again, ally themselves with many staff members in defense of middle class norms. But they are rejected by most inmates as a result. Hence it is doubtful that a majority of the inmates in any prison give their unqualified approval to either set of norms.

Finally, and in spite of the strong contemporary movement to abolish the large fortress type prison and to substitute for it community-based programs, it would be a mistake to assume that the closed, secure, total institution for convicted adult offenders is likely to disappear from the American scene in the foreseeable future. As a matter of fact, what is likely to disappear first will be the correctional schools for juveniles, prisons for women, and open institutions and camps. The reasons for this will grow out of the selection of the more tractable and less dangerous offenders for community-based programs, leaving those requiring close custody and high security to be kept in prisons. The cultural characteristics of these prisons will probably not change materially, except that they will be more difficult to manage because of the predominance of dangerous offenders and those that are thoroughly committed to criminal behavior.

NOTES

[1]Clarence Schrag, Ph.D., *Crime and Justice: American Style*, National Institute of Mental Health, 1971.

[2]Norman Johnston, *The Human Cage—A Brief History of Prison Architecture*, New York, Walker and Company, 720 Fifth Avenue, 1973.

[3]William Nagel, *The New Red Barn: A Critical Look at the Modern American Prison*, New York, Walker and Company, 720 Fifth Avenue, 1973.

[4]National Advisory Commission on Criminal Justice Standards and Goals, *Corrections*, p. 358.

[5]U.S. Bureau of Prisons, *Handbook of Correctional Institution Design and Construction*, 1949.

[6]National Clearinghouse for Criminal Justice Planning and Architecture, *Guidelines for the Planning and Design of Regional and Community Correctional Centers for Adults*, Urbana, Ill., Department of Architecture, University of Illinois, 1973.

[7]Johnston, *The Human Cage.*

[8]Nagel, *The New Red Barn.*

[9]Erving Goffman, "Characteristics of Total Institutions," pp. 15–106, in D. R. Cressey *The Prison*, New York, Holt, Rinehart, and Winston, 1961.

[10]Donald Clemmer, *The Prison Community*, New York, Holt, Rinehart, and Winston. 1958. (While this book was published originally in 1940, it must still be regarded as the classic treatise on the subject.) See also Clarence Schrag, *Crime and Justice*, pp. 202–213.

[11]Fëdor Dostoevski, *The House of the Dead*, published during the middle of the 19th century, now printed by Dell and by Dutton in paperback form in 1973.

[12]Schrag, *Crime and Justice.*

Note: For additional reference, see Norval Morris, *The Future of Imprisonment*, Chicago, University of Chicago Press, 1974.

8 Probation

The Origins of Probation

The American Correctional Association has noted that probation may be defined as a sentence, as an organization, or as a process.[1] As a sentence, probation represents a judicial disposition which establishes the convicted offender's legal status under which his freedom in the community is continued, subject to supervision by a probation organization and to conditions imposed by the court. As an organization, probation is an agency designed to assist the court and to perform specified services in the administration of criminal justice. As a process, probation involves the presentence investigation for the court and the supervision of persons in the community.

Regardless of which definition is utilized, probation is of recent origin in terms of the total history of the treatment of offenders and is a distinctly American correctional innovation. Probation is a product of century-long social trends which have consistently included a movement from those traditional punitive and repressive techniques for dealing with crime, based upon a social policy of general deterrence and retribution, to approaches which focus upon both the prevention of criminality and the rehabilitation of offenders.

Although probation is generally considered to have originated in Boston in 1841, it was not a product of a deliberate legislative or judicial act. Its antecedents are found in those features of the English common law which allowed the suspension of punishment subject to good behavior. In short, probation evolved slowly from various methods for the conditional suspension of punishment, and was a reaction to harsh and repressive criminal law including capital and corporal punishment and their almost mechanical and inhumane application. Among the judicial expedients which were the direct precursors of probation are the right of sanctuary, benefit of clergy, judicial

167

reprieve, recognizance or binding-over, provisional release on bail, and the provisional filing of cases.² The right of sanctuary dates to Biblical times and allowed transgressors to escape punishment by fleeing to designated areas, including such places of refuge as churches. The benefit of clergy was a device originally extended to the clergy by which they could, after conviction but before judgment, claim exemption from or mitigation of punishment. In practice, the benefit of clergy was a device to avoid capital punishment. The judicial reprieve was a temporary suspension by the court of either the imposition or the execution of sentence. Its purpose was to allow a convicted offender to apply for a pardon or to permit reprieve when the court was either dissatisfied with a verdict or questioned the evidence in a given case.

The recognizance, originally designed to deter the commission of crime, "consists in obliging those persons, whom there is probable ground to suspect of future misbehavior, to stipulate and to give full assurance to the public, that such offense shall not happen."³ The assurance to the public was given by entering into a recognizance or bond, with or without sureties, thus creating a debt to the state which became payable when its conditions were violated or disregarded. This procedure was utilized either to assure a defendant's appearance for trial or as a provisional suspension of a final action in a case. The jurist Blackstone noted that recognizance "must be understood rather as a caution against the repetition of the offenses, than (as) any immediate pain or punishment."⁴

The provisional release on bail was a natural extension of the recognizance process. By adding the *requirement* for bail to the provisional release aspect of the recognizance, a new process evolved which allowed accused but unconvicted defendants as well as convicted offenders to remain in the community. The element of supervision was inherent in the process. For those who had not yet stood trial, the person providing the bail insured some supervision, if only to guarantee appearance in court. For the convicted offender, the provisional release on bail served as a deferral of final action or as a suspended sentence, provided conditional freedom in place of incarceration, and some supervision. Revocation, however, remained a possibility in the event of violation of the conditions of release.

The provisional filing of cases originated in Massachusetts and consisted of the suspension of sentence "after verdict of guilty in a criminal case . . . the Court is satisfied that, by reason of extenuating circumstances, or of the pendency of a question of law in a like case before a higher court, or other sufficient reason, public justice does not require an immediate sentence."⁵ The provisional filing procedure required the consent of the offender and prosecuting attorney, with the suspension subject to those conditions which the court at its discretion might impose. The filing of a case was not the equivalent of a final judgment, and the court remained free to take action on the case at any time in the future.

Thus we can see that the recognizance, the provisional release on bail, and the provisional filing of cases were the first rudimentary steps toward probation, enabling American and English courts to suspend the imposition or execution of sentence. These practices are therefore clearly part of our common law tradition. The question as to whether courts could, based upon common law precedents, *indefinitely* suspend sentence was resolved in the United States in 1916 by the Supreme Court in the Killits case. In his opinion, Chief Justice White ruled that the English common law did not give the federal courts the power to suspend sentence indefinitely:

> It is true that, owing to the want of power in common law courts to grant new trials and to the absence of a right to review convictions in higher court, it is we think, to be conceded: (a) that both suspensions of sentence and suspensions of the enforcement of sentence, temporary in character, were often resorted to on grounds of error or miscarriage of justice which under our system would be corrected either by new trials or by the exercise of the power to review; (b) that not infrequently, where the suspension either of the imposition of a sentence or of its execution was made for the purpose of enabling a pardon to be sought or bestowed, by a failure to further proceed in the criminal cause in the future, although no pardon had been sought or obtained, the punishment fixed by law was escaped. But neither of these conditions serves to convert the mere exercise of a judicial discretion to temporarily suspend for the accomplishment of a purpose contemplated by law into the existence of an arbitrary judicial power to permanently refuse to enforce the law.[6]

The final rejection in the Killits case of an implied common law judicial power of indefinite suspension of sentence did not retard the evolution of probation, but served rather as a stimulus for the enactment of statutes expressly authorizing the suspension of sentence and probation.

The Origins of Probation in the United States

Legal considerations aside, probation in the United States is generally credited to John Augustus who, in 1841, attended a police court in Boston and posted bail for a man charged with public drunkenness. Reappearing in court three weeks later with the offender who showed "convincing" signs of reform, the judge, instead of imposing the usual penalty of imprisonment in the house of corrections, ordered payment of a nominal fine of one cent. Encouraged by this first experience, Augustus proceeded to stand bail for other offenders and offered some supervision and guidance during the period of time pending judgment. While earlier cases were confined to adult males charged with drunkenness, the scope of his activities were gradually extended to include women and children, and ultimately defendants charged with other offenses. Augustus' efforts were extended to the Boston municipal court and during the following 18 years until his death in 1859, the "father of probation" "bailed on probation" almost 2,000 offenders.

The first probation law was passed in Massachusetts in 1878 and enabled the city of Boston, through its mayor, to appoint a paid probation officer for the courts of criminal jurisdiction. Edward H. Savage, former Chief of Police of Boston, became the first statutory probation officer. The 1878 law prescribed the duties of probation officers to include court attendance, investigation of cases of persons charged with or convicted of crimes or misdemeanors, making recommendations to the courts with regard to the advisability of using probation, submission of periodic reports to the chief of police, visiting probationers, and the "rendering of such assistance and encouragement (to probationers) as will tend to prevent their again offending." The statute also gave the probation officer the power to rearrest probationers without warrant, but with the approval of the chief of police, following which the court "might proceed to sentence or make such other disposition of the case as may be authorized by law."

By a statute enacted in 1880, all cities and towns in Massachusetts were authorized to appoint probation officers. In 1891, probation was made mandatory in Massachusetts for the police and municipal courts, and the power of appointment of probation officers was transferred from municipal authorities to the courts. In 1898, probation was extended to the Massachusetts superior courts.

By the turn of the century, four additional states had enacted probation legislation. The creation of the juvenile court in Chicago in 1899 and its emphasis on the importance of the suspended sentence and adequate supervision of the probationer gave major impetus to the probation movement. By 1910, for example, 37 states and the District of Columbia had a Children's Court Act and 40 states had juvenile probation services. By 1925, probation for juveniles was available in every state; by 1956, adult probation services were available nationwide.

The Probation Process: The Presentence Investigation and Report

The two major roles of the probation officer are to conduct a presentence investigation as a basis for preparation of a presentence report and supervision of offenders on probation in the community. The first function — preparation of a detailed report based upon a complete investigation — is a critical element in judicial and correctional administration. The investigation, normally initiated immediately following a finding or admission of guilt, and the formal written report to the court, serve several important functions. Initially, the report aids the court in determining the appropriate sentence; it may also be of considerable assistance to correctional institution personnel in their classification and program activities in the event the offender is sentenced to an institution, and similarly to the paroling authority when parole is under consideration. In addition, the report is the basic source of information utilized by the probation officer in his supervision of offenders placed on probation. Finally, the report may serve as a source of relevant information for systematic research about convicted offenders.

The presentence or probation reports utilized in the United States today can trace their development and formulation to 1910. In that year, William Healy, Director of the Juvenile Psychopathic Institute in Chicago, outlined the need for "individual study of the young criminal"; he pointed to "the importance of a thorough-going study of the individual case at the period of life when something, if ever, can be done in the way of individual modification." Healy noted, "The case consequently must require careful, individual diagnosis before the rational treatment can be instituted which is really adapted to its needs."[7] Healy's observations are directly related to the purposes of the modern presentence report. For example, the Administrative Office of the United States Courts, in commenting on the presentence report model utilized in United States District Courts, observed:

> The primary objective of the presentence report is to focus light on the character and personality of the defendant, to offer insight into his problems and needs, to help understand the world in which he lives, to learn about his relationships with people, and to discover those salient factors that underlie his specific offense and his conduct in general.
>
> Probation cannot succeed unless care is exercised in selecting those who are to receive its benefits. The presentence report is an essential aid in this selective process.[8]

Healy's efforts toward classification of offenders in 1910 and 1913 and his 1915 text, *The Individual Delinquent* (sub-title: A Textbook of Diagnosis and Prognosis For All Concerned In Understanding Offenders), influenced the development of earlier models of presentence reports. He held "the deepest conviction that only through logical scientific study of the individual can there be any reasonable expectation of amendment in most delinquent careers. Those who have to do with the judging and treatment of offenders must reckon with such methods of fact as we present." Healy's system of data collection covered 11 areas: family history, developmental history, environment, mental and moral development, anthropometry, medical examination, psychological data, delinquency record, a diagnostic and prognostic summary, as well as "follow up" and "subsidiary" records.[9]

While Healy was concerned with the development of a scientific approach to delinquency, Bernard Flexner and Roger Baldwin, in a text prepared for the National Probation Association, were focusing on the use of data as gathered or suggested by Healy to improve the probation officer's performance in court. They observed, in 1914:

> Probation officers as a rule, fail to distinguish between facts and conclusions. A large portion of the evidence given by probation officers in juvenile courts is a mass of opinions and conclusions. The only way to avoid testimony so manifestly unfair and absolutely valueless, is to secure the full facts in advance as accurately as possible and put them in writing.[10]

Mary E. Richmond's 1917 text, addressed mainly to social workers, indicated a need for "social diagnosis," defined as "the attempt to make as exact a definition as possible of the situation and personality of a human being in some social need—of his situation and personality, that is, in relation to the other human beings upon whom he in any way depends or who depend upon him, and in relation also to the social institutions of his community." Cautioning the "worker to distinguish in the evidence collected what is relatively important for successful treatment from what is relatively unimportant," Miss Richmond's system of data collection included general social data, physical and mental conditions, industrial history, financial situation, education, religious affiliation, recreation, environment, relations, if any, with social agencies, and basis for treatment.[11]

In 1918, Edwin J. Cooley, Chief Probation Officer of the Court of General Sessions at New York City, observed:

> One of the current developments in our Probation work is the realization that there is a definite methodology in the making of a comprehensive diag-

nosis of a delinquent. Miss Mary E. Richmond's book *Social Diagnosis,* which, by the way, should be in the hands of every probation officer, is a very definite step in the development of social case technique.

Two years later, Cooley extended his remarks and pointed to the need for a "scientific probation technique, drawing its inspiration from the realization of the significance of the task, obtaining its information in the vast laboratory of life as a whole." In 1925, Cooley was given an opportunity to implement his ideas when he was appointed Director of the Catholic Charities Probation Bureau in New York City. In that year, Cardinal Hayes of New York, "after examining various methods proposed for the solution of the crime problem . . . came to the conclusion that in the probation system, with its study of the individual and its planning of appropriate supervision, society has developed an agency of great potential." Cooley divided his college-trained probation staff into two groups—the Investigative Corps and Supervision Corps—to insure that all "officers of each give full time to their respective duties of diagnosis and treatment." In his methodology of diagnosis, Cooley observed:

> The probation plan of *social diagnosis* should consider the legal history of the offender, the essential elements of his environment, a study of his developmental history, personality and behavior, his capacities and potentialities, and the etiology of the delinquency.
> The study of the *legal history* of the offender should comprise his previous court record, analysis of the offense, and the story and attitude of the complainant. A fingerprint system should be established and utilized to ascertain the criminal record of the delinquent.
> The diagnosis of the *social history* of the delinquent should include the personal history, education and early life, family and neighborhood conditions, employment history, recreation, habits and associates, religious observances and training, and the mitigating or aggravating circumstances of the offense.
> The diagnosis of the *personality* of the defendant should consider the following factors: heredity, physical conditions, mentality (capacity, traits, and interests), emotions, sentiments and beliefs, character and conduct, and manner and appearance.[12]

Since the pioneer classification efforts of Healy and application efforts of Cooley, presentence report usage has been extended, improved, and professionalized by leaders in the field of corrections. Indeed, in 1949, the United States Supreme Court upheld the validity of the presentence investigation and report, giving additional support to its use.[13] While there has been some minor discord concerning its format, it is obvious that the presentence report has played an increasingly greater and significant role in the administration of justice. Many authorities now advocate that presentence investigations and reports be prepared on all offenders in our courts. The National Advisory Commission on Criminal Justice Standards and Goals has adopted a position which calls for the preparation of a presentence report in every case where there is a potential sentencing disposition involving incarceration and in all cases involving felonies or minors.[14]

Format for the Presentence Report

There are many formats for the presentence report. The model adopted by the Judicial Conference Committee on the Administration of the Probation System in 1965 and used by federal probation officers is a sophisticated example. The federal model is organized into 16 sections, with the first part, Identifying Information, placed on a form. The remaining sections, prepared in narrative style, are as follows:

Offense
   Official version
   Statement of codefendants
   Statement of witnesses, complainants, and victims
Defendant's version of offense
Prior record
Family history
   Defendant
   Parents and siblings
Marital history
Home and neighborhood
Education
Religion
Interests and leisure-time activities
Health
   Physical
   Mental and emotional
Employment
Military service
Financial condition
   Assets

Financial obligations
Evaluative summary
Recommendation

Within each of these sections are "essential data" and "optional data." The former are included in all presentence reports; optional data may be used for specific cases as warranted. Adherence to the format results in increased accuracy and completeness. The essential data in the federal presentence report are:

Identifying Information

Date of report
Name of defendant
Address of defendant
Legal residence
Age and date of birth
Sex
Race
Citizenship
Education
Marital status
Dependents
Social Security number
FBI number
Docket number
Offense
Penalty
Plea: nature and date
Verdict: date
Custody status
Name of U.S. Attorney
Name of defense counsel
Detainers or charges pending
Names of codefendants
Disposition by the court
Date of sentence
Name of sentencing judge

Offense: Official Version

Nature and date of plea or verdict
Brief summary of indictment or information, including number of counts, period covered, and nature, date(s), and place(s) of offense
Extent of property or monetary loss
Extent of defendant's profit from crime
Aggravating and extenuating circumstances
Nature and status of other pending charges
Days held in jail
Reasons for inability to divert (juvenile cases)

Offense: Statement of Codefendants

Extent of their participation in offense
Present status of their case

Offense: Statement of Witnesses, Complainants, and Vicitms

All information optional

Defendant's Version of Offense

Summary of account of offense and arrest as given by defendant if different from official version
Discrepancies between defendant's version and official version
Extent to which defendant admits guilt
Defendant's attitude toward offense (e.g., remorseful, rationalizes, minimizes, experiences anxiety, etc.)
Defendant's explanation of why he became involved in the offense
Extent to which offense was impulsive or premeditated
Environmental and situational factors contributing to offense, including stressing situations, experiences, or relationships

Prior Record

Clearance with FBI, social service exchange, and police departments and sheriffs' offices in respective localities where defendant lived
Juvenile court history
List of previous convictions (date, place, offense, and disposition)

List of arrests subsequent to present offense (date, place, offense, and disposition)

Military arrests and courts martial (date, place, offense, and disposition) not covered in *Military Service*

Institutional history (dates, report of adjustment, present release status, etc.)

Previous probation and parole history (dates, adjustment, outcome)

Detainers presently lodged against defendant

Family History: Defendant

Date, place of birth, race

Early developmental influences (physical and emotional) that may have a significant bearing on defendant's present personality and behavior

Attitudes of the father and the mother toward the defendant in his formative years, including discipline, affection, rejection, etc.

By whom was defendant reared, if other than his parents

Age left home; reasons for leaving; history of truancy from home

Relationship of defendant with parents and siblings, including attitudes toward one another

Extent of family solidarity (family cohesiveness)

Relatives with whom defendant is especially close

Family History: Parents and Siblings

All information optional

Marital History

Present marriage, including common law (date, place, name and age of spouse at time of marriage)

Attitude of defendant toward spouse and children and theirs toward him

Home atmosphere

Previous marriage(s) (date, place, name of previous spouse, and outcome; if divorced, give reasons)

Children, including those from previous marriage(s) (name, age, school, custody, support)

Home and Neighborhood

Description of home (owned or rented, type, size, occupants, adequacy, and general living conditions)
Type of neighborhood, including any desirable or undesirable influences in the community
Attitude of defendant and family toward home and neighborhood

Education

Highest grade achieved
Age left school and reason for leaving
Results of psychological tests (IQ, aptitude, achievement, etc.), specify test and date

Religion

Religious affiliation and frequency of church attendance

Interests and Leisure-Time Activities

Defendant's interests and leisure-time activities (including sports, hobbies, creative work, organizations, reading)
What are his talents and accomplishments

Health: Physical

Identifying information (height, weight, complexion, eyes, hair, scars, tattoos, posture, physical proportions, tone of voice, manner of speech)
Defendant's general physical condition and health problems based on defendant's estimate of his health, medical reports, probation officer's observations
Use of narcotics, barbiturates, marihuana
Social implications of defendant's physical health (home, community, employment, associations)

Health: Mental and Emotional

Probation officer's assessment of defendant's operating level of intelligence as demonstrated in social and occupational functions
Personality characteristics as given by family members and as observed by probation officer

Attitude of defendant about himself and how he feels others feel
about him (parents, siblings, spouse, children, associates)
Social adjustment in general
Social implications of mental and emotional health (home, community,
employment, associations)

Employment

Employment history for the past 10 years (dates, nature of work,
earnings, reasons for leaving)
Employer's evaluation of defendant (immediate supervisor, where
possible), including attendance, capabilities, reliability,
adjustment, honesty, reputation, personality, attitude toward
work, and relationships with coworkers and supervisors
Occupational skills, interests, and ambitions

Military Service

Branch of service, serial number, and dates of each period of
military service
Highest grade or rank achieved and grade or rank at separation
Type and date of discharge(s)
Attitude toward military experience

Financial Condition: Assets

Statement of financial assets
General standard of living

Financial Condition: Financial Obligations

Statement of financial obligations

Evaluative Summary

Essential Data:
Highlights of body of the report
Analysis of factors contributing to present offense and
    prior convictions (motivations and circumstances)
Defendant's attitude toward offense
Evaluation of the defendant's personality, problems and
    needs, and potential for growth

Comment. Writing the evaluative summary is perhaps the most difficult and painstaking task in the entire presentence report. It has a significant bearing on the future course of the defendant's life. It is here that the probation officer calls into play his analytical ability, his diagnostic skills, and his understanding of human behavior. It is here that he brings into focus the kind of person before the court, the basic factors that brought him into trouble, and what special helps the defendant needs to resolve his difficulties.

The opening paragraph of the evaluative summary should give a concise restatement of the pertinent highlights in the body of the report. There should follow in separate paragraphs those factors which contributed in some measure to the defendant's difficulty and also an evaluation of his personality.

Recommendation

Recommendation
Basis for recommendation

Comment. Some judges ask for the probation officer's recommendation regarding probation or commitment. Where recommendations are requested, they should be a part of the presentence report. If the judge does not wish to have the recommendations included as a part of the report, they may be given on a separate sheet which may be detached if the presentence report is later sent to an institution.

If it is recommended that the defendant be placed on probation, the proposed plans for residence, employment, education, and medical and psychiatric treatment, if pertinent, should be given. The part to be played in the social adjustment of the defendant by the parental and immediate family, the pastor, close friends, and others in the community should also be shown. If commitment is recommended, the probation officer should indicate what special problems and needs should receive the attention of the institutional staff.

Where the judge asks for sentencing alternatives, they may be included in this part of the report.[15]

It is clear that comprehensive presentence reports enhance the probability of an appropriate correctional treatment being selected for individual offenders and these reports provide various judicial and correctional decision makers (judges, probation officers, institutional personnel, paroling authorities and parole officers) with sufficient data to select from among the available correctional alternatives. But it is equally clear that the preparation of detailed reports requires a large commitment of personnel and time by the probation department.

In general, and in view of the narrow range of alternatives available to judicial and correctional decision makers, current data collection efforts greatly exceed available opportunities to utilize the data. To be more specific, courts normally have three sentencing alternatives (or decisions) available — probation, jail, or imprisonment. Without commentary on the inadequacy of probation as frequently practiced, the failure of jails in achieving stated correctional goals, or the fact that prisons may produce as much criminality as they prevent, the selection of available alternatives can be made with far less information than is currently collected and made available to the decision makers.

The same holds true for probation officer decision making. Large, undifferentiated caseloads and few treatment alternatives render detailed data on offenders almost irrelevant. Institution staff, limited in number and handicapped by the lack of realistic rehabilitation programs and financial resources, have only a narrow range of options. A paroling authority with but two basic alternatives — to grant or deny parole (or to postpone this decision) — hardly benefits from sophisticated data, particularly when even that one choice is complicated, and may even be determined, by "bed-space" considerations.

In short, when viewing the very limited number of decisions or courses of action available, requirements for information are slight, at least in comparison to the data needed to select the best from a dozen possible alternatives. This suggests that while every effort be made to obtain legislative enactments which will provide more flexibility and room for maneuver, some of the current information-gathering processes might profitably be amended.

The Task Force on Corrections addressed this issue directly by noting:

> The high manpower levels required to complete reports have caused some authorities to raise questions as to the need for the kind and quantity of information that is typically gathered and presented.
> Experimentation with new and simpler forms of presentence investigation is important for reasons beyond the conservation of scarce resources of probation offices. Presentence reports in many cases have come to include a great deal of material of doubtful relevance to disposition in most cases . . . . In

many cases this kind of information is of marginal relevance to the kinds of correctional treatment actually available or called for.[16]

Innovative presentence report models are being examined and most of them emphasize not only brevity and accuracy, but also the inclusion of only those data elements which are appropriate to the decision making of judicial and correctional authorities. In general terms, the data most needed center upon the defendant's offense, his attitude about and motivation for committing it, prior criminal record, marital, family, employment, and emotional stability, and a plan for the future. Some of these data may be provided in a non-narrative or shorter narrative style than formerly; the option remains for more detailed reports for cases which are unusually complex.

Other Presentence Report Issues

There are, of course, several other issues relating to presentence report practices beside that of format. One of these concerns the "confidentiality" of the reports. Practice varies across the nation as to whether the defendant and his attorney have the right to access and review these reports on whether they are to remain confidential documents for the sole use of the judicial and correctional agencies. Strong arguments on both sides of the issue have failed to produce uniformity. It is significant to note that the National Advisory Commission on Criminal Justice Standards and Goals adopted a position of "full disclosure" and recommended that the report and all similar documents be made available to defense counsel and the prosecution at a fixed time prior to the date set for the sentencing hearing.[17]

Another issue is whether or not probation officers should make recommendations as to the disposition of a case to the court. Again, practice varies across the United States, but there appears to be an increasing consensus that recommendations concerning disposition are appropriate. Indeed, the American Correctional Association includes among its standards for the preparation of presentence reports a "recommendation for or against probation, or for other disposition according to court policy." When recommendations are made by probation officers, the courts accept the recommendations in an extremely high percentage of the cases, in some jurisdictions in excess of 95 percent. It is possible that four factors, operating independently but more probably simultaneously, account for the high proportion of agreement between probation officer recommendations and court dispositions:

1. The court, having such high regard for the professional qualities and competence of its probation staff, "follows" the probation recommendation—

a recommendation made by the person (probation officer) who best knows the defendant by reason of the presentence investigation;

2. There are many offenders who are "obviously" probation or prison cases;

3. Probation officers write their reports and make recommendations anticipating the recommendation the court desires to receive. (In this situation, the probation officer is quite accurately "second-guessing" the court disposition);

4. Probation officers in making their recommendations place great emphasis on the same factors as does the court in selecting a sentencing alternative.[18]

Operationally, some probation agencies assign the two basic probation functions—investigation and supervision—to the same officers, while other agencies separate the functions and create distinct investigation and supervision units. The issue as to whether separate or combined functions are appropriate has advocates on both sides. Those supporting the separation of functions typically argue for efficiency through specialization; those who support combined units suggest that continuity of probation services is the critical concern. To be sure, this distinction may be irrelevant in smaller agencies, particularly those with large geographic areas of responsibility, in which the probation officer must accomplish both functions, but the issue is real in larger agencies in the more urban and metropolitan areas. The dilemma is in part caused by the fact that presentence investigations and reports are generally given priority over supervision if for no other reasons than those of visibility and deadlines. The presentence report must be delivered to the court by a given time; supervision does not usually have such time constraints. Further, there is a visible product in presentence activities, a report which may be evaluated by superiors, but there is no such clear evidence of work performance in supervision.

In any event, despite variations in presentence report format on one hand through diverse organizational structures to accomplish the basic investigative and supervision functions on the other, it is clear that presentence investigations and reports are critical to the sentencing process and the correctional activities which follow. The assessment of the offender to insure a rational disposition of his case in court in terms of selection of the most appropriate correctional alternative is essential. The average of two or three weeks between a plea of guilty or a finding of guilt and sentencing—the time used by the probation agency to conduct an investigation and prepare a report—is a justifiable investment of criminal justice resources. The presentence process increases the probability of an appropriate court disposition which will serve to best meet the treatment needs of the individual offender and to protect society by minimizing the likelihood of further law violations.

The Probation Process: Supervision of Offenders

Defendants are normally placed on probation either by having the imposition of sentence suspended by the court or by having a specific sentence imposed and its execution suspended. In the latter case, a sentence (for example, five years imprisonment or six months in the county jail) is imposed on the defendant, but its execution is suspended and he is conditionally released on probation. If a violation of that probation occurs, the sentence originally imposed may be ordered or a lesser sentence may be given, but more severe sanctions than those originally ordered cannot be applied. In the other sentencing situation, in which a specific sentence was not ordered, a violation of probation may result in any sentence being given which might have been imposed at the time of the original sentencing; thus, all of the sentencing options available to the court when probation was ordered are still available if probation is violated. This sentencing distinction, although significant in the event of a violation of probation, is of lesser importance in terms of the supervision process.

The granting of probation attaches conditions to the continued freedom of the probationer and these conditions are generally the standards against which that freedom and definitions of successful or unsuccessful probation are measured. The conditions of probation generally may be divided into general and specific or special conditions, the general conditions being applicable to all probationers, the special conditions being imposed in a given case. A typical set of general conditions of probation are those found in the federal system:

> CONDITIONS OF PROBATION. It is the order of the Court that you shall comply with the following conditions of probation:
> 1. You shall refrain from violation of any law (federal, state, and local). You shall get in touch immediately with your probation officer if arrested or questioned by a law enforcement officer.
> 2. You shall associate only with law-abiding persons and maintain reasonable hours.
> 3. You shall work regularly at a lawful occupation and support your legal dependents, if any, to the best of your ability. When out of work you shall notify your probation officer at once. You shall consult him prior to job changes.
> 4. You shall not leave the judicial district without permission of the probation officer.
> 5. You shall notify your probation officer immediately of any change in your place of residence.

6. You shall follow the probation officer's instructions and advice.
7. You shall report to the probation officer as directed.[19]

Special conditions are imposed as circumstances warrant and may include, separately or in combination, the imposition of a fine, an order to make restitution to the victim of the offense, a term in the county jail, psychiatric treatment, and so on. The most controversial condition is a period of confinement in the county jail with advocates arguing that a jail sentence as a condition of probation will impress the offender with the seriousness of violating the law and serve to motivate him to successfully abide by the conditions of probation. Opponents of jail followed by probation argue that even a short period of confinement is a disruptive force, serving to interfere with successful probation treatment by disrupting employment, family, and residential patterns.

The granting of probation with its attendant conditions requires supervision to have both assistance and control functions. That these functions are clearly intertwined and have impact on probation supervision is evident, as noted by the American Correctional Association:

> *SUPERVISION OF PROBATIONERS.* The basis for probation supervision is mutual trust, cooperation, and responsibility. In providing service to a client, the probation officer is responsible for giving guidance and assistance while providing controls. The conditions of probation imposed by the court set the limits within which probation treatment occurs. The worker must balance the responsibilities of the control and treatment in his dealings with the probationer. He must, therefore, be prepared to interpret his own position and responsibility to the probationer and to interpret the probationer's status and responsibility to the court, to the probationer's family, and to the community. The exercising of authority and the setting of limits are a part of effective probation supervision.

> Four general principles usually form the foundation for attaining this balance:

> 1. Change comes from within a person; therefore, a probationer must be a participant in any treatment regime designed to help him.
> 2. The needs, problems, capacities, and limitations of the individual offender must be considered in planning a program with him.
> 3. Legally binding conditions of probation are essential and to the best interest of the offender and to the community.
> 4. The goal of supervision is to help the offender understand his own problems and enable him to deal adequately with them.

The last principle merits special emphasis. Probation's most important achievement is not control of the probationer under supervision but rather enabling the probationer to understand himself and gain strength in independent control over his own behavior.

The plan of treatment should be consistent with the findings of the presentence investigation. The intensity of supervision should be based upon the professional judgment of the probation officer. After a reasonable time, the client may be placed under minimum supervision if he is making a satisfactory adjustment. The contacts with the probationer should take place at the office, at the probationer's home, and wherever and whenever the needs of a particular case might require. Probation supervision should also include home visits with the family members and others specifically involved in the probationer's situation and plan of treatment. Visits should be unobtrusive. The role of the probation officer is that of control and supportive help when needed. The probation officer must be familiar with community agencies and social resources and be able to make proper referrals to those agencies and resources.

Probation supervision should eventuate in termination either through satisfactory completion of a period of supervision or from revocation of probation because of a violation of a condition of probation or the commission of a new offense.

A probation agency should set forth in written form its policies on violation procedures. Consultation with the court or administrative review within the probation agency may be indicated in some types of violations, particularly on conditions of probation. Written allegations should always be prepared for revocation consideration. In addition to a statement of the allegations, the judge should be furnished with a summary of the probationer's adjustment on probation, the implications of his present violation, and a prognosis for future adjustment if confined or continued on probation. The probationer should be confronted with the evidence of the alleged violation and, subject to the judge's regulation of the procedure, should be permitted to present evidence in his behalf. If the facts of the violation are not contested, the hearing may be limited to a consideration of what action is to be taken.

Termination of supervision through early discharge from probation should be initiated by the probation officer when the probationer's conduct and other circumstances warrant. No individual should be kept on probation longer than is necessary to accomplish the purpose for which probation was granted. Normally the probation officer should initiate the discharge recommendation. As a part of the termination process, the probation officer should prepare the probationer beforehand, including reducing the frequency of contact or reporting. He should inform the defendant of his legal rights such as restoration of civil rights, at the time of discharge. The probationer should receive a copy of the discharge when probation is terminated by early discharge or expiration of the sentence.[20]

Although the assistance and control elements of supervision are quite important, there are numerous other variables which have significant impact on supervision. These include caseload size, types of probation officers, offenders and treatments, and the social systems within probation agencies to include varying administrative styles. Also significant are the law enforcement, judicial, and correctional decision makers and their decisions which determine input and outgo in probation, the administrative organization of caseloads, the community itself, and cost and political considerations. These factors collectively make supervision considerably more complex than the presentence investigation and report functions of probation agencies.

Historically, and until recently, there has been considerable interest in determining the "correct" caseload size and the establishment of the "proper" numerical relationship or ratio between presentence investigation services and supervision efforts. Although some emphasis on sizes and ratios is understandable and certainly necessary in preparing budgets, providing testimony to legislative bodies, conducting probation operations in the field, projecting for future needs, planning and/or other administrative purposes, it has frequently resulted in diverting attention from other variables. These variables are more elusive; each is complex, and the manifold difficulties of supervision increase geometrically as these factors influence and act upon each other.

Caseload Size: An Historical Perspective

Caseload size has been generally established at a 50-unit level, based on the assumption that one presentence investigation is equal to five cases under supervision. This tradition dates back to the second decade of this century when Charles L. Chute of the National Probation Association observed that "fifty cases is as many as any probation officer ought to carry." The 50-unit concept was reinforced by concurring statements of authorities in the mid-1930s such as Sutherland and Tannenbaum, who suggested that 50 cases "is generally regarded as the maximum number" and, "the best practice would limit the caseload of a probation officer to 50 cases." With these and other academicians supporting Chute's original concept, professional organizations such as the American Prison Association later came to recognize that an officer "should not have more than 50 cases under continuous supervision." Indeed, the 1949 and 1954 editions of the *Manual of Correctional Standards* supported the 50-unit concept and it was not until 1966, while still suggesting a 50-unit workload, that the American Correctional Association indicated "where methods of classification for caseloads have been developed through research, varying standards of workloads may prevail."

In short, the orientation to 50-unit caseloads dates back many years and is based upon an untested assumption. The appropriate target for caseload size was recommended as 35 in 1967 by the President's Commission on Law Enforcement and Administration of Justice, but it too was without empirical basis and gave little consideration to other factors affecting supervision. Further, the 35 offenders per officer was really a ratio for staffing, not a formula for caseloads. It may be that the entire concept of caseload size may have to be dropped and a concept of workload adopted in its place.

It is significant to note that the National Advisory Commission on Criminal Justice Standards and Goals did not focus on caseload size for probation. Rather, the Commission emphasized the development of a correctional system which offers to offenders under supervision "the support and services they need so that ultimately they can live independently in a socially acceptable way."[21]

Caseload Size Research

One of the most detailed reviews of caseload size research was conducted by Stuart Adams and published in *Federal Probation* in 1967. Summarizing the findings of a dozen caseload studies conducted in California and in the federal system, Adams reported on research which included experimental or control caseloads ranging from 12 to 210 offenders. The data collectively were unable to support a consistent finding that small caseloads were superior to large, at least in terms of overall offender success and failure rates. Adams noted, however, that

> . . . it is impressive how quickly results began to emerge when emphasis turned from sheer numbers to treatment concepts: community versus institutional treatment, group and family therapy versus conventional probation supervision, and assignment to treatment by offender type. This aspect of caseload research gives point to one of the frequently voiced criticisms of the early research: We have reduced the caseloads, but we haven't told the parole agents what to do with the extra time.[22]

But even as Adams suggested a move from "sheer numbers," he provided some insight into other areas of particular concern.

> Some general concepts that have emerged from the past years of research will undoubtedly serve as guides in future years. It will continue to be important to attempt to classify offenders in ways that are relevant to treatment content and form. There will continue to be concern for the appropriate kind of treatment for particular types of clients. There will be concern about the qualifications and characteristics of treatment staff and the possibility of interaction between therapist type and offender type. Some interest will be centered on appropriate duration and intensity of treatment. Finally, there will be much attention to the locus of treatment, with increasing focus on the possibility that probation and other open-community procedures will play far more important roles in the total correctional process.
>
> It seems reasonable to assume that for a long time to come the crucial research in corrections will continue to be that which focuses on the treatment workload. This seems to be the heart of corrections—the defining situation for the continuing interaction between the agent or therapist and the client. It is an endless field of inquiry, in part because of the variety of factors involved, and in part because of the complexity of the interaction among these factors. But it is unquestionably a valuable field of inquiry, and progress in corrections will depend on how rapidly this field is mastered.[23]

Treatment

Treatment in probation is seldom defined; only slightly more often is it provided according to some predetermined plan of action. So elusive is the concept of "treatment" that almost everything which transpires between probation officer and offender during the period of supervision has at one time or another been labeled treatment. Indeed, treatment may be defined operationally as anything done to, for, or with the offender. The treatment component of supervision has on occasion been portrayed as ranging along a continuum from surveillance (protection of society) at one end and casework or therapy (rehabilitation of the offender) at the other. But these are vague concepts at best, oversimplifying a complex and frustrating problem into a dichotomous perspective of treatment.

But even as difficulties are encountered in defining and identifying treatment, probation officers maintain voluminous documents which reveal the number of treatments (direct and collateral contacts with the offender), the location of treatments (office, field, and so on), and in narrative form, the nature of treatments. This compilation of data is summarized, normally at the end of the supervision period and at other chosen intervals.

The results of treatment are carefully recorded in terms of success and failure, in part based upon the assumption that success and failure reflect simply the offender response to treatment rather than to the innumerable other influences internal and external to the offender. The probation officer and his administrator find that definitions of success and failure are sufficiently flexible to permit an individual offender to be counted in either (or some other) category. The treatment phenomenon is made more complex by noting that the successful probationer is often defined as one who responded to an appropriate treatment given by the probation agency; the probationer who failed did not so respond. That is, there is a tendency for the probation agency to accept responsibility for the application of an appropriate treatment and its resultant success and to dismiss failure as a function of the offender himself.

Further, those actions and behaviors on the part of the probation officer which are described as essential elements of a "helping relationship" may not be so viewed by the offender. Shared understandings about such helping relationships may be minimal, particularly when the relationships are typically in an authoritarian setting . . . a setting in which the terms and conditions of the conditional freedom are detailed to the offender and place more stringent requirements on his behavior than are expected from the non-offender citizenry.

Then, too, there is the matter of time available for treatment—regardless of the specific technique. If the probationer is awake 16 hours a day, a once-a-month treatment of 30 minutes' duration represents something in the nature of one-tenth of one percent of his total waking hours. This small amount of time is of doubtful significance in the complex social life of the offender, 99.9 percent of which is spent under the influence of many "significant others."

Caseload Organization

The inexactness which marks definitions of the treatment component of supervision is not found in the organization of caseloads. Across the nation, two basic types of caseloads are encountered. The most common is the balanced caseload with some weight given to geographic considerations. A second type is the single-factor specialized caseload.

The conventional method of assigning offenders to caseloads is motivated in part by administrative desires to maintain "balanced" caseloads. Theoretically, then, case 1 is assigned to officer A, case 2 to officer B, 3 to C, 4 to A, 5 to B, 6 to C, and so on. The balanced caseload must be modified somewhat because probation agencies normally consider the geographic area covered by their officers. In general terms, caseloads are equated with geography and the principle applied is that as the supervision area increases, caseload size decreases. Thus, the probation officer working in a densely populated metropolitan area has a smaller geographic area and a larger number of cases than his rural or suburban counterpart who has a greater area to cover, but fewer cases.

The second model encountered in probation supervision includes the single-factor specialized caseloads. Based upon a single factor or characteristic, such as sex, age, high-violence potential, or drug use, certain offenders are removed from the general population under supervision for placement in specialized caseloads. Thus, female offenders or drug addicts are grouped into single caseloads for supervision purposes and, on occasion, a distinct treatment or approach is utilized for these caseloads. In the main, however, it appears that there is simply an organization of some caseloads around a single offender characteristic.

It is important to note, however, that the organization of caseloads on the basis of a single factor poses a treatment dilemma in that these caseloads are not made homogeneous simply because all offenders assigned to them share a characteristic such as age or history of drug use. The traditional, balanced method of caseload organization ignores many of the important factors which comprise supervision and emphasizes administrative convenience. The single-factor caseload, whatever its deficiencies, generally is concerned at least with one type of offender and, at least in theory, allows for a matching of offender, treatment, and officer.

Offenders and Officers

In recent years, increasing attention has been devoted to offender classification systems. As an operational matter, a series of prediction or base expectancy devices have been produced which are not unlike the actuarial tables utilized by insurance companies. Typically a product of research on offenders who were under supervision during some earlier time frame, these instruments utilize a number of factors, a substantial improvement over single-factor classification systems. Although these devices generally have been geared toward prediction of success or failure on supervision rather than for determination of treatment needs, they represent a considerably more sophisticated view of the offender than simply "drug addict" or "sex offender."

Classification schemes for probation and parole officers have been neither common nor well received or publicized. The general practitioner model, the one most frequently encountered and most generally accepted by agencies, assumes that all officers, despite variations in background, training, experience, age, sex, personality, and the like, can meet the varying treatment needs of many differing types of offenders with equal ease and skill. The model is questionable, if for no other reason than the officer is not a constant while all else is a variable. However, attempts to classify officers have been limited in large measure by resistance on the part of the officers themselves to be categorized as external-internal, punitive-protective-welfare-opportunist, welfare-paternal-passive-punitive, or, for that matter, according to any other scheme. The resistance of "professional" staff to such, or similar, categorization is understandable, but unfortunate. Variations among officers in terms of capabilities and skills are somehow seen as personal deficiencies, when in fact they may be assets. Particular officer attributes might well be matched with types of offenders and treatment programs. In any event, these officer and offender variables must be considered a significant element of supervision, even if it means opening a Pandora's Box of generalist vs. specialist and casting doubts upon the advisability of the "all purpose" officer.

The Community

Of the many variables which impact upon supervision, none can be considered more significant than the community—the arena in which supervision occurs. And yet, it has only been in the past few years that the importance of the community has been recognized. The ultimate test of relevance for agencies providing supervision is within the community in which the offender lives. The question, "how important is the community?" may be answered with another question: "can an agency, even one with substantial resources, compensate for such common problems of offenders as the disadvantageousness of being in a minority group, subsistence at the poverty level, inadequate educational or vocational skills, residence in the ghetto with its feeling of hopelessness, boredom, repression, and hostility, delinquent and criminal associates, the broken-home syndrome and the welfare cycle, and the complexities of living with a set of values different from those upon which the law is based?" These and other adverse conditions exist in many communities and suggest that the traditional approaches to supervision may be irrelevant. It may well be that the dominant factor impacting upon supervision is community and that the community is of such significance that it may be necessary to reconstitute most current approaches to supervision.

But even as the role of the community is examined, attention must also be directed toward the question of whether the supervision process encourages offender dependence upon the agency or reintegration into the community. The latter role is more productive and it appears that probation agencies should become catalysts between the offender and the community, seeking to activate the community and its resources to absorb the offender as a member of the community. It may no longer be appropriate to find employment for the offender; the requirement may be to direct the offender into the normal channels of job-seeking in the community. Offenders with residential, marital, or financial problems may best be assisted by insuring that they engage those community resources which deal with these problem areas. More is suggested than a mere extension of the use of community resources. Identifying an offender as an offender, referring him as an offender to community agencies which in turn provide services because he is an offender does little to destroy the albatross of a criminal label. Indeed, such usage of community resources serves only to perpetuate the maintenance of a criminal identity and to retain the umbilical cord which links offender to agency. In short, serious attention must be given to the types of communities in which supervision services are provided, as well as to a determination of whether current and expanding usage of community resources encourage integration into community or dependence upon the agency. These are powerful variables in the supervision process, the full significance of which is as yet unknown and the examination of which has barely begun.

Decision Making and Decision Makers

Other factors impacting upon supervision include the decision makers and the decision-making process. There are substantial shortages in information about decision phenomena. Although the criminal justice system provides considerable data on various kinds of decisions, the decision scoreboard is comprised primarily of numbers, e.g., the number of arrests (police decision), the number of prosecutions (district attorney decision), the number of offenders placed on probation (judicial decision), and so on. While relevant, these data represent only a small portion of a very complex world of decision making. How many times, for example, does a probation officer decide, upon review of an offender's behavior, not to take action, or to delay action, or to take action "A" or "B" or "C"? And of these, how many do not result in an official recording of the decision in comparison to decisions to take action which will be recorded, e.g., initiation of a probation violation proceeding?

The vast majority of decisions are unrecorded; indeed, the bulk of them are not normally even thought of as decisions. Further, these decisions are not simply a function of an offender's behavior, but rather again reflect the interrelationship of many factors, some of which are explicit such as office SOP's, and some of which are considerably more complex and subtle and include the probation officer himself and the social and political system in which he operates.

Other Variables

There are still other factors which have influence on supervision. These include costs and politics, administrative styles of leadership and the social systems within agencies, and changing philosophies and practices in corrections.

Broad changes in society—technological advances and social change—affect probation. Gentle or violent mood shifts of the American people and their perspectives on crime and its correction are reflected in political structures and translated into legislation and budgets; these translations, whether accurate or not, directly affect program, policy, and personnel and may modify philosophy. Corrections, as is the case with all social agencies, reflect the prevalent belief of the people. If, for example, the general perspective on crime is that it must be "stamped out," legislative funding will be "hardware"-oriented and law enforcement-dominated. Further, the expenditures on corrections, although seen by many as inadequate, are nevertheless of sufficient magnitude to warrant requirements for cost-effectiveness studies. Demands for such studies impose additional data requirements upon correctional agencies and could mandate a business-like orientation and perspective of correctional operations.

Social systems and administrative styles are more difficult to evaluate. Even with limited data available, it is certain that the administrative environment influences probation agency functions. An authoritarian leadership structure with its resultant hierarchy, principles, and policies will have one effect; a flexible and tolerant administrative setting will have another. More than this, it has been demonstrated that performance of officers and offenders alike is affected by the administrative desires of management. Obviously, directives which state that "violation rates must be reduced" (frequently following negative comments by prominent political figures) will result in different evaluations of offender behavior. Research data have suggested that violation rates are highly correlated with management requirements. Simply put, assume three offices: Office "A" with a 40 percent violation rate, "B" with 50 percent, and "C" with a 60 percent violation rate. A transfer of administrators from office "A" to "B", from "B" to "C", and from "C" to "A" may, within a relatively short period of time, result in office "A" with a 60 percent violation rate, "B" with 40 percent, and "C" with 50 percent.

Other factors impinge directly and indirectly on supervision; these range from administrative and logistic matters to philosophical issues in corrections concerning diversion of offenders and community-based correctional operations. For example, many probation agencies have supervisory positions, theoretically to provide casework supervision to line probation officers. More often than not, the supervisor becomes an assistant administrator, assigned to special functions in the agency such as "court officer" or "intake officer." Although such usage of supervisors may ease administrative burdens within the agency, the abandonment of case supervision to meet management requirements affects caseloads and their effectiveness.

But perhaps the greatest impact on supervision will be a result of the current movement toward community corrections and the diversion of offenders from the justice system. Diversion programs which reduce the numbers of offenders entering the justice system or encourage early release from that system to community correctional systems will not only change the numbers of those under supervision, but also the nature of the offender population under supervision.

With better risk offenders diverted or absorbed into community corrections, poorer risk offenders will be under supervision or in custody; this may result in increases in probation violation rates and be followed by reactive downward adjustments in caseload sizes. Changes in the supervised population may also mandate new programs, locations, types of facilities, and personnel with considerable insight into the nature of specific communities.

Given the enormous complexity of probation supervision and the requirements for presentence services, it is evident that there cannot be an ideal organizational model or caseload size. Rather, there may be better systems for delivering services depending upon and varying with different combinations of offenders, officers, programs, and communities. The challenge is to develop these new delivery systems, to allow organizational restructuring to enhance their potential application, and to evaluate effectiveness and efficiency through experimentation and research. Flexibility in the use of resources will be the hallmark of probation agencies of the future. And resources is an all-inclusive term: personnel, management and logistic support, time, and money. Resources also include an administrative commitment to innovation and creativity, a tolerance for the errors which will inevitably occur, and a dedication to the principle that probation must serve the best interests of both society and the offender. The words flow easily; the operational activities are far more difficult and complex.

NOTES

[1]American Correctional Association, *Manual of Correctional Standards*, Washington, D.C., 1966, p. 98.

[2]United Nations, Department of Social Affairs, *Probation and Related Measures*, New York (Sales No.:1951. IV.2), E/CN/.5/230, 1951, pp. 15–26.

[3]Quoted from Robert M. Carter and Leslie T. Wilkins, eds., *Probation and Parole*, New York: John Wiley & Sons, 1970, p. 5.

[4]*Ibid.*, p. 6.

[5]*Ibid.*, p. 8.

[6]Ex parte United States, 242 U.S. 27 (1916).

[7]William Healy, "The Individual Study of the Young Criminal," *Journal of the American Institute of Criminal Law and Criminology* I (May, 1910): 50–51.

[8]Division of Probation, Administrative Office of the United States Courts, *The Presentence Investigation Report*, Washington, D.C.: U.S. Government Printing Office, 1965, p. 1.

[9]William Healy, *The Individual Delinquent*, Boston: Little, Brown and Company, 1915, pp. 8–48.

[10]Bernard Flexner and Roger Baldwin, *Juvenile Courts and Probation*, New York: The Century Company, 1914, p. 48.

[11]Mary E. Richmond, *Social Diagnosis*, New York: Russell Sage Foundation, 1917, pp. 357–381.

[12]Edwin J. Cooley, *Probation and Delinquency*, New York: Thomas Nelson and Sons, 1927, pp. vii–ix, 323–324.

[13]*Williams v. New York*, 337 U.S. 241 (1949).

[14]National Advisory Commission on Criminal Justice Standards and Goals, *Corrections*, Washington, D.C.: U.S. Government Printing Office, 1973, p. 184.

[15]Division of Probation, Administrative Office of the United States Courts, *The Presentence Investigation Report*, Washington, D.C.: U.S. Government Printing Office, 1965, pp. 1–21 (Editorial Adaptations).

[16]The President's Commission on Law Enforcement and Administration of Justice, *Task Force Report: Corrections*, Washington, D.C.: U.S. Government Printing Office, 1967, p. 19.

[17]*Corrections*, p. 188.

[18]Robert M. Carter and Leslie T. Wilkins, "Some Factors in Sentencing," *Journal of Criminal Law, Criminology and Police Science* 58 (December 1967): 503–14.

[19]Probation Form 7, United States Courts.

[20]*Manual of Correctional Standards*, pp. 107–108.

[21]*Corrections*, p. 311.

[22]Stuart Adams, "Some Findings from Correctional Caseload Research," *Federal Probation* XXXI (December 1967): 55.

[23]*Ibid.*, pp. 56–57.

9 Parole

Parole is a form of conditional release granted after a prisoner has served a portion of his sentence in a correctional institution. Parole is closely related to the indefinite or indeterminate sentence and should include careful selection, preparation for release from the institution, and supervision in the community. Parole should not be confused with probation, which is an alternative to imprisonment, or with a pardon. The pardon is an act of grace or executive clemency, normally by a governor or a state board of pardons, which results in the remission of all or part of the legal consequences of a sentence.

The Origins of Parole

Until the early nineteenth century, prisoners in the United States were sentenced to definite, fixed terms in institutions. A sentence of 10 years imprisonment meant 10 years in prison, nothing less, nothing more. Long sentences without the possibility of early release produced overcrowding and disciplinary and security problems, and these fixed sentences militated against attempts for rehabilitation or self-improvement. Political and other pressures were frequently applied to secure pardons for some inmates. Disparities in sentences generated bitterness among prisoners. Individual differences among inmates were ignored. Justice, at best, was uneven.

Although the use of the indeterminate sentence had been advocated by Dr. Benjamin Rush of Philadelphia as early as 1787, the first notable effort to provide some flexibility in sentences occurred in New York State in 1817 with the introduction of the "good time" law. This law authorized the "inspectors of the prison to reduce the sentence of any convict sentenced to imprisonment for not less than five years, one-fourth, upon certificate of the principal keeper and other satisfactory evidence that such prisoner has behaved well, and has acquired . . . in the whole, the net sum of 15 dollars or more per annum."[1] The purpose of this legislation was not only to encourage good behavior in prison, but also to promote the productivity of prison industries. Other states followed with the enactment of similar legislation. Tennessee, for example, in 1836, made it the duty of the governor "in case the conduct of any prisoner had been exceptional for a whole month" to reduce the term "not to exceed two days for each and every month he should so conduct himself." An Ohio statute in 1856 provided for a reduction of five days for each month during which a prisoner "shall not be guilty of violation of any of the rules of the prison and shall labor with diligence and fidelity."[2]

The introduction of "good time" or "time for good behavior" legislation provided some flexibility in the length of time served in prison according to a specific schedule provided by statute. The practice is still used today in the United States, the federal prison system, among others, using it. A major criticism directed toward the procedure is that it may be used primarily as a mechanism to control the inmate and assist the prison administration in obtaining conformity with its rules.

The genesis of parole may also be found in colonial America in a system which authorized indenture for juvenile offenders. Under this system, young prisoners were released from institutions and placed in the employment of private citizens to whom they were legally bound. Although the indenture system did not authorize state supervision of these offenders, they were permitted to earn a final discharge from their employers. As abuses and considerable exploitation were uncovered, it became necessary to bring about some official supervision of the indenture process. The New York House of Refuge adopted a plan in 1825 which became a model for other institutions:

> In the House of Refuge a committee of the managing society, designated as the indenturing committee, met weekly, determined which of the children should be indentured, and took full responsibility not only for the act of indenturing but also for the conditions under which the children lived as apprentices. They laid down rules for the children, for the superintendent, and for the master to whom their wards were apprenticed. They were the paroling authority in fact, though the word indenture was used instead of parole.[3]

Concurrent with these developments in America was the development of "conditional liberation" in Europe. Conditional liberation was defined by the French publicist, Bonneville de Marsangy, as "a sort of middle term between an absolute pardon and the execution of the entire sentence; the right conceded to the judiciary to release provisionally, after a sufficient period of expiatory suffering, a convict who appears to be reformed, reserving the right to return him to prison, if there is against him any well-founded complaint."[4] In 1864, de Marsangy wrote: "Society should say to the prisoner: 'Whenever you give satisfactory evidence of your genuine reformation, you will be tested, under the operation of a ticket-of-leave (parole); thus, the opportunity to abridge the term of your imprisonment is placed in your hands.' "[5]

The earliest operational example of conditional liberation was found in Spain in 1835. The governor of the prison at Valencia, Colonel Montesinos, organized the institution on the basis of semimilitary discipline, encouraged vocational training and primary education of the prisoners, and authorized a one-third reduction from the term of imprisonment by "good behavior and positive accomplishments." A similar experiment was carried out in Bavaria in the 1830s and parole was strongly advocated in France in the 1840s by de Marsangy and others; indeed, the word parole is derived from *parole d'-honneur* (word of honor) indicating the released prisoner's promise to do no wrong.

But the real credit for the development of parole is generally given to Captain Alexander Maconochie and Sir Walter Crofton. In 1790, the Governor of New South Wales was given the right to conditionally pardon prisoners who had been transported from England. His legislative authority was expanded in 1834 to include grants of land and even the assignment of newly arrived prisoners to the conditionally pardoned prisoners. This convict labor system led to substantial abuses and in 1840 the use of prisoners for domestic labor was halted; this occurred concurrently with the end of transportation to New South Wales. Maconochie was placed in charge of the English penal colony at Norfolk Island in New South Wales in 1840 and developed a plan to deal with these new conditions. The Maconochie plan was built upon the earlier European ticket-of-leave system.

The Maconochie system, initially called probation, involved a combination of the indeterminate system with provision for release on the basis of "marks" earned by good conduct, labor, and study. There were five stages through which prisoners could pass, each carrying an increasing degree of responsibility. These stages were: (1) strict imprisonment; (2) labor on government chain gangs; (3) freedom within a limited area; (4) a ticket-of-leave or parole resulting in a conditional pardon; and (5) full restoration of liberty.[6]

In the 1850s, Sir Walter Crofton, the director of Ireland's prison system, decided that there was a need for a transitional stage between confinement and liberty. Building upon the Maconochie model, Crofton evolved a classification scheme utilizing a system of marks and grading which led prisoners through three successive stages of treatment. The first stage consisted of separate confinement, with employment and training provided to the prisoners. The second was the innovation of a transition period from custody to freedom and consisted of prisoners being employed on public works projects in comparative freedom with little physical restraint. Those prisoners who successfully completed the interim step were released on "license" upon a series of conditions, a violation of which led to reimprisonment. While in this third phase, the prisoners (now actually parolees) were required to submit monthly reports, and were warned against "idle living and association with notorious criminals."[7] The innovations of periodic reports and return to prison for violations of the conditions of release were further steps on the path to modern parole.

The first legislation in the United States authorizing parole was enacted in Massachusetts in 1837. The duties of the first parole officers in that state included assisting released prisoners in finding employment and providing them with tools, clothing, and transportation. Public funds were made available for these specific purposes. The evolution of parole from that point in time was minimal until the 1870s, although from 1840 through 1870 numerous philanthropic organizations such as the Philadelphia Society for Relieving Distressed Prisoners, established by the Quakers, were active advocates of prison reform and provided aid to discharged prisoners.

In 1870, the first National Prison Conference was held in Cincinnati. From this meeting emerged a Declaration of Principles which marked the beginning of modern corrections in the United States. Two years later, 1872, an International Prison Congress exhaustively reviewed the concepts of the reformatory, parole, and the indeterminate sentence, particularly as applied in Ireland. A wave of demand for prison reform followed and in 1876 the Elmira Reformatory was opened in New York State.

The Elmira Reformatory utilized many of the principles of the Irish prison system to include a limited form of the indeterminate sentence and a method of awarding marks and parole based upon those marks. Upon release, Elmira inmates remained under the supervision of the Reformatory for a period of six months, during which time parole could be revoked if they violated any conditions attached to their release. The year 1876 marks the beginning of modern parole in the United States.

By 1880, 3 states had parole; by 1889, the number had grown to 12. With the enactment of parole legislation in Mississippi in 1944, every state had authorized parole, although the quality of parole then, as now, varied substantially.

Fixed and Indeterminate Sentences

Early American state legislatures frequently restricted judicial discretion in sentencing by prescribing a specific penalty to be applied for each kind of criminal offense. These penalties were fixed; that is, the crime of burglary carried a specified number of years of imprisonment, robbery a different but still specific number of years imprisonment as a penalty. The role of judges generally was to preside over trials and impose the sentences mandated by statute. But having a single sentence without any options failed to take into account two important considerations: varying types of behavior were classified as identical crimes and differing personal characteristics and motivations of offenders were ignored. Under this early system, robbery was robbery; a robber was a robber; all were punished equally. This system had consistency at the expense of flexibility.

Gradually, state legislatures began to distinguish differences such as robbery committed with violence and robbery committed without a weapon, or burglary committed during the day contrasted with one committed during darkness. Degrees of crimes emerged, such as robbery or burglary of the first or second degree. And, as distinctions were made between degrees of the same offense, different penalties were attached to each of them so that nighttime burglary carried a more severe and longer period of imprisonment than one committed during daylight hours. The penalties, however, were still fixed and rigid as, for example, 10 years' imprisonment for first degree robbery, 5 years for robbery of the second degree.

Over time, as legislatures began to recognize individual variations among and diversity between individual offenders, further differentiations in sentencing were allowed. Different degrees of crime were punishable by imprisonment for a specified number of years between a statutory minimum and maximum. With this kind of change, it was possible for the courts to have some discretion, even though judges still had to impose a sentence for a fixed number of years between the minimum and maximum. Thus, where the imprisonment could range from 5 to 10 years, the courts could sentence an offender to any term within this range, e.g., 7 years, 9 years.

These two changes were significant in the evolution of parole. The earlier system was altered to provide categories of each offense and a separate range of penalties for each category. The indeterminate sentence emerged and either allowed courts to specify, within statutory limits, two periods of confinement for each case, one being the minimum and the other the maximum, or mandated the courts to impose the fixed minimum and maximum prescribed by law. Thus, indeterminate sentences may be from 1 to 5 years, 5 years to life, 10 to 20 years, or some other combination.

The indeterminate sentence allows a prisoner to be released any time after completion of the minimum term, and requires release from imprisonment at the completion of the maximum term. Under the indeterminate sentence, the decision as to how much time must be served between the minimum and maximum was/is determined by nonjudicial authorities, institutional (prison) personnel during its early history, parole boards now.

The first indefinite sentence law in the United States was passed in Michigan in 1869, based in large measure on the advocacy of Z.R. Brockway, superintendent of the Detroit House of Correction. That legislation provided for the commitment of prostitutes to the House of Correction for a maximum period of three years with the Board of Managers of the facility given the authority to release inmates sooner upon evidence of reformation. This Michigan legislation was a significant move from fixed sentences and a giant step forward in correctional progress.

Both the indefinite and definite (or flat, fixed, or general) sentence systems are found in the United States in the 1970s, but the patterns vary significantly. Under the definite sentence system today, the court imposes a sentence for a given number of years, within statutory limits, and the paroling authority may release a prisoner after the minimum portion of the sentence has been served. The minimum is usually set as a fraction of the sentence, such as one-third or one-fourth, or even as a given number of months or years — for instance, the provision that parole eligibility occurs after one year.

The patterns found for indeterminate sentences vary even more widely and the total sentencing alternatives are even more complex in that some jurisdictions have different types of sentencing structures for different offenses and even the choice of alternative types of sentencing in given cases. Surveys across the country have attempted to classify these confusing and diverse patterns of sentencing, as for example, the following generalized indeterminate sentence categories, all of which are in use today:

1. Both the maximum and minimum terms are fixed by the court.

2. Both the maximum and minimum terms are fixed by the court, but the minimum is not to exceed a fraction of the maximum.

3. The maximum term is fixed by the court; the minimum is fixed by law.

4. The maximum term is fixed by law for each offense, but the minimum term is fixed by the court.

5. The maximum and minimum sentence are fixed by law for each offense.

6. The maximum term is fixed by law for each offense, and there is no minimum sentence, but the minimum term set by the parole board at an early hearing is the equivalent to a minimum sentence.

7. The maximum sentence is fixed by the court, and there is no minimum sentence.

8. The law fixes the minimum sentence, the maximum period before first parole, and the maximum sentence.

9. The law prescribes that the inmate shall be under correctional supervision until he reaches a given age, unless discharged from the sentence earlier, and he may be paroled at any time.[8]

It is clear that regardless of the nature of the sentencing structure found in a given state, the paroling authority in that state takes an active part in determining the length of time to be served by prisoners. But it is equally clear that the determination of the nature and extent of an offender's sentence is a divided task. The *legislatures* set upper and lower limits or absolute lengths of sentences which may be imposed by courts for criminal offenses. The *courts* make specific decisions on each individual case within the parameters of the law. The *paroling authorities* may exercise discretion in whatever leeway is left when the legislatures and courts are through; the amount of this discretion or decision making varies substantially by jurisdiction.

Parole Decision Making

Paroling authorities must make a variety of decisions. Depending upon the jurisdiction, the decisions may include setting the minimum date at which an inmate may be considered for parole through judgments about the actual granting of parole and the conditions attached to that conditional release to determinations about parole violation when a new offense or technical violation is reported. These decisions clearly must be made within statutory limits of a given jurisdiction and must seek out a balance between protection of the community and rehabilitation of the prisoner. These decisions are becoming more complex because they increasingly are being reviewed by the judiciary to insure that the constitutional rights of prisoners and parolees are protected.

These kinds of complex factors notwithstanding, the individuals and groups who make parole decisions must assess a wide variety of informational inputs in making decisions as, for example, the decision to grant or deny parole. While it is clear that there must be an assessment of the risk involved in releasing a prisoner to the community, there are a number of other considerations beyond the probability of success or failure on parole. True, an assessment of risk, normally involving an evaluation of the inmate's personal assets and liabilities and the assets and liabilities of the community and environment to which release is being considered, is a very significant factor. But parole decision making is not that simple; there are other considerations which help determine parole policy. Some of these are not directly related to the individual about whom a decision must be made. Available bed space, for example, may be an important latent determinant which impacts upon decisions about a specific prisoner. In terms of the total criminal justice system, it is obvious that correctional institutions do not select their populations — institutions are recipients of prisoners sentenced by courts. Should new legislation be enacted or sentencing policies be changed to produce a marked increase in the number of prisoners, overcrowded institutions may result in subtle changes in parole policy. These changes may serve to reduce institutional population pressures either by increasing the number of inmates paroled or reducing the average length of stay (shorter sentences), or both. On the other hand, there may be different adjustments in parole policies — a "toughening up" — to insure that institutions do not find themselves underpopulated. In short, institutional equilibrium and stability are bureaucratic concerns which may generate parole policies insuring that there are neither too many nor too few prisoners. Institutions and parole boards occasionally are forced into a reactive position rather than being allowed a proactive posture.

There are other significant but not well-defined factors involved in parole decision making. Particular inmates or types of inmates are "newsworthy" and decisions for or against parole may have to be at least partially assessed in terms of public opinion, political pressure, and media commentary. The assessment of risk also involves the risk to the parole board membership. The personal careers of parole board members may be jeopardized by decisions affecting prisoners who are of interest to the public, and this is true even in those instances in which the parole board membership has status beyond that of political appointment by the governor. Parole board members must also be sensitive and perhaps responsive to inputs from other members of the criminal justice system community. Comments from law-enforcement officials, prosecuting attorneys, and/or sentencing judges — and victims — cannot be ignored.

Then too, there are changes in our society, not only of a technological nature, but of a social nature which affect parole decision making. Shifts in mood of the American people and their perspectives on crime and its correction are reflected in the political structure and are translated into legislation and budgets; these translations, whether accurate or not, directly affect program, policy, and personnel, and may modify philosophy. Correctional agencies, including parole boards, as is the case with all social institutions, must somehow interpret and reflect the prevalent beliefs of the citizenry.

Beyond all of this, it is clear that parole policy affects inmate behavior, both individually and collectively, and is, in turn, affected by inmate behavior. The management and control of institutions are directly related to parole procedures and processes. It seems reasonable to assume that to the extent parole policies are known, are understood and rational, institutional management is facilitated. Ironically, this may not be completely true; indeed, there is a need for predictability *and* uncertainty. Release from imprisonment, even with parole appended to that freedom rather than a complete discharge, is perhaps the most pressing desire of inmates. Institutional control of inmates may be equated with the control of the time to be served by inmates. The reward and punishment system of American corrections is not so much the imposition of traditional penalties—isolation, segregation, "bread and water"—but rather the potential punishment of withholding freedom for failure to comply with institutional expectations of behavior. The reward system is an improved potential for release; the punishment system is the opposite—a reduced probability of release. The parole board, by virtue of its authority to parole or not parole, and in the absence of explicit criteria to guide parole decisions, has the coercive power of uncertainty to force institutional conformity.

This is not to suggest that a conspiracy exists between institutional and paroling authorities, but rather that collective behavior—a common mind—on the part of institution administrators and parole board members is a powerful force in producing institutional conformity. Further, as the parole process becomes increasingly vague, the power of correctional authorities to impose their standards of acceptable behavior on inmates is increased. As noted, the criteria for parole selection are seldom made explicit. If parole decisions were based simply upon an accumulation of a certain number of months served, participation in particular programs, and/or a certain minimum level of acceptable behavior or demonstration of remorse, or whatever, the power of the board would be enormously reduced. It would be only an administrative body with authority limited to insuring that the minimum standards for release were met.

Although it may be desirable and useful for a lack of certainty about parole criteria to exist from the perspectives of institutional staff and parole boards, uncertainty is a significant problem for the inmate who desperately searches for freedom and must seek to uncover what it is that the board wants. The inmate seeks predictability as to what kinds of behaviors, including program participation, will earn him "points" toward release. He further seeks a generalized predictability as to how much time must be served in order to "pay his debt to society." Inmates must constantly search for clues from parole board hearings as to what is appropriate institutional behavior. If, for example, the parole board begins to inquire at its hearings whether or not the applicant for parole has participated in group counseling, educational activities, or church services and then denies parole to many of those who have not participated in such programs, the inmate population will seek enrollment in those programs. Institutional staff must also search for clues about appropriate inmate behavior from parole board decisions. If for example, inmates with marginal disciplinary records in the institution are paroled, the staff may have difficulty in securing conformity with rules and regulations.

The ambiguity about the "rules" of the parole process and the absence of an appellate mechanism for parole board decisions lead to uncertainty, frustration, and hostility on the part of inmates and institutional staff. It is this precise situation which may bring about major alterations in the paroling process in the next few years. These may include not only the inmate's right to counsel and witnesses at all parole hearings, but more importantly a change in the actual authority of the parole board. The change in the authority may take a variety of forms, such as *requiring* the parole board to release an inmate on parole after a given portion of the sentence has been served, unless there are compelling reasons to deny parole and those reasons are made explicit and are a matter of record. Such a change in process from the current situation of complete discretion as to whether or not to parole an inmate on whatever criteria is deemed relevant should preclude arbitrary and capricious decisions, minimize the possibility of injustice, and remove the mystique which generally surrounds the current parole process.

Information for Parole Decision Making

A considerable amount of information about individual offenders is normally available to parole boards as they begin their deliberations about parole. Apart from considerations as to whether or not the information is either used or useful, it is available and in quantity. The sources of information are generally four in number: the presentence investigation report, correctional institution classification material, institutional progress reports, and prerelease plans.

As noted in Chapter 8, the presentence investigation report may include data on the offense, the defendant's version of the offense, prior record, family and marital history, home and neighborhood, education, religion, interests and leisure time activities, health, employment, military service, financial condition, and additionally, the probation officer's evaluation of the offender, as well as considerable identifying data such as social security number and the like. A copy of the presentence report is normally made available to the institution, as well as other relevant materials gathered during the presentence investigation.

Institutional classification materials normally begin to evolve during the reception process at the institution. An "admission summary" is generally produced which contains information on the legal aspects of the case; a summary of prior criminal or delinquent history; social history; physical condition; vocational interest, competence, and experience; educational status; religious background; recreational interests; psychological and psychiatric characteristics; initial adjustment to the prison environment; initial response to rehabilitation programs; and so on. The major purpose of these data is to develop an institutional program for the inmate, and only secondarily to begin to organize materials about parole potential. Over time, other information is added to the file including custodial status, disciplinary record, program participation, changes in status both within and outside the institution, annual or other timed-interval progress reports, special reports, legal documents, significant correspondence from such persons as the prosecuting attorney, sentencing judge, victims of the offense, and the like. These cumulative files may be quite extensive at that point in time when the inmate has a hearing with the parole board either to set the date of eligibility for parole or on the matter of parole itself.

As the time for parole consideration grows near, prerelease or preparole reports enter the information system. Parole officers or agents in the community conduct investigations to help establish a parole plan or to determine the appropriateness of a parole plan developed by the inmate and institution staff. Verification of residence, employment, living situation, family status and so on is obtained and entered into the record, as is information concerning the community situation in general.

These cumulative data from the presentence report, the institutional materials, and the prerelease investigation cannot normally be reviewed by individual parole board members. As a result, institution and/or parole staff prepare parole summaries, highlighting the individual offender's background, summarizing institutional adjustment and performance, and pointing toward potential on parole. These parole summaries, supported by extensive backup materials, may serve to facilitate parole board decision making.

Granted that a considerable amount of information is available to the parole board, at least two important issues must be surfaced. One issue centers upon the criteria for making parole decisions. The other focuses upon both the identification of the information which is used and how that information is organized to support the decisions. As relates to criteria, it is clear that the parole decision is almost entirely a matter of administrative discretion. While there may be both statutory parole eligibility restrictions and occasional procedural requirements, once these are met the parole board has almost total discretion. Across the country, statutory criteria for parole selection are the exception rather than the rule. The American Law Institute has noted:

> Under present parole practice, the release of eligible prisoners is purely discretionary and no formal criteria have been established in the statutes, aside from general principles relating to public safety. Nor has there been any standardized administrative policy in this matter; parole decisions rest on the intuition of the paroling authority, largely unguided by the laws that establish this broad grant of power or even by specific board standards.[9]

Further, there appears to be little interest in formalizing criteria or systematically assessing the policy implications of whatever criteria are used.

There is some certainty that parole boards are most concerned with the probability that an inmate will commit a criminal offense if released on parole. But probability as to an offense during the parole period may be estimated in a number of ways and by using a variety of information. O'Leary and Glaser have suggested that there are three methods by which parole board members may make an assessment of the future crime risk involved in paroling an inmate. The three methods are the intuitive conclusion, the systematic rating, and the statistical prediction.[10] The intuitive conclusion method is precisely that: after a parole board member has gathered some information about the individual on whom a decision must be made, he simply follows his intuition, a best guess.

The systematic rating method normally utilizes some kind of standardized form for releasing information. One model of the form might have a number of different entries to which plus and minus weight are appended for each entry. Another model might be one in which there is a broad outline with only a few subheadings such as the inmate's (1) assets and (2) liabilities, the

(3) assets and (4) liabilities of the community to which release is being considered. But apart from the specific format utilized, systematic rating sheets require the parole decision makers to consider both the positive and negative aspects of each case. Not infrequently, of course, this systematic approach is coupled with the intuitive method in making the final decision about parole.

Attempts to statistically predict the outcome of parole began in the 1920s. One of the first prediction tables assessed prisoners on 21 separate factors:

1. Nature of the offense
2. Number of associations in committing the offense for which convicted
3. Nationality
4. Parental status — including broken home
5. Marital status of inmate
6. Type of offender
7. Social type (gangster, socially inadequate, ne'er-do-well)
8. County from which committed
9. Size of community
10. Type of neighborhood
11. Resident or transient in community arrested
12. Statement of trial judge and prosecuting attorney with reference to recommendations for or against leniency
13. Whether or not commitment was on the acceptance of a lesser plea
14. Nature and length of sentence
15. Months of sentence actually served before parole
16. Previous criminal record
17. Previous work record
18. Punishment record at the institution
19. Age at time of parole
20. Mental age
21. Personality type and psychiatric prognosis[11]

On the basis of these factors, it was concluded that a prisoner who scored unfavorably on 15 or more factors was "definitely a poor parole risk"; a prisoner with less than 5 unfavorable ratings "will probably make a fairly adequate adjustment on parole."

The deficiencies in this early system are apparent and include ambiguity and the fact that each variable is weighted equally. As to ambiguity, what does "ne'er-do-well" (item 7) really mean? As to weighing of factors, is "nationality" of equal import with "previous criminal record"?

More recent attempts at parole prediction have utilized far more sophisticated statistical methodologies including association analysis and predictive attribute analysis. Although complex, the newer techniques are significantly better than (1) the zero-order correlations in which only the direct relationship between each item of information and outcome was measured, (2) the simple addition or subtraction of one point of score for any item found to be positively or negatively correlative with outcomes, or (3) the assignment of a weight proportional to the percentage of success in a sample to items significantly associated with outcome.[12]

The current approaches to parole prediction, apart from the specific methodology or statistical technique, utilize an "experience" or actuarial base. Records of prisoners paroled in past years are tabulated to determine the violation rate for each group into which these past parolees could have been classified at release. Thus, separate violation rates are determined for *each* age, offense, prior criminal record, educational level, and so on. These tend to be objective data, a significant improvement over vague and tenuous categories. These separate category violation rates are then combined in a fashion not unlike that used by insurance companies to determine life expectancy.

Insurance companies consider a series of objective statistical attributes, age, weight, previous health record, and occupation, among others, to determine life expectancy. Medical data reflect that the characteristic of overweight is associated with a lower life expectancy; overweight combined with a previous history of heart trouble and diabetes has an even lower life expectancy. Criminological data reflect that an extensive prior criminal record has a negative association with parole performance and that extensive prior record coupled with a history of heroin addiction an even more negative relationship with parole success. The analogy with life expectancy and parole success expectancy is useful; just as some variables are related with long life, so too are some variables related to parole success.

California's correctional system has been a pioneer in the development of prediction devices. A considerable research investment has produced "base expectancy" scores, these being generated by utilizing seven items of precommitment information which are related statistically to parole outcome and to each other. The format for calculating the California base expectancy score is:

A.   *If*   *Add*

The prisoner had, in his arrest history,   12 points
5 or more years without an arrest, or if he
was a first offender
The prisoner had no known history of opiate   13 points
drug use
The prisoner's family members had no   8 points
criminal record
The offense for which the sentence being   13 points
served is not forgery, bad checks, or burglary

B. Add:
the number of points equal to .6 of his
age at commitment and
21 points in all cases

C. Subtract, as appropriate:
3 points for each alias shown on the
prisoner's arrest record
5 points for each prior incarceration

The base expectancy score is equal to A + B − C.

Using base expectancy scores for 283 parolees from the California Medical
facility, the following data were obtained:

**Base Expectancy Table Prediction of Potential Success
Compared to Actual Adjustment of Vacaville Parolees**

Base Expectancy Score	Cases Assigned Each Score No.	%	% of Cases in Each Score Group Actually Adjusting Favorably on Parole
0 to 9	3	1	33
10 to 19	5	2	0
20 to 29	12	4	17
30 to 39	38	13	32
40 to 49	54	19	33
50 to 59	50	18	44
60 to 69	41	14	58
70 to 79	26	9	77
80 to 89	36	13	89
90 or higher	18	6	94
Total	283	100%	52%

Source: Don M. Gottfredson, "Comparing and combining subjective and objective parole predictions," California Department of Corrections Research
Newsletter, Vol. 3, No. 3–4 (Sept.–Dec., 1961), pp. 11–17.

The relationship between base expectancy scores and parole outcome is obvious, suggesting that these kinds of predictive or actuarial devices may indeed be useful to parole decision makers. Prediction scores will not replace decision makers, but as an additional piece of information for consideration by the parole board, the potential usefulness seems quite high. Some considerable amount of resistance to predictive devices will have to be overcome, and this can best be done by continued research and demonstration as to efficiency and effectiveness of such devices.

The Conditions of Parole

Parole is normally granted with a series of conditions attached to that conditional freedom. Violations of any of these terms of release may result in the return of the parolee to prison to complete the original term imposed by the court or until a subsequent parole is granted. The conditions of parole found in the United States vary from jurisdiction to jurisdiction and may comprise a bewildering set of regulations by which the parolee is expected to live.

A survey of parole rules in 1956 included the observation that:

> . . . in many states the conditions were entirely too numerous to be of much real value, that some of the statements listed as conditions were actually interpretations of policy or were included in the penal statutes of the state, that many of the regulations were unrealistic and unenforceable, and that the basic rules were not uniform through the states.[13]

A similar survey published in 1969 revealed that while some states had reduced the number of conditions of parole, most had increased the number of rules. While it is clear that conditions of parole are authorized by law and, once adopted, should have the full impact of the law, it is not at all clear that these many conditions either protect the community or assist in the rehabilitation of the offender. Further, some of the rules are prohibitions, some are compulsory, some are "advisory" or "recommended," while others deal with specifics such as distances allowed for travel away from home or curfews. In total, there are approximately 50 different parole conditions found in the 50 states and the federal system.

Utilizing data from the 1969 survey, these conditions may be grouped into 29 categories, as follows:

Parole Conditions Related to:	Number of Jurisdictions
Undesirable Associations or Correspondence	49
Liquor Usage	46
Change of Employment or Living Quarters	45
Approval of Marriage or Divorce	44
Compliance with the Law	44
Weapons	43
Motor Vehicle Registration and License	41
Filing Written Reports	41
Out-of-State Travel	40
Support of Dependents	36
First Arrival Report	36
Narcotics Usage	35
Waiver of Extradition	35
Maintaining Gainful Employment	32
Out-of-County or Community Travel	30
Indebtedness	23
Permitting Home or Job Visits and Searches	19
Curfew	10
Reporting if Arrested	7
Credit for Time on Parole if Parole is Violated	6
Civil Rights; Suffrage	4
Gambling	4
Church Attendance	4
Return to County or State of Commitment	4
Participation in Anti-narcotic Program	3
Airplane or Power Boat Licenses	3
Treatment for Venereal Disease	3
Criminal Registration	3
Acting as an Informer	2

Source: Nat R. Arluke, "A Summary of Parole Rules—Thirteen Years Later," *Crime and Delinquency* 15 (April 1969): 272–273.

Because of the variations in the conditions of parole, there is no single example that can be totally representative. However, the conditions of parole imposed by the federal system are illustrative:

1. You shall go directly to the district shown on this CERTIFICATE OF PAROLE (unless released to the custody of other authorities). Within three

days after your arrival, you shall report to your parole adviser if you have one, and to the United States Probation Officer° whose name appears on this Certificate.

2. If you are released to the custody of other authorities, and after your release from physical custody of such authorities, you are unable to report to the United States Probation Officer to whom you are assigned within three days, you shall report instead to the nearest United States Probation Officer.

3. You shall not leave the limits fixed by this CERTIFICATE OF PAROLE without written permission from the probation office.

4. You shall notify your probation officer immediately of any change in your place of residence.

5. You shall make a complete and truthful written report (on a form provided for that purpose) to your probation officer between the first and third day of each month, and on the final day of parole. You shall also report to your probation officer at other times as he directs.

6. If in any emergency you are unable to get in touch with your parole adviser, or your probation officer or his office, you shall communicate with the United States Board of Parole, Department of Justice, Washington, D.C. 20537.

7. You shall not violate any law. You shall get in touch immediately with your probation officer or his office if you are arrested or questioned by a law-enforcement officer.

8. You shall not enter into any agreement to act as an "informer" or special agent for any law-enforcement agency.

9. You shall work regularly unless excused by your probation officer, and support your legal dependents, if any, to the best of your ability. You shall report immediately to your probation officer any changes in employment.

10. You shall not drink alcoholic beverages to excess. You shall not purchase, possess, use or administer marihuana or narcotic or other habit-forming or dangerous drugs, unless prescribed or advised by a physician. You shall not frequent places where such drugs are illegally sold, dispensed, used or given away.

11. You shall not associate with persons who have a criminal record unless you have permission of your probation officer. Nor shall you associate with persons engaged in criminal activity.

12. You shall not have firearms (or other dangerous weapons) in your possession without the written permission of your probation officer, following prior approval of the United States Board of Parole.[14]

In the federal system, as in most state parole systems, the parolee signs

---

° In the federal system, the United States Probation Officer also functions as a Parole Officer.

the conditions of parole, thus acknowledging that "I understand them and know that if I violate any of them, I may be recommitted. I also understand that special conditions may be added or modifications of any conditions may be made by the Board of Parole at any time."

The need for these many conditions of parole is questionable. England's Criminal Justice Act of 1967 established five conditions for the parolee:

1. He shall report to an office indicated.
2. He shall place himself under the supervision of an officer nominated for this purpose.
3. He shall keep in touch with his officer in accordance with the officer's instructions.
4. He shall inform his officer at once if he changes his address or loses his job.
5. He shall be of good behavior and lead an industrious life.[15]

This particular set of conditions is significant for a number of reasons. First, the conditions are not a series of "do's and don'ts"; they are all written in a positive manner. Further, these conditions do not require a higher standard of behavior on the part of the parolee than would be found among the non-parolee citizenry. They are not technical in nature, e.g., curfew at 10:00 P.M., but rather suggest basically that the parolee should keep in contact with the parole officer and lead a responsible, law-abiding life. These kinds of conditions can preclude many of the problems associated with parole violation hearings based upon technical violations. For example, should a parolee face return to prison as a parole violator if he should legally marry during the period of parole without the advanced permission of the parole officer? Finally, these kinds of basic conditions may still be supplemented by specific conditions which are based upon the problems, needs, and capacities of individual parolees.

Reviewing the rules of parole, it appears that:

Some parole conditions are moralistic, most are impractical, others impinge on human rights, and all reflect obsolete criminological conceptions. On the whole, they project a precept of a man who does not exist.[16]

The conditions of release should be designed to assist in the successful re-entry of the offender into the community; the conditions should not be a list of punitive restrictions which impede, rather than aid in rehabilitation.

The Revocation of Parole

In the matter of revocation of parole, as elsewhere in the field of corrections, significant changes are occurring because of judicial review. Until the 1960s, the decisions about parole revocation for both adults and juveniles were almost entirely discretionary on the part of the paroling authority and, as a result, patterns and practices varied throughout the United States. There was an absence of procedural requirements in many states. Further, the grounds for revocation were frequently nonspecific, including such assessments as "generally poor attitude" or "failure to cooperate," rather than specific violations of the conditions of release or the commission of new offenses. Part of this entire phenomenon was due to an earlier philosophical orientation that since parole was a privilege, not a right, the privilege of parole could be terminated or withdrawn without much formality. This was particularly true in the revocation of juvenile parole, in which the decision to revoke was considered to be more of a casework determination for the benefit of the parolee than a legal matter.

A 1964 survey of American parole revocation procedure revealed that seven states did not even authorize a violation hearing, and in some states where hearings were required either by statute or policy, the alleged violator was returned directly to the institution on the basis of a parole agent report or a warrant issued by the parole board. The actual hearing or review by the board often did not take place for weeks, sometimes months, after the return to prison. As the National Advisory Commission noted: ". . . in most cases, then, revocation was a fait accompli by the time the board's representative next visited the institution to review the revocation order and officially declare the parolee a violator."[17] Even in those cases in which a violation was not sustained by the board and the parolee was released to resume his parole status, all of the earlier efforts to help were disrupted and readjustment to the community had to be restarted—family relationships, employment, residence, and so on. Legal safeguards and protections against arbitrary and vague procedures were basically absent from the parole revocation scene.

A series of court decisions has and probably will continue to change this pattern. In *Hyser* v. *Reed*, 1963, the court generally supported the traditional position that revocation was a discretionary withdrawal of a privilege not requiring an adversary hearing.[18] But the court did support the U.S. Board of Parole practice of conducting a fact-finding hearing on the site of the alleged offense or violation of a condition of parole, with a review at the institution only if the first hearing determined that the offender should be returned to prison. In 1967, the U.S. Supreme Court held in *Mempa* v. *Rhay* that a state probationer had a right to a hearing and counsel upon allegations of violations of probation.[19] Several courts interpreted the principle of the *Mempa* case as applying equally to parole and reversed part of the earlier ruling in the *Hyser* decision, finding that there *was* justification for due process at parole revocation hearings.

In 1970, in *Murray* v. *Page*, another federal case focusing upon the requirement of procedural due process at parole revocations, the court noted:

> Therefore, while a prisoner does not have a constitutional right to parole, once paroled he cannot be deprived of his freedom by means inconsistent with due process. The minimal right of the parolee to be informed of the charges and the nature of the evidence against him and to appear to be heard at the revocation hearing is inviolate. Statutory deprivation of this right is manifestly inconsistent with due process and is unconstitutional; nor can such right be lost by the subjective determination of the executive that the case for revocation is "clear."[20]

In 1972, the U.S. Supreme Court held in *Morrissey* v. *Brewer* that

> . . . the liberty of a parolee, although indeterminate, includes many of the core values of unqualified liberty and its termination inflicts a "grievous loss" on the parolee and often on others. It is hardly useful any longer to try to deal with this problem in terms of whether the parolee's liberty is a "right" or a "privilege." By whatever name the liberty is valuable and must be seen as within the protection of the Fourteenth Amendment. Its termination calls for some orderly process, however informal.[21]

The long-range implications of *Morrissey* v. *Brewer* are significant. Although the Supreme Court stated that it had no intention of creating an inflexible structure for parole revocation procedures, it did make a distinction between a *preliminary* and a *revocation* hearing. In the preliminary hearing, the Court indicated that there should be a prompt inquiry at or near the place of the alleged violation of parole by a person not directly involved in the case. Not unlike a more traditional judicial preliminary hearing, the rule was set that probable cause or reasonable grounds to believe that the parolee committed acts which would constitute a violation of parole must be established. It was further established that the parolee should be given written notice of when and why the hearing will take place, the nature of the alleged violation, and should also have the right to speak in his own behalf. The right to have witnesses who could provide relevant information was assured. Finally, the hearing officer was mandated to make a summary of the proceedings and the evidence introduced and, based upon all of the evidence, determine if there was probable cause to hold the parolee for the final decision of the parole board on the matter of revocation.

The Supreme Court further directed that the revocation hearing insure due process by mandating:

1. Written notice of the claimed violations of parole
2. Disclosure to the parolee of evidence against him
3. An opportunity to the parolee to be heard in person and to present witnesses and documentary evidence
4. The right of the parolee to confront and cross-examine adverse witnesses (unless the hearing officer specifically finds good cause for not allowing this confrontation)
5. A "neutral and detached" hearing body such as a traditional parole board, members of which need not be judicial officers or lawyers
6. A written statement by the factfinders as to the evidence relied on and reasons for revoking parole.[22]

These changes have not necessarily been met with enthusiasm by parole officials. Procedural due process requirements clearly reduce the "authority" of the parole board and place added demands on the board which may in fact be difficult to meet, given personnel and budget allocations. Resistance to change notwithstanding, there are precedents which suggest that major breakthroughs in parole revocation are at hand. The State of Washington, for example, has authorized adult parolees to have a hearing before parole board members in the community where the violation allegedly occurred, to cross-examine and subpoena witnesses, to have the assistance of counsel, including lawyers provided at state expense for indigents, and to have access to all pertinent records.

Much of the concern about parole revocation is focused upon legal issues. But at least one nonlegal issue needs to be addressed . . . that of treatment. The treatment aspect of parole suggests a need for alternatives to the current dichotomy of either violating a parolee and returning him to prison or not violating him and leaving him in the community. Clearly there must be more than these two courses of action: the challenge is to seek out the alternatives such as special restrictions, short-term confinement, the use of specialized and supportive community-based correctional programs, halfway houses, and so on. The no-action versus full-revocation model is not appropriate.

The Organization of Parole Boards and Parole Services

Although there is considerable variation in parole board organization throughout the United States, two basic models may be identified. The *institutional* model is dominant in the juvenile field; the *independent* model is common to the adult field. As is the case elsewhere in corrections, serious questions have been raised about these organizational arrangements and changes are occurring with increasing regularity.

The institutional model places parole decision making in the hands of the staff of a correctional institution. The justification most often expressed for the institutional model is that the parole decision is but one of a series of decisions affecting an inmate and that institutional staff will make a parole decision which is consistent with an overall treatment plan. The argument is basically that the institutional parole decision maker is the most familiar with the individual offender's case. Arguments against institutional parole boards focus upon the possibility that parole decisions may be made in the interest of institution management, rather than the individual offender. Concerns such as overpopulation, underpopulation, a desire to enforce one or more rules or be rid of problem cases may be operationally more significant than treatment of the individual. Further, institutional decision making is less likely to have visibility and more likely to utilize a series of informal, vague, and tenuous processes.

The independent model utilizes a parole board which is not associated with a particular institution. But it too has come under criticism on a variety of counts including statements that such independent boards are insensitive to institutional programs and fail to give the programs the support they require, that decisions are based upon inappropriate criteria, that remoteness from institutions allows little insight into the dynamics of a given case, that decisions are cursory with the end result that too often persons who should be paroled are not and those who should not be paroled are released, and finally, that such boards are frequently composed of appointees who have little training or experience in corrections. The National Advisory Commission summarized the criticisms of the independent model as follows:

Critics of the independent model assert that important decisions are being made concerning the correctional system, its programs, and the offenders in it by persons far removed from the system who have little appreciation of its true nature.[23]

In response to these criticisms and for a variety of other reasons, the *consolidation* model is emerging nationwide. This model, generated in part by a movement toward centralized administration, includes the creation of distinctive state departments of corrections which administer both institution and field programs. The consolidation model "typically results in parole decisions being made by a central decision-making authority organizationally situated in an overall department of corrections but possessing independent powers."[24] The increasing acceptance of the consolidation model is clear; in 1966, 10 of 50 state parole authorities were part of a larger state agency or department of corrections; by 1972, the number had grown to 30.

The proponents of the consolidation model argue the need for an increased concern for the entire correctional system as a system. More specifically, they suggest that consolidation will reduce the fragmentation and lack of coordination between programs by generating linkages between institutional and field staff. The need for consolidation becomes even more important as prerelease and community-based programs are initiated; such programs mandate interfaces between institution and field staff and parole decision makers. Finally, the proponents argue that the separation of parole decision making from the control of an institution may result in appropriate weight being applied to parole decision-making considerations and criteria beyond those of institutional management.

There has also been a major shift in the organizational arrangements of field parole staff. The trend — again reflecting the consolidation model — is to move parole staff away from the paroling authority and into state departments of corrections. In 1966, 31 parole boards had parole agents reporting to them through an executive. By 1972, the number had dropped to 18. The merger of parole into the larger departments of corrections has been motivated, in part, by potential savings in time and expense, administrative convenience, efficiency and effectiveness. The merger also frees the parole board from a number of complex administrative responsibilities involved in providing administrative supervision of the parole agency. Since many boards have collateral functions other than parole, such as clemency, commutation of sentences, granting or withholding "good time," the additional time made available by not having to manage a field agency may be devoted to these other tasks as well as to basic parole decision making. Given the amount of time devoted to parole decision making reported by a 1972 nationwide study, it seems imperative that the paroling authorities devote more time to parole matters. That study reflected that 11 state parole boards on average heard in excess of 40 cases per day, 14 heard between 30 and 39 cases per day, and 15 boards heard between 20 and 29 cases a day.[25] Forty cases per eight hour day means that decisions are being produced at a rate of one every twelve minutes.

In the juvenile field, as elsewhere, there are changes occurring. The creation of distinct statewide departments or divisions of juvenile corrections combining both institutions and parole is the emergent trend. Although there generally is consensus as to the need for separate juvenile corrections organizational models, there is much less agreement as to whether these juvenile correctional organizations should or should not be combined with the consolidated organizations dealing with the adult offender. To the extent that *all* correctional services, adult and juvenile, are combined in a single superagency, there is much to argue for a separate identity within that agency for juvenile and adult organizations.

Parole Supervision

Although philosophically and operationally similar to probation supervision, parole supervision has some unique features closely related to the characteristics and experiences of the parolee population. Not the least of these is the rather obvious fact that the parolee has been absent from the community for an extended period of time ranging from perhaps as little as one year through two or three decades of confinement. During that time frame, there has been change — not only in the inmate-parolee, but everywhere. The offender released from an institution finds that nothing is the same as when he entered the institution — not family or personal or social relationships, not the community, not society. Adjustment to these changes is difficult and it appears that the longer the period of confinement, the more difficult the adjustment to the free world.

In recent years, considerable attention has been devoted to "labeling theory." It is clear that the offender who serves a prison sentence will acquire one or more "labels," perhaps the best known and most debilitating being "ex-con." The label "ex-con" has at least two meanings, one for the person carrying the label, the other for those with whom the label-carrier has contact. For the carrier, the label serves as a constant and perpetual reminder of former status and it has been noted that this particular label is so important and pervasive that most other labels are secondary in significance.

Clearly, the "ex-con" label has significant impact in the free world, affecting relationships of others with the label-carrier, usually as a stigma which permeates almost every aspect of the parolee's life — personal and social, community, employment, residential, and so on.

Then too, while serving the sentence of confinement, the prisoner is subjected to experiences which are neither widely shared nor understood by the average citizen and which have elsewhere been described as dehumanizing, brutal, and destructive. The penal reality of prolonged regimentation and a regime of rigorous control without freedom is not without impact as the ex-prisoner enters parole status in the community.

Finally, the parolee possesses a set of characteristics which marked him at the time of adjudication as a marginal risk for release on probation. For reasons frequently not made explicit, the offender sentenced to prison is considered to be a poorer risk for successful adjustment or perhaps a greater threat to the community than his probationer counterpart. Whether these differences are real or imagined, the significance of being imprisoned and then paroled in contrast to being placed directly on probation adds little to the self-esteem or self-image of the parolee. And, because the parolee is considered a more marginal risk, controls imposed by the parole agency may be far more stringent and less flexible than is the case with the probationer. It is true that the probationer may have had similar experiences to those of the parolee, but the intensity or degree of difficulties generated by these experiences are significantly more disabling for the parolee.

Recognizing these factors and their impact upon the probability of parole success, correctional agencies have initiated a number of programs which attempt to bridge the gap between imprisonment and the community. Most widely known are programs involving halfway houses, work or educational release, weekend furloughs, and extended family visitation. These programs are based upon recognition that overstructured institutions cannot replicate community living and that full adjustment to the community is enhanced by transitional programs which gradually decrease the level of supervision. The halfway house, for example, provides a physical setting in which the prisoner-parolee resides during the transition period between confinement and parole. Living in the halfway house and working in the community, combined with backup support through counseling and related programs, the adjustment from prison to community is enhanced. Work and educational release programs permit inmates to leave an institution to seek employment, to work in the community with return to the institution during nonworking hours, or to participate in educational activities which are not available inside the institution. These types of programmatic activities which facilitate

223

transition between confinement and community hold great promise for increasing the likelihood of successful parole adjustment.

In addition to special program innovations and community-based facilities, there are special requirements which fall upon the parole officer. He must be particularly sensitive to the kinds of problems identified above — the confusion which may exist upon release to a community after extended confinement, the problems of personal and social adjustment brought on by changes in the community, the stigma of labeling, and so on. The parole officer has to balance two very difficult and sometimes conflicting demands: attempting to protect the community from further criminal behavior and concurrently attempting to aid in the parolee's personal rehabilitation. The American Correctional Association has observed:

> Parole supervision is a continuation of the correctional process and relies upon the parole officer's knowledge and successful application of casework principles and methods. The parole officer should be able to detect the danger signals of forthcoming criminal activity and to take prompt and appropriate action. He should make every effort to understand a parolee's personal and family problems, to help him with wise counsel toward the solution of these problems, and to bring him in touch with other state and local agencies which will be helpful to him. Parole supervision must afford protection to the community and help to the parolee without being vengeful or punitive in the enforcement of its conditions.[26]

Seeking a balance between control and assistance is difficult, particularly in an environment which may contain confusion, hostility and anger, despair and distrust. The National Advisory Commission has noted:

> Few things about parole evoke consensus, but there is some agreement that one objective and measure of success is reduction of recidivism. Even this consensus quickly becomes less firm when two specific functions are examined: (1) provision of supervision and control to reduce the likelihood of criminal acts while the offender is serving his sentence in the community (the "surveillance" function), and (2) provision of assistance and services to the parolee, so that noncriminal behavior becomes possible (the "helping" function).
> To the extent that these concerns can be integrated, conflicts are minimized, but in the day-to-day activity of parole administration they frequently clash. Decisions constantly must be made between the relative risk of a law violation at the present time and the probable long-term gain if a parolee is allowed freedom and opportunity to develop a legally approved life style. Resources are needed to clarify the choices and risks involved. Key require-

ments for this kind of assistance are development of clear definitions of recidivism and creation of information systems that make data available about the probabilities of various types of parole outcome associated with alternative decisions.[27]

Mandatory Release

Mandatory release is sometimes referred to as "conditional release." As suggested by its name, mandatory release is mandated by statute when an inmate has accumulated "time off" for good behavior or for other reasons such as work credits. This "time off" is normally deducted from the total sentence to be served. Parole officials normally do not participate in the selection of offenders to be released mandatorily, except possibly as a "reviewing authority." Indeed, it is probable that the offender who receives a mandatory release has been denied parole on one or more occasions. However, mandatory release does permit the parole staff to provide supervision for a period of time as though the offender were on parole. Conditions, not unlike those of parole, are attached to mandatory release and the released prisoner is subject to revocation and return to an institution for violation of these conditions. The mandatory release process for those denied parole does permit some degree of control and assistance in the community.

The Interstate Compact for Supervision of Parolees and Probationers

An Interstate Compact for the supervision of probationers and parolees has been enacted by every state. The Compact provides the machinery by which probationers and parolees may be transferred to other states with supervision insured and with authority for return and incarceration in the sending state should there be probation or parole violations.

This collaboration between the states has been motivated by the ever-increasing mobility of the American citizen with the resultant effect that offenders are frequently convicted away from their home states and then desire to return to their homes under probation or parole supervision. The states have found it to their mutual advantage to supervise their resident probationers and parolees even if they were convicted elsewhere.

The precedent for the Interstate Compact legislation may be traced to the Federal Crime Control Consent Act of 1934[28] which authorized two or more states to enter into agreements of mutual assistance in the prevention of crime. Since that time, the Compact has been expanded and now provides that:

1. Any state (receiving state) will supervise a parolee or probationer from any other state (sending state) if he is a resident of the receiving state and has employment there;
2. The receiving state will supervise the sending state's parolee or probationer by the same standards used for its own parolees and probationers; and
3. The sending state may revoke parole or probation in any case and retake the parolee or probationer at its discretion and with a minimum of formality.[29]

The cooperation found in the administration and operation of the Interstate Compact is further recognition of the importance of providing probation and parole supervision to assist offenders in their personal adjustment and to protect communities. Today, all states agree to serve as the agent of every other state in the supervision of offenders.

Standards for Parole

Several national organizations have recommended standards for parole. The American Correctional Association, for example, has identified nine essential elements of an adequate parole system:

1. *Flexibility in the Sentencing and Parole Laws.* There must be sufficient flexibility in the laws governing sentences and parole to permit the parole of an offender at the time when his release under supervision is in the best interests of society.

2. *A Qualified Parole Board.* The parole board must be composed of members qualified by character, intelligence, training, and experience to weigh the complex problems of human behavior involved in parole decisions, and have the knowledge, patience, and integrity required to render wise and just decisions.

3. *A Qualified Parole Staff.* It is essential that the parole services be composed of persons selected in accordance with high standards of ability, character, training, and experience, and appointed on a career-service basis. It is necessary that the administrative structure provide an adequate

number of administrative and supervisory personnel, field and institutional parole officers, employment, training, research, and other specialists,
and stenographic and clerical staff, to perform the work of the parole system.

4. Freedom from Political or Improper Influences. Complete freedom
from improper control or influence, political or otherwise.

**5. Parole Assigned to a Workable Position in the Governmental Ad-
ministrative Structure.** An administrative structure within the framework
of the government as a whole which makes it possible for the parole system, without sacrifice of proper independence, to function in complete
coordination with other departments and services, notably probation services, correctional institutions, and departments of health, mental hygiene,
welfare, and public safety.

6. Proper Parole Procedure. A parole procedure which makes provision for orienting the prisoner toward parole, preparation for the parole
board of all data pertinent to the case, a parole hearing based upon careful
study of such data, formulation, and investigation of a satisfactory parole
plan, release under adequate supervision, and return to the institution of
those who are unable to readjust satisfactorily under supervision. For
young offenders, especially, a facility to house prisoners temporarily after
release from a correctional institution (such as a halfway house) in cases
where the releasee has no suitable home or other residence available, or
who needs assistance in making a gradual adjustment to more complete
freedom from the restrictions of close confinement.

7. Prerelease Preparation within the Institution Program. Operation
within the institution of a program which aims at utilizing the period of
confinement for preparing the inmate physically, vocationally, mentally,
and spiritually for his return to society, and puts forth intensive effort,
at the close of the term, toward effecting his release under optimum
conditions as far as he, his dependents, and the community are concerned.

8. Parole Research. A system of gathering, presenting, and interpreting
data concerning the practical operations of the parole system and the effectiveness of the system. Such a system should be kept up-to-date and be
used as a guide for the evaluation of the operations and decisions of the
parole board.

9. A Proper Public Attitude toward the Parolee. A proper public attitude toward the parolee so that he may be accorded fair and helpful
treatment in his efforts to make good, especially in matters of employment
and social integration.[30]

The National Advisory Commission on Criminal Justice Standards and Goals has established eight standards covering organization of paroling authorities, parole authority personnel, the parole grant hearing, revocation hearings, the organization of field services, community services for parolees, measures of control, and manpower for parole.[31] The standards are contained in Appendix II.

Although it is clear that the recommendations of the National Advisory Commission cannot be mandated upon the individual states, it is certain that these standards or similar standards set by the individual states will set directions for parole for the next decade. One need look no further than the recommended standard for parole legislation to find a blueprint for the future of parole in the United States.

16.15 *PAROLE LEGISLATION*

Each State should enact by 1975 legislation (1) authorizing parole for all committed offenders and (2) establishing criteria and procedures for (a) parole eligibility, (b) granting of parole, (c) parole conditions, (d) parole revocation, and (e) length of parole.

In authorizing parole for all committed offenders the legislation should:

1. Not exclude offenders from parole eligibility on account of the particular offense committed.

2. Not exclude offenders from parole eligibility because of number of convictions or past history of parole violations.

3. Authorize parole or aftercare release for adults and juveniles from all correctional institutions.

4. Authorize the parole of an offender at any time unless a minimum sentence is imposed by the court in connection with an extended term (Standard 5.3), in which event parole may be authorized prior to service of the minimum sentence with the permission of the sentencing court.

In establishing procedures for the granting of parole to both adults and juveniles the legislation should require:

1. Parole decisions by a professional board of parole, independent of the institutional staff. Hearing examiners should be empowered to hear and decide parole cases under policies established by the board.

2. Automatic periodic consideration of parole for each offender.

3. A hearing to determine whether an offender is entitled to parole at which the offender may be represented by counsel and present evidence.

4. Agency assistance to the offender in developing a plan for his parole.

5. A written statement by the board explaining decisions denying parole.

6. Authorization for judicial review of board decisions.

7. Each offender to be released prior to the expiration of his term because of the accumulation of "good time" credits to be released to parole supervision until the expiration of his term.

8. Each offender to be released on parole no later than 90 days prior to the expiration of his maximum term.

In establishing criteria for granting parole the legislation should be patterned after Sec. 305.9 of the Model Penal Code and should:

1. Require parole over continued confinement unless specified conditions exist.

2. Stipulate factors that should be considered by the parole board in arriving at its decision.

3. Direct the parole decision toward factors relating to the individual offender and his chance for successful return to the community.

4. Not require a favorable recommendation by the institutional staff, the court, the police, or the prosecutor before parole may be granted.

In establishing criteria for parole conditions, the legislation should be patterned after Sec. 305.13 of the Model Penal Code and should:

1. Authorize but not require the imposition of specified conditions.

2. Require that any condition imposed in an individual case be reasonably related to the correctional program of the defendant and not unduly restrictive of his liberty or incompatible with his constitutional rights.

3. Direct that conditions be fashioned on the basis of factors relating to the individual offender rather than to the offense committed.

In establishing criteria and procedures for parole revocation, the legislation should provide:

1. A parolee charged with a violation should not be detained unless there is a hearing at which probable cause to believe that the parolee did violate a condition of his parole is shown.

   a. Such a hearing should be held promptly near the locality to which the parolee is paroled.

   b. The hearing should be conducted by an impartial person other than the parole officer.

   c. The parolee should be granted notice of the charges against him, the right to present evidence, the right to confront and cross-examine witnesses against him, and the right to be represented by counsel or to have counsel appointed for him if he is indigent.

2. Parole should not be revoked unless:

a. There is substantial evidence of a violation of one of the conditions of parole.

b. The parolee, in advance of a hearing on revocation, is informed of the nature of the violation charged against him and is given the opportunity to examine the State's evidence against him.

c. The parolee is provided with a hearing on the charge of revocation. Hearing examiners should be empowered to hear and decide parole revocation cases under policies established by the parole board. At the hearing the parolee should be given the opportunity to present evidence on his behalf, to confront and cross-examine witnesses against him, and to be represented by counsel or to have counsel appointed for him if he is indigent.

d. The board or hearing examiner provides a written statement of findings, the reasons for the decision, and the evidence relied upon.

3. Time spent under parole supervision until the date of the violation for which parole is revoked should be credited against the sentence imposed by the court.

4. Judicial review of parole revocation decisions should be available to offenders.

In defining the term for which parole should be granted, the legislation should prohibit the term from extending beyond the maximum prison term imposed on the offender by the sentencing court and should authorize the parole board to discharge the parolee from parole at any time.[32]

The Pardon

Historically, the pardon evolved to remedy wrongful convictions and reduce unduly harsh sentences. Over the years, the pardoning power has been organized and reorganized in a variety of ways and has been used for such diverse purposes as ach eving political ends, compensating for inflexible legislation, and reducing some of the disabilities often incurred by offenders collaterally with conviction. As a result, the pardon process frequently has been marked by inconsistencies and a lack of uniform application.

In each of the 50 states, the pardoning power is given to the executive branch of government, the governor. Across the country, three basic administrative models for the exercise of the power have emerged. In some states, the pardon rests exclusively with the governor, although a pardon attorney may be available to advise on legal matters. In other states, a formal pardon advisory board exists which makes recommendations to the governor, but again the governor is the ultimate decision maker. Finally, some states have a pardon board with a decision-making role in contrast to an advisory status; in each of these states, the governor is a member of the pardon board. In the federal system, the power of pardon lies with the President.

It is important to note that the pardon as a process in the justice system was developed to correct deficiencies in the system. The use of the pardon may be seen as confirming the need for alterations in the system which precedes its use. For example, a criminal conviction has collateral consequences which add disqualifications and disabilities to the convicted offender in addition to those penalties imposed by a specific sentence. A number of "civil rights" are normally forfeited by a felony or serious misdemeanor conviction including the right to hold office, to vote, to serve as a juror, or to testify in court. Conviction may also bring barriers to employment or admission to particular occupations, preclusion from possession of some licenses, and so on. Although many of these rights may be restored by pardon, it seems appropriate to develop other methods for their restoration. The pardon process then could be utilized to correct errors in the administration of justice and as a final review of law enforcement, judicial and correctional decision making. To this end, the National Advisory Commission has recommended that each state enact legislation detailing the procedures governing the application by an offender for pardon and explicit guidelines for the exercise of the pardon powers by the appropriate authorities.

NOTES

[1]*Attorney General's Survey of Release Procedures, Volume IV, Parole*, U.S. Department of Justice, Washington, D.C.: U.S. Government Printing Office, 1939, p. 15.

[2]*Ibid.*

[3]*Ibid.*, p. 7.

[4]Frederick H. Wines, *Punishment and Reformation*, New York: Crowell, 1895, pp. 218–219.

[5]*Ibid.*

[6]Harry Elmer Barnes and Negley K. Teeters, *New Horizons in Criminology*, 2d ed., New York: Prentice-Hall, p. 780.

[7]*Attorney General's Survey*, p. 13.

[8]Daniel Glaser, Fred Cohen, and Vincent O'Leary, *The Sentencing and Parole Process*, Parole Decision-Making Series, U.S. Department of Health, Education, and Welfare, Washington, D.C.: U.S. Government Printing Office, 1966, pp. 10–15.

[9]Robert O. Dawson, *Sentencing: The Decision as to Type, Length, and Conditions of Sentence*, Boston: Little, Brown and Co., 1969, p. 262.

[10]Vincent O'Leary and Daniel Glaser, "The Assessment of Risk," in *The Future of*

Parole, edited by D.J. West, London: Gerald Duckworth and Co., 1972, pp. 179–82.

[11]Clark Tibbitts, "Success and Failure on Parole Can Be Predicted," *Journal of Criminal Law and Criminology,* May, 1931, quoted in Barnes and Teeters, *New Horizons in Criminology,* p. 797.

[12]Leslie T. Wilkins and P. MacNaughton-Smith, "New Prediction and Classification Methods in Criminology," *Journal of Research in Crime and Delinquency* 1 (January 1964): 19–32.

[13]Nat R. Arluke, "A Summary of Parole Rules," *NPPA Journal* 2 (January 1956): 6–13.

[14]*Certificate of Parole,* parole form H-8, U.S. Board of Parole.

[15]Nat R. Arluke, "A Summary of Parole Rules–Thirteen Years Later," *Crime and Delinquency* 15 (April, 1969): 274.

[16]*Ibid.,* p. 269.

[17]*Corrections,* National Advisory Commission on Criminal Justice Standards and Goals, Washington, D.C.: U.S. Government Printing Office, 1973, p. 405.

[18]*Ibid.*

[19]*Ibid.*

[20]Quoted in *Ibid.,* pp. 405–406.

[21]*Ibid.,* pp. 406–407.

[22]*Ibid.,* p. 407.

[23]*Ibid.,* p. 396.

[24]*Ibid.,* p. 396.

[25]Vincent O'Leary and Joan Nuffield, "A National Survey of Parole Decision-Making," *Crime and Delinquency* 19 (July 1973): 378–393.

[26]*Manual of Correctional Standards,* American Correctional Association, Washington, D. C., 1966, pp. 127–128.

[27]*Corrections,* p. 393.

[28]Public Law 293, 73d Cong., 2d Sess.: Title 4, USC 3.

[29]Ralph C. Brendes, "Interstate Supervision of Parole and Probation," *Crime and Delinquency* 14 (July 1968): 253–260.

[30]*Manual of Correctional Standards,* pp. 115–116.

[31]*Corrections,* pp. 417–436.

[32]*Ibid.,* pp. 587–590.

10 The Organization of Correctional Services

Correctional services are provided by a wide range of agencies, and except for a limited number of private volunteer organizations, these agencies are supported by public tax funds and are embedded in a variety of ways in federal, state, county, and city governments. From the very inception of our Republic there has been a confusing diversity in the ways in which governments at all levels provided for the organizational structure for managing persons charged with or convicted of violations of the criminal law. In the beginning local communities managed in informal ways as best they could the small numbers of incorrigible youths and adult criminals.[1]

With the virtual abandonment of capital and corporal punishment for most felons it obviously would have become difficult, if not impossible, for small towns and rural counties to provide for the long-term imprisonment of the occasional convicted felon. The obvious need for some centralized facility for these cases was first recognized in Pennsylvania in 1790.

McKelvey describes the Pennsylvania transition as follows:

> The [Pennsylvania] legislature in 1790 ordered the erection of a cell house in the yard of the Walnut Street Jail for the solitary confinement of men convicted of felonies, designating the old building for the separate detention of suspects, witnesses, and misdemeanants. The act directed the Walnut Street Jail authorities to receive convicts from other counties until similar provisions could be made in their jails, thus providing a state prison without committing the legislature to that policy.[2]

Barnes comments:

> The subsequent growth in population and increase in the number of delinquents made additional facilities necessary. In 1818, the Pennsylvania legislature appropriated $60,000 for erecting in Allegheny County a state peni-

233

tentiary. The first permanent achievement in the establishment of the state prison system was completed.[3]

Correctional Administration in Transition

After the State of New York authorized the erection of the State Prison at Auburn in 1816, and Pennsylvania passed the enabling legislation for the Eastern Penitentiary in Philadelphia in 1821, several other states followed quickly with the establishment of prisons for adult felons. While these institutions were authorized by state legislatures and supported from state funds, the administrative arrangements for their relationships to the states' elective officials assumed many forms. To attempt to trace the development of these administrative arrangements for each of the states would involve one in an almost unbelievable thicket of political expediences. Some general administrative patterns evolved, however. They are mentioned and discussed briefly here, chiefly because some of them persist to the present day.

Institution Board of Trustees

A board of trustees for each institution appointed by the governor of the state was the most common pattern in the beginning. The board usually had from 5 to 11 members and was authorized to appoint the prison warden, formulate general policy, and approve the budget submitted to the legislature. The state of Nevada, which has only one state prison, still has such a board known as the Board of Prison Commissioners. As time went on and state governments became larger and more centralized, these local boards were either abolished or reduced to limited advisory functions with the actual power and authority passing to a central board or a single administrator. In some of the smaller states this change has taken place only in the last decade.

Centralized State Boards

These boards have been of two kinds, ex officio boards and appointed boards. The ex officio boards were composed of officials occupying constitutional offices or cabinet posts. The membership was usually made up of such officials as the governor, the lieutenant governor, the state treasurer, the attorney general, or some other elective or appointed state official. These boards usually had general administrative authority over other state institutions and agencies as well as the prisons and reformatories.

Appointed central boards were often called by such names as The Board of Charities and Corrections. In California, the Constitution of 1879 provided for a 5-member Board of Prison Directors appointed by the governor for 10-year terms. This Board was the governing body of the state's prisons until it was replaced by a single Director of Corrections in 1944. The Correctional Schools for Juveniles were included in a State Department of Institutions until they were transferred to the Youth Authority in 1943. The Department of Institutions was preceded by a centralized Board.

Some states also created "Boards of Control" which were given broad administrative control over most of the operating agencies of state government, such as prisons, correctional schools for juveniles, mental hospitals, public health, public welfare, and similar agencies and functions.

The Single Administrator

By the 1950s, most states had created administrative departments headed by single administrators for most functions of state government. Under this general scheme, state correctional institutions normally were either under the jurisdiction of a separate department of corrections or were under a division of corrections included within a department of public institutions, or a department of public welfare.

Beginning in the early 1960s, many of the states began grouping departments of government under the "umbrella" or "super agency" plan. This concept was intended to reduce the number of state executives responsible directly to the governor and to foster closer working relationships between state departments which had common or closely related interests. For example, there are, on the surface at least, close relationships between adult corrections and youth corrections, and between each of them and public welfare, mental hygiene, public health, and vocational rehabilitation.

Consequently, we are seeing now more and more states creating "umbrella" type agencies with the state correctional institutions and agencies being grouped together as a department or a division *but* as a part of a larger administrative agency under names like Department of Health and Welfare, Department of Mental Health and Corrections, or Department of Health and Rehabilitative Services.

These organizational patterns at the state level of government have been changing rapidly in recent years, influenced partly by the American Correctional Association's *Manual of Correctional Standards* which has recommended consistently for many years that "The correctional system should be administered by a *separate* state department," and that "The department should have a single administrative head."[4]

The other influences toward grouping the state correction department with other related state agencies come from those professional experts in government who would make state government more logical, better coordinated, and responsive to the total needs of the people rather than to a complex multiplicity of unrelated special interests.

The trend toward centralization of correctional administration and the related one of grouping corrections with other agencies under a single cabinet officer are not necessarily in conflict, but since both changes are taking place at the same time, it is important that they not be confused.

The Present Scene

The term corrections encompasses all of the activities, functions, and services which government supplies or should provide for all juvenile and adult offenders from the time a court orders them confined or placed under correctional supervision until they are legally discharged. Starting with this definition, it is clear that in no state of the Union with the possible exception of Vermont does the state government provide all the services, and in many cases even the state services are fragmented and distributed among several state agencies. There are many authorities and national organizations pressing for a unification of correctional services at the state level and for a stronger role for state government in direct services, standard setting, and financial support of those services now supplied principally by cities and counties.

The Advisory Commission on Intergovernmental Relations surveyed this confused and fragmented picture as of October, 1971.[5] In summary, the nine general functions most likely to be seen as separate correctional entities are listed in the following table with the distribution of jurisdiction amongst local government, local and state government combined, and state government.

It is apparent that prisons, parole, and juvenile correctional schools are almost exclusively state functions. Juvenile detention and jails are still principally local, but some states are beginning to move but not strongly into this area. Next to jails, probation processes by far the greatest number of correctional cases, and in view of that fact, it is interesting to note that state governments are partially involved in adult probation supervision in 13 states, and in 26 states adult probation administration is exclusively a state function. Juvenile probation which is most often attached to the juvenile courts is a local or a state/local function in all but 6 of the 50 states. It is important in this connection to remember that the decision to grant or revoke proba-

Function	Local	State/Local	State
Juvenile Detention	40	2	8
Juvenile Probation	24	20	6
Juvenile Institutions	0	0	50
Juvenile Aftercare	2	5	43
Misdemeanant Probation	11	13	26
Adult Probation	11	13	26
Jails and Adult Institutions for Misdemeanants	43	1	6
Institutions for Adult Felons	0	0	50
Parole	0	0	50

tion in each case is a judicial prerogative. The supervision of persons under probation on the contrary is an executive function just as is the management of jails and prisons.

Where the state government and local governments are both involved the patterns vary. In some, the state provides part of the funds and sets minimum standards, but the operations are local; in others the populous metropolitan counties maintain jurisdiction, leaving the less populated jurisdictions to state support and state administration.

Fragmentation by Function

We have seen that there is great organizational fragmentation of correctional operations among the various levels of government, but this is further compounded by the fact that within each state, city, or county government there are examples of Balkanization at its worst. Some of this is merely historical and continues for no better reason than the inertia found in most bureaucracies. We have pointed out earlier that there is little logic in a city police department maintaining a jail a few blocks or a few minutes away from the county jail. Modern municipal police administrators are beginning to accept the idea that they should get out of the jail business, but when it is suggested that an elective county sheriff who is basically a police official is urged to turn his jail over to a county or state department of corrections, the response is quite different. The jail is too often a substantial part of the sheriff's administrative principality and political patronage.

When one looks at the community supervision of probationers and parolees, the situation seems even more illogical from an organizational and efficiency standpoint. Since the clients of the correctional system come principally from poor families and poor neighborhoods, they tend to be geographically concentrated in the poorer sections of large cities. To illustrate the point in a specific jurisdiction consider these facts in the City and County of San Francisco:

Population	715,674 (1970)
Area	45 square miles
Federal Probationers	300
Federal Parolees	150
Juvenile Court Probationers	2,200
Adult Probationers (Superior Court)	5,300
State Youth Authority Parolees	380
State Prison Parolees	1,600
Total	9,930

Here we have the spectacle of nearly ten thousand committed juveniles and convicted adult law violators living in 45 square miles who are presumed to be supervised by *five* different public agencies sometimes operating in the same square block and occasionally in the same family, the same school, the same employment agencies, the same courts, and the same police agencies. Here it is not as the old saying has it, that the "left hand doesn't know what the right is doing," but that the index finger doesn't even work with the thumb.

Another urban jurisdiction studied a few years ago shall be nameless because some improvement has taken place since, but there, in an area of 50 square miles and a population of 800,000 people, there were over 5,000 adjudicated but not confined offenders supervised by 6 independent and separate agencies of government.

This kind of irrational fragmentation can be contrasted with the State of Wisconsin where all probation and parole services for both juveniles and adults are under the administrative direction of a single unit in the State Division of Corrections which in turn is a part of the State Department of Health and Social Services.

In those states in which the state's correctional functions are limited almost exclusively to the administration of adult and juvenile correctional institutions and the aftercare supervision of inmates paroled from them, one continues to find an administrative separation between the state agency responsible for juveniles and young adults on the one hand, and the department charged with the operation of the prisons on the other. A still further

238

separation is often found wherein the agency which administers the prisons is a state department of corrections and the parole services are administratively responsible to an independent parole board.

Need for Centralization

The National Advisory Commission on Criminal Justice Standards and Goals recommends the following on the question of administrative structure for correctional services in the states:

> Each state should enact legislation by 1978 to unify all correctional facilities and programs. The board of parole may be administratively part of an overall statewide correctional services agency, but it should be autonomous in its decisionmaking authority and separate from field services. Programs for adult, juvenile, and youthful offenders that should be within the agency include:
> 1. Services for persons awaiting trial.
> 2. Probation supervision.
> 3. Institutional confinement.
> 4. Community-based programs, whether prior to or during institutional confinement.
> 5. Parole and other aftercare programs.
> 6. All programs for misdemeanants including probation, confinement, community-based programs, and parole.[6]

A state government undertaking to assume complete responsibility for all correctional functions within its jurisdiction must address certain problems of singular difficulty. Among them are:

a. Fiscal Support

As it now stands, the states pay out of their tax revenues the total cost for both capital outlay and operation of those institutions and services which the law places under the control of its executive branch. If jails or probation services were made state rather than local functions, the state budget would be increased accordingly and the local budgets relieved of the burden. This shift in costs from one tax base to another is likely always to be the most serious obstacle.

Resistance to change from the state political decision makers will be chiefly based on monetary factors.

Opposition from local sources will arise from the vested interests of local political figures and from local employees who fear that their salaries, retirement, and status may be adversely affected. There will also be much rhetoric about the sacredness of local control and the fear of centralized bureaucracy, but the real obstacles will be essentially economic self-interest.

Local politicians and administrators are almost invariably more than willing to accept state or federal funds, but at the same time almost as invariably resist having these higher levels of government control how they use the money. State subsidies to local government normally carry with them the requirement that certain minimum standards of performance be met in order to qualify for the grants. In all kinds of public services from education to social welfare, local governments are looking more and more to sources of support other than their local tax revenues. Correctional services have been slow to seek subsidy support, but there is now a clear trend in that direction. The operation of local corrections may be turned over gradually to state government, but more probably the compromise plan of accepting partial support and the enforcement of state standards will occur.

b. The Juvenile/Adult Dichotomy

The care and management of delinquent and incorrigible children and youths historically have been a concern of both private and public welfare agencies. The philosophy that holds that these young people need protection and sympathetic care rather than punishment and legalistic controls is generally supported by most citizens and political leaders. In practice, the real problem arises because a child does not automatically become a responsible adult by reaching some arbitrary age. Most people would agree that a person under fourteen ought to be dealt with as a child, and if circumstances require, should be a social welfare case rather than one for the criminal justice system. Most would also agree, now that the voting age has been reduced to eighteen, that after that age an offender should be considered to be personally responsible for his acts and while youth and inexperience should be taken into account, the law, nevertheless, should treat him as an adult.

On the other hand, the most crime-prone age group is now made up of boys fourteen, fifteen, sixteen, and seventeen years of age. It is in these years that criminal careers are launched. Strong, well-financed, and intelligently led programs of delinquency prevention and corrections are or should be the first priority of the correctional mission of the society. There are continuing arguments against placing these particular services in the same agencies which deal with adults. There are equally persuasive voices saying that while adolescent delinquency should be given special emphasis, it is nonetheless part and parcel of a bigger set of problems and that those who would split it apart from the rest of the criminal justice system are pursuing a self-defeating course which is motivated more by emotion than by administrative logic.

c. Penalty Decision Making

The citizenry and the local police make most of the minor and many of the larger decisions as to whether or not a particular person at a particular time and under specific circumstances is to be received as a client for the criminal justice process. If the victim of an offense does not make a complaint and the police do not make an arrest or issue a citation, the process ordinarily goes no farther even though there has been an unquestioned violation of the law. Once the accused offender is arrested and charged, a more formal and complex process of decision making begins. At each decision point from the filing of a complaint to the finding of guilt some of the cases are cycled out of the process until the few who are held to be guilty and responsible face the bench for imposition of sentence.

It is at this point that the finely structured legal processes resolve into limbo, and an amorphous mixture of custom, personal bias, politics, and human uncertainty take over.[7] Sentencing, term fixing, and paroling are part and parcel of the case decision-making process. Just where judicial decision making leaves off and correctional decisions begin is a crucial issue in the management of convicted defendants. The trial judge, except in a few jurisdictions, has wide latitude within statutory limits to fix a sentence which, as long as it is legal, cannot be appealed. As a consequence, the disparity in the severity of trial court sentences has been nothing less than a national scandal for many years.[8] There have been several approaches to alleviating, if not solving, this problem. None of these has been notably successful. Briefly, they are:

1. Annual Sentencing Institutes for criminal trial court judges. That these have been useful as an educational process is unquestioned but each judge is still left free to exercise his personal discretion without review or supervision in individual cases.

2. Statutory provision in a few states permitting a defendant to appeal his sentence to a higher court entirely on the grounds of excessive severity of the penalty. Since appeals cost money and most defendants are poor, this remedy has not had far-reaching effects, even in the few states where the law makes it possible.

3. Sentencing panels[9] of three or more judges have been recommended

and are in use in a few jurisdictions. This concept is intended to overcome to a limited degree the personal biases of the single judge who tried the case or accepted the guilty plea. The process is better, no doubt, than to leave sentencing entirely to a single human being. This approach is not widely practiced and even if it were, it could not do more than place a very limited curb on the few judges who are either excessively severe or inordinately lenient.

4. The indeterminate sentence for those felony defendants committed to state and federal prisons is perhaps the most time-honored alleged remedy for the disparity problem. In those jurisdictions in which a degree of indefiniteness is permitted by law, it should be pointed out that it applies only to those committed to prison and not to the much larger number of defendants who receive probationary sentences. It is also important to note that legislators in most states insist upon statutory minimum terms for most felonies, thus removing much of whatever discretion might have been left to the term-fixing and paroling authority, except to permit them on balance to be even more punitive than probably was intended by most of the legislators.

In states with a very large volume of cases, like New York and California, it has been necessary for a number of years past to enlarge the membership of parole boards to as many as 11 members who then operate in panels of 2 or 3. Accordingly, the criticism is now made that disparity arises even between panels of the same board. With a few exceptions the members of these boards are essentially laymen and often are chosen for political reasons quite extraneous to their personal or professional qualifications. For a variety of reasons the indeterminate or indefinite sentence is now coming under general attack, not only in the United States but elsewhere in the world.

5. Appellate monitoring and review of the entire sentencing process on a routine basis may be the solution. For a more extensive discussion of this concept the reader is referred to *A New Look at Sentencing* by Richard A. McGee.[10] Parole boards which have had delegated to them a large share of the decision-making power in felony cases now may be on their way out, but if so, the judicial system of each state must find ways to overcome irrational and erratic sentencing and releasing practices.

d. Community-Based Programs v. Central State Institutions

It may seem at first blush that should state governments assume full administrative and fiscal responsibility for all correctional services that such a change might operate against the current movement toward the so-called "community-based" alternatives to institutional incarceration. This would be a very superficial view. We have only to look for a parallel development in the mental health field. The massive overpopulated state mental hospitals are being replaced all over the country with local mental hygiene clinics, day care centers, and night hospitals located in the communities where the patients and their families and friends reside. This does not mean that central mental hospitals necessarily will ever be entirely abandoned any more than a few centralized state prisons will become unnecessary.

What is more likely to happen in corrections, as in mental health programs, is a statewide unified system with the state government providing most of the financial support, regional planning, research, a central information system, statewide personnel training, administrative and professional standards and such central institutions as cannot be efficiently operated in local communities. Regional correctional administrations could be set up in the large counties and groups of smaller counties, and as much of the direct operational functions as possible could be contracted out by the state government to local agencies already existing or to be created according to need.

If the community-based concept in corrections is ever to meet its potentialities it must be a part of a well-coordinated statewide plan designed to deal with the total constellation of correctional services rather than as a fragmented and sometimes competing component of the whole.

The Organization of a State Department of Correctional Services

Whether a state department of corrections has the limited responsibility for operating state prisons, reformatories, and parole aftercare, or whether its jurisdiction extends to juvenile programs, local detention, and probation, it must have certain organizational characteristics. Space does not permit anything more than an extended outline here rather than an elaborate exposition which might require a full-length book.

1. Placement of the State Department of Corrections in State Government

A department of state government is merely a grouping of related executive functions provided for by law and placed under the direction of an administrative board or an appointed executive.

Normally, the director or commissioner heading a state department of corrections will be appointed by the governor of the state and will report directly to him. In a few states there is a state board of corrections, the members of which are appointed by the governor usually for fixed and overlapping terms. In some situations this board is merely advisory to the director, and in others, its role is similar to that of the board of directors of a private corporation, in which case the board has the authority under the law to appoint the director, usually with the approval of the governor, and often with the additional provision that the appointment be confirmed by the state senate. If the state board is the actual governing body, a director or commissioner is then in effect the executive officer of the board.

In states where there is considerable political instability and the heads of state departments are regarded as political patronage positions it is believed by some students of the problem that the existence of a part-time lay board between the governor and the director is a protection for the director against partisan political interference. Whether the director is appointed directly by the governor or by a board probably makes no essential difference, provided the board is made up of responsible members who will limit themselves to the formulation of broad policy and refrain from interfering in routine matters of administration; and further, that the governor avoids using the position of director as a vehicle for partisan political patronage.

In those states in which the executive branch of government is divided into a limited number of cabinet level (umbrella type) departments or agencies there continues to be some debate as to which grouping of state departments the correctional department should belong. In states where this plan has been adopted the department of corrections is usually grouped with such other departments as mental hygiene, public health, public welfare, health care services, and vocational rehabilitation. On the other hand, because the correctional agency is a part of the total criminal justice system of the state there are those who argue that corrections should be grouped with the public safety agencies which usually include the state police or state highway patrol, the state fire marshal, state department of criminal identification and investigation, and state department of emergency services (civil defense) and the state militia.

In those states in which the attorney general is an elective officer rather than one appointed by the governor, it is sometimes argued that the correctional function should be placed in the department of justice, headed by the attorney general, rather than in the governor's cabinet. This may seem logical on the surface, but in view of the fact that a state governor has a great deal more power and influence with the legislature and over the state budget than any other elective officer, correctional departments are much more likely to prosper if they are placed directly or indirectly under the state's chief executive, the governor, rather than under some lesser elective official.

If the recommendations of the National Advisory Commission on Criminal Justice Standards and Goals (referred to on page 239) were to be adopted in their entirety in any of the major states, the very size and complexity of the problems and services encompassed in such a unified department of corrections (including programs for adults and juveniles, local detention, and probation), would almost dictate that the correctional agency be a cabinet-level department with a direct rather than an indirect line to the governor.

2. The Head of the State Correctional Agency

This officer usually bears the title of director or commissioner, depending on the practices of the state involved. Whether he reports directly to the governor, through an intervening policy board, or through another cabinet officer who has oversight over a group of state agencies, it is important that the statutes of the state be framed in such a way as to provide some assurance that this state official be a person with substantial direct experience in the correctional field, and that he be a person of proven administrative ability. The various states have attempted to safeguard the qualifications and tenure of the head of the correctional services in different ways. One method is to provide by law that the director be appointed for a term of years, usually from four to seven. This has an advantage to the occupant of the position, but it has a disadvantage in the event that the incumbent is or becomes, while in office, incompetent or ineffective. More often than not, the heads of state agencies are appointed by the governor to serve "at the pleasure of the governor" and usually with the advice and consent of the senate. In such cases the legislature may write into the statute certain minimum qualifications for the appointee, thus limiting to some extent the discretion of the appointing power. A third method that has sometimes been employed is to provide by law that some appropriate ex officio body, such as the civil service commission or a panel of citizens made up of the presidents of state voluntary associations, like the state correctional association, the state teachers association, the state medical association, and the state peace officers association, be empowered to submit a list of three to five qualified candidates from which the governor would be required to select one for appointment.

In all honesty it must be said that none of these methods which attempt to limit the discretion of the appointing power of the governor ever work perfectly. There is also a school of thought in government which holds that, since the appointing power is elected by the people, and since he is responsible for the performance of his appointees, that no more obstacles than are absolutely necessary should be placed in the way of his having a free choice of his appointees with the possible exception of confirmation by the senate.

It should also be mentioned that in the few states that do have a board of corrections which has the power to appoint the administrative head of the department, and where there is a strong merit system in the state service, that the executive head of the department might well be a civil servant and subject to the selection processes and tenure provided by that system.

In the end, custom and tradition are likely to have more influence than any of the artificial proposals designed to prevent the appointing power from making unwise appointments.

3. The Paroling Authority

As we have previously discussed, most states have either a full-time or a part-time board ordinarily made up of three or more persons who have certain powers defined in the law to release on parole persons committed to the state prisons. The jurisdiction and the administrative placement of this board is a matter of continuing debate. The parole boards themselves are usually strong advocates of the idea that they should be completely independent and separate from any other state agency. There is usually no question about the board's independence with respect to its decision-making authority in individual cases. On the other hand, there is disagreement on the question of whether or not the board's power should be limited to granting and revoking parole or whether, in addition, it should be the administrative head of the personnel responsible for the supervision of parolees. As pointed out earlier, the National Advisory Commission on Criminal Justice Standards and Goals recommends that the board be placed for fiscal and housekeeping purposes within the state department of corrections, that it not have administrative jurisdiction over the parole officers, and that it be independent only insofar as its case decision-making powers are concerned. It is important to note that since the *Morrissey* v. *Brewer* decision of the U.S. Supreme Court in 1971, there has been a veritable explosion of court decisions limiting the arbitrary powers of parole boards. These decisions go principally to the constitutional issues of "due process" and the right of the defendant to be represented by counsel when decisions are being made affecting the prisoner's or parolee's liberty. As was pointed out earlier in the discussion of the indeterminate sentence, parole boards are being pressed more and more into the judicial rather than the executive mold, and it may be that many, if not most, of the functions now vested in parole boards will have to be returned to the judicial branch of government.

Parole board members in all but a handful of states are appointed by the governor, and almost invariably are appointed to serve terms fixed by statute. The most common term is four years, but this varies from state to state, usually in the direction of the terms being longer. The relatively long terms of office of parole board members are intended to insure as much political independence in terms of their decision-making powers as is feasible. On the other hand, when parole board members are appointed they usually get some general advice with respect to broad policies from the appointing power. Furthermore, with rare exceptions, when a parole board member is nearing the end of his term he will begin thinking about reappointment. Since the governor who appointed him may not be in office, it is only normal human behavior for him to attempt to implement parole policies which for one reason or another he is led to believe will be pleasing to the man who will have the power to reappoint. As a consequence, the concept of a completely independent parole board is to a large extent a myth. Their independence can only be assured if the governor and other members of his administration assume a sincere stance that they want the board to be independent and that they will maintain a hands-off policy. Since governors are both politicians and human beings, this is rather too much to expect in most cases.

Parole boards are under two opposite kinds of pressures in terms of policy. The "get tough on crime" advocates watch for every opportunity to criticize the parole board for releasing prisoners too soon. This can be a very persuasive influence from the political standpoint. The reverse pressure, which is not as visible but nevertheless quite as potent, comes from those who wish to maintain the state budget at a minimum level. The director of the corrections department and the parole board will both feel this pressure, chiefly from the fiscal officers of the administration and from the finance committees of the legislature.

Some states have more than one parole board. California, for example, has the Adult Authority responsible for parole decisions for men committed to the jurisdiction of the director of corrections and sentenced to prison. The Women's Board of Prison Terms and Paroles has the same function with respect to women committed to state prisons. The Youth Authority Board generally speaking has the same powers with respect to persons committed to the California Youth Authority. In that state, criminal court cases in which the accused is under 21 years of age at the time of apprehension may, if the sentencing judge chooses, commit the convicted defendant either to prison or to the Youth Authority. These youthful cases may be released to parole supervision at any time after they have been received and processed by the Youth Authority. The Youth Authority Board also has the power to revoke paroles if the defendant has not reached the age of 25 and has not been discharged.

Juvenile Court cases under the age of 18 years committed to the California Youth Authority also come under the releasing and revocation powers of the Youth Authority Board. This is an unusual situation, since juvenile court commitments are regarded as civil rather than criminal commitments. The power to release them and place them under community supervision or to discharge them entirely in most states rests with the responsible director of the agency or with the juvenile court which committed them.

The general practice in most of the states is that there be only one parole board for adults of both sexes, and that there be no such board for juvenile court commitments.

4. Qualifications of Parole Board Members

The statutes providing for parole boards usually include some broad language intended to guide the governor in selecting qualified persons for appointment as members of parole boards. In most jurisdictions this language is so general that it is more advisory than effectively limiting on the governor's selections. Also, in an effort to maintain a nonpartisan policy toward parole some state laws provide that the board be bipartisan; in other words, in a board of five members not more than three shall be of one political party. This provision is also of questionable value, because if the appointing power is a member of one political party and is required to make an appointment of a person who is a member of another party, the selection of that person may turn out to be part of a political bargain with some influential politician of the other party.

Other efforts to control by law the membership and representation on parole boards include requiring at least one member or two members of a board be women. It has also become common practice, if not required by law, for the governor to select some of the members of a parole board because of their racial or ethnic origin, or their religious affiliations. It has also been observed in some jurisdictions that if there is an influential body of opinion impinging on parole and correctional practices that some member of that group will be appointed to the board. This is especially common with respect to police and labor organizations.

Correctional Policy—Origins and Enforcement

Policy in the administrative context is defined as a settled or agreed upon course of action. One of the most important roles of the administrative head of a department of corrections is to set policy in a wide variety of general and specific areas and to enforce adherence to these policies by all members of the total organization.

In the broader sweep of governmental responsibility in a democracy, policy derives from a consensus of the beliefs and customs of the people. The appointive head of a state department must have a sense of what is right and acceptable, but generations before him have settled most of the broader issues through the instrumentality of the law. The basic law of the land in broad-stroke language is contained, as we all know, in our federal Constitution. Even constitutional law, however, is dynamic and subject to interpretation and reinterpretation by the courts as social and political conditions and public attitudes change. Each state of the Union also has its own constitution which cannot be inconsistent with that of the federal government.

As a consequence, the first cut at public policy in terms of law in our country is constitutional. Built on this basic framework, there has developed a massive collection of court decisions based on constitutional issues. This "case law" has an unusually powerful impact on criminal justice practitioners and especially upon police and correctional administrators, because our federal and state constitutions were framed with particular concern for the protection of the rights of individual private citizens and for the curbing of the arbitrary exercise of power by the agents of government. A society cannot be governed without the exercise of power, but the abuse of power can be just as destructive as its absence.

Statutory law generated almost continuously by the federal Congress and state legislatures is the next level of policy making of direct concern to the responsible head of a state department of corrections. These statutes in turn are subject to judicial interpretation as their application is questioned in case litigation.

There is still another level of policy based upon law interpretation which is of special import to state directors of corrections. Each state has an attorney general who in effect is the legal counsel of the executive branch of state government. When an executive of a state department has doubts as to what the law is on some specific issue he may formulate his question and ask the attorney general for a formal opinion. It has been said that these interpretations are "only the opinions of another lawyer" but to the state official they have the effect of law, unless or until the issue is tried in court or the law is amended by the legislature.

A straightforward example in the correctional area illustrates the situation. The sheriff of a populous county found that the state department of corrections was keeping an average of about 20 state parolees in his jail for periods ranging from a few days to a month, pending decisions on charges of parole violation. The sheriff argued that these men were state wards and therefore an unfair burden on the county budget. He asked two questions of the attorney general: 1) Was he required by law to accept custody of these men on a warrant from the state parole board? and 2) If so, should the state not be required to pay his county for the cost of their maintenance? The attorney general ruled that the sheriff was indeed required to accept custody of the parolees and that there was no law requiring the state to reimburse the county for the costs. The attorney general, however, added the gratuitous comment that, while there was no legal obligation for the state to reimburse the county, it seemed to him that there did exist a "moral" obligation to do so.

As a consequence, the county was joined by several other counties and submitted invoices of substantial magnitude to the state department of corrections. The state refused to pay. The counties brought suit in a state court. The counties lost. The counties had an obvious alternative. They might have attempted to have the legislature amend the law in such a way as to place the financial burden on the state. Undoubtedly, they chose the lawsuit because of a conviction that the governor who was concerned about another burden on his budget would veto the bill, even if the legislature passed it.

So we have seen that state corrections administrators are hedged about by laws and customs of more than usual complexity. A director is further limited and guided by the requirements which may be laid down for his guidance by the elective officer (usually the state's governor) who appointed him and who has an inherent right to insist that his appointive department heads conform not only to the law but to the broad policies which he believes were persuasive to the voters in selecting him for office.

Governors being human beings like everyone else tend to give more emphasis to some aspects of government than others. Also, since they have risen to their present positions by the political process, they usually have a keen sense of what the public wants of state government at any given time. Conversely, a governor needs to know what the public does *not* want. The development of the finest penal and correctional system in the land is unlikely to be the top priority of a gubernatorial campaign platform, but conversely, a scandal involving early parole of a politically powerful gangster or a destructive prison riot may be the rock on which a governor's political career is wrecked.

Whatever a governor's policies affecting corrections may be, they are an important factor in the policy framework within which more technical and specific policies and programs must operate.

Having read thus far, one might wonder what is left for the correctional administrator except to carry on the routine business of implementing established policy and maintaining the system. Fortunately, for the vitality of the system both legal and political policy in corrections have been stated in rather broad general terms until very recently. Traditionally, the courts had assumed a "hands off" policy with respect to the powers of administrators and parole boards in the internal management of prisons and the discipline of offenders on parole. It was inevitable, no doubt, that the arbitrary and sometimes indiscreet exercise of authority over correctional wards should have brought on a veritable flood of judicial interventions aimed at protecting the basic rights of convicted persons.[11]

This "outside" concern with correctional policy is currently forcing responsible administrators to define their policies more precisely, to reduce more of them to written statements, and to institute procedures to enforce careful adherence to policies.

No modern correctional department can operate any longer according to vague customs or upon the personal caprice of institution superintendents or parole supervisors.

Within the framework of the law a correctional agency needs to have some broad philosophical convictions about its role in the social and political scheme of human affairs. Some agencies assume that this is a nebulous set of general ideas which do not need to be stated in explicit language. Others treat the subject in a formal written *Statement of Policy* or merely include it as an introduction to the departmental rule book.

Rules, regulations, and manuals of procedure are as essential to orderly correctional administration as is the basic body of law upon which they are based. Such a book of regulations is composed not only of general guides for subordinate managers and personnel, but is in effect a kind of compilation of specific *dos* and *don'ts* covering a complete range of subject matter, from prisoner visiting to regulation of the food services, and from the procedures for administering prisoner discipline to minimum standards for medical treatment. For a quick overview of the subjects covered in a well-developed set of rules and regulations of a state department of corrections, the table of contents of the "Director's Rules" for the State of California in 1974 are reproduced below:

TABLE OF CONTENTS

Rules and Regulations of the Director
of Corrections
State of California

Section I. INMATE RULE BOOK

General Information—Laws Applicable to Inmates and Visitors.

The Organization of Correctional Services

Section II. GENERAL INSTITUTIONAL REGULATIONS

Chapter 4. General Institutional Regulations

Article 1. Public Information and Community Relations
Article 2. Security
Article 3. Escapes
Article 4. Disorders and Emergencies
Article 5. Inmate Discipline
Article 6. Segregation and Isolation
Article 7. Medical Services

Chapter 5. Personnel

Article 1. Institution Heads
Article 2. Employee Rules
Article 3. Services to Employees
Article 4. General Personnel Regulations
Article 5. Camp Regulations

There can be no general or fixed pattern for the organization of the central or headquarters office of the director of a state department of corrections, because state governments vary so much in size, as well as in the provisions of the law which created them. There are certain basic functions, however, which are common to all. The differences from one state to another in the ways in which these functions are administered will depend in part on the style and preferences of the director himself, and in a larger sense, by the numbers and kinds of deputies, assistants, and functional staff specialists the total operation can support.

The director himself, whether he reports to a board, to the governor, or to an intervening cabinet officer, is the person in command in the military sense. He will normally be the appointing power of all subordinate personnel and is in all respects the chief administrative officer of the department. He will ordinarily have at least one deputy director who is his "alter ego," and who carries any duties, responsibilities, or powers the director wishes to assign to him. The administrative "chain of command" extends from the director and his chief deputy to all heads of institutions, directors of field service units and staff services divisions.

Normally, all other headquarters staff are employed to supervise operational functions but they derive their influence from their specialized knowl-

253

edge and skill and not because any official power is vested in them.

The principal functions requiring central departmental supervision may be grouped and labeled as follows:

A. Business Management Functions
 1) Budget planning and control
 2) Accounting
 3) Property control
 4) Procurement
 5) Plant maintenance
 6) Building construction
 7) Food services and controls
B. Inmate Custody and Institutional Security
 1) Inmate discipline
 2) Inmate records
 3) Visiting
 4) Security and sanitation inspections
C. Industries and Production
 1) Factory management
 2) Farm operations
 3) Camp operations
 4) Product marketing
 5) Hobby work management

D. Inmate Care and Welfare
 1) Medical and health care services
 2) Education and training
 3) Recreation
 4) Religion
 5) Classification and counseling
 6) Release services and placement
 7) Social services
E. General Administration
 1) Personnel management
 2) Personnel training and education
 3) Public relations
 4) Research and statistics
 5) Program planning
 6) Legislative and control agency liaison
 7) Relations with local correctional agencies, such as jails, probation departments, and courts.

In the five groupings listed above there are 30 more or less specific functions and many of these might be subdivided even further. It can be seen readily enough that only in the very largest and best supported departments could one expect to find a full-time staff specialist for every function. Conversely, a function like budget control or accounting even in a very small operation will require the work of several persons.

Ideally, each function which represents an occupational specialty should be supervised by at least one qualified staff person. In practice this very seldom will be the case. The strength of the director's staff in this respect will depend on the workload and on the priority order in which the various staff functions are placed by the director and other policymakers in the state government.

Societal Relationships

As we have seen, a state department of corrections is involved in a complex set of relationships within itself and within the state government and its political subdivisions. These relationships are imperatives, but there is a whole world of other forces surrounding the system which in a variety of subtle or sometimes arbitrary ways affect the department's well-being.

At the risk of appearing to explain an extraordinarily complex set of administrative and political relationships by a mathematical-mechanical model, the diagram in Figure 10-1 is presented in an effort to give the reader a superficial view of the kind of working environment or "force field" in which the director of a state department of corrections must operate. Any such diagram has several limitations. In addition to being a static skeletal picture of a moving, ever-shifting scene, it is only two dimensional, while the real situation actually has four dimensions. The other two are depth and time. The intensity of the relationships varies, depending on current circumstances and timing. For example, there is a continuous relationship with the legislature, its committees and individual members, but these are more intense during budget hearings or at times when a special committee may be investigating some activity or problem in the department.

Going back to Figure 10-1 we see the director at the apex of a hierarchical pyramid with the conventional arrangement of senior executives and staff specialists near the top, the subordinate operating executives and employees below, and the wards (prisoners and parolees) of the system at the bottom. What such graphic depictions of an organizational structure usually omit is a representation of the more important and less formalized conglomerate of outside forces which impinge upon the director and the organization which he heads.

We have chosen to represent this external force field by an enclosing but open-ended curve known as a parabola. This curve is especially appropriate because instead of an apex it has a focus (a point) and a directrix (a straight line). The curve is plotted so that the distance from any point on the curve to the focus is equal to the shortest distance from that point to the directrix line. The relevant characteristic of this curve is that any signal (light beam or sound) originating at the focus (director) is reflected from the curve and projected in parallel lines out to infinity. Conversely, any signal entering the curve from without is reflected with great intensity to the focus. Hence, the director is officially at the *apex* of his own hierarchical pyramid and at the same time is the *focus* of the larger world whose inhabitants from time to time attempt to make the director's affairs their particular business. In re-

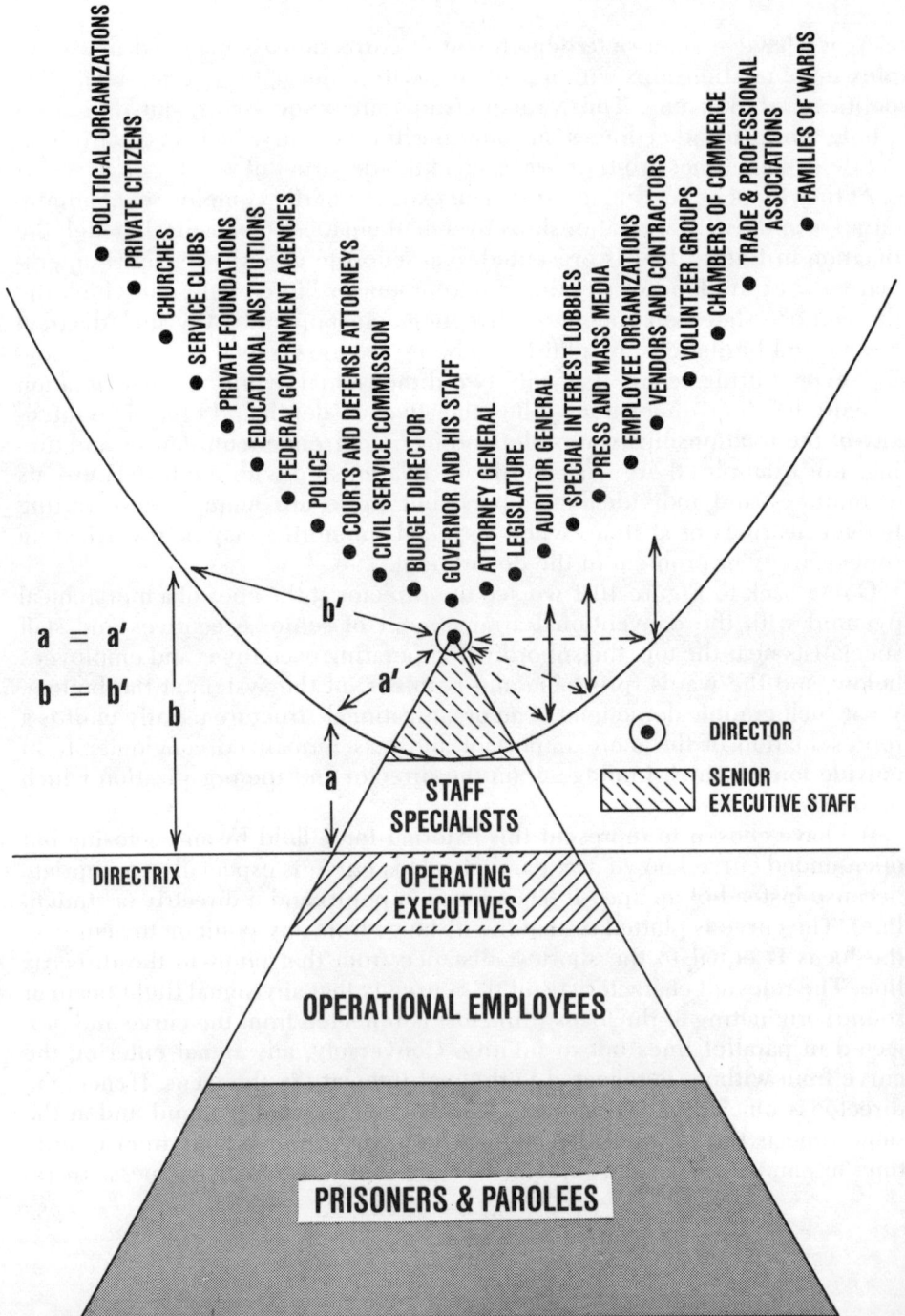

FIGURE 10–1
The Executive Pyramid and the Political Parabola

POLITICAL ORGANIZATIONS
PRIVATE CITIZENS
CHURCHES
SERVICE CLUBS
PRIVATE FOUNDATIONS
EDUCATIONAL INSTITUTIONS
FEDERAL GOVERNMENT AGENCIES
POLICE
COURTS AND DEFENSE ATTORNEYS
CIVIL SERVICE COMMISSION
BUDGET DIRECTOR
GOVERNOR AND HIS STAFF
ATTORNEY GENERAL
LEGISLATURE
AUDITOR GENERAL
SPECIAL INTEREST LOBBIES
PRESS AND MASS MEDIA
EMPLOYEE ORGANIZATIONS
VENDORS AND CONTRACTORS
VOLUNTEER GROUPS
CHAMBERS OF COMMERCE
TRADE & PROFESSIONAL ASSOCIATIONS
FAMILIES OF WARDS

a = a'
b = b'

b

a

DIRECTRIX

b'

a'

DIRECTOR

SENIOR EXECUTIVE STAFF

STAFF SPECIALISTS

OPERATING EXECUTIVES

OPERATIONAL EMPLOYEES

PRISONERS & PAROLEES

verse, the director and his associates may choose to influence, positively or negatively, some particular segment of the forces within the parabolic dish.

To discuss in detail the relationships, communications, and negotiations between the management of the corrections department and each of the entities represented in the diagram would go far beyond the scope of this chapter, but it is very important for the reader to understand something of the nature and extent of the outside "force field" as it applies to a state department of corrections. It is worthy of note also that this concept has general applications in other governmental fields and the basic idea is as valid for a small organization as for a very large one; and has its applications in federal, county, and city government as well.

Penal and Correctional Systems of the Federal Government

The federal government of the United States has maintained two criminal justice systems distinct from the states since the very beginning of the Republic. One of these maintains jurisdiction over the active members of the military forces, and the other is the federal civil jurisdiction which administers the criminal laws enacted by the Congress.

The Federal Criminal Jurisdiction—Nonmilitary

There is a substantial growing body of federal criminal law which applies where no state has jurisdiction, as for example, in the District of Columbia, on federal reservations, on the high seas, in interstate commerce, or in situations in which the federal government has an overriding interest such as in counterfeiting of currency, smuggling, violation of the internal revenue laws, and even in bank robberies where the deposits are insured by the federal government.

Persons charged with violations of the federal criminal law are tried in the United States District Courts. The judicial system is composed of 89 District Courts, 9 Circuit Courts (regional Courts of Appeal), and the United States Supreme Court.

The administrative functions of the federal criminal justice system are under the jurisdiction of the United States Department of Justice headed by the Attorney General. The Criminal Division of the Department of Justice is responsible for the United States prosecutors and the United States marshals. The investigative branch of the system is the Federal Bureau of Investigation (FBI) and the prison system is administered by the United States

Bureau of Prisons. Also, there is in the Department of Justice a separate Parole Board composed of eight members. The probation service is supervised by the Administrative Office of the Federal Courts in Washington, D.C., but as a practical matter, the probation officers are under the control of the U.S. District Court judges. These probation officers also supervise parolees released from the federal prisons.

Most defendants awaiting judicial processing who are confined in jail in lieu of bail are kept in local county jails. Those convicted defendants who receive jail sentences of one year or less are also confined in local jails. Because of the relatively small numbers of "jail" cases in any court district, the federal government normally enters into contracts with local governments for the confinement of these cases.

Until about the turn of the century all federal defendants sentenced to prison terms of one year and a day to life normally served their sentences in state prisons under contractual arrangements with the several states. This is still the case in a limited number of special cases, including some of the women and occasional cases of persons condemned to death.

Beginning with the opening of the U.S. Penitentiary at McNeil Island, Washington, in 1889,* the U.S. Department of Justice began developing its own civil prison system for felons convicted and sentenced by the U.S. District Courts. By the mid-1920s the expansion of the federal government into the criminal field had put such a strain on the capacities of Leavenworth, Atlanta, and McNeil Island Penitentiaries that Congress, after an investigation, authorized in 1930 the creation of the U.S. Bureau of Prisons in the Department of Justice. By 1929, the federal government was operating seven institutions with a resident population of about 12,000 and an equal number in state and local institutions. Before the creation and activation of the Bureau of Prisons, each prison warden operated his institution with little guidance or direction from the Department of Justice. Such fiscal and administrative control as existed was provided by an assistant attorney general who possessed no special qualifications in prison administration.

The Bureau of Prisons, U.S. Department of Justice

The first director of the new Bureau was the Honorable Sanford Bates who had been Commissioner of the Massachusetts Department of Corrections from 1919 to 1929. The Bureau continues to be headed by a director who is among that class of federal executives known as "career bureau chiefs." He

---

*The Penitentiary at Leavenworth, Kansas, was opened in 1895, and the Atlanta, Georgia, institution was activated in 1902.

' is appointed by the attorney general and holds office at his pleasure, but while not protected by civil service, the position has not been regarded so far as political or partisan in nature.

The headquarters office of the Bureau is located in Washington, D.C., and is manned by assistant directors and staff specialists in a manner similar to the arrangement found in the very large state departments of corrections. As of 1973, the Bureau's institutions held a total of about 23,000 inmates.

The institutional establishment consisted of the following:

Six Penitentiaries	(long-term adults)
Six Correctional Institutions	(intermediate-term adults)
Six Correctional Institutions	(young adults)
Six Correctional Institutions	(short-term adults)
Three Youth Centers	(youths and juveniles)
One Women's Reformatory	(adult women)
One Medical Center	(mentally ill or abnormal males)
Fourteen Community Treatment Centers	(chiefly for youthful offenders)

In addition to the Federal Women's Reformatory at Alderson, West Virginia, two of the intermediate-term adult institutions have separate divisions for women prisoners, and one of the three Youth Centers also has a women's facility.

The Community Treatment Centers are "halfway houses" located in metropolitan areas and serve as a short-term bridge from institutional confinement to release on parole. Those eligible for placement in these facilities must be under 35 years of age with expected release dates within 90 to 120 days. The Bureau provides this kind of prerelease service to from 25 percent to 30 percent of those released. It also contracts for some of these services with some 70 public and private residential agencies located in 20 states.

The nonmilitary federal correctional system, like many of the states, is, from the organizational standpoint, fragmented and largely uncoordinated. The prisons and correctional institutions for adults are well-run and, comparatively, are generously supported. Pretrial detention and jail confinement of misdemeanants are the weakest parts of the system, because they suffer from the well-known shortcomings of local jails throughout the country. The Bureau attempts to alleviate this problem by providing for federal inspection of all jails in which federal prisoners are confined, but no such arrangement can prevent the use, in some localities, of substandard facilities.

The Federal Parole Board is situated for administrative purposes in the

Department of Justice, but it is essentially a separate and independent body. The supervision of parolees is delegated to the probation officers of the United States District Courts and, as has been mentioned earlier, the probation function is entirely an adjunct of these same courts.

Under such a system, unified nationwide planning, policy formulation, and administrative direction are impractical. At the present writing many suggestions are being advanced for revamping the federal system. One idea calls for abolishing the Bureau of Prisons as an operating agency and for the confinement of prisoners and the supervision of parolees to be contracted out to state systems, and further, for the probation officers of the federal courts to be limited to making presentence reports for the judges and for the supervision of federal probationers likewise to be contracted out to state and local probation agencies. Another idea has suggested that the Bureau of Prisons change its name and that its functions be expanded to include the supervision and management of all federal defendants, prisoners, probationers and parolees.

None of these changes appears to be imminent at this writing and in fairness it must be said that the separate parts of the federal correctional "non-system" maintain relatively high professional standards and continue to occupy positions of leadership in the correctional field.

The Military Correctional System

While the military forces of the United States are subject to the civilian control of the federal government, it has always been considered necessary for the Army, Navy, and other branches of the service to maintain an internal system of disciplinary controls for the management of their own officer and enlisted personnel. This has meant, therefore, the development of a body of codified military law and a system of police, courts, and corrections to support the law.

There are many offenses such as homicide, theft, and assault which are prohibited by both the military and the civil law, but conversely, many of the offenses most common among military personnel are violations of military law only. Some of these include unauthorized absence, desertion, willful disobedience of a superior officer, misbehavior before the enemy, and mutiny.

The total criminal justice system of the military is too complex to describe in detail at this point. Suffice it to say that there is a *Uniform Code of Military Justice* (Title 10) which applies to all personnel in the military forces under the general direction of the Department of Defense and the Joint

Chiefs of Staff. The Departments of the Army, the Air Force, and the Navy each have an elaborate set of regulations in implementation of the Code.

Since the Army is the largest branch of the service, we will discuss its criminal justice system without attempting to differentiate between the services in terminology and organization. The Army, like the other two major branches, is subject to the provisions of the U.S. Constitution and the Uniform Code of Military Justice. Beyond that, the Navy, which includes the Marine Corps, operates its own courts-martial, police, and correctional facilities. This is also true of the Air Force, except that it frequently makes joint use of the Army's principal places of confinement.

At the Department of the Army level at the Pentagon the Office of the Adjutant General has responsibility for the judicial functions of the system in all commands in the continental United States, Hawaii, island outposts, and in foreign countries. The actual convening of a court-martial for purposes of trying accused personnel, however, is the prerogative of the senior officer of each major command unit.

The Provost Marshal General of the Department of the Army has general responsibility for the military police. Within the Provost Marshal General's staff there is a corrections unit usually headed by a colonel who has staff supervision over the correctional functions of the Department of the Army and its operational commands. Each fort or major command has its own Provost Marshal who is responsible through channels to the commanding general of the post for all military police officers and men assigned to him. Included in his command is the stockade or confinement facility of the post. The officer in charge of the stockade is usually a captain or a major and in some instances may be a lieutenant colonel. In the table of organization he is called the Correctional Officer.

The stockade is the army equivalent of the county jail in the civilian system. Its inmates are either persons awaiting judicial processing or are serving very short terms for relatively minor violations. Many other defendants after initial hearing by officers of the post adjutant general are assigned to a special processing detachment (not under the provost marshal) where they are held pending disposition. This is somewhat similar to "release on own recognizance" in lieu of bail in the civilian systems.

Most of the defendants convicted of minor violations are restored to regular service after punishment by such sanctions as short sentences to stockade confinement, fines and forfeiture of pay, or reduction in grade. A few others are dismissed from the service with one of the several "less than honorable discharges."

The Army also provides for a special correctional establishment known as a "Correctional Training Facility." As of 1974, only one such facility was in active operation in the United States at Fort Riley, Kansas. The purpose of this facility is to retrain men transferred to it from the stockades. They are required by Army regulations to have been convicted only of a military offense and to have at least 40 days remaining in whatever sentence may have been imposed if they have completed "basic training" and 70 days if such training had not been completed at the time of the offense — usually unauthorized absence. The mission of the Correctional Training Facility is to motivate, retrain, and restore to regular service as many of its charges as possible. The Facility has a rated capacity of 2,400 men, but operated during the period of maximum mobilization in 1968, 1969, and 1970 at from 900 to 1,800 trainees. About five out of six of those received appear to have completed the program and to have been restored to duty. How many of these actually went on to eventually complete an honorable term of service is not known.

Of those who failed to complete the retraining program a considerable proportion were given administrative discharges and a few ran away (AWOL). A few others were transferred to the U.S. Disciplinary Barracks at Fort Leavenworth, Kansas, to complete their sentences. The program is considered by the Army on balance to have been a success and worth the economic expenditure both in terms of conservation of military manpower and in the intangibles of human values.

The Disciplinary Barracks at Fort Leavenworth is now the only prison maintained by the Department of the Army for the service of sentences for offenses usually equivalent to felonies in the civilian society.* It was first designated a military prison by Congress in 1873. Until 1934, Alcatraz in San Francisco Bay was the Western Military Prison and Castle William on Governors Island in New York was the Atlantic equivalent until it was deactivated in 1940.

During World War II the Army's population of general courts-martial prisoners rose to an all-time high. At its peak in October, 1945, there were 34,766[12] general prisoners confined as follows:

Disciplinary Barracks	13,873
Rehabilitation Centers	5,873
Federal Bureau of Prisons	2,712
Guardhouses (Stockades)	808
Overseas Installations	11,500

*The Navy still maintains a similar facility at Portsmouth, New Hampshire.

Most of the Army-operated facilities were either leased state facilities or army barracks surrounded by wire fences and guard towers. There were actually three high-security Disciplinary Barracks, including Fort Leavenworth, and nine improvised medium-security installations located on Army reservations.*

The unique characteristic of the military correctional system is its erratic fluctuation in numbers, depending first, upon the total number of personnel in the armed services and second, upon the intensity of active combat engagements abroad. The principal military offense has always been unauthorized absences. An analysis of these offenders always reveals a striking similarity between them and the older adolescent population of civilian correctional schools and reformatories. They tend to come from unstable social and economic backgrounds, are school dropouts and without job skills. They are emotionally immature and are predominantly volunteers who appear to have joined the Army because they were faced with what seemed like something worse at home. Contrary to uninformed speculation it is not the conscripted unwilling soldier who causes much of the Army's disciplinary and correctional problem. It is rather the very young first-term volunteer who often runs away from "boot camp" before his uniform gets soiled.

The Special Civilian Committee for the Study of the U.S. Army Confinement System in its report, submitted to the Undersecretary of the Army in May 1970, among its many recommendations had this to say on the subject: "The majority of the group comprising this large corps of ineffective soldiers are young Regular Army soldiers who have volunteered before reaching their eighteenth birthday," and hence, "It is recommended that the Army take steps to review its standards, criteria and procedures for induction and enlistment with a view to initiating new screening methods aimed at eliminating at the point of intake a larger proportion of men unsuitable for service."

NOTES

[1] David Rothman, *Discovery of the Asylum,* Boston: Little Brown, 1971.

[2] Blake McKelvey, *American Prisons,* Chicago: University of Chicago Press, 1936.

[3] Harry Elmer Barnes, *The Evolution of Penology in Pennsylvania,* Indianapolis: Bobbs-Merrill, 1927, p. 117.

[4] American Correctional Association, *Manual of Correctional Standards,* 3rd ed., Washington, 1966.

---

*As an item of related interest it is estimated that the total prisoner population of all branches of the military service at the close of World War II approximated 50,000 persons.

[5]Advisory Commission on Intergovernmental Relations, *State-Local Relations in Criminal Justice,* Washington, D.C.: U.S. Government Printing Office, 1971, pp. 282–286.

[6]National Advisory Commission on Criminal Justice Standards and Goals, *Corrections, Standard 16.4, Unifying Correctional Programs,*1973, p. 560.

[7]Marvin E. Frankel, Judge of the U.S. Court, Southern District of New York, *Criminal Sentences—Law Without Order,* New York: Hill and Wang, 1973.

[8]Ibid., pp. 17–18, and "The Sentence–Its Relation to Crime and Rehabilitation," in *Of Prisons and Justice,* S. Doc. No. 70, 88th Cong., 2d sess., p. 311, 1964.

[9]National Council on Crime and Delinquency, *Model Sentencing Act,* 2nd ed., Hackensack: NCCD, 1972.

[10]Richard A. McGee, *A New Look at Sentencing,* Part I, Federal Probation, June, 1974, and Part II, September, 1974.

[11]Ronald L. Goldfarb and Linda R. Singer, *After Conviction,* New York: Simon and Schuster, 1973.

[12]Report of the Special Civilian Committee for the Study of the United States Army Confinement System, 1970.

11 The Management of Correctional Services

(Note to the Reader: Much of the material in the chapter which follows has been drawn from a research monograph, *Developing Correctional Administrators*, prepared under the direction of one of the writers of this book. This material represents the only national survey ever conducted of correctional administrators and is being disseminated widely outside the field of corrections for the first time in this textbook. Appendix IV also contains material drawn from this study. The study was originally funded and the results published by the Joint Commission on Correctional Manpower and Training.)

In Chapter 10 we dealt with the organization of American corrections—the structural arrangements through which agencies and governments have attempted to carry out the missions assigned to them by law and public policy. The present chapter focuses upon the dynamics of leadership and management which have characterized the correctional field in this country. Attention will be given to such functions as planning, staffing, and directing the work of correctional organizations. Information will be presented on the characteristics and the "management styles" of administrators in this field, and certain of the problems and dilemmas which impinge upon those individuals will be highlighted.

It will quickly become apparent that today's correctional administrator works at the center of a volatile field of forces which he must comprehend and deal with skillfully if he is to be successful. Not only must he relate effectively to his own staff, and to the offenders committed to his care, but he must transact with such varied other groups as the legislature, the press, labor unions and employee organizations, other segments of the criminal justice system, and a broad range of special interest groups in the community. Most challenging of all is the fact that the administrator's negotiations within this web of relationships must be pursued not only in the interests of maintaining and protecting his organization, but with the constant goal of changing and developing it toward a more optimal model of practice.

The Evolution of Administrative Theory

In Chapter 1 we noted that the field of corrections has evolved and changed as public policy has set new and different goals for it to address. We saw that the movement from revenge to restraint to reform occurred in such a fashion that historically significant goals were not abandoned when new goals were adopted. Thus, the present system is a bewildering mix of different, and often contradictory, philosophies.

The evolution of thinking about administration and management has followed a somewhat similar course. Early approaches to management were highly authoritarian and coercive, stemming from belief in the divine right of monarchs to govern according to whatever precepts pleased them. Shortly after the turn of the century, we entered a period of "scientific management" through which the theorists of that day sought to develop a rational and orderly frame of reference for defining the nature of organizations and the role of administrators.[1] This development, in its reliance on logic and rationality, was rather like the effort to use measured doses of incarceration as a correctional device in the place of corporal and capital punishment.

Following the scientific management movement, administrative theory became increasingly concerned with the experience of those who function within large, formal organizations, and a "human relations" school of administration emerged as a kind of antidote to the mechanistic and impersonal strictures of scientific management.[2] The philosophic content of this development was perhaps similar to the reform movement (the second "R") in corrections, because it emphasized the importance of understanding and meeting the highly individualistic needs of people, rather than imposing upon them an arbitrary system of rules concerning their conduct.

Finally, in contemporary theorizing concerning administration, we see an emphasis on what is sometimes called "general systems theory," an approach which stresses the sociological nature of large-scale organizations, viewing them as extraordinarily complex systems, and pointing out the need to understand linkages and interdependencies between different organizational units.[3] This emphasis on the broad context of organizational life somewhat resembles the fourth "R", reintegration, which we described in the first chapter as a correctional modality of the future. General systems theory is compatible with the correctional concept of reintegration because it focuses not only upon the individual involved (the offender or the worker or the administrator himself) but upon the complex and ever-changing social network in which all of them are embedded.

The major ethos for reforming and improving the management of American corrections during the past several decades has been the scientific management movement, somewhat tempered and modified by proposals for the improvement of the human relationships within correctional organizations. As was suggested above, scientific management was at its very essence a "rational" theory of administration. It saw organizations as machines, "human machines" it is true, but still structures created to perform prescribed tasks.

The "best" structure, according to scientific management dogma, was a pyramid or hierarchy, in which authority originated at the top of the organization and was delegated down through increasingly broad layers of subordinate administrators and supervisors, eventually reaching the work force at the bottom of the pyramid where compliance was expected to take place. This concern for the anatomy or form of the organization led to conceptions of the administrator as an omnipotent "engineer," as the designer, driver, and sometimes the mechanic who functioned within this human machine.

The central value of the scientific management position was predictability of outcomes. Organizational units were supposed to deliver according to the prescriptions established when they were created. Individual members of the organization were supposed to perform according to their job descriptions.

It seems somewhat ironic that the influence of the human relations school of management made itself felt in the handling of offenders before it had any significant impact on the handling of correctional staff by their administrators. Even after programs of education and psychotherapy for inmates made their appearance within American prisons, the employees of those institutions, primarily guards and custodians, still were organized and supervised in quite authoritarian and hierarchical ways.

As the reform movement within corrections gained greater strength, penal organizations changed somewhat to accommodate it. The traditional prison had a straight line of authority running from the warden through his deputy warden and thence down to captains, lieutenants, sergeants, and guards in a highly militaristic model. As programs for rehabilitating inmates were added to the custodial functions of prisons and reformatories, a trend developed to create a new organizational form, typically a "treatment division" alongside the custodial division which theretofore had been the heart of the prison organizational structure.

Thus, the philosophic polarities of reform and restraint were institutional-

267

ized in organization structure. These arrangements tended to generate a great deal of conflict between the custodial and treatment staff members who thus were pitted against each other. Inmates became quite skillful in playing custody forces off against treatment forces, and the reverse. Fascinating and quite elaborate alliances and reciprocities grew up between the inmate world and the staff world, which maintained some stability within the bleak and often volatile society of the prison.[4]

The collaborative and participative forms of management associated with general systems conceptualization have not had great impact in the correctional field. These approaches have been more influential in determining the nature of probation and parole organizations than in the world of correctional institutions, but even in community-based programs there has been a tendency to maintain some kind of mix between scientific management and human relations modalities. Some experimental programs in corrections have gone a considerable distance toward developing unified, collaborative regimes. The tendency in these forward-looking, experimental efforts has been to blur the line between custody and treatment, to develop a "therapeutic community" in which efforts could be made to integrate the function of controlling and containing offenders with the function of rehabilitating and reintegrating them into community life.[5]

The more innovative of these experiments represent striking examples of what can be done to create an organizational context suited to changing the attitudes and behavior of the people present therein. These programs, which are at the cutting edge of change and experimentation in the correctional field, are described in other chapters of this book. For now, however, it must be said that most correctional organizations and the administrators who manage them have not reflected the most recent contributions to administrative theory, which we have categorized here as general systems theory.

The Correctional Administrator

Profile of the Administrator

What are the characteristics of the men and women who lead American corrections? What are their needs for training and development? How can their capability to produce essential changes in the status quo be increased?

The most definitive answers to these questions are contained in a study carried out in 1968–1969 for the Joint Commission on Correctional Manpower and Training by the University of Southern California.[6]

This research, while exploratory, contacted a national sample of top and middle managers working in both institutions and community-based corrections. Organizations responsible for juvenile and adult, as well as male and female offenders were included. The profile which follows is summarized and paraphrased from that study.

Correctional administrators generally reach their managerial posts through a slow upward progression within quite narrow organizational pathways such as a juvenile probation office, an adult institution, or a parole agency. There is little crossing of the boundaries between different correctional functions and jurisdictions, much less lateral entry into correctional management from other fields such as law enforcement or corporate enterprise.

Because of this pattern of selection based on seniority, the managers tend to be of mature years. Of the top administrators studied, 75 percent were over 45 years of age, as were 55 percent of those in middle management roles. Perhaps surprisingly, the USC research discovered that administrators working in probation and parole, the community programs which offer the greatest hope for correctional innovation and reform, were older and had been in their positions longer than those working in prisons and youth institutions.

Women made up less than 19 percent of the sample. They were especially under-represented in headquarters or "central office" settings and in probation and parole agencies. In a field like corrections, which needs new and imaginative managerial talent, greater utilization of women seems an obvious step to take. Although no empirical data are available to support the point, it seems clear that the same prescription could be made with regard to the use of representatives of racial minorities and economically disadvantaged persons. The preponderance of such individuals in the offender population is an additional reason to recruit administrators whose personal background increases sensitivity to their problems.

To what extent are correctional managers prepared for their demanding duties by appropriate education and continuing in-service training? The answer, apparently, is not a reassuring one. The USC data indicate that the education of correctional managers typically does not relate directly to their work, and that in-service training tends to be sparse and of dubious quality. The most conspicuous gap in learning experiences relates to management. Figure 11–1, taken from the USC study, provides interesting documentation of this point. The data show the educational background of the administrators in the study.

A somewhat similar pattern exists with respect to the professional organizations which correctional administrators join and the publications which

FIGURE 11–1
Major Areas of Study for Degrees

AREA OF STUDY	NO.		PER CENT
AGRICULTURAL SCIENCES	7		2.2
ANTHROPOLOGY	2		0.6
BIOLOGICAL SCIENCES	3		0.9
BUSINESS	24		7.5
CRIMINOLOGY/CORRECTIONS	11		3.4
ECONOMICS	9		2.8
EDUCATION	33		11.9
ENGINEERING	2		0.6
ENGLISH	13		4.2
HISTORY	10		3.1
LAW	14		4.4
MATHEMATICS	3		0.9
MEDICINE	5		1.6
MUSIC	3		0.9
PHYSICAL SCIENCES	3		0.9
PHYSICAL EDUCATION	5		1.6
POLICE SCI/LAW ENF	2		0.6
POLITICAL SCI/GOVERNMENT	4		1.2
PSYCHOLOGY	42		13.2
PUBLIC ADMINISTRATION	5		1.6
SOCIAL WORK	36		11.3
SOCIOLOGY	47		14.8
OTHER	31		9.7
	319		100.0

Source: Elmer K. Nelson, Jr. and Catherine H. Lovell, *Developing Correctional Administrators*, research report of the Joint Commission on Correctional Manpower and Training, Washington, D.C., November, 1969, p. 27.

they read. Noting the parochial nature of their reading and the organizations
to which they belonged, the researchers said:

> It seems clear from the data the correctional administrators are for the most
> part "locals" in organization life. The majority face inward toward the orga-
> nization, responding to the norms and loyalities which it imposes as a sys-
> tem; they are very little in touch with the fast-moving "outside" world.
> Correctional administrators seem little involved with the efforts of the social
> and behavioral sciences to understand and explain deviant behavior and to
> develop concepts to guide intervention in that complex set of problems.
> They are also isolated from organized efforts to advance and refine general
> understanding of administration, especially public administration.[7]

This profile of those who organize and direct American correctional organizations should not be interpreted as demeaning their abilities and skills.
It documents more than anything else the paucity of public interest and concern for the functions which they carry out. If the administrators tend to be
parochial, does this not reflect an historic societal tendency to isolate the
correctional establishment, together with the offenders committed to it? If
they are ill-prepared for their work by education and training, does not lack
of such developmental opportunities again underscore public apathy and
neglect?

There is recent evidence that the conditions reported above are slowly beginning to change, that correctional managers are becoming more professional, competent, and more capable of serving as the leaders of needed
reforms and innovations in their organizations. Far more management workshops have been made available to this group in the past few years than ever
before. The curricula of colleges and universities have expanded under the
impact of federal funding to include courses on corrections administration
and other justice related programs. There are, however, reasons to question
both the quality of many of the new curricula and the degree of commitment
by the colleges involved to carry them on when outside funding no longer is
available.

The Job of the Administrator

The writers view the correctional administrator as occupying a focal point
within a complex and always changing field of forces. He feels himself to be,
and in reality he frequently is, "the man in the middle." John Conrad has

graphically portrayed some of the forces which bear upon administrators in the correctional field, as indicated in Figure 11–2.

Another way of thinking about the field within which correctional administrators function is to picture the relationships which they must establish and maintain if they are to accomplish their purposes. Of course these relationships differ from one correctional setting to another. The warden of a large, maximum-custody prison works within a vastly different context than the head of a small residential treatment center located within an urban complex. Nevertheless there are commonalities.

All correctional administrators, regardless of the level at which they func-

FIGURE 11–2
The Field of Forces of Correctional Administration

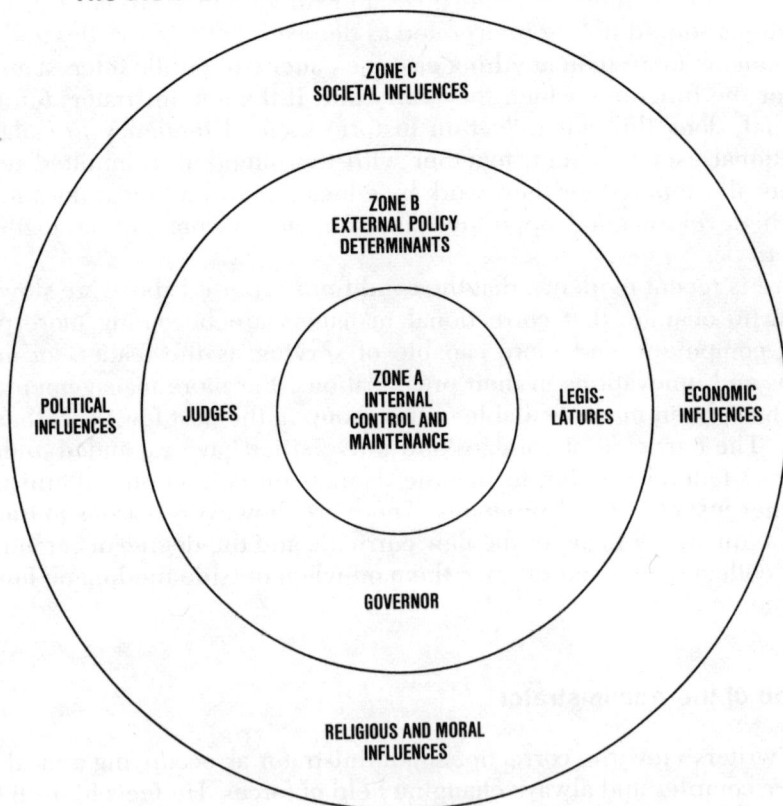

ZONE C
SOCIETAL INFLUENCES

ZONE B
EXTERNAL POLICY
DETERMINANTS

ZONE A
INTERNAL
CONTROL AND
MAINTENANCE

POLITICAL
INFLUENCES

JUDGES

LEGIS-
LATURES

ECONOMIC
INFLUENCES

GOVERNOR

RELIGIOUS AND MORAL
INFLUENCES

Source: John P. Conrad, "Research and the Knowledge Base of Corrections," *Crime and Delinquency*, 12 (1967), p. 448, fig. 2.

tion or the type of organization for which they have responsibility, must deal with their own subordinates and hierarchical superiors. Almost all of them must relate to individuals who are peers in status and authority. Most of them need to relate directly or indirectly to the offenders whom they have been assigned to manage. Such relationships might be thought of as comprising an internal circle immediately around the administrator and requiring close and constant attention day in and day out.

Other relationships exist in the external environment of the administrator and, while often critical to success in the achievement of his goals, are considerably more remote in both a physical and a social or psychological sense. For example, many correctional administrators must deal with other segments of the criminal justice system, the judiciary and the police. In order to secure resources to carry out their programs, they must relate to some legislative authority which of course varies by level of government. Like it or not, they frequently find themselves in contact with reporters and other representatives of the mass media. Correctional administrators who are seeking to implement the reintegration concept need an enormous amount of assistance from varied community interests and groups, so these too become an important part of their working field of forces.

The USC research which was previously referred to collected information on how correctional administrators in various types of settings perceived the relationships which made up their work life. Figure 11-3 presents the results of this inquiry. The administrator's perception of the significance of each relationship is indicated by its closeness to him on the chart.

This way of thinking about the job of the correctional administrator immediately suggests that he must learn to endure and work with conflict. Typically, when faced with a difficult decision in which he must choose from among alternative courses of action, it will almost inevitably be true that different people will expect different things from him. If, for example, there is a need for a new policy with regard to inmate discipline, it is probable that custodial officers would expect the warden to be strict and rigorous. Those concerned with inmate counseling and treatment might have an opposite expectation, while the inmates themselves could be predicted to advocate still other positions.

Of course the presence of conflict and dissonance is not peculiar to the correctional field. Administrators working in other arenas experience similar difficulties. In fact, management literature contains many treatises on role conflict.[8] As indicated above, conflict may occur when two or more persons expect different things of the administrator. It may arise from the fact that he plays more than one role, and, for example, might easily please his superior

JUVENILE INSTITUTIONS

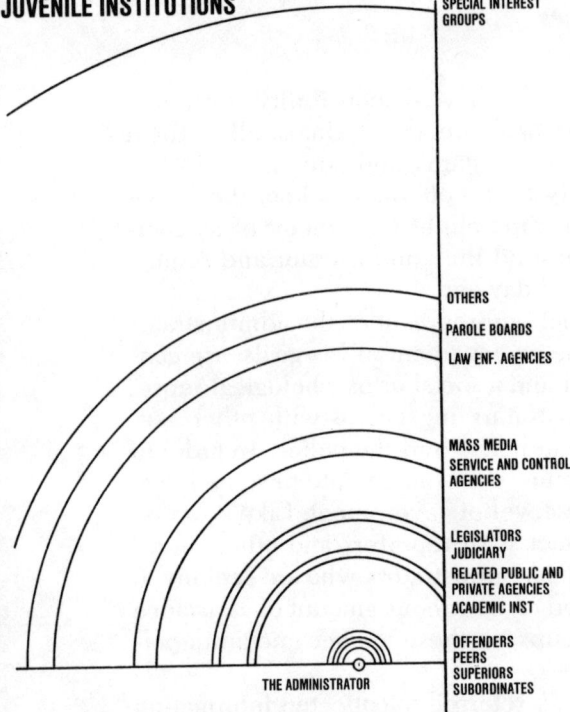

SPECIAL INTEREST
GROUPS

OTHERS
PAROLE BOARDS
LAW ENF. AGENCIES

MASS MEDIA
SERVICE AND CONTROL
AGENCIES

LEGISLATORS
JUDICIARY
RELATED PUBLIC AND
PRIVATE AGENCIES
ACADEMIC INST

OFFENDERS
PEERS
SUPERIORS
SUBORDINATES

THE ADMINISTRATOR

ADULT INSTITUTIONS

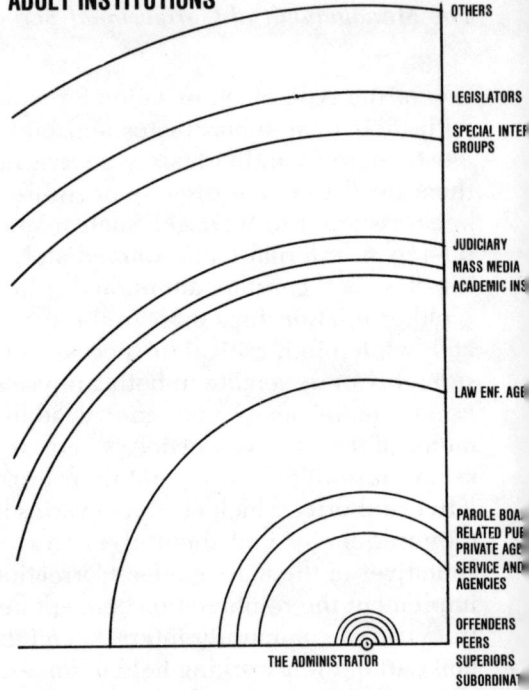

OTHERS

LEGISLATORS

SPECIAL INTEF
GROUPS

JUDICIARY
MASS MEDIA
ACADEMIC INS

LAW ENF. AGE

PAROLE BOA.
RELATED PUE
PRIVATE AGE
SERVICE AND
AGENCIES

OFFENDERS
PEERS
SUPERIORS
SUBORDINAT

THE ADMINISTRATOR

**PROBATION-
PAROLE**

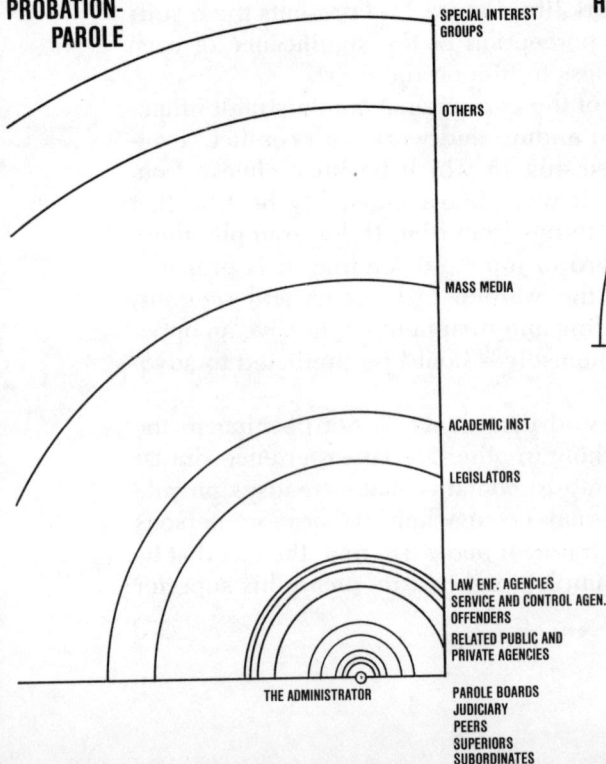

SPECIAL INTEREST
GROUPS

OTHERS

MASS MEDIA

ACADEMIC INST

LEGISLATORS

LAW ENF. AGENCIES
SERVICE AND CONTROL AGEN.
OFFENDERS
RELATED PUBLIC AND
PRIVATE AGENCIES

PAROLE BOARDS
JUDICIARY
PEERS
SUPERIORS
SUBORDINATES

THE ADMINISTRATOR

HEADQUARTERS

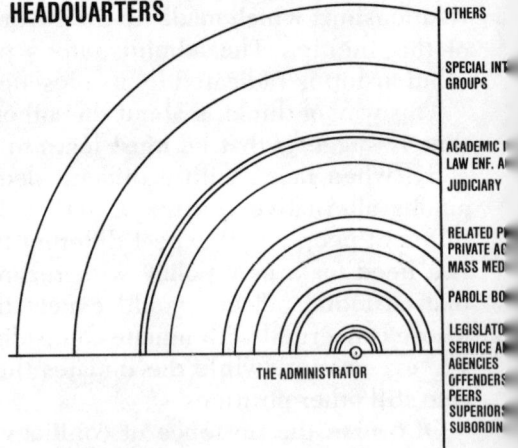

OTHERS

SPECIAL INT
GROUPS

ACADEMIC I
LAW ENF. A
JUDICIARY

RELATED P
PRIVATE AC
MASS MED

PAROLE BO

LEGISLATO
SERVICE A
AGENCIES
OFFENDERS
PEERS
SUPERIORS
SUBORDIN

THE ADMINISTRATOR

FIGURE 11-3
Force Fields of Significant[1] Relation

(Note [1]: Significance as perceived
administrator; where proximity equals
tance.)

Source: Elmer K. Nelson, Jr. and Cathe
Lovell, *Developing Correctional Adminis*
research report of the Joint Commiss
Correctional Manpower and Training, W.
ton, D.C., November, 1969, p. 34.

by long hours of work while alienating his wife for exactly the same reason. Conflict may also occur when the expectations of other people are contradictory to the values and beliefs of the individual himself.

Given the universality of role conflict as an aspect of administrative experience, it nevertheless seems safe to say that correctional administrators are more subject to this phenomenon than most other managers in either the public or the private sphere. This is true because of the many and sharply differing beliefs concerning what should be done with offenders, and the lack of any dependable empirical information to use in subscribing to one instead of another. Correctional administrators are buffeted by conflict precisely because the constituencies to which they need to relate in order to accomplish their purposes are committed to highly conflicting ideologies and norms.

It is the belief of the writers that the manner in which the correctional administrator handles conflict is highly indicative of his managerial capacity. This is especially true in regard to the administrative function of facilitating needed changes. While the tensions produced by conflict can be damaging to an organization and individuals in it, the same tensions may at times provide the only effective force for bringing about change. This is particularly true of the correctional field where the "out of sight, out of mind" syndrome makes it enormously difficult for administrators to secure the visibility and access needed to convince legislators and other holders of essential resources that help is needed. Given the flare-up of conflict and controversy, however, attention is focused upon the administrator and his problems, at least for a short time. The ability to make good use of such opportunities in moving toward goals which the administrator believes "make sense" certainly is a prime requirement of the correctional manager in the present day.

A second basic conception concerning the job of the correctional administrator is that he is a problem solver and a strategist. If you were to talk for an hour or so with the head of a correctional institution or a probation office, asking him to tell you how he spends his time, you would quickly determine that he is preoccupied with problems of different kinds. Some of these problems he assigns to himself in terms of goals which he would like to reach, goals which can only be obtained if he is able to bring about support and obtain the required resources. Other problems are thrust upon him from his internal or external environment, and in these cases too he must concern himself with how to achieve desired outcomes and avoid undesired outcomes.

The manner in which administrators seek to solve their problems and reach their goals differs greatly from individual to individual. Harold Leavitt has suggested that there are three basic ways in which administrators attempt to influence those around them: direct authority, manipulation, and collaboration.⁹ Correctional administrators develop their own individualistic styles in dealing with the difficult issues which they face every day. Far more than he perhaps realizes, each individual administrator behaves according to patterns which are fairly predictable to those around him.

The scientific management tradition of early American corrections dictated an authoritarian style, and certainly this was the dominant mode in the correctional world for most of the history which is behind us. The use of covert, manipulative techniques has always been a part of correctional management, no doubt influenced to some extent by the mutually exploitative relationships which have characterized interactions between offenders and staff members in their efforts to control and co-opt each other.

The use of collaborative and participative management methods is a much more recent aspect of correctional administration. Some modern administrators, especially those working in programs which seek to reintegrate inmates and offenders into community life, are coming to believe that a high level of trust and candor is desirable in working with all of the relationships which are critical to them. Moreover, they conclude that a strategic style based on such a premise is not only possible but highly desirable if the field of corrections is to perform its tasks more effectively than it does today.

The USC research produced some interesting information on the nature of the problems which correctional administrators perceive as significant, and toward which their strategic, problem-solving efforts were directed. The following lists summarize the results of the interview data in this regard.¹⁰ The table below sorts out the problems as seen by the administrators in terms of whether they were perceived to be primarily "internal," i.e., within the administrator's own organization, or "external," i.e., generated within the external environment.

We have presented the correctional administrator as the man in the middle of complex and potentially conflicting forces. We have pictured him as an individual whose daily work is made up of efforts to solve problems, some of which arise in his immediate environment and others from locations which are more remote from him. We have suggested that he needs to be effective in managing and using conflict if he is to be successful, and have indicated that he requires strategic skills in his problem-solving activities.

These generalizations may be helpful in providing a frame of reference for thinking about the correctional administrator, but we would like to go beyond such abstract ideas in an effort to help the reader to gain some understanding of the actual problems, dilemmas, and dynamics which make up the "real world" of correctional management. Of course it is impossible to

Internal Problems	External Problems
Relating costs to effectiveness	Sufficient data on effectiveness
Effective evaluative research	Feedback on past offenders
Adequate methods for collecting data	Adequate methods for collecting data
Familiarity with modern budgeting	Contradictions in outsiders' expectations
Assessing performance of subordinates	Political interference
Turnover of competent staff	Pursuing programs with inadequate laws
Recruiting qualified personnel	Securing approval by legislators
In-service training programs	Sufficient funds for programs
Competitive salaries for staff	Fieldwork, placements, and internships
Creating opportunities for advancement	hindering work of organization
Long-term financial planning	Adequate university course work
Sufficient time for planning	Availability of academic courses
Use of university-trained personnel	
Separating functions in organization	
Securing approval from supervisors	
Staff resistance to change	
Geographic isolation of units	
Compliance by subordinates	
Obsolete facilities and equipment	
Involving subordinates in decisions	

capture in written words the ambience of existence within correctional organizations. As is true of all efforts to comprehend complex human phenomena, there is no substitute for being there, for experiencing the sights and sounds, and more particularly the nuances of the transactions between people who occupy different roles and seek different ends within the total system for which the administrator is responsible. In the following section, however, an effort is made to focus upon concrete and specific aspects of the administrator's work.

The Administrator in Action

The USC research which has supplied an empirical basis for much of this chapter postulated nine strategies or problem-solving methods which correctional administrators typically use, as listed and defined below:[11]

1. Compromise: Adjustment and concession among the parties involved.

2. Involvement-commitment: Gaining the participation and cooperation of the parties involved and thus securing their commitment to the solution.

3. Direct Authority: Using the rewards and penalities attached to a formal position and rank in the organization.

4. Dilemma Management: Using the increased attention generated by a problem or crisis as a means of bringing about a desirable solution.

5. Expertise: Introducing new information or calling upon persons with specialized knowledge or skills.

6. Integration: Using a new approach which recognizes the competing interests involved and seeks to avoid diminishing any legitimate ones.

7. Manipulation: Not fully revealing all the purposes sought while skillfully influencing others to achieve the desired goal.

8. Invoking Standards and Norms: Calling upon widely accepted standards and beliefs to bring about the desired result.

9. Timing: Delaying action until a more opportune time or until a natural solution emerges.

Obviously some of these approaches are highly favored by modern management theory, i.e., involvement-commitment and integration, while others would be regarded negatively by many contemporary theorists, e.g., direct authority and manipulation. The research left no doubt, however, that all nine methods are frequently used under varying circumstances, and in differing combinations. Platitudinous injunctions about the virtues or deficiencies of particular methods probably have small meaning to an administrator who finds himself "on the line," confronting and having somehow to deal with a difficult, stressful problem situation.

In an effort to capture some of the operating realities of correctional administration and subject them to analysis, we present below a description of recent events in the Massachusetts Department of Youth Services, as recorded in a case study prepared by Ohlin, Coates and Miller at the Harvard Law School Center for Criminal Justice.[12] The events described, all of which took place since 1969, comprise an extremely interesting effort to reform juvenile corrections in Massachusetts. The first thrust of the reform effort concentrated on changing the juvenile institutions of the state from traditional, coercive regimes to therapeutic communities. Disenchanted with the results, the administrator involved turned his energies to the closing of these institutions and the development of alternative community-based programs.

Although the ultimate effects of these efforts are not yet known, the preliminary study of the Harvard researchers makes clear some of the consequences, especially the traumas, involved in authentic efforts to move from the Revenge, Restraint and Reform mix of modern corrections into a Reintegration model of practice. Particularly interesting, from the standpoint of the present chapter, are questions having to do with the role of the administrator in the induction and management of change. The concepts which we have been considering thus far about administration should lead the reader to keep a number of questions in mind as he studies the Massachusetts experience. One might ask, for example, how the administrator involved perceived the force field in which he was working (as we have defined and used that term) and which relationships were most significant to him. Did he misperceive the importance of some constituencies? The old-time staff? The press? The Governor? The potency of outside experts, such as Maxwell Jones who was called in to legitimate the idea of an institutional therapeutic community?

It might also be useful to consider the strategic approaches of the administrator. How much did he seek to accelerate change by obtaining the involvement and commitment of staff and others? To what extent did he rely on the use of direct authority and with what consequences? Was he manipulative at times? Did he time his moves carefully? Was he able to turn adversity to advantage at critical junctures in the situation? To what extent did he attempt to sanction the desired changes by invoking the normative standards and goals of modern correctional philosophy? Was his use of outside expertise functional, or might it have had a boomerang effect?

Of course any "answers" you discover to such questions will be highly speculative. We are in no position to judge the outcome of the Massachusetts effort or to evaluate the effectiveness of the administrator whose behavior is described in the case. Our purpose is only to apply some abstract formulations about correctional administration (the device of force field analysis and the concept of managers as strategists) to an actual situation and thus seek to solidify our understanding of these ideas.

Radical Correctional Reform:
A Case Study of the Massachusetts
Youth Correctional System*

Lloyd E. Ohlin
Robert B. Coates
Alden D. Miller
Harvard University

The most fundamental assumptions in the field of youth corrections are under attack. The Massachusetts Department of Youth Services has become the most visible national symbol of a new philosophy of corrections through its repudiation of the public training school approach and its advocacy of therapeutic communities and alternative community-based services.

The radical symbolism of the Massachusetts reforms is heightened by the fact that the first public training school for boys in the United States was established at Westboro, Massachusetts, in 1846, and the first public training school for girls at Lancaster, Massachusetts, in 1854. Since then the public training school has become the last resort for dealing with delinquent youth, though a small number may face adult criminal court and confinement in adult prisons.

A key organizing principle of traditional training schools is punishment.

Lloyd E. Ohlin, Robert Coates, and Alden D. Miller, "Radical Correctional Reform: A Case Study of the Massachusetts Youth Correctional System," *Harvard Educational Review*, 44 (February, 1974), pp. 74–111. Copyright © by President and Fellows of Harvard College.

*Prepared under grants from the National Institute of Law Enforcement and Criminal Justice, Law Enforcement Assistance Administration, Department of Justice, and from the Massachusetts Governor's Committee on Law Enforcement and Administration of Criminal Justice. Points of view or opinions stated in this document are those of the authors and do not necessarily represent the official positions or policies of the funding agencies.

The authors wish to express appreciation to John Albach, Judy Caldwell, Barry Feld, Robert Fitzgerald, David Garwood, Paula Garwood, Alan Johnson, Arlette Klein, Cliff Robinson, Barbara Stolz, Arthur Swann, Christian Teichgraeber, Ann Yates, Alma Young for their work in collecting data for the project on which this article is based.

There are efforts at vocational and general education in the training schools, but the institutions are basically custodial and authoritarian. Resocialization efforts are commonly reduced to instruments for creating conformity, deference to adult authority, and obedience to rules. Regimented marching formations, shaved heads and close haircuts, omnipresent officials, and punitive disciplinary measures have been the authoritative marks of the training school, along with the manipulation of privileges, such as cigarette smoking, T.V. watching, home visits, or release to reward compliance.

Criticism of the traditional training school comes from three major sources. For many years the documentation of high rates of recidivism among training school graduates has created pressure for new solutions. For example, the pioneering studies of Sheldon and Eleanor Glueck offered painstakingly assembled evidence of the high rates of arrest and conviction of new offenses among those exposed to training school experiences.[1] The classical studies by Shaw and McKay in the Chicago area project and the Illinois Institute of Juvenile Research documented the role of traditional training schools as agencies for socializing young people into adult criminal careers.[2] They showed how exposure to these institutions labeled young people as "delinquent" or "criminal," and how family, school, neighborhood, job market, and criminal justice agencies reinforced the stigma, resulting in high rates of recidivism.[3] These early studies have been supported by more recent work.[4]

A second source of criticism comes from the development of new ideologies of treatment in the human services. These approaches argue that individual and group counseling and therapy will lead to personal insight and better social adjustment. They urge that the problems of youth offenders be considered in the context of family and communal relations where preparation for law-abiding adulthood ordinarily occurs.[5] This search for community based treatment resources has derived support from research studies

---

[1]Sheldon Glueck and Eleanor Glueck, *Criminal Careers in Retrospect* (New York: Commonwealth Fund, 1943).

[2]Clifford R. Shaw, *The Jack Roller, A Delinquent Boy's Own Story* (Chicago: University of Chicago Press, 1930); Clifford R. Shaw *et al.*, *Social Factors in Juvenile Delinquency, A Study for the National Commission on Law Observance and Enforcement*, Vol. 2, No. 13 (Washington, D.C.: U.S. Government Printing Office, 1931).

[3]Henry D. McKay, "Report on the Criminal Careers of Male Delinquents in Chicago," in President's Commission on Law Enforcement and Administration of Justice, *Task Force on Juvenile Delinquency Report: Juvenile Delinquency and Youth Crime* (Washington, D.C.: U.S. Government Printing Office, 1967).

[4]Paul Lerman, "Evaluative Studies of Institutions for Delinquents: Implications for Research and Social Policy," *Social Work*, 13 (July 1968), 55–64.

[5]President's Commission on Law Enforcement and Administration of Justice, *Task Force on Juvenile Delinquency, Report*, Ch. 2.

that document the pervasiveness of delinquent conduct throughout all social classes.[6] These studies have underscored the bias involved in employing public training schools as a principal means of control and treatment for primarily lower class offenders.[7] Practitioners have accordingly begun to stress the efficacy of benign non-intervention, diversion to non-criminal justice treatment programs, or privately purchased services for the poor as more constructive and less stigmatizing solutions to the authority problems of lower class youthful offenders, and more nearly equivalent to solutions employed extensively in the middle class for similar problems.[8]

A third major source of challenge to the traditional training school has come from those concerned with protecting the civil rights of children. The U.S. Supreme Court decision *in re Gault* in 1967 stimulated test cases exploring the constitutionally protected rights of children.[9] These cases are beginning to focus on what due process means for children and to raise issues relating to a "right to treatment" as well as a "right to be let alone."[10] They have called greater attention to whether treatment programs adequately take account of the best interests of the child. Given this new critical exploration of the rights of children, it is understandable that the concepts and practices of the traditional training school have come under increasing attack.

These challenges to training schools have posed problems for Massachusetts and many other states. What new system of services or intervention criteria should replace the existing system? How is it possible to change the system into one which relies primarily on community based treatment? What programs should be created? How should resources be re-allocated, staff developed, and appropriate distributions of private and public responsibilities for service be arranged? Finally, how can we be sure that the new system produces better results than the one it supplants?

The response in Massachusetts to these questions is discussed in the fol-

---

[6]James F. Short, Jr., and F. Ivan Nye, "Extent of Unrecorded Delinquency, Tentative Conclusions," *Journal of Criminal Law, Criminology and Police Science,* 49 (November-December 1958), pp. 296–302; Ronald L. Akers, "Socio-Economic Status and Delinquent Behavior: A Retest," *Journal of Research in Crime and Delinquency,* 1 (January 1964), pp. 38–46.

[7]President's Commission on Law Enforcement and Administration of Criminal Justice, *Task Force on Juvenile Delinquency Report: Juvenile Delinquency and Youth Crime* (Washington, D.C.: U.S. Government Printing Office, 1967).

[8]Elizabeth Vorenberg and James Vorenberg, "Early Diversion from the Criminal Justice System: Practice in Search of a Theory," in Lloyd E. Ohlin, ed., *Prisoners in America* (Englewood Cliffs, N. J.: Prentice-Hall, 1973).

[9]Sanford J. Fox, *Cases and Materials on Modern Juvenile Justice* (St. Paul, Minn.: West Publishing, 1972).

[10]Ted Rubin, *Law as an Agent of Delinquency Prevention* (Washington, D.C.: U.S. Department of Health, Education and Welfare, Social and Rehabilitation Service, Youth Development and Delinquency Prevention Administration, 1971).

lowing account. It draws freely on a variety of evaluation studies of the Massachusetts Department of Youth Services conducted by the Center for Criminal Justice at the Harvard Law School over the past three and one half years.[11] It is a preliminary report. A final appraisal must await more complete analysis, but the widespread interest in the Massachusetts experiment justifies at this time a review of the reform effort and some of the problems it encountered.

Phase I: Emergence of a Mandate for Reform

A series of crises in youth correctional services in Massachusetts culminated in March, 1969, with the resignation of the Director of Youth Services and prepared the way for reform. Prior to 1948 Massachusetts judges committed children directly to individual institutions for the care of delinquent boys and girls. New legislation in 1948 and 1952 created a Youth Service Board and a Division of Youth Services (DYS) nominally within the Department of Education but administratively autonomous. The Youth Service Board, whose chairman was also director of DYS, made decisions concerning the placement of youth within the institutions, their transfer, parole, and discharge.

The Director from 1952 to 1969, Dr. John D. Coughlin, was an articulate and vigorous advocate of the philosophy of youth training schools. Over these years the rhetoric of rehabilitation and conspicuous successes in such programs as the forestry camp and other helpful enterprises obscured the basically custodial and authoritarian grounding of this system. The available results of earlier studies are fragmentary but the rates of recidivism varied from 40 to 70 percent depending upon the age group, length of follow-up, and criteria of recidivism employed.[12] At the time of Coughlin's resignation in 1969 the DYS included a unit for delinquency prevention, an office for the supervision of parole for boys and one for girls, and ten institutions including four detention and reception centers, a forestry camp, a school for pre-adolescent boys at Oakdale, a school for younger male adolescents at Lyman, an industrial school for older boys at Shirley, the Institution for Juvenile Guidance for troublesome and emotionally disturbed boys at Bridgewater, and an industrial school for girls at Lancaster.

---

[11]We will not attempt to describe here the nature of these studies or the methodology employed. For those wishing a more complete account of the methodology, copies of a descriptive statement entitled "Evaluation of the Effects of Alternatives to Incarceration of Juvenile Offenders," unpublished document dated August, 1973, are available from the National Institute on Law Enforcement and Administration of Justice, Law Enforcement Assistance Administration U.S. Department of Justice, Washington, D.C.

[12]Estimates provided in interviews with DYS officials and former DYS officials.

From 1965 to 1968 the DYS was the subject of six major critical studies. The initial investigations were stimulated by reports of brutal and punitive treatment of youth at the Institution for Juvenile Guidance at Bridgewater. The publicity attending these charges led Governor John A. Volpe to request a study and recommendations from technical experts in the Children's Bureau of the U.S. Department of Health, Education and Welfare.

The HEW study found many deficiencies in the Massachusetts system.[13] It pointed to the dominance of custodial goals and practices over those of treatment, the lack of effective centralized supervision and direction of child care, the absence of an adequate diagnostic and classification system, the failure to develop flexible and professional personnel practices, and the ineffectiveness of parole supervision. These findings were confirmed by a blue ribbon committee of local experts appointed by Governor Volpe in 1967 under the sponsorship of Dr. Martha Elliot, Chairman of the Massachusetts Committee on Children and Youth and former Director of the Children's Bureau in HEW. The criticisms developed in these studies and their recommendations were supported by further investigations initiated by the Attorney General and by Senate Committees. These investigations crystalized the formation of a coalition of civic and professional groups in support of major reforms. Periodic crises in the DYS became increasingly the focus of newspaper attention and mobilized a critical audience in the general public.[14]

The liberal coalition led by the Massachusetts Committee on Children and Youth introduced reform legislation in 1968, but passage was deferred until the following year. In the interim a new major crisis developed at the Institute for Juvenile Guidance at Bridgewater. Staff factions developed within the institution around clinical as opposed to punitive treatment of youth behavior problems and this conflict was documented in the public press. A local community group, the Committee for Youth in Trouble, organized to support the clinical services faction. It joined with the Massachusetts Committee on Children and Youth to broaden the attack on the goals and policies of the DYS and the ability of the Director and his staff to administer an effective treatment program.[15]

In January, 1969, Governor Francis Sargent was inaugurated to complete

---

[13]U.S. Department of Health, Education and Welfare, Welfare Administration, Children's Bureau, "A Study of the Division of Youth Service and Youth Service Board, Commonwealth of Massachusetts" (Washington, D.C.: U.S. Government Printing Office, 1966).

[14]The exploitation of crises for the formation of coalitions of criticism and defense of public agencies in the process of reform is described more fully in Lloyd E. Ohlin, "Organizational Reform in Correctional Agencies" in Daniel Glaser, ed., A Handbook on Criminology (New York: Rand McNally, 1974).

[15]For a more detailed statement of these events see Yitzhak Bakal, ed., Closing Correctional Institutions (Lexington, Mass.: D. C. Heath, 1973), pp. 151–180.

the unexpired term of Governor Volpe. Governor Sargent expressed his strong support for the reform legislation. He secured the resignation of the Director, appointed an interim Director and a blue ribbon committee to undertake a national search for a new commissioner, signed into law new legislation reorganizing the DYS in September, 1969, and appointed Dr. Jerome Miller as Commissioner of the reorganized Department of Youth Services in October, 1969, on the recommendation of the search committee.

Commissioner Miller took charge of the new Department with a mandate from the legislative and executive branches of the state government and the liberal reform groups to intitiate more progressive policies and treatment of delinquent youth. Though some specific recommendations for change in the goals of the Department had been proposed in the earlier investigations, primarily in the direction of more effective clinical and diagnostic services and community supervision, the mandate was in the main broad and undefined.

Phase II: Reforming Institutional Treatment
Commissioner Miller had earned his doctoral degree in social work while in military service, and subsequently had organized a new institution for the disturbed or delinquent children of American Air Force personnel in England. For a brief period following his service discharge he served as training officer in the Department of Youth Corrections in Maryland. He then taught in the School of Social Work at Ohio State University where he helped develop training and treatment programs in both the juvenile and adult correctional services in Ohio.

The search committee was especially impressed with Miller's deep concern for youth in trouble and his sense of urgency, as well as confidence, that better ways could be developed to help them. He expressed special attraction to a post as commissioner where a commitment to reform had already been made. He thought that the effectiveness of institutional services for youth could be greatly increased by applying the treatment principles developed in therapeutic communities for adults by Maxwell Jones in England and Scotland.[16] These strengths overcame the search committee's two major reservations about Miller's administrative and political competence. First, his professional career had not tested his capacity to administer a human service agency of this size and scope. Second, he had not had experience dealing with the political considerations that deeply penetrate the organization and operation of state bureaus in Massachusetts.

---

[16]Maxwell Jones *et al., The Therapeutic Community* (New York: Basic Books, 1953).

During the first two years of his administration, Miller sought to humanize services for delinquent children, and to build a more therapeutic climate within the institutions. Throughout this period his efforts were severely hampered by financial and personnel constraints. First, it was almost a year before he obtained appropriations to staff the new positions and services authorized by the reform legislation. Appropriations were still allocated within the line budget of the DYS to particular institutions, staff positions, and services. To reallocate funds was a very cumbersome and lengthy process that wound its way through the state Administration and Finance Office and the legislative appropriations committee. Second, the rigidity of the civil service system made it virtually impossible to transfer personnel between institutions and services except on a voluntary basis. Massachusetts personnel practices mix political patronage with civil service procedures for recruiting and protecting employees in the positions to which they are certified. With few staff vacancies and without new or transferable funds the prospects of effecting major reforms during the first year appeared remote indeed. Even with additional funds during the second year the pervasive wait-and-see attitude of entrenched staff promised little change. The challenge confronting Miller was to mobilize and release energy for change.

Articulation of Goals

Shortly after his appointment the new Commissioner began to define the goals of his administration. He stated to the staff, the press, and civic, professional, and religious groups that he intended to humanize the treatment of offenders and to build therapeutic communities within existing institutional facilities. This model of treatment would require a democratic relationship between staff and youth in small units. A social climate had to be created in which both staff and youth were encouraged to express their feelings and concerns freely and honestly. Decisions relating to housekeeping problems, discipline, privileges, home visits, and release were to be made openly in cottage meetings after full discussion.

This treatment model challenged the basic features of the traditional training school system. Little change could be expected until the differences in philosophy, goals, staff and youth roles, and the processes of decision-making could be dramatized, justified, and enforced.

One of the first directives, issued by the new Commissioner in November, 1969, ordered that henceforth youth in the institutions would be allowed to wear their hair as they chose. The "haircut edict" raised a storm of protest and cries of permissiveness among staff long accustomed to shaving boys' heads on admission, regulating length, and using haircuts as punishment. It is doubtful that Miller fully recognized at first the sensitivity of this issue. In the emerging youth style of the times thirty-eight-year-old Miller wore his own hair longer than most state officials. Hair style and length were hotly contested in many families, schools, and business establishments as a visible symbol of youth revolt against adult regulations. Miller vigorously defended the edict to dramatize the new administration's desire to accord committed youth greater freedom and shrugged off derogatory staff references to the "hippy commissioner." The resonance of this issue with a large number of moral issues relating to authority, allocation of discretion, responsibility, initiative, and self-expression gave the directive a symbolic value of great importance. It clearly cast Miller as a youth advocate in opposition to traditional expectations and established the basic issues and roles of future dramas.

As the protest simmered down, other directives followed. It was ordered that youth should be allowed to wear their own street clothes rather than institutional garments. The practice of marching in silent formation from one activity to another was discontinued. Staff protested: greater freedom of movement made running away easier and street clothes made committed youth more difficult to identify if they had run away. The edicts signified to staff that custodial concerns would increasingly be subordinated to treatment objectives.

Miller became convinced that he could not successfully establish the therapeutic community model until he had removed the basic supports of the traditional system. He looked especially to the fear of greater punishment, deprivation, or personal degradation that constituted the keystone of the authority system throughout the institutions. He immediately turned, then, to the Institute for Juvenile Guidance at Bridgewater and Cottage #9 at Shirley, reserved for those youngsters seen as most disturbed or rebellious. These institutions represented the final sanctions in a graduated set of possible control measures to induce conformity by restrictions on freedom of movement, denial of privileges, physical abuse, enforced idleness, silence, and gestures of deference toward adult authorities. Miller initiated measures to humanize both sites. A general order forbade any staff member to strike or physically abuse youth. Other directives tried to eliminate the stultifying routines of enforced idleness and silence in the punishment units and the use of strip cells and other measures of extreme isolation. An effort was made to introduce more constructive activities. Greater controls were imposed on screening and assignment to these units and the duration of stay. Frequent, unannounced inspection visits were used to discourage evasions of the new directives. Even these measures did not seem sufficient. By mid-summer of 1970 the Commissioner had paroled or transferred the youth committed to Bridgewater and he then closed the Institution. Cottage #9 at Shirley remained in some measure a symbol of the old system until in the winter of 1971–72 it, too, was closed.

The difficulty the Commissioner encountered in changing procedures in these facilities testified to the tenacity of the principles of punishment and enforced adult authority. Cottage and program staff over the years had come to accept them as indispensable to preserving order and inducing conformity. Other methods of establishing adult authority through superior knowledge, mutual trust and respect, admiration, emulation, and affection were also occasionally evident. The new administration sought to encourage these more difficult and demanding forms of authority relationships with youth. However, to achieve this, they felt convenient resort to traditional punishment measures had to be removed or made much more difficult.

The new administration took other steps to alter the control system. For example, a new directive authorized youth eligible to smoke to carry their own cigarettes. Previously, youth surrendered their cigarettes to staff members who issued them as a reward for doing chores or withheld them as punishment. Doling out cigarettes or denying access to them constituted for staff a simple but very useful control measure for enforcing authority. Like the "haircut edict," the "cigarette edict" both dramatized a change in goals and altered control alternatives available to staff.

All of these administrative actions led to strong protests by line staff members to institution superintendents and friends in the legislature. For a time resistant staff members or their friends appeared regularly when Miller gave speeches to community groups to raise questions about the loss of control and the threat of mass runaways to local communities. To the extent that staff capacity to control youth relied on these traditional control measures, their complaints were indeed justified. It was not clear when these directives were issued whether the administration could retrain staff in the uses of authority.

New Treatment Programs and Policies

The new administration sought to demonstrate the value and feasibility of new models of treatment. As funds became available staff was recruited and assigned to the newly created bureaus of institutions, education, clinical services, and aftercare. Assistant commissioners were appointed to direct each of the four bureaus. By the end of Miller's first year, his central office staff exercised a more definitive role in the development of programs to implement the new philosophy of treatment. Despite the hostility of conservative staff members, many youth and especially younger professional staff members expressed a desire to experiment with a therapeutic community model. However, no one except Miller seemed to know how such a treatment program should be operated and what it would require of staff and youth.

To help answer some of these questions the Commissioner persuaded Dr. Maxwell Jones, whose methods he had observed in England, to lead a three-day conference of staff and youth at the Shirley Institution. Jones explained the principles of a therapeutic community and directed a series of demonstrations involving youth and staff. The demonstration groups created an open climate for staff and youth to express feelings and concerns and to direct them toward constructive ends. Jones' personal skill and warmth during these demonstrations drew applause from most staff and youth, but it was clear that for many staff members the shift from traditional staff roles would not only be very difficult and slow but in many cases impossible to achieve.

The conference, however, reinforced the new policy of decentralization at Shirley so that not only cottage life experiences but also educational, vocational, and other forms of counseling or therapy would be self-contained within each cottage unit. The pressure from the new Boston Office administrators to adopt the new group treatment policies spread from Shirley to Lyman and Lancaster during the new year and a half, reinforced by dramatic changes in staff assignments, described below. Many cottages continued to operate in the traditional manner, but others experimented, sometimes with remarkable success, in establishing a therapeutic community.

In the summer and fall of 1971 the Center for Criminal Justice at Harvard University conducted studies in cottages at Shirley, Lyman, Lancaster, and Topsfield. These studies compared the attitudes of staff and youth in traditional cottages to those trying the therapeutic model. Table 1 shows differences in youth reactions to the social climate of experimental and traditional cottages just prior to the closing of the major institutions in the late fall of 1971 and early 1972. These, and results of related studies, demonstrate consistently that decentralized cottage treatment and group therapy could lead to remarkably better reactions and experiences even for youth within the same institution. The reactions of the youth reveal significant differences between the therapeutic community and the traditional custodial model. The idea of the therapeutic community is to restructure the authority system of the cottage, with youth taking new responsibilities for decisions affecting themselves and each other, on matters ranging from privileges in the cottage to home visits and ultimately release on parole. It seeks to culti-

Table 1
Youth Response to Social Climate Items in Experimental and Traditional Cottages

Social Climate Item°	Cottage Type	
	Experimental (Percent)	Traditional (Percent)
If the kids really want to, they can share in decisions about how this cottage is run.	94	85
Kids in the cottage will help a new kid get along.	91	65
Kids in this cottage usually tell someone when they think he's done something wrong.	89	77
I feel very much that I fit here.	82	52
The cottage staff deals fairly and squarely with everyone	80	57
If a kid messes up, the staff will punish her/him.	66	81
Most kids here are just interested in doing their time.	65	81
If a kid does well, other kids will tell him so personally.	61	34
Other kids will reward a kid for good behavior.	60	37
Other kids here give you a bad name if you insist on being different.	38	61
The kids in this cottage have their own set of rules on how to behave that are different from those of the staff.	36	57
There are a few kids here who run everything.	35	59
There are too many kids here who push other kids around.	33	62
This cottage is more concerned with keeping kids under control than with helping them with their problems.	30	61
Real friends are hard to find in this cottage.	25	44
This cottage is pretty much split into two different groups, with staff in one and kids in the other.	19	55

°The items in this table differentiate between the Experimental and Traditional cottages more strongly than one would expect to be the case by chance at the .05 level. In the Experimental cottages, the number of youth responding to each question varies from 85–89; and the Traditional cottages, from 82–86.

vate a sense of group cohesiveness to offset the usual tendency for the cottage to splinter into "tough," "punk," "good kid" and staff cliques, that achieve control by allowing the toughest youth to dominate the others.

Several attempts were made to create programs for girls and boys in the same institution and even the same cottage. The first such program set up a cottage for girls transferred from Lancaster at the Lyman School for Boys. A cottage was also created at Lancaster for young boys from Oakdale for whom home placements were difficult to find. This made it possible to train older girls in the care and management of younger children. After a serious fire at the girls' detention and reception center in Boston, girls were housed in the same building as boys there and later at a new detention and reception cottage for girls at Lyman. Coed cottages were established on the grounds of the Shirley Institution and later at Lancaster and Topsfield. It was expected that if boys and girls shared the same institution or the same cottage, their demeanor, grooming, speech, and conduct would improve. Stereotypic sex role beliefs and attitudes on the part of both boys and girls might be changed. Comparative data on youth reactions in coed and noncoed settings are not yet available but staff reports suggest that many of these expectations were realized and a high level of staff acceptance emerged despite initial fears of sexual promiscuity and lack of discipline.

When Miller came into office the average length of stay for youth in the institutions was eight months. Since he had become convinced that the traditional training school programs ordinarily did more harm than good he began to encourage a more rapid turnover. By the end of the first year, the more liberal parole policies had begun to create tension with the courts, probation, and police departments in a number of communities, especially urban ones. Many staff members in these agencies felt that confinement for less than nine months was too short to realize the benefits of reeducation or community protection for which commitment had been ordered. To deal with these concerns, while the new treatment programs were being developed, the Commissioner ordered that committed youth be kept in the institutions a minimum of three months before becoming eligible for parole, except in unusual cases. Youth and staff rather quickly interpreted the three month minimum as a maximum, and so the normal institutional confinement dropped to around three months.

The more rapid turnover meant that educational and vocational training programs patterned on an academic year had to be redefined and reorganized. The emphasis shifted to tutorial programs involving community volunteers and paid professionals. The former vocational training programs that continued were used for basic maintenance services within the institution or for the occupation of idle time.

The STEP program illustrates the effect of changing policies on the organization of retraining programs. STEP (Student Tutor Educational Program) used trained tutors for small group programs to create an interest in learning among imprisoned offenders and a desire to pursue higher levels of education. The program had been developed in adult correctional institutions but was introduced for youth at Shirley in 1970. Subject matter included both formal and informal instruction in such subjects as English, arithmetic, social problems, photography, and auto mechanics. Reading and arithmetic skills were taught in the context of auto mechanics, which interested many boys.

As the new administration policies shifted from centralized institutional programs to decentralized cottage programs, the STEP instructors confined their tutorial activities to particular cottages. They began to integrate their work into the counseling and therapy programs of the cottages. The shorter periods of confinements shifted emphasis from the assimilation of organized learning materials to the redirection of attitudes, motivation, and training in social interaction. The STEP instructors gradually became full-time cottage treatment staff members and STEP as a special institutional program was discontinued.

The new Commissioner urged staff members throughout DYS to suggest and implement ideas for better treatment programs. While some staff members enjoyed the new freedom to try out their ideas, they complained, sometimes bitterly, that their efforts were not sufficiently supported by the administration. For example, the STEP tutors complained on several occasions about the lack of adequate support for their program and particularly the lack of direction or a "broad master-plan."

The Commissioner firmly believed the traditional training school practices would not be tolerated if they were fully exposed to public view. He therefore encouraged community visitors and volunteers to help run the programs in the institutions, advocated a much more active use of local community facilities and programs suitable for young offenders, and used people from universities and civic groups throughout the state in volunteer programs. In addition, youth left institution grounds for various educational and recreational field trips. In general, these efforts to involve the community were not promoted vigorously by institutional staff. Perhaps one of the most successful programs was developed between the Westfield Reception and Detention Center and the School of Education at the University of Massachusetts. The Westfield institution was becoming severely overcrowded, and the staff saw community programs as a means of relief. The use of student and faculty volunteers as teachers and counselors was incorporated into the curriculum of the School of Education with students receiving academic credit for their work at Westfield.

The Problem of Staff Development

The new program ideas could not be realized without the help of staff committed to the new philosophy of treatment and competent to develop programs to implement it. Miller's problem of recruiting or retraining staff for this purpose was formidable. The civil service system in Massachusetts was grafted onto a system of political patronage grounded in an ethnically based structure of political power. The legal requirement to give absolute preference to veterans, in addition to the tradition of political sponsorship, had served on the whole to subordinate merit as a qualification for state employment. Once past the probationary period, employees obtained virtually absolute security in their civil service positions. Miller could not bring in many new staff members unless he secured new funds and created new positions or unless voluntary retirement and resignation became widespread.

Miller's options were limited. He could fill job vacancies with new staff members of his own choosing while searching for loyal adherents of the new philosophy within the existing staff; he could reassign authority and responsibility without regard to civil service classification; or, he could retrain and educate older staff members to the new philosophies of treatment. He pursued all three options, tentatively during the first year, and more vigorously during the second year as new funds became available.

A survey of staff members of the Department of Youth Services during the summer of 1970 showed that many of them, especially those in academic, clinical, or Boston Office assignments, wanted to give the new policies and philosophy of treatment a chance. Table 2 shows the percentage among various staff groups and committed youth who strongly approved of new or proposed policies and programs in the Department. The vocational staff was least approving, followed by general staff (i.e., cottage parents or supervisors) and field administrators of the institutions. The parole staff members usually had little contact with the institutions. Predictably, therefore, they favored reorganization in general, since it pointed to institutional reforms primarily, but did not approve of cottage groups making decisions, especially about release on parole, furlough, or work in the community, which would affect the normal range of the parole officer's responsibilities. Youth responses were most enthusiastic about policies allowing personal discretion about hair style, clothing, smoking, and coeducational programs.

Table 2
Percentage in Each Interest Group "Strongly Approving" Reforms

Item		Interest Group							
	General Staff	Academics	Clinicians	Vocational	Parole	Field Administrators	Boston Office	Committed Youth	Other
Reorganization of the Department by the legislature in 1969	12	16	32	16	33	22	33	—	6
Decision to transfer or parole boys (girls) up to the staff of the institution (instead of Boston Office)	24	48	48	20	0	28	21	17	28
Allowing cottage groups of staff and boys (girls) to make decisions about:									
Discipline	18	33	53	4	19	17	35	20	20
Release	8	22	38	8	5	12	21	22	13
Furlough and home visits	12	33	41	4	5	12	32	28	19
Assignments to work details	15	33	48	4	10	12	27	13	19
Permitting boys (girls) to make individual decisions about:									
Hair styles	11	44	59	4	35	11	38	49	15
Clothes	7	44	56	4	25	11	38	50	13
Smoking	5	26	34	0	14	0	29	45	13
Elimination of severe disciplinary measures such as long confinement									

create a "therapeutic community"	19	13	29	12	20	4	41	41	12
Expanding the Outward Bound program and forestry camps	34	16	49	28	40	20	37	41	26
Introducing STEP type of educational programs such as the one at Shirley	11	8	29	12	43	12	26	22	7
The following three plans suggested for development of Topsfield as:									
A staff training center	21	—	53	33	29	16	34	37	18
A special drug treatment center	30	—	38	22	33	20	28	52	32
An experimental center for group therapy programs	21	—	50	17	24	4	32	48	20
Expansion of use of volunteers in institutional program activities	19	18	44	22	14	8	44	41	26
Closing Bridgewater and allowing each institution to deal with its own security problems	15	21	47	19	14	8	22	26	20
Making some institutions coeducational	13	52	59	12	19	4	55	26	15
Number	53	166	34	18	21	25	31	27	76

These responses sensitively reflect the new directions of DYS and the resulting internal distributions of power, responsibility, and reward.[17] Later, for example, one institution's barber reminisced about the days he taught his trade to a few boys well enough so they could obtain certification, because they stayed long enough to learn and short hair styles were mandatory. A printing shop instructor felt the same way. The general staff and field administrators also sensed the emerging challenge to their authority by program innovators from the Boston Office and the greater familiarity that academic and clinical staff seemed to have with the new cottage-based treatment programs. Parole staff were reluctant to share decision making with youth—an essential requirement for negotiating successful placements in new community-based programs. Most of the parole staff defined themselves as much like juvenile bureau police officers: their job was to keep paroled youth out of trouble by advice, surveillance, and threats of official sanctions. The new image of the parole officer as a youth advocate and organizer of community services and opportunities for youth represented a radical and threatening change.

The Commissioner relied on members of the existing staff able to relate to the new philosophy of treatment. At the same time he recruited new top aides among youth workers in Ohio and in Massachusetts who had both professional credentials and enthusiasm for the job. As appropriated funds became available in the second year Miller appointed these aides to posts with program and policy development responsibilities.

The Commissioner circumvented civil service constraints by assigning authority and responsibility without regard to formal civil service rank. This caused insecurity and administrative confusion when job titles and pay assignments bore little relationship to effective responsibility. At one point a new administrator functioning in effect as Superintendent of the Industrial School for Boys at Shirley was in fact assigned and paid from the job category of maintenance worker.

The third tactic, retraining and reeducating the staff, met with relatively little success despite considerable staff interest. The three-day conference with Maxwell Jones, which gave staff for the first time a clear inkling of what Miller had in mind, was followed in September, 1970, with a training session run by Dr. Harry Vorrath, Superintendent of the Red Wing Reformatory in Minnesota. At this point some staff members had accepted the inevitability of training and were responsive to the mixture of control and treat-

[17]For the theoretical analysis relating the new goals of the Department and the internal distribution of power responsibility and reward, see Alden C. Miller, Lloyd E. Ohlin, and Robert B. Coates, "A Theoretical Synthesis for Promoting Change in Social Service Systems," (Unpublished paper, Center for Criminal Justice, Harvard Law School, October, 1973).

296

ment ideology which Dr. Vorrath espoused. An effort to routinize staff re-training at a new training center at Topsfield faltered when community re-sistance to this new Topsfield facility, acquired by DYS shortly before Miller's appointment, prevented its full use. These difficulties led to a gradual phasing out of this retraining effort. It demonstrated, however, that retraining would be at best a very gradual process. It would be financially costly and divisive since it would involve the articulation and resolution of fundamental differences in attitudes, values, and beliefs about the reeducation of youth in trouble. It would also have to be undertaken within each institution for all staff members to have lasting effect.

The Development of Fiscal Resources

Money was a constant problem. Unless funds could be freed from the support of traditional institutional programs, practices, and facilities, the chance to develop alternative treatment measures would be severely limited. The appropriation process in Massachusetts for all state agencies relies on supplemental and deficiency budgets to pick up and support commitments not adequately covered in the initial appropriation. This process is deeply immersed in political considerations and bargaining; whether a state Department or subunit gets the funds it wants rests on its own capacity to influence the legislative process. For a newcomer like Miller, despite public support from the Governor and his staff, acquiring these skills took time.

The Commissioner did not rely exclusively on the state but requested federal support. He secured grants from the Federal Law Enforcement Assistance Administration in the U.S. Department of Justice both directly and through the Massachusetts Governor's Committee on Law Enforcement and Administration of Justice, from Title I of the Federal Education Act, and Title IV of the Office of Manpower Development and Training in the U.S. Department of Labor. This federal funding permitted Miller to bring in top staff committed to his philosophy, without the restrictions of the civil service system and to establish new types of community based treatment services and supportive summertime educational, recreational, and training services in the institution. The new funds underwrote a planning unit directed by a vigorous advocate of community based treatment for youth. This unit grew rapidly as a cadre of sensitive and dedicated people. In the Spring of 1971, it worked with the key departmental administrators to produce a seven point plan setting out the direction of reform. It called for a) regionalization; b) community based treatment centers; c) expansion of the forestry program; d) relocation of detention; e) increased placement alternatives; f) grants-in-aid to cities and towns; and g) an intensive care security unit. These became the chief goals of DYS during the third year of the new administration. The planning unit and the top staff dealt with constant crises in the progress toward those goals. They also carried major responsibility for procuring new federal funds. Without this articulate infusion of new thought and ideas, the funds they procured and the crises they helped to solve, the rapid transition from the training school structure to noninstitutional alternatives would have been most difficult to achieve.

The Results of Phase II
The first two years of the new administration was a period of constant crisis, confrontation, and confusion. The Commissioner possessed neither a blueprint, nor the staff and financial resources to impose a new model of treatment services. The only stable guidelines were the broad goals of the new system, i.e., that confinement of children should be as humane as possible and their treatment as therapeutic and responsive as staff could devise. The needs of children rather than administrative orderliness or staff prerogatives and preferments were to be given top priority.

The Commissioner regarded most of the existing administrative rules and staff protections as major obstacles to change and believed the new philosophy of treatment could not be effectively established until the punitive aspects of the older system had been fully exposed and the system for distributing responsibility, authority, and rewards reconstituted. For twenty years under the previous administration, staff had acquired a set of beliefs about delinquent youth, conceptions of appropriate staff and youth relationships, and career expectations consistent with the traditional training school philosophy. Many felt rejected and threatened by the new philosophy of treatment and responded with hostility, acts of sabotage, passivity, or apathetic compliance. They magnified the confusion resulting from many of the new directives, passively endured or even encouraged runaways, and complained constantly of permissiveness and loss of authority. Although some older staff members were excited by the new philosophy and joined in with the new recruits, the first two years of the new administration were characterized by a progressive intensification of conflict and polarization of views. During the first year the new Commissioner was largely dependent on converts to his philosophy among older staff members to implement his directives. The fiscal and civil service constraints gradually produced a chaotic pattern for the assignment of administrative responsibility and authority. Former administrators placed on leave status were replaced in effective authority by adherents to the new philosophy without much regard for rank or civil service status. A fluid pattern of staff assignment developed. Staff from the Boston Office and from the institutions were reassigned to new positions as crises developed. The frequent shift of staff members to new administrative positions undermined expectations and created insecurity about career advancement based on traditional criteria of promotion.

Deposed and alienated adherents of the older philosophy were not without resources for fighting back. Most of them had long periods of service in the DYS, relatives or friends in the legislature, and influential associations in the small towns in which they resided close to the institutions. They also had long established working relationships with many judges, probation officers, and public officials who shared their views about the function and operation of training schools. Stories about policies and case decisions that documented the permissive and chaotic state of administrative practices were magnified and circulated. Many judges, probation officers, and police officials, even those initially sympathetic to the idea of reform, began to oppose the new administration. And by the fall of 1971, two legislative investigations of DYS were underway.

The results of this phase of the reform movement are difficult to assess apart from a longer range evaluation of the total movement toward community based treatment services. It is clear, however, that the concept of small group therapeutic communities had some success. This experiment showed that traditional training school environments based on a cottage system could be decentralized. One could organize within some cottages a group therapy approach creating for both youth and staff a new set of rules, expectations, and practices. The data revealed reactions from youth and staff that justifies such efforts elsewhere and are consistent with previous studies in other setting.

Whether the favorable responses of youth to the group therapy approach is translated into better adjustment in the home, school, or neighborhood cannot yet be determined. The data on recidivism rates and community adjustment of youth in these different programs are still being assembled.

Phase III: From Institutions to Community Corrections

The new administration found itself unable to change staff attitudes and beliefs or to impose a therapeutic community in all of the cottages. Table 3 provides some evidence of this; it shows a consistent pattern of differences in staff response to the items on custody and treatment as one moves from the most traditional to the most treatment oriented cottages. Miller was aware of the entrenched resistance thus reflected in many traditional cottages, and was impatient with the slow pace of change. He suggested late in 1970 that, despite the storminess of the preceding year and the feeling of traditional staff that DYS was being turned completely upside down, there had really been little or no fundamental change. He felt the same way a year later, even after some of the therapeutic community oriented cottages began to achieve conspicuous success.

Table 3
Staff Selection of Statements They Feel Best Reflect the Purposes of the Institutions

Tools of Institutions	Custody-Oriented Cottages				Treatment-Oriented Cottages			
	Cottage Nine	Cottage Eight	Elms Cottage	Westview Cottage	Sunset Cottage	Shirley Cottage	Tops-Field	I Belong
Percent of staff choosing three custodial purposes	47	33	32	37	13	21	15	9
			34			16		
Percent of staff choosing three treatment purposes	42	50	58	52	80	67	69	81
			51			72		
N	(27)	(15)	(40)	(29)	(15)	(16)	(15)	(8)

Source: Barry Feld, *Subcultures of Selected Boys' Cottages in Massachusetts Department of Youth Services Institutions in 1971*, Center for Criminal Justice, Harvard Law School, October, 1972. Staff were asked to choose three from a list of eleven statements of possible goals commonly associated with institutions for delinquents.

Miller finally concluded that therapeutic communities could be run successfully in only a few cottages within the institutions. However, he felt they might be much more successful outside the existing institutions. In community settings greater professional resources would be available to provide volunteer and purchased services in relation to which traditional expectations about juvenile prisons might no longer have force. The successful treatment cottages could then be redefined as staging cottages which would later be moved off the institutional grounds to become community-based facilities.

Closing the institutions raised the problems of building a new structure of services more closely integrated with community life. This would be the challenge of the third phase of reform. It came to involve the decentralization or regionalization of services into seven regions; the development of new court liaison staff working with juvenile judges and probation personnel to coordinate detention, diagnostic and referral policies, and individual case decisions; a new network of community services including residential and non-residential placements for individuals and small groups; some centralized services for the institutional treatment of dangerous and disturbed offenders; ways to monitor the quality of the services increasingly purchased from private agencies; and staff development programs to reassign, retrain, or discharge former staff members in ways minimizing personal hardship and injustice.

Deinstitutionalization

In the winter of 1971–72 DYS closed two major institutions, Shirley and Lyman. Lancaster was converted partly to privately run programs on the institutional grounds later in 1972. Oakdale, originally an institution for very young boys, and then a reception center, was finally closed in late 1972. No strong public reaction immediately appeared in response to the closing of the institutions. The Commissioner had succeeded in exposing these facilities as brutalizing environments for youth and staff alike. When Shirley closed, the press featured stories and pictures of Miller, members of the legislature, staff, and youth formerly confined at Shirley sledge hammering the bars and locks of the segregation cells of Cottage #9. The Commissioner emerged as an advocate in the public eye of new opportunities for youth, his opponents as advocates of punishment and repression. The staff and supporters of the now "evil" institutions reacted with stunned disbelief and feelings of betrayal for their years of work. The radical shift in correctional philosophy seemed too swift and uncompromising to accord them their due. How could the new approach suddenly be so right and the older one, in which they had staked their careers and future, so wrong?

Closing the institutions involved finding alternative placements for the youth and reassignment for the staff. The University of Massachusetts Conference was organized to transfer a large number of youth out of the institutions into the community quickly enough to avoid excessive disruption and to get the job done before crippling opposition could develop.[18] Ninety-nine boys and girls from Lyman, Lancaster, and two detention centers were taken to the University of Massachusetts for a month in January and February, 1972. College students served as advocates for the DYS youth while placements for them were worked out at the Conference. The college students were selected from three colleges and universities in the area by members of the Juvenile Opportunities Extension, a University of Massachusetts student organization that had been participating extensively in the program at the Westfield institution. Arrangements for future placement of youth, e.g., sending the youth home, placing youth in a foster home or in a group home, were worked out in a collaborative manner between the DYS staff, the advocate, and the youth themselves by considering the range of program alternatives and the needs of specific youth.

The move was accomplished with much fanfare involving a caravan of cars from Lyman to the University of Massachusetts at Amherst. The Gover-

---

[18]For a fuller discussion of this Conference see, Robert B. Coates, Alden D. Miller, and Lloyd E. Ohlin, "A Strategic Innovation in the Process of Deinstitutionalization: The University of Massachusetts Conference," in Bakal, *Closing Correctional Institutions*, pp. 127–148.

nor appeared later at the Conference to lend his support. The Conference, through the student advocates, succeeded in placing sixty-five youth in other than institutional settings. Approximately equal proportions of those remaining were placed in other institutions, ran away, or remained unplaced.

The drama of the Conference as a way of quickly closing institutions is suggested by reactions of staff members at the Lyman Institution. Staff there had been told months before that the institution would be closed but simply could not believe it. A cottage which had burned was painstakingly rebuilt by staff who were standing at the door waiting for youth to be assigned the day the motorcade to Amherst virtually emptied the institution in a matter of hours. A few weeks later staff members were exchanging rumors of mass escapes, chaos, and widespread sexual misconduct at the Conference, which would soon result in the youth being brought back to the institution. In contrast, one university official, after the Conference, remarked that the DYS youth had actually been less trouble to the university than a convention of the American Legion.

Recidivism data obtained from the central probation office records after an eleven month follow-up period yielded an overall official court appearance rate after the Conference of 48 percent with most of the appearances (79 percent) occurring during the first four months. While calculations on the rates of reappearance in court on new charges are not yet completed for the various samples of youth in the research study, the recidivism rates reported here for youth in the Conference are probably somewhat lower than court appearance recidivism rates characterizing youth from the traditional training school programs.

The youths relocated and the staff reassigned, the grounds and buildings of the large institutions which have been closed still remain with the haunting possibility that they may be used again as a primary treatment resource. Planners and administrators in DYS are convinced that DYS must divest itself of these institutions to consolidate the new policies. In addition, the Lancaster Training School is still in use although over half of the population there is in programs privately administered. The actual use of this institution probably constitutes a more serious threat to the stability of reform than the mere continuing existence of other facilities.

Regionalization

The shift from a custodial to treatment orientation had already abridged institutional autonomy, lodging greater control in the central office; with the movement toward highly decentralized community based services, control had to be reallocated to the new regional offices.

Each of these regional units consists of a small suite of business offices to serve the administrative need to coordinate and implement services for youth in each region. Unlike an institution, a regional office cannot house youth in the premises. Youth must be referred quickly to appropriate residential or non-residential programs.

With support from the Boston Office, the seven regional offices have developed placement opportunities for youth referred or sentenced to the DYS by the courts. They make contractual arrangements, usually within the region, for these services. They also handle detention, so that a youth's contact with DYS now is always at least nominally through some regional office. DYS is also trying to organize the budget by regions, somewhat as it was organized around the institutions in the past, but with less stringent controls over intradepartmental transfers.

For the youth in the DYS, regionalization has immeasurably improved service since regional offices know more about possible placements in the communities, where the youth are, and how they are doing. This now makes successive trial placements feasible, if necessary, so that ultimately youth can hope to get the best possible placement. For example, a youth might be placed in one or more foster homes before assignment to a group home, perhaps with a program of group therapy better suited to his needs. Sometimes a trial period in a particular program is explicitly agreed on by the youth and the staff with the option of trying something else if it does not work out. In other cases, evidence of poor adjustment such as a recurrent tendency to run away or persistent defiance of authority, signals the need for a change. Most staff members in interviews expressed their belief that regionalization provides new opportunities to work more effectively with youth—ways that simply did not seem available under the old system. For planners and administrators, regionalization has meant a closer fit between programs and the needs and resources of each region. The University of Massachusetts Conference placement staff had felt hampered by having to work on a statewide level.

There are still signs of newness in the work of the regions. Records and current operating information systems are only gradually developing to link the regions with the Boston Office. Perhaps the greatest continuing need, associated with the transition from the institutional structure, is to divert funds from excess staff positions left in the institution budgets to the new regional programs.

Development of New Detention, Court Liaison, and Referral Programs
Before 1972 nearly all youth detained prior to trial were held in high security institutions. DYS regards this as unnecessary for most youth and even destructive for those who are not dangerous.

Alternatives have been developed with the help of private agencies. Foster care has been greatly expanded for detention purposes. Shelter care units have been set up in several regions, each generally housing between twelve and twenty youth. These are group homes with program activities which allow for rapid turnover. Local YMCA's have proved to be the most productive private resource for such facilities. The units are staffed with a combination of YMCA and DYS personnel to involve youth in constructive activities and to discharge DYS's custodial responsibilities to the courts.

DYS created the court liaison role to deal more effectively with needs of youth while they are still under the care of the court. The court liaison officer recommends placement possibilities within the DYS system and sometimes, as well, other alternatives to conventional detention. Thus, if a youth is referred or committed to the Department of Youth Services the time between such action and placement is minimized, and the reception phase in many instances is no longer distinct from detention. In seeking other options to commitment and to reduce labeling effects, DYS has encouraged the courts to *refer* youth on a voluntary basis prior to or after adjudication instead of formally sentencing or *committing* them to DYS. From a legal standpoint *referred* youth are still within the jurisdiction of the court while *committed* youth are released to the jurisdictional authority of the Department. The services available to both groups are much the same. The principal advantage of a referral status is that the youth avoids having a formal commitment on his record. Referrals have increased greatly throughout the system, with, of course, regional variations. It is estimated that between one-fourth and one-third of all youth in both residential and nonresidential programs are now referrals instead of commitments.

The DYS staff regard the detention, court liaison, and referral programs as important components in consolidating regionalization. The regional offices have largely taken over development of these programs while quality control, monitoring, and general administrative matters have remained in the Boston Office. The court liaison and referral programs also appear to have created more constructive working relationships with the courts. DYS is providing services which the courts did not previously have readily available and is able to draw on a state-wide referral and quality control system difficult for the courts to develop themselves.

Private contracting agencies, especially the YMCA's, find these new programs an opportunity to expand their own services. A number of judges and probation staff have made effective use of the new referral opportunities and the assistance of the court liaison officers in utilizing these alternatives. In other instances they have been critical of the resistance of the DYS staff to high security facilities for a greater number of youth.

While the range of detention alternatives has been greatly increased, the older large security facilities, such as Roslindale, continue to be used. The inability of DYS to find a substitute for Roslindale or to make it a decent, habitable facility has puzzled visitors supportive of the Massachusetts reforms. A detailed history of Miller's efforts to humanize this institution — and their failure — would reveal the whole spectrum of forces (conflicting conceptions of the delinquent and appropriate treatment, the abuses of authority, untrained staff, overcrowding, civil service constraints, court and police demands for security, community resistance to new shelters or secure facilities, boredom, idleness, fear, and violence) that turns large institutions for juvenile delinquents into prisons. Physically secure units are necessary for certain youth, but such units should probably be small in size, administer a diversified program, and provide responsive care.

As in the past, detention services for girls lag somewhat behind the alternatives available for boys. The court liaison program, while providing benefits to some courts and some regions, is still not operating across the entire state.

The new referral system is not without potentially serious policy problems. It is sound to reduce the harmful results of a youth being committed. However, if youth are now being referred who otherwise would not have been committed to DYS, the risk of labeling youth earlier is also enhanced. There is some evidence that referrals to DYS are increasing without compensating statewide reductions in commitments. Whether the additional youth will unnecessarily acquire invidious labels, or whether their presence will lessen the degree to which the youth who had always been in DYS acquire such labels, is a question demanding urgent concern and investigation. There are many issues to be resolved. If the DYS programs become less punitive, more therapeutic, and more readily available they will be used more often. Yet if they provide a treatment of last resort for the most dangerous and disturbed youth, all of the youth serviced may be perceived in the same way unless clear and possibly harmful distinctions are maintained.

Development of New Residential and Non-Residential Placements
One of the most pressing problems confronting the Department of Youth Services as the institutions were closing was the development of alterna-

tives to institutional confinement.[19] The Boston Office had begun exploring placement alternatives in 1971, and stepped up its activities with the University of Massachusetts Conference in January, 1972. At first this activity focused on the development of group homes, but when it became obvious that many youth might be stranded as the institutions closed, emphasis was shifted to the development of non-residential alternatives, day or night programs in which youth participate while living at home or in some other setting. Since 1972 developing placements has become almost exclusively the responsibility of the regions.

There are roughly 80 non-residential programs across the state, in which DYS places youth, about 120 residential programs, and about 200 foster homes. About 700 youth are placed in residential group homes, and about 250 in foster homes. About 700 youth are in the non-residential programs such as Neighborhood Youth Corps, a recreation program at Massachusetts Maritime Academy, and programs at community colleges. The two most heavily used programs for committed and referred youth are group homes and non-residential services, with foster homes being considerably less used, and the use of traditional parole varying greatly from region to region. The group homes represent an alternative of moderate cost, while the non-residential services are inexpensive (see Table 4). If problems of providing prompt payment to vendors are worked out soon, the use of foster care, even less expensive than non-residential services, will probably expand.

One of the serious problems plaguing placement in general is the time lag between provision of services and payment for services. It has sometimes become so great that contracting agencies question whether regional direc-

Table 4
Cost of Program Types per Youth per Week

Type of Program	Costs per Youth per Week
Residential:	
Intensive Care	$145–$290
Group Homes	$145–$150
Foster Care	$ 30–$ 40
Non-residential	$50

---

[19]For a report on problems in overcoming community resistance to the establishment of community based residential facilities see, Robert B. Coates and Alden D. Miller, "Neutralization of Community Resistance to Group Homes," in Bakal, pp. 67–84.

tors really have the authority to contract for the DYS; as a consequence some smaller agencies are threatened with bankruptcy. The problem of long delayed payments is endemic to all the state services and especially in those departments which make substantial use of private vendors. The legislature has been reluctant to appropriate funds for purchased services especially when the somewhat unpredictable costs require deficiency appropriations. Even where funds are available, payments are delayed by a complicated system for setting rates, approving contracts, or authorizing payments in each case. All of these difficulties were aggravated in the case of DYS. Insufficient funds were available from the state, and the federal grants contained program and accounting requirements which DYS had difficulty meeting in time to establish the needed group homes. The rapid closing of the institutions created an immediate demand for alternatives which the cumbersome funding process could not meet.

No phase of Miller's administration has come under stronger criticism than his decision to initiate new programs before the resources to back them up were in hand. He took the calculated risk that the support of reform by federal funding agencies and the state executive and legislative leadership was strong enough to fulfill his promises of reimbursement in the end. In doing so he exposed his administration to a series of investigations and charges of fiscal mismanagement, irresponsibility, and administrative incompetence. In response, he has charged that the system had to be forced to meet the legitimate needs of youth for appropriate services or the development of these services would have been delayed many years.

There is ample justification for the charges on both sides. Miller's driving ambition to create a more flexible and responsive set of services for delinquent youth was reinforced by his impatience with red tape and his ability to tolerate a lot of administrative confusion as long as "helping kids" came first in every decision. His critics acknowledged his concern for youth and his credibility with them, but felt at the same time that the pace of change was harmful to both staff and youth. They argued that many youth committed to DYS needed more prolonged, professional, and intensive care than the hastily contrived new programs could furnish. DYS's readiness to place youth in newly created, untried programs might do more harm than good for many of them. The neglect of the legitimate needs of staff members showed a callous disregard for years of service and acquired skills which could still find fulfillment in the new system of services. In the new programs exploitation of staff idealism and commitment to youth services ought not to preclude provision for their economic survival and career investments.

It is still too soon to judge fairly these claims and countercharges. Short-run assessments may lack fair consideration of the long range goals which these changes were designed to achieve in terms of economic and social adjustment and community protection.

Development of New Special Programs for Dangerous and Disturbed Offenders

There is widespread agreement that most people, both youth and adult, who are now locked up need not be. There is also widespread agreement that some of those now routinely locked up, both youth and adult, really must continue to be confined. It is also widely recognized that it is extremely difficult to separate out with a tolerable margin of error those who need to be locked up from those who do not. However, recent experience in DYS with community placements has shown that with youth this problem is not as difficult as is generally assumed. Many youth clearly and obviously belong in community placements. Some clearly belong in secure settings. A few are problematic. An obvious need that emerged as the institutions closed was the provision of secure settings with intensive treatment for dangerous and disturbed youth, coupled with safeguards that would prevent misuse of these facilities.

DYS distinguishes youth who are behavior problems from youth who need psychiatric care. For both sorts of youth the Department has tried to purchase services and in December, 1973, approximately 125 youth were in intensive care placements. For the youth with behavior problems, a program run by ex-offenders who relate directly to these youth while "taking no nonsense" has had some success. This program stresses use of community resources within a framework of appropriate custodial security. For youth needing psychiatric care, DYS has purchased services from private agencies. It has also tried to coordinate more closely with the Department of Mental Health. For example, in October, 1973, it finally opened a special unit for up to six youths needing intensive psychological services at the Medfield State Hospital. Safeguards for the youth in these different settings rely on advance agreements about decision making and frequent case review.

One danger is that the courts, lacking what they believe to be secure commitment facilities, will bind over youth considered dangerous or disturbed to adult courts. These might result in confinement in an adult jail or prison. So far (up to April, 1973) this has not happened. The commitment of persons seventeen or younger from 1966 to 1973 remained very stable in the state correctional system (see Table 5). For the county jails there has been a slight rise in the percentage of all commitments represented by youth but lower numbers of youth committed in 1971 and 1972 than in pre-

Table 5
Number and Percentage of Persons Committed to the State Adult
Correctional System and County Correctional System by Year and Age

Year	State Correctional System			County Correctional System		
	Total Commitments	17 and Younger	Percent	Total Commitments	17 and Younger	Percent
Jan-March						
1973	199	6	3.0%	— *	— *	— *
1972	1,127	50	4.4%	5,499	252	4.6%
1971	1,091	47	4.3%	6,474	240	3.7%
1970	859	38	4.4%	8,119	287	3.5%
1969	875	30	3.4%	8,108	247	3.0%
1968	855	42	4.9%	8,467	283	3.3%
1967	739	32	4.3%	8,550	263	3.1%
1966	826	39	4.7%	8,990	275	3.1%
TOTAL	6,571	284	4.3%	54,207	1,847	3.4%

*Data not available.
Source: Massachusetts Department of Corrections, May 30, 1973.

vious years, except for 1969.

DYS has continuing needs in this area. It needs a program for girls, and it may need more funds for psychiatric treatment alternatives. And it needs to work with all juvenile judges to implement better ways of treating these youth than binding them over to adult courts, or relying excessively on maximum security facilities.

Development of New Quality Control Procedures

Quality control of detention, residential, and non-residential placements, and high security programs received little attention in DYS until the development of new programs made the issue inescapable. The basic problem is how to maintain control over the quality of programs contracted to private agencies. Private groups have not been accustomed to account for program quality to a public agency.

Three units have become involved in evaluation of ongoing programs. Two units in the Bureau of Aftercare have monitored some of the non-residential and residential programs. Another evaluation unit more recently organized has been more systematic. Programs are now rated on such dimensions as quality of facilities, administration and staff, controls, program, clinical services, diversion, and budget. Information from all three units has been used by the Boston Office and regional staff for recommending program changes, and in some instances program termination.

The Boston Office staff acknowledges that quality control is not fully operational, but the fact that some programs have been terminated on the basis of evaluations has encouraged staff in their belief that DYS can collect evaluative data and make decisions on the basis of it. Regional directors, a number of whom were at first skeptical of the evaluation and information system, are now calling for more evaluation to improve their own placement decisons.

The development of a fully operational quality control unit is the most essential requirement of a system relying primarily on the purchase of services from private vendors. The latter are free from the rigid constraints of public civil service and line budgets dependent on the political process of legislative approval. However, this freedom does not in itself guarantee quality programs. DYS terminated placement at several group homes. In one case the facility was found to be structurally unsound and the treatment of youth inhumane, i.e. the building had broken windows which were not being replaced and youth were being fed only once a day to cut costs. In a second instance a project was terminated because the promised services, counseling, education, and work experiences, were not being provided. In yet another case the project was stopped because the program was administered in an overly regimented, institutional manner.

The experience of other states also justifies vigorous and powerful quality control procedures. The professional or sectarian orthodoxies of private agencies may prove as inflexible and ultimately as harmful to youth as the regimen of the traditional training school. Furthermore, their tendency to admit only those youth most amenable and acceptable for treatment leaves the public agency responsible ultimately for the care of the most difficult and most economically and socially disadvantaged youth. Great care must be taken in drawing up contract requirements for the purchase of private services to guarantee access for the quality control unit. DYS seems cognizant of these problems and has demonstrated its ability to evaluate programs and eliminate those that do not perform adequately. However, it has not allocated enough resources to build a quality control system capable of monitoring all programs regularly.

The Problem of Personnel Development

Early state-wide attempts at staff retraining programs were not very successful. With regionalization and deinstitutionalization, staff training programs also changed and are now handled regionally. Deinstitutionalization and the new practice of purchasing service has put old staff members in positions where they have had to learn new skills on the job. The Boston Office has attempted to provide displaced staff with opportunities to transfer to different work, including new casework and other alternatives under the regional offices, or to join private non-profit treatment agencies that contract services to DYS. The problem nonetheless remains serious; half or more of the staff of DYS could be transferred out of the Department without impairing its functioning since most of the services provided by staff in the past are now purchased from the private sector. DYS records for 1969 show that 531 employees were assigned to the major institutions that have since been closed or converted partly to private programs. The number currently assigned to these institutions is 120; of these, 61 provide maintenance services and care for 25 youth in two cottages at Lancaster, while 59 simply maintain the facilities of two other institutions. Forty-four of the 59 will be transferred to other departments in state government destined to take over those institutions in the near future. Many of the original institutional staff not thus accounted for are associated with regional offices, which did not exist in 1969, and now employ 269 persons. The central administration in Boston has dropped from 160 to 94 employees.

Many staff members who have involved themselves in the new system have been satisfied with it. Others who have been unable or unwilling to break with past traditions have found the experience distressing. Still, the staff union leadership, with increased understanding of what is being done and why, has not opposed the changes as it did in earlier years.

The staff development problem has also been hindered by the organization of the budget. The majority of the staff that actually operates programs for youth are now in private agencies contracting services to the state; this should be reflected in the budget if staff development is to continue successfully.

The Results of Phase III
Data on youth adjustment to the new community settings are being collected through cross-sectional surveys of youth in programs and by longitudinal cohort analysis involving periodic interviews with a sample of youth as they pass through programs of the DYS. Preliminary data from the cross-sectional survey of youth in representative residential settings in two regions compared with data obtained from youth in traditional and experimental cottages before the institutions were closed suggests progress in creating better environments.

Probably one of the more salient concerns in socialization, whether in the

Table 6
Youth Perception of Reward and Punishment by Type of Program

Question	Traditional Institutional Cottage (%)	Experimental Cottage in Institution (%)	Community Based Program (%)
The staff will reward a kid for good behavior			
Agree	77	78	76°°
Disagree or DK	23	22	24
Total	100	100	100
N	85	89	34
If you do well, will the staff reward you?			
No			33°
Include me in things			7
Additional privileges			26
Make me look good in front of others			7
Make me feel good about what I am doing			28
Total			100
N			43
Other kids will reward a kid for good behavior			
Agree	37	60	80°°
Disagree or DK	63	40	20
Total	100	100	100
N	82	87	35
If a kid messes up, the staff will punish him/her			
Agree	81	66	44°°
Disagree or DK	19	34	56
Total	100	100	100
N	83	86	39
If you screw up, will staff here punish you?			
No			21°
Separate from group			13
Take away privileges			45
Hit			16
Embarrass in front of others			3
Make me feel guilty			3
Total			100
N			38

°°Source: Cross-sectional survey of youth in programs   °Source: Cohort Analysis context of the family, the school, or a program designed to aid youth in trouble, is the distribution of rewards and punishments. The development of a reward-based system is documented in Table 6. Youth in the three types of cottage environments agreed that they would be rewarded by staff for good behavior. The initial cohort data shows specifically *how* they think they will be rewarded in the community based programs. The most frequently mentioned response was "staff will make me feel good about what I am doing." The second most frequently mentioned response was "staff will give me additional privileges."

The role of youth themselves in the distribution of rewards provides some of the most striking contrasts across the three cottage environments. Only 37 percent of the youth in the traditional cottages believed that other youth would reward them for good behavior. In the experimental cottages the figure was 60 percent. This is a dramatic change which suggests that youth in community based programs are learning how to support others in a positive manner, and are in turn being supported by their peers. If this contrast between the cottage types is supported by data we are still collecting, it will be a strong indication that the new programs are producing some important, positive, and immediate effects.

While reward patterns are important in any context of socialization, punishment patterns are equally important. Again, there are contrasts across cottage environments, here in the perceived frequency of staff punishing kids who "mess up." In the traditional cottages, 81 percent of the youth believed that staff would punish. Sixty-six percent of youth in the experimental cottages indicated that staff would punish. And 44 percent of the youth in the community based programs reported that staff would punish. Punishment seems less salient in the community based programs than in the other cottage environments; discipline relies more on reward. It is also possible that punishment in the newer programs is more sophisticated and less likely to be perceived as punishment *per se* by the youth. This may often be the case in more "caring" situations. On the basis of the preliminary cohort data the type of punishment most often perceived by youth in the community based programs is the taking away of privileges.

Youth in the experimental and traditional cottages and in the community based programs saw different purposes in their respective programs. Sixty-one percent of the youth in traditional cottages believed that the cottage staff were more concerned with keeping kids under control than with helping them with their problems. Only 30 percent of the youth in the experimental cottages reported that that was the case, and only 14 percent of the youth in the community based programs believe that control is a greater concern of the staff than helping to solve problems.

Table 7
Youth Perception of Staff Control and Support by Type of Program

Question	Traditional Institutional Cottage (%)	Experimental Cottage in Institution (%)	Community Based Program (%)
This cottage is more concerned with keeping kids under control than with helping them with their problems			
Agree	61	30	14°°
Disagree or DK	39	70	86
Total	100	100	100
N	85	87	35
Do the staff here help you stay out of trouble?			
No			23°
Encourage			53
Help get jobs, into school, groups, etc.			23
Total			100
N			43

°°Source: Cross-sectional survey of youth in programs
°Source: Cohort Analysis

Youth in the cohort study have been asked how staff in the community-based programs try to help them stay out of trouble. The majority of respondents indicate that the staff encourage them by telling them that they can make it. Over twenty percent of the youth reported that staff helped them to get jobs, to join youth groups, to obtain placement in new school programs and things like that. We will be able to say more about the relative impact of moral support or encouragement and concrete support such as finding jobs as the cohort analysis proceeds.

In order to know how youth in the cohort analysis perceive relationships with others after they have been through a program, we have tabulated responses from the semantic differential test on two items, good-bad and fair-unfair, with respect to the youth's perceptions of each of nine categories of persons. The two items, good-bad and fair-unfair, are strongly related and are reliable indicators of a generally positive evaluation of a category. We have ordered the objects of evaluation in Table 8 by the ratings given them by our cohort youth on the good-bad item, and presented the average scale response to the good-bad item and the fair-unfair item. The scale range possible on each item was one to seven. Higher scores mean ratings indicating better or fairer.

"Mother" and "Program Staff" received the highest evaluations, while the "Department of Youth Services" and the "Police" receive the lowest, both on goodness and fairness. "Me" and "My Friends" are in the middle, along with "School Teacher." "My Friends" would rank higher in the ordering if the ordering were based on fairness instead of goodness.

Particularly noteworthy is the difference in evaluation given Program Staff and the DYS. Program Staff are, of course, the direct personal contact between DYS and the youth, so the concept of DYS which is rated so negatively must signify something to the youth other than their immediate experiences in programs. The similarity of DYS and police evaluations suggests that youth see the DYS in general, as opposed to program staff, as linked with the police and the courts as agents of the youth's loss of freedom. It is also possible that the youth simply associate DYS with the old, unreformed system. The youths' ranking of categories of persons corresponds loosely to what we might expect a ranking of closeness and personalness of relationships to look like. In this context it is significant that Program Staff in the community-based programs are ranked second from the top, after Mother, on both goodness and fairness.

Conclusion
The traditional training school system that existed in Massachusetts prior to

Table 8
Mean Response Scores on Two Semantic Differential Items

Category of Persons Being Described	"Goodness"	"Fairness"
Mother	6.0	5.7
Program Staff	5.2	5.3
Father	5.1	4.9
Me	4.9	4.9
My Friends	4.7	5.1
Schoolteacher	4.7	4.6
Other Kids Here	4.6	4.4
DYS	3.6	3.6
Police	3.0	2.4

N = 39.

the recent reforms is still the dominant pattern for youth corrections throughout the country. In fact, preliminary results of a national survey of juvenile correctional practices reveal that there are as many states increasing the number of delinquent youth confined in institutions as there are showing decreases.[20] For many of these states the Massachusetts experience will provide useful guidance to the problems major reforms must confront.

The Massachusetts reforms have closed the traditional training schools and developed a variety of alternative residential and non-residential services based in the new state regions. Our research in these reforms, however, is not yet complete. There has not yet been sufficient exposure time in the community for those in the new programs to provide a valid, follow-up comparison with those treated in institutions. In addition, the collection of recidivism information has been delayed pending the development of approved regulations for access by research personnel to criminal history information of juvenile and adult offenders. These arrangements have just been completed.

Additional issues need further analysis and study. One is whether the same broad changes could have been pursued as successfully more gradually. Miller and his aides have expressed the view that gradual implementation of such major changes would permit the mobilization of conservative groups inside and ouside the agency to block changes. This view is not easily discounted, given other states' experiences in reform efforts.

Another issue concerns administrative confusion and neglect of staff development in the transitional period. The rapid changes in staff assignments and responsibilities created a highly fluid administrative situation. It provided greater freedom to experiment with new treatment methods, stimulated staff members to considerable creativity and initiative, and enabled the administration to avoid premature commitment and consolidation of insufficiently tested programs. However, it has been charged that this approach unnecessarily alienated both old and new staff members.

Commissioner Miller has also been criticized for leaving Massachusetts in January, 1973, to become the new Director of Family and Children's Services in Illinois. He left before financial and personnel problems had been resolved and before a new alternative system of residential and non-residential services had fully replaced the old. He believed that reform commissioners are inevitably expendable since the hostility aroused by major

---

[20]Wolfgang I. Grichting, *Sampling Plans and Results, The University of Michigan National Assessment of Juvenile Corrections Project* (Ann Arbor: University of Michigan, Institute of Continuing Legal Education, School of Social Work, 1973).

changes becomes too great a barrier to further progress. He thinks that the consolidation of the Massachusetts community based services will now proceed faster with his successor, Commissioner Joseph Leavy, in charge.[21] It is too soon yet to know if he is right. The 1974 Departmental budget, with additional support from federal funds, enables the Department to catch up with its financial commitments on purchased services. The budget also provides more time for staff transfers and retraining. This should greatly aid in consolidating a new consensus.

The Massachusetts Department of Youth Services has undertaken a major pioneering step in correctional reform. It has demonstrated that radical changes in the official ideology, policies, and programs of treatment for delinquent youth can be achieved in a short period of time. Evidence thus far indicates that youth perceive the new system as more helpful and staff more responsive. There is widespread agreement that it encourages more humane treatment of youth and offers staff more resources for reintegrating youth into their home communities. Whether in the long run these new policies and programs will result in better protection for the community and more effective help for troubled youth is still to be determined.

---

[21]Interview with Jerome Miller by research staff, February, 1973.

Certainly the Massachusetts experience provides much food for thought on the part of those interested in correctional management. Clearly the administrator involved did seek to understand and influence the force field within which he was attempting to bring about change. He was concerned, whether consciously or otherwise, with the strategic dimensions of problem-solving, showing in fact a flair for dramatic and attention-getting devices (witness the inclusion of legislators in pictures of the highly symbolic sledge-hammering of old cell blocks and the caravan of cars carrying youth to the University of Massachusetts, and thus to a new correctional era).

Moreover, behind these highly visible gestures there seemed to be a well-conceptualized design of the new community-based program which was intended to replace the old system. Decentralization and regionalization obviously were key features of the new model, with use of service-purchase relied upon to develop the varied community resources required to implement the reintegration concept of corrections.

On the other hand, we might conjecture from the facts presented that some strategic concerns were neglected or that there was a miscalculation of their importance. The question of timing and pacing the movement of change seems particularly significant. Perhaps a more incremental approach might have avoided some problems and established a firmer base upon which to build. In this way the legitimate needs of old-time staff members might have been met more adequately, and it might have been possible to secure the resources and the public support required to implement the new model. Of course, hindsight is cheap. It could as easily be argued that old and deeply entrenched patterns of behavior will not give way to rational, incremental change efforts. Perhaps, as the administrator himself suggested, the first manager to assault traditional bulwarks must be regarded as expendable, with other, less threatening administrators taking up where he left off to solidify and institutionalize the changes which he began.[13]

We shall not attempt a more detailed analysis of the Massachusetts case, leaving it to the reader to make his own interpretations and reach his own judgments on the issues involved. We have, however, reproduced in Appendix IV a discussion of the nine administrative strategies examined in the USC research which has been referred to throughout this chapter. The reader may find it useful to reflect upon the Massachusetts events in the light of that information.[14]

"Profile of the Change-Capable Administrator"

We will close this chapter with a final excerpt from the USC research study in the form of a summary profile of what the researchers termed a

"Profile of the Change-Capable Administrator." Combining various kinds of research data, this profile highlights the managerial characteristics which seem to accompany the ability to bring about change in a field which, perhaps as much as any other, needs profound alteration if it is to approximate the goals established for it.[15]

> The purpose of this section is to identify the attributes which characterize correctional administrators who are effective in bringing about changes within their organizations. These findings have been derived mainly from an analysis of the varied descriptive data on administrators who appeared to be especially effective as agents of change. It must be admitted that the criteria of effectiveness which we employed are not only subjective but somewhat circular. Certain administrators were classified as change-capable when their administrative styles and protocols of strategic behavior reflected both concern for change and skill in bringing it about. To some extent, we also considered the reputation of some of these administrators within the correctional community for effectiveness in introducing needed change. Granting the limitations imposed by these criteria, we feel reasonably confident of our ability to offer a tentative prototype of the change-capable administrator. The profile presented below is divided into two major parts: (1) factors affecting the readiness of the administrator to bring about change; (2) factors associated with the implementation of change.

> *THE READINESS PROFILE.* Careful scrutiny of the interview data made it clear that effectiveness in the induction of change consists of more than actionist skills. Equally critical are the orientation of the administrator toward events which open up possibilities for change and his characteristic way of working with the people and forces around him. The most important of these "readiness" variables are discussed below.

> *The Conceptualizing Mind.* An important but somewhat hazy attribute of the change-capable administrator seemed to lie in his having a durable conception of his organization, its mission, and its long-range goals. This attribute appeared in the data as a kind of intellectual frame of reference which enabled the administrator to look at what was going on in the force field around him, to "make sense" of it, and thus to formulate premises for action in meeting particular problems. Such an administrator might say to himself, for example, "Morale is getting bad in the juvenile hall because . . ." The *because* in such a case would have to do with a well-established and consistently applied set of beliefs about human behavior and the forces which affect it, about the "mission" of a juvenile hall, and about the function of leadership.

> This capacity to understand, to integrate disparate pieces of information, and to envision the consequences of projected courses of action may be the most fundamental of all cognitive prerequisites to change capability. The ad-

ministrators in our sample who lacked at least a modicum of this capacity appeared in numerous critical incidents to be at the mercy of events which they seemed incapable of interpreting, much less influencing.

The Power of Knowledge. The previous paragraphs stressed the importance of the administrator's having an intellectual frame of reference within which to process information and form judgments about cause-and-effect relationships. The interview data also documented another cognitive attribute—that of being thoroughly informed about and up to date on the myriad activities which join together to make up the dynamic life of the organization. It would appear that a commitment to desirable goals may accomplish little unless the administrator also has the facts not only about current operations but about trends which help to forecast the future.

Again and again in the interview incidents, advantage seemed to go to the administrator who did his homework consistently and conscientiously. It was not so much that he needed to be better informed than all others in the situation (for this, of course, is impossible) but that he needed to be able to probe, test, and validate the positions taken by others on the basis of his own reach and grasp of the situation. Obviously a sizable amount of interest and curiosity was required to keep the administrators informed about their operations and about the environmental events which helped to determine opportunities for and constraints on change. Relevant were such diverse kinds of information as crime rates, governmental budgets, population movements, political campaigns, research on correctional innovations, and union negotiations with public organizations. It was our impression that many administrators who might otherwise have been effective changers became impotent in that role because they had insufficient knowledge to deal competently with the problems confronting them.

Scanning Alternatives and Developing Plans. Many of the descriptions of problem-solving activity which we collected associated the successful accomplishment of change with the timely development of workable plans. The change-capable administrator characteristically would report that "I could not have taken advantage of that opportunity if I had not already developed a plan of action and a set of justifications." The picture that emerged was one in which such administrators constantly scanned the needs of their organizations for change and developed plans for meeting needs which were well buttressed by relevant supporting data. Typically, these plans were tentative and, more often than not, they were never formally proposed. Sometimes they served as trial balloons through which efforts to secure essential support were given a rigorous provisional testing before any public commitment to the program was made.

Maintaining Credibility and Good Will. An important aspect of readiness to induce change for the correctional administrator seemed to be his ability to develop and sustain personal credibility throughout the force field around him. The incidents and case studies collected in our interviewing indicated that this capacity had a number of dimensions.

First, it seemed that the credibility of the administrator depended partly upon his reputation for openness. The converse of this was the apparent proclivity of many administrators to be secretive, "hiding" their operations from view as evidenced by reluctance to share information with such outsiders as members of the press, interested legislators, and special interest groups from the community.

Some change-capable administrators, on the other hand, almost made a fetish out of communicating the idea that "we have nothing to hide." Typically this approach took the form of saying that the administrator's organization was afflicted with numerous problems and limitations. This, then, became a basis for arguing that something needed to be done in order to remedy these difficulties, which might include additional staff, a new facility, or whatever might be on his agenda.

A second and quite different dimension of credibility might be described as "protecting the flanks" of the organization while awaiting opportunities to move toward change goals. In part, this function was served simply by good housekeeping. It was important to keep the process of financial administration in good order, to observe accepted norms in recruiting and selecting personnel, and generally to keep open the channels of communication with service and control agencies. In a different and more strategic sense, the function of protecting flanks also involved not being outmaneuvered in establishing and maintaining good relationships with those who influence decisions vital to the survival of the organization. Particularly in the competition for operating budgets, it seemed imperative for the administrators to be aware of the actions of potentially competitive agencies, to stay in touch with the political echelon and the key legislators involved, and to keep the needs of their organization before the public intermittently through favorable stories in the press.

A final aspect of credibility which appeared frequently in the interview data had to do with the personal image of the administrator. This variable is difficult to define because it took many forms. To some extent, it seemed related to the quality of charisma, but it also included more mundane elements such as the ability to project a reputation for not letting things get out of hand and for not "going overboard on far-fetched ideas." Later, in the implementation of change, the ability to make otherwise "far-fetched ideas" palatable as respectable innovations seemed equally important. Charisma seemed especially important for the maintenance of the administrator's credibility in the eyes of his staff. Their sense of hope and their belief that change was possible appeared to turn significantly upon whether they perceived the administrator as able to accomplish notable gains in the face of difficult odds. In this respect the stance of "happy warrior" sometimes seemed more important than a record of pragmatic achievement in winning battles.

The Developmental Approach. Still another attribute of administrators associated with the capacity to bring about change was concern for the growth and development of organization members. This was much in contrast to non-change-oriented administrators, who seemed preoccupied with their own status and power. The developmental approach manifested itself in involving subordinates in a variety of tasks which allowed them to try their wings, to play unfamiliar roles, and to make unorthodox contributions to the solution of problems. A tolerance for human error often appeared to underlie this ability.

Behind this approach to subordinate staff (and sometimes offenders as well) seemed to be a flexible view of the things people might do to advance the common cause. The business manager was not assumed to be mechanistic in his approach to people simply because he was a business manager, and this prophecy sometimes seemed to be self-fulfilling. Similarly, junior staff far down the hierarchy were assumed to have insights and capabilities which those near the top of the ladder did not have. And some administrators clearly wished to make offenders participants in the people-changing work of the organization rather than mere recipients of staff effort directed toward that goal.

We could not help but feel, as the interview data related to this point were reviewed, that this characteristic was greatly determined by the personality of the administrator. Those who were genuinely warm in their relationships with other people, and consequently interested in their development, gravitated naturally toward this approach. The administrators who were relatively isolated and self-centered in their interactions with others did not make much headway along this line despite giving lip service to the idea. In any event, when opportunities for change presented themselves, a clear advantage seemed to go to the administrator who was able quickly to mobilize human energy toward implementation of the new idea. And this could not be done unless a groundwork for it had been laid. There were numerous incidents in which administrators who apparently had not been developmental or participative in their approach to staff and offenders inaugurated an innovation, only to have it falter and eventually disappear. Change of the kind defined as significant in this study, it would seem, cannot be preemptorily "ordered in."

The Quality of Impatience. A final characteristic associated with readiness for the induction of change, as reflected in the study findings, was a persistently nagging dissatisfaction with the status quo and a corresponding impatience to find a better way. It is difficult, perhaps impossible, to determine the extent to which impatience is a constitutional or an acquired trait. That it is central to the induction of change, however, seemed little in doubt. The descriptions of problems, the portrayal of strategies, the remembrance of incidents which seemed critical to given administrators—almost inevitably seemed to lead to such a dichotomy. Many of the administrators interviewed were essentially content with the system as it was. Their efforts were bent mainly toward protection and conservation. The others, those who were "impatient," seemed chronically discontent. In this, they demonstrated a prime qualification to act as the leaders of change. Nevertheless, it was the combination of impatience with at least a minimal supply of the skills associated with conservation of the organization which seemed to create optimal qualifications to serve as leaders of change.

THE IMPLEMENTATION PROFILE. The line between qualities associated with readiness to bring about change and those required for the actual implementation of change cannot be sharply drawn. Typically, the readiness factors continued to stand the change-capable administrator in good stead during the frequently more stressful events leading to change. Nevertheless, certain variables seemed much more closely associated with action than preparedness.

Capitalizing on Opportunity. A common characteristic of the change-capable administrators seemed to be their capacity to take advantage of opportunities for innovation created by forces within the organization or in its environment. Frequently this was the mechanism through which the scanning process described in the previous section was translated into action. Administrators who were less oriented to change tended to make adjustments aimed at maintaining equilibrium. The change-capable administrators, by contrast, more often acted decisively to turn temporary disequilibrium into action of a kind previously identified as desirable.

For example, the retirement of a long-entrenched institution superintendent was seen by one departmental director as an opportunity to "make changes from top to bottom in that program." As had been anticipated in interviewing concerning the dilemma management strategy, the change-capable administrators frequently turned adversity to advantage. Mutinous behavior among prison inmates was used to persuade the legislature that additional funds for staff were required. An attack on the organization from unfriendly sources was used to command space in the mass media for affirmative declarations of program goals. It is not suggested that change was never self-initiated by the administrators. But even when it was, the change-capable group seemed much more concerned with timing and assessment of potential support and resistance than were the less change-oriented administrators.

Risk-Taking. A related characteristic was the tendency for the change-capable administrators to take risks and, in a real sense, to gamble in order to bring about change. It must be added that some of the incidents collected in the research described risk-taking which ended in disastrous losses. The most successful form of risk-taking, by contrast, seemed to be one in which there was a calculation of danger and an effort to protect against the most unacceptable consequences. Such calculations also seemed to attach considerable importance to the amount of payoff perceived by the administrator. Risks were ventured in high-gain situations which would have been considered unacceptable under low- or zero-gain circumstances.

Even in the light of such qualification, however, the change-capable administrators as a group clearly seemed willing to take chances which their less change-oriented counterparts were not prepared to take. This appeared in many ways: the appointment of an inexperienced but gifted subordinate to a key post; the reduction of severe custodial restraints in the face of predictions of calamity from old-line staff; the frank communication to the public of problems and failures; a candid and assertive confrontation with an unfriendly legislator in a public hearing; the placement in community treatment of youngsters previously defined as "too dangerous to be released." All of these are examples of risk-taking which appeared in the critical incidents.

Catalyzing. The change-capable group of administrators seemed often to act as catalysts once the process of change was under way. Frequently different parts of the organization, or forces in its environment, were opposed or indifferent to the proposed change. This problem was dealt with much of the time by getting people together to talk it out, identifying payoff for those who previously had seen no reason to participate in the change effort, or making clear that the administrator himself was thoroughly and authentically committed to change.

Somewhat different catalytic skills seemed to be required when the administrator sought to co-opt those outside his own organization. In dealing with the press, the legislature, the special interest groups within the community, where the administrator had few sanctions to employ, persuasion was much more used. And knowledge of the force field and credibility with those in key power positions were extremely important. Several administrators spoke of arranging to be introduced by some mutual friend to someone whose help was required in the solution of a problem. Others called attention to the importance of "knowing where the bodies are buried" in different power systems. It was clear that influence was exerted in a variety of ways by the more ingenious of the interviewees. One head of a large correctional organization, for example, kept careful records of the familial and friendship connections of all of his staff members with legislators and others who were influential in state government, and he put this information to good use in myriad legislative encounters.

Buffering The process of change seemed to be accompanied by tension and anxiety on the part of those who were entangled in it. The upsetting of familiar ways of doing things, the dislocation of organization members from their accustomed roles, the general fear of unknown consequences—these factors created considerable human travail when the process of change was inexorably under way.

While the change-capable administrators seemed to believe that innovation could not be achieved without a certain amount of tension, they often took action to keep it within bounds. They were aware that fear can become endemic in an organization and that it can reach levels at which those affected become either destructive or immobilized in their dealings with each other.

Buffering often was achieved by approaching the change goal in an incremental fashion and making clear to those involved that their personal problems would be worked out as events moved along. At time, buffering consisted of the administrator himself absorbing the pressures of unknown consequences while maintaining an optimistic front with his staff. At other times, buffering took the form of systematically provided opportunities for ventilation of the tensions generated by change. Some administrators described their behavior during stressful episodes in a way which made them appear clinical and therapeutic in their relationships with the others involved. It seemed equally clear that these same administrators could have benefitted from opportunities to express their own concerns, and that the loneliness of their roles often constituted a heavy burden for them.

Integrating. Several of the most impressive incidents of change involved a high level of integrative ability on the part of the administrator. The ability to satisfy seemingly contradictory needs through some previously unseen solution was an important element of successful change, albeit not a common one in our data.

Of course all administrators face the problem of facilitating disparate needs and strivings within the force field which they occupy. The management grid which was given to the administrators in our sample tapped the contradictory pulls of concern for people and concern for production (See Chapter 4.) In addition to this generic conflict, however, correctional administrators seemed to be faced with a much larger than ordinary number of dilemmas and contradictions of purpose. This, no doubt, is part and parcel of the problem of multiple goals toward which the field is oriented. The effort to reconcile punishment with treatment of offenders appeared in numerous incidents. The difficulty of blending control with treatment was a related problem. To some extent, dilemmas of this kind were more a problem of satisfying highly differing expectations from the force field than of actually devising appropriate programs of intervention.

The majority of solutions to the conflicts which appeared in the interviews were characterized more by compromise than integration. Faced with pressures to both help and punish inmates, institutional staff typically tried to provide a little of each. But many incidents did portray an administrator struggling seriously with the task of integration, of finding optimal solutions to all legitimate needs without diminishing any of them.

One attribute of the administrators who worked toward integration seemed to be flexibility. Such administrators were not locked into programmed solutions to all problems. They looked about them, seeking stimulation and guidance from a variety of sources, and sometimes produced quite unconventional answers to long-standing problems. This quality of open-mindedness and of desire to find creative solutions may also be near the apex of administrative talents related to change-capability. We did note that administrators who felt a desire to seek integrative solutions worked very hard and were deeply concerned at all times about outcomes. In the total universe of activity samples, it seemed much easier for the administrator to compromise than to integrate.

Institutionalizing. The implementation profile of the change-capable administrator may be completed, so far as our findings are concerned, by noting capacity for bringing the innovation into the main stream of organizational activity, a function which we have described as "institutionalizing." Many of the interviewees spoke with an air of frustration about the fact that encouraging changes sometimes were brought about, only to disappear within a relatively short time. An examination of their interview responses tended to reveal that little had been done to diffuse the new approach throughout the organization or to provide the manpower, funding, and management attention required to make sure that it remained ongoing after the aura of newness had evaporated.

A variety of institutionalizing devices appeared in the data. Some administrators inaugurated training programs to bring a new program or technique to the attention of staff members who had not been involved in initial experimentation with it, and to work through the problems encountered in adapting it to the requirements of different situations. Some administrators pointed out the importance of bringing those concerned with budgeting for future operations into the discussion of program innovations "early in the game." Thus, questions of forward financing on a larger scale were addressed well ahead of the presentation of a new program to the legislature, and the staff (both within and outside the organization) who had responsibility for review of budgets were allowed to participate in the excitement of starting a new program. Perhaps most fundamental of all, so far as the institutionalization of innovations was concerned, was the tendency of change-capable administrators themselves to "carry the word" about new ideas throughout the organization and into its environment. The personal support and enthusiasm of the administrator for the innovation seemed to be a highly significant factor in eliciting the support of others who previously had been content to remain uncommitted spectators.

NOTES

[1]Frederick W. Taylor, *The Principles of Scientific Management,* New York: Harper, 1911.

[2]Douglas McGregar, *The Human Side of Enterprise,* New York: McGraw-Hill, 1960.

[3]Amitai Etzioni, *A Comparative Analysis of Complex Organizations,* New York: Free Press, 1961.

[4]Gresham M. Sykes, "The Corruption of Authority and Rehabilitation," *Social Forces,* 34 (1956); pp. 257–262.

[5]See LaMar T. Empey, *Alternatives to Incarceration,* Office of Juvenile Delinquency and Youth Development Studies in Delinquency, Washington, D.C.: U.S. Government Printing Office, 1967.

[6]Elmer K. Nelson, Jr. and Catherine H. Lovell, *Developing Correctional Administrators,* research report of the Joint Commission on Correctional Manpower and Training, Washington, D.C., November, 1969.

[7]*Ibid.,* pp. 31–32.

[8]Daniel Katz, "Approaches to Managing Conflict," in *Conflict Management in Organizations,* Elsie Boulding, ed., Ann Arbor, Michigan: Brown and Brumfield, 1961, p. 12.

[9]Harold J. Leavitt, *Management Psychology,* Chicago: University of Chicago Press, 1967, p. 74.

[10]Nelson and Lovell, op. cit., p. 36.

[11]*Ibid.,* p. 55.

[12]Lloyd E. Ohlin, Robert Coates, and Alden D. Miller, "Radical Correctional Reform: A Case Study of the Massachusetts Youth Correctional System," *Harvard Educational Review,* 44, no. 1 (February, 1974), pp. 75–111.

[13]For a further appraisal of these events, see Andrew Rutherford, *The Dissolution of the Training Schools in Massachusetts,* The Academy for Contemporary Problems, 1501 Neil Avenue, Columbus, Ohio, 1974.

[14]Nelson and Lovell, op. cit., pp. 58–75.

[15]The following quote is taken from Elmer K. Nelson, Jr. and Catherine H. Lovell, *Developing Correctional Administrators,* research report of the Joint Commission on Correctional Manpower and Training, Washington, D.C., November, 1969, pp. 80–84.

12 The Legal Context of Corrections

The isolated and encapsulated nature of American corrections has been noted in different contexts throughout this book. Correctional agencies have been walled off from the larger society by bureaucratic and social boundaries. A beginning point for the present chapter is the recognition that these boundaries have been especially, indeed enormously strong and impervious in separating offenders under correctional control from the rights and remedies assured to other citizens by the Constitution and the intricate, constantly changing web of statutes and case precedents which make up the "law of the land."

Today, however, as the field of corrections gradually is opening to public scrutiny, it is also coming under increasingly sharp examination by the courts and by various interest groups concerned with the legal rights of offenders.[1] Just as American law enforcement was challenged during the 1960s by such landmark decisions as Mapp v. Ohio,[2] Escabedo v. Illinois,[3] and Miranda v. Arizona,[4] so today corrections is being asked, perhaps more accurately *instructed*, to reconsider not only its traditional practices but the legal-philosophical premises on which they rest.

Correctional administrators frequently exhibit irritation and defensiveness concerning this type of intrusion. They argue that their work, already extraordinarily demanding, becomes virtually impossible when their decisions are "second-guessed" or "undercut" by judges "who have never seen the inside of a prison." Nevertheless, the handwriting seems to be clearly on the wall. Corrections must adapt to the new legal norms voluntarily or it will be forced to do so by increasingly severe judicial sanctions. Indeed, this would seem to be a time for leadership from within, bringing about the mandated requirements of fairness and even-handed protection of individual rights through administrative action rather than judicial sanctions.

The present situation must be understood in its historical context. We

328

Americans like to refer to our Constitution in describing certain rights as inalienable, as attaching to each of us throughout his lifetime, and offering protection against arbitrary, frivolous, and inequitable uses of authority. Yet this concept, which is at the heart of the Bill of Rights, has never been recognized for those under correctional supervision. They have been protected constitutionally only against cruel and unusual punishment, a highly dubious shield considering the impossibility of precise definition of the term, and the opportunities for evasion of its requirements which abound in a correctional system well concealed from public view.

The rule of law, more implicit than explicit, for those under correctional supervision (especially those who are incarcerated) has been that they have forfeited their "inalienable" rights through criminal activity, that the rights of other citizens become at best privileges for them, matters of grace rather than obligations of the governmental agencies which have charge of their lives. This led long ago to the idea that there is a separate law for corrections, that it represents an enclave into which constitutional guarantees should not be extended or recognized. The courts adopted a "hands off" policy, tacitly agreeing with the dogma that only penal administrators have the requisite expertise in setting and administering policies affecting the rights of offenders. It is symbolic that the California statutes dealing with this area have referred for decades to the "civil death" of prison inmates.

The issues around which controversy flares today include such diverse matters as access by inmates to the courts, freedom to engage in religious cults and practices (some of which penal officials correctly point out have heavy anti-authority overtones), prison disciplinary procedures and the methods for determining whether they should be applied, the censoring of mail and the screening of prison visitors, the granting and revocation of probation and parole, the establishment of inmate grievance procedures, and a relatively new alleged right, access to rehabilitative treatment.

The literature of criminology and penology has been barren of material relevant to the legal rights of offenders until the last few years, except for highly rhetorical essays by some criminologists who indicted the correctional system for dehumanizing its charges by stripping them of their constitutional defenses. Within the past five years, however, this area has been given a great deal of attention.

It has been written and editorialized about in the journals which provide a forum for discussing the views and problems of correctional administrators.[5] It has been a subject of contention and sometimes quite impassioned verbiage in written materials generated by the growing labor union movement within the ranks of correctional guards and officers. The first comprehensive analysis of the subject was prepared by Professor Fred Cohen of the University of Texas for the Joint Commission on Correctional Manpower and Training in 1969.[6] In his monograph Professor Cohen compared developments in corrections to other fields in which the rights of those who are being dealt with through bureaucratic processes are being emphasized as never before: the public welfare system, the fields of mental health and social welfare, poverty-fighting agencies, and the military.

Cohen gives special attention to the juvenile justice system, discussing at some length the landmark case, in Re Gault.[7] The Gault decision produced a profound upheaval in the juvenile court and corrections network of America during the late 1960s by holding that juveniles had the right to notice of charges, confrontation and cross examination of witnesses, advice from legal counsel, and the protection of the constitutional privilege against self-incrimination.

What was challenged basically was the operating philosophy of juvenile corrections called *parens patrae,* the belief that the state acting through its appropriate agencies is comparable to a wise parent benevolently concerned with protecting the interests of the juvenile. In challenging this premise for dealing with juvenile offenders, the Supreme Court of the United States in effect asserted that the role of the state in fact is not always benevolent and protective when it deals with young offenders. Punishments and sanctions of various kinds typically are involved. The term "juvenile delinquent" itself represents a label and usually a stigma which has legal and social consequences throughout the life of the individual to whom it becomes attached. Thus the substantive and procedural guarantees of due process and other elements of equity and fairness were said to apply to the adjudication and correctional management of juveniles just as they do to adults.

Some of the recent publications dealing with the legal rights of offenders have taken a more pragmatic or operational form. The various jurisdictions and agencies charged with administering correctional programs have begun to face the challenge of modifying their own operating procedures in accordance with new judicial and statutory guidelines. For examples, the South Carolina Department of Corrections, with the assistance of the National Institute of Law Enforcement and Criminal Justice, has produced an excellent monograph which analyzes legal issues in a variety of areas (for example, prisoner correspondence and visitation, access to media, grooming and attire, inmate safety, administrators' liability, and the use of punitive isolation) while also setting forth recommended operating procedures to guide officials who have responsibility for such functions.[8] Similarly, a useful publication on *Model Rules and Regulations on Prisoners' Rights and Responsibilities* was prepared in 1973 by Professor Sheldon Krantz of the Boston University School of Law for the Commissioner of Corrections of the State of Massachusetts.[9]

Still another and dramatically different source of written materials is being produced by a variegated category of persons and interest groups whose approach to the topic reflects a more activistic and reformist spirit. While representing a broad spectrum of ideology and political persuasion, these analysts tend to perceive corrections as an ultimate and extraordinarily desolate enclave within which the American social, economic, and political system works systematic discrimination upon those who are legally defined and classified as offenders. It is pointed out that offenders as a group draw disproportionately from other categories of the disadvantaged — the poor, the undereducated, and underemployed, the ethnic minorities, the inner-city ghetto dwellers, and other sub-groups which are denied access to the opportunity pathways leading to "respectable" and legitimate lives in the larger society.

As might be expected, the writings which emerge from those who hold this point of view tend to be militant and usually analyze corrections in terms of alleged dysfunctions and perversities of the social system in which it is imbedded. Some of these critics call for an end to prisons, asserting that they are hopelessly bankrupt as devices for either punishment or rehabilitation. There are numerous attacks on those who make decisions about the conditions under which offenders are supervised, typically including the administrators of prisons, the members of parole boards and the judiciary.

Much of the writing in this category reflects the "muck-raking" tradition of American journalism. Some of it is very forceful and incisive, proceeding from well-documented analyses of the contemporary scene. Other writing in this large and diffuse category is sadly lacking in factual foundation and proceeds through polemical and broad-brush assertions about the current situation to unsupported conclusions about reform or abolition of existing practices. The most recent work in this area, and one which includes references to many other related writings, is the book entitled *Kind and Usual Punishment — the Prison Business*, by Jessica Mitford.[10]

Ms. Mitford mounts a strong attack on the American correctional system. One interesting theme which runs through her writings is the belief that modern rehabilitative trends within American corrections have worsened rather than improved the situation. She argues that the traditional approaches achieved only a physical degradation and mortification of the inmate, whereas modern techniques, especially those defined as behavior modification or operant conditioning, vitiate the mental and emotional faculties of the individual. She is especially critical of exploitive medical experiments with inmates who may be led to participate because of dependency and subtle pressures, or simply hopes for early release. Also included in her indictment, however, are treatment programs which seek to "program" prisoners into correct modes of behavior and away from deviant ones. Such manipulations of individual behavior in her view are grossly unethical and damaging to individual rights. In this area, however, Mitford is perhaps proceeding with less than complete knowledge since the techniques to which she refers are diverse and some may well represent valuable innovations in correctional treatment along lines which do *not* in fact warrant the spectre of human exploitation which she summons up.

Finally, we will make reference to an extremely important document which was published during the time when the present text was being prepared. It is the report of the National Advisory Commission on Criminal Justice Standards and Goals, and particularly the volume on corrections. This definitive effort to prescribe for the future of the American correctional system places a strong emphasis on the legal rights of offenders and, indeed, sets forth 18 standards in that area. It may be expected that these standards will become orienting points for correctional officials throughout the country and that they will influence practice in important and pervasive ways. The standards which relate to the legal rights of offenders are numbers 2.1 to 2.18 and are included in Appendix II of this book.

Special Areas of Concern

Because of the technical nature of the subject under discussion, and the burgeoning literature related to it, we can only attempt a broad overview in the present chapter. However, there are some topics of such importance as to require special, if necessarily brief comment. These are dealt with below.

Forms of Legal Intervention

The growing legal challenge to corrections has been accelerated by new forms and bases for judicial intervention, and by increasing willingness on the part of the federal courts to intervene even though all remedies have not been exhausted in the state courts as traditionally required.

The traditional manner of challenging the legality of correctional supervision has been the writ of habeas corpus filed by an individual petitioner. In effect, such a writ asserts that the imposition of correctional control is illegal, and asks the court to order the correctional administrator involved (typically a prison warden or superintendent) to release or deliver him from custody. Every prison has inmates who consider themselves experts in the preparation of writs (frequently providing advisory service to their less-skilled fellows), and most correctional administrators speak invectively of the "flood" of such pleas with which they are deluged each year.

Historically, the writ of habeas corpus has been used primarily to challenge the legality of correctional control on the basis of alleged error in the process of adjudicating the case by the courts. The trend, however, is to use such writs additionally to challenge the legality of the *conditions* under which correctional supervision is carried on, e.g., provision for the protection of life and health within prisons, access to the courts (and related opportunities to communicate with counsel and use legal materials), and protection against excessive or unfair use of segregation and isolation.

Cohen points out that more flexible interpretations of the use of habeas corpus increased the number of such petitions to the federal courts from 814 in 1957 to 4,845 in 1965, with the upward trend continuing.[11] Of course, there must be some constitutional basis for the writ if it is to be successfully pursued at the federal level.

Unlike some other remedies, which are discussed below, habeas corpus produces action only in individual cases, and does not provide for class actions or injunctive relief through which a correctional administrator might be required to cease certain practices or, affirmatively, to carry out others which he has neglected to perform. On the other hand, once a given inmate has succeeded in challenging the legality of his confinement on a particular ground, the way is open and precedent has been established for serial challenges by others similarly aggrieved.

A type of legal action of more immediate concern to correctional administrators consists of personal suits against them for damages based on tort liability. Such actions can be successful only if the plaintiff establishes a breach by the defendant of a duty (perhaps a statutory obligation attaching to his job), with subsequent injury or damage to the plaintiff. Moreover, there must be a "proximate" causal relationship between the breach and the injury, a requirement which has been heavily litigated and defined in case law.

In order to be found liable for personal damages in this type of action, it must be established that the defendant was negligent (or perhaps grossly negligent) in his breach of duty. Again, the question of what constitutes negligence, and the degree or standard of negligence required for tort liability to be present, are highly technical questions which have been elaborated more in case decisions than statutory law.

Correctional personnel are no more subject to tort actions than anyone else, for we all owe many duties to others and can be made the object of civil suits for breaches in those duties. The increasing number of such actions against correctional officials, however, reflects the great sensitivity of the roles they play contemporarily, as well as the sometimes volatile and adversarial nature of their relationships with offenders. While more attention is now being given to laws which indemnify penal administrators against personal liability, and to public insurance protecting them against heavy financial penalties, there is no question but that those who work in corrections (especially administrators) need to be very sensitive to their legal obligations. Examples of actions which fit this category are contained in the following statement:[12]

> Prison administrators have been subject to tort liability suits for negligence in allowing harm to come to an inmate in his care. There have been several cases involving a wrongful death action brought by a relative of an inmate who died or was killed while in the administrator's custody. For example, a warden has been held liable for the death of an inmate where adequate medical aid was not given for the treatment of smallpox,* and where death was caused by the unsanitary conditions of the inmate's cell.†
> *Hunt v. Rowton, 143 Okla. 181, 288 p. 342 (1930).
> †Smith v. Slack, 125 W. Va. 812, 26 S.E. 2d 387 (1943).
>
> Both of these cases involved the breach of a specific statutory duty. Most of the litigation involving wrongful deaths has centered around a prison official's alleged negligence in placing the decedent inmate in a cell with violent inmates who caused his death. Liability has been found in situations where the asaulting inmate was of known propensity for violence,* where the decedent was a juvenile placed with hardened criminals,† and where the inmate's cellmate was violently insane.‡ Liability was also found where the inmate was beaten to death with blackjacks after being summarily treated by an inmate kangaroo court, where the practice was not completely unknown to the sheriff in charge of the jail.§ All of these courts required only negligence as necessary for liability, although some of the officials' lack of concern for the proper placement of the inmates seemed almost malicious. Other courts, faced with similar circumstances, have found the prison official not liable because there was no malice shown.‖
> *Barlett v. Commonwealth, 418 S.W. 2d 255 (Ky. 1967).
> †People v. Guthner, 105 Colo. 37, 94 P. 2d 699 (1939).
> ‡Dunn v. Swanson, 217 N.C. 279, 7 S.E. 2d 563 (1940).
> §Browning v. Graves, 152 S.W. 2d 515 (Tex. Cir. App. 1941).
> ‖Sheffield v. Turner, 21 Utah 2d 314, 445 P. 2d 367 (1968).

A special and highly important form of tort liability is that which arises under Title 42, U.S.C. § 1983, the Federal Civil Rights Act of 1871, which requires:[13]

> Every person who, under color of any statute, ordinance, regulation, custom, or usage, of any State or Territory, subjects, or causes to be subject, any citizen of the United States or other person within the jurisdiction thereof to the deprivation of any rights, privileges, or immunities secured by the Constitution and laws shall be liable to the party injured in an action at law, suit in equity, or other proper proceeding for redress.

The recent expanded use of this federal law to redress the problems of prisoners under the jurisdiction of state and local, as well as federal control requires comment because of its uniquely constructive potentialities. While this form of legal action typically is against a specific official, that official need not suffer personal damages unless his violations were carried out with full knowledge and in bad faith. Moreover, it is possible through this mode of intervention to take preventive instead of punitive action, e.g., attacking a discriminatory or onerous regulation through a *class action,* and obtaining injunctive or *declaratory* relief which prohibits such policies, rather than merely penalizing the official who promulgated them.

Lawyers work constantly with abstract formulation in their efforts to achieve particular "justice" in an adversarial context, abstractions which they frequently admit to each other are "fictions" or perhaps even ploys. The requirement that state remedies must be exhausted before federal relief can be sought, and the doctrine of *comity* (the respect shown by one jurisdiction for the laws of another) were abstractions which long formed a wall against federal intervention in the developing sense of injustice generated by the plight of prisoners in America. Thus it was necessary to develop other fictions, counteracting ploys. The doctrine of state sovereignty, and the consequent immunity of state authorities from federal prosecution for their official acts, was overcome by asserting that such persons were only acting "under the color of state law" and therefore vulnerable as individuals to suit in the federal courts. The future use of such forms of relief seems clearly prescribed in a commentary section of the Corrections volume of the 1973 National Advisory Commission on Criminal Justice Standards and Goals:[14]

> Courts should be authorized to grant injunctions to protect offenders' rights. This would include injunctions prohibiting conduct that violates offenders' rights as well as requiring affirmative acts to assure an offender's rights are

preserved. Violation of such orders should be subjected to contempt charges as in other cases.

Civil liability for violating a person's rights is a particularly effective remedy and should be more widely utilized. In many instances, persons clothed with governmental authority have little incentive to comply with the rights of persons subject to their jurisdiction because they have no personal stake in compliance. Making governmental officials personally liable for money damages to the person whose rights are violated provides such an incentive. Where a governmental employee intentionally violates an offender's rights or the agency engages in tactics designed solely to make the attainment of offender's rights more difficult, civil liability is an appropriate remedy. Such liability is provided, but rarely utilized, in federal civil rights statutes.

The Concern for Due Process

Due process concerns run through the entire spectrum of legal issues in corrections. The term has many technical ramifications, including both procedural and substantive elements, but its essential focus is upon *fairness* in decision making which affects the conditions of individual life and liberty as indicated in the following quotation from Cohen:[15]

Perhaps the most basic explanation of the independent content aspect of due process—and clearly the most open-ended—is fundamental fairness. From the term, "fundamental fairness" flow such concepts as "impartiality," "honesty," "conformity with existing rules," "objectivity," and "proper balancing of competing interests." Although these overlapping concepts give almost no direction on solving a specific problem, they do set a tone; they emphasize the need to seek normative guidance as opposed to the most logical or efficient solution. Functionally, due process norms assume that there are and must be limits on the power of government.* Where due process has not received specific application, as Justice Douglas has said, it serves as a healthy reminder to officials that power is a heady thing and that there are limits beyond which it is not safe to go.†

By way of contrast, spokesmen for the correctional process often emphasize the *conclusion* (e.g., a "bad risk," "immature," "unfit to remain at large") and the *good faith* or *expertise* of the person making a decision.‡ While facts and conclusions need not be at war with each other, too often this is the case. Conclusions, particularly when couched in diagnostic or legal terms—or when used as manipulative labels—easily may divert our attention from an inquiry into the factual foundation for the conclusion. It is much more convenient to say that a person is "sick" or "dangerous" or "not ready for parole" than to establish the facts and the steps used to arrive at such a conclusion.

*Packer, "Two Models of the Criminal Process," 113 University of Pennsylvania Law Review 1, 13–23 (1964).

†Douglas, "The Bill of Rights is Not Enough," 38 New York University Law Review, 211 (1963).

‡Ex parte Young, 121 Cal. App. 711, 714, 10 P. 2d 154, 156 (1932).

While most of us have not had the experience of being incarcerated or otherwise under correctional supervision, we have all been subject to the regulations and the decisons of large, bureaucratic systems, e.g., the educational bureaucracy, the military, hospitals, or a motor vehicles control agency. Almost everyone, therefore, knows what it means to be dealt with arbitrarily in some matter central to his physical or psychological well-being, or to feel manipulated by omnipotent others who are insensitive to his view of the "facts" and the imperatives of the situation. And yet it may not be possible for us to imagine the state of dependency, the feeling of powerlessness and consequent alienation which correctional organizations frequently engender in offenders today.

Goffman has pointed out that communications and the use of sanctions within "total institutions" such as prisons are calculated to produce feelings of mortification and depersonalization within the inmate.[16] The stripping away of his civilian garb and grooming habits, the endless standing in line, the absolute power of officials in determining such crucial matters as time of release on parole and penalties for disciplinary infractions, these and countless other features of the correctional society place due process concerns in a far different context than that supplied by the ordinary experience of most of us. As Selznick points out:[17]

> A concern for fairness and wise validation should permeate the entire administration of criminal law, including the daily life of the prisoner. That treatment will be most effective which does the most for the inmate's sense of self-worth and responsibility. Nothing contributes more to these feelings than a social environment whose constitutive principle is justice.

What are the key elements of due process in the chain of correctional decision making? Once legal jargon is removed, they are not highly complicated. Moreover, most of them can be implemented through administrative rather than technical-legal action.

Decisions should be based upon adequate information, and that information should be shared as fully as possible with the offender who is the object of the decision. Since "facts" vary according to the perspective of the individual who supplies them, the perceptions of the offender and those sympathetic to him should be included in the information set upon which a decision is based. For example, if an inmate is charged with violating a prison regulation, the supporting evidence should not be limited to testimony by the officer who brought the charge.

There should be an objective review of important decisions by some party or parties who were not involved in the making of those decisions. And this review should be authentic, not merely a perfunctory action the outcome of which is in actuality already known to everyone involved. Thus, for example, if an offender is found to have violated a condition of his parole and ordered back to prison, the review of that critical decision should be searching and rigorous, *not* merely a bureaucratic reflex.

Some elements of due process were formulated within the legal arena, but fit administrative situations equally well. The requirement that adequate notice be given of a decision, and that the individual charged be present when charges are made and allowed not only to offer his side of the matter, but to confront and rebut evidence of others, are examples of familiar due process requirements in the adjudication of legal guilt or innocence which also are appropriate for such ministerial decisions as the granting and revocation of parole, or the disposal of an alleged breach of an institutional rule.

One of the most controversial questions within this area is whether offenders under correctional control should be allowed the types of assistance which they are constitutionally guaranteed in the courtroom. Should an inmate be allowed to be represented by legal counsel at his parole hearing? No, say most parole board members, emphatically, for such a hearing is not an adversarial, legalistic process. But does it not appear so to the would-be parolee? If right to counsel is not allowed at the parole-granting hearing, should it still be allowed at a hearing which will determine whether parole should be revoked because of an alleged new offense or violation? Parole boards tend to oppose arming the parolee with legal representation, and such related rights as the opportunity to cross-examine witnesses, but an increasing number of jurisdictions are moving in the direction of a more liberal set of standards.

The model rules on prisoners' rights prepared for the State of Massachusetts in 1973 reflect this trend, as illustrated in the following excerpts drawn from their summary of proposed rules.[18]

> The rules on freedom of expression and association balance the constitutional guarantees of the First Amendment with the legitimate security needs of the institution. Furthermore, when restrictions are necessary, the rules at-

tempt to utilize the least restrictive means possible in order that the freest expression, consistent with reasonable security needs, may be permitted.

Further the rules permit formation of inmate groups and circulation of petitions but they place reasonable limits on them.

Similarly, the usual rules are widened by permitting publication of inmate newspapers which criticize the institution, but articles which are libelous, inflammatory, or contemptuous of specific ethnic groups will be rejected.

These rules follow recent court decisions to broaden the scope of inmate contact with the outside world. They eliminate all inspection of outgoing letters as well as restrictions on potential correspondents. All complaints of illegal use of the mail are referred to postal authorities for action. Incoming mail may be opened for examination but not read.

The next rule of this section limits access to confidential inmate information to corrections, parole, and probation authorities responsible for the inmate and other government and social welfare agencies working with the inmate. Representatives of other organizations may obtain access to the inmate's files with his permission. Second, the inmate or his counsel may obtain access to all information included in the files except information derived from communications intended to be privileged or where revelation of the information would be damaging to the inmate and the informant. The rule is designed to ensure that confidential information about inmates will only be revealed to employees of agencies working with the inmate or authorized by the inmate to see the information. Inmate access to his own files is recommended as a means for ensuring that the information is accurate.

These rules attempt to make the process of work, security and other forms of inmate classifications more visible and less arbitrary. Qualifications and conditions for programs which can admit limited numbers of inmates must be clearly stated. Inmates must be told why they are receiving particular jobs and other assignments. Inmates must be given an opportunity to recommend programming for themselves and may, if they request, appear before the classification committee to argue for a particular placement.

In addition to attempting to make the classification process more visible and to involve the inmate in the process, these rules aim to ensure that the classification information about an inmate is kept current. These rules require periodic progress reports from work and housing officers and encourage social workers to seek out relevant information about inmates from sources outside the institution.

339

The comprehensive code of inmate offenses attempts to remedy both difficulties. In the first place, each offense is carefully defined so that there should be prior notice to all parties of which behavior is prescribed. Second, a specified range of punishments has been developed for each offense to eliminate the wide disparities in offenses which has existed in the past. To our knowledge, this is the first comprehensive code of offenses which has ever been proposed for a correctional system.

The rules on disciplinary procedures attempt to formulate standards of due process of law which have been required for disciplinary procedures by the federal courts or which seem necessary to ensure fairness in a manner which does not unduly burden the correctional system or threaten legitimate security interests.

The rules have several general purposes. In the first place, they seek to make the disciplinary process comprehensible to inmates and staff. For that reason, it is required that a rulebook containing the code of offenses and the disciplinary procedures be given to each inmate and each staff member.

Second, the rules seek to ensure accountability and consistency. Thus, the rules require that superior officers investigate each proposed complaint to be brought against inmates to ensure that the complaint is proper. In addition, superior officers must authorize detention of inmates prior to a hearing. Finally, the procedures seek to provide a fair hearing. Inmates must be given written notice of all charges and notice of the time for the hearing. Hearings must normally be held within three to five days of the bringing of charges to ensure that undue delays do not obscure the opportunity to prove the facts but that an adequate time for preparation exists. The hearing board would be reconstituted under the proposed rules to exclude members of the custodial staff and to include an outside member selected from a rotating panel of citizens as chairman.

For isolation and separate confinement, increased security arrangements imposed at the institutional level, these rules provide some discretion. Isolation is to be used only for major violations of disciplinary rules (or a persistent pattern of minor violations) and is limited to ten days rather than the current fifteen. The change follows trends in several states.

This section creates procedures within the Department of Corrections for consideration of inmate complaints about institutional conditions and policies. In the first place, it permits groups of inmates to submit petitions to the Commissioner who may hold hearings on the subject matter of the petition except that he must hold a hearing if twenty-five percent of the inmates or a majority of an inmate council have signed the petition. The Commissioner must also set forth his reasons for denial of the petition.

In addition to the provision on petitions, these rules create a formal mechanism for consideration of inmate complaints at both the institutional and departmental level.

It would not be realistic to predict in the period immediately ahead an amicable settlement of the differences between correctional officials and those who are strong advocates for the civil rights of offenders. There must be a balancing of individual rights and organizational or societal requirements, and polemical arguments from both sides tend to obscure operational solutions. There is little doubt, however, that correctional staff and administrators will need to understand the norms of due process much better than they do today.

The Right to Rehabilitation

Standard 2.9 of the National Advisory Commission on Criminal Justice Standards and Goals, which is reproduced in Appendix 2, probably is the most advanced of the "rights" espoused by the Commission. Indeed, their own commentary refers to it as, "the most elusive and ephemeral of the offender rights being asserted."[19]

Proposed is an affirmative and enforceable duty for correctional agencies to fulfill the right of offenders to rehabilitative programs. Sub-sections of the standard define the elements of such programs to include education, vocational training, and counseling. Interestingly, a presumption is created in favor of using community-based programs to "the maximum extent possible." Sub-section 6, however, makes a statement which might be expected to please Jessica Mitford:

> No offender should be required or coerced to participate in programs of rehabilitation or treatment nor should the failure or refusal to participate be used to penalize an inmate in any way in the institution.[20]

One of the major reasons American corrections has lacked credibility is the gap between expansive rhetoric about rehabilitation and actual availability of rehabilitative programs. Frequently judges include in their sentencing comments such phrases as, "I am sending you to prison where you will receive intensive psychiatric treatment," or "At the institution you will have an opportunity to learn a trade so that you can support yourself when you are released." The anti-social inclinations of the offender can only be reinforced if, after hearing such statements, he discovers that only a miniscule proportion of inmates receive any kind of psychotherapy, and that the little vocational training available tends to be obsolete in terms of current market requirements. The due process norms discussed in the previous section certainly require some reasonable relationship between the correctional program provided and the purpose for which the court committed the individual.[21]

The low credibility of correctional rehabilitation also stems from the statutory language which creates both institutions and community-based programs. Almost always the enabling legislation embraces the concept of rehabilitation and in effect commits the state to supply the requisite resources to implement that philosophy. But unhappily legislators' deeds in this regard have seldom matched their words. In fact, some social scientists have suggested that the prison riots which swept across the country in the 1950s, and appeared again in recent years, reflected in part a gross disparity between what was promised and what was delivered, a failure to meet the expectations generated by authoritative statements.[22]

Therefore, Standard 2.9 seems highly significant and, if implemented, could have far-reaching effects on the correctional scene. Already a few case precedents are leading in this direction, sometimes supported by the logic that the public is denied adequate protection if mandated rehabilitative programs are not in fact made available.[23] We may find an increasing number of cases in which the court terminates its sentence because the ordered treatment is not available; and perhaps situations in which the use of entire correctional facilities or programs is judicially suspended until minimal rehabilitative services (consistent with legislative intent) are supplied.

However, we shall close this section on a note of moderation and skepticism. Granted that resources should be provided to make real the promise of rehabilitation. It also seems appropriate to examine the promise, to scale down the glowing rhetoric which originated at a time when corrections was a crusading movement, given to the excesses of verbiage which characterize crusaders.[24]

Perhaps the time has come to recognize, and make explicit in law and public policy, that not all offenders need or can benefit from rehabilitative services. Some may be criminalistic because of attributes of personality or life style which simply are not accessible to even the most modern techniques of correctional treatment. Others, heretical though this may seem to some reformists, may not be suited for rehabilitation because they do not require it. Their lapse into criminal behavior may have derived from moral

342

rather than social-psychological breakdown, and therefore the role of corrections is to supply deterrent custody within humane limits. What is needed, then, is refinement of the concept of rehabilitation and more realistic statements of public policy concerning it.

The Future

The original purpose of American prisons, and the elaborate correctional apparatus that developed around them, was benevolent in nature. Isolation in socially "antiseptic" surroundings was conceived as an alternative to the brutality of corporal and capital punishment.[25] But none of the social organizations contrived by man remains antiseptic, least of all perhaps the prison. Thus we developed a sub-society of prisoners, probationers, and parolees, individuals without rights whose status made them vulnerable to gross misuse of official authority. Prisons, some have claimed, became more cruel and destructive than the barbaric methods which preceded them.

The present chapter has described recent efforts by jurists and others concerned with the legal rights of offenders to intervene in corrections systems, to define and enforce minimum standards of human welfare and dignity on behalf of those subject to correctional supervision. As we close this discussion it seems appropriate to ask whether these interventions will increase or fade, to inquire as to the future significance of the trend to build a structure of legal rights for offenders.

It is our belief that standards and norms concerning the rights of offenders (as well as machinery for their enforcement) will increase in the 1970s and 1980s. However, it seems likely that the responsibility for this process will be assumed increasingly by administrative officers, and that the judiciary will play a somewhat less active though still critically important role.

Major precedents already have been established. The old belief that offenders have no rights, only privileges, has been challenged and overcome. The courts have developed powerful sanctions with which to enforce the new norms. But obtaining compliance in a huge, fragmented corrections system is a formidable task, and only the smallest of beginnings has been made.

The administrative standards promulgated by the National Commission on Criminal Justice Standards and Goals should be widely influential, particularly if backed by funds to assist systematic change from the Law Enforcement Assistance Administration. Many states are drafting correctional codes which create statutory obligations for inmate grievance procedures and for due process in correctional decision making regarding offenders.

343

Perhaps the greatest enemy of change in this area is the continued relative isolation and "invisibility" of large penal institutions. There will continue to be innumerable violations of prisoner's rights so long as there are insufficient methods for monitoring and correcting such abuses. Bureaucracy inevitably gravitates toward preoccupation with its own convenience and survival, which conflict with the rights of individuals subject to such systems.

Needed are administrative equivalents of judicial safeguards. We may expect, then, to see ombudsmen appear in correctional settings, to find an increase in the formality of administrative hearings, and to have offenders become more vocal and more effectively assertive in advocating their own interests.

The ultimate effect of this movement will be of profound importance. Just as slaves were emancipated in the Civil War, and workers given new rights in the confrontation between labor and management which attended the industrial revolution, so also will offenders come to be regarded as valuable enough to be protected by the society of which they are a part. But, as with other such evolutionary trends, this will not happen easily or rapidly.

Conclusion

The present chapter has emphasized the rights of sentenced prisoners, but the reader should bear in mind that there are also important issues and trends with respect to the rights of probationers and parolees. One aspect of this matter has to do with the abrogation of constitutional protection against search and seizure in the case of such individuals, as well as rights with respect to probation and parole revocation hearings. Another area of importance is the imposition of conditions of probation and parole, a highly controversial matter.

Still another subject which has not been taken up in this chapter is the rights of those who have passed through the courts to appeal extremely harsh sentences. A number of states have special statutes covering this matter. The large problem of disparities in the sentencing should also be a matter of concern to all of those who are interested in improving American corrections.

Finally, the reader should be aware that we have not addressed the rights of unsentenced prisoners who are confined in local jails. Although theoretically innocent until proven guilty, it is obvious that these individuals are denied many "rights" which other citizens have. Perhaps most important of all is the defendent's constitutional right to a speedy trial, a right which all too often is made unavailable by the overloading of our judicial system.

For those interested in a more thorough and detailed examination of the subject matter dealt with in this chapter, a comprehensive treatment is now available, entitled *Legal Rights of the Convicted* by Kerper and Kerper.[26]

NOTES

[1]Fred Cohen, "The Legal Challenge to Corrections," Joint Commission on Correctional Manpower and Training, Washington, D.C., March, 1969.

[2]367 U.S. 643 (1961).

[3]378 U.S. 478 (1964).

[4]384 U.S. 436 (1966).

[5]Such as the *American Journal of Correction*, published bimonthly jointly by the American Correctional Association and the Bruce Publishing Co., 2117 W. River Road, No. Minneapolis, Minnesota 55411.

[6]Cohen, op. cit.

[7]387 U.S. 1 (1967).

[8]William D. Leeke, Director, South Carolina Department of Corrections, *The Emerging Rights of the Confined*, 1972, The Correctional Development Foundation, Inc., P. O. Box 752, Columbia, South Carolina 29202.

[9]Sheldon Krantz, Robert A. Bell, Jonathan Brant, Michael Magruder, *Model Rules and Regulations on Prisoners' Rights and Responsibilities*, Boston, Mass., 1973, Center for Criminal Justice, Boston University, School of Law, West Publishing Co., St. Paul, Minnesota.

[10]Jessica Mitford, *Kind and Usual Punishment: The Prison Business*, New York: Alfred A. Knopf, 1973.

[11]Cohen, op. cit., p. 67.

[12]Leeke, op. cit., p. 161.

[13]42 U.S.C. 1893 (Federal Civil Rights Act).

[14]National Advisory Commission on Criminal Justice Standards and Goals, *Corrections*, Washington, D.C., January 23, 1973, p. 71.

[15]Cohen, op. cit., pp. 12–13.

[16]Erving Goffman, "On the Characteristics of Total Institutions: The Inmate World," *The Prison: Studies in Institutional Organization and Change,* Donald R. Cressey, ed., Holt, Rinehart and Winston, Inc., New York, 1961, pp. 23–48.

[17]Philip Selznick, foreword to *C–Unit: Search for Community in Prison*, Elliott Studt, Sheldon L. Messinger and Thomas P. Wilson, Russell Sage Foundation, New York, 1968, p. viii.

[18]Krantz, et al., op. cit., pp. 5–11.

[19]National Advisory Commission on Criminal Justice Standards and Goals, *Corrections*, op. cit., p. 44.

[20]Ibid., p. 44.

[21]Jackson v. Indiana, 406 U.S. 715 (1972).

[22]Comment, "A Statutory Right to Treatment for Prisoners: Society's Right of Self-Defense," *Nebraska Law Review,* 50 (1971), 543. See also Note, So. Calif. Law Review, 45 (1972), 616. See also Sol Rubin, "Symposium: A Model Act for the Protection of Rights of Prisoners," Washington University Law Quarterly, Volume 1973, Summer 1973, Number 3.

[23]35 U.S. v. Allsbrook, 10 Crim. L. Rptr. 2185 (Oct. D.C. 1971).

[24]See David Rothman, *The Discovery of the Asylum* (Boston, Little Brown, 1971), for a fascinating treatment of relevant history.

[25]"Prisoners' Rights: Some Hopes and Realities," Herman Schwartz, *A Program for Prison Reform,* The Final Report, Annual Conference on Advocacy in the U.S., Chief Justice Earl Warren, June 9–10, 1972, pp. 47–62, printed by Moss Committee on Labor Enforcement and Administration of Justice.

[26]Hazel B. Kerper and Janeen Kerper, *Legal Rights of the Convicted,* West Publishing Co., St. Paul, Minn., 1974.

13 The Political Context of Corrections

As we have seen in previous chapters, correctional institutions and agencies in the United States are integral parts of political units of government—some local, some state, and some federal. Within each of these units of government a correctional agency is surrounded by a mass of influences, some of which are relatively inflexible, such as the laws defining its mission or the regulations and orders of a superior authority. Other influences and pressures are flexible and variable from time to time. These include the annual budget, which is relatively firm, but for only one year at a time, or the pressures of employee organizations, which tend to exert a continuing campaign for improved rewards for their memberships. Outside the official circles there is a series of concentric circles of community influences such as reform groups, professional associations, client advocates, the public press, and political parties.

Ideally, correctional managers and decision makers are expected to be "nonpolitical" which really should be interpreted to mean "nonpartisan." Like commissioned officers in the military service, they must serve all of the people, not just the members of a single political party. Conversely, they must be responsive to the broad policies and programs of the government in power at any given time.

Webster's dictionary defines "politics" in part as follows: "(a) the art or science of government: a science dealing with the regulation and control of men living in a society, (b) the art or science concerned with guiding or influencing government policy."

In this dictionary sense correctional managers must be skilled in the "art and science" of politics but should not be politicians in the popular meaning of the term. They are workers, managers, and executives in the government service and, therefore, must operate in a *political context*. The power and influence of the political environment works in both directions. The forces

347

in the "context" influence the correctional agency and conversely, the correctional leaders have need from time to time to "influence government policy" outside the areas wherein they have direct control. This chapter will discuss within the constraints of these few pages some of the ways in which this highly specialized social system of interacting forces operates.

Let us first identify some of the most evident spheres of influence and particularize them insofar as practicable to the field of corrections.

Intra-agency Forces

One might assume that relationships within a state department of corrections or a county probation department are essentially administrative rather than political. The relationship between the director of a state department of corrections and the superintendents, wardens, and subordinate personnel in the system is clearly an administrative one. On the other hand, if a group of employees are members of a union or a voluntary employees' association, these employees are quite clearly organized for the purpose of "influencing government policy" and hence, the relationship between the union and the management becomes a political one. Both sides exercise some power and the resolution of differences over such matters as compensation, "fringe benefits," and working conditions must be settled either by negotiation or by appealing to forces outside the immediate system. It is precisely this relationship between workers and management in the public service that brings about a large share of the intraagency political activity. Unlike private enterprise, the director of a state department of corrections has very limited powers to grant or withhold benefits for his subordinates.

For example, suppose the custodial officers of the prison system are clamoring for an increase in pay. Even if the director recognizes the justice of the request, he has no authority in most instances to make such a decision. The money must come from legislative appropriation and be approved by the governor. Beyond that, the civil service commission or its equivalent must determine how the money for salaries is to be distributed among the various ranks and classifications of employees in the prisons. Not only that, the commission must keep these rates in balance with other classifications of employees in other state departments as well as with related groups of public employees in county, city, and federal government and with workers in private enterprise who come from the same general labor market. Because of this diffusion of power it can be seen quite readily that both the rank-and-file workers and the managers must work out the best compromises they can within the political arena of the governmental jurisdiction of which they are a part.

Beyond issues of a pecuniary nature such as pay rates, retirement benefits, insurance, meals on the job, uniforms, tools and weapons, there is still some room for direct negotiations between worker organizations and agency administrators. The warden of a prison can hire and fire individual workers, but he is sharply limited by the civil service law and by the amount of discretion the warden's superior may have delegated to him. He can assign correctional officers to shifts and determine when they shall take their vacations and days off, but if this is done arbitrarily and without some concern for the human problems of his staff he can expect organized efforts to be made through political channels to circumscribe his powers even in this limited area of administrative discretion.

In short, what we have been saying above is that even in a public agency like a state prison system where the outward form is that of a quasi-military organization with a traditional "chain of command" type of structure, political forces are constantly at work. Whether the equilibrium resulting from the operation of balancing forces is good or bad is measured by the effectiveness of the agency in carrying out its mission as defined by law and public expectation.

In order to keep this chapter within the bounds of limited space the plan will be to name the principal forces within the governmental and political context and discuss each very briefly. Also, in order to keep the discussion in focus most examples will be chosen from state government, recognizing that the laws of all the states are not the same and that large county and city governments and the federal government present some unique features. Nevertheless, on balance, the political context of corrections will be found to have surprisingly similar features throughout America.

The Chief Executive

The state governor or the mayor of a great city like New York or Chicago can and usually does have more real influence upon the quality of the correctional functions of his administration than any other single political figure. A state governor's power lies principally in three areas. First, he appoints the administrator (director, commissioner, or board) to fill the position(s) which the law has provided to head the system. This administrator must be responsive to such general policies as the governor may wish to impose unless he is prepared to resign or be removed. Second, he has great power over the department's budget. This arises because the state's chief fiscal officer or budget director is also his appointee, and further, because he has the power to veto legislative bills and to "blue pencil" items of the budget after it is passed by the legislature. This veto power operates not only in matters of direct concern to the corrections agency, but it gives the governor great leverage when negotiating other related issues with legislative leaders.

The third area in which the chief executive can have great influence on correctional policy is in his role as a leader in molding public opinion. His public utterances, especially during his pre-election campaign and early in his term of office, are particularly significant. The assumption usually will be made that since the voters elected him knowing his position, it must follow that the majority of the people agree with him. That this is not necessarily altogether true is irrelevant from the political viewpoint because legislators and other decision makers will assume that it is true if such an assumption cannot be refuted.

It is unfortunate from the standpoint of improved correctional programs that only occasionally will corrections be very high on the priority list of candidates for high-level executive office. Public education, health, highways, mass transit, tax reform, and similar subjects attract far more public interest.

Governors come from many professional backgrounds in terms of education and experience, but the legal profession supplies the lion's share of the successful candidates. If as a lawyer the governor has' had any criminal law experience, it is most likely to have been as a prosecutor. The prosecutor's role in the criminal justice system is an important one but nonetheless a narrow one, and unless he is a very rare person his emphasis is likely to be on the enforcement of law in the community and on the judicial process rather than on programs which deal with the offender after conviction. The lesson in this for leaders in the correctional field is that they need to establish channels of communication with gubernatorial candidates during the campaign and immediately after a new governor takes office so that he will be less likely to get committed to unacceptable programs before he has heard from responsible persons concerned about the needs of corrections. This can be accomplished in a variety of ways — sometimes through prominent individual citizens, through professional associations of correctional workers and leaders, through public service organizations like the League of Women Voters, or any other channel which can get the respectful attention of a man whose ear is being sought by scores of other interests.

Aside from policy and program commitments the most important acts of the governor are the appointments of the administrators and decision makers of the correctional system. No matter how sound "program and policy" may be, the practical results can be disappointment and even tragedy unless the executives charged with implementation are experienced, energetic, and competent persons. The governor who assumes that the correctional system under his jurisdiction is relatively unimportant and that almost any loyal member of his party can administer it is headed for almost certain disaster. It may be true from the political standpoint that a good state prison, parole, and youth corrections program will not win many "brownie points" for a governor, but conversely, a bad operation resulting in riots, scandals, and bloodshed may be the basis for electing the governor's opponent at the next election.

The "Kitchen Cabinet"

No elective chief executive, including the President, the states' governors, city mayors, or boards of county commissioners, can run his office without some assistants and advisors who operate in direct and constant association with him. Someone must deal with the press, with the mail, with travel arrangements, with speaking engagements, with appointments to office, with extradition and executive clemency, with routine relationships with other units of government, with the political leaders of his party, with legislative matters, and with scores of miscellaneous demands for the chief's time and attention.

In state capitols the number and kinds of persons comprising this staff of the governor will depend in part on the size of the state, and in a more important way on the administrative style and experience of the governor. If the staff is large, i.e., more than a dozen or so secretaries and clerks, there will usually be an "executive secretary" whose duties normally involve the general supervision and coordination of the other members of the group. If the staff is large there will be a more complex organization. In 1974, the staff of the California Governor's Office was composed of 96 employees; that of the White House in Washington, D.C., was reported to include 5,395 employees.

This proliferation of staff specialists and functionaries of all kinds presents special problems for the heads of operating agencies, such as a state department of corrections. For example, suppose a department head has an urgent need for guidance on some problem or even a desire to warn his chief confidentially of impending trouble. The question is, how does he get through this army of staff personnel who have their own games to play and who intentionally or inadvertently may misunderstand or garble the communication in either direction?

Governors have a perfectly legitimate need for their "kitchen cabinets" and related personnel services, but if a governor dislikes routine administration, as many of them do, he runs the risk of delegating too much power to his immediate staff, and of insulating himself from his responsible cabinet officers and department heads. This also provides the opportunity for his principal staff members to take unto themselves powers which neither the law nor the system intended. This has its dangers both for the governor himself and for the departmental administrators. The events associated with the "Watergate" scandals during the administration of President Richard Nixon illustrate as no other example could the risks of permitting the executive's staff to assume too much power. The problem is not a new one and countless examples could be found in many capitols of the states.

The human tendency of persons closely associated with persons in power to arrogate unto themselves a measure of that power needs to be guarded against both by the governor himself and by his responsible administrators. Where great power resides by law in one person some of it must of necessity be delegated, but this is or should be a conscious, planned procedure. The alternative may be the assumption of power by an informal process growing out of mere proximity. The chameleons of power can turn out to be leeches on the body politic.

Earl Warren, when Governor of California, was keenly aware of the problem. When he appointed Richard A. McGee Director of the newly created Department of Corrections in 1944, he gave his new appointee this instruction: "Now, Mr. McGee, you are new in this State, and you will be operating in an unusually sensitive area of State government. From time to time someone may come to you and say, 'I have reason to believe the Governor would like you to do thus and so but probably won't want to give you his personal order.' If that should ever occur," said the Governor, "you come straight to me. If I have any instructions for you, I'll give them to you myself."

McGee was to discover as the years went by and other governors succeeded Warren that efforts to direct the policies of the Department from the Governor's Office very often originated in the minds of members of the Gover-

352

nor's secretariat or of persons close to one of them. His defense, when need-ed, was simply to say, "Let's go and discuss it with the Governor."

The Parole Board(s)

Most state correctional systems in America have one or more multiple-member boards which have varying degrees of statutory authority to release inmates of prisons and state correctional institutions, to keep them in after they are eligible, or to return them to custody after release under certain conditions. This part of the system has been discussed in terms of function and organization in previous chapters, but the political aspects of parole deserve special attention in this context.

Members of such boards in the states are normally appointed by the state's governor. In concept, the board is always regarded as "nonpartisan" and at least semiprofessional in character. Unfortunately, this arrangement offers an opportunity for political patronage which can strike at the very foundations of the board's need to be impartial, fair to all concerned, and free from ad-ministrative pressures to satisfy the current political needs of the appointing power. When one considers the fact that in spite of any system yet devised a substantial percentage of persons released on parole will commit new crimes, it can be seen readily enough that a small number of these will commit sensational crimes of a very aggravated nature. When only one such case gets unusual and widespread publicity the cry will be raised by some-one blaming the parole board for releasing the person when he might have been kept longer.

The most cogent political reason for this authority being vested in a board rather than in one official is that three or five or nine members can absorb the criticism more easily than one. Unfortunately, however, the political "heat" often will be focused on the appointing power and he will be impor-tuned to "whip the board into line." Some governors will be wise enough to respond by assuring themselves that the board had acted reasonably and in good faith and to assert that it is not their role to assume the function of the allegedly "independent" board which has been provided by law to exercise a quasi-judicial function. On the other hand, many governors and members of the "palace guard" in the governor's politically sensitive secretariat will chastise the board or even make a public statement deploring the board's "bad judgment."

As a consequence of the very nature of their task and the political climate in which they operate parole boards tend to become increasingly conservative. A board runs great risk of public and political censure if it makes an occasional honest mistake by releasing a person too soon. It runs little or no risk of criticism for keeping hundreds of others longer than just or necessary in terms of public protection. As a consequence of this political climate, especially when general crime rates are high, the whole correctional system is kept in a turmoil. Prison populations seethe with unrest, operational costs rise, institutions are overcrowded. Politicians, on one hand, demand mandatory prison sentences and longer minimum terms, while at the other extreme, agitation is rife calling for "tearing down the walls" and the substitution of "community-based programs" for all except the ovbiously "dangerous."

It is this virtually untenable political situation which has led some experienced and reputable correctional leaders to advocate the abolition of lay parole boards in the executive branch of government and the return of the sentencing, releasing, and revocation functions to the judicial branch.

The internal relationships between the parole board and the directors and managers of the institutions and parole supervision services present a somewhat different aspect of the politics of corrections. Half or more of the disciplinary and control problems of a prison warden arise directly or indirectly from having to handle too many inmates in too little space with narrow programs and too few employees. Very simply, this is called *overcrowding*. The warden has no control over the intake or the outgo. The parole board by its parole revocation practices and its releasing policies controls a substantial part of the flow of inmates both into and out of custody. The managers have to live with the total result of the parole board's policies. They complain that the board is not held accountable for its effect on the system but is more concerned with avoiding public criticism and political censure. The board in turn argues that the very reason the law has separated its decision-making powers from those of the director and his wardens is to prevent the operational administrators from releasing inmates either to save money or to reduce overcrowding without due regard for public safety.

The result of these built-in conflicts is continuing controversy between the paroling authorities and the operational administrators. Division of powers among the executive, legislative, and judicial branches in our system of government is accepted by Americans as a sound concept. A further division of powers within the very limited sphere of corrections within the executive branch by introducing a decision-making body between the courts and the administrators now is being called up for reexamination. This is one of the more troublesome phases of the political context within the correctional establishment.

The Attorney General

As stated earlier, the state's attorney general is officially the chief law officer of the executive branch of government. Hence, he is not only the official source of legal advice to department heads, but he is charged with the duty of defending the correctional administrator in lawsuits arising out of the administrator's official position. These suits are most often simply writs of habeas corpus in which prisoners allege illegal imprisonment. These will usually be handled routinely by a deputy attorney general.

On the other hand, occasionally a suit will be brought by a prisoner charging brutality, neglect, or some other violation of law. Such suits can sometimes have far-reaching administrative and political results. If the circumstances surrounding the charges attract substantial and continuing publicity, the whole political establishment of the government may get involved. The governor's office will become concerned that the governor's appointees and hence, the governor himself, may be found responsible for bad conduct or neglect. The legislature, and especially members of the opposing political party, may feel impelled to mount an extended investigation not only of the particulars of the lawsuit but of the whole department or institution involved.

If the state's attorney general is appointed by the governor, as is the case in a few states, there probably will be no political complications as far as that office is concerned. In many states, however, the attorney general is what is known as a constitutional officer; that is, his is an elective office. Because he is elected and therefore a partisan political figure, he may or may not be on friendly terms with the governor, and in some states where there are frequent shifts from one political party to another, he may even be a member of a different party from that of the governor. Under these circumstances it is understandable if the governor and his appointee who is under attack should become more than a little nervous at having a political rival serving as their defense counsel. Under these circumstances there are many cases on record in which a governor has insisted that special counsel of his own choosing be selected to defend a particularly sensitive case.

Aside from writs and lawsuits, there are few state departments which will have need for more services and ongoing relationships with the office of the attorney general than the state correctional agencies. If there is a bureau of criminal statistics or a unit of criminal investigation and identification in the state government, they are often incorporated in a state department of justice headed by the attorney general. There will be an obvious need for a close working relationship between the correctional agencies and these special service bureaus.

The Budget Director and Fiscal Control Agencies

The chief fiscal officer in the governor's cabinet can be and usually is the most powerful member of the governor's official family. He may be called budget director, director of finance, or by some similar title. He and his staff prepare the governor's budget to be presented to each regular session of the legislature. The details of the budget originate in the numerous state departments, boards, institutions, and agencies, including the department of corrections and its subordinate parts. The budget director must try to keep expenditures for all state services within the limits of anticipated revenues. Failing in that, he will be faced with the unpopular prospect of recommending increased taxes. The budget director is then not only a budget planner in a board sense, he is also a kind of referee in the competition among all the state's programs for larger shares of the available tax dollars.

As has been pointed out before, correctional programs are not high on the priority list in this struggle for a fair share of the public revenues. This is the place where the director of corrections must bring to bear all the administrative and political skills at his command if he is to survive as a successful administrator. He is not only an "underdog" in this competition but often finds himself in the position of taking "half a bone" because the decision makers are afraid of the consequences of giving him none at all. Or worse yet for his pride some budget analysts and legislators give a little more than they want to because they feel sorry for him.

Once the correctional budget gets cut down to size and fitted into the governor's budget the battle is only half won, because it still has to be adopted by the finance committees of the two houses of the legislature, voted on by both houses, adjusted for differences in "free conference," and finally signed by the governor. The director of corrections like all the other heads of agencies must defend each section of his budget before the committees in tedious hearings which may go on for days. He will almost never come out without losing some items if not whole programs in these legislative hearings. Then, even after the legislature has acted and the governor has signed the final budget bills, the director will still be subject to constant monitoring by the state's various fiscal agents before and after appropriated funds are spent.

A new fiscal year with its new budget will hardly have begun before budget planning and negotiations for the following year must begin. In short, fiscal planning and control are a continuous process. The department head may delegate much of the routine work to subordinates, but if he delegates the related political negotiations he will do so at the risk of heavy cuts in his budget requests, because legislators ordinarily want the responsible official to face them in person.

Merit System and Personnel Organizations

Most state governments and large cities and counties now have "merit systems" for all but a limited number of their employees. The laws establishing these systems were originally enacted to prevent political officeholders from using the public payroll to reward the "party faithfuls" by appointing them to all manner of positions in the public service with little regard for their qualifications and competence. It was not uncommon a relatively short time ago for a newly elected administration to replace a large proportion of the incumbents with "patronage" appointments. This often included not only key management positions, but also clerks, mechanics, guards, janitors, and any other appointment where a party supporter wanted the job.

It was this practice that degraded the public service in all of its aspects and discouraged young people from entering an occupation where tenure and promotion had little relationship to competence. In one state in which this writer had a brief experience it reached the point where the state budget document containing the roster of state employees with their positions and salaries revealed was a "best seller" just after an election in which the party and the governor in control of the state capitol were about to change. The book sold for $5.00 and served as a kind of catalog of political job opportunities.

The Civil Service Commission or the State Personnel Board, as it is known in some states, is a body, usually with five members appointed for long terms, which has the relatively independent responsibility for administering the civil service laws. The commission, through its staff, writes the job specifications for each position or class of positions authorized by the legislature, holds qualifying and promotion examinations for applicants, sets salary scales, decides disputes over disciplinary actions, and generally determines overall personnel policy and enforces the civil service law.

Some administrators in correctional agencies as well as other branches of government deplore the rigidity of the system and complain bitterly about the limitations placed upon their power to hire and fire according to their own judgment. Experienced executives in the public service usually recognize

357

that even though the system has its shortcomings it is without doubt the lesser of the two evils, if the latter one is the old system of political patronage.

The merit system has produced its own brand of politics, but it is not patronage politics. Now, the political interchange between the executives of the operating agencies and the civil service establishment relates to obtaining appropriate classifications of employees, salary scales, examination and recruitment procedures, promotional ladders, and training programs.

A far more viral form of political action has now developed in most large jurisdictions in the form of employee organizations which may either be independent voluntary associations or may be affiliated with one of the national or international labor unions, such as the AFL-CIO or the Teamsters. These associations or unions tend to cut across departmental lines and to go directly to the political power structure of the state or other political jurisdiction. In other words in a state government their paid representatives and officers exert such influence as they can directly on the governor, the legislature, and the civil service commission. It is from these sources that they must seek such "bread and butter" rewards as increased pay rates, overtime rules, vacation, sick leave and holiday allowances, provision for retirement, and collective bargaining agreements. The heads of operating departments under this new set of practices are left outside the contractual relationship except to advise the political decision makers.

The department head still has some room to move within the system, but it becomes more and more narrow as the employee groups become stronger politically. Aside from the "bread and butter" items, he still has some limited disciplinary control, power to assign workers to specific jobs and to administer grievance procedures. Even these powers are being challenged by advocates of independent ombudsmen and by employee pressures to control workloads and work assignments on the basis of worker preferences rather than by administrative judgment. As stated earlier in this chapter, the politics of management-employee relationships is becoming one of the most challenging areas in the correctional field. Most old-line correctional administrators and especially wardens of prisons are finding it difficult to adjust to this new realignment of power. When one considers that the management of a maximum security prison is faced with the constant risk of crises wherein it may become necessary to establish for short periods what would be equivalent to martial law in a free community, the apprehensions of the men in the command post are understandable. As both administrators and union leaders become more accustomed to mature negotiation, a balance between employee and client rights on the one hand and the necessity for orderly, responsible government on the other will no doubt emerge in this field, just as it appears to have in private industry.

Sister Agencies of State Government

The correctional agency, whether in state or local government, has a variety of interrelationships with other departments in the same jurisdiction. These kinds of contacts are not so much a sharing of power and authority, as with the budget director or the civil service commission as they are cooperative and service relationships. They are too numerous to elaborate on here, but mention of a few will illustrate the situation.

In a department of general services or a department of administration there will usually be a division of central purchasing which does all the buying of merchandise from buses to beans and from beds to beef. This is one of the most continuous and often troublesome responsibilities for institution administrators because of the endless variety of goods which must be acquired. The general services department may also be responsible for the allocation of office space and maintenance of state public buildings.

There is usually a department of public works which will have the supervision of contracts for the planning and construction of new buildings and the remodeling of existing structures. The state fire marshal will inspect for fire safety in all state buildings, including the prisons. In the interests of public health the department of health will do the same for sewage disposal and water supply.

The department of public welfare will often have clients in the families of probationers, parolees, and prisoners. The same is true of the department of mental hygiene and the department of vocational rehabilitation. The public school system often carries on education and training programs in correctional institutions, and parolees and their families may be taking courses in the regular school system. All of these agencies share in rendering services to clients and the managers and workers involved must find ways to cooperate.

One of the most important of the sister agencies is the department of employment or its equivalent. The thousands of clients of the correctional system have a special need for job training and job placement. This department has a direct tie to both labor and management in the private sector of the free community. The whole correctional establishment (parole, probation, and institutions) within the boundaries of a given state may have more than one percent of its entire population under correctional supervision at one time. When this is reduced to the adult male population it may be 4 or 5 percent. Furthermore, there is a continuous turnover amongst them. No one knows what percentage of working-age males are processed through the systems of corrections in say a five-year period. It can hardly be fewer than 15 percent and may be twice that many. The significance of the employment and employability of this segment of the population needs no elaboration. The correctional administrator or worker who takes his mission seriously must give attention to this need. The two public agencies which should be his greatest allies are the schools and the employment service.

In a few states where prisoners and wards of correctional schools are employed on public works, especially in reforestation and wild-land fire prevention, another partner to the correctional service may be the forest and park services. In California, at one time during the 1960s, approximately 3,000 men were employed in conservation camps operated jointly by the Department of Corrections and the State Division of Forestry. The internal political forces in the two state agencies were further complicated by the public relations aspects of having that many convicted felons located in over 40 camps scattered over the state.

Most states maintain some police agencies as functions of state government in spite of the fact that it continues to be accepted public policy in America to leave the major share of the police function to municipalities and counties. The uniformed state police force in a few states like Pennsylvania and New York have general police powers. In others, this agency is known as the highway patrol and limits its activities primarily to enforcing the traffic laws on state highways. The relationship between state correctional institutions and agencies and the state police forces is largely one of calling upon them on order of the governor as a backup force if needed in cases of emergency, such as prison riots, escapes, or disasters involving fire, earthquake, or flood, when an institution may have to be wholly or partially evacuated.

Aside from emergencies, there are numerous ways in which the state correctional agencies and state police can cooperate in such other matters as the joint use of personnel training facilities and communications networks.

The National Guard, which is the state militia in each state, is under the general command of the governor in times of peace and may also be called out on his order if it should be needed in emergencies of such magnitude as to appear to be beyond the control of the police and the correctional system.

The use of the military in cases of prison mutiny and riot has been very rare, and the experiences with doing so have almost invariably resulted in disaster if the troops engage in the actual use of lethal force against rebels armed only with clubs and homemade knives. The accidental killing and wounding of hostages and prisoners not involved in the rebellion is seldom excused by impartial investigators or by the general public. The political aftermath of such affairs can be devastating.

Riots must be suppressed and the safety of hostages protected if at all possible, but the lessons of experience at Attica, New York[2] in 1971, and the Thanksgiving Day riot at Folsom, California in 1927 (10 convicts killed, 5 wounded, 1 guard dead of a heart attack) among others, are convincing enough to dictate limiting the use of both police and the military to backup and support roles. The security forces of the prison system should be trained[3] first to prevent, second to contain, and finally to suppress mass rebellions without direct intervention by outside police and military force.

Legislative Relationships

As every schoolboy should know, each state government has a legislature made up of two houses, save Nebraska which has only one. The so-called upper house is normally termed "senate" after the federal pattern, and a lower and usually larger body goes by different names, but is most often called "assembly." Until the "One man, one vote"[4] decision of the United States Supreme Court in 1964, senators were elected from geographical senatorial districts which often contained wide differences in the number of residents from district to district. This enabled the predominantly rural districts to exert a disproportionate amount of power, thus denying the fundamental concept of representative government. Now both houses of state legislatures must be reapportioned according to population after each decennial census. The number of senators and assemblymen and the length of their terms are fixed by the constitution of each state.

Some states still follow the practice of holding biennial sessions and then only for a few months. Others have annual sessions of limited length, and others, like California, now operate much like the United States Congress, and except for recesses are for all intents and purposes in session continuously.

The head of a state correctional system probably has no more important political relationship than with the legislature and the bureaucracies employed by that branch of state government. The governor usually has a high-ranking secretary on his staff who is the direct link between his administration and the legislature. For the department head this person is an important one because he will not want to support or oppose bills in which he is interested without first consulting the governor's legislative liaison person. This secretary is, of course, a staff person, and while he has no intrinsic authority himself, he can exert great influence both on the governor and on individual legislators.

All legislatures have a system of committees in both houses organized along broad subject-matter lines. For example, there will normally be a committee on education, one on public health, one on transportation, and so on. The correctional system will have frequent matters before the finance committee of each house, because its budget is heard by these committees or subcommittees of them. Also, any bill which has a special appropriation attached to it will also be heard and voted on by these groups. An example might be a bill authorizing the establishment of a new institution requiring a substantial appropriation for planning and construction.

Other important committees found in most legislatures will include one on criminal law and procedure and one on government organization. These are likely to be the kinds of committees to which bills affecting corrections will be assigned. This is not to say that some such bill might not be assigned to almost any committee if the person or committee that assigns bills thinks the subject matter of a particular bill warrants it.

The correctional administrator who knows the importance of the legislative relationship will follow certain strategies which can only be mentioned here because of space limitation. Briefly, the correctional administrator will

1. Know the rules established by the legislature which affect the introduction, hearing, and passage of bills.

2. Know personally the chairmen of all or most of the committees.

3. Know personally all the members of the committees in which he may expect legislation in his field to be heard. This takes time and effort, especially because there tends to be considerable turnover from session to session, particularly in the lower house.

4. Know as much as possible about all of these key legislators, not only as lawmakers but as human beings who have families, hobbies, occupations, biases, ambitions, and constituents.

5. Know the real leaders in each house. Conversely, know who the ones are that are held in low repute by their fellows. To have one of the latter as the author of a bill one wants enacted may be the single factor most likely to defeat it.

6. Know the secretaries of key legislators and especially those who are

chairmen of the committees most likely to handle the legislation. They are the gatekeepers to the legislator's private audience and the managers of his calendar and telephone calls.

7. Be of service to individual legislators whenever it can be done without compromising himself. This may involve supplying information, interviewing a constituent, providing a speaker for his home service club or taking him on a trip to an institution.

8. Know and work with the staff of relevant committees. They are often bright young men or women seeking political experience, however, their very inexperience may cause them to supply their employers with inadequate or even distorted information.

9. Know his enemies who are either legislators or legislative staff persons. One cannot expect to promote and carry out positive programs in a political context without "goring somebody's ox" occasionally. Be sure to keep such enmities as are inevitable on an impersonal level.

10. If possible, cultivate at least one important and respected leader in each house who will take a special interest in his programs and with whom he can discuss legislative strategies and tactics on a confidential basis.

If all this seems like a full-time job for a man who is already overtaxed, one must candidly admit that it is. The load can be lightened somewhat, however, by having an assistant with human relations skills to do much of the footwork, the interminable waiting in committee rooms, and matters of that kind. It is nevertheless essential that the responsible top administrator be always available in the "clutches." Also, it is fortunate for him that the legislature even in the most active jurisdictions is not in session all the time.

So far, we have dealt only with direct relationships between the correctional administrator, the governor's office, and the legislative establishment itself. There is around every "state house" in the country a rather indefinable group of individuals which is often referred to in the jargon of state politics as the "Third House." It is made up of a wide variety of legislative advocates known as "lobbyists." During the height of a legislative session this group may outnumber the entire legislature. It is not necessarily made up of shadowy figures lurking in the corridors of the legislative halls and the lobbies and bars of the capital hotels as many people suppose. There are, unfortunately, some of these, but most of the legislative advocates are honorable persons of intelligence and substance. Among them will be representatives of such interests as the state chamber of commerce, the state labor organizations, the manufacturers' association, the state medical association, the chiropractors, the state league of cities, the governments of the principal cities and counties, the peace officers' association, the state correctional association, the bar association, the insurance industry, the bankers, the building contractors, the teachers' association, the race tracks, the liquor distillers, the breweries, the Catholic Church, the taxpayers' association, the telephone company, and so on and on.

Why are people in the "Third House" important to the head of the correction agency? Simply because they do influence votes for better or for worse. They may help to pass or defeat legislation in which they have some direct or peripheral interest. They are part of the correctional administrator's political context. He will do well to know as much about them and their relationships with the legislators as he can.

Local Government Agencies

In states with one or more large metropolitan centers (for instance, Illinois, New York, California, and Pennsylvania) it is these centers which provide the lion's share of the clients of the state's correctional system. It is important for the state correctional administrator to establish direct or indirect communications with such key figures as the mayor or the county executive, the chief of police, the presiding judge of the criminal court, the county or city prosecutor, the sheriff, and the chief probation officer. Many of these officials are prone to criticize state operations whenever something goes wrong. Being human, they are less prone to unload a public barrage on a state official they know and respect than on a stranger. Furthermore, the cities and counties are, in spite of much local pride, political subdivisions of state government. As such, they operate under the state's laws and often receive substantial financial aid from the state.

These local officials, agencies, and departments really cannot operate without state government and vice versa. The relationships must of necessity be that of working partners in the general business of governing the state as a total community. This partnership concept can operate effectively only if communication and a spirit of mutual help is fostered by the professional administrators. At the political level it is not uncommon to find bitter rivalries between a governor and the mayor of a major city in the state. In spite of this, both the politicians and the administrators of police and corrections need to keep partisan politics from damaging the effectiveness of the total

system. To do otherwise only gives aid and comfort to the common enemy —
crime.

The Press and the Mass Media

Newspapers, magazines, radio, and television are of profound political
importance in the United States, because of the constitutional guarantee
under the First Amendment of freedom of the press. This is not the place to
elaborate on that thesis except to make the point that the readers, listeners,
and viewers of the output of these media of mass information obviously
seem to have an insatiable and even morbid appetite for crime news and
crime entertainment. As a consequence, the police, prosecutors, and correctional agencies are the daily, even hourly, source of the raw material for
crime news and related information.

For convenience and simplicity all the mass media will be referred to
hereafter as the *press.*

Many public agencies who feel the need to get information about their
programs out to the general public have great difficulty getting the attention
of the press, except in times of trouble and scandal. In the case of a correctional agency, reporters and other representatives of the press will be seeking constantly to cultivate sources of information from the system. Many
correctional administrators have failed to realize the advantages inherent in
the fact that the gatherers of "news" need their cooperation and that because
of this fact, there is a built-in opportunity for a symbiotic relationship.

The relationship is a delicate one because by definition the word symbio-
sis means the living together of two unlike organisms with independent
needs but to the mutual but limited advantage of both. To give the press unlimited access to the records of inmates of a prison would give a reporter a
rich and almost unlimited resource for news and human interest stories. It
also would be grossly unfair to the prisoners and their families and would be
considered an unpardonable breach of professional ethics by the prison
management. On the other hand, except for some confidential personal information, much of what is in a prisoner's file is already on the public record coming out of his arrest, prosecution, and trial. There is no reason why
this kind of information cannot be given to the press, if it is requested, but
without allowing the reporter to go on a "fishing trip" through the record
files.

Many correctional administrators and especially prison wardens have
been so reluctant to give information to the press that some reporters even

have gone to the extreme of actually entering into agreements with subordinate employees to pay them a fee for any tip about an occurrence which might make news but which for real or imagined reasons the warden had not reported. The unfortunate results of this practice are threefold and all to the disadvantage of the warden. First, the tipster probably had incomplete information picked up in the guards' locker room and hence a garbled news account results. Second, since only one news outlet got the story early, it was a "scoop" and, therefore, would get a "front page" billing when it deserved a place among the want ads. Third, the reporter and his fellows would see the incident as further evidence of a public official concealing legitimate news and would carry into future situations the suspicion that the warden could not be trusted to give out the true facts.

Concealing or delaying "spot" news from the press is a sure way to guarantee a public official an unfriendly press, and when he needs press cooperation in "selling" his programs and himself to the public it may be unavailable. A well-managed correctional institution or agency will have an established and written policy about its relationship with the press so that there will be a clear understanding on the part of both the press and the managers and submanagers of the correctional system as to just what is acceptable and what is not.

A common complaint of administrators is that when news and information is given the press the resulting reporting in newspapers or newscasts is written or edited down so as to distort the original meaning. There is no complete defense against this, but there are some precautions. First, whenever time permits, news releases should be written out in a news format containing the essential facts in the first few lines. Releases should be given simultaneously to all the local outlets and wire services at the same time. Then, when facts are not reported correctly, call it to the attention of the responsible persons, and if the error is a serious one, ask for a correction in the next issue.

Sensational news about riots, stabbings, escapes, and intrigue tends to detract from the constructive elements of the program, but the very fact that the correctional agency is the source of such news gives the administrator a readier access to the press through its reporters, writers, and publishers. Unless the administrator takes advantage of this relationship, the public will soon develop a distorted image of the operation which may work to the disadvantage of everyone concerned. Unless the correctional leaders make an aggressive effort to carry their message to the public, the press generally will feel little responsibility to do it for them.

Voluntary Associations

In industrialized societies, with the concentration of populations in urban centers and the occupational specialization of workers and of industries, there has been a phenomenal growth and proliferation of voluntary associations whose members have some social, economic, or political reason for joining together. They represent a variety of spheres of power and influence of which any manager of a public agency must be aware. These associations may be made up of members of a profession, such as medicine, dentistry, law, engineering, and so on through the long list of professional occupations. There are also associations of various kinds of businesses. Almost every urban area has a chamber of commerce made up of representatives of the businesses in the area. There are associations of various specialized businesses, such as building contractors, retail merchants, and manufacturers. In addition to these, other kinds of voluntary associations include labor unions, fraternal organizations, service clubs such as Rotary, Kiwanis, and Lions, religious organizations including not only the churches, but the Salvation Army, Volunteers of America, and the Society of Friends.

There are other associations, which often have a special interest in corrections, such as the peace officers' associations, judges' associations, the NAACP and Urban League, the Parent Teachers Association, women's clubs such as the League of Women Voters, veterans' organizations such as the American Legion, and so on through an almost endless list.

It is obvious that correctional workers and managers will have frequent relationships with some of these organizations, very occasional contacts with others, and with some none at all. Nevertheless, all of these voluntary associations of citizen groups are a part of the political context in which correctional agencies must operate. Considering the diversity of relationships which impinge upon the correctional operation, it would be futile to suggest that any effort be made to establish ongoing contacts, acquaintanceships, and understandings with all of these groups. On the other hand, a few will have a particular interest in crime prevention and control and in government generally. For example, because of their interest in children, most of the women's clubs and the Parent Teachers Associations will have a special concern for juvenile corrections and delinquency prevention programs.

The administrator in charge of prisons for adults will have two kinds of built-in relationships with organized labor. First, organized labor has always been suspicious and apprehensive about the presumed competition with their membership by prison labor. On the other side of the coin, most prison systems will have about a 50 percent turnover per year, which means that if there is a standing population of 10,000 prisoners in the system about 5,000 of these will be released into the community by discharge or parole each 12 months. In highly industrialized areas of the country most of them will have to join a union in order to get employment. As a consequence, the relationship between vocational training in the institutions and the placement of parolees brings the two operations into direct contact with each other. Unless there is understanding and cooperation, inevitably there will be conflict. By the same token, the adults released from the system either by parole or probation will not only have to have union membership but they also will have to be on someone's payroll, which means a relationship with employers who are engaged in private business.

Historically, as has been pointed out in an earlier chapter, the churches and organized religious groups have had a longstanding concern for the welfare and reform of the clients of a correctional system, ranging from those condemned to death to delinquent boys and girls. Practically all institutions have a chaplaincy service which again provides a linkage between corrections and the churches. The Salvation Army and Volunteers of America have always had a deep concern, not only for the people in prisons and jails, but also for all unfortunates who live on the outer fringes of the normal social and economic life of the community. Some of the early leaders and founders of the American Prison Association, which is now known as the American Correctional Association, were clergymen. In 1950, Mr. J. Stanley Sheppard, an officer of the Salvation Army, was elected President of the American Prison Association.

Almost every community, even of a few thousand population, has its classification service clubs made up of a variety of business and professional leaders in the area. Rotary, Kiwanis, Lions, 20–30 Clubs, Optimists, Soroptimists, Zonta International, Business and Professional Women, and so on, are all well-known examples of this kind of organization. Most of them have charity funds and sometimes become involved in volunteer correctional and prevention programs. Aside from their direct involvement, each of them represents a cross section of the community, and hence, provides an opportunity for correctional leaders to discuss their programs by providing speakers for the weekly meetings.

The relevant spheres of influence represented by voluntary associations will vary from community to community, and region to region. For our present purpose, it is important only to point out and emphasize the potentialities for constructive relationships with these organizations for the correction

worker or leader who recognizes the importance of obtaining the cooperation and involvement of responsible citizens.

Conclusion

Much of what has been said in this chapter may seem to the uninitiated to
be a discussion of public and community relations rather than of the political
context of corrections. The simple truth is that the two are so intertwined
that they cannot be separated either in theory or practice. In the beginning
we made the distinction between competitive partisan politics and the
broader meaning of politics as the art and science of government and of influencing government policy. Many citizens and public officials have great
difficulty in keeping these two concepts separated.

In a representative government based on democratic principles one must
always keep in mind that *political power* derives from the people and their
social institutions. *Political authority,* on the other hand, is delegated
through the ballot and related political processes to executives, legislators,
and judges. This delegation of authority is always limited, first by existing
law, and second by time. The *power* of the citizenry is as permanent as the
government itself—the *authority* of persons in public office is temporary.
Those who occupy these posts of temporary authority to exercise political
power cannot expect to have a benign and comfortable official life. They are
actors in a living drama in which they play major or minor, but transitory,
roles. They cannot endure or achieve their missions except by understanding the political contexts of their positions and by interacting with the forces
within that environment. Correctional workers and leaders are faced with
unique challenges in this context, but the rewards can be great for those
steadfast men and women whose values call for a constructive concern for
the predicament of man.

> You must give some time to your fellow man. Even if it's a little thing, do
> something for those who have need of help, something for which you get no
> pay but the privilege of doing it. For remember, you don't live in a world all
> your own. Your brothers are here, too.[5]

NOTES

[1]*Webster's New Collegiate Dictionary,* Springfield, Mass., G. & C. Merriam Company, 1973, p. 890.

[2]*The Official Report of the New York State Special Commission on Attica,* New York, Bantam Books, September 1972.

[3]American Correctional Association, *Causes, Preventive Measures and Methods of Controlling Riots and Disturbances in Correctional Institutions,* Washington, D. C., 1970.

[4]Wesberry v. Sanders, 376 U.S., page 1, 1964.

[5]Albert Schweitzer, quoted in *Federal Probation* 20, 2 (June 1956):9.

14 The Future of American Corrections

Most efforts to predict the future shape of American corrections have been reflections of the hopes and beliefs of the would-be prophets much more than analytical projections of present trends to some distant time horizon. Indeed it could be argued with some force that the nature of corrections today greatly reflects the self-fulfilling prophecies, the hopes and beliefs of reformists from the past. One approach to prediction, then, would be through an examination of what various advocates and critics of corrections *wish* to happen, and an assessment of their respective capacities to influence coming events.

However, there is reason to believe that such a mode of prediction would have less utility in predicting some future tomorrow than have past predictions concerning today. Alvin Toffler refers to change as "avalanching upon our heads," and offers an arresting opinion of Kenneth Boulding that, "Almost as much has happened since I was born as happened before."[1] Corrections will change as a result of accelerating technology, urbanization, and myriad other changes in its social and political context. But *how* will it change? Will it become more unified philosophically? Will it become more coherent organizationally? Most important of all, will it become more effective in protecting society? If so, how?

Our thoughts on such formidable questions are necessarily speculative. In the main, we shall suggest future conditions on the basis of trends which are already discernible, but some predictions or perhaps more accurately guesses, are not greatly constrained by present realities. The time horizon used for most of the projects is the year 2000, unless modified downward by such phases as, "in the short run," or upward by, "in the distant future." No doubt our personal beliefs about what *ought* to be will find expression in these statements, a caveat the reader should not underestimate.

Before attempting to characterize the corrections of the future, it seems useful to discuss some underlying assumptions about probable changes in the crime problem, in the composition of the offender population, and in the noncorrectional alternatives to the present system. This is the purpose of the following section.

Bases for Prediction

Changes in the Crime Problem

While there is great uncertainty about the magnitude of the crime problem, and well-based doubt concerning the accuracy of existing techniques for measuring it, almost all authorities would agree that it has increased steadily since World War II. Recently the Law Enforcement Assistance Administration announced a plan to conduct victimization studies periodically in four regions of the country, i.e., scientific samplings of the experience of citizens as the *victims* of crime. Until this important development (except for a household study of the victims of crime sponsored by The President's Commission on Law Enforcement and the Administration of Justice in 1966), we have been limited to statistics on the response of criminal justice officials to criminal acts, e.g., arrests, bookings, arraignments, convictions, and so on. Thus, one prediction which can be made with some confidence for the near future is the presence of much more valid and reliable information about the size and nature of the crime problem in the United States.

Will that problem increase or decrease? No doubt it will increase as the general population increases, but we are prepared to predict that the *rate* of crime (incidence per 100,000 population) will level and then go down, slowly and unevenly (varying by type of crime and locale) over the next several years.

The factors involved in this projection are complex, but a major one is the known decrease in the proportion of the total population made up of late adolescents and young adults, especially males. Young men and youth are well known to be the age group most prone to criminal and delinquent behavior, and their numbers in the American population have been inordinately high for some years because of the "baby boom" which followed World War II, a condition which is only now leveling out. We may expect a declining birth rate in the decades ahead, according to many demographers.

A second major factor which may be expected to produce changes in the nature and size of the crime problem is the movement to decriminalize various types of conduct for which individuals are now legally convicted and made a part of the offender population. The policy of regarding alcoholics as ill rather than criminal, the liberalization of laws on marijuana possession and use, the legalization of prostitution under controlled conditions, the removal from the criminal statutes of penalties for private, homosexual acts between consenting adults—all of these are examples of a growing tendency, if not toward increased tolerance for certain forms of deviant behavior, at least toward a public policy of dealing with them outside of the orbit of the criminal justice system.

It may be inaccurate to refer to such conduct as "victimless crimes," as many commentators have, for they frequently victimize both the perpetrator and others around him in tragic ways. But society is discovering that criminal sanctions often exacerbate rather than ameliorate problems of this kind, and that solutions may better be found through other services such as health, welfare, or employment. In any case, the removal of criminal sanctions in such areas will gradually reduce the overall workload of corrections, and relieve it of certain responsibilities, such as the treatment of alcoholics and drug addicts, which not only have interferred greatly with other correctional tasks, but never have been successfully achieved. The general effect of the decriminalization movement should be reduction and simplification of the work of the American correctional system.

Changes in the Offender Population

Daniel Glaser, in a perceptive paper on the future of American corrections, has predicted that the years immediately ahead will see major changes in the makeup of the population under correctional supervision.[2] He argues, in brief, that this group will become more and more similar to the general population from which it is drawn, except that it will continue to be made up disproportionately of young persons, perhaps even more so than today.

As we have seen, the offender profile has long been configured to include disproportionate numbers of males, youths, ethnic minorities, and the poor and the undereducated, underemployed residents of the inner city. Glaser believes that those committed to corrections will come to include more affluent, more white, and more female elements, and that it will be less composed of those with handicaps in the areas of education and employability. He asserts that these outcomes will occur as a result of increasingly successful efforts to reduce poverty in the United States (through welfare reforms and economic opportunity programs), and through eradication of racial and ethnic discrimination. Thus, fewer and fewer persons would become criminals because of economic hardship and class discrimination; offenders would become more middle class and more white.

The increase of females in the mix, Glaser believes, will arise from the same dynamics which have produced the Women's Liberation Movement, the emancipation of the female from sex-segregated statuses. Just as women are finding their way into legitimate roles long reserved to males, we may expect to see them opt more often for criminal roles and "opportunities" which have long been regarded as the special preserve of males. If true, this would mean that females would shift from relatively self-destructive modes of crime (e.g., prostitution and acting as passive cohorts to aggressive male offenders), and themselves undertake such offenses as robbery, burglary, and "confidence games."

Current statistical data on offenders in corrections lend some credence to Glaser's statements, for all of the trends he mentions are now apparent in some degree. However, it seems wise not to over-predict changes in these categories. The correction of class and racial inequities is at best a slow process, and filled with unanticipated consequences. And it is to be hoped that the intelligence behind the "liberation" of women will not often regard crime as a desirable expression of freedom.

It seems most realistic to expect that the bulk of offenders will continue to be those with multiple disadvantages. Unhappily, the experience of failure, the acquisition of "trouble," is a cumulative process. Most of those who occupy our jails and prisons in the year 2000 will still wear other identities than that of criminal. They will more often than not be poor and/or alcoholic and/or members of an ethnic minority, and so on through an all-too-familiar list of interlocking factors which contribute to a criminal career.

The identity of *criminal*, itself, the labeling stigmata, will continue to be a powerful factor in increasing the probability that the individual involved will be a criminal in the future.

One predictive statement which seems well supported by present evidence is that the higher the frequency and the longer the duration of contacts with corrections, the more apt the individual involved will be to continue as a "client" of the correctional system. This will be as true in the year 2000 as it is today, for the self-fulfilling capacity of invidious labels, and of membership in a deviant group, will not change in the foreseeable future.

The Development of Alternatives to Corrections

As was indicated in an earlier chapter, recent years have seen a major emphasis on the diversion of offenders away from the criminal justice system. The underlying concept on which such strategies are based is that individuals who violate the law will be less apt to do so in the future if they are not officially defined as "delinquent" or "criminal" and made to associate with others who wear that same label. The major weakness of the diversion approach thus far has been the lack of viable alternatives to correctional supervision. It does little good to speak of "alternate tracks" to those which lead into our prisons and jails unless one develops at the end of those tracks realistic forms of assistance and control to meet the needs of those involved.

A series of enormously difficult questions present themselves in this connection. If the individual who is chronically inebriated and thereby presents a danger to himself and others is not to be sent to jail, where should he be sent? If the youngster who is experiencing a disorganized home life, and is beginning to show rebellious and unacceptable behavior in school, is not to be sent to the juvenile hall, where should he be sent? If the individual with complex emotional problems (e.g., sexual aberrations or episodes of pre-psychotic rage) should receive treatment instead of incarceration, who should be assigned responsibility for supplying that form of assistance? Such questions could be extended through a long chronicle of heretofore unmet needs.

While the development of the idea is relatively new, we may reasonably expect that the task of discovering and developing alternatives to correctional management will be addressed seriously in the next one to two decades. In fact, small, pilot programs meeting a great variety of human needs already are to be found around the country. More and more federal money is going into the development of such programs and we are beginning to see a more effective dissemination of information about their successes and failures so that other communities may consider utilizing them. Detoxication centers for alcoholics, community programs for youths who are drifting away from parental control, community psychiatric programs for emotionally disturbed individuals, intensive vocational training for those with severe employment problems — these are examples of the types of alternatives which are needed and are gradually appearing.

Thus far we have tended to delay response until the problems of crime and delinquency become severe. The extremely expensive use of incarceration is reserved for those who have demonstrated their dangerousness in clear and dramatic ways. What is needed and hopefully will be supplied by the year 2000 is a sizeable investment of resources in more preventive types of programs which anticipate and intercept individuals who are developing a pattern of anti-social behavior.

The fact that these programs are developing more and more under the auspices of agencies which do not label the recipients of assistance as criminal or delinquent is highly important. Hopefully we will *not* have more programs of formal prediction of crime and delinquency, since the labeling effects of such predictions may do more harm than good. What is needed is an early warning system to respond to the clear indications of people whose troubled lives are carrying them irrevocably toward the correctional system. The net effect of developing such alternative programs should reduce the workload of corrections and focus it much more sharply upon the individual whose problems cannot be met more appropriately by other agencies.

Foci for Change

We have discussed some assumptions about the future of the crime problem, the makeup of the offender population, and the development of alternatives to the use of corrections which will provide a context for what follows. Now an effort will be made to indicate what American corrections will be like circa the year 2000. Our predictions will be made under four headings: 1) the philosophic bases for correctional services; 2) the organization and delivery of correctional services; 3) the programmatic content of correctional services; 4) the development and dissemination of new knowledge.

The Philosophic Bases for Correctional Services

A major theme of this book has been the belief that American corrections is caught, and often immobilized, in the binds of multiple, conflicting goals: punishment vs. rehabilitation, free will vs. determinism, institutional incapacitation of offenders vs. their reintegration into community life. Will these ambivalent and vitiating pressures continue into the future? Or is there hope for a more integrated philosophy for corrections, one which would direct the field along a reasonably straight line of improvement and refinement of its operating methodologies?

We cannot discern any global synthesis or overarching metamorphosis of existing philosophies in the foreseeable future. Those who are concerned with the construction of new theories tend to be divided from each other by academic and disciplinary boundaries (e.g., sociology, psychology, political science) much as practitioners are divided by the bureaucratic boundaries which run through the criminal justice field. As Malcolm W. Klein points out:

> If we are to advance beyond our current very limited abilities to devise more effective correctional approaches, we must become more organized around the nature of the problem not the nature of our several professions.[3]

However, becoming organized around the nature of the problem, even if we can overcome the divisive manner in which knowledge is territorialized, is no easy task. The "problem," as we have seen, is enormously varied. Offenders are not a monolithic group, no matter how much members of the public would like to believe them to be. In fact a major reason for defeating and polemical arguments about correctional philosophy is the tendency to speak in all-inclusive, broad-brush terms: "Criminals are psychopathic predators and should be executed or imprisoned"; or alternatively, "offenders are the victims of inadequate families and diminished opportunities, and should be afforded rehabilitative assistance in the community." Both statements could be accurate, but with regard to different sub-groups or one individual at different times.

What may be predicted, then, is the development and sharpening of theoretical positions which refer to discrete parts of the offender population, positions which address both the nature of their problems and the type of intervention which should be employed to deal with them. A beginning has been made on this complex task through the pioneering work of Marguerite Warren and her colleagues.[4]

Thus, we may expect to see in the years ahead a sorting out of the premises for correctional service. Instead of the present mishmash of competing purposes, offenders will more and more be programmed around a particular primary purpose, e.g., intensive reintegrative treatment in the community, intensive psychological treatment in an appropriate institution, intensive custodial treatment in a different kind of institution, and so on. Within such major modalities will be sub-programs designed to meet particular requirements of particular individuals. There will be a capability for flexible sequencing from one mode to another, e.g., from confinement designed for punitive deterrence to community treatment designed for reintegration.

Well before the year 2000, correctional philosophy will have become less diffuse and more rationally differentiated by type of offender and type of intervention. It will be more forthright and explicit. Perhaps punishment will even be called punishment, instead of more euphemistic terms, and it will be possible to think through the humanitarian limits which should be placed upon it and the ways in which it can be made more effective as an individual and a general deterrent.

The penultimate social policy for responding to "deviance" and "evil" in mankind probably will be as elusive and ephemeral in 2000 as it is today. The forces which make men creative and innovative are intertwined with those which make them degenerate and destructive. Crime and punishment, too, are reciprocal in the affairs of men.

What we can hope for, and work to achieve, is a social policy which brings the management of offenders out into the light of day, where brutality and neglect will not be tolerated, where the ways of dealing with each other that make us civilized are extended to the greatest possible extent to those who violate the law; and where the use of punitive sanctions, when they need to be used, is done openly and unambiguously. While correctional dilemmas will still be present in 2000, we believe that the field will be approached by the public more as an object of responsible concern, and less in a spirit of morbid fascination.

The Organization and Delivery of Correctional Services

We have seen that the problems which afflict American corrections are not limited to philosophical conflict and impasse. They are also manifest in an administrative system which is so Balkanized, and so diffuse, as to further confound the implementation of system improvement efforts. The present capacity of correctional administrators to serve as the leaders of needed changes seems limited, according to information presented in Chapter 11.

It is tempting to forecast the drawing together of the organizational bits and pieces which make up American corrections into a single comprehensive system by 2000, but there is no realistic basis for believing that such a development will take place. Our federal system of government requires distribution rather than concentration of authority. The correctional mission will continue to be performed, therefore, at all levels of government and "efficiency" considerations will exert only a moderate unifying and rationalizing influence in the face of that basic political reality. Moreover, the increasingly accepted idea that reintegrative programs for offenders should be administered locally will reinforce continued fragmentation of services, though hopefully not in such a random and discursive manner as in the past.

What we may hope to see by the year 2000, however, and the trend in this direction already is well established, is a knitting together of the disparate pieces which make up corrections into a reasonably well connected and integrated system. Similarly, we may predict with some assurance that the interfaces between corrections and other bureaucratic systems (e.g., the judiciary, law enforcement, mental health, and social welfare) also will contain much more effective linkage of information and exchange of resources than is possible today. One writer in addressing this subject made the following forecasts:[5]

The correctional system of the future will have a configuration of numerous, quite autonomous subsystems operating to maximize cooperation and inter-change . . . we ought not to expect a monolithic correctional apparatus for the United States in the future. But remedies must and will be found for the present problems of fragmentation. They will take the form, we predict, of a large repertoire of reciprocal arrangements between the parts of the total system. These new arrangements will be used flexibly and with much less reverence for the sanctity of organizational and governmental boundaries than is evident today.

Offenders with special requirements will be sent to specialized facilities capable of meeting their needs, regardless of the jurisdictional niceties involved. Offenders whose primary requirement is to reestablish themselves in their home communities will be routed there and supervised by local authorities. The federal and state governments will facilitate the efforts of local governments to develop strong community-based programs and will back-stop them with resources they cannot provide; for example, a fully staffed center for screening and diagnosis of offenders or an institution for mentally ill offenders.

The administrators of a cooperative correctional system would need to understand the national network of services of which their particular program would be an integral part. They would need to be aware of the laws, policies, and procedures through which cross-jurisdictional cooperation could be implemented. They would need to participate in those public and private organizations which address the problems of coordinating correctional efforts across the country and carry out planning and information-gathering activities. In sum, they would need to be outwardly directed, rather than concerned only with local activities. They would need to work with the totality of corrections-related activities rather than with the happenings of their own organizational enclave.

This movement toward a more unified and effective correctional system has three major dimensions which will determine the nature of organizational arrangements in 2000. Principal among these is the evolution and acceptance of distinctive roles for each of the various levels of government. Also of considerable importance is the refinement and implementation of comprehensive and automated information systems on offenders and on correctional programs. A final theme of change which will significantly influence the shape of corrections in the future is the movement toward more open and collaborative forms of correctional organization.

The major shift in the roles played by the various levels of government will be toward assumption of responsibility for *operating* correctional programs by local government, and toward assumption of responsibility for *financing* and *facilitating* such programs by state and federal government. This trend will act to reverse the historical pattern under which offenders have been committed to penal institutions and subsequent parole programs operated under state and federal authority. Put in a less formal way, we will increasingly send the money where the problem is rather than sending the problem where the money is.

In this new mode of dividing responsibility for the correctional mission, the federal government and the larger of the state governments will concentrate upon indirect services. They will do long-range planning, coordinating corrections with other criminal justice services. They will set standards for local correctional agencies and monitor their operations to bring about conformity to those standards. They will provide financial subsidies and revenue sharing for the localities as well as funds for pilot efforts to develop better techniques for managing offenders. They will provide manpower development services, including various types of education and training, and will disseminate information concerning the effectiveness of correctional methods as well as technical assistance for jurisdictions which wish to implement new programs. They will, in short, stimulate, guide, and assist local correctional agencies in improving their correctional services.

The larger states and the federal government will continue to directly administer only those programs which are uneconomic and unproductive for local operation; perhaps highly specialized institutions (e.g., for mentally ill offenders) and prisons for recidivists who are serving long terms and for whom there is little hope of rehabilitation. The latter type of institution will provide austere but humane conditions of confinement and will emphasize work programs for inmates.

Local governments, on the other hand, will develop community-based correctional *systems* representing a range of services which hopefully will be used in concert: jails and short-term institutions, "halfway houses" and other residential facilities, work furlough and educational release programs, probation and parole services. The thrust of such programs will be toward reintegrating the offender in the community.

The major unit of local government responsible for community-based correctional services will be the county. However, counties which are not populous enough to support a complete range of correctional resources may contract with each other to share such resources on a regional basis. Large cities may decide to operate their own community correctional systems. There are no simple rules for determining which governmental auspices would be best, except that the population base should be large enough to support a comprehensive system, and the political and administrative mandate should be clear to make that system operate as an integrated whole.

Turning to another organizational issue, in a recent article, Richard A. McGee has addressed the long-standing problem of inadequacy in parole granting and supervision functions. He illustrates this problem with the following anecdote:[6]

> Juan Gonsalez, a convicted burglar, sat opposite a panel of the Parole Board at San Quentin Prison. This was his second appearance in the same room in a little over 2 years. He was obviously bitter because the Board had denied him parole the first time. The interview had been brief, and the Chairman asked him the customary closing question: "Now, Mr. Gonsalez, is there anything you'd like to say in your own behalf?" With thinly disguised belligerence in his voice Juan answered, "Yes, Sir! I'm now 24 years old and my crime partner, Jimmy Schneider, who was 19 at the time got sent to the Youth Authority and now has been out on the street already for nearly a year. All I ask is justice—just *justice*." He got up on his feet and stalked defiantly toward the door. Just as he was about to reach for the knob he stopped and turning slowly around he said in quite a different tone, "Mr. Chairman, could I change that statement? What I really meant to ask for was *mercy*. I think I've had about all the justice I can take."
>
> Perhaps no phase of the administration of criminal justice is so murky and ill-defined as the question of the assessment of individual criminal cases and the decision, by whomever has the power, as to what the appropriate penalty is to be. The Sixth Amendment guarantees "the right to a speedy and public trial. . . ." But since most defendants in criminal proceedings plead guilty, the sentencing function becomes the most substantive part of the event. Also, the decision is usually arrived at in private negotiation and once made is subject to little or no review by higher authority.

McGee's recommendation for improvement in this area represents a major redistribution of governmental responsibilities. In effect, he calls for the elimination of parole boards as quasi-judicial entities, and the assumption of the functions they now perform by the judiciary. His proposal includes the following elements:[7]

1. All powers of sentencing convicted criminals, including length of confinement, release to community supervision, and revocation of such releases is placed by statute under the direct purview and control of the State's judicial system.

2. The management of prisons and correctional schools is retained in the executive branch within the State Department of Correctional Services.

3. The management of agencies responsible for the supervision and control of persons placed on probation or conditionally released from State penal or correctional institutions is placed in the executive branch, but this group of functions would be unified at the local level. Whether the organizational structure is State, county, or regional is irrelevant to the basic plan except that if administered by local governments the State would set standards and contribute to fiscal support.

4. All sentencing, term fixing, releasing, discharging, and revoking of releases is done by trial court judges subject to law and to standards, guidelines, and review by a special division of the State Court of Appeal.

We include the proposal summarized above as a part of our predictions for the year 2000. Recognizing the controversial nature of such a recommendation (especially among parole board members) it nevertheless seems a sound solution to the problem of how best to make decisions about parole release and revocation (vesting them in the judiciary) and how best to carry out the supervision of parolees (vesting that function in local government and integrating it with probation supervision).

A final aspect to the organization and delivery of correctional services on which we should like to make a futuristic statement is that of manpower for the field, especially for performing the tasks of leadership and the facilitation of change. Previous chapters have noted numerous problems and limitations in this area. The Joint Commission on Correctional Manpower and Training, of 1966–1969, made clear the paucity of well-trained and highly competent personnel throughout corrections.

Polls conducted for the Commission documented the low opinion held by the public regarding the desirability of entering corrections as an occupational field. The lack of horizontal mobility of correctional staff was verified, as well as the lack of entry to the field by outsiders who might bring fresh and useful perspectives with them. We have seen that contemporary corrections is an insular field, greatly in need of competent, motivated, and variously prepared workers to move it toward new goals.

It is extremely difficult to predict the extent to which these problems will have been overcome by 2000. But societal and economic trends are taking place which seem relevant to the question. In a paper prepared for Project STAR, Perry Rosove makes the following comments upon the characteristics of a post-industrial economy in America:[8]

Of more recent vintage than worldwide population growth, but no less well documented, is the long-range trend of industrialization. As societies become industrialized, an increasing proportion of the population gives up agriculture and engages in the production of finished goods from raw materials and in their distribution to consumers. During the 100 years from 1750 to 1850 technological developments occurred that profoundly affected the whole pattern of civilization, first in Britain, then in continental Europe and in the North American continent, and ultimately in much of the rest of the world. This transformation is referred to as the Industrial Revolution. It is a revolution that is still going on all over the world. In the United States and other highly industrialized nations, the continuing process of industrialization is taking on new characteristics, referred to in the sociological literature as the "post-industrial society."

Whereas the first Industrial Revolution was symbolized by the factory town, armies of blue-collar workers, and such industries as coal mining, textiles, iron-making, and railroading, the post-industrial society is characterized by new types of industries such as plastics and electronics based on new and different technologies, science, and logic, and new types of workers—knowledge workers rather than manual workers. As C. Wright Mills put it: "Fewer individuals manipulate things, more handle people and symbols."

According to Daniel Bell, the United States is now in the first stages of a post-industrial society. We are, he writes, "the first nation in the history of the world in which more than half of the employed population is not involved in the production of food, clothing, houses, automobiles, and other tangible goods." The symbolic turning point came in 1956 when for the first time the number of white-collar workers (professional, managerial, office and sales personnel) outnumbered the blue-collar workers (craftsmen, semi-skilled operatives, and laborers) in the occupational structure.

Data comparing the relative growth of the goods-producing industries with the services-producing industries from the U.S. Department of Labor indicate very slow growth for the former and rapid growth for the latter. For example, starting from a comparable base in 1947 with about 27 million workers in both types of industries, the Department projects only about 30 million workers in the goods-producing industries by 1980 in contrast to about 60 million workers in the services-producing industries. Associated with the growth of the services-producing industries, we find the white-collar occupations growing faster than any other occupational group. As the demand for white-collar workers has increased, the educational qualifications of the labor force have also risen steadily.

As the role of manufacturing declines in the post-industrial society, other types of activities grow in relative importance, such as services, research, education, and amenities. The professional-technical class becomes the major occupational group and, most importantly for our purposes here, innovation in society and material success become increasingly dependent upon theoretical rather than practical knowledge. Thus, education, particularly higher education, increasingly provides access to employment and privilege in the society.

It would appear that a much larger manpower pool will be available to corrections in the years ahead, and that it will include many of the talents and aptitudes required to renovate the field. The more imponderable question is whether the field can make itself attractive to those who might be interested in putting their creative energies into an area which has historically been stereotyped (largely because of the clientele involved) as dismal and hopeless of improvement. Will people enter corrections in the future as some entered the Peace Corps in the past, out of a feeling that a once insoluble problem can indeed be solved?

We are inclined toward optimism in answering this question. Young and socially conscious people have become "aware" of corrections in recent years as never before. They have tended, it is true, to seek change from the outside, feeling that the corrections bureaucracy is more a part of the problem than of the solution. But this seems to be changing. The presence of LEEP scholarships has dramatically increased the number of persons preparing for careers in criminal justice, including corrections, within the last few years. It is to be hoped that a larger proportion of LEEP students in the future will be drawn from the pre-service category, thus increasing the flow into corrections and other parts of the criminal justice field of individuals with a lifetime of work ahead of them, and no parochial habits to overcome.

In any case, we predict that well before the year 2000 corrections will be staffed, not only by more people, but by a more diversified and generally more competent work force. There will be proportionally more women, more members of ethnic minorities, more ex-offenders. There will be more persons with experience from other fields, and more new graduates who have been prepared in a greater variety of disciplines, e.g., the social sciences, law, social work, public administration, and criminal justice studies programs.

The organizational procedures for recruiting, developing, and utilizing personnel will be much more effective and much more flexible than they are today. There will be much more mobility between as well as within agencies, both horizontally and vertically. Rigid civil service requirements which constrain the movement and growth of workers will be modified in favor of planned programs to provide staff with new and challenging responsibilities which renew their sense of purpose and fulfillment.

The trend to tie together the agencies which make up our federated corrections network through automated information exchange is already well underway. By the year 2000 it should be operating quite effectively. A major obstacle to coordinated use of correctional services has been the lack of readily available information on the services which are available and the background of the offenders who are candidates for them. Correctional officials faced with making decisions about where to send offenders and what kind of program to prescribe for them have been necessarily myopic, limited to a narrow set of information about the individual involved and constrained by the programming alternatives extant within their own institution or agency.

By 2000, however, correctional decision makers should have almost instantly available to them such information as the following: A sophisticated and computerized profile of the offender involved, including his response to earlier correctional supervision; a display of statistical probabilities concerning the expected response of individuals "like" the one involved to various program alternatives; a display of available "openings" within the correctional system involved, or other systems with which it has made arrangements for reciprocal use of services, e.g., openings for vocational training in electronics or for a particular kind of psychiatric treatment.

The technology needed to develop, store, and transmit data of this kind with great speed and efficiency is already available. The more difficult problems lie in working out cooperative arrangements between agencies and governmental units through which they can share information and program resources flexibly and efficiently. The insularity and parochialism of the present system will make progress in this area slow. The fact that offenders typically are sentenced under the laws of a particular jurisdiction, to a facility operated by that jurisdiction, and paid for by tax revenues which it receives, makes inter-governmental and multi-governmental cooperation laborious at best. Much of the energy of those involved tends to go into the protection of organizational boundaries and the segregation and control of financial resources.

Nevertheless, there are encouraging developments on the scene today, especially the establishment of the Law Enforcement Assistance Administration as a federal agency with responsibility for rendering facilitative services to state and local governments, and the resultant development of state planning agencies designed to play a similar role. By the year 2000 the great majority of offenders should be evaluated on the basis of adequate information and assigned to a reasonably optimal program of management and assistance.

The prediction that correctional organizations will be much more open and participative by 2000 is based upon a clearly discernible movement in that direction, not only in corrections but in the administration of a great variety of public and business enterprises in this country. In their book *Tomorrow's Organizations,* Jun and Storm summarize the attributes of traditional and bureaucratic organizations (the dominant system today) in the following list:[9]

1. A pyramidal arrangement of its hierarchy
2. Formal division of work, based on task specialization
3. Clearly defined authority, chain of command and communication
4. A merit system based on technical competence
5. Prescribed rules and regulations
6. Accountability
7. Decision-making power centered at the top.

The same authors then attempt to specify the nature of future organizations which are emerging from the present amalgam. Referring to the new models as nonhierarchical and integrated, they describe them as having the following important characteristics:[10]

1. Participative management
2. New, nonauthoritarian leadership styles
3. Risk taking and mutual trust
4. The accounting of both technical skill and interpersonal competence
5. More power and control to lower levels of the hierarchy
6. Adaptive change capability in relation to the turbulent environment.

Doubtless there are many persons who would scoff at the idea that organizations created to manage and punish criminals can or should become open and collaborative in the sense suggested above. They might argue that the important values to be achieved through such organizations are order and control, efficiency and predictability, rigor and compliance. The idea that inmates, probationers, and parolees should be involved in the formulation of policy and the making of decisions might well seem outrageous to them. How realistic, then, is it to predict such changes in organizational climate and management style?

Our answer is somewhat mixed. It seems likely that those correctional agencies which are committed to the rehabilitation and reintegration of offenders will move fairly rapidly toward open and participative approaches, while those whose function continues to be control and deterrence will remain hierarchical in format and operation. We have already suggested that the future will see a more frank and definite separation of the "helping" and the "punishing" functions.

As this occurs, it appears likely that the institutions designed for punishment will solidify themselves around formalistic, authoritarian regimes. There will be little or no pretension of sharing power with inmates, and only minor efforts to do so with rank-and-file staff members. There will, however, be strong organizational safeguards against cruel, arbitrary, and inconsistent methods of handling both inmates and staff. The norm will be fairness within an admittedly austere and rigorous environment. Minimum rights of physical and mental health will be scrupulously protected. Nevertheless, everyone will understand that the primary purpose of such organizations is to punish law violators.

On the other hand, organizations which have a mandate to rehabilitate and reintegrate offenders will move rather rapidly toward participative styles. Included will be probation and parole agencies, community residential facilities, and some small institutions which carry on intensive treatment programs and emphasize linkages with the community. Those administering such programs will recognize increasingly that offenders can best learn socially acceptable modes of behavior in a context which gives them both influence and choice.

The basic organizational strategy will be to move from viewing the offender as a dependent and controlled recipient of services, to viewing him as a vital and authentic *participant* in the process of changing himself. The traditional and self-defeating dichotomy of "we" and "they" which has long separated staff and their correctional "clients" will break down as those involved come to see themselves as members of a common effort.

Similarly, we may expect the rigid separation of "custody staff" and "treatment staff" to become much less significant as the line between them becomes functionally blurred. The reintegrative programs of the future will emphasize *teams* of individuals (staff and offenders), possessing varied competences and working together in an equalitarian social context.

The movement of reintegrative correctional services toward openness and participativeness will occur to a great extent because of public concern for the *delivery* of services and for *accountability* on the part of those administratively responsible for providing such services. The present system emphasizes process rather than product (indeed tends to re-cycle the same individual through the same process), and, in its closed, protective manner of operating frustrates accountability efforts by way of bureaucratic camouflage. It is a classic case of original organizational purpose (making offenders noncriminal in their future conduct) being displaced by organizational strivings for maintenance and survival. Many correctional organizations, while espousing the rhetoric of rehabilitation, allocate almost no energy or resources to tasks which might sensibly be related to that purpose.

Bertrand de Jouvenel, in an essay "On Attending to the Future," suggests that planning for the future requires concern not only for "more" but for "better" uses of energy. He terms those who are effective leaders of change "forwardists," and considers it a prime function of such persons "to raise questions of *orientation*."[11] This perspective is most helpful in considering the value premises and the resultant structural design of correctional organizations of the future.

We would assert, in this context, that the corrections of the future must establish its credibility by developing a much-increased capability of changing offenders into nonoffenders. To do so it must streamline its operations in order to deliver the greatest possible "offender-changing" impact for the lowest possible cost. The system should (and we believe will) come to think of its activities in cost-benefit terms and account to the public in the same way.

The consequences of this line of analysis seem fairly clear so far as organization design is concerned. Those programs which define their goals as punishment and deterrence will utilize large, layered organization structures, and will deal with the offenders assigned to them in relatively impersonal authority-oriented ways. By contrast, those programs which define their goals as rehabilitating and reintegrating the offenders assigned to them will utilize small groups within relatively small systems. They will emphasize collaborative processes and will seek to maximize those activities through which people learn best to know and change themselves.

The Programmatic Content of Correctional Services

What types of rehabilitative services will prevail in the year 2000? How will inmates be treated in large prisons? In halfway houses? As members of a probation officer's caseload? What will be the status of behavior modification as a correctional therapy technique? Of group counseling? Of vocational training? Will the general strategy of reintegrating offenders into community life have been made operational? If so, how? If this strategy does not stand the test of time, what will replace it?

Answers to such questions must either be brave or foolhardy. There is not much experience to go on in predicting the program modalities of the future. Corrections typically has selected its "interventions" with offenders on an impulsive, almost frivolous basis. As previously noted, the movement often has been circular rather than in a straight line of additive development and refinement of treatment and control methods. Aware of the bankrupt character of the revenge and restraint philosophies of the past, and perhaps bemused by the faddism of people-changing ideas in the present era, correctional officials have embraced a succession of seemingly omnipotent experts who purported to hold the answer to the riddle of crime.

"Experts" on the immorality of man, and its correction, prescribed the silent penitence of the Pennsylvania system of confinement, and the more economically feasible work ethic of the Auburn system which contested with it. The thoroughly American belief that men's faults and deficiencies could be cured by education found its way into the prisons, and was briefly dominant as *the* correctional technique. Simple humanitarianism inspired the initiation of probation by John Augustus.

Freudian concepts of a malignant unconscious gave rise to the correctional therapy movement, the concept of psychopathic behavior, and millions of manhours of individual and group psychotherapy. Sociologists and their followers analyzed offender social structures and advocated, with evangelical zeal, the concept of the therapeutic community. The exponents of classical learning theory, and the laboratory techniques of experimental psychology, presented behavior modification and programmed environments as "answers" to the elusive question of how to make criminals noncriminal.

Meantime, the advocates of punishment, preferably quick and certain punishment (though neither has recently been achievable), have never given up their campaign. So corrections became, and remains, a peculiar admixture of moralistic, psychiatric, humanitarian, sociological, and economically pragmatic approaches, none dominant for long, and none ever permanently repudiated. How can we predict the future from that?

Perhaps, however, some kind of pattern which permits extrapolation to the future is in fact evident in this confusing mosaic of beliefs about the reasons for criminality and the cures thereto. Perhaps the movement is not really circular but rather in zigs and zags toward some more generalized concept of what is needed and what might work reasonably well in the long run. Certain propositions do seem to provide a durable foundation for correctional programs in the year 2000.

First, to repeat a point made in other places, it seems abundantly clear that the correctional programs of the future will be highly differentiated. Criminals are as varied as noncriminals, misbehavior is as complex and many-faceted as conforming behavior. In 2000 there should be a much wider repertoire of correctional management programs than exists today, including not only very intensive forms, but others in which there is little or no intervention at all. As diagnosis and classification become more advanced, interventions will be developed to match the problem categories so defined.

A second and related building block for correctional programming in the future will be the interrelating of theories of crime causation with theories of correctional intervention. One of the major obstacles to more effective programs for the rehabilitation and reintegration of offenders today is the fact that theories about crime causation have evolved rather independently of theories about treatment.

Explanations of crime have ranged across a broad spectrum of variables: those which operate deep in the psyche of the individual (e.g., neurotic conflicts and psychotic aberrations); those which operate in interactions between people (e.g., a "bad" parent-child relationship); and those which operate in the larger culture (e.g., poverty and "a lack of moral standards").

Correctional interventions, on the other hand, typically have been vague as to their suppositions about what underlying problem the treatment is expected to redress. By 2000 we may expect to see much clearer and more explicit linkage between theories of causation and theories of treatment. Consequently, there should be more practical and logical connections between diagnosis and intervention in individual cases.

Another feature of correctional programs in the future, we predict, will be a comprehensive implementation of the concept of diversion. The system for processing offenders will be seen as a series of screens. Beginning with pretrial diversion (and even further back in the case of crime prevention programs), each stage will be regarded as a "line of defense," a point at which as many offenders as possible will be kept from penetrating more deeply into the system.

The diversion strategy will be made real through the gradual creation of noncorrectional treatment resources. The following categories of individuals, now routinely routed into corrections, will be provided assistance through other auspices: alcoholics, many sex offenders, many victims of drug abuse, adolescents struggling against adverse family and neighborhood circumstances, large numbers of people whose primary need is for a satisfying work role, and a heterogenous population of "misfits" who now fill the jails for relatively minor offenses.

Thus, differential treatment, interrelating of diagnosis and treatment, and operationalizing of the diversion concept are three general forecasts of the future.

390

In an article entitled, "What's Past is Prologue," one of the authors made the following additional predictions:[12]

1. Fewer offenders, and especially the younger ones, will be confined for long periods in custodial institutions.

2. The programs of these institutions will place greater emphasis on preparation for release and reintegration into normal society and less on the prevention of escapes and on economic production, unless it contributes to occupational competence.

3. The new correctional institutions for both youths and adults will be much smaller, perhaps less than a hundred residents each, and will be located in cities, not on farms as has been our tradition.

4. There will be less and less of the sharp dichotomy between incarceration and parole- or probation-supervision. Offenders will move in and out among varying degrees of restraint. Work and training furloughs, week-end sentences, halfway houses, and similar community-based programs will become more common and more varied.

5. Probation services will expand, but they will be better supported and will include a much wider variety of programs, including hostels, group homes, training programs, job placements, sheltered workshops, psychiatric services, and special counseling.

6. Postinstitutional supervision (parole) will also exhibit changes in variety and character similar to those in the community programs for probationers.

7. The character, composition, and function of parole boards will change. These boards, made up largely of lay persons appointed by state governors, are seldom well qualified for their decision-making tasks, and, to compound the problem, they are peculiarly vulnerable to the most reactionary influences in the society, which do not support the majority concept of rehabilitation as opposed to retribution.

8. New forms of disposition tribunals, as substitutes for the conventional "sentencing" by judges and the term-fixing and paroling functions of lay parole boards, will be developed.

9. Community-based programs must make more and more use of related community resources, both public and private. To do this, the organization and management of the correctional services must be consolidated and coordinated in each community. It is now the rule rather than the exception in major cities, in an area, say, ten miles square, to find from five to ten separate governmental agencies (federal, state, county, and city), supervising several thousand probationers and parolees of all ages and both sexes. There is no valid excuse for the cost, confusion, and inefficiency of this arrangement.

10. More and more attention will be given to the development of informa-

tion systems making use of modern computer technology so that decision-makers throughout the justice system can operate on a basis of facts instead of opinion and guesswork.

11. Empirical research methods will be employed more and more as the means of defining and refining the problems of crime and delinquency and of evaluating and testing the effectiveness of programs.

12. From the standpoint of the offender who would seek to escape the consequences of his behavior, the "New Corrections" will be far more difficult to evade than is the case under our present system; conversely, for those who need help, professionally competent assistance will be provided. And the long-term needs for public correction will be better served.

To these predictions, we would add the following:

1. The modus operandi of community corrections will be developed and refined around the reintegration concept. Essentially, this will mean the achievement of a capability for mobilizing a great variety of community resources. Community correctional workers will shift from being "office-bound" and therapy-oriented to becoming catalysts, brokers, facilitators and advocates for the interest and needs of offenders. Offenders who have served time in penal institutions will be regarded as "returnees," finding their way into channels of community life which do not stigmatize them and prohibit their acceptance as conforming individuals. There will be a much greater use of volunteers, family members of offenders and the social circle of friends and interested other people who can assist the reintegration process.

2. There will be a major concentration of resources for the treatment and control of offenders at the level of the misdemeanant system. Instead of being receptacles for individuals who are outcasts from society but have not presented serious enough problems to be committed to state prisons, the jails will be regarded as a point of opportunity for intervention in the lives of individuals who are apt to become serious social casualties if not provided assistance.

3. The field of corrections will play a major role in programs for the prevention of crime and delinquency. Corrections will become the spokesman for needs in the area, stimulating other community systems (particularly the schools, family services and mental health services) to intervene at an earlier time and in a more appropriate way in the case of youth and adults who are clearly "at risk" of becoming criminal offenders.

4. A large portion of those who are committed to the correctional system will not receive any intervention at all, i.e., they will merely be "accepted" as adjudicated and defined as persons whose opportunities to return to a

legitimate way of life are best reinforced by allowing them to pursue that goal without any contacts or official attention from the system itself.

5. The model of causation and intervention which revolves around the idea that offenders are emotionally or mentally ill will have a significantly lower impact in the year 2000 than it does today. Only a small proportion of offenders will be regarded as properly defined in terms of that model. The great majority of offenders will be regarded as individuals who have "learned" an unacceptable mode of solving their problems. The task of helping them to return to an acceptable way of life will also be regarded as primarily a learning function.

The Discovery and Dissemination of New Information

During the last 15 to 20 years there have been a number of efforts to develop action-research information concerning correctional programs. The Ford Foundation established a number of university centers for research and demonstration during the late 1950s and early 1960s. The National Institute of Mental Health initiated funding for research in crime and delinquency at about the same time. However, the research findings which have been generated thus far have not been brought together and communicated in a form which is understandable and useful to workers in the field. As one of the writers observed in an earlier publication:[13]

> Practitioners, on the whole, regard researchers as completely impractical and almost incapable of addressing or even recognizing the "real" questions. One researcher tells the story of seeing the title "Research and Reality" on a delinquency prevention conference program. Upon asking about this, he learned that the planners of the meeting felt a need to counteract much talk about research with some talk about "reality." He reports being somewhat disturbed by this, because for some time he had nourished the belief that research was a systematic way of approaching and illuminating the realities of life.
>
> The theoretician and the practitioner tend to develop stereotyped impressions of each other which inhibit open and constructive cooperation. Each may be at once too admiring and too condemning of the other. The theoretician tends to romanticize the practitioner's "fight in the front lines" while underestimating his capacity to conceptualize and innovate. The practitioner, in turn, frequently exaggerates the theoretician's academic capabilities while defensively belittling his capacity to be sensible and down-to-earth. Obviously the negative stereotypes impede effective cooperation between action and research in correction.
>
> Social scientists have a great deal of trouble communicating with one another. They face an even more difficult task when they seek to communicate

393

with those engaged in action of some kind. This is partly a problem of "jargon" on both sides. But it also derives from the fact that we simply don't talk to one another very much across professional and occupational barriers. Behind these failures, no doubt, is a great deal of defensiveness on all sides. One result of this situation is that researchers frequently are denied opportunity to study significant problems.

Even when communication has been established, there remains the intricate and never-ending task of achieving effective collaboration. There are constant problems when researchers from different disciplines work together on a particular study. But, again, the most troublesome collaboration problem seems to lie in interactions between researchers and action personnel. Requirements that seem imperative for good research, (e.g., a control group, adherence to the research design) often seem onerous to those engaged in action. On the other hand, the imperative of vigorous and efficient action sometimes turns out to be a grave obstacle to the researcher. The dilemma faced by correctional workers in formulating their attitudes toward evaluative research was described by Cressey a decade ago. He points out that they are supposed to be in favor of such research while recognizing that its findings may threaten the very existence of their program. Schiff contends that a program must go through some developmental stages before it can provide a congenial atmosphere for research activities that seek to evaluate its methods and goals. In one study of this matter, in a large agency of the federal government, he concluded that such research has little chance while the program is in its crusading period — i.e., while those involved have a heavy emotional investment in proving that their approach is the right one and therefore have little tolerance for the sometimes discordant findings that attend objective inquiry. Klein notes the emotional involvement also of the researcher in such programs. The researcher, too, knows that program failure may reflect on his prestige.

The Law Enforcement Assistance Administration showed little interest in funding research during the first few years of its existence. At the time of this writing, there are signs that this agency may be prepared to allocate a significant amount of the monies available to it in the interest of discovering better methods for dealing with offenders. One plan under consideration by LEAA is the establishment of a number of on-going programs of research within major universities which have special competence in this area among their faculties.

Unhappily, there are few signs at present of interest in developing a national informational network which would collect research information, translated into a form usable to practitioners and disseminated widely. The

Ford Foundation has discussed this need and indicated some interest in funding it, but no actual programs in this area have been initiated, to the knowledge of the writers. Indeed, it may be said that we "know" a great deal more at the present time than we are able to use because of gaps in communication and understanding. Knowledge about correctional techniques is scattered in bits and pieces throughout the world and it represents an extremely difficult task to bring these pieces of knowledge together, evaluate them in terms of their comparability, and recommunicate them in a form which those who are in charge of correctional programs can make use of.

There is a danger of defining the problem of putting research knowledge to work in simplistic terms. It is not merely a matter of translating academic jargon into practical, programmatic terms. Most of the research which has been done has not been oriented to the problem of utilizing its findings. In fact, many academic researchers are negative to this possibility, arguing that their task is to illuminate the complex world of reality rather than to prescribe "better ways" for practitioners to operate. We need to establish much closer communication between those concerned with research and those concerned with action. Also needed, perhaps, is a new breed of individual who works as a mediator and a catalyst between the world of research and the world of action. Such "marginal" people would be extremely useful in moving back and forth across the boundary which separates these two worlds, and helping each to understand the other better.

Also needed is organizational machinery to insure that research information is in fact "heard" and listened to within the operating programs which need to know about it. Correctional administrators, especially, need to set aside time in their busy days to be briefed on research information and to consider its implications for the work they are doing. This requires routines and organizational sanctions since such activity is all too apt to be defined as "esoteric" and to be crowded off the calendar by more urgent and seemingly more important matters. The truth, however, is that in a field in which very little is known about what works and what does not work, nothing is more important than providing for incremental increases in understanding relative to the effectiveness of existing programs.

We predict that by the year 2000 there will be an on-going and reasonably effective informational network which will tie practitioners together with correctional researchers and facilitate their communications with each other. It seems probable that the federal government will play a leading role in funding and maintaining this network. Perhaps the National Council on Crime and Delinquency (which has done good work in a preliminary way through its Information Clearing House) will also play a significant role. It also seems likely that efforts along this line in the United States will be combined with similar efforts elsewhere in the world.

Conclusion

In this chapter we have resisted the temptation to speculate on the long-range future of corrections and have concentrated on an extrapolation of current trends to a time horizon of about 25 years from now. As Rick Carlsen has stated in his paper "Crime in the Future: 1980–2000,"[14] "forecasting is a very imprecise business." We will be subject to sufficient error in this limited effort. It does not seem appropriate in this book to conjure up our personal visions of the "ultimate" correctional scheme.

Perhaps, in fact, there is no such thing and never will be. New ideas about what conduct should be defined as deviant and subject to legal sanctions will constantly be introduced. The societal response which we call corrections also will constantly be modified, and always with unanticipated consequences.

Crime and its correction will forever be relative to the views and mores of the era, as made clear in Kai Erikson's *Wayward Puritans*, here referred to by Carlsen:[15]

> A concrete example of the relative nature of crime was depicted in Kai Erikson's book, *Wayward Puritans*, when he examined puritan Massachusetts prior to, at the height of, and after the Salem witch trials. Erikson's hypothesis is that there was a relatively fixed line between what societies viewed as normal and what those same societies viewed as deviant. He further hypothesized that the "content" of the deviant population changes in order to meet the "needs" of a given society. In examining historical records, Erikson found that his hypotheses were largely confirmed. There was a relatively constant "supply" of deviants over the sixty year period he examined. But the nature of that deviance changed throughout the period.
>
> Thus, for example, prior to the witch trials, the citizens of Salem legally proscribed activities then found objectionable including vagrancy, public drunkenness, fornication, and so on. But when the community became exercised about witches, its jails were then filled with persons charged with witchcraft, displacing persons charged with crimes of vagrancy, fornication, public drunkenness, etc. After the witch trial phenomenon had abated, once again the jails in Salem were occupied with persons charged with vagrancy, fornication, public drunkenness, etc.

In spite of these somewhat skeptical observations about the value of prediction, we wish to end on a note of positivism about futurist perspectives. Just as there are many, often unrealized, uses of the past, there is great importance in addressing the future as masterable, as amenable to change through our wisest and most determined efforts. Certainly the troubled enterprise of corrections in America deserves that order of concern.

NOTES

[1]Alvin Toffler, *Future Shock*, New York: Random House, p. 15.

[2]Daniel Glaser, "Changes in Corrections During the Next Twenty Years," *Future Roles of Criminal Justice Personnel: Position Papers*, American Justice Institute, March 2, 1972.

[3]Malcolm W. Klein, "Collaboration Between Practitioners and Researchers: Relevant Knowledge in Corrections," *Federal Probation*, December, 1973, p. 46.

[4]See California Youth Authority, Division of Research, "Community Treatment Reports," Sacramento, 1962–1973.

[5]Elmer K. Nelson, Jr. and Catherine H. Lovell, *Developing Correctional Administrators*, Washington, D. C.: Joint Commission on Correctional Manpower and Training, November, 1969, p. 15.

[6]Richard A. McGee, "A New Look at Sentencing," *Federal Probation*, June, 1974, p. 3.

[7]Richard A. McGee, "A New Look at Sentencing," *Federal Probation*, September, 1974, pp. 3–11.

[8]Perry Rosove, "Implications of Social Trends for Crime and Criminal Justice," Lesson Module No. 5, Criminal Justice Planning Institute, Center for the Administration of Justice, University of Southern California, 1974, pp. 10, 11.

[9]Jong S. Jun and William B. Storm, *Tomorrow's Organizations: Challenges and Strategies*, Glenview, Illinois: Scott, Foresman & Company, 1973, p. 20.

[10]*Ibid.*, p. 22.

[11]Bertrand de Jouvenel, "On Attending to the Future," *Environment and Change: The Next Fifty Years*, edited by William R. Ewald, Jr., Bloomington: Indiana University Press, 1968.

[12]Richard A. McGee, "What's Past Is Prologue," Philadelphia: *The Annals of the American Academy of Political and Social Science*, 381 (January, 1969): 9, 10.

[13]E. K. Nelson, Jr. and Fred Richardson, "Perennial Problems in Criminological Research," *Crime and Delinquency*, January, 1971, pp. 26, 27.

[14]Rick Carlsen, "Lesson Module No. 4," Criminal Justice Planning Institute, Center for the Administration of Justice, University of Southern California, 1974, p. 8.

[15]*Ibid.*, pp. 7, 8.

APPENDICES

On October 20, 1971, the Administrator of the Law Enforcement Assistance Administration (LEAA) appointed a National Advisory Commission on Criminal Justice Standards and Goals, with Russell W. Peterson, Governor of Delaware, as chairman. The purpose of the Commission was to formulate national criminal justice standards and goals for crime reduction and prevention at the state and local levels. Although LEAA provided $1.75 million in discretionary grants for the work of the Commission, it did not direct the work of or have voting participation in the Commission. Indeed, the Standards established by the Commission do not necessarily represent the views of LEAA or its parent organization, the United States Department of Justice. In 1973, seven reports were issued by the Commission:

A National Strategy to Reduce Crime
Criminal Justice System
Police
Courts
Corrections
Community Crime Prevention
Proceedings of the National Conference on Criminal Justice

These reports, collectively, may represent the future of criminal justice in the United States. Although there is no mandate that the Standards and Goals be adopted by the individual states or at local levels, it seems certain that they will have significant impact as a blueprint or road map for tomorrow. Clearly, there will be changes in them . . . additions, modifications and deletions . . . and these will be generated by an ongoing dialogue and interchange of ideas between criminal justice academicians, administrators, practitioners and researchers, and the citizenry. To the extent that there is closure on appropriate Standards and Goals for the American justice system, there can be an orderly progression toward their achievement.

The first three appendices which follow are drawn from the *Corrections* report of the Commission. Appendix I reproduces the first chapter of the report, "Corrections and the Criminal Justice System." Appendix II provides a summary of the major recommendations of the Commission as relate to corrections. Space limitations here have precluded reproducing the complete Standards. Appendix II contains either the lead paragraph or an edited summary of each standard. The reader is urged to refer to the basic report for the complete text as well as for the extensive commentary accompanying each standard. Appendix III summarizes the national data on correctional organization, state by state.

Appendix IV reproduces part of the USC study referred to in Chapter 11, which was originally funded by the Joint Commission on Correctional Manpower and Training and published by that Commission in November, 1969, as *Developing Correctional Administrators*. Appendix IV is meant to be used in conjunction with and as a supplement to Chapter 11, "The Management of Correctional Services."

Appendix I

Corrections and the Criminal Justice System

The pressures for change in the American correctional system today are building so fast that even the most complacent are finding them impossible to ignore. The pressures come not only from prisoners but also from the press, the courts, the rest of the criminal justice system, and even practicing correctional personnel.

During the past decade, conditions in several prison systems have been found by the courts to constitute cruel and unusual punishment in violation of the Constitution. In its 1971–72 term, the U.S. Supreme Court decided eight cases directly affecting offenders, and in each of them the offender's contention prevailed.

The riots and other disturbances that continue to occur in the Nation's prisons and jails confirm the feeling of thoughtful citizens that such institutions contribute little to the national effort to reduce crime. Some maintain that time spent in prisons is in fact counterproductive.

It is clear that a dramatic realignment of correctional methods is called for. It is essential to abate use of institutions. Meanwhile much can be done to eliminate the worst effects of the institution—its crippling idleness, anomymous brutality, and destructive impact. Insofar as the institution has to be relied on, it must be small enough, so located, and so operated that it can relate to the problems offenders pose for themselves and the community.

These changes must not be made out of sympathy for the criminal or disregard of the threat of crime to society. They must be made precisely because that threat is too serious to be countered by ineffective methods.

Source: National Advisory Commission on Criminal Justice Standards and Goals, *Corrections*, Washington, D.C.: U.S. Government Printing Office, 1973, pp. 1–14.

Many arguments for correctional programs that deal with offenders in the community — probation, parole, and others — meet the test of common sense on their own merits. Such arguments are greatly strengthened by the failing record of prisons, reformatories, and the like. The mega-institution, holding more than a thousand adult inmates, has been built in larger number and variety in this country than anywhere else in the world. Large institutions for young offenders have also proliferated here. In such surroundings, inmates become faceless people living out routine and meaningless lives. And where institutions are racially skewed and filled with a disproportionate number of ill-educated and vocationally inept persons, they magnify tensions already existing in our society.

The failure of major institutions to reduce crime is incontestable. Recidivism rates are notoriously high. Institutions do succeed in punishing, but they do not deter. They protect the community, but that protection is only temporary. They relieve the community of responsibility by removing the offender, but they make successful reintegration into the community unlikely. They change the committed offender, but the change is more likely to be negative than positive.

It is no surprise that institutions have not been successful in reducing crime. The mystery is that they have not contributed even more to increasing crime. Correctional history has demonstrated clearly that tinkering with the system by changing specific program areas without attention to the larger problems can achieve only incidental and haphazard improvement.

Today's practitioners are forced to use the means of an older time. And dissatisfaction with correctional programs is related to the permanence of yesterday's institutions. We are saddled with the physical remains of last century's prisons and with an ideological legacy that has implicitly accepted the objectives of isolation, control, and punishment, as evidenced by correctional operations, policies, and programs.

Corrections must seek ways to become more attuned to its role of reducing criminal behavior. Changing corrections' role from one of merely housing society's rejects to one of sharing responsibility for their reintegration requires a major commitment on the part of correctional personnel and the rest of the criminal justice system.

Behind these clear imperatives lies the achievable principle of a much greater selectivity and sophistication in the use of crime control and correctional methods. These great powers should be reserved for controlling persons who seriously threaten others. They should not be applied to the nuisances, the troublesome, and the rejected who now clutter our prisons and reformatories and fill our jails and youth detention facilities.

The criminal justice system should become the agency of last resort for social problems. The institution should be the last resort for correctional problems.

Of primary importance as the pressures for change gain force are definition of corrections' goals and objectives, articulation of standards to measure achievement, and establishment of benchmarks to judge progress. That is the purpose of this report on corrections.

DEFINITION AND PURPOSES OF CORRECTIONS

Technical terms can be defined as they arise later in this report, but to begin with a definition of corrections is needed. Corrections is defined here as the community's official reactions to the convicted offender, whether adult or juvenile.

This is a broad definition and it suffers, as most definitions do, from several shortcomings. The implications of the definition for the management of juveniles and for pretrial detention require further discussion. So does the fact that it states no purpose for corrections.

Juvenile Corrections

Use of the term "convicted offender" in a definition of corrections would seem to exclude all juveniles who pass through the juvenile court process, since that process is noncriminal and no conviction may result from it. Juvenile court operations are based on the parens patriae concept in which the state assumes responsibility for a juvenile only to protect "the child's best interests." There is no charge or conviction; rather there is a hearing and a finding as to what action is in the child's interests. Only when the juvenile is tried as an adult on a criminal charge can he be termed a "convicted offender."

But the definition is worded with full understanding of the problem it creates. Juveniles who have not committed acts considered criminal for adults should not be subject to the coercive treatment that vague labels such as "juvenile delinquency" now allow. This is most obvious in the case of such categories as "minors in need of supervision," "dependent and neglected" children, or youths "lapsing into moral danger." The distinction is less clear for the groupings of "delinquent," "beyond parental control," or "habitually unruly." The point here, however, is that if we are concerned with helping the child rather than with the child's noncriminal act, then such help is not a proper function of the criminal justice system.

To define away corrections' role in the treatment of juveniles, however, is not automatically to change the current situation in which correctional systems are deeply enmeshed in juvenile programs, both in the community and in institutions. Regardless of propriety, corrections has accepted the role of "treating" and "helping" juveniles. By so doing, corrections has assumed a responsibility it cannot now evade, responsibility for reforming the manner and processes of treating juveniles. Such an assumption implies that reform must be approached realistically, recognizing current practice and the systems supporting it.

This report, therefore, will discuss the diversion of juveniles from the criminal justice system, juvenile intake and detention, juvenile institutions, and community programs for youth. As a long-range objective, juveniles not tried as adults for criminal acts should be removed from the purview of corrections. However, the current investment in juvenile corrections and the attitudes acquired by correctional staff over the years indicate that the ultimate goal is not immediately feasible.

402

Jails and Pretrial Detention

The second major difficulty raised by the definition used here is that it would seem to include the jailing of convicted misdemeanants but would not cover pretrial detention. Again, the wording is intentional. This report does discuss the elimination of jails in their present form and the development of community correctional centers. These centers would serve some functions traditionally performed by jails and some new ones, with most functions being "correctional." Jails have not traditionally been part of the correctional system but rather have been run by law enforcement agencies. Still, as long as convicted offenders require services, provision of those services should be the responsibility of the correctional system, regardless of the type of conviction or sentencing disposition.

In addition, what happens to the offender through every step of the criminal justice process has an effect on corrections. If he has been detained before conviction, the nature and quality of that detention may affect his attitude toward the system and his participation in correctional programs. Corrections, therefore, has a very real interest in how pretrial detention is conducted and should make its concerns known.

Detention before trial should be used only in extreme circumstances and then only under careful judicial control. The function of detention prior to trial is not correctional. However, as long as pretrial detention is used at all, it should be carried out in the recommended community correctional centers because of the resources that will be available there. Thus, by implication, corrections is assuming responsibility for the pretrial detainee, even through this is not properly its function as defined here.

Varying Purposes of Corrections

The definition of corrections as the community's official reactions to convicted adult and juvenile offenders neither states nor implies what corrections should try to achieve. This is essential if realism is to replace rhetoric in the field. In particular, corrections is not defined here as being directed exclusively toward the rehabilitation (or habilitation, which is more often the case) of the convicted offender.

If correctional processes were, or could be, truly rehabilitative, it is hard to see why they should be restricted to the convicted. Corrections is limited to the convicted because there are other justifications for coercively intervening in their lives in addition to helping them. Clearly, the penal sanctions imposed on convicted offenders serve a multiplicity of purposes, of which rehabilitation is only one.

Even when correctional purposes are both benevolent and rehabilitative, there is no reason to assume they are so viewed and experienced by the convicted offender. He may believe our intent is to punish, to deter others from crime, or merely to shut him up while he grows older and the fires of violence or criminality die down. Furthermore, insofar as the word "rehabilitation" suggests compulsory cure or coercive retraining, there is an impressive and growing body of opinion that such a purpose is a mistaken sidetrack that corrections has too long pretended to follow.

In the new view, crime and delinquency are symptoms of failure and disorganization in the community as well as in the offender himself. He has had too little contact with the positive forces that develop law-abiding conduct—among them good schools, gainful employment, adequate housing, and rewarding leisure-time activities. So a fundamental objective of corrections must be to secure for the offender contacts, experiences, and opportunities that provide a means and a stimulus for pursuing a lawful style of living in the community. Thus, both the offender and the community become the focus of correctional activity. With this thrust, reintegration of the offender into the community comes to the fore as a major purpose of corrections.

Corrections clearly has many purposes. It is important to recognize that correctional purposes can differ for various types of offenders. In sentencing the convicted murderer we usually are serving punitive and deterrent rather than rehabilitative purposes. Precisely the contrary is true with respect to the deprived, ill-educated, vocationally incompetent youth who is adjudged delinquent; with him, rehabilitative and reintegrative purposes predominate.

There is no doubt that corrections can contribute more than it does to the reduction and control of crime, and this is clearly one of its purposes. What is done in corrections may reduce recidivism. To the extent that recidivist crime is a substantial proportion of all crime, corrections should be able to reduce crime. A swift and effective criminal justice system, respectful of due process and containing a firm and humane corrections component, may provide useful deterrents to crime. Through these mechanisms corrections can contribute to the overall objective of crime reduction. This is an entirely worthy objective if it can be achieved without sacrificing other important human values to which this society is dedicated.

There are other limits to the overarching purpose of reducing crime and the extent to which it can be accomplished. The report of the President's Task Force on Prisoner Rehabilitation (April 1970) was surely correct when it stressed that:

> . . . some of the toughest roots of crime lie buried in the social conditions, especially poverty and racial discrimination, that prevail in the nation's inner cities. These conditions not only make it difficult for millions of Americans to share in America's well-being, but make them doubt society's good faith toward them, leaving them disposed to flout society. America's benefits must be made accessible to all Americans. How successfully America reduces and controls crime depends, in the end, upon what it does about employment and education, housing and health, areas far outside our present mandate or, for that matter, our particular competence. This is not to say that improvements in the correctional system are beside the point. . . . Our point is that improvements in the correctional system are necessarily tactical maneuvers that can lead to no more than small and short-term victories unless they are executed as part of a grand strategy of improving all the nation's systems and institutions.[1]

It is a mistake to expect massive social advance to flow either from corrections or from the criminal justice system as a whole. That system can be fair; it can be humane; it can be efficient and expeditious. To an appreciable extent it can reduce crime. Alone, it cannot substantially improve the quality and opportunity of life. It cannot save men from themselves. It can be a hallmark of a harmonious and decent community life, not a means of achieving it. There is another limitation on corrections' potential to reduce and control crime. Corrections is only a small part of a social control system applied to define, inhibit, reduce, and treat crime and criminals. It is but a subsystem of the criminal justice system. And it is the inheritor of problems created by the many defects in the other subsystems.

Corrections alone cannot solve the diverse problems of crime and delinquency confronting America, but it can make a much more significant contribution to that task. Correctional planning and programs must be closely related to the planning and programs of police and courts. Corrections' goals must be defined realistically and pursued with determination by application of achievable and measurable standards.

STANDARDS AND GOALS IN CORRECTIONS

It may be objected: Here is still another list of uplifting aspirations for corrections. Will they never learn that rhetoric is not self-fulfilling? It will be argued: More emphatic reaffirmations of the obvious are not needed; the need is for implementation of what we already know. The argument has force, but it misses the distinction between general principles that abound in corrections and specific standards that have been dismally scarce. Precise definition of goals, and of standards marking steps toward their achievement, is no waste of energy. Operating without them invites, if it does not guarantee, failure.

Standards vs. Principles

A comprehensive and soundly based body of guiding principles to direct correctional reform has existed ever since the American Prison Association's "Declaration of Principles" in 1870. The principles, revised in 1930 and reformulated in more modern language in 1960 and 1970, still remain a contemporary document. We have yet to achieve the aspirations of 1870. And there have been many subsequent attempts in this country to guide those who would improve corrections.

Both the Wickersham Commission's report in 1931 and the report in 1967 of the President's Commission on Law Enforcement and Administration of Justice (often referred to as the Crime Commission) contain a wealth of recommendations. Many of them continue to attract substantial support but have yet to be implemented. With such a treasury of past recommendations, why should there be further effort to articulate standards and goals for corrections? Quite apart from the need to be clearer in purpose and direction in a time of rapid change, there is a compelling practical reason for the present definition of standards and goals.

The reason is this: Principles and recommendations are neither self-fulfilling nor self-interpreting. Standards and goals may be much more precise, while retaining sufficient flexibility to allow agencies some freedom. When clearly formulated and precisely stated in measurable terms, they can serve as the basis for objective evaluation of programs as well as development of statutes and regulations relating to correctional services.

Standards and goals set forth in this report may lack automatic enforcing machinery, but it has been the Commission's intention to minimize vagueness in definition. Correctional administrators can readily discern whether or not standards have been achieved. All concerned with running or observing an institution, agency, or program will know whether the standard has been applied or the goal achieved. That was not true of the 1870 Declaration of Principles or of the several series of Commission recommendations that followed. The range for individual interpretation has been too great in view of endemic political and social problems confronting correctional administrators.

The standard has another important practical advantage over the principle and the recommendation. It supports more strongly and authoritatively the passage of legislation, promulgation of regulations, and development of other quality control mechanisms that provide an element of enforcement. It encourages public opinion to focus on and press for correctional reform. It prevents all of us from concluding that what we have is right simply because we have it. It reduces room for rationalization.

Achieving Standards

As a State moves from accepting these standards and goals to achieving them, new legislation may be required. More often, merely administrative and regulatory expression will be needed. The recent promulgation by the State of Illinois of an extensive system of administrative regulations for adult correctional institutions is a step of great significance toward the introduction of an enforceable rule of law into a penal system. The regulations were discussed with the staff before adoption and made readily available to the prisoners when instituted. They contain what are in effect self-enforcement mechanisms. For example, they include well-defined provisions concerning disciplinary offenses and hearings and a grievance procedure available to all prisoners. Indeed, one of the most effective methods of attaining standards and achieving goals is to add to them mechanisms for their enforcement.

Standards and goals must be realistic and achievable, but that certainly does not mean that they need to be modest. The American culture has not only a bursting energy but also a remarkable capacity for adapting to change. What was unthinkable yesterday may be accepted as common practice today. In the criminal justice system, such changes have been observable in recent years with respect to the treatment of narcotics addiction and in the law's attitude toward a range of victimless crimes. They have been seen in the remarkable sweep of the movement toward procedural due process in all judicial and quasi-judicial hearings within the criminal justice system. When the courts abandoned the "hands-off" doctrine that led them to avoid inquiry into prison conditions, this was another aspect of change.

In recent years the Federal Government and many of the States have begun to demonstrate in budgets their seriousness of purpose in correctional reform. For whatever reason, more money is now being allocated to this task. The low priority traditionally assigned to budgetary support for the penal system and to prisoners generally is being changed. It is being supplanted by realization that the quality of life depends in part on creation of a humane, just, and efficient criminal justice system. Coupled with this realization is the knowledge that achievement of such a system must entail substantial correctional reform.

On the other hand, it must be recognized that the road to correctional reform is littered with discarded panaceas. Politically, there has been no great incentive to invest in correctional reform. Until quite recently, there was scant public recognition of the importance of the criminal justice system to community life, and so fiscal support for corrections was little more than a pittance grudgingly doled out. These attitudes have not disappeared completely. Simple solutions are still offered with the promise of dramatic consequences. Correctional reform has lacked both a constituency and a sound political base. Such support as it is now attracting flows in part from the increasing recognition that, if there is to be an effective criminal justice system, an integral part of it must be an effective, humane correctional system.

Formulation and specification of standards and goals can be a step of permanent significance in moving from admirable rhetoric toward a working blueprint for correctional reform with built-in quantitative and qualitative yardsticks of progress.

CORRECTIONS IN THE CRIMINAL JUSTICE SYSTEM

A substantial obstacle to development of effective corrections lies in its relationship to police and courts, the other subsystems of the criminal justice system. Corrections inherits any inefficiency, inequity, and improper discrimination that may have occurred in any earlier step of the criminal justice process. Its clients come to it from the other subsystems; it is the consistent heir to their defects.

The contemporary view is to consider society's institutionalized response to crime as the criminal justice system and its activities as the criminal justice process. This model envisions interdependent and interrelated agencies and programs that will provide a coordinated and consistent response to crime. The model, however, remains a model—it does not exist in fact. Although cooperation between the various components has improved noticeably in some localities, it cannot be said that a criminal justice "system" really exists.

Even under the model, each element of the system would have a specialized function to perform. The modern systems concept recognizes, however, that none of the elements can perform its tasks without directly affecting the efforts of the others. Thus, while each component must continue to concentrate on improving the performance of its specialized function, it also must be aware of its interrelationships with the other components. Likewise, when functions overlap, each component must be willing to appreciate and utilize the expertise of the others.

The interrelationships of the various elements must be understood in the context of the purposes for which the system is designed. It is generally agreed that the major goal of criminal law administration is to reduce crime through use of procedures consistent with protection of individual liberty. There is less agreement on the specific means of achieving that goal and the relative priority when one set of means conflicts with another.

For example, the criminal justice system must act in relation to two sets of individuals—those who commit crimes and those who do not. Sanctions thought to deter potential lawbreakers may be destructive to offenders actually convicted. Long sentences of confinement in maximum security penitentiaries once were thought to deter other individuals from committing criminal offenses. It is now recognized that long periods of imprisonment not only breed hostility and resentment but also make it more difficult for the offender to avoid further law violations. Long sentences likewise fuel the tension within prisons and make constructive programs there more difficult. Thus, whatever weight may be given to the deterrent effect of a long prison sentence, the benefits are outweighed by the suffering and alienation of committed offenders beyond any hope of rehabilitation or reintegration.

Offenders, perhaps long before the reformers, viewed the criminal justice apparatus as a system. The "they-versus-us" attitude is symptomatic of their feeling that police, courts, and corrections all represent society. Thus it is critically important that all elements of the system follow procedures which insure that offenders are, and believe themselves to be, treated fairly, if corrections is to release individuals who will not return to crime.

Corrections and the Police

The police and corrections are the two elements of the criminal justice system that are farthest apart, both in the sequence of their operations and, very often, in their attitudes toward crime and criminal offenders. Yet police and corrections serve critical functions in society's response to crime. And cooperation between police and correctional personnel is essential if the criminal justice system is to operate effectively.

Police because of their law enforcement and order maintenance role often take the view that shutting up an offender is an excellent, if temporary, answer to a "police problem." The police view the community at large as their responsibility, and removal of known offenders from it shifts the problem to someone else's shoulders.

Police are more intimately involved than correctional staff are with a specific criminal offense. They often spend more time with the victim than with the offender. They are subjected to and influenced by the emotional reactions of the community. It is thus understandable that police may reflect, and be more receptive to, concepts of retribution and incapacitation rather than rehabilitation and reintegration as objectives of corrections.

Correctional personnel more often take a longer view. They seldom are confronted with the victim and the emotions surrounding him. While the police can hope for, and often achieve, a short-range objective—the arrest of a criminal—the correctional staff can only hope for success in the long run. Corrections seeks to assure that an offender will not commit crimes in the future.

Corrections with its long-range perspective is required, if not always willing, to take short-run risks. The release of an offender into the community always contains some risks, whether it is at the end of his sentence or at some time before. These risks, although worth taking from the long-range perspective, are sometimes unacceptable to the police in the short run.

For the most part the released offenders whom police encounter are those who have turned out to be bad risks. As a result the police acquire an imprecise and inaccurate view of the risks correctional officials take. With correctional failures—the parole or probation violator, the individual who fails to return from a furlough—adding a burden to already overtaxed police resources, misunderstanding increases between police and corrections.

If many of the standards proposed in this report are adopted, the police will perhaps take an even dimmer view of correctional adequacy. If local jails and other misdemeanant institutions are brought within the correctional system and removed from police jurisdiction, corrections will bear the responsibility for a substantially larger number of problems that would otherwise fall to the police. Likewise, as additional techniques are implemented that divert more apparently salvageable offenders out of the criminal justice system at an early stage, those offenders who remain within the system will be the most dangerous and the poorest risks. Obviously, a higher percentage of these offenders are likely to fail in their readjustment to society.

The impact of police practices on corrections, while not so dramatic and tangible as the effects of correctional risk-taking on the police, nonetheless is important and often critical to the correctional system's ability to perform its functions properly. The policeman is the first point of contact with the law for most offenders. He is the initiator of the relationship between the offender and the criminal justice system. He is likewise the ambassador and representative of the society that system serves. To the extent that the offender's attitude toward society and its institutions will affect his willingness to respect society's laws, the police in their initial and continued contact with an offender may have substantial influence on his future behavior.

It is recognized widely that the police make a number of policy decisions. Obviously, they do not arrest everyone found violating the criminal law. Police exercise broad discretion in the decision to arrest, and the exercise of that discretion determines to a large extent the clientele of the correctional system. In fact, police arrest decisions may have a greater impact on the nature of the correctional clientele than do the legislative decisions delineating what kinds of conduct are criminal.

Police decisions to concentrate on particular types of offenses will directly affect correctional programming. A large number of arrests for offenses that do not involve a significant danger to the community may result in misallocation and improper distribution of scarce correctional resources. The correctional system may be ill-prepared to cope with a larger than normal influx of certain types of offenders.

The existence of broad, all-encompassing criminal statutes including dangerous, nondangerous, and merely annoying offenders assures broad police arrest discretion. Real or imagined discrimination against racial minorities, youth, or other groups breeds hostility and resentment against the police, which inevitably is reflected when these individuals enter the correctional system.

Carefully developed, written criteria for the use of police discretion in making arrests of criminal offenders would relieve the present uncertainties and misunderstandings between police and correctional personnel. If the goals and purposes of the police in making these decisions are publicized, correctional staff should be able to work more effectively with police departments in arriving at meaningful standards and policies.

Similarly, community-based correctional programs cannot hope to be successful without police understanding and cooperation. Offenders in these programs are likely to come in contact with the police. The nature of the contact and the police response may directly affect an offender's adjustment.

Police understandably keep close surveillance on released felons, since they are a more easily identifiable risk than the average citizen. Where police make a practice of checking ex-offenders first whenever a crime is committed, the ex-offenders may begin to feel that the presumption of innocence has been altered to a presumption of guilt.

When a felon returning to a community is required to register with the police and his name and address are published in police journals, his difficulties in readjusting to community life are compounded. Mass roundups of ex-offenders or continued street surveillance have limited or questionable advantages for the police and significant disadvantages for correctional programs.

Where evidence suggests that an ex-offender is involved in criminal activity, the police obviously must take action. However, the police should recognize that the nature of their contact with ex-offenders, as with citizens in general, is critically important in developing respect for law and legal institutions. To conduct contacts with the least possible notoriety and embarrassment is good police practice and a help to corrections as well.

It should also be noted that the police can make affirmative contributions to the success of community-based programs. The police officer knows his community; he knows where resources useful for the offender are available; he knows the pitfalls that may tempt the offender. The police officer is himself a valuable community resource that should be available for correctional programs. This of course requires the police to take a view of their function as one of preventing future crime as well as enforcing the law and maintaining public order.

Bringing about a better working relationship between the police and corrections will not be an easy task. Progress can be made only if both recognize that they are performing mutually supportive, rather than conflicting, functions. Corrections has been long in explaining the purposes of its programs to the police. Today corrections is beginning to realize that much of its isolation in the criminal justice system has been self-imposed. Closer working relationships are developed through mutual understanding, and both police and corrections should immediately increase their efforts in this regard. Recruit and inservice training programs for each group should contain discussions of the other's programs. Police should designate certain officers to maintain liaison between correctional agencies and law enforcement and thus help to assure better police-corrections coordination. The problems and recommendations discussed in this section are addressed in the Commission's report on the Police. Standards set out in that report's chapter on criminal justice relations, if fully implemented, would materially enhance the working relationships between police and corrections.

Corrections and the Courts

The court has a dual role in the criminal justice system: it is both a participant in the criminal justice process and the supervisor of its practices. As participant, the court and its officers determine guilt or innocence and impose sanctions. In many jurisdictions, the court also serves as a correctional agency by administering the probation system.

In addition to being a participant, the court plays another important role. When practices of the criminal justice system conflict with other values in society, the courts must determine which takes precedence over the other.

In recent years the courts have increasingly found that values reflected in the Constitution take precedence over efficient administration of correctional programs. Some difficulties presently encountered in the relationship between corrections and the courts result primarily from the dual role that courts must play.

The relationship between courts and corrections is clearly understood by both parties when the court is viewed as a participant in the administration of the criminal law. Correctional officers and sentencing judges recognize each other's viewpoints, although they may not always agree. Those practices of the courts that affect corrections adversely are recognized by the courts themselves as areas needing reform.

Both recognize that sentencing decisions by the courts affect the discretion of correctional administrators in applying correctional programs. Sentencing courts generally have accepted the concept of the indeterminate sentence, which grants correctional administrators broad discretion in individualizing programs for particular offenders.

There is growing recognition that disparity in sentencing limits corrections' ability to develop sound attitudes in offenders. The man who is serving a 10-year sentence for the same act for which a fellow prisoner is serving 3 years is not likely to be receptive to correctional programs. He is in fact unlikely to respect any of society's institutions. Some courts have attempted to solve the problem of disparity in sentencing through the use of sentencing councils and other devices. Appellate review of sentencing would further diminish the possibility of disparity.

The appropriateness of the sentence imposed by the court will determine in large measure the effectiveness of the correctional program. This report recognizes that prison confinement is an inappropriate sanction for the vast majority of criminal offenders. Use of probation and other community-based programs will continue to grow. The essential ingredient in the integration of courts and corrections into a compatible system of criminal justice is the free flow of information regarding sentencing and its effect on individual offenders.

The traditional attitude of the sentencing judge was that his responsibility ended with the imposition of sentence. Many criminal court judges, often with great personal uneasiness, sentenced offenders to confinement without fully recognizing what would occur after sentence was imposed. In recent years, primarily because of the growing number of lawsuits by prisoners, courts have become increasingly aware of the conditions of prison confinement. Continuing judicial supervision of correctional practices to assure that the program applied is consistent with the court's sentence should result in increased interaction between courts and corrections.

Correctional personnel must recognize that they are to some extent officers of the court. They are carrying out a court order and, like other court officers, are subject to the court's continuing supervision. Corrections has little to lose by this development and may gain a powerful new force for correctional reform.

Legal Rights, the Courts, and Corrections

The United States has a strong and abiding attachment to the rule of law, with a rich inheritance of a government of law rather than men. This high regard for the rule of law has been applied extensively in the criminal justice system up to the point of conviction. But beyond conviction, until recently, largely unsupervised and arbitrary discretion held sway. This was true of sentencing, for which criteria were absent and from which appeals were both rare and difficult. It was true of the discretion exercised by the institutional administrator concerning prison conditions and disciplinary sanctions. It applied to the exercise by the parole board of discretion to release and revoke.

Within the last decade, however, the movement to bring the law, judges, and lawyers into relationships with the correctional system has grown apace. The Commission welcomes this development, and many of the standards and goals prescribed in this report rely heavily on increasing substantive and procedural due process in the authoritative exercise of correctional discretion. Since this is a contentious issue, introductory comments may be appropriate.

The American Law Institute took legal initiative in the criminal justice field in drafting the Model Penal Code, which has stimulated widespread recodifications of substantive criminal law at the Federal and State levels. An important subsequent step was extension of legal aid to the indigent accused, a development achieved by a series of Supreme Court decisions and by the Criminal Justice Act of 1964 and similar State legislation. This move brought more lawyers of skill and sensitivity into contact with the criminal justice system. Then the remarkable project on Minimum Standards for Criminal Justice, pursued over many years to completion by the American Bar Association, began to have a similar widespread influence.

But for the correctional system, historically and repeatedly wracked by riot and rebellion, the most dramatic impact has been made by the courts' abandonment of their hands-off doctrine in relation to the exercise of discretion by correctional administrators and parole boards.

It was inevitable that the correctional immunity from constitutional requirements should end. The Constitution does not exempt prisoners from its protections. As courts began to examine many social institutions from schools to welfare agencies, prisons and other correctional programs naturally were considered. Once the courts agreed to review correctional decisions, it was predictable that an increasing number of offenders would ask the court for relief. The courts' willingness to become involved in prison administration resulted from intolerable conditions within the prisons.

Over the past decade in particular, a new and politically important professional group, the lawyers, has in effect been added to corrections, and it is not likely to go away. The Supreme Court of the United States has manifested its powerful concern that correctional processes avoid the infliction of needless suffering and achieve standards of decency and efficiency of which the community need not be ashamed and by which it will be better protected. Stimulated by the initiative of Chief Justice Burger, the American Bar Association has embarked on an ambitious series of programs to involve lawyers in correctional processes, both in institutions and in the community.

Federal and State legislatures have concerned themselves increasingly with correctional codes and other correctional legislation. The National Council on Crime and Delinquency in 1972 drafted its Model Act for the Protection of Rights of Prisoners. But more important than all these, lawyers and prisoners are bringing—and courts are hearing and determining—constitutional and civil rights actions alleging unequal protection of the law, imposition of cruel and unusual punishments, and abuse of administrative discretion.

A series of cases has begun to hold correctional administrators accountable for their decisionmaking, especially where such decisions affect first amendment rights (religion, speech, communication), the means of enforcing other rights (access to counsel or legal advice, access to legal materials), cruel and unusual punishments, denial of civil rights, and equal protection of the law. The emerging view, steadily gaining support since it was enunciated in 1944 in *Coffin* v. *Reichard*,[2] is that the convicted offender retains all rights that citizens in general have, except those that must be limited or forfeited in order to make it possible to administer a correctional institution or agency—and no generous sweep will be given to pleas of administrative inconvenience. The pace and range of such litigation recently has increased sharply. The hands-off doctrine that used to insulate the correctional administrator from judicial accountability is fast disappearing.

Correctional administrators have been slow to accept this role of the courts and many of the specific decisions. It is understandably difficult to give up years of unquestioned authority. Yet the courts, in intervening, required correctional administrators to reevaluate past policies and practices that had proved unsuccessful. Without the courts' intervention and the resulting public awareness of prison conditions, it is unlikely that the present public concern for the treatment of criminal offenders would have developed. Thus, the courts' intervention has provided corrections with public attention and concern. In the long run, these cases bring new and influential allies to correctional reform.

Increasingly, these new allies of corrections are fitting themselves better for this collaboration. The law schools begin to provide training in correctional law. The American Bar Association provides energetic leadership. The Law Enforcement Assistance Administration supports these initiatives. The Federal Judicial Center develops creative judicial training programs, and judicial administration finally is acknowledged as an important organizational problem. Federal and State judges in increasing number attend sentencing institutes. Bridges are being built between the lawyers and corrections.

What it comes to is this: Convicted offenders remain within the constitutional and legislative protection of the legal system. The illogic of attempting to train lawbreakers to obey the law in a system unresponsive to law should have been recognized long ago. Forcing an offender to live in a situation in which all decisions are made for him is no training for life in a free society. Thus the two sets of alternatives before the judiciary in most cases involving correctional practices are the choice between constitutional principle and correctional expediency, and the choice between an insitution that runs smoothly and one that really helps the offender. In exercising their proper function as supervisors of the criminal justice system, the courts have upset practices that have stifled any real correctional progress.

The courts will and should continue to monitor correctional decisions and practices. The Constitution requires it. The nature of the judicial process dictates that this supervision will be done case by case. A period of uneven and abrupt change and uncertainty will inevitably result. Some court rulings will indeed make administration of correctional programs more difficult. To hold hearings before making decisions that seriously affect an offender is a time-consuming task. Allowing free correspondence and access to the press by offenders creates the risk of unjustified criticism and negative publicity. Eliminating inmate guards (trusties) requires the expenditure of additional funds for staff. Correctional administrators could ease the transition by adopting on their own initiative new comprehensive procedures and practices that reflect constitutional requirements and progressive correctional policy.

The Need for Cooperation in the System

It is unrealistic to believe that the tensions and misunderstandings among the components of the criminal justice system will quickly disappear. There are—and will continue to be—unavoidable conflicts of view. The police officer who must subdue an offender by force will never see him in the same light as the correctional officer who must win him with reason. The courts, which must retain their independence in order to oversee the practices of both police and corrections, are unlikely to be seen by either as a totally sympathetic partner.

On the other hand, the governmental institutions designed to control and prevent crime are closely and irrevocably interrelated, whether they function cooperatively or at cross-purposes. The success of each component in its specific function depends on the actions of the other two. Most areas of disagreement are the result of inadequate understanding both of the need for cooperation and of the existing interrelationships. The extent to which this misunderstanding can be minimized will determine in large measure the future course of our efforts against crime.

The Commission recognizes that correctional progress will be made only in the context of a criminal justice system operating as an integrated and coordinated response to crime. Thus corrections must cooperate fully with the other components in developing a system that uses its resources more effectively. If there are persons who have committed legally proscribed acts but who can be better served outside the criminal justice system at lower cost and little or no increased risk, then police, courts, corrections, legislators, and the public must work together to establish effective diversion programs for such persons. If persons are being detained unnecessarily or for too long awaiting trial, the elements of the system must work together to remedy that situation. If sentencing practices are counterproductive to their intended purposes, a comprehensive restructuring of sentencing procedures and alternatives must be undertaken.

This perspective is in large measure responsible for the broad scope of this report on corrections. The time is ripe for corrections to provide the benefits of its knowledge and experience to the other components of the system. Such issues as diversion, pretrial release and detention, jails, juvenile intake, and sentencing, traditionally have not been considered within the scope of correctional concern. But corrections can no longer afford to remain silent on issues that so vitally affect it. Thus this report on corrections addresses these and other issues that have previously been considered problems of other components of the criminal justice system. It could be said that they are addressed from a correctional perspective, but in a broader sense they are presented from a criminal justice system point of view.

OBSTACLES TO CORRECTIONAL REFORM

Fragmentation of Corrections

One of the leading obstacles to reforming the criminal justice system is the range and variety of governmental authorities — Federal, State, and local — that are responsible for it. This balkanization complicates police planning, impedes development of expeditious court processes, and divides responsibility for convicted offenders among a multiplicity of overlapping but barely intercommunicating agencies. The organizational structure of the criminal justice system was well-suited to the frontier society in which it was implanted. It has survived in a complex, mobile, urban society for which it is grossly unsuited. Accordingly, this report seriously addresses large-scale organizational and administrative restructuring of corrections.

One set of solutions is to accept the present balkanization of corrections, recognizing its strong political support in systems of local patronage, and to prescribe defined standards, buttressed by statewide inspection systems to attain those standards. Local jails provide a good example. At the very least, if they are to be retained for the un-convicted, they must be subject to State-controlled inspection processes, to insure the attainment of minimum standards of decency and efficiency. A further control and support that might be added is State subsidy to facilitate attainment of defined standards and goals by the local jails, the carrot of subsidy being added to the stick of threatened condemnation and closure. However, these measures are but compromises.

The contrasting mode of organizational restructuring of corrections is an integrated State correctional system. There is much support for movement in that direction. For example, it is recommended in this report that supervision of offenders under probation should be separated from the courts' administrative control and integrated with the State correctional system.

If prisons, probation, parole, and other community programs for adult and juvenile offenders are brought under one departmental structure, there is no doubt of that department's improved bargaining position in competition for resources in cabinet and legislature. Other flexibilities are opened up; career lines for promising staff are expanded, to say nothing of interdepartmental inservice training possibilities. Above all, such a structure matches the developing realities of correctional processes.

An increasing interdependence between institutional and community-based programs arises as their processes increasingly overlap; as furlough and work-release programs are expanded; as institutional release procedures grow more sophisticated and graduated; and as more intensive supervisory arrangements are added to probation and parole supervision. Institutional placement, probation, and parole or after-care grow closer together and structurally intertwine. This is true for both adult and juvenile offenders.

Development of further alternatives to the traditional institution, and diversion of offenders from it, will increase this pressure toward an integrated statewide correctional system, regionalized to match the demography and distribution of offenders in the State. Administrative regionalization of such structurally integrated statewide correctional systems may be necessary in the more populous or larger States to link each regional system with the needs, opportunities, and social milieu of the particular offender group. Regionalization greatly facilitates maintaining closer ties between the offender and his family (as by visits, furloughs, and work release) than is possible otherwise.

In sum, the task of achieving an effective functional balance between State and local correctional authorities is complex and uncertain, yet it offers opportunity. It will require political statesmanship that transcends partisan, parochial, and patronage interests. But whatever the interagency relationships may be, the enunciation of precisely defined standards and goals for those agencies will aid in attainment of effective and humane correctional processes.

Overview of Corrections

The correctional administrator (and for the present purposes, the sentencing judge too) is the servant of a criminal justice system quite remarkable in its lack of restraint.

Historically, the criminal law has been used not only in an effort to protect citizens but also to coerce men to private virtue. Criminal law overreaches itself in a host of "victimless" crimes; that is, crimes without an effective complainant other than the authorities. This application of the law is a major obstacle to development of a rational and effective correctional system.

When criminal law invades the sphere of private morality and social welfare, it often proves ineffective and criminogenic. What is worse, the law then diverts corrections from its clear, socially protective function. The result is unwise legislation that extends the law's reach beyond its competence. Manifestations are seen in relation to gambling, the use of drugs, public drunkenness, vagrancy, disorderly conduct, and the noncriminal aspects of troublesome juvenile behavior. This overreach of criminal law has made hypocrites of us all and has confused the mission of corrections. It has overloaded the entire criminal justice system with inappropriate cases and saddled corrections with tasks it is unsuited to perform.

The unmaking of law is more difficult than the making; to express moral outrage at objectionable conduct and to urge legislative proscription is politically popular. On the other hand, to urge the repeal of sanctions against any objectionable conduct is politically risky since it can be equated in the popular mind with approval of that conduct. But corrections, like the rest of the criminal justice system, must reduce its load to what it has some chance of carrying. Too often we are fighting the wrong war, on the wrong front, at the wrong time, so that our ability to protect the community and serve the needs of the convicted offender is attenuated. It is for this reason that a major emphasis in this report is placed on developing diversions from and alternatives to the correctional system.

It is particularly urgent to evict from corrections many of the alcoholics and drug addicts who now clutter that system. They should be brought under the aegis of more appropriate and less punitive mechanisms of social control. The same is true of truants and other juveniles who are in need of care and protection and have not committed criminal offenses. They should be removed from the delinquency jurisdiction of the courts as well as corrections.

At the same time, the rapid expansion of those diverse community-based supervisory programs called probation and parole is needed. Most States still lack probation and parole programs that are more than gestures toward effective supervision and assistance for convicted offenders. Standards and goals for correctional reform depend largely on the swift, substantial improvement of probation and parole practices.

Overemphasis on Custody

The pervasive overemphasis on custody that remains in corrections creates more problems than it solves. Our institutions are so large that their operational needs take precedence over the needs of the people they hold. The very scale of these institutions dehumanizes, denies privacy, encourages violence, and defies decent control. A moratorium should be placed on the construction of any large correctional institution. We already have too many prisons. If there is any need at all for more institutions, it is for small, community-related facilities in or near the communities they serve.

There is also urgent need for reducing the population of jails and juvenile detention facilities. By using group homes, foster care arrangements, day residence facilities, and similar community-based resources, it should be possible to eliminate entirely the need for institutions to hold young persons prior to court disposition of their cases. Likewise, by other methods discussed in this report, it will be practicable to greatly reduce the use of jails for the adult accused. By placing limitations on detention time and by freely allowing community resources, agencies, and individuals to percolate the walls of the jail, it will be possible to minimize the social isolation of those who must be jailed.

Nevertheless, it must be recognized that at our present level of knowledge (certainly of adult offenders) we lack the ability to empty prisons and jails entirely. There are confirmed and dangerous offenders who require protracted confinement because we lack alternative and more effective methods of controlling or modifying their behavior. At least for the period of incarceration, they are capable of no injury to the community.

Even so, far too many offenders are classified as dangerous. We have not developed a means of dealing with them except in the closed institution. Too often we have perceived them as the stereotype of "prisoner" and applied to all offenders the institutional conditions essential only for relatively few. Hence, this report stresses the need for development of a broader range of alternatives to the institution, and for the input of greater resources of manpower, money, and materials to that end.

Community-based programs are not merely a substitute for the institution. Often they will divert offenders from entering the institution. But they also have important functions as part of the correctional process. They facilitate a continuum of services from the institution through graduated release procedures—such as furloughs and work release—to community-based programs.

Large institutions for adult and juvenile offenders have become places of endemic violence. Overcrowding and the admixture of diverse ethnic groups, thrown together in idleness and boredom, is the basic condition. Race relations tend to be hostile and ferocious in the racially skewed prisons and jails.

Increasing political activism complicates inmate-staff relations. Knives and other weapons proliferate and are used. Diversion of the less violent and more stable from institutions will leave in the prisons and jails a larger proportion of hardened, dangerous, and explosive prisoners. The correctional administrator thus confronts a stark reality. While making needed changes to benefit the great majority of inmates, he must cope with a volatile concentration of the most difficult offenders, whose hostility is directed against the staff.

For these reasons and others, continuing attention must be paid to conditions within the remaining institutions. Although the institution must be used only as a last resort, its programs must not be neglected. Such attention is essential if the institution is to serve as the beginning place for reintegration and not as the end of the line for the offender.

418

The principle of community-based corrections also extends to prisons and jails. We must make those institutions smaller, for only then can they cease to hold the anonymous. We must make them more open and responsive to community influences, for only thus can we make it possible for prisoners and staff alike to see what the community expects of them.

Lack of Financial Support

The reforms envisioned in this report will not be achieved without substantially increased government funds being allocated to the criminal justice system and without a larger portion of the total being allocated to corrections. There is little sense in the police arresting more offenders if the courts lack the resources to bring them to trial and corrections lacks the resources to deal with them efficiently and fairly. Happily, the Federal Government, followed by many States, already is providing important leadership here.

Budgetary recognition is being given to the significance of crime and the fear it produces in the social fabric. For example, statutory provisions now require that at least 20 percent of the Federal funds disbursed by the Law Enforcement Assistance Administration to the States to aid crime control be allocated to corrections. It is clearly a proper role for the Federal Government to assist States by funds and direct services to increase the momentum of the movement toward community-based corrections and to remedy existing organizational inefficiencies.

Two other obstacles to reform merit mention in this litany of adversity and the means of overcoming it. Like the other impediments to change, these obstacles are not intractable, but, like the rest, they must be recognized as genuine problems to be reckoned with if they are not to frustrate progress. They are, first, the community's ambivalence, and second, the lack of knowledge on which planning for the criminal justice system can be firmly based.

Ambivalence of the Community

If asked, a clear majority of the community would probably support halfway houses for those offenders who are not a serious criminal threat but still require some residential control. But repeated experience has shown that a proposal to establish such a facility in the neighborhood is likely to rouse profound opposition. The criminal offender, adult or juvenile, is accorded a low level of community tolerance when he no longer is an abstract idea but a real person. Planning must be done, and goals and standards drafted, in recognition of this fact.

Responsible community relations must be built into all correctional plans. The antidote to intolerance of convicted offenders is the active involvement of wide segments of the community in support of correctional processes. With imagination and a willingness to take some risks, members of minority groups, ex-offenders, and other highly motivated citizens can play an effective supporting role in correctional programs.

Part of this process of opening up the institution to outside influences is the creation of a wider base for staff selection. Obviously, recruitment of members of minority groups is vitally important and must be energetically pursued. Of parallel importance, women must be employed in community-based programs and at every level of the institution (for men and women, for adults and youths) from top administration to line guard. Corrections must become a full equal opportunity employer.

Correctional administrators have tended to isolate corrections from the general public—by high walls and locked doors. In light of the community's ambivalence toward corrections, lack of effort at collaboration with community groups and individual citizens is particularly unfortunate. In almost every community there are individuals and social groups with exceptional concern for problems of social welfare whose energies must be called upon. A lobby for corrections lies at hand, to be mobilized not merely by public information and persuasion, but also by encouraging the active participation of the public in correctional work.

There are yet other advantages in such a determined community involvement in corrections. Obstacles to the employment of ex-offenders will be lowered. Probation and parole caseloads could be reduced if paraprofessionals and volunteers, including ex-offenders, assist. And the "nine-to-five on weekdays" syndrome of some probation and parole services can be cured, so that supervision and support can be available when most needed.

Lack of Knowledge Base for Planning

In this catalog of problems in corrections to be solved, the need for a knowledge base must be seriously considered. Research is the indispensable tool by which future needs are measured and met. Chapter 15 surveys present correctional knowledge and prescribes means to determine which of our correctional practices are effective and with which categories of offenders.

Lack of adequate data about crime and delinquency, the consequences of sentencing practices, and the outcome of correctional programs is a major obstacle to planning for better community protection. It is a sad commentary on our social priorities that every conceivable statistic concerning sports is collected and available to all who are interested. One can readily find out how many lefthanders hit triples in the 1927 World Series. Yet if we wish to know how many one-to-life sentences were handed out to the 1927 crop of burglars—or the 1972 crop for that matter—the facts are nowhere to be found.

Baseline data and outcome data are not self-generating; no computer is self-activating. Research is of central significance to every correctional agency. It is not, as it so often is regarded, merely a public relations gimmick to be manipulated for political and budgetary purposes. It is an indispensible tool for intelligent decision making and deployment of resources.

It is time we stopped giving mere lip service to research and to the critical evaluation of correctional practices. To fail to propound and to achieve ambitious research and data-gathering goals is to condemn corrections to the perpetual continuance of its present ineptitude.

NOTES

1. President's Task Force on Prisoner Rehabilitation, *The Criminal Offender—What Should Be Done?* Washington, D.C.: Government Printing Office, 1970, p. 7.
2. 143 F. 2d 443 (6th Cir. 1944). Cert. denied 325 U.S. 887 (1945).

Appendix II

A Summary of Standards
for Corrections

RIGHTS OF OFFENDERS

Standard 2.1 Access to Courts

Each correctional agency should immediately develop and implement policies and procedures to fulfill the right of persons under correctional supervision to have access to courts to present any issue cognizable therein, including (1) challenging the legality of their conviction or confinement; (2) seeking redress for illegal conditions or treatment while incarcerated or under correctional control; (3) pursuing remedies in connection with civil legal problems; and (4) asserting against correctional or other governmental authority any other rights protected by constitutional or statutory provision or common law.

Standard 2.2 Access to Legal Services

Each correctional agency should immediately develop and implement policies and procedures to fulfill the right of offenders to have access to legal assistance, through counsel or counsel substitute, with problems or proceedings relating to their custody, control, management, or legal affairs while under correctional authority. Correctional authorities should facilitate access to such assistance and assist offenders affirmatively in pursuing their legal rights. Governmental authority should furnish adequate attorney representation and, where appropriate, lay representation to meet the needs of offenders without the financial resources to retain such assistance privately.

Standard 2.3 Access to Legal Materials

Each correctional agency, as part of its responsibility to facilitate access to courts for each person under its custody, should immediately establish policies and pro-

Source: National Advisory Commission on Criminal Justice Standards and Goals, *Corrections*, Washington, D.C.: U.S. Government Printing Office, 1973, editorial adaptations.

cedures to fulfill the right of offenders to have reasonable access to legal materials.

Standard 2.4 Protection Against Personal Abuse

Each correctional agency should establish immediately policies and procedures to fulfill the right of offenders to be free from personal abuse by correctional staff or other offenders.

Standard 2.5 Healthful Surroundings

Each correctional agency should immediately examine and take action to fulfill the right of each person in its custody to a healthful place in which to live. After a reasonable time to make changes, a residential facility that does not meet the requirements set forth in state health and sanitation laws should be deemed a nuisance and abated.

Standard 2.6 Medical Care

Each correctional agency should take immediate steps to fulfill the right of offenders to medical care. This should include services guaranteeing physical, mental, and social well-being as well as treatment for specific diseases or infirmities. Such medical care should be comparable in quality and availability to that obtainable by the general public.

Standard 2.7 Searches

Each correctional agency should immediately develop and implement policies and procedures governing searches and seizures to insure that the rights of persons under their authority are observed.

Standard 2.8 Nondiscriminatory Treatment

Each correctional agency should immediately develop and implement policies and procedures assuring the right of offenders not to be subjected to discriminatory treatment based on race, religion, nationality, sex, or political beliefs.

Standard 2.9 Rehabilitation

Each correctional agency should immediately develop and implement policies, procedures, and practices to fulfill the right of offenders to rehabilitation programs. A rehabilitative purpose is or ought to be implicit in every sentence of an offender unless ordered otherwise by the sentencing court. A correctional authority should have the affirmative and enforceable duty to provide programs appropriate to the purpose for which a person was sentenced. Where such programs are absent, the correctional authority should (1) establish or provide access to such programs or (2) inform the sentencing court of its inability to comply with the purpose for which sentence was imposed.

Standard 2.10 Retention and Restoration of Rights

Each State should enact legislation immediately to assure that no person is deprived of any license, permit, employment, office, post of trust or confidence, or political or judicial rights based solely on an accusation of criminal behavior. Also, in the implementation of Standard 16.17 . . . legislation depriving convicted persons of civil rights should be repealed. This legislation should provide further that a convicted and incarcerated person should have restored to him on release all rights not otherwise retained.

Standard 2.11 Rules of Conduct

Each correctional agency should immediately promulgate rules of conduct for offenders under its jurisdiction. Correctional agencies should provide offenders under their jurisdiction with an up-to-date written statement of rules of conduct applicable to them. Correctional agencies in promulgating rules of conduct should not attempt generally to duplicate the criminal law.

Standard 2.12 Disciplinary Procedures

Each correctional agency immediately should adopt, consistent with Standard 16.2, disciplinary procedures for each type of residential facility it operates and for the persons residing therein.

Minor violations of rules of conduct are those punishable by no more than a reprimand, or loss of commissary, entertainment, or recreation privileges for not more than 24 hours.

Major violations of rules of conduct are those punishable by sanctions more stringent than those for minor violations, including but not limited to, loss of good time, transfer to segregation or solitary confinement, transfer to a higher level of institutional custody or any other change in status which may tend to affect adversely an offender's time of release or discharge.

Rules governing major violations should provide for a hearing on the alleged violation and should provide for internal review of the hearing officer's or board's decision. Such review should be automatic. The reviewing authority should be authorized to accept the decision, order further proceedings, or reduce the sanction imposed.

Standard 2.13 Procedures for Nondisciplinary Changes of Status

Each correctional agency should immediately promulgate written rules and regulations to prescribe the procedures for determining and changing offender status, including classification, transfers, and major changes or decisions on participation in treatment, education, and work programs within the same facility.

Standard 2.14 Grievance Procedure

Each correctional agency immediately should develop and implement a grievance procedure. Each person should be able to report a grievance which should be transmitted without alteration, interference, or delay to the person or entity responsible for receiving and investigating grievances, and (a) such person or entity preferably should be independent of the correctional authority. It should not, in any case, be concerned with the day-to-day administration of the corrections function that is the subject of the grievance, and (b) the person reporting the grievance should not be subject to any adverse action as a result of filing the report. Each grievance not patently frivolous should be investigated. A written report should be prepared for the correctional authority and the complaining person. The report should set forth the findings of the investigation and the recommendations of the person or entity responsible for making the investigation. The correctional authority should respond to each such report, indicating what disposition will be made of the recommendations received.

Standard 2.15 Free Expression and Association

Each correctional agency should immediately develop policies and procedures to assure that individual offenders are able to exercise their constitutional rights of free expression and association to the same extent and subject to the same limitations as the public at large. Regulations limiting an offender's right of expression and association should be justified by a compelling state interest requiring such limitation. Where such justification exists, the agency should adopt regulations which effectuate the state interest with as little interference with an offender's rights as possible.

Standard 2.16 Exercise of Religious Beliefs and Practices

Each correctional agency immediately should develop and implement policies and procedures that will fulfill the right of offenders to exercise their own religious beliefs. These policies and procedures should allow and facilitate the practice of these beliefs to the maximum extent possible, within reason, consistent with Standard 2.15.

Standard 2.17 Access to the Public

Each correctional agency should develop and implement immediately policies and procedures to fulfill the right of offenders to communicate with the public. Correctional regulations limiting such communication should be consistent with Standard 2.15. Questions of right of access to the public arise primarily in the context of regulations affecting mail, personal visitation, and the communications media.

Standard 2.18 Remedies for Violation of an Offender's Rights

Each correctional agency immediately should adopt policies and procedures, and where applicable should seek legislation, to insure proper redress where an offender's rights as enumerated in this chapter are abridged.

DIVERSION FROM THE CRIMINAL JUSTICE PROCESS
Standard 3.1 Use of Diversion

Each local jurisdiction, in cooperation with related State agencies, should develop and implement by 1975 formally organized programs of diversion that can be applied in the criminal justice process from the time an illegal act occurs to adjudication.

The planning process and the identification of diversion services to be provided should follow generally and be associated with "total system planning" as outlined in Standard 9.1. Each diversion program should operate under a set of written guidelines that insure periodic review of policies and decisions.

PRETRIAL RELEASE AND DETENTION
Standard 4.1 Comprehensive Pretrial Process Planning

Each criminal justice jurisdiction immediately should begin to develop a comprehensive plan for improving the pretrial process.

Standard 4.2 Construction Policy for Pretrial Detention Facilities

Each criminal justice jurisdiction, State or local as appropriate, should immediately adopt a policy that no new physical facility for detaining persons awaiting trial should be constructed and no funds should be appropriated or made available for such construction until a comprehensive plan is developed in accordance with Standard 4.1, alternative means of handling persons awaiting trial as recommended in Standards 4.3 and 4.4 are implemented, adequately funded, and properly evaluated, the constitutional requirements for a pretrial detention facility are fully examined and planned for, and the possibilities of regionalization of pretrial detention facilities are pursued.

Standard 4.3 Alternatives to Arrest

Each criminal justice jurisdiction, State or local as appropriate, should immediately develop a policy, and seek enabling legislation where necessary, to encourage the use of citations in lieu of arrest and detention.

Standard 4.4 Alternatives to Pretrial Detention

Each criminal justice jurisdiction, State or local as appropriate, should immediately seek enabling legislation and develop, authorize, and encourage the use of a variety of alternatives to the detention of persons awaiting trial.

Standard 4.5 Procedures Relating to Pretrial Release and Detention Decisions

Each criminal justice jurisdiction, State or local as appropriate, should immediately develop procedures governing pretrial release and detention decisions.

426

Standard 4.6 Organization of Pretrial Services

Each State should enact by 1975 legislation specifically establishing the administrative authority over and responsibility for persons awaiting trial.

Standard 4.7 Persons Incompetent to Stand Trial

Each criminal justice jurisdiction, State or local as appropriate, should immediately develop procedures and seek enabling legislation, if needed, governing persons awaiting trial who are alleged to be or are adjudicated incompetent to stand trial.

Standard 4.8 Rights of Pretrial Detainees

Each State, criminal justice jurisdiction, and facility for the detention of adults should immediately develop policies and procedures to insure that the rights of persons detained while awaiting trial are observed.

Standard 4.9 Programs for Pretrial Detainees

Each State, criminal justice jurisdiction, and agency responsible for the detention of persons awaiting trial immediately should develop and implement programs for these persons.

Standard 4.10 Expediting Criminal Trials

Each State should enact legislation, and each criminal justice jurisdiction should develop policies and procedures, to expedite criminal trials and thus minimize pretrial detention.

SENTENCING

Standard 5.1 The Sentencing Agency

States should enact by 1975 legislation abolishing jury sentencing in all cases and authorizing the trial judge to bear full responsibility for sentence imposition within the guidelines established by the legislature.

Standard 5.2 Sentencing the Nondangerous Offender

State penal code revisions should include a provision that the maximum sentence for any offender not specifically found to represent a substantial danger to others should not exceed five years for felonies other than murder. No minimum sentence should be authorized by the legislature. The sentencing court should be authorized to impose a maximum sentence less than that provided by statute. Criteria should be established for sentencing offenders.

Standard 5.3 Sentencing to Extended Terms

State penal code revisions should contain separate provision for sentencing offenders when, in the interest of public protection, it is considered necessary to incapacitate them for substantial periods of time.

Standard 5.4 Probation

Each sentencing court immediately should revise its policies, procedures, and practices concerning probation, and where necessary, enabling legislation should be enacted.

A sentence to probation should be for a specific term not exceeding the maximum sentence authorized by law, except that probation for misdemeanants may be for a period not exceeding one year.

The court should be authorized to impose such conditions as are necessary to provide a benefit to the offender and protection to the public safety.

The offender should be provided with a written statement of the conditions imposed and should be granted an explanation of such conditions.

Procedures should be adopted authorizing the revocation of a sentence of probation for violation of specific conditions imposed.

Probation should not be revoked for the commission of a new crime until the offender has been tried and convicted of that crime.

Standard 5.5 Fines

In enacting penal code revisions, State legislatures should determine the categories of offenses for which a fine is an appropriate sanction and provide a maximum fine for each category.

Standard 5.6 Multiple Sentences

State legislatures should authorize sentencing courts to make disposition of offenders convicted of multiple offenses.

Under normal circumstances, when an offender is convicted of multiple offenses separately punishable, or when an offender is convicted of an offense while under sentence on a previous conviction, the court should be authorized to impose concurrent sentences.

Where the court finds on substantial evidence that the public safety requires a longer sentence, the court should be authorized to impose consecutive sentences.

Standard 5.7 Effect of Guilty Plea in Sentencing

Sentencing courts immediately should adopt a policy that the court in imposing sentence should not consider, as a mitigating factor, that the defendant pleaded guilty or, as an aggravating factor that the defendant sought the protections of right to trial assured him by the Constitution.

This policy should not prevent the court, on substantial evidence, from considering

428

the defendant's contrition, his cooperation with authorities, or his consideration for the victims of his criminal activity, whether demonstrated through a desire to afford restitution or to prevent unseemly public scrutiny and embarrassment to them. The fact that a defendant has pleaded guilty, however, should be considered in no way probative of any of these elements.

Standard 5.8 Credit for Time Served

Sentencing courts immediately should adopt a policy of giving credit to defendants against their maximum terms and against their minimum terms, if any, for time spent in custody and "good time" earned.

The court should assume the responsibility for assuring that the record reveals in all instances the amount of time to be credited against the offender's sentence and that such record is delivered to the correctional authorities. The correctional authorities should assume the responsibility of granting all credit due an offender at the earliest possible time and of notifying the offender that such credit has been granted.

Credit as recommended in this standard should be automatic and a matter of right and not subject to the discretion of the sentencing court or the correctional authorities.

Standard 5.9 Continuing Jurisdiction of Sentencing Court

Legislatures by 1975 should authorize sentencing courts to exercise continuing jurisdiction over sentenced offenders to insure that the correctional program is consistent with the purpose for which the sentence was imposed. Courts should retain jurisdiction also to determine whether an offender is subjected to conditions, requirements, or authority that are unconstitutional, undesirable, or not rationally related to the purpose of the sentence, when an offender raises these issues.

Standard 5.10 Judicial Visits to Institutions

Court systems should adopt immediately, and correctional agencies should cooperate fully in the implementation of, a policy and practice to acquaint judges with the correctional facilities and programs to which they sentence offenders, so that the judges may obtain firsthand knowledge of the consequences of their sentencing decisions.

Standard 5.11 Sentencing Equality

The following procedures should be implemented by 1975 by court rule or legislation to promote equality in sentencing:

1. Use of sentencing councils for individual sentences. (See Standard 5.13)
2. Periodic sentencing institutes for all sentencing and appellate judges. (See Standard 5.12.)
3. Continuing sentencing court jurisdiction over the offender until the sentence is completed. (See Standard 5.9.)
4. Appellate review of sentencing decisions.

Standard 5.12 Sentencing Institutes

Court systems immediately should adopt the practice of conducting sentencing institutes to provide judges with the background of information they need to fulfill their sentencing responsibilities knowledgeably.

Standard 5.13 Sentencing Councils

Judges in courts with more than one judge immediately should adopt a policy of meeting regularly in sentencing councils to discuss individuals awaiting sentence, in order to assist the trial judge in arriving at an appropriate sentence.

Standard 5.14 Requirements for Presentence Report and Content Specification

Sentencing courts immediately should develop standards for determining when a presentence report should be required and the kind and quantity of information needed to insure more equitable and correctionally appropriate dispositions.

Standard 5.15 Preparation of Presentence Report Prior to Adjudication

Sentencing courts immediately should develop guidelines as to the preparation of presentence reports prior to adjudication, in order to prevent possible prejudice to the defendant's case and to avoid undue incarceration prior to sentencing.

Standard 5.16 Disclosure of Presentence Report

Sentencing courts immediately should adopt a procedure to inform the defendant of the basis for his sentence and afford him the opportunity to challenge it.

Standard 5.17 Sentencing Hearing—Rights of Defendant

Sentencing courts should adopt immediately the practice of holding a hearing prior to imposition of sentence. At the hearing the defendant should have the right to be represented by counsel or appointed counsel, to present evidence on his own behalf, to subpoena witnesses, to call or cross-examine the person who prepared the presentence report and any persons whose information, contained in the presentence report, may be highly damaging to the defendant, and to present arguments as to sentencing alternatives. Guidelines should be provided as to the evidence that may be considered by the sentencing court for purposes of determining sentences.

Standard 5.18 Sentencing Hearing—Role of Counsel

Sentencing courts immediately should develop and implement guidelines as to the role of defense counsel and prosecution in achieving sentencing objectives. It should be the duty of both the prosecutor and defense counsel to avoid any undue publicity about the defendant's background, challenge and correct, at the hearing, any inaccuracies contained in the presentence report, inform the court of any plea discussion which resulted in the defendant's guilty plea, and verify, to the extent possible, any information in the presentence report.

Standard 5.19 Imposition of Sentence

Sentencing courts immediately should adopt the policy and practice of basing all sentencing decisions on an official record of the sentencing hearing. The record should be similar in form to the trial record.

CLASSIFICATION OF OFFENDERS

Standard 6.1 Comprehensive Classification Systems

Each correctional agency, whether community-based or institutional, should immediately reexamine its classification system and reorganize it so that no offender should receive more surveillance or "help" than he requires and no offender should be kept in a more secure condition or status than his potential risk dictates. The classification system should be issued in written form so that it can be made public and shared.

The system should provide full coverage of the offender population, consistent with individual dignity and basic concepts of fairness, provide for maximum involvement of the individual in determining the nature and direction of his own goals, be adequately staffed, and sufficiently objective and quantifiable to facilitate research, demonstration, model building, intrasystem comparisons, and administrative decision making.

Standard 6.2 Classification for Inmate Management

Each correctional agency operating insitutions for committed offenders, in connection with and in addition to implementation of Standard 6.1, should reexamine and reorganize its classification system immediately. The purpose of initial classification should be to screen inmates for safe and appropriate placements and to determine whether these programs will accomplish the purposes for which inmates are placed in the correctional system, and through orientation to give new inmates an opportunity to learn of the programs available to them and of the performance expected to gain their release.

The purpose of reclassification should be the increasing involvement of offenders in community-based programs as set forth in Standard 7.4 . . . .

Standard 6.3 Community Classification Teams

State and local correctional agencies should establish jointly and cooperatively by 1978, in connection with the planning of community-based programs, classification teams in the larger cities of the State for the purpose of encouraging the diversion of selected offenders from the criminal justice system, minimizing the use of institutions for convicted or adjudicated offenders, and programming individual offenders for community-based programs.

The planning and operation of community classification teams should involve State and local correctional personnel, personnel of specific community-based programs, police, court, and public representatives.

CORRECTIONS AND THE COMMUNITY

Standard 7.1 Development Plan for Community-Based Alternatives to Confinement

Each State correctional system or correctional system of other units of government should begin immediately to analyze its needs, resources, and gaps in service and to develop by 1978 a systematic plan with timetable and scheme for implementing a range of alternatives to institutionalization. The plan should specify the services to be provided directly by the correctional authority and those to be offered through other community resources. Community advisory assistance is essential. The plan should be developed within the framework of total system planning.

Standard 7.2 Marshaling and Coordinating Community Resources

Each State correctional system or the systems of other units of government should take appropriate action immediately to establish effective working relationships with the major social institutions, organizations, and agencies of the community, including employment and educational resources, social welfare services, the law enforcement system, and other relevant community organizations and groups.

Standard 7.3 Corrections' Responsibility for Citizen Involvement

Each State correctional system should create immediately: (a) a multipurpose public information and education unit, to inform the general public on correctional issues and to organize support for and overcome resistance to general reform efforts and specific community-based projects; and (b) an administrative unit responsible for securing citizen involvement in a variety of ways within corrections, including advisory and policymaking roles, direct service roles, and cooperative endeavors with correctional clients.

Standard 7.4 Inmate Involvement in Community Programs

Correctional agencies should begin immediately to develop arrangements and procedures for offenders sentenced to correctional institutions to assume increasing individual responsibility and community contact. A variety of levels of individual choice, supervision, and community contact should be specified in these arrangements, with explicit statements as to how the transitions between levels are to be accomplished. Progress from one level to another should be based on specified behavioral criteria rather than on sentence, time served, or subjective judgments regarding attitudes. The arrangements and procedures should be incorporated in the classification system to be used at an institution.

JUVENILE INTAKE AND DETENTION

Standard 8.1 Role of Police in Intake and Detention

Each juvenile court jurisdiction immediately should take the leadership in working out with local police agencies policies and procedures governing the discretionary diversion authority of police officers and separating police officers from the detention decision in dealing with juveniles.

Police agencies should establish written policies and guidelines to support police discretionary authority, at the point of first contact as well as at the police station, to divert juveniles to alternative community-based programs and human resource agencies outside the juvenile justice system, when the safety of the community is not jeopardized.

Police should not have discretionary authority to make detention decisions. This responsibility rests with the court, which should assume control over admissions on a 24-hour basis.

Standard 8.2 Juvenile Intake Services

Each juvenile court jurisdiction immediately should take action, including the pursuit of enabling legislation where necessary, to establish within the court organized intake services operating as a part of or in conjunction with the detention center. Intake services should be geared to the provision of screening and referral intended to divert as many youngsters as possible from the juvenile justice system and to reduce the detention of youngsters to an absolute minimum.

Standard 8.3 Juvenile Detention Center Planning

When total system planning indicates need for renovation of existing detention facilities or for construction of a new juvenile detention facility, each jurisdiction should take the following principles into consideration in planning the indicated renovations or new construction:

> The detention facility should be located in a residential area in the community and near court and community resources; population of detention centers should not exceed 30 residents; living area capacities within the center should not exceed 10 or 12 youngsters each; security should be based on a combination of staffing patterns, technological devices, and physical design; facility programming should utilize community resources; new construction and renovation of existing facilities should be based on consideration of the functional interrelationships between program activities and program participants; detention facilities should be coeducational and should have access to a full range of supportive programs; and citizen advisory boards should be established to pursue development of in-house and community-based programs and alternatives to detention.

Standard 8.4 Juvenile Intake and Detention Personnel Planning

Each jurisdiction immediately should reexamine its personnel policies and procedures for juvenile intake and detention personnel and make such adjustments as may be indicated to insure that they are compatible with and contribute toward the goal of reintegrating juvenile offenders into the community without unnecessary involvement with the juvenile justice system.

LOCAL ADULT INSTITUTIONS

Standard 9.1 Total System Planning

State and local corrections systems and planning agencies should immediately undertake, on a cooperative basis, planning for community corrections based on a total system concept that encompasses the full range of offenders' needs and the overall goal of crime reduction.

Standard 9.2 State Operation and Control of Local Institutions

All local detention and correctional functions, both pre- and postconviction, should be incorporated within the appropriate State system by 1982.

Standard 9.3 State Inspection of Local Facilities

Pending implementation of Standard 9.2, State legislatures should immediately authorize the formulation of State standards for correctional facilities and operational procedures and State inspection to insure compliance.

Standard 9.4 Adult Intake Services

Each judicial jurisdiction should immediately take action, including the pursuit of enabling legislation where necessary, to establish centrally coordinated and directed adult intake services to perform investigative services for pretrial intake screening, emphasize diversion of alleged offenders from the criminal justice system and referral to alternative community-based programs, offer initial and ongoing assessment, evaluation, and classification services to other agencies as requested, provide assessment, evaluation, and classification services that assist program planning for sentenced offenders, and arrange secure residential detention for pretrial detainees at an existing community or regional correctional center or jail, or at a separate facility for pretrial detainees where feasible.

Standard 9.5 Pretrial Detention Admission Process

County, city, or regional jails or community correctional centers should immediately reorganize their admission processing for residential care so that in addition to providing appropriate safeguards for the community, admission processing for pretrial detention has conditions and qualities conducive to overall correctional goals.

Standard 9.6 Staffing Patterns

Every jurisdiction operating locally based correctional institutions and programs should have their personnel on a merit or civil service status with salaries equal to those of persons with comparable qualifications and seniority in the jurisdiction's police department. Law enforcement personnel should not be assigned to these institutions. Qualifications for correctional staff members should be set at the State level and include a high school diploma. A program of preservice and inservice staff training should be given all personnel and these personnel should be responsible for maintenance and security operations as well as the bulk of in-house correctional programming, to include classification of inmates.

Standard 9.7 Internal Policies

Every jurisdiction operating locally based correctional institutions and programs for adults should immediately adopt these internal policies: a system of classification should be used to provide the basis for residential assignment and program planning for individuals; detention rules and regulations should be provided each new admission and posted in each separate area of the facility; every inmate has the right to visits from family and friends; the institution's medical program should obtain assistance from external medical and health resources; three meals daily should be provided at regular and reasonable hours; the inmates' lives and health are the responsibility of the facility; each detention facility should have written provisions that deal with its management and administration; and the use of an inmate trustee system should be prohibited.

Standard 9.8 Local Correctional Facility Programming

Every jurisdiction operating locally based correctional facilities and programs for adults should immediately adopt the following programming practices: a decisionmaking body should be established to follow and direct the inmate's progress through the local correctional system, either as a part of or in conjunction with the community classification team concept set forth in Standard 6.3; educational programs should be available to all residents in cooperation with the local school district; vocational programs should be provided by the appropriate state agency; a job placement program should be operated at all community correctional centers as part of the vocational training program; each local institution should provide counseling services; volunteers should be recruited and trained to serve as counselors, instructors, teachers, and recreational therapists; a range of activities to provide physical exercise should be available both in the facility and through the use of local recreational resources; in general, internal programs should be aimed only at that part of the institutional population unable to take advantage of ongoing programs in the community; and meetings with the administrator or appropriate staff of the institution should be available to all individuals and groups.

Standard 9.9 Jail Release Programs

Every jurisdiction operating locally based correctional facilities and programs for convicted adults immediately should develop release programs drawing community leadership, social agencies, and business interest into action with the criminal justice system.

Standard 9.10 Local Facility Evaluation and Planning

Jurisdictions evaluating the physical plants of existing local facilities for adults or planning new facilities should have a comprehensive survey and analysis made of criminal justice needs and projections in a particular service area.

Facility planning, location, and construction should develop, maintain, and strengthen offenders' ties with the community; increase the likelihood of community acceptance, the availability of contracted programs and purchased professional services, and attractiveness to volunteers, paraprofessionals, and professional staff; and afford easy access to the courts and legal services to facilitate intake screening, presentence investigations, postsentence programming, and pretrial detention.

PROBATION

Standard 10.1 Organization of Probation

Each State with locally or judicially administered probation should take action, in implementing Standard 16.4, Unifying Correctional Programs, to place probation organizationally in the executive branch of State government. The State correctional agency should be given responsibility for establishing statewide goals, policies, and priorities that can be translated into measurable objectives by those delivering services; program planning and development of innovative service strategies; staff development and training; planning for manpower needs and recruitment; collecting statistics, monitoring services, and conducting research and evaluation; offering consultation to courts, legislative bodies, and local executives; and, coordinating the activities of separate systems for delivery of services to the courts and to probationers until separate staffs to perform services to the courts are established within the courts system.

Standard 10.2 Services to Probationers

Each probation system should develop by 1975 a goal-oriented service delivery system that seeks to remove or reduce barriers confronting probationers. The needs of probationers should be identified, priorities established, and resources allocated based on established goals of the probation system.

Standard 10.3 Misdemeanant Probation

Each State should develop additional probation manpower and resources to assure that the courts may use probation for persons convicted of misdemeanors in all cases for which this disposition may be appropriate. All standards of this report that apply to probation are intended to cover both misdemeanant and felony probation. Other than the possible length of probation terms, there should be no distinction between misdemeanant and felony probation as to organization, manpower, or services.

Standard 10.4 Probation Manpower

Each State immediately should develop a comprehensive manpower development and training program to recruit, screen, utilize, train, educate, and evaluate a full range of probation personnel, including volunteers, women, and ex-offenders. The program should range from entry level to top level positions.

Standard 10.5 Probation in Release on Recognizance Programs

Each probation office serving a community or metropolitan area of more than 100,000 persons that does not already have an effective release on recognizance program should immediately develop, in cooperation with the court, additional staff and procedures to investigate arrested adult defendants for possible release on recognizance while awaiting trial, to avoid unnecessary use of detention in jail.

MAJOR INSTITUTIONS

Standard 11.1 Planning New Correctional Institutions

Each correctional agency administering State institutions for juvenile or adult offenders should adopt immediately a policy of not building new major institutions for juveniles under any circumstances, and not building new institutions for adults unless an analysis of the total criminal justice and adult corrections systems produces a clear finding that no alternative is possible.

Standard 11.2 Modification of Existing Institutions

Each correctional agency administering State institutions for juvenile or adult offenders should undertake immediately a five-year program of reexamining existing institutions to minimize their use, and, for those who must be incarcerated, modifying the institutions to minimize the deleterious effects of excessive regimentation and harmful physical environments imposed by physical plants.

Standard 11.3 Social Environment of Institutions

Each correctional agency operating juvenile or adult institutions, and each institution, should undertake immediately to reexamine and revise its policies, procedures, and practices to bring about an institutional social setting that will stimulate offenders to change their behavior and to participate on their own initiative in programs intended to assist them in reintegrating into the community.

Security and disciplinary policies and methods should be geared to support the objective of social reintegration of the offender rather than simply to maintain order and serve administrative convenience.

Standard 11.4 Education and Vocational Training

Each institution for juveniles or adults should reexamine immediately its educational and vocational training programs to insure that they meet standards that will individualize education and training. These programs should be geared directly to the reintegration of the offender into the community. It is recognized that techniques and practices for juveniles may be somewhat different from those required for adults, but the principles are similar. Usually the programs for juveniles and youths are more adequately equipped and staffed, but this distinction should not continue. It is assumed that intensive efforts will be made to upgrade adult institutions and that juvenile institutions will be phased out in favor of community programs and facilities.

Standard 11.5 Special Offender Types

Each correctional agency operating major institutions, and each institution, should reexamine immediately its policies, procedures, and programs for the handling of special problem offenders — the addict, the recalcitrant offender, the emotionally disturbed, and those associated with organized crime.

The commitment of addicts to correctional institutions should be discouraged, and correctional administrators should actively press for the development of alternative methods of dealing with addicts, preferably community-based alternatives.

Each institution should make special provisions other than mere segregation for inmates who are serious behavior problems and an immediate danger to others.

Each correctional agency should provide for the psychiatric treatment of emotionally disturbed offenders.

Each correctional agency and institution to which convicted offenders associated with organized crime are committed should adopt special policies governing their management during the time they are incarcerated.

Standard 11.6 Women in Major Institutions

Each State correctional agency operating institutions to which women offenders are committed should reexamine immediately its policies, procedures, and programs for women offenders, and make such adjustments as may be indicated to make these policies, procedures, and programs more relevant to the problems and needs of women.

Standard 11.7 Religious Programs

Each institution should immediately adopt policies and practices to insure the development of a full range of religious programs.

Standard 11.8 Recreation Programs

Each institution should develop and implement immediately policies and practices for the provision of recreation activities as an important resource for changing behavior patterns of offenders.

Standard 11.9 Counseling Programs

Each institution should begin immediately to develop planned, organized, ongoing counseling programs, in conjunction with the implementation of Standard 11.3 . . ., which is intended to provide a social-emotional climate conducive to the motivation of behavioral change and interpersonal growth.

Standard 11.10 Prison Labor and Industries

Each correctional agency and each institution operating industrial and labor programs should take steps immediately to reorganize their programs to support the reintegrative purpose of correctional institutions.

PAROLE

Standard 12.1 Organization of Paroling Authorities

Each State that has not already done so should, by 1975, establish parole decision-making bodies for adult and juvenile offenders that are independent of correctional institutions. These boards may be administratively part of an overall statewide correctional services agency, but they should be autonomous in their decision-making authority and separate from field services. The board responsible for the parole of adult offenders should have jurisdiction over both felons and misdemeanants.

Standard 12.2 Parole Authority Personnel

Each State should specify by statute by 1975 the qualifications and conditions of appointment of parole board members.

Standard 12.3 The Parole Grant Hearing

Each parole jurisdiction immediately should develop policies for parole release hearings that include opportunities for personal and adequate participation by the inmates concerned; procedural guidelines to insure proper, fair, and thorough consideration of every case; prompt decisions and personal notification of decisions to inmates; and provision for accurate records of deliberations and conclusions.

Standard 12.4 Revocation Hearings

Each parole jurisdiction immediately should develop and implement a system of revocation procedures to permit the prompt confinement of parolees exhibiting behavior that poses a serious threat to others. At the same time, it should provide careful controls, methods of fact-finding, and possible alternatives to keep as many offenders as possible in the community. Return to the institution should be used as a last resort, even when a factual basis for revocation can be demonstrated.

Standard 12.5 Organization of Field Services

Each State should provide by 1978 for the consolidation of institutional and parole field services in departments or divisions of correctional services. Such consolidations should occur as closely as possible to operational levels.

Standard 12.6 Community Services for Parolees

Each State should begin immediately to develop a diverse range of programs to meet the needs of parolees. These services should be drawn to the greatest extent possible from community programs available to all citizens, with parole staff providing linkage between services and the parolees needing or desiring them.

Standard 12.7 Measures of Control

Each State should take immediate action to reduce parole rules to an absolute minimum, retaining only those critical in the individual case, and to provide for effective means of enforcing the conditions established.

Standard 12.8 Manpower for Parole

By 1975, each State should develop a comprehensive manpower and training program which would make it possible to recruit persons with a wide variety of skills, including significant numbers of minority group members and volunteers, and use them effectively in parole programs.

ORGANIZATION AND ADMINISTRATION

Standard 13.1 Professional Correctional Management

Each corrections agency should begin immediately to train a management staff that can provide managerial attitude and adminstrative procedures permitting each employee to have more say about what he does; a management philosophy encouraging delegation of work-related authority to the employee level and acceptance of employee decisions; administrative flexibility to organize employees into teams or groups concerned with helping their teammates and achieving common goals; desire and administrative capacity to eliminate consciously as many as possible of the visible distinctions between employee categories; and, the capability of accomplishing promotion from within the system through a carefully designed and properly implemented career development program.

Standard 13.2 Planning and Organization

Each correctional agency should begin immediately to develop an operational, integrated process of long-, intermediate-, and short-range planning for administrative and operation functions. This should include an established procedure open to as many employees as possible for establishing and reviewing organizational goals and objectives at least annually; a research capability for adequately identifying the key social, economic, and functional influences impinging on that agency and for predicting the future impact of each influence; the capability to monitor, at least annually, progress toward previously specified objectives; and an administrative capability for properly assessing the future support services required for effective implementation of formulated plans.

These functions should be combined in one organizational unit responsible to the chief executive officer but drawing heavily on objectives, plans, and information from each organizational subunit.

Standard 13.3 Employee-Management Relations

Each correctional agency should begin immediately to develop the capability to relate effectively to and negotiate with employees and offenders.

Standard 13.4 Work Stoppages and Job Actions

Correctional administrators should immediately make preparations to be able to deal with any concerted work stoppage or job action by correctional employees. Such planning should have the principles outlined in Standard 13.3 as its primary components. In addition, further steps may be necessary to insure that the public, other correctional staff, or inmates are not endangered or denied necessary services because of a work stoppage.

MANPOWER FOR CORRECTIONS

Standard 14.1 Recruitment of Correctional Staff

Correctional agencies should begin immediately to develop personnel policies and practices that will improve the image of corrections and facilitate the fair and effective selection of the best persons for correctional positions.

Standard 14.2 Recruitment from Minority Groups

Correctional agencies should take immediate, affirmative action to recruit and employ minority group individuals (black, Chicano, American Indian, Puerto Rican, and others) for all positions.

Standard 14.3 Employment of Women

Correctional agencies immediately should develop policies and implement practices to recruit and hire more women for all types of positions in corrections.

Standard 14.4 Employment of Ex-Offenders

Correctional agencies should take immediate and affirmative action to recruit and employ capable and qualified ex-offenders in correctional roles.

Standard 14.5 Employment of Volunteers

Correctional agencies immediately should begin to recruit and use volunteers from all ranks of life as a valuable additional resource in correctional programs and operations.

Standard 14.6 Personnel Practices for Retaining Staff

Correctional agencies should immediately reexamine and revise personnel practices to create a favorable organizational climate and eliminate legitimate causes of employee dissatisfaction in order to retain capable staff.

Standard 14.7 Participatory Management

Correctional agencies should adopt immediately a program of participatory management in which everyone involved—managers, staff, and offenders—shares in identifying problems, finding mutually agreeable solutions, setting goals and objectives, defining new roles for participants, and evaluating effectiveness of these processes.

Standard 14.8 Redistribution of Correctional Manpower Resources to Community-Based Programs

Correctional and other agencies, in implementing the recommendations of Chapters 7 and 11 for reducing the use of major institutions and increasing the use of community resources for correctional purposes, should undertake immediate cooperative studies to determine proper redistribution of manpower from institutional to community-based programs.

Standard 14.9 Coordinated State Plan for Criminal Justice Education

Each State should establish by 1975 a State plan for coordinating criminal justice education to assure a sound academic continuum from an associate of arts through graduate studies in criminal justice, to allocate education resources to sections of the State with defined needs, and to work toward proper placement of persons completing these programs.

Standard 14.10 Intern and Work-Study Programs

Correctional agencies should immediately begin to plan, support, and implement internship and work-study programs to attract students to corrections as a career and improve the relationship between educational institutions and the field of practice.

Standard 14.11 Staff Development

Correctional agencies immediately should plan and implement a staff development program that prepares and sustains all staff members.

RESEARCH AND DEVELOPMENT, INFORMATION, AND STATISTICS

Standard 15.1 State Correctional Information Systems

Each State by 1978 should develop and maintain, or cooperate with other States in the development and maintenance of, a correctional information system to collect, store, analyze, and display information for planning, operational control, offender tracking, and program review for all State and county correctional programs and agencies.

Standard 15.2 Staffing for Correctional Research and Information Systems

Each State, in the implementation of Standard 15.1, should provide minimum capabilities for analysis and interpretation of information. For all but the largest components (facilities, branch offices, programs), a small information and statistics section capable of periodic reports on the consequences of policy and decision making will suffice. Larger components will benefit from having a professional staff capable of designing and executing special assessment studies to amplify and explicate reports generated by the information system.

Standard 15.3 Design Characteristics of a Correctional Information System

Each State, in the establishment of its information system under Standard 15.1, should design it to facilitate four distinct functions: offender accounting, administrative-management decision making, ongoing departmental research, and rapid response to ad hoc inquiries.

Standard 15.4 Development of a Correctional Data Base

Each State, in the establishment of its information system under Standard 15.1, should design its data base to satisfy the following requirements: the information-statistics functions of offender accounting, administrative decision making, ongoing research, and rapid response to questions should be reflected in the design; the data base should allow easy compilation of an annual statistical report; the data base should include all data required at decision points; the requirements of other criminal justice information systems for corrections data should be considered in the design; all data base records should be individual-based and contain elements that are objectively codable; the integrity and quality of data in each record is the responsibility of the information group; the corrections information-statistics system should be designed and implemented modularly to accommodate expansion of the data base; data bases should be designed for future analyses; the results of policies (in terms of evaluation) should be reported to administrators; and, the initial design of the corrections data base should recognize that change will be continual.

Standard 15.5 Evaluating the Performance of the Correctional System

Each correctional agency immediately should begin to make performance measurements on two evaluative levels – overall performance or system reviews as measured by recidivism, and program reviews that emphasize measurement of more immediate program goal achievement. Agencies allocating funds for correctional programs should require such measurements.

THE STATUTORY FRAMEWORK OF CORRECTIONS

Standard 16.1 Comprehensive Correctional Legislation

Each State, by 1978, should enact a comprehensive correctional code, which should include statutes governing: services for persons awaiting trial; sentencing criteria, alternatives, and procedures; probation and other programs short of institutional confinement; institutional programs; community-based programs; parole; pardon.

The code should include statutes governing the preceding programs for: felons, misdemeanants, and delinquents; adults, juveniles, and youth offenders; male and female offenders. Each legislature should state the "public policy" governing the correctional system.

Standard 16.2 Administrative Justice

Each State should enact by 1975 legislation patterned after the Model State Administrative Procedure Act, to regulate the administrative procedures of correctional agencies.

Standard 16.3 Code of Offenders' Rights

Each State should immediately enact legislation that defines and implements the substantive rights of offenders.

Standard 16.4 Unifying Correctional Programs

Each State should enact legislation by 1978 to unify all correctional facilities and programs. The board of parole may be adminstratively part of an overall statewide correctional services agency, but it should be autonomous in its decision making authority and separate from field services. Programs for adult, juvenile, and youthful offenders that should be within the agency include: services for persons awaiting trial; probation supervision; institutional confinement; community-based programs, whether prior to or during institutional confinement; parole and other aftercare programs; all programs for misdemeanants including probation, confinement, community-based programs, and parole.

Standard 16.5 Recruiting and Retaining Professional Personnel

Each State, by 1975, should enact legislation entrusting the operation of correctional facilities and programs to professionally trained individuals.

Legislation creating top management correctional positions should be designed to protect the position from political pressure and to attract professionals.

Standard 16.6 Regional Cooperation

Each State that has not already done so should immediately adopt legislation specifically ratifying the following interstate agreements: Interstate Compact for the

Supervision of Parolees and Probationers, Interstate Compact on Corrections, Interstate Compact on Juveniles, Agreement on Detainers, Mentally Disordered Offender Compact.

In addition, statutory authority should be given to the chief executive officer of the correctional agency to enter into agreements with local jurisdictions, other States, and the Federal Government for cooperative correctional activities.

Standard 16.7 Sentencing Legislation

Each State, in enacting sentencing legislation (as proposed in Chapter 5) should classify all crimes into not more than 10 categories based on the gravity of the offense. The legislature should state for each category, a maximum term for state control over the offender that should not exceed 5 years — except for the crime of murder and except that, where necessary for the protection of the public, extended terms of up to 25 years may be imposed on the following categories of offenders: persistent felony offenders, dangerous offenders, and professional criminals.

Standard 16.8 Sentencing Alternatives

By 1975 each State should enact sentencing legislation reflecting the following major provisions: all sentences should be determined by the court rather than by a jury; the court should be authorized to utilize a variety of sentencing alternatives; the court should be authorized to recommend to the board of parole that the offender not be paroled until a given period of time has been served, or impose a minimum sentence to be served prior to eligibility for parole, not to exceed one-third of the maximum sentence imposed or be more than three years, or allow the parole of an offender sentenced to a minimum term prior to service of the minimum upon the request of the board of parole; the legislature should delineate specific criteria patterned after the Model Penal Code for imposition of the alternatives available; the sentencing court should be required to make specific findings and state specific reasons for the imposition of a particular sentence; and, the court should be required to grant the offender credit for all time served in jail awaiting trial or appeal arising out of the conduct for which he is sentenced.

Standard 16.9 Detention and Disposition of Juveniles

Each State should enact legislation by 1975 limiting the delinquency jurisdiction of the courts to those juveniles who commit acts that if committed by an adult would be crimes.

Standard 16.10 Presentence Reports

Each State should enact by 1975 legislation authorizing a presentence investigation in all cases and requiring it in all felonies, in all cases where the offender is a minor, and, as a prerequisite to a sentence of confinement in any case.

The legislation should require disclosure of the presentence report to the defendant, his counsel, and the prosecutor.

Standard 16.11 Probation Legislation

Each State should enact by 1975 probation legislation (1) providing probation as an alternative for all offenders; and (2) establishing criteria for (a) the granting of probation, (b) probation conditions, (c) the revocation of probation, and (d) the length of probation.

Standard 16.12 Commitment Legislation

Each State should enact, in conjunction with the implementation of Standard 16.1, legislation governing the commitment, classification, and transfer of offenders sentenced to confinement.

Standard 16.13 Prison Industries

By 1975, each State with industrial programs operated by or for correctional agencies should amend its statutory authorization for these programs so that, as applicable, they do not prohibit specific types of industrial activity from being carried on by a correctional institution, the sale of products of prison industries on the open market, the transport or sale of products produced by prisoners, the employment of offenders by private enterprise at full market wages and comparable working conditions, and the payment of full market wages to offenders working in state-operated prison industries.

Standard 16.14 Community-Based Programs

Legislation should be enacted immediately authorizing the chief executive officer of the correctional agency to extend the limits of confinement of a committed offender so the offender can participate in a wide variety of community-based programs.

Standard 16.15 Parole Legislation

Each State should enact by 1975 legislation (1) authorizing parole for all committed offenders and (2) establishing criteria and procedures for (a) parole eligibility, (b) granting of parole, (c) parole conditions, (d) parole revocation, and (e) length of parole.

Standard 16.16 Pardon Legislation

Each State by 1975 should enact legislation detailing the procedures (1) governing the application by an offender for the exercise of the pardon powers, and (2) for exercise of the pardon powers.

446

Standard 16.17 Collateral Consequences of a Criminal Conviction

Each State should enact by 1975 legislation repealing all mandatory provisions depriving persons convicted of criminal offenses of civil rights or other attributes of citizenship.

Appendix III

Data on Correctional Organization

Parent Agency Responsibility for Administering Correctional Services, by State,[1]
January 1971

State	Juvenile Detention	Juvenile Probation	Juvenile Institutions	Juvenile Aftercare
Alabama	Local	Local	3 Separate & Independent Boards	Dept. of Pensions & Security & Local
Alaska	Dept. of Health & Welfare	Dept. of Health & Welfare	Dept. of Health & Welfare	Dept. of Health & Welfare
Arizona	Local	Local	Dept. of Corrections	Dept. of Corrections
Arkansas	Local	Dept. of Welfare & Local	Juvenile Training School Dept.	Juvenile Training School Dept
California	Local	Local	Dept. of Youth Authority	Dept. of Youth Authority
Colorado	Local	Local & District	Dept. of Institutions	Dept. of Institutions
Connecticut	Juvenile Court Districts	Juvenile Court Districts	Dept. of Youth Services	Dept. of Youth Services
Delaware	Dept. of Health & Soc. Servs.	Local	Dept. of Health & Soc. Servs.	Dept. of Health & Soc. Servs.
Florida	Local	Local	Dept. of Health & Rehabilitative Services	Dept. of Health & Rehabilitative Service

Source: Table reproduced from Advisory Commission on Intergovernmental Relations, St Local Relations in the Criminal Justice System, Washington: Government Printing Office, 1 pp. 282–286.
[1]Some states have local services in addition to state services.

Misde-meanant Probation	Adult Probation	Local Adult Institutions and Jails	Adult Institutions	Parole
oard of ardons : Paroles	Board of Pardons & Paroles	Local	Board of Corrections	Board of Pardons & Paroles
ept. of ealth & 'elfare	Dept. of Health & Welfare	Dept. of Health & Welfare	Dept. of Health & Welfare	Dept. of Health & Welfare
one	Local	Local	Dept. of Corrections	Dept. of Corrections
one	Local	Local	Dept. of Corrections	Board of Pardons & Parole
cal	Local	Local	Dept. of Corrections	Dept. of Corrections
cal	Local	Local	Dept. of Institutions	Dept. of Institutions
ept. of dult obation	Dept. of Adult Probation	Dept. of Corrections	Dept. of Corrections	Dept. of Corrections
ept. of alth & c. Servs.	Dept. of Health & Soc. Servs. & Local	Dept. of Health & Soc. Servs.	Dept. of Health & Soc. Servs.	Dept. of Health & Soc. Servs.
cal & obation Parole mmission	Local & Probation & Parole Commission	Local	Dept. of Health & Rehabilitative Services	Probation & Parole Commission

continued

449

Parent Agency Responsibility for Administering Correctional Services, by State, January 1971 (Continued)

State	Juvenile Detention	Juvenile Probation	Juvenile Institutions	Juvenile Aftercare
Georgia	Division of Children & Youth & Loc.	Division of Children & Youth & Loc.	Division of Children & Youth	Division of Children & Youth
Hawaii	Local	Local	Dept. of Social Service	Dept. of Social Service
Idaho	State Board of Health & Local	State Board of Health & Local	State Board of Health	State Board of Health
Illinois	Local	Local	Dept. of Corrections	Dept. of Corrections
Indiana	Local	Dept. of Welfare & Local	Dept. of Corrections	Dept. of Corrections
Iowa	Local	Local	Dept. of Social Services	Dept. of Social Services
Kansas	Local	Local	Dept. of Social Welfare	Dept. of Social Welfare
Kentucky	Local	Dept. of Child Welfare & Loc.	Dept. of Child Welfare	Dept. of Child Welfare
Louisiana	Local	Dept. of Public Welfare & Local	Dept. of Corrections	Dept. of Public Welfare & Loca
Maine	Local	Dept. of Mental Health & Corrections & Loc.	Dept. of Mental Health & Corrections	Dept. of Mental Hea & Corrections

Misde-meanant Probation	Adult Probation	Local Adult Institutions and Jails	Adult Institutions	Parole
ept. of obation & cal	Dept. of Probation & Local	Local	Dept. of Corrections	Board of Pardons & Parole
cal	Local	Local	Dept. of Social Service	Board of Parole & Pardons
ne	Board of Correction	Local	Board of Correction	Commission for Pardons & Parole
cal	Local	Local	Dept. of Corrections	Dept. of Corrections
al	Local	Local	Dept. of Corrections	Dept. of Corrections
ne	Dept. of Social Services	Local	Dept. of Social Services	Dept. of Social Services
al	Loc. & Board of Probation & Parole	Local	Director of Penal Institutions	Board of Probation & Parole
ot. of rections	Dept. of Corrections	Local	Dept. of Corrections	Dept. of Corrections
e	Dept. of Corrections	Local	Dept. of Corrections	Dept. of Corrections
ot. of tal Health orrec- s	Dept. of Mental Health & Corrections	Local	Dept. of Mental Health & Corrections	Dept. of Mental Health & Corrections

continued

Parent Agency Responsibility for Administering Correctional Services, by State, January 1971 (Continued)

State	Juvenile Detention	Juvenile Probation	Juvenile Institutions	Juvenile Aftercare
Maryland	Dept. of Juvenile Services	Dept. of Juvenile Services	Dept. of Juvenile Services	Dept. of Juvenile Services
Massachusetts	Youth Service Board	Local	Youth Service Board	Dept. of Youth Services
Michigan	Local	Local	Dept. of Social Services	Dept. of Social Services
Minnesota	Local	Dept. of Corrections & Local	Dept. of Corrections	Dept. of Corrections
Mississippi	Local	Local	Board of Trustees	State DPW and Local
Missouri	Local	Local	Board of Training Schools	Board of Training Schools
Montana	Local	Local	Dept. of Institutions	Dept. of Institutions
Nebraska	Local	District Courts & Local	Dept. of Public Institutions	Dept. of Public Institutions
Nevada	Local	Local	Dept. of Health & Welfare	Dept. of Health & Welfare
New Hampshire	Board of Parole	Dept. of Probation & Local	Board of Parole	State Industrial School

Misdemeanant Probation	Adult Probation	Local Adult Institutions and Jails	Adult Institutions	Parole
ept. of role & obation & cal	Dept. of Parole & Probation & Local	Local	Dept. of Correctional Services	Dept. of Parole & Probation
cal	Local	Local	Dept. of Correction	Parole Board
pt. of rrections Local	Dept. of Corrections & Local	Local	Dept. of Corrections	Dept. of Corrections
pt. of rrections Local	Dept. of Corrections & Local	Local	Dept. of Corrections	Dept. of Corrections
ne	Board of Probation & Parole	Local	Dept. of Correction	Board of Probation & Parole
al	Board of Probation & Parole	Local	Dept. of Correction	Board of Probation & Parole
ne	Board of Pardons	Local	Dept. of Institutions	Board of Pardons
trict rts & al	District Courts	Local	Dept. of Public Institutions	Board of Parole
pt. of ole & bation	Dept. of Parole & Probation	Local	Board Prison Commissioners	Dept. of Parole & Probation
ot. of bation ocal	Dept. of Probation & Local	Local	Board of Parole	Board of Parole

continued

Parent Agency Responsibility for Administering Correctional Services, by State, January 1971 (Continued)

State	Juvenile Detention	Juvenile Probation	Juvenile Institutions	Juvenile Aftercare
New Jersey	Local	Local	Dept. of Institutions & Agencies	Dept. of Institutions & Agencies
New Mexico	Local	Local	Dept. of Corrections	Local
New York	Local	Local	Dept. of Social Services	Dept. of Social Services
North Carolina	Local	District & Local	Board of Juvenile Correction	Local
North Dakota	Local	DPW & Local	Dept. of Institutions	Public Welfare Board
Ohio	Local	Local	Youth Commission	Youth Commission
Oklahoma	Local	Loc. & Dept. of Welfare & Institutions	Dept. of Welfare & Institutions	Dept. of Welfare & Institutions
Oregon	Local	Corrections Division & Local	Corrections Division	Corrections Division
Pennsylvania	Local	Local	Board of Training Schools	Board of Training Schools & Local
Rhode Island	Dept. of Social Welfare	Dept. of Social Welfare	Dept. of Social Welfare	Dept. of Social Welfare
South Carolina	Local	Local	Dept. of Juvenile Corrections	Dept. of Juvenile Corrections

Misde-meanant Probation	*Adult Probation*	*Local Adult Institutions and Jails*	*Adult Institutions*	*Parole*
cal	Local	Local	Dept. of Institutions & Agencies	Dept. of Institutions & Agencies
pt. of rrections	Dept. of Corrections	Local	Dept. of Corrections	Parole Board
vision of bation ocal	Division of Probation & Local	Local	Dept. of Correctional Services	Dept. of Correctional Services
bation mmission	Probation Commission	Dept. of Corrections	Dept. of Corrections	Board of Parole
ne	Board of Pardons	Local	Dept. of Institutions	Board of Pardons
al	Local	Local	Dept. Mental Hygiene & Correction	Dept. Mental Hygiene & Correction
ne	Local & Dept. of Corrections	Local	Dept. of Corrections	Pardon & Parole Board
rections ision	Corrections Division	Local	Corrections Division	Parole Board
rd of oations & le & al	Board of Probations & Parole & Local	Dept. of Justice & Local	Dept. of Justice	Board of Probations & Parole
t. of al fare	Dept. of Social Welfare	Dept. of Social Welfare	Dept. of Social Welfare	Dept. of Social Welfare
oation, le & on Board	Probation, Parole & Pardon Board	Local	Dept. of Corrections	Probation, Parole & Pardon Board

continued

455

Parent Agency Responsibility for Administering Correctional Services, by State, January 1971 (Continued)

State	Juvenile Detention	Juvenile Probation	Juvenile Institutions	Juvenile Aftercare
South Dakota	Local	Local	Board of Charities & Corrections	Board of Pardons & Parole
Tennessee	Local	Dept. of Corrections & Local	Dept. of Corrections	Dept. of Corrections
Texas	Local	Local	Youth Council	Youth Council
Utah	Local	Juvenile Court Districts	Dept. of Social Services	Juvenile Court Districts
Vermont	Dept. of Corrections	Dept. of Corrections	Dept. of Corrections	Dept. of Corrections
Virginia	Local	Dept. of Welfare & Institutions & Local	Dept. of Welfare & Institutions	Dept. of Welfare & Institutions & Local
Washington	Local	Local	Dept. of Social & Health Services	Dept. of Social & Health Services
West Virginia	Local	Dept. of Welfare & Local	Commissioner of Public Institutions	Commissioner of Public Institutions
Wisconsin	Local	Dept. of Health & Soc. Services & Local	Dept. of Health & Social Services	Dept. of Health & Social Services
Wyoming	Local	Dept. of Probation & Parole & Local	Board of Charities & Reform	Dept. of Probation & Parole

Misde-meanant Probation	Adult Probation	Local Adult Institutions and Jails	Adult Institutions	Parole
ne	Board of Pardons & Parole	Local	Board of Charities & Corrections	Board of Pardons & Parole
cal	Dept. of Corrections	Local	Dept. of Corrections	Dept. of Corrections
cal	Local	Local	Dept. of Corrections	Board of Pardons & Paroles
vision of rrections	Division of Corrections	Local	Division of Corrections	Division of Corrections
pt. of rrections	Dept. of Corrections	Dept. of Corrections	Dept. of Corrections	Dept. of Corrections
pt. of lfare & titutions	Dept. of Welfare & Institutions	Local	Dept. of Welfare & Institutions	Dept. of Welfare & Institutions
cal	Dept. of Social & Health Services	Local	Dept. of Institutions	Board of Prison Terms & Paroles
cal & Div. robation arole	Local & Div. of Probation & Parole	Local	Commissioner of Public Institutions	Div. of Probation & Parole
pt. of alth & Soc. vices & al	Dept. of Health & Soc. Services & Local	Local	Dept. of Health & Social Services	Dept. of Health & Social Services
pt. of bation arole	Dept. of Probation & Parole	Local	Board of Charities & Reform	Dept. of Probation & Parole

continued

457

Parent Agency Responsibility for Administering Correctional Services, by State, January 1971 (Continued)

State	Juvenile Detention	Juvenile Probation	Juvenile Institutions	Juvenile Aftercare
Local	40	24	0	2
State Local	2	20	0	5
State	8	6	50	43

Misde-meanant Probation	Adult Probation	Local Adult Institutions and Jails	Adult Institutions	Parole
	11	43	0	0
	13	1	0	0
	26	6	50	50

Appendix IV

Developing Correctional Administrators

THE METHOD OF COMPROMISE

Adjustment and concession as an approach to problem-solving appeared much more heavily in the incidents than in the generalized self-perceptions of the interviewees. The administrators disliked the label of compromise but made frequent use of the method, an outcome which seemed connected with their view of correctional management as having to satisfy multiple and often contradictory goals. Believing that it was impossible to maximize any single goal at the absolute expense of others, the administrators inevitably found themselves operating as arbiters of conflicting forces.

The foci of conflict reported in the incidents were numerous and varied, but one predominated: the traditional struggle between treatment and control in the management of offenders, as described in Chapter 1. This was not a particular problem for the administrators of agencies in which the rehabilitation of offenders was addressed only in token ways, but it was a continuing and often a volatile problem in the programs which had made major commitments to both goals. The following are examples of types of problems in which compromise solutions frequently occurred.

1. A plan is developed to send institutionalized boys out to a nearby community for work and recreation. Some members of the community, including the press, react with alarm and opposition. Some of the older members of the custodial force of the institution also oppose the plan and seek in covert ways to subvert it.

2. The newly appointed administrator of treatment services in an institution launches a group therapy program, believing it can go far toward changing nega-

Source: Elmer K. Nelson, Jr. and Catherine H. Lovell, *Developing Correctional Administrators*, research report of the Joint Commission on Correctional Manpower and Training, Washington, D.C.: Government Printing Office, November, 1969, pp. 58–75.

tive attitudes and behavior among the offenders who participate and that it can help to bridge a very wide gap between staff and offenders. In the first few weeks of the new program much opposition and criticism develops. Schedules are dislocated as the new program competes for the time of the offenders with established programs. The movement of offenders within the institution is changed and complicated, to the dismay of the custodial personnel.

3. A parole administrator determines that his staff are spending far too much time in their offices writing reports and fulfilling bureaucratic requirements. Offenders are dealt with in routinized ways which are not varied according to their individual needs. In fact, very little counseling and help is actually being provided to parolees. In his effort to restructure the work of the parole officers, the administrator encounters a great deal of adverse reaction from those who have a vested interest in the ongoing system. The issue becomes polarized around the assertion that the new plan is "social work oriented," while the old system was commendable in that it took a realistic and firm approach to offenders. Some members of the parole board identify with this position and bring pressure to bear upon the administrator involved.

A study of the approaches taken toward solving problems such as those reconstructed above revealed that the administrators involved used compromise frequently in very different ways. For some it seemed to be the dominant approach to problem-solving. Not only did they meet crises by trying to placate and satisfy the minimal requirements of those involved, but they allocated rewards and penalties in such a fashion that no interest prevailed but no interest ever really lost out entirely. This type of administrative behavior often seemed to be used together with direct authority and manipulation. It appeared to be most effective at system maintenance and quite ineffective in producing significant changes.

Another pattern involving the use of compromise was conspicuously different. Here concession and negotiation appeared as a "fallback" strategy to be used when preferred approaches became ineffectual. Typically, the adminstrator would move aggressively toward change goals and draw back only when mounting resistance instructed him that he had lost momentum. Then, however, he would scan the resistance, send out "feelers" to ascertain what the most imperative needs of opposing forces were, and enter into compromise in a manner calculated to consolidate his gains. The resulting pattern was a combination of integration and compromise.

In this second pattern, compromise seemed to be accompanied by a variety of other strategies. Though the data are unclear on this point, it would seem that integration was the major preferred strategy in such cases and that all of the other strategies (perhaps unhappily including manipulation) were brought to bear on the problem according to the administrator's perception of which method would serve his purposes most effectively and expeditiously.

There were some administrators in the interview sample who both rejected compromise as a label for their strategy and described their behavior in a manner which indicated that they actually avoided adjustment and concession in the real-life arena.

Like the "moralist" administrators in the study of school superintendents by Gross, Mason, and McEachern,[1] these interviewees seemed to believe that they knew what was best for all involved and inferred, therefore, that compromise was both ethically and psychologically unacceptable. Not unsurprisingly, these individuals tended to nominate the use of direct authority as their most preferred strategy for problem-solving. We cannot help but believe that such inflexibility most often hinders effective administrative action.

THE METHOD OF INVOLVEMENT-COMMITMENT

As has been stated, the interviewees selected the strategy of involvement-commitment in describing their own behavior more frequently than any other problem-solving method when confronted with a forced choice. With very few exceptions, they seemed to be aware of the concept of "participative management" which is so much in vogue in the literature today and regarded it as a prestigious style of administration.

In contrast to the findings regarding compromise, however, the critical incidents revealed much less use of involvement-commitment than did the statistical data based on generalized self-perceptions of the interviewees. Examination of the incidents made it clear that we must distinguish between many different kinds of involvement in the problem-solving process. It was possible to place the incidents in which the involvement-commitment strategy was reported into four rough categories differentiated with regard to the depth and authenticity of the involvement process.

The first level of involvement, the most superficial, consisted of bringing people together to inform them of decisions already made. This category could be subdivided into two groups. In the first, it was made clear that the only involvement expected was to hear the decisions which had been made unilaterally by the administrator and then take part in the process of dissemination and implementation. In the second (and this appeared quite frequently in the incidents), there was ritual involvement of others in discussing the desirability of decisions which in fact had already been made. In these cases, it would appear that a very small amount of involvement-commitment was combined with a large amount of manipulation. When this approach was observed in staff meetings we attended, however, it appeared that the manipulation aspect usually was ineffectual, since those involved were well aware that the decision-making was unilateral.

A second level at which the involvement-commitment strategy was used consisted of the involvement of others, usually subordinates, in devising and carrying out a plan for the implementation of decisions which were made unilaterally. An interesting feature of this strategy was that some of the time the administrators who reported it seemed convinced that the process had been fully democratic, even though what they described clearly was a limited use of the principle of participation.

A third level in the use of the involvement-commitment strategy consisted of those cases in which the administrator did in fact involve others in the making of decisions about change. Some of the interviewees, in fact, tended to look upon their managerial careers as evolutionary in the sense that they started at what we have defined here as level 1 and progressed to level 3. In such cases, there tended to be expressions of satisfaction with the greater utilization of others in the problem-solving process. A typical comment would be:

> In the beginning I thought I had to do it all myself and went around acting like the great leader. It was a great relief when I found out that I could get others to help in making the decisions, and I think the place runs a lot better this way because everybody has a stake in what we decide to do.

The fourth level of involvement of others was similar to the category just described but has the additional feature of the involvement of others in the diagnosis of problems and change needs. This did not appear very clearly in specific incidents, but in the case of some of the interviewees was an essential aspect of their administrative styles. One top administrator described his approach to problem-solving cogently:

> I try to make everyone feel that they have as much at stake in what goes on in this agency as I do and that they have as much responsibility for finding out how to get the job done better. We are working in a very primitive field in corrections and have a lot to learn. No one should feel that he has all the answers, especially the top man.

As observed in staff meetings, this administrator did in fact not only allow participation by his immediate subordinates but required it. And, though it is proper that we should avoid evaluative statements as to effectiveness since our data do not permit them, it did seem clear to the two interviewers involved that there was a high level of commitment to organizational goals in this management team.

It also seemed useful to classify the incidents in which the strategy of involvement-commitment was employed on the basis of who was involved. The great preponderance of those who were brought into the problem-solving process by the reporting adminstrator were subordinates. In fact, the "mind set" of most interviewees with respect to the involvement of others was that this method was appropriate only for subordinates. In particular, second level managers usually avoided involving their peers and tended to approach their superiors very cautiously about unsolved problems. The most obvious gap in the incident data on involvement-commitment was in the area of including offenders in problem-solving. Here we had few incidents indeed! Nevertheless there were incidents reporting the use of involvement-commitment with all relationships, indicating perhaps that it is an extremely valuable and versatile strategy which could be used much more widely than it is today.

A few administrators whose work brought them into close contact with offenders described revealing examples of involving them in problem-solving at all of the four levels defined above. These examples made it clear that the gulf between staff and offenders is so wide and so imbedded in the social structure of the two groups that involvement-commitment is extremely difficult to implement. The typical inmate advisory council seemed to operate at levels 1 and 2 as described above. But there were examples of staff-offender interaction in living units in which decisions vital to the life of the institution were made collaboratively. Clearly, in such cases, the interviewees were reporting the evolution of new roles for both staff and offenders. The vested interests of staff in retaining the roles of superior and treater (interests of which apparently they are not fully conscious) raise provocative questions for those concerned with professional training and development.

The limited number of incidents in which the involvement-commitment strategy was employed in dealing with superiors was interesting. Administrators working in headquarters settings sometimes sought to involve the governor or other political executive above them in the activities of the correctional system. Similar approaches were attempted with legislators who served on key committees and whose understanding and support were required for the funding of new programs. The incidents reported in this area were not always successful, and indeed it would appear that correctional administrators often feel frustrated by their inability to make effective calls on the time and attention of their superiors, at least until a crisis occurs.

One top administrator in a headquarters setting described a lengthy process through which a work furlough plan for inmates to return to community life was enacted into law. Much learning and development were involved for the administrator, since this represented his first major attempt at change and brought him into contact with the governor and the legislature for the first time in his role as director. His approach to the task of obtaining new and, for his state, unprecedented legislation depended heavily upon the involvement-commitment strategy. He contacted citizen groups concerned with community welfare and, while he presented the work furlough idea to them as an already conceived goal, he solicited their support in getting it enacted into law. He contacted numerous legislators with explanations of the proposed legislation and its probable benefits in reducing costs of the correctional process while increasing opportunities for rehabilitation of offenders. Some legislators who were already friendly to the proposal were asked to contact others who were not. Similarly, the governor was persuaded of the desirability of the idea at an early stage, and he was asked to make personal contact with a limited number of legislators whose support was regarded as critical. The director spent a great deal of time working on these contacts himself and, when the time came for legislative hearings, devoted almost all of his time in advocacy for the bill and neutralizing hard centers of resistance.

The director of this incident spoke of his own development along two major dimensions. First, he admitted that in the beginning he was ill at ease and somewhat anxious about contacts with the governor and the legislators. He gained confidence and self-assurance by "becoming immersed in the battle." In addition to this psychological dimension, a cognitive factor was involved. In the beginning, the world of partisan politics and the legislative process were unfamiliar to the director. He simply did not understand very much about the ways in which influence is exercised in order to achieve desired changes in public policy. He felt not only that he was "desensitized" emotionally by the rough-and-tumble involved in playing the advocate role but that he learned a great deal by doing so. This last point seems important because most of the administrators in the study appeared to enter the political arena only reluctantly and tended to feel vulnerable while in it.

In general, the involvement-commitment strategy was used much more in the internal force field than in the external one. Administrators who were comfortable and felt that they had experienced success in working collaboratively with external interests such as legislators, the press, and special community groups appeared to have a much higher capability for bringing change about than did those who either avoided such relationships or used less preferred strategies in them.

Several administrators reported spending large proportions of their time in efforts to mobilize a wider base of support for correctional programs. Examples of such efforts were: the development of trade advisory councils through which both management and labor unions were brought into contact with the training of inmates and their placement on jobs in the community; the development of an extensive program for the use of lay volunteers in the probation supervision process; and the cooptation of employers and employment service agencies in a substantial effort to open up job opportunities for released offenders.

One interesting aspect of the use of involvement-commitment by the administrators in our sample was that they often viewed staff members in their organizations as potential links to points in the surrounding force field where support or assistance was required. The director of food services in one institution became extremely effective at placing offenders in jobs in the food service industry because he had entree with the "gatekeepers" to those jobs. His superior was quite prepared to have him spend a large part of his time in the community rather than performing the tasks listed in his job description, because the superior saw the major goal of the institution being better served in that manner.

The involvement-commitment strategy seemed most satisfying and appeared to be practiced most authentically when it was accompanied by the strategy of integration. It appeared to be superficial and unauthentic when accompanied by the strategy of manipulation. Paradoxically, some of the administrators who made good use of the involvement-commitment approach also used direct authority at times. One such administrator spoke of the relationship between the two strategies in an insightful manner when he said:

> It has seemed to me that the idea of participation sometimes gets to be an excuse for avoiding your responsibility as the administrator. At times one can't get the involvement he would like because time and circumstances make it impossible. And even when there has been a lot of involvement and people have contributed a great deal to the working out of a plan, a decision still has to be made.

The substantial gap between how administrators would like to behave with respect to involvement of others and the way in which they actually behave reveals major opportunities for executive development. Dependence on less preferred methods of problem-solving needs to be understood in terms of felt inadequacy to practice the art of involving others and gaining their commitment to goals of change. An upgrading of both personal skills and knowledge of the groups and individuals whose cooperation is needed seems necessary.

THE METHOD OF DIRECT AUTHORITY

The majority of interviewees seemed highly ambivalent about the exercise of influence through the use of rewards and penalties attached to their administrative positions. A minority of those interviewed voiced no such concern and seemed comfortable with the idea that authority and responsibility should be commensurate and that the administrator who shrinks from exercising the former thus abdicates the latter. Such conceptions may seem simplistic or plainly inaccurate in the light of modern management theory, yet the incidents which we collected indicated that such theory, at its present stage of development, does not give sufficient attention to distinctions between positive and negative uses of authority.

Some interesting incidents on the use of authority were reported by administrators who worked in the more traditional and custodial programs. These incidents help us realize that authority is a major variable in correctional administration. The maintenance of control over captive offenders in such settings (where participative management is wholly alien to the normative structuring of social interaction) appears to involve quite delicate judgments, a deft hand, and a measure of good luck. In incidents involving the reestablishment of formal authority over mutinous inmates, the frequency with which certain vignettes appeared made them seem almost apocryphal.

Typically, inmates involved in a work stoppage, a sitdown strike, or a refusal to eat the prison food were approached on the basis of "divide and conquer." The more amenable inmates were first brought under control and were well rewarded for their conformity (e.g., by a steak dinner), while those who continued on strike went hungry. Through such a process the hard core of the dissidents was separated out and eventually brought under control. Those who reported such stories seemed much more preoccupied with the tactical aspects of maintaining or regaining control than in understanding the dynamics through which it was threatened or lost. Nevertheless, the feeling came through that administrators who were seasoned by such difficult experiences developed a shrewd, if unevenly tempered, insight into the human fabric of their organizations.

Incidents involving the direct use of authority as the only or the primary method of solving problems occurred almost entirely in settings where revenge and restraint were the major goals of organizational activity. When reform and reintegration were legitimated as goals, direct authority did not seem sufficient even to maintain the system, much less to change it in ways congruent with those goals. In fact, it appeared that some of the most powerful tensions and conflicts reported in the incidents were generated by the continuation of authoritarian regimes in programs wherein both staff and inmates had come to believe that participative methods of management would be introduced. This point can be illustrated through combining elements from a series of connected incidents collected in our research.

The resulting fabricated case study involved the appointment of a new warden in an old and highly repressive prison. The new appointee was described as an extremely dynamic, articulate, and charismatic individual. Coming to his post with a mandate to reform the system and develop rehabilitative programs, he received a great deal of attention from the press. He spoke out against capital and corporal punishment, both of which had been administered for many years in his institution. He called for community volunteers to help with educational and recreational activities for inmates. He embarked upon a program of staff training through which university faculty members came to the institution to instruct the custodial force in a variety of subjects generally associated with the reform model of correctional practice. Needless to say, the inmates were keen observers of both the publicity and the actual changes which took place. The power elite of the inmate population consisted of a group of individuals on the "max unit," almost all of whom had long been committed to criminal careers.

Within only a few months it became clear that the new warden's efforts to supply leadership toward a changed system were not well understood or imitated by subordinate administrators and certainly not by the most influential inmate leaders. The method of direct and coercive authority which had been practiced for decades in the institution continued to be the dominant approach to securing compliance from those within the system. Rewards and penalties were meted out in well-elaborated ways. The small number of "treatment staff" whom the warden had brought with him to his new assignment were accorded superficial respect but were actually viewed with considerable amusement and condescension by the informal coalition of staff and inmates which maintained control over the belief system of the institution.

As the disparity between the original statements about change and the actual results became more evident, considerable tension and dissatisfaction began to develop among both staff and inmates. They were no longer sure that familiar principles would govern their efforts to "make out" in the system, but it seemed to most of them that the new approach was not making much headway either. One of the old-time guards said: "It's like trying to conquer China; the invaders get enveloped in the old system and disappear."

The new warden was reported to have shifted his own administrative style as these developments occurred. He still remained an extremely active and charismatic figure, involving himself deeply in many aspects of the program. Nevertheless, his own problem-solving behavior began to shift more and more toward the direct use of authority, often in punitive ways which reflected the long-standing norms of the institution. While still holding to his original goals in public pronouncements, he was sometimes heard to say that he had tried to move too fast and that some of the old approaches "make pretty good sense." He told the professional associates from outside the prison, "You just don't change these people right away by bringing social work into the place."

Never very skillful in the participative involvement of subordinates in problem-solving, nevertheless the warden had established numerous committees and endorsed the use of group process; e.g., including "every inmate on any unit who wants to get involved" as a way of changing from the old regime to a modern, treatment-oriented program. Now, however, he sometimes showed impatience with the slowness of committee work and at times impulsively issued terse, unilateral orders much in the tradition of the previous warden.

The behavior of the new warden shifted somewhat in still other ways which were highly visible to the inmates and the line custodial staff and were laden with strong symbolic meaning for them. While continuing to oppose corporal punishment as a governmental policy, he made increasing use of it as a punishment for violation of institutional rules. He adopted the policy of personally attending sessions where the paddle was applied, saying that he did so as a way of protecting inmates against excessive brutality. He explained the difference between his public position and his operating policy on the rationale that tradition-bound systems must be changed incrementally rather than precipitously.

The end result of this sequence of events was an explosive and highly destructive riot in which costly property damage occurred and a number of personal injuries were sustained. The leaders of the riot were the hard core of inmates who previously had shared power with the old-line custodians and felt their influence slipping in the new regime. The followers, however, were the mass of inmates who (although confused and largely unable to articulate the reasons for their hostility) plainly felt that they had been promised benefits which were not forthcoming.

Most of the incidents involving the use of authority were not so dramatic as the one recounted above but perhaps have more relevance for everyday practice in modern correctional programs. A number of patterns of authority use appeared in the incidents, varying to a great extent in the way in which authority was combined with other strategies to obtain desired results.

A majority of administrators at the second echelon considered the use of authority as an essentially undesirable approach to problem-solving and believed that involvement-participation was the preferred method. One interviewee asserted, "Once you have to resort to authority, you have lost the game. The trick of administration is to bring people together to decide what needs to be done and then give them their heads in doing it." This attitude seemed particularly prevalent among administrators with professional training, especially those whose backgrounds were in social work. We wonder, however, whether such a complete avoidance of the use of formal sanctions might not constitute an abdication of certain kinds of administrative responsibility. In fact, incidents collected from management teams composed of members holding such a view and others favoring the use of authority suggested that, when an administrator denies sanctioning as a part of his role, that function is assumed by others. One division head described the situation of an administrative peer by saying: "John thinks he is operating completely democratically, but what is really happening is that his assistant cracks the whip and gets things done. And he is the fellow everyone knows really runs the division."

Another pattern appeared to be the combination of authority with manipulation, the latter often flying under false colors as involvement-commitment. One top administrator, in incidents reported both by himself and by others in his management team, demonstrated a clear and apparently long-standing tendency to shift back and forth between arbitrary order-giving (backed up by equally arbitrary rewarding and penalizing) and an affectation of commitment to democratic management. In the "democratic" phase, the administrator would call numerous meetings in which he spoke at length and quite repetitiously about the virtues of staff participation, then finished by instructing his division heads on what to do. It was said that his sense of timing was so finely developed that "to his regret" there was never any time left for questions and certainly none for critical reactions to his edicts.

A much preferred pattern of authority use, on the basis of precepts set forth in Chapters 1 and 2 (that management should establish participative conditions and view men as self-actualizing), was one in which that approach to problem-solving was combined with the method of integration. The use of outside expertise and the invoking of standards and norms also appeared as a part of this pattern in some incidents. Frequently involvement-commitment (without the unauthentic overtone introduced by manipulation) constituted an intervening phase during which the goal of integrating diverse interests was pursued and the direct use of authority was avoided.

An example of this more complicated method of problem-solving behavior occurred in a large institution which had moved by fits and starts over the years from a totally repressive regime to one in which, while the excess of sadism and mortification of inmates were relinquished, only the smallest beginnings had been made in working toward the goals of reform and integration. At this juncture a new superintendent was appointed who had demonstrated unusual competence in a previous assignment as an institutional administrator and who, while quite pragmatic and eclectic in his approach to management, was generally committed to the idea of involving staff in problem-solving. He was also committed to the reform model of correctional practice and had begun to move toward the reintegration model through his experiences in working with community interests near the institutions which he had headed.

The major problem perceived by the new administrator when he arrived to assume his duties at the institution was that most of the staff, including second-level managers, had been nurtured in the old system and had little understanding of the use of rehabilitative methods with offenders. Moreover, they were used to an adminstrative climate in which hierarchy and the use of direct authority were the prime ingredients.

The newly arrived superintendent took his time about making changes and used the early weeks of his administration to get acquainted with the people and the traditions of the institution. In this way, he identified a number of "rough gems" who, he felt, could assume or continue in administrative roles if they could be helped to catch the vision and understand the content of modern correctional practice. He then proceeded to set up a number of committees to plan for long-needed and quite basic changes in the programs of the institution. He made it clear to the people participating (including the offenders who were involved in this process) that his request for assistance was not "phony" and that he would take their recommendations seriously.

While staff members were moving into the task of planning a new approach, and thus learning skills and behavior which were quite unfamiliar to most of them, the superintendent brought to the institution a number of outsiders whom he regarded as "carriers" of the new ideas which he wanted to see better understood and adopted by his staff. He sent a number of key subordinates on visits to correctional programs in other jurisdictions and carefully paved the way for them to be cordially received by the administrators there. He circulated literature which was relevant to the planning being done. He involved himself deeply in the committee work and was apt to walk in unexpectedly at almost any meeting, sit for a time, and perhaps make a few comments. Never, however, did he assume the role of chairman at these meetings.

While all of this was going on, the superintendent was also communicating widely the policy that the planning process would lead to decisions and that these decisions were ultimately his personal responsibility. He established some rather severe time deadlines for different phases of the planning operation and indicated that he expected to receive specific recommendations which could quickly be translated into action. When the first wave of planning was over, he moved expeditiously to issue policy directives and called meetings (including an unprecedented meeting of all staff and inmates in the institution) at which he expressed appreciation for their participation in developing a new program, indicated what his decisions were with respect to their recommendations, and talked about the responsibility everyone would have for implementation.

This incident, which combined involvement with authority, and other data suggest that currently popular formulations about participative management do not sufficiently address the problem of how authority may be well used and used in a way which is compatible with more prestigious management styles. Perhaps the correctional field presents unusual opportunities for study of the use of authority because of the great disparities in power and influence which exist within correctional systems. In any case, it seems to us that further study should not proceed from the simplistic dichotomy that authority is bad and democracy is good; rather it should seek to understand the subtle and elusive attributes which distinguish "good" from "bad" use of authority, and to examine its relationship to other management techniques.

THE METHOD OF DILEMMA MANAGEMENT

Almost all of the interviewees quickly grasped and responded to the idea that at times problems can be solved only by turning adversity to advantage, the method which we have designated dilemma management.[2]

The quantitative data on strategic behavior indicated that administrators working in juvenile institutions used dilemma management as their most preferred method of problem-solving when interacting with legislators, representatives of the mass media, and special interest groups from the community. Probation and parole administrators also ranked it as their most preferred strategy in dealing with legislators. Interestingly, administrators working in headquarters settings designated dilemma management as their most preferred strategy in dealing with offenders, an outcome which perhaps reflects the fact that they work directly with offenders only under conditions of adversity or crisis. It is equally interesting that administrators working in institutions for adult offenders reported usng this method least of all, in no case placing it above the fifth priority in their ranking of strategies except in contacts with administrative superiors, where they ranked it third. Perhaps this group of administrators is so inured to adversity in the internal force field that its management and utilization is perceived as an everyday process rather than a strategy to be called upon under unusual circumstances.

Several of the incidents seem to combine dilemma management with delay as problem-solving methods. The reporting administrator would explain that he had identified a major problem which stood in the way of movement toward established goals. However, he would report, it was impossible to take any significant action aimed at the solution of the problem because of his inability to generate the resources or support required for its solution. Under these circumstances, he would play a waiting game until some crisis or highly visible problem attracted attention toward his needs and permitted him to obtain assistance which heretofore had been impossible to acquire.

For example, one director of a state correctional system described his long-standing interest in developing an in-service training program for institutional staff members. His efforts to develop rehabilitative programs and to achieve a more compatible relationship between treatment and custodial staff were long thwarted because the custodial personnel were uninformed about and unsympathetic toward modern methods of working with offenders. Furthermore, the state legislature repeatedly demonstrated an unwillingness to appropriate funds for training. Thus the department's efforts in this area were far below the optimal level.

Then came a mild scandal in one of the institutions within the system. A number of correctional officers failed to observe institutional regulations in handling of inmate property and mail. Contraband was allowed to enter the institution. Word of these matters which leaked out to the press was given wide publicity. Standing in an elevator in the state capitol, the director of the department found himself the butt of some ill-tempered jokes from three legislators who were standing near him. He considered that they were "kidding on the square" and took the initiative by asking, "Well, if you really want to do something constructive to end such incidents, why don't you give us the money for training correctional officers which we have been asking for?" One of the legislators took the request seriously, later talked to the director, and worked out a legislative program which was "sold" on the basis of the malperformance of the officers in the reported episode.

In our analysis of the incidents in dilemma management, we found it desirable to make a distinction between those administrators who carefully prepared to take advantage of a crisis should it occur and those who appeared simply to "luck out" when trouble arrived. In the incident reported above, careful staff work had been done to develop an in-service training plan and to specify its costs. When the time arrived for action, it was necessary only to make small adjustments in the plan and bring it to the attention of legislators who, while once uninterested, now were ready to give it sympathetic attention.

In other incidents, however, the reporting administrators seemed to be in reality rewriting history by claiming the use of dilemma management when in actuality they had only landed on their feet after a crisis and discovered that crucial groups in their force field were prepared to meet their needs more adequately than before. Thus, a prison riot in one state led to a doubling of staff within the institution where it occurred, even though the warden had gone along for a considerable time without attempting to assess his staff needs or to secure the support needed to meet them. Without suggesting that virtue always wins out under these circumstances, the stories told to us about crisis and adversity contained many examples of administrators who were dismissed after the crisis episode. The benefits of increased attention and support, if any, went to their successors. While qualifying as one method of systemic change in corrections, this does not meet our concept of strategic behavior.

A number of the incidents which we classified as involving the use of dilemma-management were not nearly so dramatic as those involving prison riots and scandals. Some of them seemed related to an axiom of psychotherapy, that it is frequently necessary for latent problems to become manifest before they can be confronted and resolved. Some of the second-level administrators who were interviewed talked about long-standing organizational problems which they were able to "get some leverage on" only when events forced them out into the open. There were numerous examples. A "personality clash" between two subordinate supervisors, which had both of them "sulking" and refusing to communicate for months, was finally ameliorated when the two lost their tempers while with the reporting administrator. A growing tendency for staff on the night shift to arrive late for duty was quickly dealt with when inmates on a living unit which was temporarily unsupervised broke out a reserve of well-fermented fruit juice and held a raucous party. A tendency for parole officers working out of one office to make only superficial contacts with their parolees (or even to record contacts which had not been made) was dealt with rigorously when a parolee who had committed a serious new offense told newspaper reporters that he had not seen his parole officer for many months and the supervisor's explanation to the press (based on office records) proved to be inaccurate.

It seemed clear to us that the use of dilemma management as an approach to the solving of administrative problems could be effective only if it were part of a repertoire of other strategies and if it were used with skill and careful preparation which predated what one interviewee called "the time of trouble and tribulation which tries the mettle of the administrator." Nevertheless, the incident data on this strategy seemed to have implications for executive development. Case studies or actual field experiences with crises and trouble could be important vehicles for education and individual growth. Although some of our interviewees who had long experience in administrative positions were inclined to say that there is no substitute for personal occupancy of the "lonely" executive role, we were persuaded that at least some of the learning involved therein could be achieved through imaginative simulation of real events.

THE METHOD OF INTRODUCING EXPERTISE

The importation of specialized knowledge or skill whether in the form of human resources or some inanimate carrier such as literary or visual materials, was frequently nominated as an approach to problem-solving and was given a relatively high priority in the forced-choice rankings made by all interviewees. Moreover, it was spread rather uniformly across a wide range of relationships.

Expertise was employed in a wide variety of ways in the incidents. Correctional administrators often find themselves in at least nominal control of services which affect every aspect of human life. Institutional managers in particular, must provide and maintain quality control over the feeding, housing, recreation, training, employment, and protection of the inmates under their charge. Beyond these functions, many administrators also seek to provide psychological and spiritual retraining. And all of this must be done in the potentially incongruous context of custodial containment and control.

Even the administrators of probation and parole programs must have concern for this same broad spectrum of services. While not working in encapsulated environments such as correctional institutions, the community-based administrators have the added problem of mobilizing a variety of resources over which they have no direct authority. Thus the securing of needed employment, training, and medical assistance requires that their staff (the supervising probation and parole officers) be knowledgeable about these resources, skillful in determining which are needed, and most of all, able to secure them. To say that a great deal of specialized expertise is required in the performance of these functions is something of an understatement.

Many of the institutional administrators who reported incidents expressed frustration in their efforts to attract needed expertise from typically indifferent outsiders. This was particularly the case with respect to consultation related to rehabilitative programs. In part, this reflected an uncertainty about the relative effectiveness of different rehabilitative techniques. There was a tendency for many administrators to have on their desks some of the recent works concerning crime or delinquency, and to refer to them in conversation, but we found few examples of well organized and implemented programs to bring such materials to the attention of staff or to help them consider the implications of current research and theory for local operations. Some of the incidents concerned the development of staff training programs and libraries, but in general it did not seem that such activities made a vital difference in

473

the direction or velocity of change in the general programming of the agency. Most staff libraries which we saw were dusty and out of date.

The introduction of needed expertise seemed to be more relevant to actual needs when it arose out of a particular, vexing problem. In one incident a panel of experts on dietetics and nutrition redesigned the food service program of an institution after it had come under severe criticism from inmates and their families. In another incident an interdenominational committee of clergymen was called in to help deal with a charge that time and physical space in an institution were inequitably allocated as between Protestant and Roman Catholic interests. Thus, expertise injected with the purpose of solving a specific problem seemed more potent than expertise introduced for the general good of the organization.

In incidents reported by community-based administrators, the successful co-optation of needed expertise seemed at times to depend upon the administrator's ability to identify intersections of interest between his own agency and others in the force field. One parole administrator described a situation in which his staff needed psychiatric consultation in order to deal more effectively with emotionally disabled clients. Budget constraints made it impossible to meet this need through the employment of qualified psychiatrists. In scanning alternative solutions, the administrator discovered that the psychiatric training program of his state university needed real-life opportunities for psychiatric interns to apply their generic skills to the problems of crime and delinquency. The discovery of these intersecting needs provided a basis for a series of workshops and seminars in which parole officers interacted with young psychiatrists to the considerable satisfaction of all parties involved.

We obtained additional insights through an examination of incidents which were designated as "ineffective" by the interviewee. Two factors contributed to unsuccessful outcomes: the lack of relevance of the available expertise to the problem which needed solution, and the low quality of the "expert" input. Demonstrations of the irrelevance of "experts" occurred during incidents where otherwise competent and well-intentioned outsiders simply could not develop solutions that were really pertinent to specific problems. For example, a parole administrator described a large-scale effort of his department to enlist the efforts of service clubs in obtaining employment for offenders. A number of such organizations were contacted and persuaded to define this activity as having a high priority for their clubs. Parole officers attended meetings to give carefully prepared talks. Parolees were called in to describe the problems encountered by offenders in obtaining jobs. All of this resulted in a sizable effort on the part of service club members to open up job opportunities for probationers.

The difficulty, however, was that the membership of the service clubs did not really constitute an appropriate power base for significantly changing the employment system for ex-offenders. In retrospect, the reporting administrator somewhat ruefully recognized that "most of those who set out to help us were small businessmen who had a highly limited number of jobs available within their own organizations." This experience, he said, helped him to recognize that "the real breakthrough" would have to come through obtaining advice and subsequently active assistance (a combination of expertise and involvement-commitment) from such authentic "gatekeepers" as the officials of large industrial unions, the heads of organizations employing hundreds or even thousands of workers, the personnel directors of these same organizations and, finally, the public employment agencies which provide a large and highly bureaucratized network of contact points between potential employers and those in need of employment.

The factor of quality, as illuminated by the "unsuccessful" incidents, seemed to reflect the fact that our society is replete with "experts" of all kinds, not a few of whom turn out to be duds or frauds, however invincible their "paper" qualifications seem to be. If the tone of this comment seems unduly sour, it is because our interviewees had a number of convincing stories to tell about entreprenurial outsiders who assured the solution of complex problems concerning which they had only the most meager understanding. Some interviewees may have been resentful partly because the correctional field tends to shift its allegiance in decidedly fickle fashion from one "omipotent" source of expertise to another—education, psychiatry, sociology, management consultation, and, most recently, computerized information-processing.

In any case, many of the incidents involving the use of outside expertise were rather sad tales of flirtation with outsiders who, as it turned out, possessed no magic solution to long-standing problems. So numerous and diverse are the purported experts around the correctional field that a plausible goal of executive development might be to increase the sophistication and awareness of administrators concerning ther relative strengths and limitations.

A final observation is in order concerning the introduction of expertise as an approach to problem-solving. Some of the incidents made it clear that in dealing with outside experts the administrator must be sensitive to the reactions of such inside power centers as the legislature, service and control agencies, and others who might be negative to the influence of the "expert" or the "consultant." Indeed, it appeared that rather delicate judgment may be required to distinguish between the times when "expert" evidence carries the day and the times when it alienates those whose cooperation is most needed. The importance of this variable is reflected in the fact that perennial consultants to correctional agencies, such as representatives of the National Council on Crime and Delinquency, have learned to defer to the overriding importance of local needs and traditions and have become skillful in adapting their conceptions of "the best way" to indigenous circumstances.

Some of the incidents which were judged as less than successful by those who reported them involved events in which legislators, control agency officials, representatives of the local press, or others concluded that "our situation is special and we really don't care how they do it in some other place." The lack of sure and proven knowledge concerning what works and does not work in correctional practice suggests that this may not be an unreasonable position much of the time.

The problem for executive development lies in developing an ability to identify forms of outside assistance which are both relevant and of good quality. Even when these criteria are met, however, the problem remains of using the influence of outside experts in such a fashion as to persuade rather than alienate "inside" decision-makers. Viewing this function as a task for executive development, the administrator might be seen as playing the role of mediator between local and outside forces. The great limitation apparent in our sample of administrators with respect to the performance of this task was their parochialism and lack of contact with authoritative opinion, research data, and experience in other jurisdictions. There seemed to be a clear contrast between those administrators who were knowledgeable and in touch with developments relevant to their work, and those who were essentially insular in outlook. The former seemed to generate in their staffs a spirit of inquiry and an appetite for finding connections between their correctional enclave and the outside world. In such settings, small talk at coffee breaks included, for example, references to a professor's comments at an evening lecture, a book on management read over the weekend, a newspaper story about efforts to change programming for mentally ill patients from an institutional to a community-based approach. In the settings in which management did not provide models for such "reaching out" behavior, discussion over coffee tended to revolve more around local gossip and intrigue, preoccupation with such concerns seemingly substituting for the harder questions of program policy that were left unaddressed.

THE METHOD OF INTEGRATION

Within our conceptual scheme the integration of disparate interests and goals was a highly preferred approach to administrative problem-solving. (See Chapter 2.) Our use of the term integration in the classification of incidents is based upon Mary Parker Follett's work in distinguishing integration (contrasted with domination and compromise) as an administrative strategy.[3]

Administrators who were skillful in integrating legitimate but seemingly irreconcilable interests usually did so by probing the context within which the problem was moving rather than through a rigid application of predetermined values and priorities. This is not to say that such administrators had no concern for values and goals; the opposite seemed to be true. But the administrators with integrative capability seemed to bring their value positions to the problem situation as general referents rather than as polarizing influences. In the case of nonintegrative interviewees, predetermined positions were rigidly applied, with the result that solutions could only be achieved either through an authoritative edict (domination, in Follett's terms) or a scaling down of legitimate aspirations on the part of the parties involved, i.e., compromise.

The incidents classified under the heading of integration included a variety of types of conflict. The great majority, however, fall under the following headings: (1) conflicts about the management of offenders between treatment and control orientations; (2) conflicts between those who favored the conservation and maintenance of the organization within its force field and those who perceived a need to change its direction or mode of operation; and (3) conflict between concern for production and task performance versus concern for the morale, welfare, and development of the human participants in the situation. Conflicts of the last type presented particularly difficult problems of definition. The social worker attached to an institutional living unit tended to think of production as a change in inmate attitudes and behaviors. The custodial officer attached to the same unit thought of production as cleanliness, order, and discipline on the unit and argued that the creation of these conditions amounted to exactly what the social worker was seeking. Conflicts in this case centered not so much around long-term images of desired change as around the intervening processes which were thought likely to produce those results.

Treatment vs. Control

The incidents which revolved around conflicts between the goals of helping and controlling offenders provided more examples of compromise than of integration. Many of the organizations studied seemed to have institutionalized these functions in a way that insured their separateness. Periodic skirmishes occurred along divisional boundaries when one side or the other considered its interests to be in jeopardy, but the paucity of collaborative problem-solving between administrators in peer rank was notable.

However, the relatively rare instances of integrative problem-solving in which the functions of control and treatment were merged rather than compromised were extremely interesting. One institutional administrator, for example, described a series of events in which disciplinary infractions by inmates escalated sharply and feelings between the custodial staff and the inmates became exacerbated. Many representatives of the treatment-training component sympathized with the inmates and at times subverted the custodians in their efforts to enforce rules.

In discussion with the staff involved and with members of the inmate advisory council, the warden found opinions so polarized and feelings so strained that there seemed little basis for fact-finding and negotiation. The inmates asserted angrily that the officers were "always on our back," while the officers maintained that "the place has been getting completely out of hand and we have to make it clear who is in charge here."

Members of the treatment division seemed torn by the conflict between hierarchical loyalties to the institutional rule system and the dicta of their profession which moved them to oppose, as one of them put it, "authoritarian handling which aggravates the inmate's tendency to be hostile and reinforces his tendency to be immature and dependent."

Almost everyone involved seemed to be talking in terms of slogans and abstract principles, all of which sounded high-minded and virtuous. The warden was angered by the extent to which all parties seemed bent on frustrating each other rather than working out a solution to the problem. He confessed that he also felt somewhat afraid because he could feel tension building and believed that there might be a series of explosive incidents before long in which people would be seriously injured.

One morning the warden received a request for an interview from an "old con" who, although not on the inmate advisory council and certainly not much involved in rehabilitative programs, had prestige in the inmate society because of his accomplishments in crime and because he was a "loner" who always said what he meant. This inmate told the warden that he and "other old timers like myself" were interested in doing "quiet time." He said that the continuing animosity between the young "orangutangs" and the "stupid screws" was making life very difficult, and he thought that something should be done about it. Asked for advice on what steps might be taken, he offered to serve on a small committee of inmates and staff who would study the situation and bring in recommendations to the warden.

After a night's thought, the warden decided to move along the lines suggested by the inmate. He appointed to the study committee the inmate who had made the suggestion, the head of the inmate advisory council, and two middle-management staffers (one from custody and one from treatment) who tended to be moderate and reasonable in their approach to other people. The warden announced this move publicly at an evening movie attended by most of the inmates, and subsequently he gave considerable personal attention to the work of the committee.

This process did not suddenly solve the problem, but it set in motion a series of events which eventually led to a much more satisfactory disciplinary program. One of the major features of the new program was strong participation of the inmates in defining, modifying, and implementing the rule system of the institution. Eventually inmates actually sat on disciplinary boards and, at a living-unit level, made the major decisions about penalties to be imposed for rule infractions by their fellows, subject only to general review by designated staff members. There seemed, in this situation, good reason to believe that the goal of maintaining reasonable order and control had indeed been integrated with the goal of helping the offenders involved to learn about self-control, not only at an individual level but in terms of the institutionalization of this function within a miniature society.

Incidents involving the integration of control and treatment within community-based correctional programs were somewhat more obscure. Elliot Studt has referred to parole officers as "Janus figures" because they face both ways on the status passage which the offender is expected to traverse from the position of prison inmate to that of responsible citizen. The strain experienced by the officers in their efforts to police the conduct of the offender, thus protecting the public while still assisting him in making a successful adjustment to community life, appeared to be exceedingly severe in several incidents reported to us.

The ways in which these officers managed at times to integrate the function of control with that of treatment were human rather than bureaucratic. The rules and conditions of probation and parole stood as a kind of formal structure for both officers and offenders, but the real-life struggles through which the offenders attempted to come to terms with the expectations of their families, employers, friends, and acquaintances obviously presented continuing dilemmas for all involved.

One probation officer told of approaching his job in an unconventional way which allowed him to monitor and set limits on the behavior of his juvenile charges while still providing them essential emotional support and much-needed opportunities for ventilating pent-up feelings. He explained that he was then working in an area where most of the juvenile probationers came from middle- or upper-class families. He said that the parents, and particularly the fathers, tended to be neglectful of their sons and out of touch with them. Therefore he made himself available to boys in this situation, only some of whom were probationers. Being a relaxed person and genuinely interested in young people, he spent long hours talking with them at drive-in restaurants, recreation spots, and around school. He felt that not only was he able to fill some of the gaps left open by indifferent parents but that he found opportunities to help the youngsters evaluate the feelings of anger and deprivation generated in previous inadequate relationships.

The probation officer's close contacts with the boys at times made him privy to their interest in law-violating activities. He was "tested" by them numerous times with reference to his own commitment to societal rules and quickly learned that he could be a useful model for the boys only if his own attitudes were clear and unambiguous around the need to support authority.

He cited this experience as an exception to the usual process of probation supervision, pointing out that the high caseloads and the bureaucratic requirements for reporting that were established by administrative decree tend to make officers act as surveillance agents (with occasional office interviews, defined as "therapy") rather than true integrators of help and control.

System Maintenance vs. Change

Turning now to the integration of system maintenance with change, as revealed in the incidents, we may note first that the capacity to blend the two seemed to be present more often at top administrative levels than at the second level. Perhaps this is more a matter of role than aptitude, since it seems reasonable to believe that top administrators are better positioned to comprehend needs for both conservation and innovation than are subordinates whose responsibility is limited to particular sectors of the organization.

Two major types of integration appeared in the incidents. The first involved instances in which an administrator managed to blend maintenance and change concerns through the direct exercise of his own influence. The second consisted of efforts to institutionalize the integration of these two concerns within appropriate organizational structures.

With respect to the exercise of personal influence, there were a number of incidents in which administrators reported a conscious avoidance of "oversell" in presenting proposed new programs to the legislature, fiscal control agencies, or other groups whose support was required for approval. Obviously, such restraint was difficult, since administrators are conditioned to fight hard for a share of the public revenue in a highly competitive environment. Nevertheless, certain administrators told us that in the long run it was better to justify proposed new programming on the basis that "we don't know for sure how effective it will be, but the best evidence we can obtain suggests that it will substantially improve our operations." It was admitted that often it is possible to coax or force a particular program through with grandiose promises, but the integration-minded administrators suggested that eventually they might pay a heavy price for such action. Legislative and other relevant reviewing authorities might become cynical about the administrator's "puffing" statements and discount them in the future. They asserted that the administrator who oversells for short-term gains loses his credibility in the very parts of his force field where he needs it most.

It seemed clear that maintaining the reputation and integrity of the agency while still being an effective advocate for needed changes is an extremely difficult function. The neophyte administrator, particularly, faces many seductions when he is cast in the role of correctional expert and asked to defend his proposals for a better system. It is much more satisfying to claim unequivocally that a proposed innovation will work than to place qualifications upon its possible success. The administrators who sought to integrate the functions of system maintenance and system change seemed at times to define themselves as teachers, in the broadest meaning of the term. They saw as essential the need to provide key legislators, budget reviewers, members of the press, and others with opportunities to gain a more sophisticated understanding of the crime problem and of the tentative character of present knowledge about correctional techniques. They were well armed with facts about the inadequacy and costliness of the present system and argued that we must take risks in moving toward a better system but that these risks should be calculated ones and that we should continually evaluate the success of new and experimental ventures.

Some administrators who approached change in this fashion spoke of developing satisfying partnerships with those in the external force field who had previously been regarded as critics. Long-term change, in fact, seemed to depend upon establishing a coalition of interests in which the administrator was no longer a lone voice for needed reforms but had developed commitment on the part of numerous others capable of exercising influence at key decision points.

With regard to activities taking place within their own organizations, the administrators who sought to combine system maintenance with change appeared to exercise considerable personal influence in the sense of providing models for a "strategy of search". During contacts with staff who represented particular program interests, these administrators communicated the idea that it is not neccessary to maintain a facade about effectiveness and that it is highly desirable to seek better ways of doing the job.

One administrator told at length of his contacts with a group of subordinates who were overzealous in their advocacy of a vocational training program for offenders. They bombarded visitors to the institution with glowing statements about the training and with "success stories" about ex-inmates who had obtained highly paid jobs. While still maintaining a generally supportive attitude toward the program, the administrator began to ask for "hard data" on the number of trainees who obtained employment in their specialty, the length of time they held such jobs, and other information related to success. Gradually the staff involved began to ask such questions themselves and reportedly experienced a sense of relief in discovering that their program did not have to be a total success so long as it was being reviewed objectively. They then became more capable of devising ways of improving training and job placement. The same administrator also indicated that he made it a practice to move staff about to different jobs in order to keep them from developing too much vested interest in a particular program.

The incidents which involved an effort to institutionalize the integration of system maintenance and change were typically not reported as highly effective. Rather, they seemed to represent somewhat primitive efforts to build change dynamics into organizations in which the idea of change was basically alien and threatening.

A long incident (really a case study) about the development of an action research program within a large correctional system provided many insights about the difficulties involved in such efforts. Defensiveness and suspicion between researchers and those in action roles appeared very clearly. An early tendency for the researchers to proceed unilaterally rather than in collaboration with program operators in defining research questions led to serious consequences in the form of lack of cooperation from those in action roles when data collection was carried on. The most successful integration of action and inquiry seemed to occur when the researchers became deeply involved in the real-life problems of program staff and the latter became involved in research activities. Such collaborative activities developed mutual trust and support as well as greater awareness by all involved of the problems and dilemmas of inquiry and evaluation. Nevertheless, it appeared to us that research as a way of institutionalizing change in corrections has made only a small beginning and that the problem of integrating concerns for system maintenance with the hard questioning of system operations which is implicit in research activities has not been satisfactorily resolved in any operating agency.

Another institutionalized approach to the integration of system maintenance and change in corrections was the establishment of special organizational units for planning and development. Some of the interviewees in our sample reported assigning specially qualified staff to the task of looking ahead, assessing the adequacy of available resources in terms of the projected workload, and thinking generally about the future without being overly constrained by present realities. It appeared to us that some of these efforts were not making much headway, that the staff involved in planning and development were relatively remote, not only from ongoing operations but also from the information required to make realistic projections into the future.

Nevertheless, there were incidents in which important changes apparently came about through such arrangements. In one case, the head of planning and development in a department of corrections was brought to that role from many years of varied experience in both institutional and community-based correctional programs. Long an outspoken and intelligent critic of agency programs, he was asked to evaluate the entire system, talk to anyone he wished to, and make recommendations to the director for new legislation and for policy changes. His rapport with operating personnel and his intimate knowledge of the system prepared him to make recommendations which, although far-reaching in nature, were congruent with the basic commitments and goals of the organization. By contrast, some planning and development efforts seemed ineffectual because they were carried on by persons who made their recommendations on the basis of extremely superficial understanding of the existing system.

A general and quite basic limitation of studies and surveys as instruments for introducing needed change appeared to be that ideas about change were largely formulated within the framework of current ideology. It seemed difficult for those identified with the reform movement in corrections to take a fresh and objective look at ongoing operations. Perhaps a consortium of insiders and outsiders might make a more effective planning and development team than most of those which have operated thus far on the correctional scene.

Production vs. Human Welfare

The integration of concern for production and concern for human welfare and morale was revealed in a number of incidents, although as previously stated, there was a good deal of "muddiness" in the data with regard to the meaning of the terms. Perhaps the best way to approach a discussion of this dimension would be to note that much of the incident data reflected no effort to integrate these two concerns. Some business managers, for example, seemed totally oriented to the maintenance of good fiscal records and the balancing of the budget. But one "elder statesman" in this group offered a number of ingenious examples of ways in which he was able to advance the treatment and training program for the offenders in his agency by his handling of the fiscal system. He said, "The job really started to be fun when I decided that these young fellows involved in treatment [meaning both the staff and the offenders] were not my enemies and there were lots of ways that I could help them." He seemed to derive his major job satisfaction from being able to supply fiscal support for needed innovations rather than, in typical fiscal management behavior, playing a role of denying and restricting. It did appear, it must be added, that he made personal and perhaps quite arbitrary judgments about which treatment programs were worthy and which were not.

If the major "production" of a correctional organization really is the changing of offender attitudes and behaviors, then it is apparent that lesser production goals, which are really only means to that end, need to be subordinated. Problems occur when these lesser goals are made dominant. Thus, great tension and animosity developed in one institution when the farm manager became so preoccupied with crop production that he neglected opportunities for inmates assigned to this activity to learn skills which might have helped them to secure employment after release. The ability of administrators both in institutions and in the community to establish the goal of reintegration of offenders as a major orientating point for all staff seemed critical. With the reintegration goal as the major reference point for all participants, there was a basis for determining which priorities were more justified than others. Without it, diverse interests tended to compete with each other in ways which were frequently destructive, and the climate and morale of the organization was adversely affected. In this sense the integration of production with human welfare seemed to depend very greatly upon the administrator's ability to use the strategy of invoking standards and norms in such a manner as to generate consensus about and commitment to the goals of the agency.

THE METHOD OF MANIPULATION

While many of the interviewees were reluctant to identify themselves with use of manipulation, as operationally defined in our research, the incidents which they reported frequently revealed intricate manipulation strategies. Some of the interviewees were refreshingly blunt in saying, in effect, that in a competitive, pluralistic system there is sometimes great advantage in "concealing part of your hand." Still others spoke of this practice in more bland terms; e.g., "It is wise to cultivate goodwill from people whose help you will need later."

It is difficult to assess this strategy, or the possibilities for refining it through developmental experience, because it is so negatively stereotyped in our society. The interviews indicated that manipulation is most appropriate and effective when used in relationships in which the parties deal at arm's length and the caveat of potential exploitation is well understood on both sides. Yet the quantitative data based on forced-choice rankings of strategies show the use of manipulation slightly more frequently with relationships in the internal force field than in the external one.

Paradoxically, even those administrators who were predominantly oriented toward a preferred set of strategies, such as involvement-commitment, integration, and use of expertise, seemed to make use of manipulation when the problem context was highly competitive or antagonistic. In these situations, problem-solving was so structured that in order for the administrator to win, someone else would have to lose. Just as a good chess player does not tell his opponent the moves he expects to make ahead of time, the administrators who reported manipulation strategies seemed to regard concealment as a major advantage. An example may help to clarify this point.

One day an administrator received a call from a newspaper reporter who told him that the head of a newly formed private association which purported to help offenders reestablish themselves in the community had been sharply critical of the correctional organization headed by the administrator. The group had charged that the policies of his organization were antagonistic to the purposes of the private program and demanded a public explanation. The administrator, while irritated and somewhat threatened by the communication, affected an unruffled manner and said that he would like an opportunity to study the charges and meet with those who had made them in order to see what might be done. Having already formulated a negative opinion of the private group, however, he instead proceeded to make a number of telephone calls to officials in other jurisdictions where groups affiliated with the same private organization were operating. In this way he obtained anecdotal information from credible sources which cast doubt upon the integrity and responsibility of the group. He then called in the reporter who had contacted him and in an "off the record" interview made available to him the new sources of information, saying that he did not want to be quoted since he had no firsthand knowledge of the allegations. With the reporter following these new and more attractive lures, the administrator engaged in delaying tactics with the private association, whose originally clamorous demands for attention subsided after a few days.

It may be helpful to consider our data on manipulation in the light of management literature associated with the concept of social exchange.[4] If we assume, as does the concept of social exchange, that those operating in the administrative arena interact with each other in terms of complex desires to achieve gains and avoid losses, it becomes clear that certain of these interactions will be competitive or even antagonistic in nature. Our incidents tended to bear this out. The administrators dealt more openly with legislators with whom there was a prospect of mutual gain (e.g., securing approval of a new institution to be located in the district of a friendly assemblyman) than with those who had no particular reason to be supportive of correctional program expansion. While openness and candor might be advocated as general principles by an administrator, he was much more apt to practice them with a newspaper reporter who was friendly than with one who was "looking for trouble." We heard many references to such tactics; e.g., "protecting our flanks against that young assistant in the governor's office who wants to build his empire," or "Tom Jones [a subordinate working in one of the institutions] is a troublemaker and would discredit his superiors if we put him into a position where he could do so."

In final appraisal of our incident data on manipulation, two contradictory themes predominated. First, it seemed clear that there were numerous occasions when all of the administrators believed it necessary to be guarded rather than open and to use influence indirectly rather than directly. At the same time, several ineffective incidents (some of them reported about other administrators rather than the interviewees themselves) indicated that it is disastrous for an administrator to become known as deceptive and as one who works behind the scenes to undercut others. We heard a great many approving descriptions of other managers who were admired because "you can trust him," or "even if he disagrees with you, you always know where he stands," or "he always operates out in the open."

While our data do not provide a basis for reconciling the basic inconsistency of such attitudes toward manipulation and the practice of it, they do suggest some plausible explanations. First, certain relationships seem to require a higher level of openness than do others. An administrator who amiably supplied critics of his program with ammunition to use in a legislative hearing was perceived by his associates as "naive" rather than as possessed of great integrity. Secondly, openness seemed to depend greatly upon individual personality and style. Some administrators naturally operated in an open and spontaneous way which apparently was contagious and allowed them to deal directly and above board in a wide range of relationships. Others were much more cautious and reserved, becoming relatively open only as a result of long-term contact with other individuals. A style which generated universal disapproval among our interviewees, however, was that in which a facade of openness masked calculative and manipulative stratagems for dealing with others.

THE METHOD OF INVOKING STANDARDS AND NORMS

We found that the administrators studied, particularly those with innovative capacity, made wide and varied use of the strategy of invoking standards and norms. "Authoritative" standards such as those promulgated by the American Correctional Association, the National Council on Crime and Delinquency, and the U.S. Children's Bureau frequently constituted the primary basis for requesting a better staffing ratio, a new institution, or some other desideratum. The administrators who were orientated toward change tended to speak about their operations in comparative terms; e.g., "we have better job placement services than the Employment Service" or "our school program has been accredited in the top category for this county."

It was obvious, however, that most of the standards and norms which are pertinent to the rehabilitation or reintegration of offenders rest on rather flimsy evidence, and most of the administrators seemed well aware of this limitation. One interviewee said:

> I stand up in front of the Ways and Means Committee and tell them that we simply have to hire enough additional officers to get the caseload size down to that recommended by NCCD, but I know damn well that if they ask me for proof that this would reduce recidivism, I wouldn't have much to say.

The administrators who were most attracted to the idea of building a research capability into their organizations seemed to be most skeptical of the sanctity of existing standards.

We identified a small number of interviewees for whom the invoking of standards and norms seemed to be the primary strategy used in problem-solving. For every problem, with these individuals, there seemed to be an appropriate axiom or principle to produce the answer. Frequently in these cases the invoking of norms was at a highly abstract level and at times seemed to have a pontifical tone. Without exception, all of the incidents which we obtained from administrators who appeared to depend primarily upon the invoking of standards and norms had to do with organizational maintenance rather than change. The following incident is illustrative.

One interviewee described a situation in which boys committed to a forestry camp became recalcitrant and difficult to manage. Responsibility for their supervision and programming was divided between paid staff and volunteers from a nearby community. It was reported that the problems started when volunteer supervisors allowed the boys to get out of hand during the evening recreational period. Work efficiency in reforestation projects then dropped sharply. Liquor (possibly stolen from nearby vacation cottages) appeared in the camp and there was furtive drinking in the barracks. Boys began to run away. Word that all was not well found its way back to the headquarters and also came to the attention of a number of private citizens who, as a result, became critical of the correctional system.

The administrator's description of his resolution of these difficulties was paternalistic in tone. He indicated that his subordinates had chosen volunteer workers who were "goodhearted, but didn't understand how to handle these boys." In subsequent meetings with both professional staff and volunteers, the administrator reported "educating" them along lines which seemed clear-cut to him. There is a "right way" to handle rebellious boys, he explained, indicating that a combination of firmness and paternally allocated benevolence was the correct formula. He also detailed a number of specific standards for the conduct of work and recreation programs, standards which "have to be observed if you are going to avoid problems."

The troubling aspect of this and related incidents was that those administrators who depended so heavily upon preformulated axioms frequently were regarded by their associates as "rigid" and lacking in capacity to introduce truly significant innovations. We gained the impression that some correctional organizations make a token display of rehabilitative programs but in major substance retain the practices and the climate of authoritarian regimes. One key to such conditions may be the presence of administrators who, in seeing themselves as the source of all legitimate prescription and authority, keep hierarchically subordinate staff and offenders in dependent and relatively uncreative roles.

A seemingly preferable use of standards and norms in problem-solving appeared in instances of administrative behavior which emphasized search for more effective methods rather than treating existing dogma as immutable. Administrators conforming to this pattern made much use of standards and norms to solve particular problems (in some cases tending to be somewhat manipulative when seeking to influence naive interest groups) but tended to regard them as tentative "rules of thumb" which can be improved upon as knowledge about correctional intervention techniques advances. In this pattern the invoking of standards and norms tended to be combined with integration, involvement-commitment, the use of expertise and, at times, manipulation.

THE METHOD OF DELAY

The use of delay was reported persistently, though with a relatively low frequency, by administrators in discussing many relationships. An amusingly constant response to the interviewer's suggestion that deciding not to decide was a possibility, came in such statements as "Yes, I've learned that's so, and I don't charge in like I used to in the beginning."

It appeared that some respondents actually were reporting an avoidance of problems rather than a well conceived strategy of solving them through delay. On the other hand, a few administrators had given a great deal of thought to the timing of efforts to bring about change and reported quite elaborate strategies in which delay was combined with such other methods as dilemma management and involvement-commitment. These administrators placed a great deal of importance upon preparatory work which enabled them to move strongly and decisively when the time for action finally arrived. Activities carried on in the preparatory period included gathering facts and arguments to support a change when the time came to advocate it openly, helping staff to be ready to implement a major new program by a prior period of development and training, and "softening up the public" as, for example, in preparation for a work furlough law, through a series of educational programs about the causes of crime and the potentiality of many offenders for successful reintegration in the community.

It seemed to us that the use of delay was especially characteristic of administrators who had been seasoned in bureaucratic battles and, while still preserving a zeal for reform and change, had learned to bide their time and develop needed support. Some of the ineffective incidents reported by such administrators from their earlier careers were intended to document the idea that ill-considered efforts to introduce change which result in failure are more harmful than no effort at all.

One crusty elder in correctional management suggested that there has been a tendency for administrators in the field to move impulsively on the belief that "the guys with the white hats always win." He spoke at some length about the disadvantages which correctional executives face in competing with a multitude of other more attractive programs for public funds. He argued for long-term planning (consistent with the "mixed-scanning model" described in Chapter 2) and urged that administrators desiring to develop and change their programs should be objective in calculating the chances of success before taking overt action.

In our incidents, successful use of the strategy of delay seemed to depend more than anything else on a shrewd ability to appraise the movement of forces which might be mobilized for or against a given project and on a fine sense of timing in moving from preparation into action. It appeared that the skillful use of delay in the interest of change objectives was closely related to the strategy of compromise employed for the same purpose. Trygve Lie is reported to have observed that "you have to make compromises that in the long run will serve the principles for which you stand." Change-minded administrators seemed to be stoic about delay on the same premise. We will close this section with an episode of administrative behavior which illustrates this point.

An administrator who had responsibility for both institutional and community-based correctional programs was visited one day by a prominent businessman who said that he "want to do something serious about getting offenders back on the right track." He explained that he had read publicity released by the President's Crime Commission concerning the woeful condition of the nation's institutions and the lack of personnel for effective rehabilitative work in the community. Explaining his concern for human predicaments by saying that he was an alcoholic who had "learned to handle the problem," he indicated that he would like to organize a select committee

487

of business leaders who would work to open up job opportunities for ex-offenders and promote better understanding of their problems "in the respectable part of town."

The administrator was delighted with this opportunity. The two men proceeded to lay out a plan of action which involved launching the new program at a press conference with the governor and a series of supportive news stories based on cases of men who had made a successful transition from the role of prison inmate to that of responsible citizen.

In moving to implement the plan in the following days, however, the administrator encountered two rather discouraging reactions. First, his enthusiastic explanation of the plan to the governor elicited only a lukewarm response. The governor made it clear that, while he himself was not campaigning for reelection, nevertheless he was involved with the campaigns of lesser officials within his party. He pointed out that the issue of law and order was "touchy," with "a lot of real idiots" doing most of the talking about the need to get tough with criminals. He said to the administrator. "You know that I've always been on the right side of these questions, but just be sure you don't put me in a spot which will be embarrassing to my friends in the party."

The second negative reaction came from a reporter on the staff of the major newspaper in the area where the committee of businessmen was to be formed. He had always been more or less friendly to the administrator, and they had worked together effectively in the past. This time, however, he listened to the "pitch" of the administrator in a rather perfunctory manner and indicated that his paper already had plans for a major series about crime. Somewhat in the same vein as the governor's comments, he said that he would be glad to stop by and talk further if the administrator wished him to but added that "this may not be the best time to do what you want." Only two days later the first of the series to which the reporter had referred appeared in the press, and the administrator discovered to his discomfort that it was to consist of interviews with a number of prominent law enforcement officials who were highly critical of recent Supreme Court decisions concerning the investigation and adjudication of crimes, and generally were negative to correctional programs.

The administrator then asked the businessman who had suggested the new program to come in for further discussion. They quickly agreed that it would be a bad time to launch a major effort of the kind proposed and addressed themselves to the problem of laying a solid groundwork for later implementation of the plan. The businessman agreed to talk informally with a number of his friends and solicit their support. The administrator indicated that he would assign some staff members to work out more effective liaison with employment agencies and to identify a number of inmates who might be suited for the kind of help which later would be furnished.

At the time of the interview, the select committee had still to be appointed and the program was being held in abeyance. But the administrator already was "reading the signs up ahead" and had concluded that the time was nearing when the governor would see considerable payoff in identifying himself with an alliance of businessmen interested in helping ex-offenders. The administrator also had little doubt that the press would be willing to give good coverage to the new program. He roughly paraphrased the old adage by saying, "There are times when you have to back away in order to fight again another day."

NOTES

1. Neal Gross, Ward S. Mason, Alexander W. McEachern, *Exploration in Role Analysis: Studies of the School Superintendency Role*, New York: Wiley, 1958, pp. 281–318.
2. We are indebted to Richard A. McGee for the articulation of this idea and for numerous pointed examples of its application in various relationships and problem areas.
3. See *Dynamic Administration: The Collected Papers of Mary Parker Follett*, Henry C. Metcalf and L. Urwick, eds., New York: Harper, 1940, pp. 30–49.
4. For a further discussion of this concept, see Peter M. Blau, "Social Exchange" (under "Interaction"), in *International Encyclopedia of Social Sciences*, 1968, VII, 452–457; James A. Davis and Kenneth Boulding, "Two Critiques of Homans' Social Behavior: Its Elementary Forms," *American Journal of Sociology*, LXVII (1961), 454–461; Frank Sherwood, "Social Exchange in the Institution-Building Process" (paper prepared for the Comparative Administration Group, American Society for Public Administration, June 1967).

Index *

*Note: Numerals set in bold type refer to figures or tables.

Index

Index

495